The International Institute
for Strategic Studies

The Military Balance 2002•2003

Published by **Oxford University Press** for
The International Institute for Strategic Studies
Arundel House, 13–15 Arundel Street,
London WC2R 3DX, UK

The Military Balance 2002·**2003**

Published by Oxford University Press for
The International Institute
for Strategic Studies
Arundel House, 13–15 Arundel Street,
London WC2R 3DX, UK
http://www.iiss.org

This publication has been prepared by the Director of the Institute and his staff, who accept full responsibility for its contents.

First published October 2002

ISBN 0-19-851672-X
ISSN 0459-7222

The Military Balance (ISSN 0459-7222) is published annually in October by Oxford University Press, Great Clarendon Street, Oxford OX2 6DP, UK. The 2002 annual subscription rate is: UK£80 (individual rate), UK£108 (institution rate); overseas US$132 (individual rate), US$185 (institution rate).

Payment is required with all orders and subscriptions are accepted and entered by the volume (one issue). Please add sales tax to the prices quoted. Prices include air-speeded delivery to Australia, Canada, India, Japan, New Zealand and the USA. Delivery elsewhere is by surface mail. Air-mail rates are available on request. Payment may be made by cheque or Eurocheque (payable to Oxford University Press), National Girobank (account 500 1056), credit card (Mastercard, Visa, American Express, JCB), direct debit (please send for details) or UNESCO coupons. Bankers: Barclays Bank plc, PO Box 333, Oxford, UK, code 20-65-18, account 00715654. Claims for non-receipt must be made within four months of dispatch/order (whichever is later).

Please send subscription orders to the Journals Subscription Department, Oxford University Press, Great Clarendon Street, Oxford, OX2 6DP, UK
tel +44 (0)1865 353907 *fax* +44 (0)1865 353485
e-mail jnl.orders@oup.co.uk.

In North America, *The Military Balance* is distributed by Mercury International, 365 Blair Road, Avenel, NJ 07001, USA. Periodical postage paid at Rahway, NJ, and additional entry points.

US POSTMASTER: Send address corrections to *The Military Balance*, c/o Mercury International, 365 Blair Road, Avenel, NJ 07001, USA.

Printed in Great Britain by Bell & Bain Ltd, Glasgow.

Contents

The Military Balance 2002·2003 Preface

The Military Balance is updated each year to provide an accurate assessment of the military forces and defence expenditures of 169 countries. The data in the current edition is according to IISS assessments as at 1 August 2002. Inclusion of a country or state in *The Military Balance* does not imply legal recognition or indicate support for a particular government.

GENERAL ARRANGEMENT

Part I of *The Military Balance* comprises the regional trends and military capabilities of countries grouped by region. Regional groupings are preceded by a short introduction describing the military issues facing the region. There are tables depicting nuclear delivery and warhead holdings as well as high readiness capabilities and military satellites. In addition there is a table of selected non-state armed groups. Also, an analytical essay explores the issue of emerging military counter-terrorist responses.

Part II contains macro-economic and defence economic data of countries grouped by region. Tables show comparisons of defence expenditure, and military manpower for the years of 1985, 2000 and 2001. Conventional Forces in Europe Treaty data is shown as well as arms-trade data.

The loose wall-map is updated from 2001 to show data on recent and current armed conflicts, including fatalities and costs.

USING THE MILITARY BALANCE

The country entries in *The Military Balance* are a quantitative assessment of the personnel strengths and equipment holdings of the world's armed forces. The strengths of forces and the numbers of weapons held are based on the most accurate data available or, failing that, on the best estimate that can be made with reasonable confidence. The data presented each year reflect judgements based on information available to the IISS at the time the book is compiled. Where information differs from previous editions, this is mainly because of substantive changes in national forces, but it is sometimes because the IISS has reassessed the evidence supporting past entries. An attempt is made to distinguish between these reasons for change in the text that introduces each regional section, but care must be taken in constructing time-series comparisons from information given in successive editions.

In order to interpret the data in the country entries correctly, it is essential to read the explanatory notes beginning on page 5.

The large quantity of data in *The Military Balance* has been compressed into a portable volume by extensive employment of abbreviations. An essential tool is therefore the alphabetical index of abbreviations, which appears on the laminated card at the back of the book. For ease of reference, this may be detached and used as a bookmark.

ATTRIBUTION AND ACKNOWLEDGEMENTS

The International Institute for Strategic Studies owes no allegiance to any government, group of governments, or any political or other organisation. Its assessments are its own, based on the material available to it from a wide variety of sources. The cooperation of governments has been sought and, in many cases, received. However, some data in *The Military Balance* are estimates. Care is taken to ensure that these are as accurate and free from bias as possible. The Institute owes a considerable debt to a number of its own members, consultants and all those who helped compile and check material. The Director and staff of the Institute assume full responsibility for the data and judgements in this book. Comments and suggestions on the data presented are welcomed. Suggestions on the style and method of presentation are also much appreciated.

Readers may use data from *The Military Balance* without applying for permission from the Institute on condition that the IISS and *The Military Balance* are cited as the source in any published work. However, applications to reproduce portions of text, complete country entries or complete tables from *The Military Balance* must be referred to the publishers. Prior to publication, applications should be addressed to: Journals Rights and Permissions, Oxford University Press, Great Clarendon Street, Oxford OX2 6DP, UK, with a copy to the Editor of *The Military Balance.*

Explanatory Notes

ABBREVIATIONS AND DEFINITIONS

Abbreviations are used throughout to save space and avoid repetition. The abbreviations may have both singular or plural meanings; for example, 'elm' = 'element' or 'elements'. The qualification 'some' means *up to*, while 'about' means *the total could be higher than given*. In financial data, '$' refers to US dollars unless otherwise stated; billion (bn) signifies 1,000 million (m). Footnotes particular to a country entry or table are indicated by letters, while those that apply throughout the book are marked by symbols (* for training aircraft counted by the IISS as combat-capable, and where serviceability of equipment is in doubt). A full list of abbreviations appears on the detachable laminated card at the back of the book.

COUNTRY ENTRIES

Information on each country is shown in a standard format, although the differing availability of information results in some variations. Each entry includes economic, demographic and military data. Military data include manpower, length of conscript service, outline organisation, number of formations and units and an inventory of the major equipment of each service. This is followed, where applicable, by a description of the deployment of each service. Details of national forces stationed abroad and of foreign-stationed forces are also given.

ARMS ORDERS AND DELIVERIES

Tables in the regional texts show arms orders and deliveries listed by country buyer for the past and current years, together with country supplier and delivery dates, if known. Every effort has been made to ensure accuracy, but some transactions may not be fulfilled or may differ from those reported.

GENERAL MILITARY DATA

Manpower

The 'Active' total comprises all servicemen and women on full-time duty (including conscripts and long-term assignments from the Reserves). Under the heading 'Terms of Service', only the length of conscript service is shown; where service is voluntary there is no entry. 'Reserve' describes formations and units not fully manned or operational in peacetime, but which can be mobilised by recalling reservists in an emergency. Unless otherwise indicated, the 'Reserves' entry includes all reservists committed to rejoining the armed forces in an emergency, except when national reserve service obligations following conscription last almost a lifetime. *The Military Balance* bases its estimates of effective reservist strengths on the numbers available within five years of completing full-time service, unless there is good evidence that obligations are enforced for longer. Some countries have more than one category of 'Reserves', often kept at varying degrees of readiness. Where possible, these differences are denoted using the national descriptive title, but always under the heading of 'Reserves' to distinguish them from full-time active forces.

Other Forces

Many countries maintain paramilitary forces whose training, organisation, equipment and control suggest they may be used to support or replace regular military forces. These are listed, and their roles described, after the military forces of each country. Their manpower is not normally included in the Armed Forces totals at the start of each entry. Home Guard units are counted as paramilitary. Where paramilitary groups are not on full-time active duty, '(R)' is added after the title to indicate that they have reserve status. When internal opposition forces are armed and appear to pose a significant threat to a state's security, their details are listed separately after national paramilitary forces.

Equipment

Quantities are shown by function and type, and represent what are believed to be total holdings, including active and reserve operational and training units and 'in store' stocks. Inventory totals for missile systems – such as surface-to-surface missiles (SSM), surface-to-air missiles (SAM) and anti-tank guided weapons (ATGW) – relate to launchers and not to missiles. Stocks of equipment held in reserve and not assigned to either active or reserve units are listed as 'in store'. However, aircraft in excess of unit establishment holdings, held to allow for repair and modification or immediate replacement, are not shown 'in store'. This accounts for apparent disparities between unit strengths and aircraft inventory strengths.

Operational Deployments

Where deployments are overseas, *The Military Balance* lists permanent bases and does not normally list short-term operational deployments, particularly where military operations are in progress. An exception is made in the case of peacekeeping operations. Recent developments are also described in the text for each regional section.

GROUND FORCES

The national designation is normally used for army formations. The term 'regiment' can be misleading. It can mean essentially a brigade of all arms; a grouping of battalions of a single arm; or (as in some instances in the UK) a battalion-sized unit. The sense intended is indicated in each case. Where there is no standard organisation, the intermediate levels of command are shown as headquarters (HQs), followed by the total numbers of units that could be allocated to them. Where a unit's title overstates its real capability, the title is given in inverted commas, with an estimate given in parentheses of the comparable unit size typical of countries with substantial armed forces. For guidelines for unit and formation strengths, see box.

Equipment

The Military Balance uses the following definitions of equipment:

Main Battle Tank (MBT) An armoured, tracked combat vehicle, weighing at least 16.5 metric tonnes unladen, that may be armed with a 360° traverse gun of at least 75mm calibre. Any new-wheeled combat vehicles that meet the latter two criteria will be considered MBTs.

Armoured Combat Vehicle (ACV) A self-propelled vehicle with armoured protection and cross-country capability. ACVs include:

Heavy Armoured Combat Vehicle (HACV) An armoured combat vehicle weighing more than six metric tonnes unladen, with an integral/organic direct-fire gun of at least 75mm (which does not fall within the definitions of APC, AIFV or MBT). *The Military Balance* does not list HACVs separately, but under their equipment type (light tank, reconnaissance or assault gun), and where appropriate annotates them as HACV.

Armoured Infantry Fighting Vehicle (AIFV) An armoured combat vehicle designed and equipped to transport an infantry squad, armed with an integral/organic cannon of at least 20mm calibre. Variants of AIFVs are also included and indicated as such.

Armoured Personnel Carrier (APC) A lightly armoured combat vehicle, designed and equipped to transport an infantry squad and armed with integral/organic weapons of less than 20mm calibre. Variants of APCs converted for other uses (such as weapons platforms, command posts and communications vehicles) are included and indicated as such.

Artillery A weapon with a calibre of 100mm and above, capable of engaging ground targets by delivering primarily indirect fire. The definition covers guns, howitzers, gun/howitzers, multiple-rocket launchers and mortars.

Military Formation Strengths

The manpower strength, equipment holdings and organisation of formations such as brigades and divisions differ widely from country to country. Where possible, the normal composition of formations is given in parentheses. It should be noted that where both divisions and brigades are listed, only separate brigades are counted and not those included in divisions.

Units and formation strength	
Company	100–200
Battalion	500–800
Brigade (Regiment)	3,000–5,000
Division	15,000–20,000
Corps (Army)	60,000–80,000

NAVAL FORCES

Categorisation is based on operational role, weapon fit and displacement. Ship classes are identified by the name of the first ship of that class, except where a class is recognised by another name (such as *Udalay*, *Petya*). Where the class is based on a foreign design or has been acquired from another country, the original class name is added in parentheses. Each class is given an acronym. All such designators are included in the list of abbreviations. The term 'ship' refers to vessels with over 1,000 tonnes full-load displacement that are more than 60 metres (m) in overall length; vessels of lesser displacement, but of 16m or more overall length, are termed 'craft'. Vessels of less than 16m overall length are not included. The term 'commissioning' of a ship is used to mean the ship has completed fitting out and initial sea trials, and has a naval crew; operational training may not have been completed, but otherwise the ship is available for service. 'Decommissioning' means that a ship has been removed from operational duty and the bulk of its naval crew transferred. Removing equipment and stores and dismantling weapons, however, may not have started. Where known, ships in long-term refit are shown as such.

Definitions

To aid comparison between fleets, the following definitions, which do not necessarily conform to national definitions, are used:

Submarines All vessels equipped for military operations and designed to operate primarily below the surface. Those vessels with submarine-launched ballistic missiles are listed separately under 'Strategic Nuclear Forces'.

Principal Surface Combatant This term includes all surface ships with both 1,000 tonnes full load displacement and a weapons system for other than self-protection. All such ships are assumed to have an anti-surface ship capability. They comprise: aircraft carriers (defined below); cruisers (over 8,000 tonnes) and destroyers (less than 8,000 tonnes), both of which normally have an anti-air role and may also have an anti-submarine capability; and frigates (less than 8,000 tonnes) which normally have an anti-submarine role. Only ships with a flight deck that extends beyond two-thirds of the vessel's length are classified as aircraft carriers. Ships with shorter flight decks are shown as helicopter carriers.

Patrol and Coastal Combatants These are ships and craft whose primary role is protecting a state's sea approaches and coastline. Included are corvettes (500–1,500 tonnes with an attack capability), missile craft (with permanently fitted missile-launcher ramps and control equipment) and torpedo craft (with anti-surface-ship torpedoes). Ships and craft that fall outside these definitions are classified as 'patrol' and divided into 'offshore' (over 500 tonnes),'coastal' (75–500 tonnes), 'inshore' (less than 75 tonnes) and 'riverine'. The adjective 'fast' indicates that the ship's speed is greater than 30 knots.

Mine Warfare This term covers surface vessels configured primarily for mine laying or mine countermeasures (such as mine-hunters, minesweepers or dual-capable vessels). They are further classified into 'offshore', 'coastal', 'inshore' and 'riverine' with the same tonnage definitions as for 'patrol' vessels shown above.

Amphibious This term includes ships specifically procured and employed to disembark troops and their equipment onto unprepared beachheads by means such as landing craft or helicopters, or directly supporting amphibious operations. The term 'Landing Ship' (as opposed to 'Landing Craft') refers to vessels capable of an ocean passage that can deliver their troops and equipment in a fit state to fight. Vessels with an amphibious capability but not assigned to amphibious duties are not included. Amphibious craft are listed at the end of each entry.

Support and Miscellaneous This term covers auxiliary military ships. It covers four broad categories: 'underway support' (e.g., tankers and stores ships), 'maintenance and logistic' (e.g., sealift ships), 'special purposes' (e.g., intelligence collection ships) and 'survey and research' ships.

Merchant Fleet This category is included in a state's inventory when it can make a significant contribution to the state's military sealift capability.

Weapons Systems Weapons are listed in the following order: land-attack missiles, anti-surface ship missiles, surface-to-air missiles, guns, torpedo tubes, other anti-submarine weapons, and helicopters. Missiles with a range of less than 5km, and guns with a calibre of less than 76mm, are not included. Exceptions may be made in the case of some minor combatants with a primary gun armament of a lesser calibre.

Aircraft All armed aircraft, including anti-submarine warfare and maritime-reconnaissance aircraft, are included as combat aircraft in naval inventories.

Organisations Naval groupings such as fleets and squadrons frequently change and are often temporary; organisations are shown only where it is meaningful.

AIR FORCES

The term 'combat aircraft' refers to aircraft normally equipped to deliver air-to-air or air-to-surface ordnance. The 'combat' totals include aircraft in operational conversion units whose main role is weapons training, and training aircraft of the same type as those in front-line squadrons that are assumed to be available for operations at short notice. Training aircraft considered to be combat capable are marked with an asterisk (*). Armed maritime aircraft are included in combat aircraft totals. Operational groupings of air forces are shown where known. Squadron aircraft strengths vary with aircraft types and from country to country.

Definitions

Different countries often use the same basic aircraft in different roles; the key to determining these roles lies mainly in aircrew training. In *The Military Balance* the following definitions are used as a guide:

Fixed Wing Aircraft

Fighter This term is used to describe aircraft with the weapons, avionics and performance capacity for aerial combat. Multi-role aircraft are shown as fighter ground attack (FGA), fighter, reconnaissance and so on, according to the role in which they are deployed.

Bombers These aircraft are categorised according to their designed range and payload as follows:

Long-range Capable of delivering a weapons payload of more than 10,000kg over an unrefuelled radius of action of over 5,000km;

Medium-range Capable of delivering weapons of more than 10,000kg over an unrefuelled radius of action of between 1,000km and 5,000km;

Short-range Capable of delivering a weapons payload of more than 10,000kg over an unrefuelled radius of action of less than 1,000km.

A few bombers with the radius of action described above, but designed to deliver a payload of less than 10,000kg, and which do not fall into the category of FGA, are described as **light bombers**.

Helicopters

Armed Helicopters This term is used to cover helicopters equipped to deliver ordnance, including for anti-submarine warfare. They may be further defined as:

Attack Helicopters with an integrated fire control and aiming system, designed to deliver anti-armour, air-to-ground or air-to-air weapons;

Combat Support Helicopters equipped with area suppression or self-defence weapons, but without an integrated fire control and aiming system;

Assault Armed helicopters designed to deliver troops to the battlefield.

Transport Helicopters The term describes unarmed helicopters designed to transport personnel or cargo in support of military operations.

DEFENCE ECONOMICS

Country entries in **Part II** show defence expenditure, selected economic performance indicators and demographic aggregates. **Part II** also contains an international comparison of defence expenditure and military manpower, giving expenditure figures for the past two years against a bench-mark year in constant US dollars. The aim is to provide an accurate measure of military expenditure and of the allocation of economic resources to defence. All country entries are subject to revision each year, as new information, particularly that regarding defence expenditure, becomes available. The information is necessarily selective. A wider range of statistics is available to IISS members on request.

Individual country entries typically show economic performance over the past two years, and current-year demographic data. Where these data are unavailable, information from the last available year is provided. Defence expenditure is generally shown for the past two years where official outlays are available, or sufficient data for reliable estimates exist. Current-year defence budgets and, where available, defence budgets for the following year are also listed. All financial data in the country entries are shown both in national currency and US dollars at current year, not constant, prices. US dollar conversions are generally, but not invariably, calculated from the exchange rates listed in the entry. In a few cases, notably Russia and China, a US dollar purchasing power-parity (PPP) rate is used in preference to official or market-exchange rates.

Definitions of terms

To avoid errors in interpretation, an understanding of the definition of defence expenditure is important. Both the UN and NATO have developed standardised definitions, but in many cases countries prefer to use their own definitions (which are not in the public domain). For consistency, the IISS uses the NATO definition (which is also the most comprehensive) throughout.

In *The Military Balance,* military expenditure is defined as the cash outlays of central or federal government to meet the costs of national armed forces. The term 'armed forces' includes strategic, land, naval, air, command, administration and support forces. It also includes paramilitary forces such as the *gendarmerie,* customs service and border guard if these are trained in military tactics, equipped as a military force and operate under military authority in the event of war. Defence expenditures are reported in four categories: Operating Costs, Procurement and Construction, Research and Development (R&D) and Other Expenditure. Operating Costs include: salaries and pensions for military and civilian personnel; the cost of maintaining and training units, service organisations, headquarters and support elements; and the cost of servicing and repairing military equipment and infrastructure. Procurement and Construction expenditure covers national equipment and infrastructure spending, as well as common infrastructure programmes. It also includes financial contributions to multinational military organisations, host-nation support in cash and in kind, and payments made to other countries under bilateral agreements. FMA counts as expenditure by the donor, and not the recipient, government. R&D is defence expenditure up to the point at which new equipment can be put in service, regardless of whether new equipment is actually procured. The fact that the IISS definitions of military expenditure are generally more inclusive than those applied by national governments and the standardised UN format means that our calculated expenditure figures may be higher than national and UN equivalents.

The issue of transparency in reporting military expenditures is a fundamental one. Only a minority of the governments of UN member-states report defence expenditures to their electorates, the UN, the International Monetary Fund (IMF) and other multilateral organisations. In the case of governments with a proven record of transparency, official figures generally conform to a standardised definition of defence expenditure, and consistency problems are not usually a major issue. Where these conditions of transparency and consistency are met, the IISS cites official defence budgets and outlays as reported by national governments, NATO, the UN, the Organisation for Security and Cooperation in Europe (OSCE) and the IMF. On the other hand, some governments do not report defence expenditures until several years have elapsed, while others understate these expenditures in their reports. Where these reporting conditions exist, *The Military Balance* gives IISS estimates of military expenditures for the country concerned. Official defence budgets are also shown, in order to provide a measure of the discrepancy between official figures and what the IISS estimates real defence outlays to be. In these cases *The Military Balance* does not cite official defence expenditures (actual outlays), as these rarely differ significantly from official budgetary data. The IISS defence-expenditure estimates are based on information from several sources, and are marked 'ε'. The most frequent instances of budgetary manipulation or falsification typically involve equipment procurement, R&D, defence industrial investment, covert weapons programmes, pensions for retired military and civilian personnel, paramilitary forces and non-budgetary sources of revenue for the military arising from ownership of industrial, property and land assets.

The principal sources for economic statistics cited in the country entries are the IMF, the Organisation for Economic Cooperation and Development (OECD), the World Bank and three regional banks (the Inter-American, Asian and African Development Banks). For some countries basic economic data are difficult to obtain. This is the case in a few former command economies in transition and countries currently or recently involved in armed conflict. The Gross Domestic Product (GDP) figures are nominal (current) values at market prices. GDP growth is real not nominal growth, and inflation is the year-on-year change in consumer prices. Two different measures of debt are used to distinguish between OECD and non-OECD countries: for OECD countries, debt is gross public debt (or, more exactly, general government gross financial liabilities) expressed as a proportion of GDP. For all other countries, debt is gross foreign debt denominated in current US dollars. Dollar exchange rates relate to the last two years plus the current year. Values for the past two years are annual averages, while current values are the latest monthly value.

Calculating exchange rates

Typically, but not invariably, the exchange rates shown in the country entries are also used to calculate GDP and defence-expenditure dollar conversions. Where they are not used, it is because the use of exchange rate dollar conversions can misrepresent both GDP and defence expenditure. This may arise when: the official exchange rate is overvalued (as with some Latin American and African countries); relatively large currency fluctuations occur over the short-to-medium term; or when a substantial medium-to-long-term discrepancy between the exchange rate and the dollar PPP exists. Where exchange-rate fluctuations are the problem, dollar values are converted using lagged exchange rates (generally by no more than six months). For former communist countries, PPP rather than market exchange rates are sometimes used for dollar conversions of both GDP and defence expenditures, and this is marked.

The arguments for using PPP are strongest for Russia and China. Both the UN and IMF have issued caveats concerning the reliability of official economic statistics on transitional economies, particularly those of Russia and some Eastern European and Central Asian countries. Non-reporting, lags in the publication of current statistics and frequent revisions of recent data (not always accompanied by timely revision of previously published figures in the same series) pose transparency and consistency problems. Another problem arises with certain transitional economies whose productive capabilities are similar to those of developed economies, but where cost and price structures are often much lower than world levels. PPP dollar values are used in preference to market exchange rates in cases where using such exchange rates may result in excessively low dollar-conversion values for GDP and defence expenditure.

Demographic data

Population aggregates are based on the most recent official census data or, in their absence, demographic statistics taken from *World Population Projections* published annually by the World Bank. Data on ethnic and religious minorities are also provided under country entries where a related security issue exists.

United States

CHANGING POSTURES AND REVIEWING CAPABILITIES

Since 11 September 2001, the US military establishment has been engaged on a number of operations to deal with the terrorist threat, while at the same time carrying out reforms to current force structures, and changes to existing deployments. The essay on page 232 of this year's *Military Balance* looks in more detail at some aspects of the reforms that are taking place, while issues concerning expenditure are explored in Section II.

The attacks on the World Trade Center and the Pentagon came at a time when the Quadrennial Defense Review (QDR) was close to completion. The review, which was announced on 30 September, had already set itself the objective of generating a strategy that was flexible, and which would extend US influence, while preserving US homeland security. The four goals of the new defence policy, as laid out in the QDR, are:

- assuring allies and friends of the United States' steadiness of purpose and its capability to fulfil its security commitments;
- dissuading adversaries from undertaking programmes or operations that could threaten US interests or those of its allies and friends;
- deterring aggression and coercion by forward deploying the capacity to swiftly defeat attacks and impose severe penalties for aggression on an adversary's military capability and supporting infrastructure; and
- decisively defeating any adversary, if deterrence fails.

The review was keen to shift strategic thinking away from the existing 'threat-based' model to a forward-looking, 'capabilities-based' approach, which would examine the means a potential adversary may use to fight the US. To accommodate this move, US planners were tasked with 'transforming' the military to extend Washington's strategic advantage. Key to this was the need to generate force-planning options that would give strategic planners a wider set of military alternatives to cope with both existing and future threats. Changes to force structures have the following aims:

- defend the United States;
- deter aggression and coercion forward in critical regions;
- swiftly defeat aggression in overlapping major conflicts while preserving for the president the option to call for a decisive victory in one of those conflicts – including the possibility of regime change or occupation; and
- conduct a limited number of smaller-scale contingency operations.

These aims were reiterated by Secretary of Defense Rumsfeld in his Annual Report to Congress on 15 August 2002. Revealing developing priorities, he said that the military has six operational goals. 'Protect the US homeland and defeat WMD and means of delivery; protect and sustain power in distant anti-access and area denial environments; deny enemy sanctuary by developing capabilities for persistent surveillance, tracking and rapid engagement; leverage information technologies and innovative network-centric concepts to link joint forces; protect information systems from attack; maintain unhindered access to space and protect US space capabilities.' A *Unified Command Plan* has also been developed to enhance homeland security.

The QDR's organisational impact

One of the key changes generated by the QDR will be the creation of Standing Joint Task Force (SJTF) Headquarters. These will provide common standard operating procedures, tactics, techniques and technical system requirements, and will have the ability to move expertise among commands. Standing Joint Task Forces, which will be structured to meet both asymmetric and symmetric threats by exploiting US asymmetric military advantages and joint force options, are also under development. Also, by 1 October 2002, changes to the Unified Command Plan (UCP), which were announced on 17 April, will have begun. The UCP establishes the missions and geographic responsibilities of commanders and assigns, where required, the responsibility for security cooperation and military coordination with all countries in a particular region. The revised plan includes the formation of a fifth regional command, Northern Command (NORTHCOM), with responsibilities covering Canada, the US and Mexico. President Bush has selected the current commander of US Space Command (SPACECOM), US Air Force (USAF) General Ralph E. Eberhart, as the first C-in-C NORTHCOM. In his new post, Eberhart will command the US element to North American Aerospace Defense Command (NORAD), although he will relinquish command of SPACECOM. Eberhart will be responsible for land, aerospace and sea defences of the US, and will also command US forces that operate in support of US civil authorities, not only in response to attacks but also in the event of natural disasters.

Meanwhile, SPACECOM and US Strategic Command (STRATCOM) are set to merge in a bid to enhance combat effectiveness, limit duplication and streamline and accelerate strategic decision-making. Currently, STRATCOM is the command-and-control centre for US nuclear forces, while SPACECOM handles US military space operations, information operations, computer network defence and space campaign planning. Both are concerned with countering the threat from weapons of mass destruction (WMD). The merger is scheduled for October 2002, and the resultant command will be responsible for both early warning of, and defence against, missile attack as well as long-range conventional attacks. The merger will increase the standing of the USAF as the lead space authority, although it could result in the disbandment of the army's Space and Missile Defense Command.

One of the QDR's recommendations that affects all of the armed services is the development of the concept of 'network-centric' warfare, in which all relevant systems within the battlespace are utilised to best advantage. The main aim of this concept is to cut the time taken to make high-level tactical and operational decisions – curtailing the 'sensor to shooter' cycle or 'kill cycle' and is particularly related to the integration into frontline military use of new developments in C4ISTAR.

In a sense, the QDR was addressing new asymmetric threats before 11 September, and little had to be altered in the aftermath of the terrorist attacks. The main focus of change for the US was in the area of homeland security rather than in the traditional military sphere. The homeland security issue focused specifically on the need for the inter-agency coordination (explored further in the essay on page 232). A major development has been the creation of the Office of Homeland Security within the White House, a move dovetailed by the Department of Defense, which has created its own interim Office of Homeland Defense (the QDR had earlier instituted a Homeland Security Working Group), with the intention of establishing a permanent office in late 2002. There are now 27 Weapons of Mass Destruction Civil Support Teams, which were first formed in 1998, with another five in the planning stages. These teams are composed of National Guard personnel.

However, with much attention presently focused on asymmetric threats, it is noteworthy that the Pentagon is still taking account of traditional threats. Indeed, in the future, there may be a further change, moving away from a concentration on asymmetric threats back towards a more strategic, symmetric threat. In this context, the Department of Defense has published the Report to Congress of the US–China Security Review Commission, Chapter 9 of which argues that China may be the next major threat to US strategic interests in the future.

Current military force developments

The US Marine Corps has formed a new brigade to counter terrorism, the 4th Marine Expeditionary Brigade (Anti-Terrorism). This is a crisis force capable of deploying two platoons anywhere in the US in six hours, with a further 1,000 Marines in the following three days. The new unit unifies the Marine Corps Security Forces Battalion, Marine Security Guard Battalion, Chemical-Biological Incident Response Force and a specially trained infantry battalion under a single command.

The army, meanwhile, has formed two prototype Brigade Combat Teams (BCT), a concept which has been part of the army's vision for future forces since 1999. A further four BCTs are to form by 2007 with the intention of adjusting forward-deployed forces to better reflect regional concerns. BCTs are intended to provide a fast deployment force that is better armed and protected than the army's current light forces. As for the air force, the USAF is now concentrating on weapon systems rather than platforms, reflecting the QDR's emphasis on transformation. To fund new C4ISTAR, precision-strike and air-defence systems, a major re-examination of F-22 roles and numbers, and the proposed lease of 100 modified Boeing 767 tankers can be expected. Also, the *Crusader* artillery system, one notable 'legacy system' project, which has been in development for some time has been shelved to provide more money for new projects.

In June 2002, reacting to the new post 11-September strategic environment, the US Navy (USN) made first mention of its new operational concept, entitled Sea Power 21. At the core of the concept, which will shape the medium-term future of the navy, are three major tasks: 'sea strike'; 'sea shield'; and 'sea basing'. 'Sea strike' is defined as the projection of dominant and decisive power against key enemy targets. As such, it will probably require the USN to place considerable emphasis on carrier-borne aircraft, UCAVs and UAVs, land-attack missiles and long-range ship-borne guns, together with platforms capable of operating in littoral areas. 'Sea shield' is the projection of defensive power from the sea – on behalf of the US and its allies – in order to dissuade and deter potential adversaries in multiple theatres. It covers a range of naval capabilities, from the existing ability to secure sea lines of communication, to the current naval nuclear deterrent and future sea-based missile defence. The third task, 'sea basing', is defined as the projection of power around the world and includes the routine forward deployment and regular overseas deployments of US naval platforms, in addition to possession of the necessary logistic capability.

The global war on terror, as the Pentagon termed the military response to the terrorist threat, first manifested itself in deployments to Uzbekistan, Kyrgyzstan, Tajikistan and Afghanistan, all of which are governed by Status of Forces Agreements. The US presence in these countries and *Operation Enduring Freedom* are explored further in the Central and South Asia section, beginning on page 122. An important component of US military involvement in that region has been the deployment of HQAB Corps as the in-theatre operational command headquarters. Titled Combined Joint Task Force 180, this is the first example of the new Joint Task Force concept envisaged in the QDR. The anti-terror campaign has also extended into Southeast Asia, with the deployment of some 150 US Special Forces personnel to the Philippines. The task was to advise and train the Philippines armed forces in counterinsurgency techniques. A further 500 troops, including engineers and aviation assets, provided additional support. In early-to-mid 2002, around 1,000 US troops also participated in joint US–Philippine *Balikatan* training exercises, a number of which had taken place in previous years. By July 2002, however, US forces had begun to pull out of the Philippines. In general, the focus of US force planning is shifting away from Europe to planning for conflicts in two particular regions – Northeast and Southwest Asia.

Strategic policy

In the strategic arena, the Nuclear Posture Review (NPR), which was submitted to Congress in January 2002 – and leaked in March – contained a mixture of old and new elements when compared to the most recent NPR in 1994. Conceptually, the new NPR proposed to replace the familiar strategic triad of land-, sea- and air-based nuclear forces with a new triad composed of: nuclear and non-nuclear offensive systems; active and passive defences (including missile defence); and a revitalised nuclear infrastructure. In practical terms, the NPR called for a reduction in operationally deployed strategic weapons to a level of between 1,700 and 2,200 weapons by 2012, while maintaining most decommissioned weapons in active and inactive strategic reserves. (These numbers, and a timetable for the reductions, were later codified in the Strategic Offensive Reduction Treaty signed by Presidents Bush and Putin in Moscow on 24 May 2002.) The NPR also proposed an ambitious programme to extend the life of existing delivery vehicles and restore facilities for the production of nuclear weapons components.

The overall numbers of, and the breakdown between ICBMs, *Trident* submarines and bombers in the 2002 NPR, are virtually identical to the recommendations of its 1994 predecessor. Unlike this earlier NPR, however, which sized strategic forces against a potential Russian threat, the new NPR based its recommendations on a 'capabilities-based approach' involving 'immediate, potential, or unexpected contingencies', which included Russia, China, North Korea, Iran, Iraq, Syria and Libya. To meet such contingencies, the NPR suggested the possibility of using nuclear weapons to destroy deep underground facilities or in response to chemical and biological weapon (CBW) attacks. While some critics argued that this represented a significant shift in US doctrine governing the use of nuclear weapons, Washington has long refused to rule out the option of using such weapons in response to non-nuclear attacks.

Most press headlines and commentary focused on the NPR's proposal to study the development of a new generation of earth-penetrating nuclear weapons (so called mini-nukes) designed to destroy hardened or deeply buried targets. At some point, the development of such weapons could require a resumption of nuclear testing, and the NPR proposed to shorten the lead-time necessary to resume testing. However, the administration emphasised that it had no plans 'at this time' to resume nuclear testing. Notwithstanding that some administration officials believed nuclear testing would eventually be necessary to validate existing weapons and develop new ones, Washington did not want to suffer the political consequences of triggering a new round of nuclear testing by other powers.

The 11 September attacks created domestic and international political conditions that assisted Washington's preference to pursue missile defence without legal constraints. The administration announced its intention to withdraw from the Anti-Ballistic Missile (ABM) Treaty on 13 December 2001, and the withdrawal took effect six months later on 13 June 2002. However, the demise of the ABM Treaty did not substantially increase political tensions between Washington, Moscow and Beijing – in large measure because both Russia and China sought to emphasise their solidarity with the US in the 'war against terrorism'. With Russia and China acquiescing to the US move, opposition to missile defence in Europe and the US Senate has largely evaporated.

As outlined in the Nuclear Posture Review and the Quadrennial Defense Review, the administration proposed to refocus and expand the existing missile-defence programme from a single-site 'national' missile defence to a broad-based research, development and testing effort aimed at deploying 'layered' missile defences – to include ground-, sea-, air- and possibly space-based systems. As a practical matter, however, the Pentagon's immediate plans focused on establishing, by 2004, a land-based test facility in Alaska with five interceptors, which could serve as an emergency missile defence system against North Korea. Other options under consideration, such as deployment of a sea-based missile, mounted on *Aegis*-class destroyers and the Airborne Laser, both of which are intended to intercept target missiles in their boost-phase, could probably not be deployed until the end of the decade at the earliest.

The attacks on New York and Washington also stimulated greater administration support for Cooperative Threat Reduction (CTR) programmes with Russia, designed to prevent the leak of nuclear, chemical and biological materials, technology and expertise to rogue states or terrorists groups. While initially somewhat sceptical about such programmes, the administration embraced CTR efforts in the wake of 11 September, due to closer US–Russian relations and greater concern about terrorist attacks using WMD. Reflecting these developments, the administration sought $1.04 billion for CTR programmes in its FY2003 budget request (a 37% increase over the FY2002 appropriation), and set up working groups between the Department of Energy and the Russian Ministry of Atomic Energy to establish a programme for securing radiological materials and to study options for accelerating programmes to dispose of surplus nuclear materials that could be used in weapons. At the same time, funding for programmes to help destroy Russian chemical weapons and to assist in converting former biological-weapons-related facilities was suspended because of administration concerns that Moscow was withholding information and cooperation concerning its past CBW programmes.

Along with increased US spending, the administration successfully spearheaded efforts to persuade its European allies to increase their support for CTR programmes with Russia. As a result, the June 2002 Group of Eight (G8) meeting in Canada agreed on a 'Global Partnership Against the Spread of Weapons of Mass Destruction', in which they committed to raise up to $20bn over the next ten years to support CTR programmes, such as the destruction of chemical weapons, the dismantlement of decommissioned nuclear submarines, the disposition of fissile materials and the employment of former weapons scientists. In return, Russia agreed to a new set of guidelines to ensure effective and efficient implementation of the new projects. Given the reluctance of the Russian government to carry out these new guidelines and the reluctance of most European governments to devote substantial new funds to CTR projects, considerable work lies ahead to realise the 'Global Partnership'.

United States US

Total Armed Forces

ACTIVE 1,414,000
(incl 196,100 women; excl Coast Guard)
RESERVES 1,259,300
(incl Stand-by Reserve)

READY RESERVE 1,235,900
Selected Reserve and Individual Ready Reserve to augment active units and provide reserve formations and units
NATIONAL GUARD 464,300
Army (ARNG) 355,900 **Air Force** (ANG) 108,400
RESERVE 771,600
Army 358,100 **Navy** 174,100 **Marines** 99,900
Air Force 139,500
STAND-BY RESERVE 23,400
Trained individuals for mob **Army** 700 **Navy** 5,600 **Marines** 600 **Air Force** 16,500

US Strategic Command (US STRATCOM)

HQ: Offutt AFB, NE (manpower incl in Navy and Air Force totals)

NAVY up to 432 SLBM in 18 SSBN
(Plus 16 *Poseidon* C-3 launchers in one op ex-SSBN redesignated SSN (32 msl), START accountable)

SSBN 18 *Ohio*
10 (SSBN-734) with up to 24 UGM-133A *Trident* D-5 (240 msl)
8 (SSBN-726) with up to 24 UGM-93A *Trident* C-4 (192 msl)

AIR FORCE
ICBM (Air Force Space Command) 550
11 msl sqn
500 *Minuteman* III (LGM-30G)
50 *Peacekeeper* (MX; LGM-118A)
AC (Air Combat Command (ACC)):
115 active hy bbr
5 sqn (1 AFR) with 94 B-52H (56 combat ready, including 44 combat-coded and 12 dual-tasked)
2 sqn with 21 B-2A (16 combat ready)
FLIGHT TEST CENTRE 3
2 B-52, 1 B-2

Strategic Recce/Intelligence Collection (Satellites)

IMAGERY Improved *Crystal* (advanced **KH-11**) visible and infra-red imagery (perhaps 3 op, resolution 6in) ***Lacrosse*** (formerly ***Indigo***) radar-imaging sat (resolution 1–2m)
ELECTRONIC OCEAN RECCE SATELLITE (EORSAT) to detect ships by infra-red and radar
NAVIGATIONAL SATELLITE TIMING AND RANGING (NAVSTAR) 24 sat, components of Global Positioning System (GPS); block 2R system with accuracy to 1m replacing expired sat

ELINT/SIGINT 2 *Orion* (formerly *Magnum*), 2 *Trumpet* (successor to *Jumpseat*), 3 name n.k., launched Aug 1994, May 1995, Apr 1996

NUCLEAR DETONATION DETECTION SYSTEM detects and evaluates nuclear detonations; sensors to be deployed in NAVSTAR sat

Strategic Defences

US Space Command (HQ: Peterson AFB, CO)
North American Aerospace Defense Command (NORAD), a combined US–Ca org (HQ: Peterson AFB, CO)
US Strategic Command (HQ: Offutt AFB, NE)

EARLY WARNING

DEFENSE SUPPORT PROGRAM (DSP) infra-red surv and warning system. Detects msl launches, nuclear detonations, ac in after burner, spacecraft and terrestrial infra-red events. Approved constellation: 3 op sat and 1 op on-orbit spare

BALLISTIC-MISSILE EARLY-WARNING SYSTEM (BMEWS) 3 stations: Clear (AK), Thule (Greenland), Fylingdales Moor (UK). Primary mission to track ICBM and SLBM; also used to track sat

SPACETRACK USAF radars at Incirlik (Tu), Eglin (FL), Cavalier AFS (ND), Clear, Thule, Fylingdales Moor (UK), Beale AFB (CA), Cape Cod (MA); optical tracking systems in Socorro (NM), Maui (HI), Diego Garcia (Indian Ocean)

USN SPACE SURVEILLANCE SYSTEM (NAVSPASUR) 3 transmitting, 6 receiving-site field stations in south-east US

PERIMETER ACQUISITION RADAR ATTACK CHARACTERISATION SYSTEM (PARCS) 1 north-facing phased-array system at Cavalier AFS (ND); 2,800km range

PAVE PAWS phased-array radars in MA, GA; 5,500km range

MISCELLANEOUS DETECTION AND TRACKING RADARS US Army Kwajalein Atoll (Pacific) **USAF** Ascension Island (Atlantic), Antigua (Caribbean), Kaena Point (HI), MIT Lincoln Laboratory (MA)

GROUND-BASED ELECTRO-OPTICAL DEEP SPACE SURVEILLANCE SYSTEM (GEODSS) Socorro, Maui (HI), Diego Garcia

AIR DEFENCE

RADARS

OVER-THE-HORIZON-BACKSCATTER RADAR (OTH-B) 1 in ME (mothballed), 1 in Mountain Home AFB (mothballed); range 500nm (minimum) to 3,000nm

NORTH WARNING SYSTEM to replace DEW line
15 automated long-range (200nm) radar stations
40 short-range (110–150km) stations

DEW LINE system deactivated

Army 485,500

(incl 71,400 women)
3 Army HQ, 4 Corps HQ (1 AB)
2 armd div (3 bde HQ, 5 tk, 4 mech inf, 3 SP arty bn; 1 MLRS bn, 1 AD bn; 1 avn bde)
2 mech div (3 bde HQ, 5 tk, 4 mech inf, 3 SP arty bn; 1 MLRS bn, 1 ADA bn, 1 cav sqn; 1 avn bde)
1 mech div (3 bde HQ, 4 tk, 5 mech inf, 3 SP arty bn; 1 MLRS bn, 1 ADA bn, 1 cav sqn; 1 avn bde)
1 mech div (2 bde HQ, 1 bct HQ, 2 tk, 2 mech inf, 2 bct bn, 2 air aslt inf, 3 SP arty bn; 1 AD bn; 1 avn bde)
2 lt inf div (1 with 2 bde HQ, 1 bct HQ, 8 inf, 1 bct, 3 arty bn; 1 avn bde
1 with 2 bde HQ, 6 inf, 2 arty, 1 AD bn; 1 avn bde)
1 air aslt div (3 bde HQ, 9 air aslt, 3 arty bn; 2 avn bde (8 hel bn: 3 ATK, 3 aslt, 1 comd, 1 med tpt))
1 AB div (3 bde HQ, 9 AB, 3 arty, 1 AD, 1 air cav, 1 avn bde)
1 indep inf bde
1 AB Task Force (bde)
5 avn bde (1 army, 3 corps, 1 trg)
3 armd cav regt (1 hy, 1 lt, 1 trg (OPFOR))
6 arty bde (3 with 1 SP arty, 2 MLRS bn; 1 with 3 arty, 1 MLRS bn; 1 with 3 MLRS bn; 1 with 1 MLRS bn)
1 indep inf bn, 1 inf bn (OPFOR)
10 *Patriot* SAM bn
2 Integrated Div HQ (peacetime trg with 6 enhanced ARNG bde - 3 per div)
Special Operations Forces (see page 23)

READY RESERVE

ARMY NATIONAL GUARD (ARNG) (355,900) capable after mob of manning 8 div (1 armd, 3 mech, 3 med, 1 lt inf) • 15 indep bde, incl 14 enhanced (1 armd, 5 mech, 7 inf, 1 cav) • 1 armd cav regt • 17 fd arty bde HQ • 1 Scout gp • Indep bn: 1 inf, 42 arty, 32 avn, 11 AD (2 *Patriot*, 9 *Avenger*), 40 engr

ARMY RESERVE (AR) (358,100) 7 trg div, 5 exercise div, 13 AR/Regional Spt Comd, 4 hel bn (2 AH-64, 2 CH-47), 3 hel coy (2 UH-60, 1 CH-47), 2 ATK ac bn

(Of these, 205,000 Standing Reservists receive regular trg and have mob assignment; the remainder receive limited trg, but as former active-duty soldiers could be recalled in an emergency.)

EQUIPMENT

MBT some 7,620 M-1 *Abrams* incl M-1A1, M-1A2
RECCE 96 Tpz-1 *Fuchs*
AIFV 6,710 M-2/-3 *Bradley*
APC 15,910 M-113A2/A3 incl variants
TOTAL ARTY 5,396
TOWED 1,547: **105mm**: 434 M-102, 416 M-119; **155mm**: 697 M-198
SP 155mm: 2,087 M-109A1/A2/A6
MRL 227mm: 830 MLRS (all ATACMS-capable)
MOR 120mm: 932 M-120/121; plus **81mm**: 624 M-252
ATGW 8,715 TOW (incl 1,379 HMMWV, 626 M-901,

6,710 M-2/M-3 *Bradley*), 19,000 *Dragon*, 950 *Javelin*
RL 84mm: AT-4
SAM FIM-92A *Stinger*, 703 *Avenger* (veh-mounted *Stinger*), 95 *Linebacker* (4 *Stinger* plus 25mm gun), 483 *Patriot*
SURV Ground 98 AN/TPQ-36 (arty), 56 AN/TPQ-37 (arty), 68 AN/TRQ-32 (COMINT), 16 AN/TSQ-138 (COMINT), 5 AN/TSQ-138A **Airborne** 4 *Guardrail* (RC-12D/H/K, 3 RU-21H ac), 7 EO-5ARL (DHC-7)
AMPH 51 ships:
6 *Frank Besson* LST: capacity 32 tk
34 LCU-2000
11 LCU-1600
Plus craft: some 73 LCM-8
UAV 7 *Hunter* (5 in store)
AC some 282: 46 **C-12C/R**, 90 **C-12D/F/J**, 3 **C-20**, 47 **C-23A/B**, 8 **C-26**, 1 **C-37**, 2 **C-182**, 2 **O-2**, 1 **PA-31**, 37 **RC-12D/H/K**, 12 **RC-12P/Q**, 2 **T-34**, 26 **UC-35**, 4 **UV-18A**, 1 **UV-20A**
HEL some 4,813 (1,294 armed): 370 **AH-1S**, 694 **AH-64A/D**, 36 **AH-6/MH-6**, 650 **UH-1H/V**, 1,539 **UH-60AL/MH-60L/K**, 4 **UH-60Q**, 63 **EH-60A (ECM)**, 421 **CH/-47D**, 21 **CH-47E**, 513 **OH-58A/C**, 350 **OH-58D** (incl 194 armed), 150 **TH-67** *Creek*, 2 **RAH-66**

Navy (USN) 385,400

(incl 57,800 women)
2 Fleets: Pacific, Atlantic
Surface combatants further divided into:
5 Fleets: **2nd** Atlantic, **3rd** Pacific, **5th** Indian Ocean, Persian Gulf, Red Sea, **6th** Mediterranean, **7th** W. Pacific; plus Military Sealift Command (MSC), Naval Special Warfare Command, Naval Reserve Force (NRF)

SUBMARINES 72

STRATEGIC SUBMARINES 18 (see page 16)
TACTICAL SUBMARINES 54 (incl about 8 in refit)
SSGN 33
2 *Seawolf* (SSN-21) with up to 45 *Tomahawk* LAM/ASSM plus 8 × 660mm TT (Mk 48 HWT)
23 imp *Los Angeles* (SSN-751) with 12 *Tomahawk* LAM/ASSM (VLS), 4 × 533mm TT (Mk 48 HWT, *Harpoon* ASSM)
8 mod *Los Angeles* (SSN-719) with 12 *Tomahawk* LAM/ASSM (VLS), 4 × 533mm TT (Mk 48 HWT, *Harpoon* ASSM)
SSN 21
20 *Los Angeles* (SSN-688) with 4 × 533mm TT (*Tomahawk* LAM/ASSM, *Harpoon* ASSM Mk 48 HWT)
1 *Sturgeon* (SSN-637) with 4 × 533mm TT (*Tomahawk* SLCM, Mk48 HWT)

PRINCIPAL SURFACE COMBATANTS 129

AIRCRAFT CARRIERS 12
CVN 9
8 *Nimitz* (CVN-68) (one in refit)
1 *Enterprise* (CVN-65)
CV 3
2 *Kitty Hawk* (CV-63)
1 *J. F. Kennedy* (CV-67) (in reserve)
AIR WING 11 (10 active, 1 reserve); average Air Wing comprises 9 sqn
3 with 12 F/A-18C, 1 with 14 F-14, 1 with 8 S-3B and 2 ES-3, 1 with 6 SH-60, 1 with 4 EA-6B, 1 with 4 E-2C, 1 spt with C-2
CRUISERS 27
CG 27 *Ticonderoga* (CG-47 *Aegis*)
5 *Baseline* 1 (CG-47–51) with 2 × 2 SM-2 MR SAM/ASROC, 2 × 4 *Harpoon* SSM, 2 × 127mm guns, 2 × 3 ASTT (Mk 46 LWT), 2 SH-2F or SH-60B hel
22 *Baseline* 2/3 (CG-52) with 2 VLS Mk 41 (61 tubes each) for combination of SM-2 ER SAM, and *Tomahawk* LAM/ASSM; other wpns as *Baseline* 1
DESTROYERS 55
DDG 55
28 *Arleigh Burke* (DDG-51 *Aegis*) Flight I/II with 2 VLS Mk 41 (32 tubes fwd, 64 tubes aft) for combination of *Tomahawk* LAM/ASSM, SM-2 ER SAM and ASROC, 2 × 4 *Harpoon* SSM, 1 × 127mm gun, 2 × 3 ASTT (Mk 46 LWT)
5 *Arleigh Burke* (DDG-79 *Aegis*) Flight IIA, armament as above plus 2 SH-60B hel
20 *Spruance* (DD-963) with 2 VLS Mark 41 for combination of *Tomahawk* LAM/ASSM and ASROC, 2 x 4 *Harpoon* SSM, *Sea Sparrow* SAM, 2 × 127mm gun, 2 × 3 ASTT (Mk 46 LWT), 2 SH-60B hel
FRIGATES 35
FFG 35 *Oliver Hazard Perry* (FFG-7) (incl 7 in reserve) all with *Harpoon* SSM, 1 SM-1 MR SAM, 2 × 3 ASTT (Mk 46 LWT), 1 × 76mm gun; plus either 2 × SH-60 or 1 × SH-2F hel

PATROL AND COASTAL COMBATANTS 21

PATROL, COASTAL 13 *Cyclone* PFC with SEAL team
PATROL, INSHORE 8<

MINE WARFARE 27

MINELAYERS none dedicated, but mines can be laid from attack SSN, ac and surface ships.
MINE COUNTERMEASURES 27
1 *Inchon* MCCS (in reserve) with 2 UH-46D and 8 MH-53E hel
2 *Osprey* (MHC-51) MHC (plus 10 *Osprey* in reserve)
9 *Avenger* (MCM-1) MCO (plus 5 *Avenger* in reserve)

AMPHIBIOUS 41

LCC 2 *Blue Ridge*, capacity 700 tp
LHD 7 *Wasp*, capacity 1,890 tp, 60 tk; with 5 AV-8B ac, 42 CH-46E, 6 SH-60B hel; plus 3 LCAC
LHA 5 *Tarawa*, capacity 1,900 tp, 100 tk; with 6 AV-8B ac, 12 CH-46E, 9 CH-53; plus 4 LCU
LPD 11 *Austin*, capacity 900 tp, 4 tk; with 6 CH-46E hel;

plus 2 LCAC

LSD 15

8 *Whidbey Island*, capacity 500 tp, 40 tk; with 4 LCAC
4 *Harpers Ferry*, capacity 500 tp, 40 tk; with 2 LCAC
3 *Anchorage*, capacity 330 tp, 38 tk; with 3 LCAC

LST 1 *Newport*, capacity 347 tp, 10 tk (in reserve) plus

CRAFT about 200

72 LCAC, capacity 1 MBT; about 37 LCU-1610, capacity 1 MBT; 8 LCVP; 75 LCM; plus numerous LCU

COMBAT LOGISTICS Force 6

2 *Supply* AOE with 3 CH-46E hel
4 *Sacramento* AOE with 2 CH-46E hel

NAVAL RESERVE SURFACE FORCES 26 (counted in the active totals)

1 CV (*J. F. Kennedy*) fully op with assigned air wg, 8 FFG, 5 MCM, 10 MHC, 1 MCCS (*Inchon*), 1 LST generally crewed by 70% active and 30% reserve, plus 22 MIUW units

NAVAL INACTIVE FLEET about 28

3 CV, 2 BB, 4 DD, 5 LST, 5 LKA, 2 AO, 2 AF, 5 AG plus misc service craft

MILITARY SEALIFT COMMAND (MSC)

MSC operates about 110 ships around the world carrying the designation 'USNS' (US Naval Ships). They are not commissioned ships and are manned by civilians. Some also have small mil depts assigned to carry out specialised mil functions such as comm and supply ops. MSC ships carry the prefix 'T' before their normal hull numbers.

Naval Fleet Auxiliary Force 34

7 AE • 6 AF • 2 AH • 13 AO • 5 AT/F • 1 AOE

Special Mission Ships 23

AG • 1 AR/C • 3 AGOS (counter-drug ops) • 8 AGOS • 9 AGHS • 2 AGM

Prepositioning Program/Maritime Prepositioning Program 32

1 ro-ro AK • 3 hy ro-ro AK • 1 flo-flo AK • 4 AK • 13 MPS AK • 4 LASH • 2 AOT • 2 AVB • 1 AG • 1 AO

Sealift Force 30

8 AKR • 17 ro-ro AKR • 5 AOT

ADDITIONAL MILITARY SEALIFT

(crewed and maintained by US Maritime Administration, when activated, come under operational control of MSC)

Ready Reserve Force (RRF) 74

(ships at readiness of 4/5/10/20 days)
31 ro-ro, 15 breakbulk, 9 AR/C, 7 hy lift, 8 tkrs, 2 AVB, 2 trp ships

National Defense Reserve Fleet (NDRF) 41

31 breakbulk, 7 tkrs, 3 heavy lift ships

COMMERCIAL SEALIFT about 315

US-flag (198) and effective US-controlled (EUSC, 117) ships potentially available to augment mil sealift

AUGMENT FORCES 13

13 Cargo Handling Bns (1 active, 12 reserve)

NAVAL AVIATION 70,230

(incl 6,300 women)
incl 12 carriers, 11 air wg (10 active, 1 reserve) **Flying hours** F-14: 252; F-18: 252
Average air wg comprises 9 sqn
3 with 12 F/A-18C, 1 with 10 F-14, 1 with 8 S-3B, 1 with 6 SH-60, 1 with 4 EA-6B, 1 with 4 E-2C, 1 spt with C-2

ORGANISATION

AIRCRAFT

Ftr 12 sqn
4 with F-14A, 5 with F-14B, 3 with F-14D

FGA/attack 24 sqn
23 with F/A-18C, 1 with F/A-18A

ELINT 4 sqn
2 with EP-3, 2 with EA-6B

ECM 14 sqn with EA-6B

MR 12 land-based sqn with P-3CIII

ASW 10 sqn with S-3B

AEW 10 sqn with E-2C

COMD 1 sqn with E-6A (TACAMO)

OTHER 2 sqn with C-2A

Trg 16 sqn
2 *Aggressor* with F/A-18, 14 trg with T-2C, T-34C, T-44, T-45A

HELICOPTERS

ASW 20 sqn
10 with SH-60B (LAMPS Mk III)
10 with SH-60F/HH-60H

MCM 1 sqn with MH-53E

MISC 5 sqn
4 with CH-46, 1 with MH-53E

Trg 2 sqn with TH-57B/C

NAVAL AVIATION RESERVE (NR) 22,220

(incl 3,000 women)

AIRCRAFT

Ftr attack 3 sqn with F-18

AEW 1 sqn with E-2C

ECM 1 sqn with EA-6B

MPA 7 sqn with P-3C/EP-3J

FLEET LOG Spt 1 wg
6 sqn with C-9B/DC-9, 4 sqn with C-130T, 1 sqn with C-40A, 3 sqn with C-20

Trg 2 *Aggressor* sqn (1 with F/A-18, 1 with F-5E/F)

HELICOPTERS 1 wg

ASW 2 sqn: 1 with SH-60F/HH-60F, 1 with SH-60B

MSC 3 sqn: 2 with HH-60H, 1 with UH-3H

EQUIPMENT

(Naval Inventory incl Marine Corps ac and hel)
1,705 cbt ac plus 207 in store; 693 armed hel plus 39 in store

AIRCRAFT

157 **F-14** (39 **-A** (ftr, incl 1 **NF-14A** trials) plus 14 in store, 69 **-B** (ftr, incl 1 **NF-14B** trials) plus 1 in store, 49 **-D** (ftr, incl 3 **NF-14D** trials)) • 854 **F/A-18** (185 **-A** (FGA, incl 46 NR, 81 MC (49 MCR), 1 **NF/A-18A** trials) plus 14 in store, 30 **-B** (incl 3 NR, 4 MC), 407 **-C** (incl 86 MC and 2 **NF/A-18C** trials), 144 **-D** (incl 95 MC and 3 **NF/18D** trials), 42 **-E** plus 4 in store, 46 **-F** plus 1 in store) • 150 **AV-8B** (134 **AV-8B** (FGA, incl 127 MC) plus 15 in store, 15 **TAV-8B** (trg, incl 14 MC) plus 3 instore, 1 **NAV-8B** (trials)) • 2 **F4** (1 **F4-S** (FGA) plus 20 in store, 1 **YF-4J** (prototype, FGA)) • 0 **A6** (FGA) plus 44 in store • 120 **EA-6B** (ELINT, incl 4 NR, 30 MC) plus 1 in store • 11 **EP-3** (11 **EP3-E** (ELINT)) plus 1 **EP-3J** in store • 246 **P-3** (2 **-B** (MR) plus 26 in store, 224 **-C** (MR incl 46 NR, 1 **NP-3C**, trials) plus 31 in store, 11 **NP-3D** (MR trials), 4 **UP-3A** (utility), 5 **VP-3A** (VIP tpt)) • 109 **S-3** (109 **-B** (ASW)) plus 1 in store, plus 4 **US-3A** (tpt), 12 **ES-3A** (recce) in store • 69 **E-2C** (67 **E-2C** (AEW, incl 9 NR) plus 8 in store, 2 **TE-2C** (trg) • 0 **A-3** (AEW) plus 12 in store • 16 **E-6** (2 **-A** (COMD) plus 1 in store, 14 **-B** (COMD) plus 1 **TE-18F** (mod E-6 trg) in store • 107 **C-130** (20 **-T** (tpt, all NR), 73 **KC-130** (tpt, 33 **-F**, incl 32 MC plus 1 in store; 9 **-J** incl 2 MC; 13 **-R**, all MC; 28 **-T**, all MCR), 1 **DC-130A** (tpt, NR) plus 1 in store, 1 **TC-130G** (display), plus 3 **LC-130** (polar ops, 2 **-F**, 1 **-R**) in store • 4 **UC-35** (2 **-C** (tpt, both MCR), 2 **-D** (tpt, incl 1 MC) • 61 **UC-12** (37 **-B** (tpt, incl 6 NR, 10 MC of which 3 MCR) plus 4 in store, 10 **-F** (tpt, 6 NR, 4 MCR), 10 **-M** (tpt, all 10 NR), 4 **RC-12** (mod UC-12 tpt, 2 **-F**, 2 **-M**) • 36 **C-2A** (tpt) plus 1 in store • 17 **C-9B** (tpt, incl 15 NR, 2 MC) • 9 **DC-9** (tpt, all 9 NR) plus 1 in store • 4 **C12-C** (tpt) • 7 **C-20** (tpt, 2 **-D**, 5 **-G** (incl 1 MC)) • 7 **C-26D** (tpt) • 4 **C-40A** (tpt) • 1 **CT-39** (VIP tpt (1 **-G**)) • 36 **F-5** (32 **-E** (trg, incl 12 MCR) plus 20 in store, 4 **-F** (trg, incl 1 MCR) • 7 **TA-4J** (trg) plus 12 in store • 96 **T-2C** (trg) plus 13 in store • 26 **T-39** (1 **-D** (trg), 8 **-G** (trg), 17 **-N** (trg)) • 55 **T-44A** (trg) • 137 **T-45** (74 **-A** (trg), 63 **-C** (trg)) • 306 **T-34C** (305 **T-34C** (trg, incl 2 MC) plus 5 in store, 1 **NT-34C** (trials)) • 9 **T-38A** (trg) • 21 **TC-12B** (trg) • 2 **U-6A** (utl) • 1 **NU-1B** (trials) • 2 **X-26A** (test) • 1 **X-31A** (test) • 23 **QF-4** (3 **-N** (drone), 20 **-S** (drone))

HELICOPTERS

195 **AH-1** (193 **-W** (atk incl 145 MC, of which 40 MCR), 2 **-Z**) plus 2 **-Z** in store • 235 **SH-60** (157 **-B** (ASW, incl 5 NR and 2 **N-SH-60B** trials), 74 **-F** (ASW, incl 6 NR), 1 **YSH-60F** (prototype), 13 **-R**) plus 1 **-B** and 1 **-F** in store • 0 **SH-2G** (ASW/ASUW) plus 14 in store • 52 **UH-3H** (ASW/SAR incl 9 NR) plus 1 in store • 1 **SH-3H** (ASW) plus 15 in store • 39 **HH-60H** (cbt spt, incl 16 NR) • 33 **MH-60** (4 **-R** (aslt/utl), 29 **-S** (aslt/utl)) plus 1 **-S** in store • 40 **MH-53E** (MCM, incl 7 NR) plus 3 in store • 98 **UH-1** (96 **-N** (utl, incl 94 MC of which 20 MCR), 2 **-Y** (utl)) plus 1 **-Y** in store • 40 **HH-46D** (utl inc 5 MC) • 11 **UH-46D** (utl) • 3 **UH-60** (3 **UH60l** (utl) plus 1 **UH-60A** in store) • 24 **HH-1N** (SAR, incl 6 MC) plus 5 in store • 191 **CH-53** (40 **-D** (tpt, all 40 MC), 151 **-E** (tpt, 150 MC of which 21 MCR)) plus 9 **-D** and 10 **-E** in store • 252 **CH-46** (24 **-D** (tpt), 228 **-E** (tpt, all MC of which 24 MCR)) • 8 **VH-60N** (VIP tpt, all 8 MC) • 14 **VH-3** (3 **-A** (2 VIP tpt, 1 trials), 11 **-D** (VIP tpt, all 11 MC)) • 3 **OH-58C** (observer) • 118 **TH-57** (44 **-B** (trg), 74 **-C** (trg)) plus 9 **-C** in store • 6 **TH-6B** (test)

TILT ROTOR 7 V-22 (MC)

MISSILES

AAM AIM-120 AMRAAM, AIM-7 *Sparrow*, AIM-54A/C *Phoenix*, AIM-9 *Sidewinder*

ASM AGM-45 *Shrike*, AGM-88A HARM; AGM-84 *Harpoon*, AGM-119 *Penguin* Mk-3, AGM-114 *Hellfire*

Marine Corps (USMC) 173,400

(incl 10,500 women)

GROUND

ORGANISATION

3 Marine Expeditionary Forces (MEF); 2 Marine Expeditionary Brigade (MEB) drawn from:

3 div
- 1 with 3 inf regt (9 bn), 1 tk, 2 lt armd recce (LAV-25), 1 aslt amph, 1 cbt engr bn, 1 arty regt (4 bn), 1 recce bn
- 1 with 3 inf regt (9 bn), 1 tk, 1 lt armd recce (LAV-25), 1 aslt amph, 1 cbt engr bn, 1 arty regt (4 bn), 1 recce bn
- 1 with 2 inf regt (6 bn), 1 cbt spt bn (1 AAV, 1 LAR coy), 1 arty regt (2 bn), 1 cbt engr bn, 1 recce bn

3 Force Service Spt Gp

1 MEB (anti-terrorism) incl
- 1 bn Marine Corps Security Force (Atlantic and Pacific)
- Marine Security Guard bn (1 HQ, 7 region coy)
- 1 Chemical and Biological Incident Response Force
- 1 anti-terrorism bn

Special Ops Forces incl 3 recce bn, 3 Force recce coy

RESERVES (MCR)

1 div (3 inf (9 bn), 1 arty regt (5 bn); 1 lt armd recce (LAV-25), 1 aslt amph, 1 recce, 1 cbt engr bn)

1 Force Service Spt Gp

Special Ops Forces incl 1 recce bn, 2 Force recce coy

EQUIPMENT

MBT 403 M-1A1 *Abrams*

LAV 400 LAV-25 (**25mm** gun) plus 334 variants incl 50 Mor, 95 ATGW (see below)

AAV 1,321 AAV-7A1 (all roles)

TOWED ARTY 105mm: 331 M-101A1; **155mm**: 596 M-198

MOR 81mm: 586 M-252 (incl 50 LAV-M)

ATGW 1,083 TOW, 1,121 *Predator*, 95 LAV-TOW

RL 83mm: 1,650 SMAW; **84mm**: 1,300 AT-4

SURV 23 AN/TPQ-36 (arty)

AVIATION 35,650

(incl 1,980 women)

Flying hours 249 fixed wing (non-tpt), 365 fixed wing (tpt), 277 (hel)

3 active air wg and 1 MCR air wg

Flying hours cbt aircrew: 270

AIR WING no standard org, but a notional wg comprises

AC 118 FW: 48 **F/A-18A/C/D**, 48 **AV-8B**, 10 **EA-6B**, 12 **KC-130**

HEL 156: 10 **CH-53D**, 32 **CH-53E**, 36 **AH-1W**, 18 **UH-1N**, 60 **CH-46E**

plus 1 MC C^2 gp, 1 wg spt gp

ORGANISATION

Aircraft

FTR 18 sqn with 208 F/A-18A/C/D (incl 4 MCR sqn)

FGA 7 sqn with 100 AV-8B

ECM 4 sqn with 20 EA-6B

TKR 5 sqn with 69 KC-130F/R/T (incl 2 MCR sqn)

TRG 4 sqn

1 with 12 AV-8B, 14 TAV-8B; 1 with 40 F/A-18A/B/C/D, 2 T-34C; 1 with 2 F-5E (MCR); 1 with 8 KC-130F

Helicopters

ARMED 6 lt attack/utl with 159 AH-1W and 86 UH-1N (incl 2 MCR sqn)

TPT 15 **med** sqn with 210 CH-46E (incl 2 MCR sqn), 4 sqn with 38 CH-53D; 6 **hy** sqn with 135 CH-53E (incl 2 MCR sqn)

TRG 4 sqn

1 with 29 AH-1W, 12 UH-1N, 4 HH-1N; 1 with 20 CH-46; 1 with 6 CH-53D; 1 with 15 CH-53E, 6 MH-53E

SAM 3+ bn

2+ bn (5 bty), 1 MCR bn with *Stinger* and *Avenger*

UAV 2 sqn with *Pioneer*

Marine Corps Aviation Reserve 11,700

(640 women); 1 air wg

Aircraft

FTR/attack 4 sqn with 47 F-18A

1 *Aggressor* sqn with 2 F5-E/F

TKR 2 tkr/tpt sqn with 28 KC-130T

Helicopters

ARMED 2 attack/utl sqn with 37 AH-1W, 20 UH-1N

TPT 4 sqn: 2 **med** with 25 CH-46E, 2 **hy** with 16 CH-53E

SAM 1 bn (2 bty) with *Stinger* and *Avenger*

EQUIPMENT

(incl MCR): 450 cbt ac; 279 armed hel

Totals included in the Navy inventory

Aircraft

266 **F/A-18** (81 **-A** (FGA, incl 49 MCR), 4 **-B** (FGA), 86 **-C** (FGA), 95 **-D** (FGA)) • 141 **AV-8B** (127 **AV-8B** (FGA), 14 **TAV-8B** (trg)) • 30 **EA-6B** (ELINT) • 75 **KC-130** (32 **-F** (tpt), 2 **-J** (tpt), 13 **-R** (tpt), 28 **-I** (tpt, all 28 MCR)) • 3 **UC-35** (2**-C** (tpt, all 2 MCR), 1 **-D** (tpt)) • 2 **C-9B** (tpt) • 1 **C-20** (1 **-G** (tpt)) • 14 **UC-12** (10 **-B** (tpt, incl 3 MCR), 4 **-F** (tpt)) • 2 **T-34C** (trg) • 13 **F-5** (12 **-E** (trg, all MCR), 1 **-F** (trg))

Helicopters

188 **AH-1** (185 **-W** (atk, incl 40 MCR)) • 94 **UH-1** (94 **-N** (utl, incl 20 MCR)) • 5 **HH-46D** (utl) • 6 **HH-1N** (SAR) • 190 **CH-53** (40 **-D** (tpt), 150 **-E** (tpt, incl 21 MCR)) • 228 **CH-46** (228 **-E** (tpt, incl 24 MCR)) • 8 **VH-60N** (VIP tpt) • 11 **VH-3** (11 **-D** (VIP tpt)) • 7 **MV-22B** (tilt rotor)

MISSILES

SAM 1,929 *Stinger*, 235 *Avenger*

AAM *Sparrow* AMRAAM, *Sidewinder*

ASM *Maverick*, *Hellfire*, TOW

Coast Guard (active duty)

34,480 military, 5,840 civilian

(incl 3,590 women)

By law a branch of the Armed Forces; in peacetime ops under, and is funded by, the Department of Transport

Bdgt Authority

Year	1995	1996	1997	1998	1999	2000	2001	2002
US$bn	3.7	3.7	3.8	3.9	4.6	4.8	5.1	5.7
								expected request

PATROL VESSELS 137

OFFSHORE 42

12 *Hamilton* high-endurance with HH-60J LAMPS/HU-65A *Dolphin* hel, all with 76mm gun

13 *Bear* med-endurance with HH-65A hel

14 *Reliance* med-endurance with 25mm gun, hel deck

1 *Alex Haley* med-endurance

2 *Mature* med-endurance

plus 19 sea-going buoy tenders

COASTAL 95

49 *Farallon*, 46 *Baracuda*, plus 15 coastal buoy tenders

INLAND, tenders only

13 inland construction tenders, 5 small inland buoy tenders, 18 small river buoy tenders, 1 inland icebreaker

SUPPORT AND MISCELLANEOUS 24

2 polar icebreakers, 9 icebreaking tugs, 2 trg, 11 tugs

AVIATION (3,730 incl 120 women)

AIRCRAFT 17 HU-25 (plus 22 supt or in store), 23 HC-130H (plus 4 spt)

HELICOPTER 83 HH-65A (plus 12 spt), 23 HH-60J (plus 7 spt), 8 MH-68

RESERVES 7,960 incl 1,150 women

Air Force (USAF) 369,700

(incl 56,400 women) **Flying hours** ftr 205, bbr 186, tkr 218, airlift 288
Air Combat Comd (ACC) 4 air forces, 23 ac wg **Air Mobility Comd** (AMC) 2 air forces, 12 ac wg
Almost the entire USAF – active force, reserve force and ANG – is divided into 10 Aerospace Expeditionary Forces (AEFs). Each AEF is on call for 90 days every 15 months, and at least 2 of the 10 AEFs is on call at any one time. Each AEF, with 10,000–15,000 personnel, comprises approx 90 multi-role ftr and bbr ac, 31 intra-theatre refuelling ac and 13 ac for intelligence, surv, recce and EW missions.

TACTICAL 55 active ftr sqn (18–24 ac/sqn) in ACC, USAFE and PACAF
8 (2 ANG) with 93 B-1B
11 with F-15, 6 with F-15E, 21 with F-16C/D, 6 with A-10/OA-10, 2 with F-117, 1 *Aggressor* with F-16C/D

SUPPORT
RECCE 3 sqn with U-2R and RC-135, 1 sqn with E-8 JSTARS
AEW 1 Airborne Warning and Control wg, 6 sqn with E-3B/C
EW 2 sqn with EC-130
FAC 7 tac air control sqn, mixed A-10A/OA-10A
TRG 46 sqn
25 fg trg (T-1, T-6, T-37, T-38)
21 mission trg (C-5, C-17, C-130, E-3, F-15, F-16, KC-135, HH-60)
TPT 29 sqn
12 strategic: 4 with C-5, 1 with C-141, 7 with C-17
9 tac airlift with C-130
8 op sup units with C-9, C-12, C-20, C-21, C-37, C-40, VC-125, UH-1
TKR 22 sqn
18 with KC-135, 4 with KC-10A
SAR 6 sqn with HH-60 and HC-130N/P
MEDICAL 3 medical evacuation sqn with C-9A
WEATHER RECCE WC-135
TRIALS weapons trg units with **ac** A-10, B-1, B-52, C-12, C-17, C-135, F-15, F-16, F-117, F-22, HH-60, KC-135, T-38, AT-38
UAV 3 sqn with *Predator*, *Global Hawk* (in test)

RESERVES
AIR NATIONAL GUARD (ANG) 108,400
(incl 19,182 women)
BBR 2 sqn with B-1B
FTR 4 AD sqn (3 F-15, 1 F-16)
FGA 33 sqn
6 with A-10/ OA-10
24 with F-16
3 with F-15A/B
TPT 26 sqn
23 tac with C-130E/H/J
3 strategic: 1 with C-5, 2 with C-141B
TKR 23 sqn with KC-135E/R (11 with KC-135E, 12 with KC-135R)
SPECIAL OPS 1 sqn with EC-130E
SAR 3 sqn with **ac** H/MC-130 **hel** HH-60
TRG 7 sqn with F-15, F-16, C-130
AIR FORCE RESERVE (AFR) 74,700
(incl 16,984 women)
BBR 1 sqn with B-52H
FGA 5 sqn
3 with F-16C/D, 2 with A-10/OA-10
TPT 19 sqn
7 strategic: 2 with C-5A, 5 with C-141B
11 tac with C-130E/H/J
1 weather recce with WC-130H/J
TKR 7 sqn with KC-135E/R (5 KC-135R, 2 KC-135E)
SAR 2 sqn with HH-60, HC-130; 1 sqn with HH-60 only
SPECIAL OPS 2 sqn with MC-130E
TRG 3 sqn with A-10, F-16, C-141
ASSOCIATE 25 sqn (personnel only)
4 for C-5, 1 for C-141, 1 aero-medical for C-9, 6 C-17, 4 for KC-10, 1 for KC-135, 1 for *Aggressor* (F-16), 1 for F-16 trg, 6 for T-37, T-38, T-1 trg

AIRCRAFT
LONG-RANGE STRIKE/ATTACK 208 cbt ac: 94 **B-52H** (92 in service, 2 test) • 93 **B-1B** (33 in store, 2 test) • 21 **B-2A** (20 in service, 1 test)
RECCE 32 **U-2S** (31 in service, 1 on lease) • 4 **TU-2 R/S** • 15 **E-8C** (JSTARS) • 2 **E-9A** • 3 **RC-135S** (*Cobra Balls*), 2 **RC-135U** (*Combat Sent*), 16 **RC-135V/W** (*Rivet Joint*) • 162 **RF-4C** in store
COMD 33 **E-3B/C** (32 in service, 1 test) • 4 **E-4B** • 26 **EC-135**
TAC 2,928 cbt ac (incl ANG, AFR); no armed hel: 248 **F-4 D/E/G** in store • 736 **F-15** (520 **-A/B/C/D** (ftr, incl 110 ANG, 11 test, 19 in store)), 216 **-E** (FGA, 4 test) • 1,769 **F-16** (415 **-A** (incl 73 ANG, 3 test, 339 in store), 83 **-B** (incl 27 ANG, 15 test, 41 in store), 1,091 **-C** (incl 425 ANG, 64 AFR, 12 test), 180 **-D** (incl 45 ANG, 12 AFR, 8 test) • 16 **F-22A** (9 test, 2 **YF-22A** in store) • 217 **F-111**/33 **EF-111A** (in store) • 51 **F-117** (1 test) • 226 **A-10A** (incl 72 ANG, 39 AFR), 2 test, 134 in store • 109* **OA-10A** (FAC incl 18 ANG, 8 AFR) • 5 **EC-18B/D** Advanced Range Instrumentation (3 in store) • 21* **AC-130H/U** (special ops, USAF) • 34 **HC-130N/P** (incl 9 ANG plus 12 AFR) • 29 **EC-130E/H** (special ops incl 8 ANG SOF, 1 test) • 66 **MC-130E/H/P** (special ops incl 41 SOF (4-Ps ANG, 14-Es AFR)) • 18 **WC-130H/J** weather recce, (10 AFR) 8 in store • 3 **WC-135C/W** (1 in store) • 3 **OC-135** ('Open Skies' Treaty) • 1 **EC-137D** (in store)
TPT 126 **C-5** (74 **-A** (strategic tpt, incl 14 ANG, 32

AFR), 50 **-B**, 2 **-C**) • 23 **C-9A/C** • 23 **C-12C/-D/-F/-J** (8 in store) • 87 **C-17A** • 13 **C-20** (5 **-B**, 3 **-C**, 2 **-H**, 3 in store) • 78 **C-21A** (2 ANG) • 3 **C-22B** (1 ANG, 2 in store) • 2 **VC-25A** • 11 **C-26B** (ANG) • 5 **C-27** in store • 4 **C-32A** • 9 **C-37A** • 2 **C-38A** (ANG) • 539 **C-130B/E/H/J** (incl 226 ANG, 114 AFR), 15 in store • 4 **C-135B/C/E** • 2 **C-137C** in store • 116 **C-141B/C** (incl 18 ANG, 50 AFR, 49 in store)

TKR 600 **KC-135A/E/R/T** (incl 216 ANG, 76 AFR, 55 in store) • 59 **KC-10A** tkr/tpt

TRG 180 **T-1A** • 112 **T-3A** in store • 79 **T-6A** • 1 **TE-8A** • 2 **TC-18E** • 3 **UV-18B** • 507 **T-37B** (152 in store) • 559 **T-38A/C** (134 in store) • 103 **AT-38B** (78 in store) • 110 **T-41** (104 in store) • 6 **T-43A** (2 in store)• 6 **CT-43A** in store • 2 **TC-135S/W**

HELICOPTERS

43 **MH-53M/J** *Pave Low* (26 special ops, 7 in store) • 11 **HH-1H** in store • 105 **HH-60G** (18 ANG, 23 AFR, 3 test) • 62 **UH-1N** • 6 **TH-53A**

UAV

High Level – 6 **RQ-4A** *Global Hawk*
Tactical – 10 **RQ-1A/B** *Predator* (1 test)

MISSILES

AAM 7,000+ AIM-9M *Sidewinder*, 4,000+ AIM-7M *Sparrow*, 5,000+ AIM-120 A/B/C AMRAAM

ASM 18,000+ AGM-65A/B/D/G *Maverick*, 7,500+ AGM-88A/B HARM, 70+ AGM-84B *Harpoon*, 978 AGM-86B ALCM, 817 AGM-86C ALCM, 406 AGM-129A, 350+ AGM-130A, 150+ AGM-142, 180+ AGM-154 *JSOW*

CIVIL RESERVE AIR FLEET (CRAF) 683

commercial ac (numbers fluctuate)

LONG-RANGE 666

passenger 460 (A-310, B-747, B -757, B-767, DC-10, L-1011, MD-11)

cargo 206 (B-747, DC-8, DC-10, L-1011, MD-11)

SHORT-RANGE 99

passenger 89 (A-300, B-727, B-737, MD-80/83)

cargo 10 (L-100, B-727, DC-9)

DOMESTIC AND AERO-MEDICAL 71

Special Operations Forces (SOF)

Units only listed

ARMY (15,300)

5 SF gp (each 3 bn) • 1 Ranger inf regt (3 bn) • 1 special ops avn regt (3 bn) • 1 Psychological Ops gp (5 bn) • 1 Civil Affairs bn (5 coy) • 1 sigs, 1 spt bn

RESERVES

2 ARNG SF gp (3 bn) • 12 AR Civil Affairs HQ (4 comd, 8 bde) • 2 AR Psychological Ops gp • 36 AR Civil Affairs 'bn' (coy)

NAVY (4,000)

1 Naval Special Warfare Comd • 1 Naval Special Warfare Centre • 3 Naval Special Warfare gp • 2 Naval Special Warfare sqn • 8 SEAL teams • 2 SEAL delivery veh teams • 2 Special Boat sqn • 6 DDS

RESERVES (1,400)

1 Naval Special Warfare Comd det • 6 Naval Special Warfare gp det • 3 Naval Special Warfare unit det • 5 SEAL team det • 2 Special Boat unit • 2 Special Boat sqn • 1 SEAL delivery veh det • 1 CINCSOC det

AIR FORCE (9,320)

1 air force HQ, 1 wg
13 sqn with 13 AC-130U, 21 MC-130H, 20 MC-130P, 33 MH-53J/M, 5 C-130E

RESERVES (AFRC 1,260, ANG 1,040)

2 sqn: 14 MC-130E

ANG

1 sqn: 5 EC-130E, 3 EC-130J

Deployment

Commanders' NATO appointments also shown (e.g., COMEUCOM is also SACEUR)

EUROPEAN COMMAND (EUCOM)

some 98,000. Plus 14,000 Mediterranean 6th Fleet: HQ Stuttgart-Vaihingen (Commander is SACEUR)

ARMY (61,000) HQ US Army Europe (USAREUR), Heidelberg

NAVY HQ US Navy Europe (USNAVEUR), London (Commander is also CINCAFSOUTH)

AIR FORCE (30,100) HQ US Air Force Europe (USAFE), Ramstein (Commander is COMAIRCENT)

USMC 950

GERMANY

ARMY 56,000

V Corps with 1 armd(-), 1 mech inf div(-), 1 arty, 1 AD (2 *Patriot* (10 bty), 1 *Avenger* bn), 1 engr, 1 avn bde

Army Prepositioned Stocks (APS) for 2 armd/mech bde, approx 57% stored in Ge

EQPT (incl APS in Ge, Be, Lux and Nl)

some 541 MBT, 760 AIFV, 852 APC, 508 arty/MRL/mor, 134 ATK hel

AIR FORCE 12,400, 60 cbt ac

1 air force HQ: USAFE

1 ftr wg: 3 sqn (2 with 42 F-16C/D, 1 with 12 A-10 and 6 OA-10)

1 airlift wg: incl 16 C-130E and 6 C-9A, 9 C-21, 2 C-20, 1 CT-43

NAVY 300

USMC 250

BELGIUM

ARMY 890; approx 22% of POMCUS

NAVY 100

AIR FORCE 300

GREECE

NAVY 240; base facilities at Soudha Bay, Makri
AIR FORCE 50; air base gp. Facilities at Iraklion

ITALY

ARMY 2,600; HQ: Vicenza. 1 AB Task Force (Bde)
EQPT for Theater Reserve Unit/Army Readiness Package South (TRU/ARPS), incl 116 MBT, 127 AIFV, 4 APC
NAVY 4,400; HQ: Gaeta; bases at Naples, La Maddalena, 1 MR sqn with 9 P-3C at Sigonella
AIR FORCE 3,620; 1 AF HQ (16th Air Force), 1 ftr wg, 2 sqn with 42 F-16C/D
USMC 170

LUXEMBOURG

ARMY approx 21% of APS

MEDITERRANEAN

NAVY some 14,000 (incl 2,100 Marines). **6th Fleet** (HQ: Gaeta, It): typically 3 SSN, 1 CVBG (1 CV, 6 surface combatants, 1 fast spt ship), 2 LHD/LPD, 2 AO, 1 AE, 1 AF, 1 AT/F. MPS-1 (4 ships with eqpt for 1 MEF (fwd)). Marine personnel: some 2,000. MEU (SOC) embarked aboard Amph Ready Group ships

NETHERLANDS

ARMY 380; approx 7% of APS
AIR FORCE 160
NAVY 10

NORWAY

ARMY 13: APS incl 18 M-109, 18 M-198 arty, no aviation assets
AIR FORCE 30
NAVY 10

PORTUGAL

(for Azores, see Atlantic Command)
NAVY 50

SPAIN

NAVY 1,760; base at Rota
AIR FORCE 360
USMC 70

TURKEY

NAVY 20, spt facilities at Izmir and Ankara
AIR FORCE 3,800; facilities at Incirlik. 1 wg (ac on det only), numbers vary (incl F-15E, F-16, EA-6B, KC-135, E-3B/C, C-12, HC-130, HH-60)
USMC 40

UNITED KINGDOM

ARMY 440
NAVY 1,220; HQ: London, admin and spt facilities
1 SEAL det
AIR FORCE 7,600
1 air force HQ (3rd Air Force): 1 ftr wg, 72 cbt ac, 2 sqn with 48 F-15E, 1 sqn with 24 F-15C/D
1 special ops gp, 1 air refuelling wg with 15 KC-135
USMC 140

PACIFIC COMMAND (USPACOM)

HQ: Hawaii

ALASKA

ARMY 6,400; 1 lt inf bde
AIR FORCE 8,000; 1 air force HQ (11th Air Force): 1 ftr wg with 2 sqn (1 with 18 F-16, 1 with 12 A-10, 6 OA-10), 1 wg with 2 sqn with 42 F-15C/D, 1 sqn with 18 F-15E, 1 sqn with 16 C-130H, 4 E-3B, 3 C-12, 1 air tkr wg with 8 KC-135R, 1 ANG rescue wg with 5 HH-60, 3 HC-130

HAWAII

ARMY 15,700; HQ: US Army Pacific (USARPAC): 1 lt inf div (2 lt inf bde)
AIR FORCE 3,550; HQ: Pacific Air Forces (PACAF): 1 wg (ANG) with 15 F-15A/B, 4 C-130H and 8 KC-135R
NAVY 7,500; HQ: US Pacific Fleet
Homeport for some 22 SSN, 3 CG, 4 DDG, 2 FFG, 4 spt and misc ships
USMC 5,760; HQ: Marine Forces Pacific

SINGAPORE

NAVY 90; log facilities
AIR FORCE 34 det spt sqn

JAPAN

ARMY 1,900; 1 corps HQ, base and spt units
AIR FORCE 11,350; 1 air force HQ (5th Air Force) 1 ftr wg, 2 sqn with 36 F-16, 1 wg, 2 sqn with 48 F-15C/D, 1 sqn with 15 KC-135, 1 SAR sqn with 8 HH-60, 1 sqn with 2 E-3 AWACS, 1 Airlift Wg with 10 C-130 E, 4 C-21, 4 C-9, 1 special ops gp
NAVY 5,200; bases: **Yokosuka** (HQ 7th Fleet) homeport for 1 CV, 9 surface combatants, 1 LCC **Sasebo** homeport for 4 amph ships, 1 MCM sqn
USMC 20,000; elm 1 MEF (-) with 1 mne div (-)

SOUTH KOREA

ARMY 29,100; 1 Army HQ (UN comd), 1 inf div (mech) with 2 bde (2 mech inf, 2 air aslt, 2 tk bn), 2 SP arty, 2 MLRS, 1 AD bn, 1 avn, 1 engr bde, 1 air cav bde (2 ATK hel bn), 1 *Patriot* SAM bn (Army tps)
EQPT incl 116 MBT, 126 AIFV, 111 APC, 45 arty/MRL/mor
AIR FORCE 7,600; 1 air force HQ (7th Air Force): 2 ftr wg, 84 cbt ac; 3 sqn with 60 F-16, 1 sqn with 12 A-10, 12 OA-10, 1 special ops sqn
NAVY 300 **USMC** 140

GUAM

ARMY 30
AIR FORCE 1,580; 1 air force HQ (13th Air Force)
NAVY 1,850; MPS-3 (4 ships with eqpt for 1 MEB)
Naval air station, comms and spt facilities

AUSTRALIA

AIR FORCE 70
NAVY some 40; comms facility at NW Cape, SEWS/SIGINT station at Pine Gap, and SEWS station at Nurrungar

DIEGO GARCIA

NAVY 650; MPS-2 (5 ships with eqpt for 1 MEB) Naval air station, spt facilities

AIR FORCE 18

THAILAND

ARMY 40 **NAVY** 10 **AIR FORCE** 30 **USMC** 28

US WEST COAST

MARINES 1 MEF formed with 1 mne div (-)

AT SEA

PACIFIC FLEET 140,400 USN, 13,470 reserve, 29,600 civilians (HQ: Pearl Harbor (HI)) **Main base**: Pearl Harbor **Other bases**: Bangor, Everett, Bremerton (WA), San Diego (CA)

Submarines 8 SSBN, 27 SSN

Surface Combatants 6 CV/CVN, 13 CG, 24 DDG, 15 FFG, 2 LCC

Amph 1 comd, 6 ARG - 3 LHA, 3 LHD, 8 LSD, 1 LST, 6 LPD plus 1 AG, 62 MSC ships

Other 2 MCM, 8 auxiliary ships

Naval Aviation 1400 Ac

Surface Forces divided between two fleets

3rd Fleet (HQ: San Diego) covers Eastern and Central Pacific, Aleutian Islands, Bering Sea; typically 3 CVBG, 4 URG, amph gp

7th Fleet (HQ: Yokosuka) covers Western Pacific, J, Pi, ANZUS responsibilities, Indian Ocean; typically 1 CVBG (1 CV, 6-9 surface combatants), 2 LHD/LPD, 2 LSD/LST, 1 LCC, 4 AO, 2 MCM; 363 tac ac, 77 P-3, 162 other ac, 200 hel

CENTRAL COMMAND (USCENTCOM)

commands all deployed forces in its region; HQ: MacDill AFB, FL

ARMY 1,100

AT SEA

5th Fleet HQ: Manama. Average US Naval Forces deployed in Indian Ocean, Persian Gulf, Red Sea; typically 1 CVBG (1 CV, 6 surface combatants), 3 amph ships, 4 MCM

BAHRAIN

NAVY/USMC/ARMY 4,200

KUWAIT

ARMY ε6,000 (incl those on short-term (6 months) duty); 1 bde HQ; prepo eqpt for 1 armd bde (2 tk, 1 mech bn, 1 arty bn)

NAVY 10

AIR FORCE 2,000 (force structure varies)

USMC 378

OMAN

AIR FORCE 200

NAVY 60

QATAR

ARMY/AIR FORCE ε3,300; prepo eqpt for 1 armd bde

SAUDI ARABIA

ARMY 300; 1 *Patriot* SAM, 1 sigs unit

AIR FORCE 4,050. Units on rotational detachment, **ac** numbers vary (incl F-15E, F-16, F-117, A-10, C-130, KC-135, U-2, E-3)

NAVY 20

USMC 38

UAE

AIR FORCE 390

TRAINING ADVISORS

NIGERIA 12

SOUTHERN COMMAND (USSOUTHCOM)

HQ: Miami, FL

ARMY 800; HQ: US Army South, Fort Buchanan, PR: 1 inf bn, plus avn, engr units

USMC 100

COLOMBIA

ARMY 15

HONDURAS

ARMY 170 **USMC** 46 **AIR FORCE** 140

NORTHERN COMMAND (USNORTHCOM)

HQ: Peterson AFB, CO (CINC has op control of all CONUS-based army and air forces)

US EAST COAST

USMC 19,140; 1 MEF formed with 1 mne div (-)

BERMUDA

NAVY 800

CUBA

ARMY 900 plus Joint Task Force - ε170

NAVY 590 (Guantánamo)

USMC 486 (Guantánamo)

AIR FORCE 63

ICELAND

NAVY 960; 1 MR sqn with 6 P-3, 1 UP-3

USMC 48

AIR FORCE 470; 4 F-15C/D, 1 KC-135, 1 HC-130, 4 HH-60G

PORTUGAL (AZORES)

NAVY 10; limited facilities at Lajes

AIR FORCE 720 periodic SAR detachments to spt space shuttle ops

UNITED KINGDOM

NAVY 1,220; comms and intelligence facilities at Edzell, Thurso

AT SEA

ATLANTIC FLEET (HQ: Norfolk, VA) 108,000 USN, 17,000 civilians **Main base** Norfolk **Other main bases** Groton (CT), King's Bay (GA), Mayport (FL)

Submarines 10 SSBN, 28 SSN

Surface Combatants 6 CV/CVN, 14 CG, 21 DDG, 20 FFG

Amph 1 LCC, 2 LHA, 4 LPH, 6 LPD, 5 LSD, 6 LST, 1 LKA
Surface Forces divided into 2 fleets:
2nd Fleet (HQ: Norfolk) covers Atlantic; typically 4–5 CVBG, amph gp, 4 URG
6th Fleet (HQ: Gaeta, Italy) under op comd of EUCOM, typically 1 CVBG, 1 amph gp

Continental United States (CONUS)

major units/formations only listed

ARMY (USACOM) 328,000

provides general reserve of cbt-ready ground forces for other comd
Active 2 Army HQ, 3 Corps HQ (1 AB), 1 armd, 2 mech, 1 lt inf, 1 AB, 1 air aslt div; 6 arty bde; 2 armd cav regt, 6 AD bn (1 *Avenger*, 5 *Patriot*)
Reserve (ARNG): 3 armd, 2 mech, 2 med, 1 lt inf div; 18 indep bde
NAVY 186,200
AIR FORCE 276,200
USMC 141,300; 2 MEF formed with 2 mne div

US STRATEGIC COMMAND (USSTRATCOM)

HQ: Offutt AFB, NE. See entry on page 16

AIR COMBAT COMMAND (ACC)

HQ: Langley AFB, VA. Provides strategic AD units and cbt-ready Air Force units for rapid deployment

AIR FORCE SPACE COMMAND (AFSPC)

HQ: Peterson AFB, CO. Provides ballistic-msl warning, space control, worldwide sat ops, and maintains ICBM force

US JOINT FORCES COMMAND (USJFCOM)

HQ: Norfolk, VA. Responsible for military training and exercises and provision of joint forces for combatant commanders

US SPECIAL OPERATIONS COMMAND (USSOCOM)

HQ: MacDill AFB, FL. Comd all active, reserve and National Guard special ops forces of all services based in CONUS. See page 23

US TRANSPORTATION COMMAND (USTRANSCOM)

HQ: Scott AFB, IL. Provides all common-user airlift, sealift and land tpt to deploy and maintain US forces on a global basis

AIR MOBILITY COMMAND (AMC)

HQ: Scott AFB, IL. Provides strategic, tac and special op airlift, aero-medical evacuation, SAR and weather recce

Forces Abroad

AFGHANISTAN (OP ENDURING FREEDOM): ε7,500

UN AND PEACEKEEPING

BOSNIA (SFOR II): ε2,000; 1 div HQ, 1 inf bde plus spt tps **EAST TIMOR** (UNMISET): 3 obs **EGYPT** (MFO): 865; 1 inf, 1 spt bn **ETHIOPIA/ERITREA** (UNMEE): 6 obs **FYROM** (KFOR): 260 **GEORGIA** (UNOMIG): 2 obs **HUNGARY** (SFOR) 350; 230 Air Force *Predator* UAV **IRAQ/KUWAIT** (UNIKOM): 11 obs **KYRGYZSTAN**: some, to be 4,000 **MIDDLE EAST** (UNTSO): 2 obs **WESTERN SAHARA** (MINURSO): 7 obs **SAUDI ARABIA** (*Southern Watch*) **Air Force** units on rotation, numbers vary (incl F-15, F-16, F-117, C-130, KC-135, E-3) **TAJIKISTAN**: ε50 **TURKEY** (*Northern Watch*) **Air Force** 1,400; 1 tac, 1 Air Base gp (ac on det only), numbers vary but include F-16, F-15, EA-6B, KC-135, E3B/C, C-12, HC-130 **UZBEKISTAN**: ε1,200 **YUGOSLAVIA** (KFOR): 5,100

Paramilitary

CIVIL AIR PATROL (CAP) 53,000

(incl 25,000 cadets); HQ, 8 geographical regions, 52 wg, 1,700 units, 535 CAP ac, plus 4,700 private ac

NATO and Non-NATO Europe

REGIONAL TRENDS

On 12 September 2001, one day after the terrorist attacks on New York and Washington, the North Atlantic Council assured the US that its 'NATO Allies stand ready to provide the assistance that may be required as a consequence of these acts', and invoked the mutual assistance clause (Article 5) of the 1949 North Atlantic (Washington) Treaty. However, such pledges served to highlight NATO's inability to conduct operations against asymmetric threats, and generated increased scrutiny of the growing gap in the US and European commitment to defence spending. Within NATO, the creation of the NATO–Russia Council on 28 May 2002 has to some extent muted Russian arguments against the alliance's expansion into eastern Europe. Meanwhile, the Prague Summit in November 2002 will decide the next round of membership.

European anti-terrorist activity is now focusing on the al-Qaeda network, which is assessed as posing the greatest terrorist threat to Europe. Thus there has been a shift of attention away from the more traditional terrorist groupings. The Basque Euskadi ta Askatasuna (ETA) group remains very active, while in Greece, the 17 November group – active since 1975 – has largely been dismantled by the Greek authorities. Meanwhile, in the UK, the Provisional Irish Republican Army (IRA), the largest and most well-armed Irish republican terrorist group, has by and large adhered to the 1998 ceasefire, despite continuing sectarian violence in Northern Ireland.

NATO

New challenges

The inability of NATO to play more than a peripheral role in the anti-terror campaign soon became a source of debate both inside and outside the organisation. NATO's most direct action was *Operation Eagle Assist*, a seven-month deployment of European NATO airborne early-warning assets to the US, in order to free up US aircraft to directly support anti-terrorist operations, along with the deployment of NATO's Standing Naval Force Mediterranean to the eastern Mediterranean. Also, an indirect benefit to operations inside Afghanistan (both the coalition *Operation Enduring Freedom* and the International Security Assistance Force) was the high level of interoperability amongst national contingents, which stemmed directly from their training within NATO.

Lord Robertson, NATO's Secretary-General, recognised the organisation's inability to play a larger role and was quick to urge change. In particular, he highlighted the excessive number of objectives within the Defence Capabilities Initiative, and proposed that the list should be reduced. With this in mind, NATO defence ministers agreed on 6 June 2002 to focus on a 'small number of capabilities essential to the full range of Alliance missions'. The capabilities are designed to contribute to NATO's ability to:

- defend against chemical, biological, radiological and nuclear attacks;
- ensure secure command, communications and information superiority;
- improve interoperability of deployed forces and key aspects of combat effectiveness; and
- ensure rapid deployment and sustainment of combat forces.

Recommendations for the initiative are due for submission at the Prague Summit, although a progress report is due in at NATO's Council in Permanent Session in Warsaw in September.

High readiness

NATO had already started to address the last item on the above list, by improving the readiness state of some of its existing force structures. Here, NATO takes the term 'high readiness' to mean the ability to deploy corps main elements within a month. In March 2002, the Allied Rapid Reaction Corps (ARRC) was certified as a High Readiness Force (Land) Headquarters (HRF(L)HQ). Five other HRF(L)HQs are to be certified by the end of 2002: Eurocorps; the 1st German/Netherlands Corps; the Italian Rapid Reaction Corps; the 3rd Turkish Corps; and one undesignated Spanish corps. Two lower readiness corps are to be certified in 2004–05. The Greek 'C' Corps and the Multinational Corps (Northeast) have been earmarked for this role.

Addressing asymmetric threats

The European members of NATO have been slow to follow the US lead in developing force structures and equipments to deal with asymmetric threats. In the short term, the UK is the only European nation to act on the requirement – identified through operations in Afghanistan – to develop a 'network-centric' capability and to reduce 'sensor-to-shooter' times. France and Greece have recognised this need, but have yet to act on it. In July 2002, the UK Ministry of Defence (MoD) published a 'New Chapter' to its 1998 Strategic Defence Review. In this document, prompted by the post 11-September realisation that asymmetric actions can have a strategic impact, the MoD identifies new threats and lays out strategies for countering them. This work includes the allocation of extra finance and an enhanced role for the UK Territorial Army. French President Jacques Chirac, in his 14 July Bastille Day speech, highlighted the need for France to follow the progress made by the UK.

On 11 October 2001, German Chancellor Gerhard Schröder declared that his country's post-war role as a supporting player was 'irrevocably over' and that he was willing to send troops abroad 'to participate in military operations in defence of freedom and human rights'. German troops had deployed to Kosovo in 1999, but Afghanistan was to prove Germany's first combat deployment outside Europe. Troops of the *Kommando Spezialkräfte*, or KSK – Germany's Special Forces unit – were involved in *Operation Enduring Freedom*, while Germany played a lead role in ISAF, providing a brigade headquarters, and heading an infantry battlegroup, among other contributions. Meanwhile, German naval units assumed command of a task force operating off the Horn of Africa in support of *Operation Enduring Freedom* in May 2002, though they are scheduled to relinquish this in late 2002.

In southern Europe, October 2001 saw the Greek government release a new national defence policy for the period to 2015. The new Strategic Defence Review concentrates on four main areas: the provision of smart weapons and new technologies; decreasing the conscript base and increasing the professional core of the armed forces; improving joint service interoperability; and preparations to confront new asymmetric threats. Under a new force structure plan, the Greek army will be reduced from thirteen to nine active divisions by 2015, plus one in reserve. The manning level for these divisions is scheduled to increase to over 70%.

Enlargement, and relations with Russia (see also page 87)

The accession to NATO of the latest round of potential member countries will be decided at the Prague Summit in November 2002. Among the nine aspirants, the three Baltic states – Estonia, Latvia and Lithuania – are expected to be the most likely to succeed in the short term. Moscow's objections to this move, which were linked to the large Russian populations in these states, their proximity to Russia's western border and the question of Kaliningrad (the Russian enclave on the Baltic coast between Poland and Lithuania that houses the Russian Baltic Fleet), have become muted.

In general, cooperation with Russia has improved in the period since 11 September, during which Moscow has not only tolerated the NATO debate on expansion into eastern Europe, but the deployment of Western forces into a number of former Soviet republics in Central Asia under the counter-terrorism banner. The NATO–Russia Permanent Joint Council – in existence since the 1997 Founding Act – held its last meeting, in Reykjavik, on 14 May 2002. This was replaced by the NATO–Russia Council (NRC), which formally came into existence on 28 May 2002 at NATO's Rome Summit. The NRC will focus on enhancing cooperation in the following key areas:

- counter terrorism and threat assessments;
- crisis management;

- non-proliferation;
- arms control and confidence-building measures;
- theatre missile defence;
- search and rescue;
- military-to-military cooperation; and
- civil emergencies.

The NRC allows for dialogue and decision-making on these specific topics, although decisions are to be taken by consensus, thus preserving NATO's prerogative to act independently.

Southeast Europe

The NATO-led military presence in the Balkans remains vital to continued peace and security, although this presence could be complicated if Bulgaria and Romania are admitted to NATO in November 2002. In the main, the region is undergoing a shift in the emphasis of military operations away from military peacekeeping towards supporting economic reconstruction and civilian policing. *Operation Essential Harvest*, designed to collect weapons from ethnic Albanian insurgents in Macedonia, bolstered the fragile, Western-brokered peace between the government and the insurgents in the autumn of 2001. The UK-led, brigade-size NATO force of some 3,000 troops, which deployed to conduct the agreed disarmament process, was originally tasked to collect 3,300 weapons. In the event, many more were gathered, including captured armour and air-defence equipment. The peace process and constitutional reform in Macedonia has been enhanced by *Task Force Fox*, a NATO mission of 700 troops charged with protecting monitors from the EU and Organisation for Security and Cooperation in Europe (OSCE).

Further north, the NATO-led Stabilisation Force (SFOR) and Kosovo Force (KFOR) deployments, in Bosnia–Herzegovina and Kosovo respectively, retain their critical importance to the success of the political reform and economic reconstruction processes. However, the post-11 September strategic environment has had an impact on Western military deployments to these two key operations. On 6 June 2002, NATO defence ministers decided a reduction in force levels, which by the end of 2002 will result in SFOR numbering 12,000 troops while KFOR will comprise some 32,000 troops. This reduction is a reflection both of the pressure on US military deployments from the needs of anti-terrorism campaign, along with the projected gradual assumption, by the EU, of leadership and responsibility for Western operations in the Balkans. Russian forces in KFOR and SFOR have reduced from 4,200 to 360 troops as part of the overall reduction.

European defence forces

Moves continue to expedite the nascent European defence capability, and there are signs of a shift towards solving some of the problems inherent in the creation of a European force of the type discussed in the 2001–2002 edition of *The Military Balance*. At the Capability Improvement Conference on 19–20 November 2001, it was clear that there are still a considerable number of capability gaps to be filled if an EU force is to be deployable by the end of 2003, despite the formal allocation of forces to meet the 'Headline Goal' of 60,000 troops and additional elements such as police units (to be deployed in less than 60 days, with the capability to sustain them for one year). Of the 55 major shortfalls which were identified, only five had been solved by the end of 2001. The European Capabilities Action Plan aims to address these. A table of possible country contributions to a future force is on page 30.

NON-NATO EUROPE

The Transdniestr issue

The separatist conflict in Transdniestr, ongoing for a decade, was discussed on 17 March 2002 by Russia's President Putin, Moldovan President Vladimir Voronin and Ukranian President Leonid Kuchma at a meeting in Odessa. In a positive statement at the meeting, President Voronin said that Moldova was ready

Table 1 Selected European Force Components Available for Crisis-Management Operations

see also Table 2

	Maritime	Ground (No. of personnel)	Air
A		1 mech inf bn for PKO only 1 lt inf bn 1 NBC unit (2,000)	1 tpt hel sqn
Be	2 frigates 6 MCMV 1 comd ship	I mech inf bde	1 sqn F-16 (24) 8 C-1302 airbus
SF		1 mech inf bn 1 tpt coy 1 Civil–Military Cooperation (CIMIC) coy (2,000)	
Fr	1 SSN 2 aircraft carriers (22 cbt ac each) 2 amph ships 4 frigates 3 spt ships	HQs and C4ISR 1 lt inf bde 1 armd div 1 AB div 1 amph div SF (12,000)	1 air-naval group 75 cbt ac 1 AWACS 8 tanker ac 3 tpt ac (long-range) 24 tpt ac (mid-range)
Ge	13 ships 1 amph tpt ship	HQ GE/NE Corps 18,000 (all elements) incl 7 cbt bns	6 sqns cbt ac 8 AD sqns
Gr	8 ships	1 op HQ 1 mech inf bde 1 lt inf bn	1 cbt hel unit 1 tpt hel unit 42 cbt ac 4 tpt ac 1 *Patriot* AD bn 1 SHORAD sqn
Irl		1 lt inf bn SF gp (850 total)	
It	1 maritime HQ 1 aircraft carrier (6 cbt ac, 8 hel) 1 destroyer 3 frigates 4 ptl ships 1 submarine 4 MCMV 2 amph ships	Op level HQ and C3I Corps level HQ 1 Civil–Military Cooperation gp SF (12,500–14,500)	26 Tornado and AMX cbt ac 6 CSAR hel 4 C-130J ac 2 tanker ac 3 MPA 2 SHORAD units
Lu		1 lt recce unit	1 A-400M
Nl	1 LPD AD and Comd frigates frigates – n.k.	HQ of 1 GE/NE Corps 1 mech inf bde 1 airmob bde 1 amph bn	1 air bde F-16 ac
Por	1 frigate 1 submarine 1 ptl boat 1 sp ship 1 svy ship	1 inf bde (4,000)	12 F-16 4 C-130 Hercules 12 C-212 tac tpt ac 3 MPA 4 Puma hel
Sp		1 div, 1 bde HQs 1 mech bde mtn units 1 lt inf gp SF	Air-navy unit 2 sqns F-1/F-18 cbt ac [24 in total] 1 tpt sqn
Swe	2 corvettes 1 sp ship	1 mec inf bn (900) 1 engr unit (175) 1 MP unit (160) 1 marine unit (206)	4 AJS 37 ac (to be 8 JAS 39 in 2004) 4 C-130
UK	1 aircraft carrier 2 SSN 4 destroyer/frigate 1 hel carrier	1 mobile Joint HQ 1 armd/mech bde 1 amph bde (12,500)	72 cbt ac 58 strat tpt ac and *Chinook*/*Merlin* hel

to grant separatists in Transdniestr 'the broadest possible autonomous status' – a statement opening the way to further talks.

Russian troops and military equipment have remained in Transdniestr since the collapse of the Soviet Union. In order to comply with obligations under the Final Act of the Agreement on Adaptation of the Conventional Forces Europe (CFE) Treaty, signed in Istanbul on 19 November 1999, Russian troops were to have been withdrawn from the region by the end of 2001. Although President Putin had earlier indicated that this withdrawal would indeed take place, it had not happened by August 2002. An additional issue concerns the removal or destruction of Russian ammunition stocks in Transdniestr, which the OSCE is tasked with facilitating. However, the separatist authorities in Tiraspol have thus far not allowed this ammunition to be transported out of the region.

Georgia (see also Russia, page 86)

In Georgia, the drawdown of Russian bases continues. The base at Vaziani was closed in 2001, and Akhalkalaki, in the Samtskhe-Javakheti region near the Armenian border, is being slowly closed. However, this is having a deleterious impact on the local economy, with a substantial proportion of the local ethnic Armenian population dependent on the base for employment. Meanwhile, the base at Batumi, in the autonomous region of Adjaria, remains open, and the Gudauta base, in the separatist region of Abkhazia, acts as an operational support base for the Russian peacekeeping contingent, which operates in the region under a CIS mandate. The Georgian government insists on an OSCE inspection of the Gudauta base, which the Russians reject. Russia says it will take 11 years for final withdrawal from the remaining bases – a position unacceptable to Georgia.

Meanwhile, following international concern over a possible al-Qaeda presence in the Pankisi Gorge in Georgia, which has been a refuge for Chechen terrorist groups, 150 US military instructors deployed to Tbilisi from May 2002 to train Georgian military units in counter-insurgency and anti-terrorism operations. By 2004, it is intended that Georgia should have 2,000 counter-insurgency troops trained and grouped in four battalions. There is also to be a National Military Command centre to coordinate operations of all types.

TERRORISM

Al-Qaeda

Several suspected al-Qaeda plots to commit terrorist operations in Western Europe, mainly against American and British assets, were uncovered and thwarted in 2000, 2001 and 2002. However, although Europe was a key recruitment, planning and staging base for the 11 September 2001 attacks on the World Trade Center and the Pentagon, the US appears to remain al-Qaeda's primary target. Nonetheless, Europe's sizable Muslim population, together with clear post-11 September evidence of heavy al-Qaeda infiltration in Europe – particularly in France, Germany and the United Kingdom – have made transnational Islamic terrorism Europe's paramount counter-terrorist concern.

Existing counter-terrorism regimes, designed to combat domestic terrorism in a number of European countries, have been re-oriented, through statutory and operational changes, to cope with al-Qaeda's transnational threat. Meanwhile, law-enforcement and intelligence cooperation between European governments and the US has been stepped up – mainly on a bilateral basis but also through the EU, NATO and G-8. Between 11 September 2001 and July 2002, suspected terrorist assets valued at $35 million were frozen, and European authorities arrested over 300 individuals with suspected links to al-Qaeda. The EU list of illegal terrorist organisations has expanded since 11 September, and as of July 2002 correlated closely with the US State Department's customarily longer list. An EU-wide arrest warrant to facilitate the transnational counter-terrorism effort is scheduled to come into full effect by 2004, although problems in implementation should be anticipated. At the same time, domestic terrorism in Western Europe has continued at roughly the same level as during 2000–01.

Northern Ireland

In Northern Ireland, the Provisional Irish Republican Army (IRA), the largest and most formidable anti-British Irish republican terrorist group, remains on cease-fire, and in October 2001 and April 2002, was certified by the Independent International Commission on Decommissioning (IICD) to have put small quantities of weapons 'beyond use' in an effort to further the faltering peace process. These weapons constitute a minuscule portion of the IRA's estimated 100-tonne arsenal. Low-level terrorism (in particular, the use of petrol bombs, blast bombs and pipe bombs) by anti-British republican groups and pro-British loyalist groups opposed to the peace process in Northern Ireland has increased. So has community sectarian violence, which is often provoked by paramilitary groups and has been especially intense in north and east Belfast.

In 2001–02, loyalists increasingly feuded, became disenchanted with the peace process and perceived British concessions to republicans, and engaged in violent political protest. In October 2001, John Reid, the Secretary of State for Northern Ireland, declared that the cease-fire of the Ulster Defence Association/Ulster Freedom Fighters, one of two main Protestant pro-British loyalist groups who had declared cease-fires in October 1994, was no longer in effect. The cease-fire of the other main loyalist group, the Ulster Volunteer Force, remained officially intact. Loyalists were suspected of killing a Catholic journalist in September 2001, and killed a Protestant informer in December 2001. Republican violence has also increased, though not to the same extent as loyalist violence. In 2001, republicans committed four murders and 40 bombings, while the respective loyalist figures were 13 and 270. In June 2002, the Police Service of Northern Ireland (PSNI, formerly the Royal Ulster Constabulary, renamed in November 2001) announced that between 1 January and 31 March 2002, another 17 people had died in Northern Ireland as a result of political violence. Dissident republicans were blamed for a bomb attack on a Catholic PSNI recruit in County Antrim in June 2002. Civil disorder surged during the April–September 'marching season', when tensions customarily grow due to parades staged by Protestant orders and, to a much lesser extent, Catholic organisations.

The dissident Real IRA and Continuity IRA have purchased light and crew-served weapons as well as explosives from suppliers in Eastern Europe. They also possess a small portion of the Provisional IRA's former stockpile following defections. In May 2002, a London court sentenced three Real IRA members to 30 years imprisonment for terrorist offences. The three had been caught, by an elaborate security operation, in the process of illegally attempting to buy arms in Slovakia. Dissident republican activity will likely continue and may rise. Furthermore, despite being officially stood down, the Provisional IRA is believed to have been involved in several non-fatal shooting incidents connected to community unrest in east Belfast.

Additional evidence of Provisional IRA restiveness has surfaced elsewhere. In August 2001, Colombian authorities arrested three suspected Provisional IRA members on charges that they helped train members of the rebel Revolutionary Armed Forces of Colombia (FARC). In April 2002, a Provisional IRA 'hit list' of senior British and Northern Irish officials was uncovered in West Belfast. Also in April, Russian security services informed British military intelligence that the Provisionals had purchased at least 20 sophisticated AN-94 armour-piercing assault rifles from Russian sources in late 2001. Finally, in April 2002, a report to Congress by the US State Department's Office of Counterterrorism substantiated suspicions that up to 15 Provisional IRA men had joined Iranian, Cuban and possibly Basque terrorists in Colombia between 1998 and 2001, and for compensation had trained the FARC in urban terror techniques, including the use of secondary explosive devices and homemade mortars – both IRA innovations.

Basque terrorism

Euskadi ta Askatasuna (ETA), the Basque separatist group, killed at least ten people and set off numerous explosions between September 2001 and July 2002. Meanwhile, Spanish Prime Minister Jose Maria Aznar showed unwillingness to make further political compromises. ETA also launched a bombing campaign in areas of Spain frequented by tourists, in an effort to cause economic problems and embarrass the government. In March 2002, two bombs were set off in Mediterranean resorts, killing a policeman. Five car-bombs were exploded in coastal areas during the weekend of 22–23 June near Seville, which at the time was hosting an EU summit. The blasts seriously injured 12 people, including three British tourists.

Spanish and French security forces have had some anti-terrorist successes between August 2001 and August 2002, and have made over 50 arrests and confiscated over 600 kilogrammes of explosives. However, ETA appears to have sufficient supplies of explosives and small arms to continue its campaign at the level seen following the end of its 14-month cease-fire in December 1999. Popular support for Herri Batasuna, ETA's political wing, seems to have shrunk. In May 2002, based on suspicions that the party foments anti-government violence and exacts a 'revolutionary tax' in the Basque region to finance ETA, the Spanish parliament passed a law empowering the government to outlaw the party and confiscate its assets. In July 2002, a Spanish judge ruled that Batasuna was required to post a $23.5m bond to pay for property damage caused by pro-ETA street violence or have property in that amount confiscated.

Turkey

In Turkey, Kurdish separatist violence fell to its lowest level for 15 years during 2002. In April 2002, the Kurdistan Workers' Party (PKK) changed its name to the Kurdish Freedom and Democracy Congress (KADEK) as part of a long-term strategy to shift the main focus of its activities from terrorism and guerrilla warfare to non-violent political agitation. Ankara is sceptical about any genuine change of heart, and KADEK remains illegal. Almost all the PKK's armed militants had withdrawn from Turkish territory, into northern Iraq, in the wake of the organisation's unilateral ceasefire in August 1999. This followed the capture, six months earlier, of PKK leader Abdullah Ocalan. However, in the first six months of 2002, the Turkish military continued to pursue and eliminate isolated groups of militants who had remained behind in Turkey. In May 2002, the army launched a large-scale operation against camps in northern Iraq, where KADEK's military wing, the People's Defence Force (HSK), still has an estimated 5,000 militants under arms. In June 2002, Ankara announced that emergency rule would be lifted in Hakkari and Tunceli provinces, but extended it for four months in Diyarbakir and Sirnak provinces, where rebels are still believed to be active. The KADEK leadership has threatened to renew military operations if Turkey executes Ocalan, who is currently under a death sentence on the Turkish prison island of Imrali, or fails to introduce greater cultural and political freedoms for the country's 12 million Kurds. However, given the logistical damage caused by Turkish raids on its camps, low morale, a shortage of funds and reluctance among neighbouring states to provide active support, it is unlikely that the organisation would be able to sustain a guerrilla campaign.

Turkish fears that KADEK would link up with non-Kurdish left-wing extremists to launch an urban terror campaign have so far proved unfounded. The largest Turkish leftist organisation, the Revolutionary Peoples Liberation Party-Front (DHKP-C), is in disarray after shifting its strategic focus from urban terrorism to a prison campaign of hunger strikes, which began in October 2000, to try to force the government to ease anti-terrorist legislation and improve conditions in the country's jails. By July 2002, over 60 hunger strikers had died, another 30 had been killed in prison riots and several hundred more had been permanently disabled, without obtaining any concessions from the Turkish government. Over the previous year, the DHKP-C had staged only one major operation – a suicide bombing on 10 September 2001 that killed four people, including an Australian tourist. In summer 2002, the DHKP-C leadership was under intense internal pressure to reassert itself by staging a high-profile bombing or assassination. But personnel losses, resulting from the hunger strikes and high levels of penetration by Turkish intelligence, has crippled the DHKP-C's cell network and severely limited its effectiveness.

In the first half of 2002, Turkish and US authorities foiled several planned attacks by al-Qaeda sympathisers on American interests in Turkey. However, local Islamic terrorist groups, such as the Islamic

Great East Raiders Front (IBDA-C) and the predominantly Kurdish group known as Hizbullah (unrelated to the Lebanese organisation of the same name) remained on the defensive, concentrating on protecting and rebuilding their networks, rather than staging new operations, after a series of police raids in 2001 resulted in the capture and imprisonment of most of their leaders. In June 2002, there was a spate of about a dozen small-scale bombings of parks and banks in Istanbul. As of July, who was responsible remained unclear. Neither KADEK nor the DHKP-C claimed credit, and the targets were not ones ordinarily associated with Islamists.

Other European threats

There is a possibility that more extreme elements of the anti-globalisation movement, coupled with the rightward tilt of traditionally left-leaning European governments, could produce a resurgence of left-wing terrorist groups. For example, on 19 March 2002, a faction of the Italian Red Brigades – which had been largely quiescent since the 1980s – assassinated Italian government economic adviser Marco Biagi in Bologna. Subsequently, the group issued a virulent 26-page communiqué by e-mail, stating that Biagi was killed for representing 'the interests of bourgeois imperialism' and praising the 11 September al-Qaeda operation as a model of effective terrorism.

There were signs in 2002 that Greek counter-terrorism authorities, anxious to bolster security for the summer Olympic Games (slated for Athens in 2004) and erase a reputation for a lax approach to terrorism, could make headway in neutralising the elusive anti-Western 17 November Revolutionary Organisation. In July 2002, following a botched 29 June bomb attack in the Greek tourist port of Piraeus, the disabled perpetrator led police to a large arms cache in central Athens. Forensic investigators also matched the fingerprints of the captured terrorist with those found on a stalled getaway van at the scene of the 1997 murder of Greek-British ship-owner Costis Peraticos. The 17 November group has killed 23 people over the course of 27 years, including CIA station chief Richard Welch in 1975 and Brigadier Stephen Saunders, a British defence attaché, in 2000.

Belgium Be

Total Armed Forces

ACTIVE 39,260
(incl 1,860 Medical Service; 3,230 women)

RESERVES 100,500
Army 71,500 **Navy** 3,300 **Air Force** 10,000 **Medical Service** 15,700

Army 26,400

(incl 1,500 women)
1 joint service territorial comd (incl 2 engr, 2 sigs bn)
1 op comd HQ
1 mech inf div with 3 mech inf bde (each 1 tk, 2 armd inf, 1 SP arty bn, 1 engr coy) (2 bde at 70%, 1 bde at 50% cbt str), 1 AD arty bn, 2 recce (incl 1 UAV), 1 MP coy; 1 recce bn (MNDC)
1 cbt spt div (5 mil schools forming, 1 arty, 1 engr bn – augment mech inf div, plus 1 inf, 1 tk bn for bde at 50% cbt str)
1 para-cdo bde (2 para, 1 cdo, 1 recce/SF bn, 1 arty, 1 AD bty, 1 engr coy)
1 lt avn gp (2 ATK, 1 obs bn)

RESERVES
Territorial Defence 11 lt inf bn (9 province, 1 gd, 1 reserve)

EQUIPMENT
MBT 132 *Leopard* 1A5
RECCE 119 *Scimitar*
AIFV 218 YPR-765 (plus 56 'look-a-likes')
APC 187 M-113 (plus 109 'look-a-likes'), 95 *Spartan* (plus 50 'look-a-likes'), 50 *Pandur* incl 'look-a-likes'
TOTAL ARTY 272
TOWED 105mm: 14 LG Mk II
SP 155mm: 108 M-109A2
MOR 107mm: 90 M-30; **120mm**: 60; plus **81mm**: 118
ATGW 420 *Milan* (incl 215 YPR-765, 2 M-113)
RL 66mm: LAW
AD GUNS 35mm: 51 *Gepard* SP
SAM 118 *Mistral*
AC 10 BN-2A *Islander*
HELICOPTERS 74
ASLT 28 A-109BA
OBS 18 A-109A
SPT 28 SA-318 (5 in store)
UAV 3 *B-Hunter* systems (18 air vehs)

Navy 2,400

(incl 280 women)
BASES Ostend, Zeebrugge. Be and Nl navies under joint op comd based at Den Helder (Nl)

PRINCIPAL SURFACE COMBATANTS 3
FRIGATES 3
FFG 3 *Wielingen* with 4 MM-38 *Exocet* SSM, 8 *Sea Sparrow* SAM, 1 × 100mm gun, 2 × ASTT (Fr L5 HWT), 1 × 6 ASW rkt

MINE WARFARE 11
MINE COUNTERMEASURES 11
4 *Van Haverbeke* MCMV (US *Aggressive* MSO) (incl 1 used for trials), 7 *Aster* (tripartite)

SUPPORT AND MISCELLANEOUS 11
2 log spt/comd with hel deck, 1 PCR, 1 sail trg, 5 AT; 1 AGOR, 1 AG

NAVAL AVIATION
EQUIPMENT
HELICOPTERS
3 SA-316B *Alouette* III

Air Force 8,600

(incl 800 women)
Flying hours 165
FGA 3 sqn with 36 F-16 MLU
FGA/RECCE 1 sqn with 12 F-16A(R)/B
FTR 2 sqn with 24 F-16A/B ADI (12 MLU ADX by 2002)
OCU with 8 F-16B
TPT 2 sqn
1 with 11 C-130H
1 with 2 Airbus A310-200, 1 *Falcon* 900, 2 *Falcon* 20, 2 ERJ-135LR, 2 ERJ-145LR
TRG 3 sqn
2 with *Alpha Jet* (1 flt with CM-170)
1 with SF-260
SAR 1 sqn with *Sea King* Mk 48

EQUIPMENT
90 cbt ac (plus 45 in store), no armed hel
AC 129 **F-16** (72 **-A**, 18 **-B**, plus 39 in store (110 to receive mid-life update)) • 6 ***Mirage* 5** (in store) • 11 **C-130** (tpt) • 2 **Airbus A310-200** (tpt) • 2 ***Falcon* 20** (VIP) • 1 ***Falcon* 900B** • 2 **ERJ-135 LR**, 2 **ERJ-145 LR** (tpt) • 10 **CM-170** (trg, liaison) • 33 **SF-260** (trg) • 29 ***Alpha Jet*** (trg)
HEL 5 (SAR) *Sea King*
MISSILES
AAM AIM-9 *Sidewinder*, AIM-120 AMRAAM
ASM AGM-65G *Maverick*
SAM 24 *Mistral*

Forces Abroad

GERMANY 2,000; 1 mech inf bde (being withdrawn)

UN AND PEACEKEEPING
BOSNIA/CROATIA (SFOR II): up to 450 (UNMOP): 1 obs **DROC** (MONUC): 5 **INDIA/PAKISTAN** (UNMOGIP): 2 obs **FYROM** (KFOR): 210 **ITALY** (SFOR Air): 4 F-16A **MIDDLE EAST** (UNTSO): 6 obs

WESTERN SAHARA (MINURSO): 1 obs
YUGOSLAVIA (KFOR): 800

Foreign Forces

NATO HQ NATO Brussels; HQ SHAPE Mons
US 1,290: **Army** 890 **Navy** 100 **Air Force** 300

Canada Ca

Total Armed Forces

ACTIVE 52,300
(incl 6,100 women). Some 10,500 are not identified by service

RESERVES 35,400
Primary 20,700 **Army** (Militia) (incl comms) 14,000 **Navy** 4,000 **Air Force** 2,100 **Primary Reserve List** 600 ***Supplementary*** **Ready Reserve** 14,700

Army (Land Forces) 19,300

(incl 1,600 women)
1 Task Force HQ • 3 mech inf bde gp, each with 1 armd regt, 3 inf bn (1 lt), 1 arty, 1 engr regt, 1 recce sqn, 1 AD bty • 1 indep AD regt • 1 indep engr spt regt • 1 cdo unit (Joint Task Force-2)

RESERVES
Militia 10 bde gp; 18 armd, 51 inf, 15 arty, 12 engr, 20 log bn level units, 14 med coy
Canadian Rangers 127 patrols

EQUIPMENT
MBT 114 *Leopard* C-2
RECCE 5 *Lynx* (in store), 195 *Cougar*, 203 *Coyote*
LAV 150 *Kodiak* (LAV-III), 269 *Grizzly*, 199 *Bison*
APC 1,214 M-113 A2 (341 to be upgraded, 82 in store), 61 M-577
TOWED ARTY 213: **105mm**: 185 C1/C3 (M-101), 28 LG1 Mk II
SP ARTY 155mm: 58 M-109A4 (plus 18 in store)
MOR 81mm: 167
ATGW 150 TOW (incl 72 TUA M-113 SP), 425 *Eryx*
RL 66mm: M-72
RCL 84mm: 1,040 *Carl Gustav*; **106mm**: 111
AD GUNS 35mm: 34 GDF-005 with *Skyguard*; **40mm**: 57 L40/60 (in store)
SAM 22 ADATS, 96 *Javelin*, *Starburst*

Navy (Maritime Command) 9,000

(incl 2,800 women)
BASES Ottawa (National), Halifax (Atlantic), Esquimalt (Pacific)

SUBMARINES 2 (commissioned, but not yet op)
2 *Victoria* SSK† (UK *Upholder*) with 6 × 533mm TT (Mk 48 HWT)

PRINCIPAL SURFACE COMBATANTS 16
DESTROYERS 4
DDG 4 modified *Iroquois* with 1 Mk-41 VLS for 29 *Standard* SM-2 MR SAM, 1 × 76mm gun, 2 × 3 ASTT (Mk 46 LWT), 2 CH-124 *Sea King* ASW hel (Mk 46 LWT)
FRIGATES 12
FFG 12 *Halifax* with 8 *Harpoon* SSM, 16 *Sea Sparrow* SAM, 2 × ASTT, 1 CH-124A *Sea King* hel (Mk 46 LWT)

PATROL AND COASTAL COMBATANTS 14
12 *Kingston* MCDV, 2 *Fundy* PCC (trg)

SUPPORT AND MISCELLANEOUS 6
2 *Protecteur* AO with 3 *Sea King* hel, 1 AOT; 1 diving spt; 2 AGOR

DEPLOYMENT
ATLANTIC Halifax (HQ): 1 SSK, 2 DDG, 7 FFG, 1 AO, 1 AK, 6 MCDV (Air Force Assets); 2 MR plus 1 MR (trg) sqn with CP-140 and 3 CP-140A, 1 general purpose and 1 (trg) hel sqn with 26 CH-125 hel
PACIFIC Esquimalt (HQ): 1 SSK, 2 DDG, 5 FFG, 1 AO, 6 MCDV (Air Force Assets); 1 MR sqn with 4 CP-140 and 1 ASW hel sqn with 6 CH-124 hel

RESERVES
HQ Quebec
4,000 in 24 div; tasks: crew 10 of the 12 MCDV; harbour defence; naval control of shipping

Air Force (Air Command) 13,500

(incl 1,700 women)
Flying hours 210
1 Air Div with 13 wg responsible for operational readiness, combat air-spt, air tpt, SAR, MR and trg
EARLY WARNING Ca NORAD Regional HQ at North Bay: 47 North Warning radar sites: 11 long-range, 36 short-range; Regional Op Control Centre (ROCC) (2 Sector Op Control Centres (SOCC)): 4 Coastal Radars and 2 Transportable Radars. Ca Component – NATO Airborne Early Warning (NAEW)

EQUIPMENT
140 (incl 18 MR) cbt **ac**, no armed **hel**
AC 122 **CF-18** (83 **-A**, 39 **-B**) - 60 op (5 sqns) and 62 fighter trg, testing and rotation • 4 sqns with 18 **CP-140** (MR) and 3 **CP-140A** (environmental patrol) • 4 sqns with 32 **CC-130E/H** (tpt) and 5 **KCC-130** (tkr) • 1 sqn with 5 **CC-150** (Airbus A-310) and 5 **Boeing CC-137** • 1 sqn with 8 **CC-144B** (VIP) • 4 sqns with 4 **CC-138** (SAR/tpt), 7 **CC-115** (SAR/tpt)
HEL 3 sqns of 29 **CH-124** (ASW, afloat) • 75 **CH-146** (tpt, SAR) • 12 **CH-113** (SAR/tpt), being replaced by 15 **CH-149**

TRG 2 Flying Schools **ac** 136 **CT-114** *Tutor*, 4 **CT-142** **hel** 9 **CH-139** *Jet Ranger*
NATO FLIGHT TRAINING CANADA 26 T-6A/ CT-156 (primary). First of 20 Hawk 115 (advanced wpns/tactics trg) delivered
AAM AIM-7M *Sparrow*, AIM-9L *Sidewinder*

Forces Abroad

UN AND PEACEKEEPING

BOSNIA (SFOR II): 1,600: 1 inf bn, 1 armd recce, 1 engr sqn **CYPRUS** (UNFICYP): 1 **DROC** (MONUC): 6 **EGYPT** (MFO): 29 **ETHIOPIA/ERITREA** (UNMEE): 6 obs **MIDDLE EAST** (UNTSO): 6 obs **SIERRA LEONE** (UNAMSIL): 5 obs **SYRIA/ISRAEL** (UNDOF): 189: log unit **YUGOSLAVIA** (KFOR): 800

Paramilitary 9,350

Canadian Coast Guard has merged with **Department of Fisheries and Oceans**. Both are civilian-manned.

CANADIAN COAST GUARD (CCG) 4,700

some 96 vessels incl 29 navaids/tender, 11 survey/ research, 5 icebreaker, 4 PCO, 18 cutter, 10 PCI, 12 fisheries research, 4 ACV, 3 trg plus numerous lifeboats; plus **hel** 6 Bell-206L, 5 Bell-212, 16 BO-105

DEPARTMENT OF FISHERIES AND OCEANS (DFO) 4,650

some 90 vessels incl 35 AGOR/AGHS, 38 patrol, 17 icebreakers

Foreign Forces

UK 643: Army 500; Air Force 143

Czech Republic Cz

Total Armed Forces

ACTIVE 49,450

(incl 1,780 Central HQ and staff elements; 25,000 conscripts)
Terms of service 12 months

Army 36,370

(incl 15,500 conscripts)
1 mech div HQ
1 rapid-reaction bde (2 mech, 1 AB, 1 recce, 1 arty, 1 engr bn)
2 mech bde (each with 3 mech, 1 recce, 1 arty, 1 AD, 1 engr bn)
1 SF gp
1 arty, 1 SAM, 1 engr regt
9 trg and mob base (incl arty, AD, engr)

RESERVES

1 territorial def HQ: 2 trg and mob base, 1 engr regt, 8 territorial def comd, 3 civilian def base

EQUIPMENT

MBT 622: 37 T-54, 44 T-55, 541 T-72M (140 to be upgraded)
RECCE some 182 BRDM, OT-65
AIFV 879: 549 BMP-1, 186 BMP-2, 129 BPzV, 15 BRM-1K
APC 345 OT-90, 17 OT-64 plus 561 AIFV and APC 'look-a-likes'
TOTAL ARTY 585
TOWED 122mm: 109 D-30
SP 298: **122mm**: 25 2S1; **152mm**: 273 *Dana* (M-77)
MRL 122mm: 85 RM-70
MOR 93: **120mm**: 85 M-1982, 8 SPM-85
SSM FROG-7, SS-21
ATGW 721 AT-3 *Sagger* (incl 621 on BMP-1, 100 on BRDM-2), 21 AT-5 *Spandrel*
AD GUNS 30mm: M-53/-59
SAM SA-7, ε140 SA-9/-13
SURV GS-13 (veh), *Small Fred/Small Yawn* (veh, arty)

Air Force 11,300

(incl AD and 8,500 conscripts); 44 cbt ac, 34 attack hel
Organised into two main structures – Tactical Air Force and Air Defence
Flying hours 60
FGA 2 sqn with 36 L-159 (further 36 deliveries in progress)
FTR 1 sqn with 8 MiG-21
IN STORE 5 MiG-23, 24 Su-22MK/UM3K, 27 MiG-21
TPT 2 sqn with 14 L-410, 8 An-24/26/30, 2 Tu-154, 2 Yak-40, 1 Challenger CL-600 **hel** 2 Mi-2, 4 Mi-8, 1 Mi-9, 10 Mi-17
HEL 3 sqn (aslt/tpt/attack) with 24 Mi-2, 9 Mi-8/20, 32 Mi-17, 34* Mi-24, 11 PZL W-3 (SAR)
TRG 1 regt with **ac** 24 L-29, 14 L-39C, 17 L-39ZO, 3 L-39MS, 8 Z-142C **hel** 8 Mi-2
AAM AA-2 *Atoll*, AA-7 *Apex*, AA-8 *Aphid*
SAM SA-2, SA-3, SA-6

Forces Abroad

KUWAIT (OP ENDURING FREEDOM): ε350; 1 NBC recce unit

UN AND PEACEKEEPING

CROATIA (UNMOP): 1 obs (SFOR): 7 **DROC** (MONUC): 5 incl 4 obs **ETHIOPIA/ERITREA** (UNMEE): 2 obs **GEORGIA** (UNOMIG): 5 obs **SIERRA LEONE** (UNAMSIL): 5 obs **YUGOSLAVIA** (KFOR): ε400

Paramilitary 5,600

BORDER GUARDS 4,000
(1,000 conscripts)
INTERNAL SECURITY FORCES 1,600
(1,500 conscripts)

Denmark Da

Total Armed Forces

ACTIVE 22,700
(incl 1,400 joint service personnel; 5,700 conscripts; 685 women; excluding some 8,000 civilians)
Terms of service 4–12 months (up to 24 months in certain ranks)

RESERVES 64,900
Army 46,000 **Navy** 7,300 **Air Force** 11,600
Home Guard (*Hjemmevaernet*) (volunteers to age 50) about 59,300 incl **Army** 46,400 **Navy** 4,500 **Air Force** 5,500 **Service Corps** 2,900

Army 12,800

(incl 5,000 conscripts, 350 women; excluding 3,000 civilians)
1 op comd • 1 mech inf div with 3 mech inf bde (each 2 mech inf, 1 tk, 1 SP arty bn), 1 regt cbt gp (1 mech inf, 1 mot inf bn, 1 engr coy), 1 recce, 1 tk, 2 AD, 1 engr bn; div arty • 1 rapid reaction bde with 2 mech inf, 1 tk, 1 SP arty bn (20% active cbt str) • 1 recce, 1 AD, 1 engr coy, 1 MLRS coy • Army avn (1 attack hel coy, 1 recce hel det) • 1 SF unit

RESERVES
5 local def region (1–2 mot inf bn), 2 regt cbt gp (3 mot inf, 1 arty bn)

EQUIPMENT
- **MBT** 230 *Leopard* 1A5, 18 *Leopard* 2A4
- **RECCE** 36 Mowag *Eagle*
- **APC** 315 M-113 (plus 369 'look-a-likes' incl 55 SP mor), 11 *Piranha* III
- **TOTAL ARTY** 417
  - **TOWED 105mm**: 72 M-101; **155mm**: 97 M-114/39
  - **SP 155mm**: 76 M-109
  - **MRL 227mm**: 12 MLRS
  - **MOR 120mm**: 160 Brandt; **81mm**: 455 (incl 53 SP)
- **ATGW** 140 TOW (incl 56 SP)
- **RL 84mm:** 10,600 AT-4
- **RCL 84mm**: 1,131 *Carl Gustav*
- **SAM** *Stinger*
- **SURV** ARTHUR
- **ATTACK HEL** 12 AS-550C2 with TOW
- **SPT HEL** 13 Hughes 500M/OH-6
- **UAV** *Sperwer*

Navy 4,000

(incl 150 women; 500 conscripts)
BASES Korsøer, Frederikshavn, Vaerloese (naval avn)
SUBMARINES 4
SSK 4
- 2 *Tumleren* (mod No *Kobben*) with Swe Type 61 HWT
- 1 *Narhvalen*, with Swe Type 61 HWT
- 1 *Kronborg* (Swe *Nacken*) with Swe Type 61 HWT (in refit)

PRINCIPAL SURFACE COMBATANTS 3
CORVETTES 3
FSG 3 *Niels Juel* with 8 *Harpoon* SSM, 8 *Sea Sparrow* SAM, 1 × 76mm gun
PATROL AND COASTAL COMBATANTS 27
MISSILE CRAFT 4 *Flyvefisken* (Stanflex 300) PFM with 2 × 4 *Harpoon* SSM, 6 *Sea Sparrow* SAM, 1 × 76mm gun, 2 × 533mm TT
TORPEDO CRAFT 3 *Flyvefisken* PFT with 6 *Sea Sparrow* SAM, 1 × 76mm gun, 2 × 533mm TT
PATROL CRAFT 20
- **OFFSHORE** 4
- 4 *Thetis* PCO with 1 × 76mm gun, 1 *Lynx* hel
- **COASTAL** 16
- 4 *Flyvefisken* (Stanflex 300) PFC with 1 × 76mm gun, 3 *Agdlek* PCC, 9 *Barsøe* PCC

MINE WARFARE 7
MINELAYERS 4
- 2 *Falster* (400 mines), 2 *Lindormen* (50 mines)

(All units of *Flyvefisken* class can also lay up to 60 mines)
MINE COUNTERMEASURES 3
- 3 *Flyvefisken* (SF300) MHC/MSC

SUPPORT AND MISCELLANEOUS 13
- 1AE, 1 tpt; 4 icebreakers, 6 environmental protection, 1 Royal Yacht plus several AT and anti-pollution craft

NAVAL AVIATION
EQUIPMENT
- **HELICOPTERS**
- 8 *Lynx* (up to 4 embarked)

COASTAL DEFENCE
1 coastal fortress; **150mm** guns, coastal radar
2 mobile coastal msl batteries: 2 × 8 *Harpoon*
RESERVES (Home Guard)
40 inshore patrol craft/boats

Air Force 4,500

(incl 125 conscripts, 185 women)
Four air bases
Flying hours 180
TACTICAL AIR COMD
FGA/FTR 3 sqn with 68 F-16A/B (60 op, 8 attritional

reserve)
TPT 1 sqn with 3 C-130H, 3 *Challenger*-604 (MR/VIP)
SAR 1 sqn with 8 S-61A hel
TRG 1 flying school with 28 SAAB T-17

CONTROL AND AIR DEFENCE GROUP

2 SAM bn: 6 bty with 36 I HAWK launchers plus STINGER
5 radar stations, one in the Faroe Islands

EQUIPMENT

68 cbt ac, no armed hel
AC 68 **F-16A/B** (FGA/ftr) • 3 **C-130H** (tpt) • 3 ***Challenger*-604** (tpt) • 28 **SAAB T-17**
HEL 8 **S-61** (SAR)

MISSILES

ASM AGM-65 *Maverick*, GBU-12 and GBU-24 LGBs
AAM AIM-9 *Sidewinder*, AIM-120A AMRAAM
SAM HAWK, *Stinger*

Forces Abroad

AFGHANISTAN (OP ENDURING FREEDOM): ε100
KYRGYZSTAN (OP ENDURING FREEDOM): 75 incl C-130 contingent

UN AND PEACEKEEPING

AFGHANISTAN (ISAF): ε50 **BOSNIA** (SFOR II):365; incl 1 tk sqn (10 *Leopard* 1A5 MBT); aircrew with NATO E-3A ops; Air Force personnel in tac air-control parties (TACP). (UNMIBH): 1 obs **CROATIA** (UNMOP): 1 obs **DROC** (MONUC): 2 obs **EAST TIMOR** (UNMISET): 4 incl 2 obs **ETHIOPIA/ERITREA** (UNMEE): 4 obs **FYROM** (OP AMBER FOX): 40 **GEORGIA** (UNOMIG): 6 obs **INDIA/PAKISTAN** (UNMOGIP): 6 obs **IRAQ/KUWAIT** (UNIKOM): 5 obs **ITALY** (BALKAN AIR OPERATION): 6 F-16 **MIDDLE EAST** (UNTSO): 10 obs **SIERRA LEONE** (UNAMSIL): 2 obs **YUGOSLAVIA** (KFOR): 540: 1 inf bn gp incl 1 scout sqn, 1 inf coy

Foreign Forces

NATO HQ Joint Comd North-East
UN HQ Standby High-Readiness Brigade (SHIRBRIG)

France Fr

Total Armed Forces

ACTIVE 260,400

(incl 5,200 **Central Staff**, 8,600 ***Service de santé*** not listed; 23,660 women)

RESERVES 100,000

Army 28,000 **Navy** 6,500 **Air Force** 8,000 **Gendarmerie** 50,000 **Medical Service** 7,000 **POL Service** 500

Strategic Nuclear Forces (7,000)

(**Navy** 3,300 **Air Force** 3,100 ***Gendarmerie*** 600)
NAVY 64 SLBM in 4 SSBN
SSBN 4
2 *L'Inflexible* each with 16 M-4/TN-71, SLBM, 4 × 533mm TT (SM-39 *Exocet* USGW, L5/F17 HWT)
2 *Le Triomphant* each with 16 M-45/TN-75 SLBM, 4 × 533mm TT (SM-39 *Exocet* USGW, L5 HWT)
AIRCRAFT
28 *Super Etendard* strike; plus 16 in store
AIR FORCE
3 sqn with 60 *Mirage* 2000 N(ASMP)
TKR 1 sqn with 11 C-135FR, 3 KC-135
RECCE 1 sqn with 5 *Mirage* IV P
AIRBORNE RELAY 4 C-160H *Astarte*
CBT TRG 6 *Mystere* 20, 6 *Jaguar* E

Army 137,000

(incl 12,500 women; excluding 30,000 civilians) regt normally bn size
1 Land Comd HQ
5 Regional, 4 Task Force HQ
2 armd bde (each 2 armd, 2 armd inf, 1 SP arty, 1 engr regt)
2 mech inf bde (each 1 armd, 1 armd inf, 1 APC inf, 1 SP arty, 1 engr regt)
2 lt armd bde (each 2 armd cav, 2 APC inf, 1 arty, 1 engr regt)
1 mtn inf bde with 1 armd cav, 3 APC inf, 1 arty, 1 engr bde)
1 AB bde with 1 armd cav, 4 para inf, 1 arty, 1 engr, 1 spt regt
1 air mobile bde with 3 cbt hel, 1 spt hel regt
1 arty bde with 2 MLRS, 3 *Roland* SAM, 1 *HAWK* SAM regt
1 arty, 1 engr, 1 sigs, 1 Int and EW bde
1 Fr/Ge bde (2,500): Fr units incl 1 armd cav, 1 APC inf regt

FOREIGN LEGION (8,000)

1 armd, 1 para, 6 inf, 2 engr regt (incl in units listed above)

MARINES (14,700)

(mainly overseas enlisted)
11 regt in Fr (incl in units listed above), 10 regt overseas

SPECIAL OPERATIONS FORCES

1 para regt, 1 hel units, 3 trg centre

RESERVES

Territorial def forces: 75 coy (all arms), 14 coy (engr, spt)

EQUIPMENT

MBT 786 (CFE: 1,084): 471 AMX-30B2, 315 *Leclerc*
RECCE 317 AMX-10RC (300 to be upgraded), 187 ERC-90F4 *Sagaie*, 1,176 VBL M-11
AIFV 384 AMX-10P/PC

APC 3,700 VAB (incl variants)
TOTAL ARTY 794
TOWED 155mm: 97 TR-F-1
SP 155mm: 273 AU-F-1
MRL 227mm: 61 MLRS
MOR 120mm: 363 RT-F1
ATGW 700 *Eryx*, 1,348 *Milan*, HOT (incl 135 VAB SP)
RL 84mm: AT-4; **89mm**: 9,850; **112mm**: 9,690 APILAS
AD GUNS 20mm: 328 53T2
SAM 26 HAWK, 98 *Roland* I/II, 331 *Mistral*
SURV RASIT-B/-E (veh, arty), RATAC (veh, arty)
AC 2 Cessna *Caravan* II , 5 PC-6, 8 TBM-700
HELICOPTERS 418
ATTACK 292: 109 SA-341F, 156 SA-342M, 27 SA-342AATCP
RECCE 4 AS-532 *Horizon*
SPT 122: 21 AS-532, 101 SA-330
UAV 8 CL-289 (AN/USD-502), 2 *Crecerelle*

Navy 45,600

(incl 1,700 Marines, 6,800 Naval Avn; 4,260 women)
COMMANDS SSBN (ALFOST) HQ Brest **Atlantic** (CECLANT) HQ Brest **North Sea/Channel** (COMAR CHERBOURG) HQ Cherbourg **Mediterranean** (CECMED) HQ Toulon **Indian Ocean** (ALINDIEN) HQ afloat **Pacific Ocean** (ALPACI) HQ Papeete
ORGANIC COMMANDS ALFAN/Toulon (Surface Ships) **ALFAN/Brest** (Surface Ships ASW) **ALFAN/Mines** (mine warfare) **ALAVIA** (naval avn) **ALFUSCO** (Marines) **ALFOST** (SS)
BASES France Cherbourg, Brest (HQ), Lorient, Toulon (HQ) **Overseas** Papeete (HQ) (Tahiti), La Réunion, Nouméa (New Caledonia), Fort de France (Martinique), Cayenne (French Guiana)

SUBMARINES 10
STRATEGIC SUBMARINES 4 SSBN (see **Strategic Nuclear Forces**)
TACTICAL SUBMARINES 6
SSN 6 *Rubis* with 4 × 533mm TT (SM-39 *Exocet* USGW, F17 HWT)

PRINCIPAL SURFACE COMBATANTS 35
AIRCRAFT CARRIERS
1 *Charles de Gaulle* CVN (40,600t), capacity 35–40 ac (typically 16 *Super Etendard*, 10 *Rafale M*, 2 E-2C *Hawkeye*, 5 hel)
CRUISERS 1 *Jeanne d'Arc* CG with 6 MM-38 *Exocet* SSM, 2 × 100mm guns, capacity 8 SA-319B hel
DESTROYERS 3
DDG 3
2 *Cassard* with 8 MM-40 *Exocet* SSM, 1 × 2 SM-1MR SAM, 1 × 100mm gun, 2 × ASTT (Fr L5 HWT), 1 *Panther* hel
1 *Suffren* (Duquesne) with 4 MM-38 *Exocet* SSM, 1 × 2 *Masurca* SAM, 2 × 100mm gun, 4 × ASTT (Fr L5 HWT)
FRIGATES 30
FFG 30
6 *Floréal* with 2 MM-38 *Exocet* SSM, 1 × 100mm gun, 1 *Panther* hel
7 *Georges Leygues* with *Crotale* SAM, 1 × 100mm gun, 2 × ASTT (Fr L5 HWT), 2 *Lynx* hel (Mk 46 LWT); 5 with 8 MM-40 *Exocet* SSM, 2 with 4 MM-38 *Exocet* SSM
2 *Tourville* with 1 × 6 MM-38 *Exocet* SSM, *Crotale* SAM, 2 × 100mm gun, 2 × ASTT (Fr L5 HWT), 2 *Lynx* hel (Mk 46 LWT)
10 *D'Estienne d'Orves* with 1 × 100mm gun, 4 ASTT, 6 ASW mor; 4 with 2 MM-38 *Exocet* SSM, 6 with 4 MM-40 *Exocet* SSM
5 *La Fayette* with 8 MM-40 *Exocet* SSM, *Crotale* SAM, 1 × 100mm gun, 1 *Panther* hel

PATROL AND COASTAL COMBATANTS 35
PATROL, OFFSHORE 1 *Albatros* PCO (Public Service Force, based in Indian Ocean)
PATROL, COASTAL 23
10 *L'Audacieuse* PCC, 8 *Léopard* PCC (instruction), 3 *Flamant* PCC (Public Service Force), 1 *Sterne* PCC, 1 *Grebe* PCC (Public Service Force)
PATROL, INSHORE 11
2 *Athos* PCI<, 2 *Patra* PCI<, 2 *Stellis* PCI<, 5 PCI< (manned by *Gendarmarie Maritime*)

MINE WARFARE 21
COMMAND AND SUPPORT 1 Loire MCCS
MINELAYERS 0, but SS and *Thetis* (trials ship) have capability
MINE COUNTERMEASURES 20
13 *Eridan* (tripartite) MHC, 4 *Vulcain* MCM diver spt, 3 *Antares* (route survey/trg)

AMPHIBIOUS 9
2 *Foudre* LPD, capacity 470 tps, 30 tk, 4 *Cougar* hel, 2 *Edic* LCT or 10 LCM
2 *Ouragan* LPD: capacity 350 tps, 25 tk, 2 *Super Frelon* hel or 4 *Puma* hel, 2 *Edic* LCT
5 *Champlain* LSM: capacity 140 tps, 12 veh
Plus craft: 5 LCT, 15 LCM

SUPPORT AND MISCELLANEOUS 26
UNDER WAY SUPPORT 4 *Durance* AO with 1 SA-319 hel
MAINTENANCE AND LOGISTIC 3
1 *Jules Verne* AR with 2 SA-319 hel, 2 *Rhin* depot/spt, with hel
SPECIAL PURPOSES 14
8 trial ships, 2 *Glycine* trg, 4 AT/F (3 civil charter)
SURVEY/RESEARCH 5
4 AGHS, 1 AGOR

NAVAL AVIATION (6,800 incl 480 women)
ORGANISATION
Flying hours *Super Etendard*: 180–220 (night qualified pilots)
AIRCRAFT
NUCLEAR STRIKE 2 flt with *Super Etendard*
STRIKE 1 flt with *Rafale M* (from 2002)
MR 1 flt with *Nord*-262

MP 2 sqn with *Atlantique*
AEW 1 flt with E-2C
TRG 3 units with *Nord*-262 *Rallye* 880, CAP 10
HELICOPTERS
ASW 2 sqn with *Lynx*
SAR/TRG 1 unit with AS-565MA*

EQUIPMENT
58 cbt ac (plus 28 in store); 30 armed hel (plus 18 in store)
AIRCRAFT
8 ***Rafale* M** • 28 ***Super Etendard*** plus 16 in store • 18 ***Atlantique** ** **2** plus 12 in store • 13 ***Nord* 262** • 8 ***Xingu*** • 7 ***Rallye* 880*** • 7 **CAP-10** • 5 ***Falcon* 10 MER** • 2 ***Falcon* 50 MER** • 2 **E2C *Hawkeye*** • 5 ***Guardian***
HELICOPTERS
17 ***Lynx*** plus 16 in store • 13 **AS-565MA** plus 2 in store • 21 ***Alouette* III** • 6 ***Super Frelon*** • 3 ***Dauphin* AS 365F**
MISSILES
ASM *Exocet* AM-39
AAM *Mica*, AS 30 *Laser*

MARINES (1,700)
COMMANDO UNITS (500) 5 groups: 2 aslt, 1 recce, 1 attack swimmer, 1 raiding
FUSILIERS-MARIN (1,200) 14 naval-base protection gp
PUBLIC SERVICE FORCE naval personnel performing general coast guard, fishery protection, SAR, anti-pollution and traffic surv duties: 1 *Albatross*, 1 *Sterne*, 1 *Grebe*, 3 *Flamant* PCC; **ac** 4 N-262 **hel** 4 SA-365 (ships incl in naval patrol and coastal totals). Comd exercised through ***Maritime Préfectures*** (Premar): ***Manche*** (Cherbourg), ***Atlantique*** (Brest), ***Méditerranée*** (Toulon)

Air Force 64,000

(incl 6,900 women, strategic nuc forces, excl 6,000 civilians)
Flying hours 180

AIR SIGNALS AND GROUND ENVIRONMENT COMMAND
CONTROL automatic *STRIDA* II, 6 radar stations, 1 sqn with 4 E3F
SAM 11 sqn (1 trg) with *Crotale*, *Aspic*, SATCP and AA gun bty (**20mm**)

AIR COMBAT COMMAND
FTR 6 sqn with *Mirage* 2000C/B/5F
FGA 6 sqn
3 with *Mirage* 2000D • 1 with *Jaguar* A • 2 with *Mirage* F1-CT
RECCE 2 sqn with *Mirage* F1-CR
TRG 2 OCU sqn
1 with *Mirage* F1-C/B • 1 with *Mirage* 2000/BC
EW 1 sqn with C-160 ELINT/ESM

AIR MOBILITY COMMAND (CFAP)
TPT 14 sqn
1 hy with DC-8F, A310-300, A319
6 tac with C-160/-160NG, C-130H
7 lt tpt/trg/SAR/misc with C-160, DHC-6, CN235, *Falcon* 20, *Falcon* 50, *Falcon* 900, TBM-700, N-262, AS-555
EW 1 sqn with DC-8 ELINT
HEL 5 sqn with AS-332, SA-330, AS-555, AS-355, SA-319
TRG 1 OCU with C-160, N-262, 1 OCU with SA-319, AS-555, SA-330

AIR TRAINING COMMAND
TRG *Alpha Jet*, EMB-121, TB-30, EMB-312, CAP-10/-20/-231, CR-100, N262

EQUIPMENT
449 cbt ac, no armed hel
AC 339 ***Mirage*** (11 **F-1B** (OCU), 26 **F-1C** (OCU plus 6 in Djibouti), 43 **F1-CR** (recce), 42 **F1-CT** (FGA), 5 **MIVP** (recce), 105 **-M-2000B/C/5F** (49 -C (ftr), 30 -5F (upgraded C), 26 -B (OCU)), 64 **-M-2000N** (strike, FGA), 43 **-M-2000D**) • 20 ***Jaguar*-E** (FGA) (plus 98 in store) • 90* ***Alpha Jet*** (trg, plus 29 in store) • 4 **E-3F** (AEW) • 2 **A 310-300** (tpt) • 2 **A319** (VIP) • 2 **DC-8F** (tpt) • 1 **DC-8 *Sarigue*** (AEW) • 14 **C-130** (**5 -H** (tpt), 9 **-H-30** (tpt)) • 11 **C-135FR** (tkr) • 72 **C-160** (tpt/9-tkr) • 3 **KC-135** • 14 **CN-235M** (tpt) • 19 **N-262** • 17 ***Falcon*** (7 **-20**), 4 **-50** (VIP), 2 **-900** (VIP)) • 17 **TBM-700** (tpt) • 6 **DHC-6** (tpt) • 32 **EMB-121** (trg) • 92 **TB-30** (trg plus 50 in store) • 9 **CAP-10B/231/232** (trg) • 48 **EMB-312** (trg) • 2 **CR-100** (trg)
HEL 3 **SA-319** (*Alouette* III) • 29 **SA-330** (26 tpt, 3 OCU) (*Puma*) • 7 **AS-332** (tpt/VIP) (*Super Puma*) • **3 AS-532** (tpt) (*Cougar*) • 4 **AS-355** (*Ecureuil*) • 43 **AS-555** (34 tpt, 9 OCU) (*Fennec*)
UAV 4 *Hunter*

MISSILES
ASM ASMP, AS-30/-30L
AAM *Super* 530F/D, R-550 *Magic* 1/II, AIM-9 *Sidewinder*, *Mica*

Forces Abroad

GERMANY 3,000: incl elm Eurocorps and Fr/Ge bde (HQ, 1 inf, 1 recce regt)
ANTILLES (HQ Fort de France): 4,000: 3 regt (incl 1 mne inf, 2 SMA), 1 air tpt unit **ac** 2 C-160 **hel** 2 SA-330, 2 AS-555, 1 FFG (1 AS-365 hel), 2 PCI, 1 LSM, 1 spt ***Gendarmerie*** 3 coy
FRENCH GUIANA (HQ Cayenne): 3,000: 3 regt (incl 1 SMA), 2 PCI 1 *Atlantic* **ac**, 1 air tpt unit **hel** 4 SA-330, 3 AS-555 ***Gendarmerie*** 3 coy
INDIAN OCEAN (Mayotte, La Réunion): 4,700: 3 regt (2 mne inf, 1 SMA), 1 spt bn, 1 air tpt unit **ac** 2 C-160 **hel** 2 AS 555, 1 LSM, 1 spt ***Gendarmerie*** 2 coy **Navy** Indian Ocean Squadron, Comd ALINDIEN (HQ afloat): 2 FFG, 1 PCO, 2 PCI, 1 AOR (comd), reinforcement 2 FFG, 1 *Atlantic* ac
NEW CALEDONIA (HQ Nouméa): 2,600: 1 mne inf

regt; 6 ERC-90 recce, 5 **120mm** mor; 1 air tpt unit, det **ac** 2 CN-235 **hel** 2 AS-555, 5 SA-330 **Navy** 1 FFG (2 AS-365 hel), 2 PCI, 1 LSM, 1 spt **ac** 2 *Guardian* MR ***Gendarmerie*** 4 coy

POLYNESIA (HQ Papeete) 2,600 (incl *Centre d'Expérimentation du Pacifique*): 1 mne inf bn, 1 Foreign Legion bn, 1 air tpt unit; 2 CN-235, **hel** 2 AS-332 **Navy** 1 FFG, 2 PC, 1 amph, 1 AGHS, 5 spt **ac** 2 *Guardian* MR

CHAD 950: 2 inf coy, 1 ERC-90 recce sqn **ac** 5 Mirage F1, 2 C-160, 1 C-130 **hel** 4 SA-330

CÔTE D'IVOIRE 550: 1 mne inf coy (1 ERC-90 recce sqn) **hel** 1 AS-555

DJIBOUTI 3,200: 2 combined regt (incl 2 inf coy, 2 recce sqn, 1 arty bty, 1 engr coy; 1 sqn with **ac** 4 *Mirage* F-1C, 5 Mirage 2000, 1 C-160 **hel** 1 SA-330, 1 AS-555

GABON 750: 2 mne inf coy, 1 ERC-90 recce platoon **ac** 2 C-160 **hel** 1 AS-555

SENEGAL 1,150: 1 mne inf coy, 1 ERC-90 recce sqn, 5 120mm mor, 1 LSM **ac** 1 C-160 tpt **hel** 1 AS-555

UN AND PEACEKEEPING

AFGHANISTAN (ISAF): 400 **BOSNIA** (SFOR II): 2,200 **CROATIA**: **SFOR Air Component** 11 *Jaguar*, 10 Mirage 2000C/D, 1 E-3F, 1 KC-135, 1 N-262 **DROC** (MONUC): 6 incl 1 obs **EGYPT** (MFO): 15; 1 DHC-6 **ETHIOPIA/ERITREA** (UNMEE): 2 **FYROM** (OP AMBER FOX): 210 **GEORGIA** (UNOMIG): 3 obs **IRAQ/KUWAIT** (UNIKOM): 11 obs **ITALY** (DELIBERATE FORGE): 3 *Jaguar* **KYRGYZSTAN** 6 *Mirage* 2000D, 3 C-135FR **LEBANON** (UNIFIL): 235: elm 1 log bn **MIDDLE EAST** (UNTSO): 3 obs **SAUDI ARABIA** (*Southern Watch*): 170; 5 *Mirage* 2000C, 3 F-1CR, 1 C-135FR **SIERRA LEONE** (UNAMSIL): 1 obs **TAJIKISTAN** 2 C-130 **WESTERN SAHARA** (MINURSO): 25 obs (*Gendarmerie*) **YUGOSLAVIA** (KFOR): 5,200

Paramilitary 101,399

GENDARMERIE 101,399

(incl 7,250 women, 1,966 civilians) **Territorial** 64,659 **Mobile** 17,715 **Schools** 4,661 **Overseas** 3,426 **Maritime**, **Air** (personnel drawn from other dept.) 3,293 **Republican Guard**, **Air tpt**, **Arsenals** 4,601 **Administration** 3,044

EQPT 28 VBC-90 armd cars; 155 VBRG-170 APC; 781 **60mm**, **81mm** mor; 5 PCIs (listed under Navy), plus 34 other patrol craft and 4 AT **hel** 12 SA-316/319, 30 AS-350 B/BA

Foreign Forces

GERMANY 254: elm EUROCORPS
SINGAPORE AIR FORCE 200; 18 TA-4SU *Skyhawks* (Cazaux AFB)

Germany Ge

Total Armed Forces

ACTIVE some 296,000
(incl 107,000 conscripts, 7,100 women)
Terms of service 9 months; 12–23 months voluntary

RESERVES 390,300
(men to age 45, officers/NCO to 60) **Army** 317,050 **Navy** 12,000 **Air Force** 61,250

Army 203,200

(incl 85,900 conscripts, 4,600 women)

ARMY FORCES COMMAND

1 special ops div with 2 AB (1 Crisis Reaction Force (CRF)), 1 cdo SF bde • 1 airmobile div with 1 air mech bde, 1 army avn bde with 5 regt • 1 SIGINT/ELINT bde • 1 spt regt

ARMY SUPPORT FORCES COMMAND

3 log bde

CORPS COMMANDS

I Ge/Nl Corps 2 armd div
II Corps 1 armd div
IV Corps 2 armd inf div
Corps Units 2 spt bde and Ge elm of Ge/Nl Corps, 1 ATGW hel regt

Summary of Corps cbt units
9 armd bde, 9 armd inf and the Ge elm of the Ge/Fr bde, 1 inf, 1 mtn bde, 7 arty regt, 7 engr bde, 7 AD regt, 6 recce bn
Bde differ in their basic org, peacetime str, eqpt and mob capability; 4 (2 armd, 1 inf and Ge/Fr bde) are allocated to the CRF, the remainder to the Main Defence Forces (MDF)
1 armd div earmarked for Eurocorps, 1 armd div bde for the Allied Rapid Reaction Corps (ARRC) incl 1 pl bde and 1 armd inf div for the Multi-National Corps North East

Military District Commands (MDC)
4 MDC. The MDC comd and control 27 Military Region Commands (MRC)

EQUIPMENT

MBT 2,490: 707 *Leopard* 1A1/A3/A4/A5, 1,783 *Leopard* 2 (350 to be upgraded to A6)
RECCE 523: 409 SPz-2 *Luchs*, 114 TPz-1 *Fuchs* (NBC)
AIFV 2,110 *Marder* A2/A3, 133 *Wiesel* (with **20mm** gun)
APC 873 TPz-1 *Fuchs* (incl variants), 2,201 M-113 (incl 317 arty obs and other variants), 56 APCV-2
TOTAL ARTY 1,735
TOWED 353: **105mm**: 16 Geb H, 140 M-101; **155mm**: 197 FH-70
SP 155mm 643: 516 M-109A3G, 127 PzH 2000

MRL 227: **110mm**: 78 LARS; **227mm**: 149 MLRS
MOR 120mm: 512 Tampella
ATGW 2,002: 1,618 *Milan*, 174 RJPz-(HOT) *Jaguar* 1, 210 *Wiesel* (TOW)
AD GUNS 1,535: **20mm**: 1,155 Rh 202 towed; **35mm**: 380 *Gepard* SP (147 being upgraded)
SAM 143 *Roland* SP, *Stinger* (incl some *Ozelot* SP)
SURV 18 *Green Archer* (mor), 110 RASIT (veh, arty), 74 RATAC (veh, arty)
HELICOPTERS 566
ATTACK 202 PAH-1 (BO-105 with HOT)
SPT 364: 122 UH-1D, 108 CH-53G, 92 BO-105M, 32 *Alouette* II, 10 EC-135
UAV CL-289 (AN/USD-502)
MARINE (River Engineers) 13 LCM

Navy 25,500

(incl 3,700 Naval Avn; 5,000 conscripts, 1,000 women)
COMMANDS Type comds SS, FF, Patrol Boat, MCMV, Naval Avn
BASES Glücksburg (Maritime HQ), Wilhelmshaven, Kiel, Olpenitz, Eckernförde, Warnemünde
SUBMARINES 14
SSK 12 Type 206/206A with 8× 533mm TT (*Seeaal* DM2 A3 HWT)
SSC 2 Type 205 with 8 × 533m TT
PRINCIPAL SURFACE COMBATANTS 14
DESTROYERS 2
DDG 2 *Lütjens* (mod US *Adams*) with 1 × 1 *Standard* SM-1 MR SAM/*Harpoon* SSM launcher, 2 × 127mm guns, 6 ASTT (Mk 45 LWT), 8 ASROC (Mk 46 LWT)
FRIGATES 12
FFG 12
8 *Bremen* with 8 *Harpoon* SSM , *Sea Sparrow* SAM, 1 × 76mm gun, 2 × 2 324mm ASTT (Mk 46 LWT), 2 *Lynx* hel
4 *Brandenburg* with 4 MM-38 *Exocet* SSM, 1 VLS Mk-41 for *Sea Sparrow* SAM, 1 × 76mm gun, 4 × 324mm ASTT (Mk 46 LWT), 2 *Lynx* hel
PATROL AND COASTAL COMBATANTS 25
MISSILE CRAFT 25
10 *Albatros* (Type 143) PFM with 4 *Exocet* SSM, and 2 × 533mm TT
10 *Gepard* (T-143A) PFM with 4 *Exocet* SSM
5 *Tiger* (Type 148) PFM with 4 *Exocet* SSM
MINE WARFARE 23
MINE COUNTERMEASURES 23
5 *Kulmback* (mod *Hameln*) MHC
12 *Frankenthal* (T-332) MHC
5 *Ensdorf* (mod *Hameln*) MSC
1 MCM/T-742A diver spt ship
AMPHIBIOUS craft only
2 T-704 LCU/LCM
SUPPORT AND MISCELLANEOUS 40
UNDER WAY SUPPORT 2 *Spessart* AO
MAINTENANCE AND LOGISTIC 14
2 *Berlin* spt
6 *Elbe* spt, 3 small (2,000t) AOT, 1 *Lüneburg* log spt, 2 AE
SPECIAL PURPOSE 20
3 AGI, 2 trials, 8 multi-purpose (T-748/745), 1 trg, 5 AT, 1 icebreaker (civil)
RESEARCH AND SURVEY 4
1 AGOR, 3 AGHS (civil-manned for Ministry of Transport)

NAVAL AVIATION (3,700)
ORGANISATION
Flying hours *Tornado*: 180
3 wgs, 7 sqn
AIRCRAFT
FGA/RECCE 2 sqn with *Tornado*
MP 2 sqn with *Atlantic*, Do-228
TRG 1 sqn with *Tornado*
HELICOPTERS
ASW 1 sqn with *Lynx* Mk 88/88A
ASUW/SAR 1 sqn with *Sea King* Mk 41
EQUIPMENT
66 cbt ac, 43 armed hel
AIRCRAFT
49 ***Tornado*** • 17 ***Atlantic*** (13 armed MR, 4 int) • 4 **Do-228** (2 polution control, 2 tpt)
HELICOPTERS
15 ***Sea Lynx* Mk 88** • 7 ***Lynx* Mk 88A** • 21 ***Sea King* Mk 41**
MISSILES
ASM *Kormoran*, *Sea Skua*, HARM
AAM AIM-9 *Sidewinder*, *Roland*

Air Force 67,300

(incl 16,100 conscripts, 1,500 women)
Flying hours 150
AIR FORCE COMMAND
4 air div
FGA 5 wg with 10 sqn *Tornado*; 1 wg operates ECR *Tornado* in SEAD role
FTR 4 wg (with 7 sqn F-4F; 1 sqn MiG-29)
RECCE 1 wg with 2 sqn *Tornado*
SAM 6 mixed wg (each 1 gp *Patriot* (6 sqn) plus 1 gp *Hawk* (4 sqn plus 2 reserve sqn)); 14 sqn *Roland*
RADAR 2 tac Air Control regts, 8 sites; 11 remote radar posts
TRANSPORT COMMAND (GAFTC)
TPT 3 wg, 4 sqn with *Transall* C-160 (incl 1 OCU), 4 sqn (incl 1 OCU) with Bell UH-1D, 1 special air mission wg with Airbus A-310, CL-601, 3 AS-532U2 (VIP)
TRAINING
FGA OCU with 37 *Tornado*
FTR OCU with 23 F-4F
NATO joint jet pilot trg (Sheppard AFB, TX) with 35 T-37B, 40 T-38A; primary trg sqn with Beech *Bonanza* (Goodyear AFB, AZ), GAF Air Defence School (Fort Bliss TX)

EQUIPMENT

446 cbt ac (60 trg (overseas)); no attack hel

AC 152 **F-4** *Phantom* II (incl 7 in store), 266 ***Tornado*** (190 FGA, 35* ECR, 41 Recce), 1 **MiG-21**, 3 **MiG-23** (2 in store) • 23 **MiG-29** (19 (ftr), 4* **-UB** (trg)) • 1 **Su-22** • 83 ***Transall* C-160** (tpt, trg) • 7 **A-310** (VIP, tpt) • 6 **CL-601** (VIP) • 35 **T-37B** • 40 **T-38A**

HEL 72 **UH-1D** (68 SAR, tpt, liaison; 4 VIP) • 3 **AS-532U2** (VIP)

MISSILES

ASM AGM-65 *Maverick*, AGM-88A HARM

AAM AIM-9 *Sidewinder*, AA-8 *Aphid*, AA-10 *Alamo*, AA-11 *Archer*

SAM *Hawk*, *Roland*, *Patriot*

Forces Abroad

FRANCE: 254; Ge elm Eurocorps
POLAND: 65; Ge elm Corps HQ (multinational)
3 MPA in ELMAS/Sardinia
US: **Army** trg area with 35 *Leopard* 2 MBT, 26 *Marder* AIFV, 12 M-109A3G **155mm** SP arty **Air Force** 812 flying trg at Goodyear, Sheppard, Holloman AFBs, NAS Pensacola, Fort Rucker with 35 T-37, 40 T-38, 23 F-4F; 37 *Tornado*, msl trg at Fort Bliss
DJIBOUTI (OP ENDURING FREEDOM): **KENYA** (OP ENDURING FREEDOM): 150, 3 MPA **KUWAIT** (OP ENDURING FREEDOM): 50; 6 Tpz-1 *Fuchs* (NBC)

UN AND PEACEKEEPING

AFGHANISTAN (ISAF): ε1,120 **BOSNIA** (SFOR II): 1,700 (to be 1,000); 28 SPz-2 *Luchs* recce, 32 TPz-1 *Fuchs* APC, hel 3 CH-53, 4 UH-1D **DJIBOUTI** hel 2 *Sea King* **FYROM** (OP AMBER FOX): 560; 2 UH-1D **GEORGIA** (UNOMIG): 11 obs **IRAQ/KUWAIT** (UNIKOM): 14 **ITALY** (SFOR II/KFOR): 200 Air Force, 3 Tornado recce **UZBEKISTAN** (ISAF): 163 **YUGOSLAVIA** (KFOR): 4,600 (to be 3,100); 63 *Leopard* 2 MBT, 31 *Marder* AIFV, 25 SPz-2 *Luchs* recce, 51 TPz-1 *Fuchs* APC, 6 *Wiesel* TOW ATGW; 3 CH-53, 8 UH-1D hel

Foreign Forces

NATO HQ Allied Rapid Reaction Corps (ARRC), HQ Allied Air Forces North (AIRNORTH), HQ Joint Command Centre (JCCENT), HQ Multi-National Division (Central) (MND(C)) to deactivate by 31 Dec 2002, Airborne Early Warning Force: 17 E-3A *Sentry*, 2 Boeing-707 (trg)
BELGIUM 2,000: 1 mech inf bde(-), being withdrawn
FRANCE 3,000: incl elm Eurocorps
NETHERLANDS 2,600: **Army** 2,300: 1 mech inf bde **Air Force** 300
UK 17,100: **Army** 17,100: 1 corps HQ (multinational), 1 armd div
US 68,950: **Army** 56,000: 1 army HQ, 1 corps HQ; 1 armd (-), 1 mech inf div (-) **Navy** 300 **USMC** 250 **Air Force** 12,400: HQ USAFE, (HQ 17th Air Force), 1 tac ftr wg with 3 sqn (2 with 42 F-16C/D, 1 with 12 A-10 and 6 OA-10), 1 tac airlift wg; incl 16 C-130E, 6 C-9A, 9 C-21, 2 C-20, 1 CT-43

Greece Gr

Total Armed Forces

ACTIVE 177,600

(incl 11,600 HQ staff and centrally controlled formations/units; 98,321 conscripts, 5,520 women)
Terms of service **Army** up to 16 months **Navy** up to 19 months **Air Force** up to 19 months

RESERVES some 291,000

(to age 50) **Army** some 235,000 (Field Army 200,000, Territorial Army/National Guard 35,000) **Navy** about 24,000 **Air Force** about 32,000

Army 114,000

(incl 81,000 conscripts, 2,700 women)

FIELD ARMY

3 Mil Regions • 1 Army, 2 comd, 5 corps HQ (incl 1 RRF) • 5 div HQ (1 armd, 3 mech, 1 inf) • 5 inf div (3 inf, 1 arty regt, 1 armd bn) • 5 indep armd bde (each 2 armd, 1 mech inf, 1 SP arty bn) • 7 mech bde (2 mech, 1 armd, 1 SP arty bn) • 5 inf bde • 1 army avn bde with 5 avn bn (incl 1 ATK, 1 tpt hel) • 1 indep avn coy • Special Forces: 1 marine bde (3 bn), 1 special ops comd (incl 1 amph cdo sqn), 1 cdo bde (3 cdo, 1 para sqn) • 4 recce bn • 5 fd arty bn • 10 AD arty bn • 2 SAM bn with I HAWK
Units are manned at 3 different levels
Cat A 85% fully ready **Cat B** 60% ready in 24 hours
Cat C 20% ready in 48 hours

RESERVES 34,000

National Guard internal security role

EQUIPMENT

MBT 1,735: 695 M-48A5, 628 M-60A1/A3, 412 *Leopard-1*

RECCE 130 M-8, 37 VBL, 8 HMMWV

AIFV 501 BMP-1

APC 131 *Leonidas* Mk1/Mk2, 1,540 M-113A1/A2

TOTAL ARTY 1,901

TOWED 729: **105mm**: 18 M-56, 445 M-101; **155mm**: 266 M-114

SP 400: **155mm**: 195 M-109A1B/A2/A3GEA1/A5, 12 *Zuzana*, **175mm**: 12 M-107; **203mm**: 181 M-110A2

MRL 122mm: 116 RM-70; **227mm**: 36 MLRS (incl ATACMS)

MOR 107mm: 620 M-30 (incl 231 SP); plus **81mm**:

2,800
ATGW 290 *Milan* (incl 42 HMMWV), 336 TOW (incl 320 M-901), 262 AT-4 *Spigot*
RL 64mm: 18,520 RPG-18; **66mm**: 10,700 M-72
RCL 84mm: 2000 *Carl Gustav*; **90mm**: 1,314 EM-67; **106mm**: 1,291 M-40A1
AD GUNS 23mm: 506 ZU-23-2
SAM 1,000 *Stinger*, 42 I HAWK, 21 SA-15, 20 SA-8B, SA-10 (S-300) in Crete, originally intended for Cy
SURV 10 AN/TPQ-36 (arty, mor), 2 AN/TPQ-37(V)3
AC 43 U-17A
HELICOPTERS
ATTACK 20 AH-64A
SPT 9 CH-47D (1 in store), 76 UH-1H, 31 AB-205A, 14 AB-206

Navy 19,000

(incl 9,800 conscripts, 1,300 women)
BASES Salamis, Patras, Soudha Bay
SUBMARINES 8
SSK 8
4 *Glavkos* (Ge T-209/1100) with 533mm TT, and *Harpoon* USGW (1 in refit)
4 *Poseidon* (Ge T-209/1200) with 533mm TT and *Harpoon* USGW
PRINCIPAL SURFACE COMBATANTS 14
DESTROYERS 2
DDG 2 *Kimon* (US *Adams*) with 6 *Harpoon* SSM, 1 × 1 *Standard* SM-1 SAM, 2 × 127mm gun, 2 × 3 ASTT, 1 × 8 *ASROC* SUGW
FRIGATES 12
FFG 12
4 *Hydra* (Ge MEKO 200) with 8 *Harpoon* SSM, 1 × 127mm gun, 6 ASTT, 1 SH-60 hel
3 *Elli* (Nl *Kortenaer* Batch 2) with 8 *Harpoon* SSM, *Sea Sparrow* SAM, 2 × 76mm gun, 4 ASTT, 2 AB-212 hel (4th to be commissioned in Nov 2002)
4 *Aegean* (Nl *Kortenaer* Batch 1) with 8 *Harpoon* SSM, *Sea Sparrow* SAM, 1 × 76mm gun, 4 ASTT, 2 AB-212 hel
1 *Makedonia* (ex-US *Knox*) (US lease) with *Harpoon* SSM (from ASROC launcher), 1 × 127mm gun, 4 ASTT, 8 *ASROC* SUGW
PATROL AND COASTAL COMBATANTS 40
CORVETTES 5 *Niki* (ex-Ge *Thetis*) FS with 4 ASW RL, 4 × 533mm TT
MISSILE CRAFT 17
11 *Laskos* (Fr *La Combattante* II, III, IIIB) PFM, all with 2 × 533mm TT; 8 with 4 MM-38 *Exocet* SSM, 5 with 6 *Penguin* SSM
4 *Votsis* (Fr *La Combattante* IIA) PFM 2 with 4 MM-38 *Exocet* SSM, 2 with *Harpoon* SSM
2 *Stamou* with 4 SS-12 SSM
TORPEDO CRAFT 8
4 *Hesperos* (Ge *Jaguar*) PFT with 4 533mm TT
4 *Andromeda* (No *Nasty*) PFT with 4 533mm TT
PATROL CRAFT 10
OFFSHORE 4
2 *Armatolos* (Dk *Osprey*) PCO, 2 *Pirpolitis* PCO
COASTAL/INSHORE 6
2 *Tolmi* PCC, 4 PCI<
MINE WARFARE 13
MINELAYERS 1 *Aktion* (US LSM-1) (100–130 mines)
MINE COUNTERMEASURES 12
2 *Europe* MHC (UK *Hunt*)
8 *Alkyon* (US MSC-294) MSC
2 *Atalanti* (US *Adjutant*) MSC
AMPHIBIOUS 6
5 *Chios* LST with hel deck: capacity 300 tps, 4 LCVP plus veh
1 *Inouse* (US *County*) LST: capacity 400 tps, 18 tk
Plus about 61 craft: 2 LCT, 6 LCU, 11 LCM, some 31 LCVP, 7 LCA, 4 *Zubr* ACV
SUPPORT AND MISCELLANEOUS 20
2 AOT, 4 AOT (small), 1 *Axios* (ex-Ge *Lüneburg*) log spt, 1 AE, 3 AGHS, 1 trg, 2 personnel tpt, 6 AWT
NAVAL AVIATION (250)
EQUIPMENT
18 armed hel
HELICOPTERS
ASW 8 AB-212, 2 SA-319, 8 S-70B
SAR 2 AB-212
MISSILES
AAM *Penguin*

Air Force 33,000

(incl 7,521 conscripts, 1,520 women)
TACTICAL AIR CMD
FGA/AD 14 sqns with A-7H, F-16CG/DG, F-4E, F-5A/B, *Mirage* F-1CG, *Mirage* 2000 EG/BG
AEW 1 sqn with 2 Saab 340H *Erieye*
RECCE 1 sqn with RF-4E
AIR SUP CMD
TPT 3 sqn with C-130H/B, YS-11, C-47, Do-28, *Gulfstream*
HEL 1 sqn with AB-205A, AB-212, Bell 47G, AS-332
CSAR First of 6 CSAR *Super Puma* to be delivered in 2003
AIR DEFENCE
2 *Nike* and 1 *Patriot* SAM sqns, twin **35mm** guns
AIR TRAINING CMD
TRG 4 sqn with T-2E, T-37B/C, T-6A, T-33
EQUIPMENT
418 cbt ac, no armed hel
AC 96 **A-7H/TA-7H** • 86 **F-5A/B**, 10 **NF-5A**, 1 **NF-5B** • 92 **F-4E/RF-4E**, of which 36 being upgraded • 74 **F-16CG** (FGA)/**DG** (trg) • 25 *Mirage* **F-1 CG** (ftr) • 34 *Mirage* **2000** (**EG** (FGA)/**BG*** (trg))-10 EG being upgraded to 2000-5 • (97 F-TF-104Gs in storage) • 2 Saab 340H *Erieye* (on loan from Swe

AF pending delivery of 4 EMB-145/*Erieye* from 2003-4) • 4 **C-47** (tpt) • 10 **C-130H** (tpt) • 5 **C-130B** (tpt) • 2 **YS-11-200** (tpt) • 13 **Do-28** (tpt) • 2 ***Gulfstream* I/V** (VIP tpt) • 35 **T-2E** (trg) • 34 **T-37B/C** (trg) • 45 **T-6A** (trg)

HEL 13 **AB-205A** (SAR) • 4 **AS-332** • 1 **AB-206** • 4 **AB-212** (VIP, tpt) • 7 **Bell 47G** (liaison)• 6 **CSAR AS-332** to be delivered

MISSILES

ASM AGM-65 *Maverick*, AGM-88 HARM

AAM AIM-7 *Sparrow*, AIM-9 *Sidewinder* L/P, R-550 *Magic* 2, AIM 120 AMRAAM, *Super* 530D

SAM 1 bn with 36 *Nike Hercules*, 6 *Patriot* PAC-3 bty, 12 bty with *Skyguard*, 40 *Sparrow*, 4 SA-15, 9 *Crotale*, **35mm** guns

Forces Abroad

CYPRUS 1,250: incl 1 mech bde and officers/NCO seconded to Greek-Cypriot forces

UN AND PEACEKEEPING

ADRIATIC (*Sharp Guard* if re-implemented): 2 MSC **AFGHANISTAN** (ISAF): ε30 **BOSNIA** (SFOR II): 250 **SFOR Air Component** 1 C-130 **ETHIOPIA/ERITREA** (UNMEE): 2 obs **GEORGIA** (UNOMIG): 4 obs **IRAQ/KUWAIT** (UNIKOM): 2 obs **WESTERN SAHARA** (MINURSO): 1 obs **YUGOSLAVIA** (KFOR): 1,700

Paramilitary 4,000

COAST GUARD AND CUSTOMS 4,000

some 100 patrol craft, **ac** 2 Cessna *Cutlass*, 2 TB-20 *Trinidad*

Foreign Forces

NATO HQ Joint Command South-Centre (SOUTHCENT). (COMMZ(S)): ε18 spt tps from 6 countries for KFOR

US 290: **Navy** 240; facilities at Soudha Bay **Air Force** 50; air base gp; facilities at Iraklion

Hungary Hu

Total Armed Forces

ACTIVE 33,400

(incl 2,100 Central HQ comd staff; 22,900 conscripts)
Terms of service 6 months

RESERVES 90,300

Army 74,900 **Air Force** 15,400 (to age 50)

Land Forces 23,600

(incl 16,500 conscripts)
1 Land Forces HQ, 1 garrison comd
1 mob and trg comd (with 5 trg school/centre)
3 mech inf bde each 2 mech, 1 armd, 1 arty bn, 1 recce coy, 1 AD bty, 1 engr coy
1 mixed arty bde, 1 SAM regt
1 engr bde
1 lt mixed, 1 MP regt
2 recce bn
1 army maritime wing, 1 counter mine bn

RESERVES

4 mech inf bde

EQUIPMENT

MBT 743: 505 T-55, 238 T-72
RECCE 104 FUG D-442
AIFV 490 BMP-1, 12 BRM-1K, 178 BTR-80A
APC 459 BTR-80, 335 PSZH D-944 (82 in store), 4 MT-LB (plus 310 APC and AIFV 'look-a-like' types)
TOTAL ARTY 834
TOWED 528: **122mm**: 227 M-1938 (M-30); **152mm**: 301 D-20
SP 122mm: 151 2S1
MRL 122mm: 56 BM-21
MOR 120mm: 99 M-120 (1 in store)
ATGW 364: 110 AT-3 *Sagger* (incl BRDM-2SP), 30 AT-4 *Spigot* (incl BRDM-2 SP), 224 AT-5 *Spandrel*
ATK GUNS 85mm: 162 D-44 (all in store); **100mm**: 106 MT-12
AD GUNS 57mm: 186 S-60 (43 in store)
SAM 243 SA-7, 60 SA-14, 45 *Mistral*
SURV PSZNR-5B, SZNAR-10

Army Maritime Wing (270)

BASE Budapest

RIVER CRAFT 50

6 *Nestin* MSI (riverine), some 44 An-2 mine warfare/patrol boats

Air Force Command 7,700

(incl conscripts)
37 cbt ac (plus 55 in store), 49 attack hel
Flying hours 50
FGA 1 tac ftr wg with 27 MiG-29A/UB (14 being upgraded), 8 MiG-21, 1 MiG-23, 1 Su-22
IN STORE 44 MiG-21, 3 MiG-23, 8 Su-22
ATTACK HEL 1 cbt hel wg with 49 Mi-24
SUPPORT HEL 23 Mi-8/17 (tpt/assault), 1 Mi-9 (Cmd Post), 2 Mi-17PP (EW)
TPT 1 mixed tpt wg, 1 mixed tpt sqn, ac 8 An-26, 4 Z-43, hel 20 Mi-2, 24 Mi-8/17
TRG 19 L-39, 12 Yak-52
AAM AA-2 *Atoll*, AA-8 *Aphid*, AA-10 *Alamo*, AA-11 *Archer*

ASM AT-2 *Swatter*, AT-6 *Spiral*
SAM 2 mixed AD msl regt with 66 SA-2/-3/-5, 12 SA-4, 20 SA-6

Forces Abroad

UN AND PEACEKEEPING

BOSNIA (SFOR II): 4 obs plus 155 tps (engr) **CYPRUS** (UNFICYP): 121 **EGYPT** (MFO): 41 mil pol **GEORGIA** (UNOMIG): 7 obs **IRAQ/KUWAIT** (UNIKOM): 6 obs **WESTERN SAHARA** (MINURSO): 6 obs **YUGOSLAVIA** (KFOR): 325; 1 mech inf bn

Paramilitary 14,000

BORDER GUARDS (Ministry of Interior) 12,000 (to reduce)

11 districts/regts plus 1 Budapest district (incl 7 rapid-reaction coy; 68 BTR-80 APC)

Iceland Icl

Total Armed Forces

ACTIVE Nil

Paramilitary 120

COAST GUARD 120

BASE Reykjavik
PATROL CRAFT 4
2 *Aegir* PCO with hel, 1 *Odinn* PCO with hel deck, 1 PCI<
AVN ac 1 F-27, **hel** 1 SA-365N, 1 SA-332, 1 AS-350B

Foreign Forces

NATO Island Commander Iceland (ISCOMICE, responsible to CINCEASTLANT)
US 1,478: **Navy** 960; MR: 1 sqn with 4 P-3C **Marines** 48 **Air Force** 470; 4 F-15C/D, 1 HC-130, 1 KC-135, 4 HH-60G
NETHERLANDS 16: **Navy** 1 P-3C

Italy It

Total Armed Forces

ACTIVE 216,800
(incl 70,200 conscripts)
Terms of service all services 10 months

RESERVES 65,200 (immediate mobilisation)
Army 11,900 (500,000 obligation to age 45) **Navy** 23,000 (to age 39 for men, variable for officers to 73) **Air Force** 30,300 (to age 25 or 45 (specialists))

Army 128,000

(incl 57,000 conscripts)
1 Op Comd HQ, 3 mil region HQ
1 Projection Force HQ with 1 sigs bde
1 mtn force with 3 mtn bde, 1 engr, 1 avn regt, 1 alpine AB bn
2 div defence force
  1 with 1 armd, 1 mech, 1 armd cav, 1 AB, 1 airmobile bde, 1 engr regt
  1 with 5 mech bde, 1 engr, 1 avn regt
1 spt comd with
  1 AD div: 2 HAWK SAM, 2 SHORAD regt
  1 arty bde: 1 hy arty, 2 arty, 1 NBC regt
  1 engr bde (3 regt)
  1 avn div: 3 avn regt, 1 avn bn

EQUIPMENT
MBT 1,018 (plus 235 in store): 440 *Leopard* 1 (320 A1, 120 A5), 378 *Centauro* B-1, 200 *Ariete*
AIFV 26 VCC-80 *Dardo*
APC 920 M-113 (incl variants), 545 VCC-1, 1,228 VCC-2, 157 Fiat 6614, 87 BV-206
AAV 14 LVTP-7
TOTAL ARTY 1,354
TOWED 325: **105mm**: 157 Model 56 pack; **155mm**: 164 FH-70, 4 M-114 (in store)
SP 155mm: 260 M-109G/L; **203mm**: 1 M-110
MRL 227mm: 22 MLRS
MOR 120mm: 724 Brandt, 22 RT-F1; **81mm**: 1,200
ATGW 426 TOW 2B, 432 I-TOW, 752 *Milan*
RL 1,860 *Panzerfaust* 3
RCL 80mm: 434 *Folgore*
AD GUNS 25mm: 120 SIDAM SP
SAM 66 HAWK, 80 *Stinger*, 46 *Skyguard*/*Aspide*
AC 6 SM-1019, 3 Do-228, 3 P-180
HELICOPTERS
ATTACK 45 A-129
ASLT 27 A-109, 61 AB-206
SPT 88 AB-205A, 66 AB-206 (obs), 14 AB-212, 22 AB-412, 36 CH-47C
UAV 5 *Mirach* 20

Navy 38,000

(incl 2,500 Naval Avn, 1,500 Marines; 5,000 conscripts)
COMMANDS 1 Fleet Commander CINCNAV (also NATO COMEDCENT) **Area Commands** 5 Upper Tyrrhenian, Ionian and Strait of Otranto, Rome, Sardinia, Sicily
BASES La Spezia (HQ), Taranto (HQ), Brindisi, Augusta

SUBMARINES 6

SSK 6

4 *Pelosi* (imp *Sauro*) with 6 × 533mm TT (Type 184 HWT)

2 *Sauro* with 6 × 533mm TT (Type 184 HWT)

PRINCIPAL SURFACE COMBATANTS 20

AIRCRAFT CARRIERS 1 *G. Garibaldi* CVS with standard composition of 6 AV-8B *Harrier* V/STOL or 4 SH-3 *Sea King* hel

CRUISERS 1 *Vittorio Veneto* CGH with 4 *Teseo* SSM, 1 × 2 *Standard* SM-1 ER SAM, 8 × 76mm gun, 2 × 3 ASTT, 6 AB-212 ASW hel (Mk 46 LWT)

DESTROYERS 4

DDG 4

2 *Luigi Durand de la Penne* (ex-*Animoso*) with 2 × 4 *Teseo* SSM, 1 *Standard* SM-1 MR SAM, 1 × 127mm gun, 6 × 324mm ASTT (Mk 46 LWT), 2 AB-312 hel

2 *Audace* with 4 *Teseo* SSM, 1 *Standard* SM-1 MR SAM, 1 × 127mm gun, 2 × 3 ASTT, 2 AB-212 hel

FRIGATES 14

FFG 14

8 *Maestrale* with 4 *Teseo* SSM, *Aspide* SAM, 1 × 127mm gun, 2 × 533mm ASTT, 2 AB-212 hel

2 *Lupo* with 8 *Teseo* SSM, *Sea Sparrow* SAM, 1 × 127mm gun, 2 × 3 ASTT, 1 AB-212 hel

4 *Artigliere* with 8 *Teseo* SSM, 8 *Aspide* SAM, 1 × 127mm gun, 1 AB-212 hel

PATROL AND COASTAL COMBATANTS 16

CORVETTES 8 *Minerva* FS with *Aspide* SAM, 1 × 76mm gun, 6 × ASTT

PATROL, OFFSHORE 5

4 *Cassiopea* PCO with 1 × 76mm gun, 1 AB-212 hel, 1 *Comandante Cigala Fuligosi* PCO with 1 × 76mm gun, 1 AB 212 hel

PATROL, COASTAL 3

3 *Esplatore* PCC

MINE WARFARE 13

MINE COUNTERMEASURES 13

1 MCCS (ex *Alpino*)

4 *Lerici* MHC/MSC

8 *Gaeta* MHC/MSC

AMPHIBIOUS 3

2 *San Giorgio* LPD: capacity 350 tps, 30 trucks, 2 SH-3D or 1 CH-47 hel, 6 landing craft

1 *San Giusto* LPD: capacity as above

Plus some 33 craft: about 3 LCU, 10 LCM and 20 LCVP

SUPPORT AND MISCELLANEOUS 28

2 *Stromboli* AO, 1 *Etna* AO; 5 AWT, 2 AR; 1 ARS, 7 sail trg, 7 AT (plus 43 coastal AT); 3 AGOR; 2 diving tender

NAVAL AVIATION (2,500)

EQUIPMENT

18 cbt ac; 79 armed hel

AIRCRAFT

FGA 16 AV-8B

TRG 2 TAV-8B*

HELICOPTERS

ASW 16 SH-3D, 40 AB-212, 9 EH-101

AMPH ASLT 8 SH-3D, 6 AB-212

MISSILES

AAM AIM-9L *Sidewinder*

AGM 65 *Maverick*

ASM *Marte* Mk 2, AS-12

SPECIAL FORCES (Special Forces Command – COMSUBIN)

4 gp; 1 diving op; 1 Navy SF op; 1 school; 1 research

MARINES (San Marco gp) (1,500)

1 bn gp, 1 trg gp, 1 log gp

EQUIPMENT

30 VCC-1, 20 VCC-2 APC, 18 LVTP-7 AAV; 4 Brandt **120mm**, 16 **81mm** mor, 8 **106mm** RCL, 6 *Milan* ATGW, *Stinger* SAM

Air Force 50,800

(incl 91 women and 8,200 conscripts)

AFHQ 2 Inspectorates (Naval Aviation, Flight Safety), 1 Op Cmd (responsible for 5 op bde), 1 Force Cmd, 1 Logs Cmd, 1 Trg Cmd

FGA 8 sqn

4 with *Tornado* IDS • 4 with AMX (50% of 1 sqn devoted to recce)

FTR 5 sqn

4 with F-104 ASA • 1 with *Tornado* ADV

MR 2 sqn with BR 1150 *Atlantic* (OPCON to Navy)

EW 1 ECM/recce sqn with G-222VS, PD-808, P-180, P-166DL-3

TPT 3 sqn

2 with G-222, C-130J • 1 with C-130H

TKR/TPT/CAL 1 sqn with B707-320, G-222 RM, PD-808

TPT/VIP 2 sqn with **ac** *Falcon* 50, *Falcon* 900EX, DC-9, A319CJ **hel** SH-3D

TRG

1 OCU with TF-104G

4 sqn with AMX-T, MB-339A, MB-339CD, SF-260M

1 sqn with MB-339A (aerobatic team)

1 sqn with hel NH-500

CSAR 1 sqn with hel HH-3F

SAR 3 det with HH-3F, 4 det with AB-212

AD 12 bty: 3 HSAM bty with *Nike Hercules*, 9 SAM bty with *Spada*

EQUIPMENT

261 cbt ac (plus 65 in store), 6 armed hel

AC 100 ***Tornado*** (77 IDS, 23 ADV) (plus 14 FGA and 1 ADV in store) • 49 **F-104ASA** (plus 4 in store) • 12 **TF-104G** • 74 **AMX** (56 (FGA), 18 **-T** (trg)) (plus 29 in store) • 69 **MB-339** (17 aero team, 52 trg) • 14* **MB-339CD** (plus 1 in store) • 12* ***Atlantic*** (MR) (plus 6 in store) • 2 **Boeing-707-320** (tkr/tpt) (plus 2 in store) • 16 **C-130H/J** (tpt/tkr) (plus 2 in store) • 22 **G-222** (tpt/tac/calibration) (plus 16 in store) • 2 **Airbus A319CJ** • 3 ***Falcon* 50** (VIP) (plus 1 in store), 2 ***Falcon* 900** (VIP) • 6 **P-166-DL3** (liaison/trg) • 4 **P-180** (liaison) (plus 2 in store) • 3 **PD-808** (ECM, cal, VIP, tpt) • 34 **SF-260M** (trg) (plus 5 in store) • 32 **SIAI-208** (liaison) (plus 7 in store)

HEL 23 **HH-3F** (17 SAR, 6*CSAR) • 1 **SH-3D** (liaison/VIP) (plus 1 in store) • 27 **AB-212** (SAR) (plus 8 in store) • 48 **NH-500D** (trg) (plus 2 in store)

UAV 4 *Predator* on order, first op by mid-2002

MISSILES

ASM AGM-88 HARM, *Kormoran*

AAM AIM-9L *Sky Flash, Aspide*

SAM *Nike Hercules, Aspide*

Forces Abroad

GERMANY 93: **Air Force, NAEW Force**
MALTA 16: **Air Force** with 2 AB-212
US 40: **Air Force** flying trg
CANADA 12: **Air Force** flying trg

UN AND PEACEKEEPING

AFGHANISTAN (ISAF): ε350 **ALBANIA** (COMMZ-W): 1,160 spt tps for KFOR **BOSNIA** (SFOR II): 1,600: 1 mech inf bde gp **DROC** (MONUC): 4 incl 1 obs **EGYPT** (MFO): 75 **ETHIOPIA/ERITREA** (UNMEE): 210 incl 4 obs **INDIA/PAKISTAN** (UNMOGIP): 8 obs **IRAQ/KUWAIT** (UNIKOM): 4 obs **LEBANON** (UNIFIL): 51; hel unit **MIDDLE EAST** (UNTSO): 7 obs **WESTERN SAHARA** (MINURSO): 5 obs **YUGOSLAVIA** (KFOR): 4,200

Paramilitary 254,300

CARABINIERI 111,800

(Ministry of Defence – under command of the Chief of Defence Staff but remain under the control of Ministry of Interior for civil police functions)

Territorial 5 inter-regional, 19 regional, 102 provincial comd, 10 territorial dept, 1 gp comd **Trg** HQ and 5 school **Mobile def** 1 div, special units with 1 Ministry of Foreign Affairs Carabinieri comd, 8 other comd with tp, 1 hel gp; 1 mobile div: 2 bde (1 with 2 mobile regt), 1 AB regt, 11 mobile bn, 1 Special Intervention Group (GIS)), 1 mounted cav regt

EQUIPMENT 48 Fiat 6616 armd cars; 10 VCC-1, 20 VCC-2 APC **hel** 24 A-109, 38 AB-206, 30 AB-412 **craft** 72 PCC, 74 PCI, 28 PCR<

PUBLIC SECURITY GUARD 79,000 (Ministry of Interior)

11 mobile units; 40 Fiat 6614 APC **ac** 5 P-68 **hel** 12 A-109, 20 AB-206, 9 AB-212

FINANCE GUARDS 63,500 (Treasury Department)

14 Zones, 20 Legions, 128 gp **ac** 5 P-166-DL3 **hel** 15 A-109, 65 Breda-Nardi NH-500M/MC/MD; 3 PCI; plus about 300 boats

HARBOUR CONTROL (*Capitanerie di Porto*)

(subordinated to Navy in emergencies): 12 PCI, 130+ boats; 4 AB-412 (SAR)

Foreign Forces

NATO HQ Allied Forces South Europe, HQ Allied Air Forces South (AIRSOUTH), HQ Allied Naval Forces South (NAVSOUTH), HQ Joint Command South (JCSOUTH), HQ 5 Allied Tactical Air Force (5 ATAF)
US 10,790: **Army** 2,600; 1 inf bn gp **Navy** 4,400 **Air Force** 3,620 **USMC** 170
DELIBERATE FORGE COMPONENTS Be 4 F-16A **Ca** 6 CF-18 **Da** 3 F-16A **Fr** 6 *Mirage* 2000C/D, 3 *Jaguar* **GE** 19 *Tornado* **Nl** 4 F-16A **Sp** 5 EF-18, 1 KC-130 **Tu** 4 F-16C **UK** 4 *Harrier* GR-7, 1 *Canberra* PR9, 2 E-3D *Sentry* **US** 32 F-16C/D, 2 E-3D, 1 AC-130, 1 KC-135, 6 UH-60, 2 U-2, 10 P-3C, 5 C-12, 5 C-21, 2 LJ-35, 1 SW4B

Luxembourg Lu

Total Armed Forces

ACTIVE 900

Army 900

1 lt inf bn, 2 recce coy (1 to Eurocorps/BE div, 1 to AMF(L))

EQUIPMENT

MOR 81mm: 6
ATGW 6 TOW
RL LAW

Air Force

(none, but for legal purposes NATO's E-3A AEW ac have Lu registration)

1 sqn with 17 E-3A *Sentry* (NATO standard), 2 Boeing 707 (trg)

Forces Abroad

UN AND PEACEKEEPING

BOSNIA (SFOR II): 23 **Deliberate Forge Air Component** 5 E-3A **YUGOSLAVIA** (KFOR): some

Paramilitary 612

GENDARMERIE 612

Netherlands Nl

Total Armed Forces

ACTIVE 49,580

(incl 2,150 HQ Staff and centrally controlled units/formations, 3,300 Royal Military Constabulary; 4,155 women; excl 20,000 civilians)

RESERVES 32,200

(men to age 35, NCOs to 40, officers to 45) **Army** 22,200 **Navy** some 5,000 **Air Force** 5,000 (immediate recall)

Army 23,150

(incl 1,630 women)
1 Corps HQ (Ge/Nl), 1 mech div HQ • 3 mech inf bde (2 cadre) • 1 air-mobile bde (3 inf bn) • 1 fd arty gp, 1 AD bn • 1 engr gp (3 bn)
Summary of cbt arm units
3 tk bn • 6 armd inf bn • 3 air-mobile bn • 1 armd recce bn • 6 arty bn • 1 AD bn • 1 SF bn • 2 MLRS bty

RESERVES

(cadre bde and corps tps completed by call-up of reservists)
National Command (incl Territorial Comd): 6 inf bn, could be mob for territorial defence
Home Guard 3 sectors; lt inf wpns

EQUIPMENT

MBT 30 *Leopard* 1, 298 *Leopard* 2
AIFV 352 YPR-765
APC 236 YPR-765 (plus 524 AIFV & APC look-a-likes), 59 XA-188 *Sisu*, 21 TPz-1 *Fuchs*
TOTAL ARTY 370
TOWED 155mm: 20 M-114, 80 M-114/39, 12 FH-70 (trg)
SP 155mm: 121 M-109A3
MRL 227mm: 22 MLRS
MOR 120mm: 115 Brandt; **81mm**: 40
ATGW 753 (incl 135 in store): 427 *Dragon*, 326 TOW (incl 96 YPR-765)
RL 84mm: AT-4
RCL 84mm: *Carl Gustav*
AD GUNS 35mm: 77 *Gepard* SP (60 to be upgraded); **40mm**: 60 L/70 towed
SAM 312 *Stinger*
SURV AN/TPQ-36 (arty, mor)
UAV *Sperwer*
MARINE 1 tk tpt, 3 coastal, 3 river patrol boats

Navy 12,130

(incl 950 Naval Avn, 3,100 Marines; 1,150 women)
BASES Netherlands Den Helder (HQ). Nl and Be Navies under joint op comd based Den Helder. Valkenburg (MPA) De Kooy (hel) **Overseas** Willemstad (Curaçao)

SUBMARINES 4

SSK 4 *Walrus* with Mk 48 HWT; plus provision for *Harpoon* USGW

PRINCIPAL SURFACE COMBATANTS 12

DESTROYERS 2
DDG (Nl desig = FFG) 2
2 *Van Heemskerck* with 8 *Harpoon* SSM, 1 *Standard* SM-1 MR SAM, 4 × 324mm ASTT
FRIGATES 9
FFG 9
8 *Karel Doorman* with 8 *Harpoon* SSM, *Sea Sparrow* SAM, 1 × 76mm gun, 4 ASTT, 1 *Lynx* hel
1 *Kortenaer* with 8 × *Harpoon* SSM, 8 × *Sea Sparrow* SAM, 1 × 76mm gun, 4 ASTT, 2 *Lynx* hel (stationed permanently in Antilles)

MINE WARFARE 12

MINELAYERS none, but *Mercuur*, listed under spt and misc, has capability
MINE COUNTERMEASURES 12
12 *Alkmaar* (tripartite) MHC
plus 4 diving vessels

AMPHIBIOUS 1

1 *Rotterdam* LPD: capacity 600 troops, 6 *Lynx* hel or 4 NH-90 plus 4 LCU/6 LCA
plus craft: 5 LCU, 6 LCA

SUPPORT AND MISCELLANEOUS 8

1 *Amsterdam* AO (4 *Lynx* or 2 NH-90), 1 *Zuideruis* AO (2 *Lynx* or 2 NH-90), 1 *Pelikaan* spt; 1 *Mercuur* torpedo tender, 2 trg; 1 AGOR, 1 AGHS

NAVAL AVIATION (950)

EQUIPMENT
10 cbt ac, 21 armed hel
AIRCRAFT
MR/ASW 10 P-3C
HELICOPTERS
ASW/SAR 21 *Lynx*

MARINES (3,100)

3 Marine bn (1 cadre); 1 spt bn (incl 1 recce, 2 mor coy) (1 bn integrated with UK 3rd Cdo Bde to form UK/NL Amph Landing Force)

EQUIPMENT

APC 22 YPR-765 (incl 11 'look-a-likes'), 20 XA-188 *Sisu*
TOWED ARTY 105mm: 8 lt
MOR 120mm: 14 Brandt; **81mm**: 18
ATGW *Dragon*
RL AT-4
RCL 84mm: *Carl Gustav*
SAM *Stinger*

Air Force 8,850

(incl 975 women)
Flying hours 180
3 Cmds - Tac Air, Support, Air Trg
CBT AC GP
FTR/FGA/RECCE swing role. 6 sqn (with 18 F-16 AM (MLU) each) at 3 air bases. 1 trg sqn
AIR TPT FLEET 1 sqn with F-50, F-60, C-130H-30, KDC-10 (tkr/tpt), *Gulfstream* IV
TAC HEL GP
2 sqn with AH-64D
1 sqn with BO-105
1 sqn with AS-532U2, SA-316
1 sqn with CH-47D
1 SAR sqn with AB-412 SP
TRG 1 sqn with PC-7
GBAD GP
AD 4 sqns (TRIAD), each with 1 *Patriot* SAM bty (TMD), 2 *Hawk* SAM bty, 7 *Stinger* teams

EQUIPMENT

143 cbt ac, 30 attack hel
AC 143 **F-16**: (138 - 92 F-16A, 21 F-16A(R) and 25 F-16B – converted under European mid-life update programme) • 2 **F-50** • 4 **F-60** • 2 **C-130H-30** • 2 **KDC-10** (tkr/tpt) • 1 *Gulfstream* IV • 13 **PC-7** (trg)
HEL 3 **AB-412 SP** (SAR) • 4 **SA-316** • 15 **BO-105** • 30 **AH-64D** • 13 **CH-47D** • 17 **AS-532U2**

MISSILES

AAM AIM-9/L/N *Sidewinder*, AIM-120B AMRAAM
ASM AGM-65G *Maverick*, AGM-114K *Hellfire*
SAM 48 HAWK, 5 *Patriot*, 100 *Stinger*
AD GUNS 25 VL 4/41 *Flycatcher* radar, 75 L/70 **40mm** systems

Forces Abroad

GERMANY 2,600: **Army** 2,300; 1 mech inf bde (1 armd inf, 1 tk bn), plus spt elms **Air Force** 300
ICELAND 16: **Navy** 1 P-3C
NETHERLANDS ANTILLES Nl, Aruba and the Netherlands Antilles operate a Coast Guard Force to combat org crime and drug smuggling. Comd by Netherlands Commander Caribbean. HQ Curaçao, bases Aruba and St Maarten **Navy** 20 (to expand); 1 FFG, 1 amph cbt det, 3 P-3C, 1 Marine bn (2 coy)

UN AND PEACEKEEPING

AFGHANISTAN (ISAF): ε150 **BOSNIA** (SFOR II): ε1,000; 1 mech inf bn gp **ETHIOPIA/ERITREA** (UNMEE): 3 **FYROM** (OP AMBER FOX): ε400 **ITALY**: 80 (DELIBERATE FORGE) 4 F-16 **MIDDLE EAST** (UNTSO): 12 obs **YUGOSLAVIA** (KFOR): 1,450

Paramilitary 3,300

ROYAL MILITARY CONSTABULARY (*Koninklijke Marechaussee*) 3,300 (incl 400 women)
6 districts with 60 'bde'. Eqpt incl 24 YPR-765 APC

Foreign Forces

NATO HQ Allied Forces North Europe
US 550: **Army** 380 **Air Force**160 **Navy** 10

Norway No

Total Armed Forces

ACTIVE 26,600
(incl 400 Joint Services org, 400 Home Guard permanent staff; 15,200 conscripts)
Terms of service **Army**, **Navy**, **Air Force**, 12 months, plus 4–5 refresher trg periods

RESERVES

219,000 on 24–72 hour readiness; obligation to 44 (conscripts remain with fd army units to age 35, officers to age 55, regulars to age 60)
Army 89,000 **Navy** 22,000 **Air Force** 25,000 **Home Guard** some 83,000 on mob

Army 14,700

(incl 8,700 conscripts)
2 Joint Comd, 4 Land Comd, 14 territorial regt
North Norway 1 ranger bn, border gd, cadre and trg units for 1 div (1 armd, 2 mot inf bde) and 1 indep mech inf bde
South Norway 2 inf bn (incl Royal Guard), indep units plus cadre units for 1 mech inf and 1 armd bde

RESERVES

17 inf, 3 ranger, 1 arty bn; AD, engr, sigs and log units

LAND HOME GUARD 73,000

18 districts each divided into 2–6 sub-districts (bn) comprising a total of 480 units (coy)

EQUIPMENT

MBT 170 *Leopard* (111 -1A5NO, 59 -1A1NO)
AIFV 53 NM-135 (M-113/**20mm**), ε104 CV 9030N
APC 109 M-113 (incl variants), ε80 XA-186/-200 *Sisu*
TOTAL ARTY 184
TOWED 155mm: 46 M-114/39
SP 155mm: 126 M-109A3GN
MRL 227mm: 12 MLRS
MOR 81mm: 450 (40 SP incl 24 M-106A1, 12 M-125A2)
ATGW 320 TOW-1/-2 incl 97 NM-142 (M-901), 424 *Eryx*
RL 66mm: M-72
RCL 84mm: 2,517 *Carl Gustav*
AD GUNS 20mm: 252 Rh-202 (192 in store)
SAM 300 RBS-70 (120 in store)
SURV *Cymberline* (mor), 12 ARTHUR

Navy 6,100

(incl 160 Coastal Defence, 270 Coast Guard; 3,300 conscripts)
COMMANDS 2 Joint Operational Comds, COMNAVSONOR (south Norway) and COMNAVNON (north Norway) with regional naval commanders and 7 regional Naval districts
BASES Horten, Haakonsvern (Bergen), Olavsvern (Tromsø)

SUBMARINES 6

SSK 6 *Ula* with 8 × 533mm TT (DM 2 A3 HWT)

PRINCIPAL SURFACE COMBATANTS 3

FRIGATES 3
FFG 3 *Oslo* with 4 *Penguin 1* SSM, *Sea Sparrow* SAM, 1 × 2 76mm gun, 6 *Terne* ASW RL, *Stingray* LWT (1 more in reserve)

PATROL AND COASTAL COMBATANTS 15

MISSILE CRAFT 15
11 *Hauk* PFM with 6 × *Penguin* 2 SSM, 2 × *Mistral* SAM, 2 (Swe TP-613) HWT
3 mod *Hauk*, wpns as above
1 *Skjold* PFM

MINE WARFARE 10

MINELAYERS 2
1 *Vidar*, coastal (300–400 mines), 1 *Tyr* (amph craft also fitted for minelaying)
MINE COUNTERMEASURES 8
4 *Oskøy* MHC, 4 *Alta* MSC, plus 2 diver spt

AMPHIBIOUS craft only
3 *Tjeldsund* LCT, 22 S90N LCA

SUPPORT AND MISCELLANEOUS 6
1 *Horten* sub/patrol craft depot ship; 1 *Valkyrien* TRV, 1 Royal Yacht, 2 *Hessa* trg, 1 *Mariata* AGI

NAVAL HOME GUARD 4,900
on mob assigned to 10 HQ sectors incl 31 areas; 235 vessels plus 77 boats

COASTAL DEFENCE
FORTRESS 6: **75mm**; 3: **120mm**; 3: **cable mine**; 3: **torpedo bty**; 5: **lt msl bty**

COAST GUARD (270)
PATROL AND COASTAL COMBATANTS 10
PATROL, OFFSHORE 3
3 *Nordkapp* with 1 *Lynx* hel (SAR/recce), fitted for 6 *Penguin* Mk 2 SSM
PATROL INSHSORE 7 PCI< (4 on lease) plus 6 cutters for fishery dept
AVN hel 6 *Lynx* Mk 86 (Air Force-manned)

Air Force 5,000

(incl 3,200 conscripts, 185 women)
Flying hours 180
OPERATIONAL COMMANDS 2 joint with COMSONOR and COMNON
FGA 4 sqn with F-16A/B
MR 1 sqn with 4 P-3C/2 P-3N *Orion*
TPT 1 sqn with C-130
CAL/ECM 1 sqn with 2 *Falcon* 20C (EW) and 1 *Falcon* 20C (Flight Inspection Service)
TRG MFI-15
SAR 1 sqn with *Sea King* Mk 43B
TAC HEL 2 sqn with Bell-412SP

EQUIPMENT
61 cbt ac (incl 4 MR), no armed hel
AC 57 **F-16A/B** • 6 **P-3** (4* **-C** UIP (MR), 2 **-N** (pilot trg)) • 6 **C-130H** (tpt) • 3 ***Falcon* 20C** (EW/FIS) • 3 **DHC-6** (tpt) • 15 **MFI-15** (trg)
HEL 18 **Bell 412 SP** (tpt) • 12 ***Sea King* Mk 43B** (SAR) • 6 ***Lynx* Mk 86** (Coast Guard)

MISSILES
ASM CRV-7, *Penguin* Mk-3
AAM AIM-9L/N *Sidewinder*, AIM 120 AMRAAM

AIR DEFENCE
SAM 6 bty NASAMS, 10 bty RB-70
AAA 8 bty L70 (with Fire-Control System 2000) org into 5 gps

AA HOME GUARD
(on mob under comd of Air Force): 2,500; 2 bn (9 bty) AA **20mm** NM45

Forces Abroad

UN AND PEACEKEEPING
AFGHANISTAN (ISAF): ε30 **BOSNIA** (SFOR II): 125 **CROATIA** (UNMOP): 1 obs **DROC** (MONUC): 5 incl 3 obs **EAST TIMOR** (UNMISET): 5 **EGYPT** (MFO): 4 Staff Officers **ETHIOPIA/ERITREA** (UNMEE): 5 obs **MIDDLE EAST** (UNTSO): 11 obs **YUGOSLAVIA** (KFOR): 980

Foreign Forces

US 53: Prepo eqpt for **Marines**: 1 MEB **Army**: 1 arty bn **Air Force**: ground handling eqpt
Ge prepositioned eqpt for 1 arty bn
NATO HQ Joint Command North Europe (JC North)

Poland Pl

Total Armed Forces

ACTIVE 163,000
(incl 8,200 centrally controlled staffs, units/formations; 81,000 conscripts)
Terms of service 12 months

RESERVES 234,000

Army 188,000 **Navy** 12,000 (to age 50) **Air Force** 19,000 (to age 60) **Supplementary** 15,000

Army 104,050

(incl 58,700 conscripts)
To reorg:
2 Mil Districts/Army HQ
1 Multi-national Corps HQ (Pl/Ge/Da)
2 Corps HQ
3 mech inf div
1 armd cav div
6 bde (incl 1 armd, 2 mech inf (1 coastal), 1 air aslt, 1 air cav, 1 mtn inf)
2 arty, 2 engr, 7 territorial def bde
1 recce, 1 SSM, 3 AD, 2 cbt hel regt
1 special ops, 1 gd regt

EQUIPMENT

MBT 262 T-55, 649 T-72/M1/M1D, 233 PT-91
RECCE 435 BRDM-2
AIFV 1,248 BMP-1, 33 BRM-1
APC 33 OT-64 plus some 693 'look-a-like' types
TOTAL ARTY 1,482
TOWED 362: **122mm**: 227 M-1938 (M-30); **152mm**: 135 M-1938 (ML-20)
SP 652: **122mm**: 533 2S1; **152mm**: 111 *Dana* (M-77); **203mm**: 8 2S7
MRL 249: **122mm**: 219 BM-21, 30 RM-70
MOR 219: **120mm**: 204 M-120, 15 2B11/2S12
SSM launchers: 4 SS-21
ATGW 258: 129 AT-3 *Sagger*, 104 AT-4 *Spigot*, 18 AT-5 *Spandrel*, 7 AT-7 *Saxhorn*
AD GUNS 644: **23mm**: 376 ZU-23-2, 44 ZSU-23-4 SP; **57mm**: 224 S-60
SAM 952: 80 SA-6, 576 SA-7, 64 SA-8, 232 SA-9 (*Grom*)
HELICOPTERS
ATTACK 43 Mi-24D/V, 22 Mi-2URP
SPT 5 Mi-2URN, 6 Mi-17T/U, 18 Mi-8T/U, 34 W-3W/A
TPT 11 Mi-8, 29 Mi-2, 1 W-3W/A-1
SURV *Big Fred* ((SNAR-10) veh, arty)

Navy 14,300

(incl 2,000 Naval Avn; 7,500 conscripts)
COMMANDS Strike (Gdynia), **Coastal Defence** (Swinoujscie, Kolobrzeg, Gdynia), **Naval Avn** (Gdynia-Babie Doly)
BASES Gdynia (HQ), Swinoujscie, Kolobrzeg, Hel, Gdynia-Babie Doly

SUBMARINES 4

SSK 4
1 *Sokol* (No *Kobben*) (1 more to commission late 2002)
1 *Orzel* SS (RF *Kilo*) with 6 × 533mm TT
2 *Wilk* (RF *Foxtrot*) with 10 × 533mm TT (expected to be decommissioned late 2002)

PRINCIPAL SURFACE COMBATANTS 4

DESTROYERS 1
DDG 1 *Warszawa* (FSU mod *Kashin*) with 4 SS-N-2C *Styx* SSM, 2 × 2 SA-N-1 *Goa* SAM, 5 × 533mm TT, 2 ASW RL
FRIGATES 3
FFG 2 *Pulawski* (US *Perry*) with *Harpoon* SSM, *Standard* SM-1MR SAM, 1 × 76mm gun, 2 × 3 324mm ASTT (A 244 Mod 3 LWT)
FF 1 *Kaszub* with SA-N-5 *Grail* SAM, 1 × 76mm gun, 2 × 2 533mm ASTT, 2 ASW RL

PATROL AND COASTAL COMBATANTS 23

CORVETTES 4 *Gornik* (FSU *Tarantul* I) FSG with 2 × 2 SS-N-2C *Styx* SSM, 1 × 4 SA-N-5 *Grail* SAM, 1 × 76mm gun
MISSILE CRAFT 5 FSU *Osa* I PFM with 4 SS-N-2A SSM
PATROL CRAFT 14
COASTAL 3 *Sassnitz* PCC with 1 × SA-N-5 *Grail* SAM and 1 × 76mm gun, 8 *Obluze* PCC
INSHORE 11
11 *Pilica* PCI<

MINE WARFARE 22

MINELAYERS none, but SSK, *Krogulec* MSC and *Lublin* LSM have minelaying capability
MINE COUNTERMEASURES 22
3 *Krogulec* MHC/MSC, 13 *Goplo* (*Notec*) MSC, 4 *Mamry* (*Notec*) MHC/MSC, 2 *Leniwka* MSI

AMPHIBIOUS 5

5 *Lublin* LSM, capacity 135 tps, 9 tk
Plus craft: 3 *Deba* LCU (none employed in amph role)

SUPPORT AND MISCELLANEOUS 18

1 AOT; 5 ARS; 1 *Polochny C* AGF, 5 trg, 1 sail trg, 2 mod *Moma* AGI; 3 AGHS

NAVAL AVIATION (2,000)

ORGANISATION
Flying hours MiG-21: 60
AIRCRAFT
FTR 2 sqn with MiG-21
RECCE 1 sqn with PZL TS-11 *Iskra*, M-28 *Bryza* R
TPT 1 sqn with An-2, M-28 *Bryza* TD
OTHER 1 sqn with M-28 *Bryza* E
HELICOPTERS
ASW 1 sqn with Mi-14PL
SAR 1 sqn with Mi-14PS, PZL *Anakonda*
TPT 1 sqn with Mi-2, PZL-W3, Mi-17
EQUIPMENT
26 cbt ac, 12 armed hel
AIRCRAFT
18 **MiG-21** • 12 **PZL TS-11 *Iskra*** • 3 **An-286** • 4 **M-28 *Bryza* E** • 4 **M-28 *Bryza* TD** • 1 **An-2**
HELICOPTERS
13 **Mi-14PL** • 3 **Mi-14PS** • 5 **Mi-2** • 5 **PZL *Anakonda*** • 2 **Mi-17** • 2 **W-3S**

Air Force 36,450

(incl 14,800 conscripts); 201 cbt ac, no attack hel
Flying hours 60–180
2 AD Corps - North and South
FTR 1 sqn with 22 MiG-29 (18 -29U, 4 -29UB)
FGA/RECCE 5 sqn with 98 Su-22 (81 -22M4, 17 -22UM3K)
4 sqn with 81 MiG-21 (28 -21 bis, 27 -21MF/M/R, 26 -21UM)
TPT 1 regt and 3 sqn with 50 AT ac (10 An-26, 2 An-28, 2 M-28 *Bryza*, 9 Yak-40, 2 Tu-154, 25 An-2)
HEL 98 hel (67 Mi-2, 12 Mi-8, 18 W-3 *Sokol*, 1 Bell 412)
TRG 105 TS-11 *Iskra*, 35 PZL-130 *Orlik*
AAM AA-2 *Atoll*, AA-3 *Anab*, AA-8 *Aphid*, AA-11 *Archer*
ASM AS-7 *Kerry*
SAM 3 bde and 1 indep regt with 25 btn (20 SA-3, 3 SA-4, 2 SA-5)

Forces Abroad

AFGHANISTAN (OP ENDURING FREEDOM): 87
UN AND PEACEKEEPING
BOSNIA (SFOR II): 287; 2 inf coy; (UNMIBH): 1 obs **CROATIA** (UNMOP): 1 obs **DROC** (MONUC): 3 obs **ETHIOPIA/ERITREA** (UNMEE): 6 obs **FYROM** (OP AMBER FOX): 25 **GEORGIA** (UNOMIG): 3 obs **IRAQ/KUWAIT** (UNIKOM): 5 obs **LEBANON** (UNIFIL): 473: 1 inf bn, mil hospital **SYRIA** (UNDOF): 357: 1 inf bn **WESTERN SAHARA** (MINURSO): 6 obs **YUGOSLAVIA** (KFOR): 574; 1 inf bn

Paramilitary 21,400

BORDER GUARDS (Ministry of Interior and Administration) 14,100
11 district units, 2 trg centres
MARITIME BORDER GUARD
about 12 patrol craft: 6 PCO, 6 PCC
PREVENTION UNITS OF POLICE (OPP–Ministry of Interior) 7,300
(1,000 conscripts)

Foreign Forces

GERMANY 65: elm Corps HQ (multinational)

Portugal Por

Total Armed Forces

ACTIVE 43,600
(8,130 conscripts, 2,875 women)
Terms of service **Army** 4–8 months **Navy** and **Air Force** 4–12 months

RESERVES 210,930
(all services) (obligation to age 35) **Army** 210,000 **Navy** 930

Army 25,400

5 Territorial Comd (2 mil region, 1 mil district, 2 mil zone)
1 mech inf bde (2 mech inf bn, 1 tk gp, 1 recce sqn, 1 SP arty, 1 AA bty, 1 engr coy)
1 rapid reaction bde (lt intervention bde) (1 inf bn , 1 recce sqn, 1 fd arty gp, 1 AA bty, 1 engr coy)
1 AB bde (2 para bn, 1 recce sqn, 1 fd arty gp, 1 AA bty, 1 ATK, 1 engr coy)
1 composite regt (3 inf bn, 2 AA bty)
1 MP regt, 1 special ops centre
RESERVES
3 territorial def bde (on mob)
2 inf bn (on mob – for rapid reaction bde)
EQUIPMENT
MBT 187: 86 M-48A5, 101 M-60 (8 -A4, 86 -A3)
RECCE 15 V-150 *Chaimite*, 25 ULTRAV M-11
APC 240 M-113, 40 M-557, 73 V-200 *Chaimite*
TOTAL ARTY 318 (excl coastal)
TOWED 134: **105mm**: 51 M-101, 24 M-56, 21 L119; **155mm**: 38 M-114A1
SP 155mm: 6 M-109A2
MOR 107mm: 62 M-30 (14 SP); **120mm**: 116 *Tampella*; **81mm**: incl 21 SP
COASTAL 21: **150mm**: 9; **152mm**: 6; **234mm**: 6 (inactive)
RCL 84mm: 162 *Carl Gustav*; **90mm**: 112; **106mm**: 128 M-40
ATGW 131 TOW (incl 18 M-113, 4 M-901), 83 *Milan* (incl 6 ULTRAV-11)
AD GUNS 95, incl **20mm**: Rh202; **40mm**: L/60
SAM 15 *Stinger*, 37 *Chaparral*

DEPLOYMENT
AZORES AND MADEIRA 2,250; 1 composite regt (3 inf bn, 2 AA bty)

Navy 10,800

(incl 1,580 Marines; 360 conscripts, 130 recalled reserves)
COMMANDS Naval Area Comd, 4 **Subordinate Comds** Azores, Madeira, North Continental, South Continental
BASES Lisbon (Alfeite), 4 spt bases Leca da Palmeira (North), Portimao (South), Funchal (Madeira), Ponta Delgada (Azores), Montido (naval aviation)
SUBMARINES 2
SSK 2 *Albacora* (Fr *Daphné*) with 12 × 550mm TT

PRINCIPAL SURFACE COMBATANTS 6
FRIGATES 6
FFG 3 *Vasco Da Gama* (MEKO 200) with 8 *Harpoon* SSM, 8 *Sea Sparrow* SAM, 1 × 100mm gun, 6 ASTT, some with 2 *Super Lynx* hel
FF 3 *Commandante João Belo* (Fr *Cdt Rivière*) with 2 × 100mm gun, 6 ASTT
PATROL AND COASTAL COMBATANTS 28
PATROL, OFFSHORE 10
6 *João Coutinho* PCO with 2 × 76mm gun, hel deck
4 *Baptista de Andrade* PCO with 1 × 100mm gun, hel deck
PATROL, COASTAL 8 *Cacine* PCC
PATROL, INSHORE 9
5 *Argos* PCI<, 4 *Centauro* PCI<
RIVERINE 1 *Rio Minho* PCR, 3 *Albatros* PCR
AMPHIBIOUS craft only
1 LCU
SUPPORT AND MISCELLANEOUS 13
1 *Berrio* (UK *Green Rover*) AO; 2 trg, 1 ocean trg, 1 div spt; 8 AGHS
NAVAL AVIATION
EQUIPMENT
HELICOPTERS
5 *Super Lynx* Mk 95

MARINES (1,580)
2 bn, 1 police, 1 special ops det
1 fire spt coy
EQUIPMENT
MOR 120mm: 36

Air Force 7,400

Flying hours F-16: 180
1 op air com (COFA), 5 op gps
FGA 2 sqn
1 with F-16A/B, 1 with *Alpha Jet*
SURVEY 1 sqn with C-212
MR 1 sqn with P-3P
TPT 3 sqn
1 with C-130H, 1 with C-212, 1 with *Falcon* 20 and *Falcon* 50
SAR 2 sqn
1 with SA-330 hel, 1 with SA-330 hel and C-212
LIAISON/UTILITY 1 sqn with Cessna FTB-337G, hel 1 sqn with SA-330
TRG 2 sqn
1 with *Socata* TB-30 *Epsilon*, 1 with *Alpha Jet*
hel and multi-engine trg provided by SA-316 and one of C-212 sqns
EQUIPMENT
50 cbt ac (plus 15 in store), no attack hel
AC 25 ***Alpha Jet*** (FGA/trg) (plus 15 in store) • 19 **F-16A/B** (16 -A, 3 -B) • 6* **P-3P** (MR) • 6 **C-130H** (tpt/SAR) • 24 **C-212** (20 **-A** (12 tpt/SAR, 1 Nav trg, 2 ECM trg, 5 fisheries protection), 4 **-B** (survey)) • 12 **Cessna 337** (utility) • 1 ***Falcon* 20** (tpt, cal) • 3 ***Falcon* 50** (tpt) • 16 ***Epsilon*** (trg)
HEL 10 **SA-330** (SAR/tpt) • 18 **SA-316** (trg, utl)
MISSILES
ASM AGM-65B/G *Maverick*, AGM-84A *Harpoon*
AAM AIM-9Li *Sidewinder*

Forces Abroad

SAO TOME & PRINCIPE 5 Air Force, 1 C-212
UN AND PEACEKEEPING
AFGHANISTAN (ISAF): ε20 **BOSNIA** (SFOR II): 330; 1 inf bn(-) **CROATIA** (UNMOP): 1 obs **EAST TIMOR** (UNMISET): 733, 24 Air Force, 1 C-130H **WESTERN SAHARA** (MINURSO): 4 obs **YUGOSLAVIA** (KFOR): 313

Paramilitary 46,400

NATIONAL REPUBLICAN GUARD 25,600
Commando Mk III APC **hel** 7 SA-315
PUBLIC SECURITY POLICE 20,800

Foreign Forces

NATO HQ South Atlantic at Lisbon (Oeiras)
US 770: **Navy** 50 **Air Force** 720

Spain Sp

Total Armed Forces

ACTIVE 177,950
(incl 9,450 not identified by service; some 9,400 women)

RESERVES 328,500
Army 265,000 **Navy** 18,500 **Air Force** 45,000

Army 118,800

6,600 women)
4 Area Defence Forces
1 rapid action div with 1 AB, 1 airmobile, 1 Legion lt inf bde, 1 Legion special ops unit
1 mech inf div with 2 mech inf, 1 armd bde, 1 lt armd cav, 1 SP arty, 1 AAA, 1 engr regt
1 mtn, 1 cav bde
1 army avn bde with 1 attack, 1 med tpt, 4 tac tpt bn
1 special ops comd with 3 special ops bn
1 fd arty comd with 4 SP arty regt and 2 AAA regt
1 engr comd with 4 engr bn

1 AD comd (2 HAWK SAM, 7 AD bn)
1 coast arty comd (2 coast arty regt)
2 Legion regt

RESERVES (cadre units)

2 mech inf bde, 1 fd arty regt, 1 engr regt

EQUIPMENT

MBT 682: 209 AMX-30 EM2, 164 M-48A5E, 184 M-60A3TTS, 108 *Leopard* 2 A4 (Ge tempy transfer), 17 *Centauro* B-1
RECCE 317 BMR-VEC (77 **90mm**, 208 **25mm**, 32 **20mm** gun)
AIFV 68 *Pizarro*
APC 2,023: 1,337 M-113 (incl variants), 686 BMR-600 (incl variants)
TOTAL ARTY 1,036 (excluding coastal)
TOWED 414: **105mm**: 170 M-56 pack, 56 L 118, 168 M-26; **155mm**: 20 M-114
SP 194: **105mm**: 34 M-108; **155mm**: 96 M-109A1/A5; **203mm**: 64 M-110A2
COASTAL ARTY 53: **6in**: 44; **305mm**: 6; **381mm**: 3
MRL 140mm: 14 *Teruel*
MOR 120mm: 414 (incl 226 SP); plus **81mm**: 1,314 (incl 102 SP)
ATGW 442 *Milan* (incl 106 SP), 28 HOT, 200 TOW (incl 68 SP)
RCL 106mm: 507
AD GUNS 20mm: 460 GAI-BO1; **35mm**: 92 GDF-002 twin; **40mm**: 183 L/70
SAM 24 I HAWK, 18 *Roland*, 13 *Skyguard/Aspide*, 108 *Mistral*
HELICOPTERS 153 (28 attack)
27 HU-21C/HU-21L (AS-532UL), 48 HU-10B, 45 HA/HR-15 (17 with **20mm** guns, 28 with HOT), 6 HU-18, 10 HR-12B, 17 HT-17D
SURV 2 AN/TPQ-36 (arty, mor)

DEPLOYMENT

CEUTA AND MELILLA 8,100; 2 armd cav, 2 Spanish Legion, 2 mot inf, 2 engr, 2 arty regt; 2 lt AD bn, 1 coast arty bn
BALEARIC ISLANDS 4,550; 1 mot inf regt: 3 mot inf bn; 1 mixed arty regt: 1 fd arty, 1 AD; 1 engr bn
CANARY ISLANDS 8,600; 3 mot inf regt each 2 mot inf bn; 1 mot inf bn, 2 mixed arty regt each: 1 fd arty, 1 AD bn; 2 engr bn

Navy 26,950

(incl 700 Naval Avn, 5,600 Marines; 1,600 women)
NAVAL ZONES Cantabrian, Strait (of Gibraltar), Mediterranean, Canary (Islands)
BASES El Ferrol (La Coruña) (Cantabrian HQ), San Fernando (Cadiz) (Strait HQ), Rota (Cadiz) (Fleet HQ), Cartagena (Murcia) (Mediterranean HQ), Las Palmas (Canary Islands HQ), Palma de Mallorca and Mahón (Menorca)

SUBMARINES 8

SSK 8
4 *Galerna* (Fr *Agosta*) with 4 × 533mm TT (L5-HWT)
4 *Delfin* (Fr *Daphné*) with 12 × 550mm TT (L5-HWT)

PRINCIPAL SURFACE COMBATANTS 16

AIRCRAFT CARRIERS 1 *Príncipe de Asturias* CVS; air gp: typically 6 to 10 AV-8/AV-8B, 4 to 6 SH-3D ASW hel, 2 SH-3D AEW hel, 2 AB 212 hel
FRIGATES 15
FFG 15
6 *Santa Maria* (US *Perry*) with 1 × 1 SM-1 MR *Standard* SAM/*Harpoon* SSM launcher, 1 × 76mm gun, 2 × 3 ASTT, 2 SH-60B hel
5 *Baleares* with 8 *Harpoon* SSM, 1 × 1 SM-1 MR *Standard* SAM, 1 × 127mm gun, 2 × 2 ASTT, 8 ASROC SUGW
4 *Descubierta* with 8 *Harpoon* SSM, *Sea Sparrow* SAM, 1 × 76mm gun, 6 ASTT, 1 × 2 ASW RL

PATROL AND COASTAL COMBATANTS 37

PATROL, OFFSHORE 8
4 *Serviola* PCO with 1 × 76mm gun, 1 *Chilreu* PCO, 1 *Descubierta* PCO, 1 *Alboran* PCO, 1 *Arnomendi* PCO
PATROL, COASTAL 10 *Anaga* PCC
PATROL, INSHORE 19
6 *Barceló* PFI<, 4 *Conejera* PCI<, 2 *Toralla* PCI, 7 PCI<

MINE WARFARE 11

MINE COUNTERMEASURES 11
1 *Descubierta* MCCS
4 *Segura* MHO
6 *Júcar* (US *Adjutant*) MSC

AMPHIBIOUS 4

2 *Hernán Cortés* (US *Newport*) LST, capacity: 400 tps, 500t veh, 1 hel plus 3 LCVP, 1 LCPL
2 *Galicia* LPD, capacity 620 tps, 2500t veh, 4 hel plus 6 LCVP/4 LCU
Plus 13 craft: 3 LCT, 2 LCU, 8 LCM

SUPPORT AND MISCELLANEOUS 27

2 AO; 3 AWT, 3 AK; 5 AT, 1 diver spt, 4 trg, 1 sail trg; 6 AGHS, 2 AGOR

NAVAL AVIATION (700)

ORGANISATION
Flying hours AV-8B: 160
AIRCRAFT
FGA 2 sqn with AV-8B/AV-8B plus
LIAISON 1 sqn with Cessna *Citation* II
HELICOPTERS
ASW 1 sqn with SH-3D/G *Sea King* (modified to SH-3H standard), 1 sqn with SH-30B
EW 1 flt with SH-30B
COMD/TPT 1 sqn with AB-212
TRG 1 sqn with Hughes 500
EQUIPMENT
17 cbt ac; 37 armed hel
AIRCRAFT
9 **AV-8B** • 8 **AV-8B** plus • 3 **Cessna** ***Citation*** **II**

HELICOPTERS
10 **AB-212** • 11 **SH-3D** (8 **-H** ASW, 3 **-D** AEW) • 10 **Hughes 500** • 6 **SH-60B**
MISSILES
AAM AIM-9 *Sidewinder*, *Maverick*, AMRAAM
ASW Mk 46 LWT
ASUW *Harpoon*

MARINES (5,600)

1 mne bde (3,000); 2 inf, 1 spt bn; 3 arty bty
5 mne garrison gp

EQUIPMENT

MBT 16 M-60A3
AFV 17 *Scorpion* lt tk, 16 LVTP-7 AAV
TOWED ARTY 105mm: 12 M-56 pack
SP ARTY 155mm: 6 M-109A
ATGW 24 TOW-2, 18 *Dragon*
RL 90mm: C-90C
SAM 12 *Mistral*

Air Force 22,750

(incl 1,200 women)
Flying hours EF-18: 160; F-5: 220; *Mirage* F-1: 160

CENTRAL AIR COMMAND (Torrejon) 4 wg

FTR 2 sqn with EF-18 (F-18 *Hornet*)
RECCE 1 sqn with RF-4C
TPT 8 sqn
2 with C-212, 1 with C-295, 2 with CN-235, 1 with *Falcon* (20, 50, 900), 1 with Boeing 707 (tkr/tpt), 1 with AS-332 (tpt)
SPT 4 sqn
1 with CL-215, 1 with Boeing 707, C-212 (EW) and *Falcon* 20, 1 with C-212, AS-332 (SAR), 1 with C-212 and Cessna *Citation* V
TRG 3 sqn
1 with C-212, 1 with C-101, 1 with Beech *Bonanza*

EASTERN AIR COMMAND (Zaragosa) 2 wg

FTR 3 sqn
2 with EF-18, 1 OCU with EF-18
TPT 2 sqn
1 with C-130H, 1 tkr/tpt with KC-130H
SPT 1 sqn with **ac** C-212 (SAR) **hel** AS-330

STRAIT AIR COMMAND (Seville) 4 wg

FTR 3 sqn
2 with *Mirage* F-1 CE/BE
1 with EF/A-18
LEAD-IN TRG 2 sqn with F-5B
MP 1 sqn with P-3A/B
TRG 6 sqn
2 hel with S-76C, EC-120B *Colibri*, 1 with C-212, 1 with E-26 (*Tamiz*), 1 with C-101, 1 with C-212

CANARY ISLANDS AIR COMMAND (Gando) 1 wg

FGA 1 sqn with EF-18
TPT 1 sqn with C-212
SAR 1 sqn with **ac** F-27 **hel** AS-332 (SAR)

LOGISTIC SUPPORT COMMAND (MALOG)

1 trials sqn with C-101, C-212 and F-5A, EF/A-18, F-1

EQUIPMENT

198 cbt ac, no armed hel
AC 91 **EF/A-18 A/B** (ftr, OCU) • 23 **F-5B** (FGA) • 65 ***Mirage* F-1CF/-BE/-EE** of which 49 (45 FIC/CE/EDA/EE and 4 FIB/BE) modernised • 12* **RF-4C** (recce) • 7* **P-3** (2 **-A** (MR), 5 **-B** (MR)) • 3 **Boeing 707** (tkr/tpt) • 7 **C-130H/H-30** (tpt), 5 **KC-130H** (tkr) • 75 **C-212** (31 tpt, 9 SAR, 6 recce, 26 trg, 2 EW, 1 trials) • 2 **C-295** (9 on order to replace some **C-212**) • 2 **Cessna 550 *Citation* V** (recce) • 78 **C-101** (trg) • 15 **CL-215** (spt) • 5 ***Falcon* 20** (3 VIP tpt, 2 EW) • 1 ***Falcon* 50** (VIP tpt) • 2 ***Falcon* 900** (VIP tpt) • 21 **Do-27** (U-9, liaison/trg) • 3 **F-27** (SAR) • 37 **E-26** (trg) • 20 **CN-235** (18 tpt, 2 VIP tpt) • 25 **E-24** (*Bonanza*) trg • 5 **E-20** (*Barón*) trg
HEL 5 **SA-330** (SAR) • 12 **AS-332** (6 SAR, 6 tpt) • 8 **S-76C** (trg) • 15 **EC 120B** *Colibri*

MISSILES

AAM AIM-7 *Sparrow*, AIM-9 *Sidewinder*, AIM-120 AMRAAM, R-530
ASM AGM-65G *Maverick*, AGM-84D *Harpoon*, AGM-88A HARM
SAM *Mistral*, *Skyguard/Aspide*

Forces Abroad

AFGHANISTAN (OP ENDURING FREEDOM): 5 C-130, 8 CN-235, 1 P-3

UN AND PEACEKEEPING

AFGHANISTAN (ISAF): 350 **BOSNIA** (SFOR II): 1,200; 2 inf coy, 1 cav sqn **DROC** (MONUC): 1 **ETHIOPIA/ERITREA** (UNMEE): 5 incl 3 obs **ITALY** (Deliberate Forge) 4 F/A-18, 1 KC-130 **YUGOSLAVIA** (KFOR): 1,300; 4 inf coy, 1 cav sqn

Paramilitary 73,360

GUARDIA CIVIL 72,600

9 regions, 19 inf *tercios* (regt) with 56 rural bn, 6 traffic security gp, 6 rural special ops gp, 1 special sy bn; 18 BLR APC, 18 Bo-105, 5 BK-117 hel

GUARDIA CIVIL DEL MAR 760

32 PCI

Foreign Forces

NATO HQ Joint Command South-West (JCSOUTHWEST)
US 2,190: **Navy** 1,760 **Air Force** 360 **USMC** 70

Turkey Tu

Total Armed Forces

ACTIVE ε514,850

(incl ε391,000 conscripts) *Terms of service* 18 months

RESERVES 378,700

(all to age 41) **Army** 258,700 **Navy** 55,000 **Air Force** 65,000

Army ε402,000

(incl ε325,000 conscripts)

4 army HQ: 9 corps HQ • 1 mech div (1 mech, 1 armd bde) • 1 mech div HQ • 1 inf div • 14 armd bde (each 2 armd, 2 mech inf, 2 arty bn) • 17 mech bde (each 2 armd, 2 mech inf, 1 arty bn) • 9 inf bde (each 4 inf, 1 arty bn) • 4 cdo bde (each 4 cdo bn) • 1 inf regt • 4 aviation regt, 1 attack hel bn, 3 avn bn (2 trg, 1 tpt), 1 Presidential Guard regt • 5 border def regt • 26 border def bn

RESERVES

4 coastal def regt • 23 coastal def bn

EQUIPMENT

Total figures in ( ) were reported to CFE on 1 Jan 2002

MBT 4,205 (2,445): 2,876 M-48 A5T1/T2 (1,300 to be stored), 932 M-60 (658 -A3, 274-A1), 397 *Leopard* (170-1A1, 227-1A3)

RECCE ε250 *Akrep*, ARSV (*Cobra*)

TOTAL AIFV/APC (2,831)

AIFV 650 AIFV

APC 830 AAPC, 2,813 M-113/-A1/-A2

TOTAL ARTY (2,990)

TOWED 105mm: M-101A1; **155mm**: 517 M-114A1\A2, 6 *Panter*; **203mm**: 162 M-115

SP 105mm: 365 M-52T, 26 M-108T; **155mm**: 222 M-44T1; **175mm**: 36 M-107; **203mm**: 219 M-110A2

MRL 70mm: 24; **107mm**: 48; **122mm**: T-122; **227mm**: 12 MLRS (incl ATACMS)

MOR 2,021: **107mm**: 1,264 M-30 (some SP); **120mm**: 757 (some 179 SP); plus **81mm**: 3,792 incl SP

ATGW 1,283: 186 *Cobra*, 365 TOW SP, 392 *Milan*, ε340 *Eryx*

RL M-72

RCL 57mm: 923 M-18; **75mm**: 617; **106mm**: 2,329 M-40A1

AD GUNS 1,664: **20mm**: 439 GAI-DO1; **35mm**: 120 GDF-001/-003; **40mm**: 803 L60/70, 40 T-1, 262 M-42A1

SAM 108 *Stinger*, 789 *Redeye* (being withdrawn)

SURV AN/TPQ-36 (arty, mor)

AC 168: 3 Cessna 421, 34 *Citabria*, 4 B-200, 4 T-42A, 98 U-17B, 25 T-41D

HELICOPTERS

ATTACK 37 (28) AH-1W/P

SPT 50 S-70A, 19 AS-532UL, 12 AB-204B, 64 AB-205A, 20 AB-206, 2 AB-212, 28 H-300C, 3 OH-58B, 94 UH-1H

UAV CL-89 (AN/USD-501), *Gnat* 750, *Falcon* 600

Navy 52,750

(incl 3,100 Marines, 1,050 Coast Guard; 34,500 conscripts)

COMMAND Naval Forces Command (Ankara) **Sub Commands** Northern Sea Area (Istanbul), Southern Sea Area (Izmir), Training (Altinovayalova), Fleet (Gölcük)

BASES Gölcük (HQ), Erdek, Istanbul, Canakkale, Eregli, Bartin, Izmir, Foca, Aksaz, Antalya, Mersin, Iskenderun

SUBMARINES 13

SSK 10

6 *Atilay* (Ge Type 209/1200) with 8 × 533mm TT (SST 4 HWT)

4 *Preveze* (Ge Type 209/1400) with 8 × 533mm TT (*Harpoon* USGW, *Tigerfish*/DM 2A-4 HWT)

SSC 3

1 *Canakkale* (US *Guppy*)† with 10 × 533mm TT

2 *Hizirreis* (US *Tang*) with 8 × 533mm TT (Mk 37 HWT)

PRINCIPAL SURFACE COMBATANTS 19

FRIGATES 19

FFG 18

6 *Gaziantep* (US *Perry*) with 4 *Harpoon* SSM, 36 *Standard* SM-1 MR SAM, 1 × 76mm gun, 2 × 3 ASTT

4 *Yavuz* (Ge MEKO 200) with 8 *Harpoon* SSM, *Sea Sparrow* SAM, 1 × 127mm gun, 2 × 3 ASTT, 1 AB-212 hel

4 *Barbaros* (MOD Ge MEKO 200) with 8 *Harpoon* SSM, 8 *Sea Sparrow* SAM, 1 × 127mm gun, 6 × 324mm TT, 1 AB-212 hel

2 *Muavenet* (US *Knox*-class) with *Harpoon* SSM (from ASROC launcher), 1 × 127mm gun, 4 ASTT, 8 ASROC SUGW, 1 AB 212 hel

2 *Burak* (Fr *d'Estienne d'Orves*) with 2 MM-38 *Exocet* SSM, *Mistral* SAM, 1 × 100mm gun, 4 ASTT (L5 HWT)

FF 1 *Berk* with 4 × 76mm guns, 6 ASTT, 2 Mk 11 *Hedgehog*

PATROL AND COASTAL COMBATANTS 49

MISSILE CRAFT 21

3 *Kilic* PFM with 8 × *Harpoon* SSM, 1 × 76mm gun

8 *Dogan* (Ge Lürssen-57) PFM with 8 *Harpoon* SSM, 1 × 76mm gun

8 *Kartal* (Ge *Jaguar*) PFM with 4 *Penguin* 2 SSM, 2 × 533mm TT

2 *Yildiz* PFM with 8 *Harpoon* SSM, 1 × 76mm gun

PATROL CRAFT 28

COASTAL 28

1 *Girne* PFC, 6 *Sultanhisar* PCC, 2 *Trabzon* PCC, 4 PGM-71 PCC, 1 *Bora* (US *Asheville*) PFC, 10 AB-25 PCC, 4 AB-21 PCC

MINE WARFARE 24

MINELAYERS 1

1 *Nusret* (400 mines) plus 3 ML tenders (*Bayraktar*, *Sarucabey* and *Çakabey* LST have minelaying capability)

MINE COUNTERMEASURES 23

5 *Edineik* (Fr *Circe*) MHC
8 *Samsun* (US *Adjutant*) MSC
6 *Karamürsel* (Ge *Vegesack*) MSC
4 *Foça* (US *Cape*) MSI (plus 8 MCM tenders)

AMPHIBIOUS 8

1 *Osman Gazi* LST: capacity 980 tps, 17 tk, 4 LCVP
2 *Ertugru* LST (US *Terrebonne Parish*): capacity 400 tps, 18 tk
2 *Bayraktar* LST (US LST-512): capacity 200 tps, 16 tk
2 *Sarucabey* LST: capacity 600 tps, 11 tk
1 *Çakabey* LSM: capacity 400 tps, 9 tk
Plus about 59 craft: 35 LCT, 2 LCU, 22 LCM

SUPPORT AND MISCELLANEOUS 27

1 *Akar* AO, 5 spt tkr, 2 Ge *Rhein* plus 3 other depot ships, 3 tpt, 2 AR; 3 ARS, 5 AT, 1 div spt; 2 AGHS

NAVAL AVIATION

EQUIPMENT

16 armed hel

HELICOPTERS

ASW 3 AB-204AS, 13 AB-212
TRG 7 TB-20

MARINES (3,100)

1 regt, HQ, 3 bn, 1 arty bn (18 guns), spt units

Air Force 60,100

(incl 31,500 conscripts) 2 tac air forces (divided between east and west), 1 tpt comd, 1 air trg comd, 1 air log comd

Flying hours 180

FGA 11 sqn

1 OCU with F-5A/B, 4 (1 OCU) with F-4E, 6 (1 OCU) with F-16C/D

FTR 7 sqn

2 with F-5A/B, 2 with F-4E, 3 with F-16C/D

RECCE 2 sqn with RF-4E

TPT 5 sqn

1 with C-130B/E, 1 with C-160D, 2 with CN-235, 1 VIP tpt unit with *Gulfstream*, *Citation* and CN 235

TKR 7 KC-135R

LIAISON 10 base flts with **hel** UH-1H

SAR hel AS-532

TRG 3 sqn

1 with T-41, 1 with SF-260D, 1 with T-37B/C and T-38A. Each base has a stn flt with **hel** UH-1H and in some cases, **ac** CN-235

SAM 4 sqn with 92 *Nike Hercules*, 2 sqn with 86 *Rapier*

EQUIPMENT

485 cbt ac, no attack hel

AC 224 **F-16C/D** (194 **-C**, 30 **-D**) • 87 **F/NF-5A/B** (FGA) (48 being upgraded as lead-in trainers) • 174 **F-4E** (90 FGA, 47 ftr, 37 **RF-4E** (recce)) (54 being upgraded to *Phantom* 2020) • 13 **C-130B/E** (tpt) • 7 **KC-135R** • 19 **C-160D** (tpt) • 2 ***Citation* VII** (VIP) • 46 **CN-235** (tpt/EW) • 40 **SF-260D** (trg) • 60 **T-37** trg • 70 **T-38** (trg) • 28 **T-41** (trg)

HEL 20 **UH-1H** (tpt, liaison, base flt, trg schools), 20 **AS-532** (14 SAR/6 CSAR) being delivered

UAV 1 ***Gnat* 750** system

MISSILES

AAM AIM-7E *Sparrow*, AIM 9 S *Sidewinder*, AIM-120 AMRAAM

ASM AGM-65 *Maverick*, AGM-88 HARM, AGM-142, *Popeye* 1

Forces Abroad

TURKISH REPUBLIC OF NORTHERN CYPRUS
ε36,000; 1 corps HQ, 2 mech inf div; 441 M-48A5 MBT; 266 M-113, 361 AAPC APC; 72 **105mm**, 18 **155mm**, 12 **203mm** towed arty; 90 **155mm** SP arty; 6 **122mm** MRL; 127 **120mm,** 148 **107mm**, 175 **81mm** mor; **20mm**, 16 **35mm**; 48 **40mm** AA guns; **ac** 3 **hel** 4 **Navy** 1 PCI

UN AND PEACEKEEPING

AFGHANISTAN (ISAF): ε1,400 **BOSNIA** (SFOR II): 1,200; 1 inf bn gp **EAST TIMOR** (UNMISET): 2 obs **GEORGIA** (UNOMIG): 5 obs **IRAQ/KUWAIT** (UNIKOM): 7 obs **ITALY** (Deliberate Forge): 4 F-16 C **YUGOSLAVIA** (KFOR): 940

Paramilitary

***GENDARMERIE*/NATIONAL GUARD** ε150,000 (Ministry of Interior, Ministry of Defence in war)

50,000 reserve; some *Akrep* recce, 535 BTR-60/-80, 25 *Condor* APC **ac** 2 Dornier 28D, 0-1E **hel** 19 Mi-17, 8 AB-240B, 6 AB-205A, 8 AB-206A, 1 AB-212, 14 S-70A

COAST GUARD 2,200

(incl 1,400 conscripts); 48 PCI, 16 PCI<, plus boats, 2 tpt

Foreign Forces

NATO HQ Joint Command South-East (JCSOUTHEAST), HQ 6 Allied Tactical Air Force (6 ATAF)

OPERATION NORTHERN WATCH

UK Air Force 160; 4 *Jaguar* GR-3A/-B, 2 VC-10 (tkr)
US 3,860: **Navy** 20 **Air Force** 3,800; 1 wg (**ac** on det only), numbers vary (incl F-16, F-15C, KC-135, E-3B/C, C-12, HC-130, HH-60) **USMC** 40
US Installations for seismic monitoring
ISRAEL Periodic det of F-16 at Akinci

United Kingdom UK

Total Armed Forces

ACTIVE 210,450
(incl 17,350 women)

RESERVES 256,750

Army 201,150 (Regular 160,800) **Territorial Army** (TA) 40,350 **Navy/Marines** 14,300 (Regular 10,200, Volunteer Reserves 4,100) **Air Force** 41,300 (Regular 39,700, Volunteer Reserves 1,600)

Strategic Forces (1,000)

SLBM 58 msl in 4 SSBN, fewer than 200 op available warheads
SSBN 4
4 *Vanguard* SSBN each capable of carrying 16 *Trident* D5; will not deploy with more than 48 warheads per boat, but each msl could carry up to 12 MIRV (some *Trident* D5 msl configured for sub-strategic role)
EARLY WARNING
Ballistic-Missile Early-Warning System (BMEWS) station at Fylingdales

Army 114,800

(incl soldiers under trg, 3,800 Gurkhas, 946 Full Time Reserve; 8,050 women)
regt normally bn size
1 Land Comd HQ • 3 (regenerative) div HQ (former mil districts) and UK Spt Comd (Germany) • 1 armd div with 3 armd bde, 3 arty, 4 engr, 1 avn, 1 AD regt • 1 mech div with 3 mech bde (*Warrior/Saxon*), 3 arty, 4 engr, 1 AD regt • ARRC Corps tps: 3 armd recce, 2 MLRS, 2 AD, 1 engr regt (EOD) • 1 tri-service joint hel comd incorporating 1 air aslt bde • 1 arty bde HQ, 1 AD bde HQ, 1 recce bde HQ • 2 log bde • 14 inf bde HQ (3 control ops in N. Ireland, remainder mixed regular and TA for trg/administrative purposes only)
1 joint NBC regt (Army/RAF)
Summary of combat arm units
6 armd regt • 4 armd recce regt • 6 mech inf bn (*Saxon*) • 9 armd inf bn (*Warrior*) • 25 lt inf bn (incl 3 AB bn (1 only in para role), 2 Gurkha) • 1 SF (SAS) regt • 11 arty regt (2 MLRS, 6 SP, 2 fd (1 cdo, 1 air aslt), 1 trg) • 4 AD regt (2 *Rapier*, 2 HVM) • 11 engr regt • 5 (incl 1 trg) army avn regt, 4 indep flt

HOME SERVICE FORCES
N. Ireland 4,500: 3 inf bn (2,200 full-time)
Gibraltar 350: 1 regt (150 full-time)
Falkland Island Defence Force 60

RESERVES
Territorial Army 4 lt recce, 15 inf bn, 2 SF (SAS), 3 arty (1 MLRS, 1 fd, 1 obs), 4 AD, 5 engr, 1 avn regt

EQUIPMENT
MBT 594: 386 *Challenger* 2, 205 *Challenger*, 3 *Chieftain*
RECCE 327 *Scimitar*, 137 *Sabre*, 11 *Fuchs*
AIFV 575 *Warrior*, 10 AFV 432 *Rarden*
APC 1,117 AFV 432, 585 FV 103 *Spartan*, 649 *Saxon*, 2 *Saracen*, 10 *Stormer*, plus 1,675 AIFV and APC 'look-a-likes'
TOTAL ARTY 457
TOWED 214: **105mm**: 166 L-118/-119; **155mm**: 48 FH-70
SP 155mm: 179 AS-90
MRL 227mm: 64 MLRS
MOR 81mm: 470 (incl 110 SP)
ATGW 787 *Milan*, 60 *Swingfire* (FV 102 *Striker* SP), TOW
RL 94mm: LAW-80
SAM 135 HVM (SP), 147 *Starstreak* (LML), 335 *Javelin*, 98 *Rapier* (some 24 SP)
SURV 19 *Cymbeline* (mor)
AC 6 BN-2
HELICOPTERS
ATTACK 14 WAH-Mk1 *Apache*, 108 *Lynx* AH-1/-7/-9
SPT 133 SA-341 *Gazelle*, 15 *Scout*
UAV 8 *Phoenix*
LANDING CRAFT 6 RCL, 4 LCVP, 4 workboats

Navy (RN) 42,350

(incl 6,200 Naval Avn, 7,000 Royal Marines Command; 3,650 women)
COMMAND: CINCFLEET (**type cmd**: ships, submarines, naval avn, RFA, marines); CINCNAVHOME (trg, spt)
BASES UK Northwood (HQ Fleet, CINCEASTLANT), Devonport, Faslane, Portsmouth (HQ); Culdrose, Prestwick, Yeovilton (all Naval Aviation); **Overseas** Gibraltar

SUBMARINES 16
STRATEGIC SUBMARINES 4 SSBN (see *Strategic Forces*)
TACTICAL SUBMARINES 12
SSN 12
5 *Swiftsure* with 5 × 533mm TT (*Sub-Harpoon* SSM, *Spearfish/Tigerfish* HWT); two (*Splendid* and *Spartan*) with *Tomahawk* Block IIIC LAM
7 *Trafalgar* with 5 × 533mm TT (*Sub-Harpoon* SSM, *Spearfish/Tigerfish* HWT); four (*Triumph*, *Trafalgar*, *Turbulent* and *Torbay*) with *Tomahawk* Block IIIC LAM

PRINCIPAL SURFACE COMBATANTS 35
AIRCRAFT CARRIERS 3: 2 mod *Invincible* CVS each with **ac** 8 FA-2 *Sea Harrier* V/STOL **hel** 12 *Sea King*, up to 9 ASW, 3 AEW; plus 1 mod *Invincible* in

extended refit
Full 'expeditionary air group' comprises 8 *Sea Harrier* FA-2, 8 RAF *Harrier* GR-7, 2 *Sea King* ASW, 4 *Sea King* AEW

DESTROYERS 11
DDG 11
7 Type 42 Batch 1/2 with 2 × *Sea Dart* SAM, 1 × 114mm gun, 6 × 324mm ASTT (*Stingray* LWT), 1 *Lynx* hel
4 Type 42 Batch 3 with wpns as above

FRIGATES 21
FFG 21
4 *Cornwall* (Type 22 Batch 3) with 8 *Harpoon* SSM, *Seawolf* SAM, 1 × 114mm gun, 6 × 324mm ASTT (*Stingray* LWT), 2 *Lynx* or 1 *Sea King* hel
1 *Broadsword* (Type 22 Batch 2) with 4 × MM 38 *Exocet* SSM, *Seawolf* SAM, 6 × 324mm ASTT (*Stingray* LWT), 2 *Lynx* or 1 *Sea King* hel
16 *Norfolk* (Type 23) with 8 *Harpoon* SSM, *Seawolf* VL SAM, 1 × 114mm gun, 4 × 324mm ASTT (*Stingray* LWT), 1 *Lynx* Mk 8 hel

PATROL AND COASTAL COMBATANTS 20
PATROL, OFFSHORE 4
1 *Castle* PCO, 3 *Island* PCO
PATROL, INSHORE 16
16 *Archer* (incl 8 trg)

MINE WARFARE 23
MINELAYER no dedicated minelayer, but all SSN have limited minelaying capability
MINE COUNTERMEASURES 23
1 mod *Castle* MCCS, 11 *Hunt* MCC (incl 4 mod *Hunt* MCC/PCC), 11 *Sandown* MHO (4 batch 1, 7 batch 2)

AMPHIBIOUS 5
1 *Ocean* LPH, capacity 800 tps, 18 hel plus 4 LCVP
4 *Sir Bedivere* LSL; capacity 340 tps, 16 tk, 1 hel (RFA manned)
Plus 23 craft: 9 LCU, 14 LCVP
(see *Army* for additional amph lift capability)

SUPPORT AND MISCELLANEOUS 20
(most manned and maintained by the **Royal Fleet Auxiliary** (RFA), a civilian fleet, owned by UK MoD, which has 2,400 manpower; type cmd under CINCFLEET)
UNDER WAY SUPPORT 7
2 *Fort Victoria* AO, 3 *Rover* AO, 2 *Fort Rosalie* AF (all RFA manned)
MAINTENANCE AND LOGISTIC 8
1 *Diligence* AR, 1 *Sea Crusader* AK, 1 *Sea Centurion* AK, 1 *Dart* AK, 4 *Leaf* AOT (all RFA manned)
SPECIAL PURPOSE 2
1 *Argus* AVB (RFA manned), 1 *Endurance* (ice patrol, RN manned)
SURVEY 3
1 *Scott* AGHS, 1 *Roebuck* AGHS, 1 *Gleaner* AGHS (all RN manned)

NAVAL AVIATION (Fleet Air Arm)
(6,200 incl 330 women)
ORGANISATION
Flying hours *Harrier*: 275
A typical CVS air group consists of 8 *Sea Harrier* FA-2, 7 *Sea King* (ASW), 3 *Sea King* (AEW) (can carry 8 RAF *Harrier* GR-7 instead of 4 *Sea King*)
AIRCRAFT
FTR 2 sqn with *Sea Harrier* FA-2 plus 1 trg sqn with *Harrier* T-8
TRG 1 sqn with *Jetstream*
FLEET SPT 13 *Mystère-Falcon* (civil registration), 1 Cessna *Conquest* (civil registration), 1 Beech *Baron* (civil registration) 5 GROB 115 (op under contract)
HELICOPTER
ASW 1 sqn with *Sea King* Mk-6, 1 sqn with EH 101 *Merlin* Mk1
ASW/ATK 1 sqn with *Lynx* Mk 3/8 (in indep flt)
AEW 1 sqn with *Sea King* Mk-2
CDO SPT 2 sqn with *Sea King* Mk-4, 1 flt with *Lynx* Mk 7
RECCE 1 flt with *Gazelle* AH-1
SAR 1 sqn with *Sea King* Mk-5
TRG 2 sqn with EH-101 *Merlin* Mk 1, 1 sqn with *Sea King* Mk-4, 1 sqn with *Lynx* Mk 3
EQUIPMENT
34 cbt ac (plus 21 in store), 180 armed hel
AIRCRAFT
29 ***Sea Harrier* FA-2** (plus 19 in store) • 5* **T-4/T-8** (trg) plus 2 in store • 14 ***Hawk*** (spt) • 13 ***Jetstream***
HELICOPTER
88 ***Sea King*** (42 **HAS-5/6**, 33 **HC-4**, 13 **AEW** [2 Mk 7, 11 Mk 2]) • 36 ***Lynx*** Mk 3 • 6 ***Lynx*** Mk 7 (incl in Marines entry) • 23 ***Lynx*** Mk 8, 38 **EH-101 *Merlin*** Mk 1 • 8 ***Gazelle*** AH-1 (incl in Marines entry)
MISSILES
ASM *Sea Skua*
AAM AIM-9 *Sidewinder*, AIM-120C AMRAAM

ROYAL MARINES COMMAND (7,000, incl RN and Army)
1 cdo bde: 3 cdo; 1 cdo arty regt (Army); 1 cdo AD bty (Army), 2 cdo engr (1 Army, 1 TA), 1 LCA sqn. Serving with RN/Other comd: 1 sy gp, Special Boat Service, 1 cdo lt hel sqn, 2 LCA sqn, 3 dets/naval parties
EQUIPMENT
MOR 81mm
ATGW *Milan*
SAM HVM
HEL 9 SA-341 (*Gazelle*); plus 3 in store, 6 *Lynx* AH-7
AMPH 24 RRC, 4 LCAC
RESERVES
About 1,000

Air Force (RAF) 53,300

(incl 5,650 women)
Flying hours *Tornado* GRI/4: 188, F3: 208; *Harrier* GR-7:

218; *Jaguar*: 215
FGA/BBR 5 sqn with *Tornado* GRI/4
FGA 5 sqn
3 with *Harrier* GR-7, 2 with *Jaguar* GR-1A/GR-3/3A
FTR 5 sqn with *Tornado* F-3 (4 by Jan 2003) plus 1 flt in the Falklands
RECCE 4 sqn
2 with *Tornado* GR-1A/4A, 1 with *Canberra* PR-9, 1 with *Jaguar* GR-1A/GR-3/3A
MR 3 sqn with *Nimrod* MR-2
AEW 2 sqn with E-3D *Sentry*
ELINT 1 sqn with *Nimrod* R-1
TPT/TKR 3 sqn
2 with VC-10 C1K, VC-10 K-3/-4, and 1 with *Tristar* K-1/KC-2A, plus 1 VC-10 flt in the Falklands
TPT 1 sqn with C-17, 4 sqn with *Hercules* C-130K/J, 1 comms sqn with **ac** BAe-125, BAe-146 **hel** AS-355 (*Twin Squirrel*)
TARGET FACILITY/CAL 1 sqn with *Hawk* T-1/T-1A
OCU 5: *Tornado* GR-1/4, *Tornado* F-3, *Jaguar* GR-3/3A/T2A, *Harrier* GR-7/-T10, *Nimrod* MR-2
TRG *Hawk* T-1/-1A/-1W, *Jetstream* T-1, *Bulldog* T-1, G.115E *Tutor*, HS-125 *Dominie* T-1, *Tucano* T-1, T-67 *Firefly*
TAC HEL 7 sqn
1 with CH-47 (*Chinook*) and SA-341 (*Gazelle* HT3), 2 with SA-330 (*Puma*), 1 with CH-47 and *Sea King* HAR-3, 2 with CH-47, 1 with *Merlin* HC3
SAR 2 hel sqn with *Sea King* HAR-3/3A, 1 with *Wessex* HC-2 in Cyprus
TRG *Sea King* (including postgraduate training on 203(R) sqn), Tri-Service Defence Helicopter School with AS-350 (*Single Squirrel*) and Bell-412

EQUIPMENT

332 cbt ac (plus 136 in store), no armed hel
AC 206 ***Tornado*** (112 **GR-1/4**), 94 **F-3** (plus 75 **GR** and 20 **F-3** in store) • 46 ***Jaguar*** (39 **GR-1A/3/3A**, 7 **T-2A/B** (plus 20 in store)) • 60 ***Harrier*** (51 **GR-7**, 9 **T-10** (plus 20 **GR-7** and 2 **T-10** in store)) • 101 ***Hawk* T-1/1-A-W** (plus 17 in store) • 5 ***Canberra*** (1 **T-4**, 4 **PR-9**) • 23 ***Nimrod*** (3 **R-1** (ECM), 20* **MR-2** (MR) (plus 1 in store) • 6 ***Sentry* (E-3D)** (AEW) • 4 **C-17A** • 9 ***Tristar*** (2 **K-1** (tkr/pax), 4 **KC-1** (tkr/pax/cgo), 2 **C-2** (pax), 1 **C-2A** (pax) • 19 **VC-10** (10 **C-1K** (tkr/cgo), 4 **K-3** (tkr), 5 **K-4** (tkr)) • 50 ***Hercules*** **C-130** (27 **-K**, 23 **-J**) • 5 **BAe-125 CC-3** (comms) • 2 **BAe-146** Mk 2 (VIP tpt) • 76 ***Tucano*** (trg) (plus 50 in store) • 9 ***Jetstream*** (trg) • 9 ***Dominie*** (trg) • 99 ***Tutor*** (trg) • 45 *Firefly* 160 (trg)
HEL 5 ***Wessex*** • 38 **CH-47** (*Chinook*) • 6 *Merlin* HC3 (22 on order) • 39 **SA-330 (*Puma*)** • 25 ***Sea King*** • 38 **AS-350B** (***Single Squirrel***) • 3 **AS-355** (***Twin Squirrel***) • 9 **Bell-412EP**

MISSILES

ASM AGM-65G2 *Maverick*, AGM-84D-1 *Harpoon*, *Paveway* II, *Paveway* III
AAM ASRAAM, AIM-9L/M *Sidewinder*, *Sky Flash* AMRAAM
ARM ALARM

ROYAL AIR FORCE REGIMENT

6 fd sqn, 4 gd based air defence sqns with 24 *Rapier* field standard C fire units; joint *Rapier* trg unit (with Army), 3 tactical Survival To Operate (STO) HQs
VOLUNTEER RESERVE AIR FORCES (Royal Auxiliary Air Force/RAF Reserve): 3 field sqns, 1 gd based AD sqn, 1 air movements sqn, 2 medical sqns, 2 intelligence sqns, 5 op support sqns covering STO duties, 1 C-130 Reserve Aircrew flt, 1 HQ augmentaion sqn, 1 mobile meteorological unit

Deployment

ARMY

LAND COMMAND
Assigned to ACE Rapid Reaction Corps **Germany** 1 armd div plus Corps cbt spt tps **UK** 1 mech inf div, 1 air aslt bde; additional TA units incl 8 inf bn, 2 SAS, 3 AD regt **Allied Command Europe Mobile Force** (*Land*) (AMF(L)): UK contribution 1 inf BG (incl 1 inf bn, 1 arty bty, 1 sigs sqn). AMF(L) will disband on 30 Oct 2002
HQ NORTHERN IRELAND
(some 7,800 (incl 200 RN, 1,100 RAF), plus 4,500 Home Service committed to N. Ireland); 3 inf bde HQ, up to 13 major units in inf role (5 in province, 1 committed reserve, up to 4 roulement inf bn, 3 Home Service inf bn), 1 engr, 1 avn regt.
The roles of the remainder of Army regular and TA units incl Home Defence and the defence of Dependent Territories, the Cy Sovereign Base Areas and Bru.

NAVY

FLEET (CinC is also CINCEASTLANT and COMNAVNORTHWEST): almost all regular RN forces are declared to NATO, split between SACLANT and SACEUR
MARINES 1 cdo bde (declared to SACLANT)

AIR FORCE

STRIKE COMMAND responsible for all RAF front-line forces. Day-to-day control delegated to 3 Gps **No. 1** (All RAF front-line fast jet ac, excl *Harrier*) **No. 2** (AT, AAR, airborne C^{3}I support and RAF regt) **No. 3** (Joint Force *Harrier*, maritime assets and HQ Augmentation sqn)

Forces Abroad

AFGHANISTAN 3 CH-47 hel
ANTARCTICA 1 ice patrol ship (in summer only)
ASCENSION ISLAND RAF 37
BELGIUM RAF 196
BELIZE Army 30
BRUNEI Army some 1,100: 1 Gurkha inf bn, 1 hel flt (3 hel)

CANADA Army 500 trg and liaison unit **RAF** 143; routine trg deployment of **ac** *Tornado, Harrier, Jaguar*
CYPRUS 3,190: **Army** 1,970; 2 inf bn, 1 engr spt sqn, 1 hel flt **RN** 20 **RAF** 1,200; 1 hel sqn (5 *Wessex* HC-2), plus **ac** and 1 AD radar on det
FALKLAND ISLANDS ε1,300: **Army** 400; **RN** 1 DDG/FFG, 1 PCO, 1 spt, 1 AR **RAF** 800 1 *Tornado* F-3, 1 *Hercules* C-130, 1 VC-10 K (tkr), 2 *Sea King* HAR-3, 2 CH-47 hel, 1 *Rapier* SAM sqn
GERMANY Army 17,100; 1 corps HQ (multinational), 1 armd div
GIBRALTAR 575: **Army** 60; Gibraltar regt 175 **RN/ Marines** 235; 2 PCI; Marine det, base unit **RAF** 105; periodic ac det
INDIAN OCEAN (*Armilla Patrol*): 1 DDG/FFG, 1 spt
Diego Garcia 1 Marine/naval party
Op Veritas RAF 720, 2 E-3D, 3 *Nimrod* MR-2, 2 *Tristar* K-1
KENYA Army 20
NEPAL Army 63 (Gurkha trg org)
NETHERLANDS RAF 137
OMAN & MUSCAT RAF 33
SIERRA LEONE Army ε100 incl Trg Team, Tri-service HQ and spt
USA RAF 162
WEST INDIES 1 DDG/FFG, 1 spt

UN AND PEACEKEEPING

AFGHANISTAN (ISAF): ε400; RAF 270 (incl fwd mounting base elm in Karachi), 3 spt hel, 2 utl hel **BAHRAIN** (*Southern Watch*): RAF 50 1 VC-10 (tkr) **BOSNIA** (SFOR II): ε1,700 (incl log and spt tps in Croatia); 1 Augmented Brigade HQ (multinational) with 1 recce sqn, 1 armd inf bn, 1 engr bn, 1 hel det **CYPRUS** (UNFICYP): 416: 1 inf bn, engr spt **DROC** (MONUC): 6 **GEORGIA** (UNOMIG): 7 obs **IRAQ/ KUWAIT** (*Southern Watch*): RAF 300; 8 *Tornado* GR4; (UNIKOM): 11 obs **ITALY** (Deliberate Forge): 350; 4 *Harrier* GR-4, 1 K-1 *Tristar* (tkr), 2 E-3D *Sentry* (periodic) **SAUDI ARABIA** (*Southern Watch*): RAF 825; 6 *Tornado* F3 **SIERRA LEONE** (UNOMSIL): 21 incl 15 obs **TURKEY** (*Northern Watch*): RAF 190; 4 *Jaguar* GR-3/3A, 2 VC-10 (tkr) **YUGOSLAVIA** (KFOR): 2,200; 1 armd bde with 1 armd inf, 1 inf bn, 1 engr regt; hel 2 SA-341 *Gazelle*
MILITARY ADVISERS 458 in 26 countries

Foreign Forces

US 9,400: **Army** 440 **Navy** 1,220 **Air Force** 7,600; 1 Air Force HQ (3rd Air Force) 1 ftr wg (2 sqn with 48 F-15E, 1 sqn with 24 F-15C/D), 1 air refuelling wg with 15 KC-135, 1 Special Ops Gp with 5 MC-130R, 5 MC-130H, 1 C-130E, 8 MH-53J, 1 naval air flt with 2 C-12
USMC 140
NATO HQ Allied Naval Forces North (HQNAVNORTH), HQ East Atlantic (HQEASTLANT) Combined Air Operations Centre (CAOC) 9, High Wycombe

Albania Alb

Total Armed Forces

ACTIVE ε27,000

The Alb armed forces are being re-constituted. The army is to consist of 5 inf divs, a cdo bde of 3 bn, 10 inf bde, 1 mech inf bde, 4 tk bde and 4 arty bde. Restructuring is now planned to be completed by 2010. Eqpt details are primarily those reported prior to the country-wide civil unrest of 1997 and should be treated with caution.

Army some 20,000

EQUIPMENT

MBT ε400: incl T-34 (in store), T-59
LT TK 35 Type-62
RECCE 15 BRDM-1
APC 103 PRC Type-531
TOWED ARTY 122mm: 425 M-1931/37, M-30, 208 PRC Type-60; **130mm**: 100 PRC Type-59-1; **152mm**: 90 PRC Type-66
MRL 107mm: 50 PRC Type-63
MOR 82mm: 259; **120mm**: 550 M-120; **160mm**: 100 M-43
RCL 82mm: T-21
ATK GUNS 45mm: M-1942; **57mm**: M-1943; **85mm**: 61 D-44 PRC Type-56; **100mm**: 50 Type-86
AD GUNS 125 incl **37mm**: M-1939; **57mm**: S-60

Navy ε2,500

BASES Durrës, Sarandë, Shëngjin, Vlorë

PATROL AND COASTAL COMBATANTS† 20

TORPEDO CRAFT 11 PRC *Huchuan* PHT with 2 533mm TT
PATROL CRAFT 9
1 PRC *Shanghai* II PCC, 3 FSU Po-2 PFI<, 5 (US) PB Mk3 (for Coast Guard use)<

MINE WARFARE 2

MINE COUNTERMEASURES† 2
2 FSU T-301 MSC, (plus 2 FSU T-43 MSO in reserve)

SUPPORT AND MISCELLANEOUS 2
1 AGOR, 1 AT†

Air Force 4,500

98 cbt ac†, no armed hel
Flying hours 10–15
FGA 1 air regt with 10 J-2 (MiG-15), 14 J-6 (MiG-17), 23 J-6 (MiG-19)
FTR 2 air regt
1 with 20 J-6 (MiG-19), 10 J-7 (MiG-21)
1 with 21 J-6 (MiG-19)
TPT 1 sqn with 10 C-5 (An-2), 3 Il-14M, 6 Li-2 (C-47)

HEL 1 regt with 20 Z-5 (Mi-4), 4 SA-316, 1 Bell 222
TRG 8 CJ-5, 15 MiG-15UTI, 6 Yak-11
SAM† some 4 SA-2 sites, 22 launchers

Forces Abroad

UN AND PEACEKEEPING

AFGHANISTAN (ISAF): 30 **BOSNIA** (SFOR II): 70 **GEORGIA** (UNOMIG): 1 obs

Paramilitary

INTERNAL SECURITY FORCE 'SPECIAL POLICE': 1 bn (Tirana) plus pl sized units in major towns

BORDER POLICE (Ministry of Public Order): e500

Foreign Forces

NATO (COMMZW): ε1,200 spt tps for KFOR

Armenia Arm

Total Armed Forces

ACTIVE 44,610
(incl about 2,550 HQ staff; 33,100 conscripts)
Terms of service conscription, 24 months

RESERVES
some mob reported, possibly 210,000 with mil service within 15 years

Army 38,900

(incl conscripts)
5 Army Corps HQ
- 1 with 2 MRR, 1 recce bn
- 1 with 5 MRR, 1 tk bn, 1 recce, 1 arty, 1 MRL, 1 maint bn
- 1 with 4 MRR, 1 SP arty regt
- 1 with 1 MRR, 1 indep special rifle regt, 2 fortified areas
- 1 with 2 MRR, 1 tk, 1 recce, 1 maint bn

1 mot rifle trg bde
2 arty regt (1 SP), 1 ATK regt
1 SAM bde, 2 SAM regt
1 mixed avn regt, 1 avn sqn
1 SF, 1 engr regt

EQUIPMENT
MBT 8 T-54, 102 T-72
AIFV 80 BMP-1, 7 BMP-1K, 5 BMP-2, 12 BRM-1K, 6 BMD-1
APC 11 BTR-60, 21 BTR-70, 4 BTR-80, plus 100 look-a-likes
TOTAL ARTY 229
TOWED 121: **122mm**: 59 D-30; **152mm**: 2 D-1, 34 D-20, 26 2A36
SP 38: **122mm**: 10 2S1; **152mm**: 28 2S3
MRL 51: **122mm**: 47 BM-21; **273mm**: 4 PRC WM-80
MOR 120mm: 19 M-120
ATK GUNS ε35: **85mm**: D-44; **100mm**: T-12
ATGW 9 AT-3 *Sagger*, 13 AT-6 *Spiral*
SAM 25 SA-2/-3, 27 SA-4, 20 SA-8, ε15 SA-9/-13
SURV GS-13 (veh), *Long Trough* ((SNAR-1) arty), *Pork Trough* ((SNAR-2/-6) arty), *Small Fred/Small Yawn* (arty), *Big Fred* ((SNAR-10) veh/arty)

Air and Defence Aviation Forces 3,160

8 cbt ac, 13 armed hel
FGA 1 sqn with 5 Su-25, 1 MiG-25, 2 L-39
HEL 1 sqn with 7 Mi-24P* (attack), 3 Mi-24K*, 3 Mi-24R*, 7 Mi-8MT (combat support), 9 Mi-2 (utility)
TPT 1 An-24, 1 An-32
TRG CENTRE 2 An-2 (plus 4 in store), 10 Yak-52 (plus 10 in store), 6 Yak-55/Yak-18T

Paramilitary 1,000

MINISTRY OF INTERNAL AFFAIRS
4 bn: 44 BMP-1, 1 BMP-1K, 5 BRM-1K, 2 BMD-1, 24 BTR-60/-70/-152

BORDER TROOPS (Ministry of National Security)
35 BMP-1, 3 BRM-1K, 2 BMD-1, 23 BTR-60/-70

Foreign Forces

RUSSIA 2,900: **Army** 1 mil base (div) with 74 MBT, 17 APC, 129 ACV, 84 arty/MRL/mor **Air Defence** 1 sqn 18 MiG-29, 2 SA-12 (S-300) bty, SA-6 bty

Austria A

Total Armed Forces

(Air Service forms part of the Army)

ACTIVE some 34,600
(incl ε17,400 active and short term; ε17,200 conscripts; excl ε9,500 civilians; some 66,000 reservists a year undergo refresher trg, a proportion at a time)
Terms of service 7 months recruit trg, 30 days reservist refresher trg during 8 years (or 8 months trg, no refresher); 60–90 days additional for officers, NCOs and specialists

RESERVES
72,000 ready (72 hrs) reserves; 990,000 with reserve trg, but no commitment. Officers, NCOs and specialists to

age 65, remainder to age 50

Army 34,600

(incl ε17,200 conscripts)
1 Land Forces Comd with
3 inf bde (each 3 inf bn)
1 mech inf bde with 2 mech inf, 1 tk, 1 recce, 1 SP arty bn
1 mech inf bde with 1 mech inf, 2 tk, 1 SP arty bn
2 SP arty regt, 2 recce, 3 engr, 1 ATK bn
1 Provincial mil comd with 1 inf regt (plus 5 inf bn on mob)
8 Provincial mil comd (15 inf bn on mob)

EQUIPMENT

MBT 160 M-60A3 (in store), 114 *Leopard* 2A4
LT TK 137 *Kuerassier* JPz SK (plus 118 in store)
APC 425 Saurer 4K4E/F (incl look-a-likes), 68 *Pandur*, some *Ulan*
TOWED ARTY 105mm: 84 IFH (M-101 deactivated); **155mm**: 20 M-2A1 (deactivated)
SP ARTY 155mm: 162 M-109A2/-A3/-A5ÖE
FORTRESS ARTY 155mm: 24 SFK M-2 (deactivated)
MRL 128mm: 16 M-51 (in store)
MOR 81mm: 497; **107mm**: 133; **120mm**: 241 M-43
ATGW 378 RBS-56 *Bill*, 87 RJPz-(HOT) *Jaguar* 1
RCL 84mm: 2,088 *Carl Gustav*; **106mm**: 374 M-40A1 (in store)
ANTI-TANK GUNS
STATIC 105mm: some 227 L7A1 (*Centurion* tk – being deactivated)
AD GUNS 20mm: 145 (plus 319 in store)

MARINE WING

(under School of Military Engineering)
2 river patrol craft<; 10 unarmed boats

Air Force (6,850)

(ε2,240 conscripts); 52 cbt ac, 11 armed hel
Flying hours 120 ftr/FGA, 180 hel/tpt
1 air div HQ (AF Comd by end 2002), 3 air regt, 3 AD regt, 1 air surv regt
FTR/FGA 1 wg with 23 SAAB J-35Oe
LIAISON 12 PC-6B
TPT 3 C-130K, 2 *Skyvan* 3M, 1 CASA 235-300 (on lease)
HEL
LIAISON/RECCE 11 OH-58B*
TPT 22 AB-212, 9 S-70A being delivered
UTILITY/SAR 23 SA-319 *Alouette* III
TRG 16 PC-7, 29* SAAB 105Oe hel 11 AB-206A
MISSILES
AAM AiM-9P3/P5
AD 36 *Mistral* with Thomson RAC 3D radars; 72 **20mm** AA guns: 72 Twin **35mm** AA towed guns with 36 *Skyguard* radars; air surv *Goldhaube* with *Selenia* MRS-403 3D radars and Thomson RAC 3D. 1 3DLRR in delivery

Forces Abroad

UN AND PEACEKEEPING

AFGHANISTAN (ISAF): 60 **BOSNIA** (SFOR II): 2 **CYPRUS** (UNFICYP): 4 **ETHIOPIA/ERITREA** (UNMEE): 1 obs **GEORGIA** (UNOMIG): 2 obs **INDIA/PAKISTAN** (UNMOGIP): 1 obs **IRAQ/KUWAIT** (UNIKOM): 2 obs **MIDDLE EAST** (UNTSO): 3 obs **SYRIA** (UNDOF): 363; 1 inf bn **WESTERN SAHARA** (MINURSO): 2 obs **YUGOSLAVIA** (KFOR): 498

Azerbaijan Az

Total Armed Forces

ACTIVE 72,100

Terms of service 17 months, but can be extended for ground forces

RESERVES

some mob 300,000 with mil service within 15 years

Army 62,000

4 Army Corps HQ • 22 MR bde • 2 arty bde, 1 ATK regt

EQUIPMENT

MBT 220: 120 T-72, 100 T-55
AIFV 135: 44 BMP-1, 41 BMP-2, 1 BMP-3, 28 BMD-1, 21 BRM-1
APC 25 BTR-60, 28 BTR-70, 11 BTR-80, 11 BTR-D plus 306 MT-LB
TOTAL ARTY 282
TOWED 141: **122mm**: 92 D-30; **152mm**: 30 D-20, 22 2A36
SP 122mm: 12 2S1
COMBINED GUN/MOR 120mm: 26 2S9
MRL 122mm: 53 BM-21
MOR 120mm: 47 PM-38
ATGW ε250: AT-3 *Sagger*, AT-4 *Spigot*, AT-5 *Spandrel*, AT-7 *Saxhorn*
SAM ε40 SA-4/-8/-13
SURV GS-13 (veh); *Long Trough* ((SNAR-1) arty), *Pork Trough* ((SNAR 2/ 6) arty), *Small Fred/Small Yawn* (veh, arty), *Big Fred* ((SNAR-10) veh, arty)

Navy 2,200

BASE Baku

PATROL AND COASTAL COMBATANTS 6

PATROL, CRAFT 6
1 *Turk*, 1 *Osa* II, 2 *Stenka* PFI<, 1 *Zhuk* PCI<, 1 *Svetlyak* PCI<

MINE WARFARE 5

MINE COUNTERMEASURES 5

3 *Sonya* MSC, 2 *Yevgenya* MSI

AMPHIBIOUS 2

2 *Polnochny* LSM capacity 180 tps

SUPPORT AND MISCELLANEOUS 3

1 *Vadim Popov* (research), 2 *Balerian Uryvayev* (research)

Air Force and Air Defence 7,900

48† cbt ac, 15 attack hel

FGA regt with 4 Su-17, 5 Su-24, 2 Su-25, 5 MiG-21

FTR sqn with 32 MiG-25 (incl 5 UB)

TPT 4 ac (1 An-12, 3 Yak-40)

TRG 26 L-29, 12 L-39, 1 Su-17

HEL 1 regt with 7 Mi-2, 13 Mi-8, 15* Mi-24

IN STORE ac 31 MiG-25, 1 MiG-21, 2 L-29

SAM 100 SA-2/-3/-5

Forces Abroad

UN AND PEACEKEEPING

YUGOSLAVIA (KFOR II): 34

Paramilitary ε15,000+

MILITIA (Ministry of Internal Affairs) 10,000+

EQPT incl 7 BTR-60/-70/-80

BORDER GUARD (Ministry of Internal Affairs) ε5,000

EQPT incl 168 BMP-1/-2 AIFV, 19 BTR-60/-70/-80 APC, 2 US PCI<

Opposition

ARMENIAN ARMED GROUPS

ε18,000 in Nagorno-Karabakh, perhaps 40,000 on mob (incl ε8,000 personnel from Arm)

EQPT (reported) 316 incl T-72, T-55 MBT; 324 ACV incl BTR-70/-80, BMP-1/-2; 322 arty incl D-44, 102 D-30, 53 D-20, 99 2A36, 44 BM-21, KS-19

Belarus Bel

Total Armed Forces

ACTIVE 79,800

(incl 28,500 in centrally controlled units and MoD staff; 4,000 women; 30,000 conscripts)

Terms of service 9–12 months

RESERVES some 289,500

with mil service within last 5 years

Army 29,300

MoD tps: 1 MRD (trg), 3 indep mob bde, 1 arty div (5 'bde'), 1 arty regt

2 SSM, 1 ATK, 1 *Spetsnaz*

3 Corps

1 with 3 indep mech, 1 SAM bde, 1 arty, 1 MRL, 1 ATK regt

1 with 1 SAM bde, 1 arty, 1 MRL regt

1 with 1 SAM bde, 1 arty, 1 ATK, 1 MRL regt

EQUIPMENT (CFE declared totals as at 1 Jan 2002)

MBT 1,608 (241 in store): 29 T-55, 1,484 T-72, 95 T-80

AIFV 1,588 (76 in store): 109 BMP-1, 1,164 BMP-2, 161 BRM, 154 BMD-1

APC 919 (261 in store): 188 BTR-60, 445 BTR-70, 194 BTR-80, 22 BTR-D, 70 MT-LB

TOTAL ARTY 1,471 (150 in store) incl

TOWED 428: **122mm**: 178 D-30; **152mm**: 6 M-1943 (D-1), 58 D-20, 136 2A65, 50 2A36

SP 568: **122mm**: 236 2S1; **152mm**: 163 2S3, 120 2S5; **152mm**: 13 2S19; **203mm**: 36 2S7

COMBINED GUN/MOR 120mm: 54 2S9

MRL 344: **122mm**: 208 BM-21, 11 9P138; **130mm**: 1 BM-13; **220mm**: 84 9P140; **300mm**: 40 9A52

MOR 120mm: 77 2S12

ATGW 480: AT-4 *Spigot*, AT-5 *Spandrel* (some SP), AT-6 *Spiral* (some SP), AT-7 *Saxhorn*

SSM 60 *Scud*, 36 FROG/SS-21

SAM 350 SA-8/-11/-12/-13

SURV GS-13 (arty), *Long Trough* ((SNAR-1) arty), *Pork Trough* ((SNAR-2/-6) arty), *Small Fred/Small Yawn* (veh, arty), *Big Fred* ((SNAR-10) veh, arty)

Air Force and Air Defence Forces 22,000 (incl 10,200 Air Defence)

212 cbt ac, 58 attack hel

Flying hours 15

FGA 35 Su-24MK/MR, 76 Su-25/UB

FTR 35 MiG-23MLD/UB, 43 MiG-29S/UB, 23 Su-27P/UB

HELICOPTERS

ATTACK 53 Mi-24, 4 Mi-24R, 1 Mi-24K

CBT SPT 29 Mi-6, 125 Mi-8, 8 Mi-24K, 4 Mi-24R

TPT ac 4 Il-76 (plus 12 Il-76 civilian but available for mil use), 3 An-12, 1 An-24, 6 An-26, 1 Tu-134 **hel** 14 Mi-26

MISSILES

AAM AA-7, AA-8, AA-10, AA-11

ASM AS-10, AS-11, AS-14

AIR DEFENCE

Consists of SAM/AAA units, ECM/ECCM units

SAM 175 SA-3/-5/-10

Paramilitary 110,000

BORDER GUARDS (Ministry of Interior) 12,000

MINISTRY OF INTERIOR TROOPS 11,000

MILITIA (Ministry of Interior) 87,000

Bosnia-Herzegovina BiH

Total Armed Forces

In accordance with the Dayton Peace Accords, **BiH** is composed of two **entities**:
• the (Muslim-Croat) 'Federation of Bosnia and Herzegovina' and
• the (Serbian) 'Republika Srpska'.

The constitution has attributed all competencies regarding defence and military matters to the two entities. There are no armed forces (except for Border Guards and the Brcko-district police) at the State level. The two entities have kept the armed forces they had established throughout the armed conflict until the 1995 Dayton Peace Accord.

The armed forces of the entities are subject to an arms-limitation regime established under the Dayton Peace Accord. An agreement signed by BiH, its two entities, Cr and FRY on 14 June 1996, established arms ceilings for the armed forces of the parties. Both entity armed forces are currently reducing their active strengths to those agreed in the Common Defence Policy signed in 2001. These are:

VF-B – 9,200, VF-H – 4,000, VRS – 6,600

ACTIVE see individual entries below

Forces of the Federation of Bosnia and Herzegovina

The Armed Forces of the federation are composed of the (predominately Muslim) 'Army of Bosnia and Herzegovina' (VF-B formerly ABiH) and the Bosnian Croat 'Croatian Defence Council' (VF-H formerly HVO). The federation's defence law indicates that the forces are to have joint institutions at the level of Ministry of Defence, General Staff and some formations directly subordinated to the General Staff incl the air force, air defence command and arty div. Integration has been limited so far. Forces are separated from the corps level downwards. The Federation Army (VF) is currently reducing to only 6 active brigades

Army (VF) some 13,200 (VF-B 9,200; VF-H 4,000) (excluding conscripts)

1 Joint HQ • 4 Corps (res) • Federal Reaction Force, 1 armd, 1 mech, 2 inf, 1 engr bde

RESERVES

VF-B: 110,000, VF-H: 40,000

EQUIPMENT (mostly held under SFOR control in weapon storage sites)

MBT 203: 20 T-34, 14 T-54, 68 T-55, 6 M-84, 50 AMX-30, 45 M-60A3

LT TK 8 PT-76

AIFV 25 AMX-10P, 10 M-80

APC 80 M-113A2, M-80, 38 OT-60, BTR-50, BTR-70, BOV

TOTAL ARTY 880 (incl ATK guns)

TOWED 105mm: 36 L-118, 28 M-2A1, 20 M-56, 4 M-18/26; **122mm:** 116 D-30, 3 M-38; **130mm:** 35 M-46; **152mm:** 18 D-20, M-84; **155mm:** 124 M-114 A2; **203mm:** 2 M-2

SP 122mm: 7 2S1

MRL 107mm: 29 Type 63; **122mm:** 36 APR-40, 5 BM-21; **128mm:** 34 M-91, M-63

MOR 120mm: 341 M-75, 15 UBM-52, M-74, M-38; **82mm**

ATGW 250 incl AT-3 *Sagger*, 52 AT-4 *Fagot*, 51 *Red Arrow* (TF-8)

ATK GUNS 100mm: 27 T-12/MT-12

AD GUNS 20mm: M-55, Bov-3; **23mm:** 19 ZU-23; **30mm:** M-53; **57mm:** S-60

SAM SA-7/-9/-14/-16

HEL 10 Mi-8/-17, 15 UH-1H

AC 3 UTVA-75

Republika Srpska Armed Forces (VRS)

Army some 6,600

to be 2 Corps HQ, 1 armd, 1 mech, 2 trg bde plus spt

RESERVES 80,000

EQUIPMENT (mostly held under SFOR control in weapon storage sites)

MBT 80 T-55, 57 M-84

AIFV 103 M-80

APC 67 M-60, 22 BOV-M, 9 BTR-50PK

TOTAL ARTY 581 (incl ATK guns)

TOWED 105mm: 82 M-56; **122mm:** 138 D-30, M-1938 (M-30); **130mm:** 38 M-46; **152mm:** 9 D-20, 3 M-84

SP 122mm: 24 2S1

MRL 122mm: 32 BM-21; **128mm:** 36 M-63, 20 M-77; **262mm:** 1 M-87 *Orkan*

MOR 120mm: 70 incl M-75, M-52, M-74

SSM FROG-7

ATGW about 150 incl AT-3 *Sagger*

ATK GUNS 100mm: 128 T-12

AD GUNS 975: incl **20mm**, **23mm** incl ZSU 23-4; **30mm:** M53/59SP; **57mm:** ZSU 57-2; **90mm**

SAM SA-2, some SA-6/-7B/-9

AC 10 *Orao*, 8 *Jastreb*, 1 *Super Galeb*

HEL 20 SA-341, 10 Mi-8, 7 HN-45

Forces Abroad

UN AND PEACEKEEPING

ETHIOPIA/ERITREA (UNMEE): 9 obs

Foreign Forces

NATO (SFOR II): about 18,000 (to be 12,000 by end 2002): Be, Ca, Da, Fr, Ge, Gr, Hu, It, Nl, No, Pl, Por, Sp, Tu, UK, US **Non-NATO** Alb, A, Bg, Ea, Irl, Lat, L, Mor, R, RF, Swe

Bulgaria Bg

Total Armed Forces

ACTIVE 68,450

(incl about 15,250 centrally controlled staff and MoD staff, but excl some 10,000 construction tps; perhaps 49,000 conscripts). Being restructured. To be 45,000 by 2004
Terms of service 9 months

RESERVES 303,000

Army 250,500 **Navy** (to age 55, officers 60 or 65) 7,500 **Air Force** (to age 60) 45,000

Army 31,050

(incl ε33,300 conscripts)
3 Mil Districts/Corps HQ
1 with 1 mech inf div, 1 tk, 1 lt inf, 2 mech (res), 1 arty bde
1 with 1 tk, 2 mech (res), 1 arty bde
1 with 2 mech, 1 arty bde
Army tps: 4 *Scud*, 1 SAM bde, 2 arty, 1 MRL, 3 ATK, 3 AD arty, 1 SAM regt
1 AB bde
1 multinational bde HQ (SEEBRIG)

RESERVES

1 mtn, 3 inf, 8 territorial def regt

EQUIPMENT

MBT 1,475: 1,042 T-55, 433 T-72
ASLT GUN 68 SU-100
RECCE 58 BRDM-1/-2
AIFV 100 BMP-1, 114 BMP-23
APC 659 BTR-60, 1,012 MT-LB (plus 1,270 'look-a-likes')
TOWED ARTY 100mm: M-1944 (BS-3); **122mm**: 195 M-30, M-1931/37 (A-19); **130mm**: 60 M-46; **152mm**: M-1937 (ML-20), 206 D-20
SP ARTY 122mm: 692 2S1
MRL 122mm: 222 BM-21
MOR 120mm: 359 2S11 *Tundzha* SP
SSM launchers: 28 FROG-7, 36 *Scud*
ATGW 200 AT-3 *Sagger*, AT-4 *Spigot*, AT-5 *Spandrel*
ATK GUNS 85mm: 150 D-44; **100mm**: 200 T-12
AD GUNS 400: **23mm**: ZU-23, ZSU-23-4 SP; **57mm**: S-60; **100mm**: KS-19
SAM SA-7, 20 SA-3, 27 SA-4, 20 SA-6
SURV GS-13 (veh), *Long Trough* ((SNAR-1) arty), *Pork Trough* ((SNAR-2/-6) arty), *Small Fred/Small Yawn* (veh, arty), *Big Fred* ((SNAR-10) veh, arty)

Navy ε4,370

(incl ε2,000 conscripts)
COMMAND Northern Varna; **Southern** Burgas
BASES Varna, Burgas, Atya, Vidin, Balchik, Sozopol

SUBMARINES 1

SSK 1 *Pobeda* (FSU *Romeo*)-class with 533mm TT†

PRINCIPAL SURFACE COMBATANTS 1

FRIGATES 1
FF 1 *Smeli* (FSU *Koni*) with 1 × 2 SA-N-4 *Gecko* SAM, 2 × 2 76mm guns, 2 × 12 ASW RL

PATROL AND COASTAL COMBATANTS 23

CORVETTES 7
1 *Tarantul* II FSG with 2 × 2 SS-N-2C *Styx* SSM, 2 × 4 SA-N-5 *Grail* SAM, 1 × 76mm gun
4 *Poti* FS with 2 ASW RL, 4 ASTT
2 *Pauk* I FS with 1 SA-N-5 *Grail* SAM, 2 × 5 ASW RL, 4 × 406mm TT, 2 × 5 ASW RL
MISSILE CRAFT 6 *Osa* I/II PFM with 4 SS-N-2A/B *Styx* SSM
PATROL, INSHORE 10
10 *Zhuk* PFI<

MINE WARFARE 20

MINE COUNTERMEASURES 20
4 *Sonya* MSC, 4 *Vanya* MSC, 4 *Yevgenya* MSI<, 6 *Olya* MSI<, 2 PO-2 MSI<

AMPHIBIOUS 2 FSU *Polnocny A* LSM, capacity 150 tps, 6 tk
Plus 6 LCU

SUPPORT AND MISCELLANEOUS 16

3 AO, 1 diving tender, 1 degaussing, 1 AT, 7 AG; 3 AGHS

NAVAL AVIATION

EQUIPMENT
9 armed hel
HELICOPTERS
ASW 9 Mi-14

COASTAL ARTY 2 regt, 20 bty
GUNS 130mm: 4 SM-4-1
SSM SS-C-1B *Sepal*, SSC-3 *Styx*

NAVAL GUARD

3 coy

Air Force 17,780

232 cbt ac, 43 attack hel, 1 AD Corps, 1 Tactical Aviation corps
Flying hours 30–40
FGA 1 regt with 39 Su-25 (35 -A, 4 -UB)
FTR 3 regt with 64 MiG-23, 77 MiG-21 bis, 21 MiG-29 (17 -A, 4 -UB)

RECCE 1 regt with 21 Su-22* (18 -M4, 3 -UM3), 10 MiG-21MF/UM*
TARGET FACILITIES 12 L-29 operated by front-line sqns
TPT 1 regt with 2 Tu-134, 2 An-24, 5 An-26, 6 L-410, 1 Yak-40 (VIP)
SURVEY 1 An-30 (*Open Skies*)
HEL 2 regt
1 with 43 Mi-24 (attack)
1 with 8 Mi-8, 31 Mi-17, 6 Bell-206, 1 Bell 430
TRG 2 trg schools with 12 L-29 (basic), 30 L-39ZA (advanced)
MISSILES
ASM AS-7 *Kerry*, AS-14 *Kedge*
AAM AA-2 *Atoll*, AA-7 *Apex*, AA-8 *Aphid*, AA-11 *Archer*
SAM SA-2/-3/-5/-10 (20 sites, some 110 launchers)

Forces Abroad

UN AND PEACEKEEPING
BOSNIA (SFOR II): 1 pl **ETHIOPIA/ERITREA** (UNMEE): 7 incl 2 obs

Paramilitary 34,000

BORDER GUARDS (Ministry of Interior) 12,000
12 regt; some 50 craft incl about 12 FSU PO2 PCI<
SECURITY POLICE 4,000
RAILWAY AND CONSTRUCTION TROOPS 18,000

Croatia Cr

Total Armed Forces

The armed forces of Croatia are subject to an arms limitation regime established under the Dayton Peace Accord. An agreement signed by BiH, its two entitites, Cr and FRY on 14 June 1996, established ceilings for the holdings of the armed forces of the parties

ACTIVE ε51,000
(incl ε18–20,000 conscripts)
Terms of service 6 months

RESERVES 140,000
Army 100,000 **Home Defence** 40,000

Army ε45,000

(incl conscripts)
6 Mil Districts • 7 Guard bde (org varies) • 1 mixed arty/MRL bde • 1 ATK bde • 4 AD bde • 1 engr bde

RESERVES
33 inf 'bde' (incl 1 trg), 6 mixed arty/MRL bde, 2 ATK bde, 1 engr bde
EQUIPMENT
MBT 280: 222 T-55, 55 M-84, 3 T-72M
RECCE 17 BRDM-2
AIFV 106 M-80
APC 15 BTR-50, 13 M-60PB, 9 BOV-VP plus 23 'look-a-likes'
TOTAL ARTY some 975 incl
TOWED 76mm: ZIS-3; **105mm**: 50 M-56, 6 M-56H1, 90 M-2A1; **122mm**: 45 M-1938, 42 D-30; **130mm**: 79 M-46; **152mm**: 20 D-20, 18 M-84, 3 M-84H1; **155mm:** 19 M-1, 18 M-1H1; **203mm**: 22 M-2
SP 122mm: 8 2S1
MRL 122mm: 40 BM-21; **128mm**: 8 M-63, 182 M-91; **262mm**: 2 M-87 *Orkan*
MOR 120mm: 317 M-75, 6 UBM-52; plus **82mm**: 489
ATGW AT-3 *Sagger* (10 on BRDM-2), AT-4 *Spigot*, AT-7 *Saxhorn*, *Milan* reported
RL 73mm: RPG-7/-22. **90mm**: M-79
ATK GUNS 100mm: 142 T-12
AD GUNS 600+: **14.5mm**: ZPU-2/-4; **20mm**: BOV-1 SP, M-55; **30mm**: M-53/59, BOV-3SP

Navy 3,000

BASES Split (HQ), Pula, Sibenik, Ploce, Dubrovnik
Minor facilities Lastovo, Vis
SUBMARINES 1
SSI 1 *Velebit* (Mod *Una*) for SF ops (4 SDV or 4 mines)
PATROL AND COASTAL COMBATANTS 8
MISSILE CRAFT 2
1 *Kralj Petar* PFM with 4 or 8 RBS-15 SSM
1 *Rade Koncar* PFM with 4 RBS-15 SSM
PATROL, COASTAL/INSHORE 6
1 *Dubrovnik* (Mod FSU *Osa* 1) PFC, can lay mines
4 *Mirna* PCC, 1 RLM-301 PCI< plus 5 PCR
AMPHIBIOUS craft only
2 *Silba* LCT, and 9 LCU
SUPPORT AND MISCELLANEOUS 4
2 AT, 1 *Spasilac* ARS, 1 FSU *Moma* AGHS

MARINES
2 indep inf coy

COASTAL DEFENCE
some 10 coast arty bty, 3 RBS-15 SSM bty

Air Force 3,000

(incl AD forces, conscripts)
24 cbt ac, 22 armed hel
Flying hours 50
FGA/FTR 2 sqn with 20 MiG-21 bis/4 MiG-21 UM
TPT 1 An-2, 2 An-32, 3 CL-415, 2 CL-215 (fire fighting)

HEL 6 Mi-8, 13* Mi-8MTV-1, 9* Mi-24
TRG 20 PC-9, 5 UTVA, 9 Bell 206B
AAM AA-2 *Atoll*, AA-8 *Aphid*
AIR DEFENCE FORCE (2,000)
SAM SA-7, SA-9, SA-10, SA-14/-16

Forces Abroad

UN AND PEACEKEEPING
ETHIOPIA/ERITREA (UNMEE): 5 obs **SIERRA LEONE** (UNAMSIL): 10 obs

Paramilitary 10,000

POLICE 10,000 armed
COAST GUARD boats only

Foreign Forces

UN (UNMOP): 27 obs from 22 countries; (SFOR II): ε500

Cyprus Cy

Total Armed Forces

ACTIVE 10,000
(incl 8,700 conscripts; 500+ women)
Terms of service conscription, 26 months, then reserve to age 50 (officers 65)

RESERVES
60,000 all services

National Guard 10,000

(incl 8,700 conscripts) (all units classified non-active under Vienna Document)
1 Corps HQ, 1 air comd, 1 naval comd • 2 lt inf div HQ • 2 lt inf bde HQ • 1 armd bde (3 bn) • 1 svc spt bde • 1 arty comd (regt) • 1 Home Guard comd • 1 SF comd (regt of 3 bn)

EQUIPMENT
MBT 113 AMX-30 (incl 52 -B2), 41 T-80U
RECCE 124 EE-9 *Cascavel*, 15 EE-3 *Jararaca*
AIFV 43 BMP-3
APC 165 *Leonidas*, 126 VAB (incl variants), 16 AMX-VCI
TOWED ARTY 75mm: 4 M-116A1 pack; **88mm**: 36 25-pdr (in store); **100mm**: 20 M-1944; **105mm**: 72 M-56; **155mm**: 12 TR F1
SP ARTY 155mm: 12 F3, 12 *Zuzana*
MRL 122mm: 4 BM-21; **128mm**: 18 FRY M-63
MOR 376+: **81mm**: 170 E-44, 70+ M1/M29 (in store); **107mm**: 20 M-30/M-2; **120mm**: 116 RT61
ATGW 45 *Milan* (15 on EE-3 *Jararaca*), 22 HOT (18 on VAB)
RL 66mm: M-72 LAW; **73mm**: 850 RPG-7; **112mm**: 1,000 *Apilas*
RCL 90mm: 40 EM-67; **106mm**: 144 M-40A1
AD GUNS 20mm: 36 M-55; **35mm**: 24 GDF-003 with *Skyguard*; **40mm**: 20 M-1 (in store)
SAM 60 *Mistral* (some SP), 24 *Aspide*, 6 SA-15

MARITIME WING
1 *Kyrenia* (Gr *Dilos*) PCC
1 *Salamis* PCC< (plus 11 boats)
1 coastal def SSM bty with 3 MM-40 *Exocet*

AIR WING
No cbt ac, 6 armed hel
AC 1 BN-2 *Islander*, 2 PC-9
HEL 6 Mi-24VK-2*, 2 Bell UH-1H, 2 Bell 206C, 4 SA-342 *Gazelle* (with HOT), 2 Mi-2 (in store)

Paramilitary some 750

ARMED POLICE about 500
1 mech rapid-reaction unit (350), 2 VAB/VTT APC, 1 BN-2A *Maritime Defender* ac, 2 Bell 412 hel
MARITIME POLICE 250
2 *Evagoras* PFI, 1 *Shaltag* PFI, 5 SAB-12 PCC

Foreign Forces

GREECE 1,250: 1 mech inf bde incl 950 (ELDYK) (Army); 2 mech inf, 1 armd, 1 arty bn, plus ε200 officers/NCO seconded to Greek-Cypriot National Guard
EQPT 61 M-48A5 MOLF MBT, 80 *Leonidas* APC (from National Guard), 12 M-114 155mm towed arty, 6 M-110A2 203mm SP arty
UK (in Sovereign Base Areas) 3,190: **Army** 1,970; 2 inf bn, 1 eng spt sqn, 1 hel flt **Air Force** 1,200; 1 hel sqn, plus ac on det
UN (UNFICYP) some 1,206; 3 inf bn (Arg, Slvk, UK), tps from A, Ca, SF, Hu, Irl, ROK, plus 35 civ pol from 2 countries

'Turkish Republic of Northern Cyprus'

Total Armed Forces

ACTIVE ε5,000
Terms of service conscription, 24 months, then reserve to age 50

RESERVES 26,000
11,000 **first-line** 10,000 **second-line** 5,000 **third-line**

Army ε5,000

7 inf bn

EQUIPMENT

MOR 120mm: 73
ATGW 6 *Milan*
RCL 106mm: 36

Paramilitary

ARMED POLICE ε150

1 Police SF unit

COAST GUARD

(operated by TRNC Security Forces)
1 *Raif Denktash* PCC • 2 ex-US Mk5 PCC • 2 SG45/SG46 PCC • 1 PCI

Foreign Forces

TURKEY

ARMY ε36,000 (mainly conscripts)

1 Corps HQ, 2 mech inf div, 1 armd bde, 1 indep mech inf bde, 1 arty, 1 SF regt, 1 army air comd

EQUIPMENT

MBT 441 M-48A5 T1/T2, 8 M-48A2 (trg)
APC 361 AAPC (incl variants), 266 M-113 (incl variants)
TOWED ARTY 105mm: 72 M-101A1; **155mm**: 18 M-114A2; **203mm:** 12 M-115
SP ARTY 155mm: 90 M-44T
MRL 122mm: 6 T-122
MOR 81mm: 175; **107mm**: 148 M-30; **120mm**: 54 HY-12
ATGW 66 *Milan*, 48 TOW
RL 66mm: M-72 LAW
RCL 90mm: M-67; **106mm**: 192 M-40A1
AD GUNS 20mm: Rh 202; **35mm**: 16 GDF-003; **40mm**: 48 M-1
SAM 50+ *Stinger*
SURV AN/TPQ-36
AC 3 U-17. Periodic det of F-16C/D, F-4E
HEL 3 UH-1H, 1 AS-532UL

NAVY

1 *Caner Goyneli* PCI<

Estonia Ea

Total Armed Forces

ACTIVE 5,510

(incl 2,300 HQ staff and centrally controlled units; 1,310 conscripts; excl some 390 civilians)
Terms of service 8 months; officers, NCOs and some specialists 11 months

RESERVES some 24,000

Army some 2,550

(incl 1,030 conscripts)
4 Defence Regions, 14 Defence Districts, 5 inf, 1 arty • 1 guard, 1 recce bn • 1 peace ops centre, 1 peacekeeping bn(-)

RESERVES

Militia 8,500, 15 *Kaitseliit* (Defence League) units

EQUIPMENT

RECCE 7 BRDM-2
APC 25 BTR-60/-70/-80
TOWED ARTY 105mm: 19 M 61-37
MOR 81mm: 44; **120mm**: 14 2S11
ATGW 10 *Mapats*, 3 RB-56 *Bill*
RL 82mm: 200 B-300
RCL 84mm: 109 *Carl Gustav*; **90mm**: 100 PV-1110; **106mm**: 30 M-40A1
AD GUNS 23mm: 100 ZU-23-2

Navy 440

(incl 230 conscripts)
Lat, Ea and L have set up a joint Naval unit BALTRON with bases at Liepaja, Riga, Ventspils (Lat), Tallinn (Ea), Klaipeda (L)
BASES Tallinn (HQ BALTRON), Miinisadam (Navy and BALTRON)

PATROL AND COASTAL COMBATANTS 3

CORVETTE 1
1 *Admiral Pitka* (Da *Beskytteren*) FS with 1 × 76mm gun
PATROL CRAFT 2
2 *Rihtiniemi* PCC

MINE WARFARE 4

MINELAYERS 0
But *Rihtiniemi* can lay mines
MINE COUNTERMEASURES 4
2 *Lindau* (Ge) MHC
2 *Kalev* (Ge *Frauenlob*) MSI

SUPPORT AND MISCELLANEOUS 1

1 *Laine* (Ru *Mayak*) AK

Air Force 220

(incl 50 conscripts)
1 air base and 1 air surv div
Flying hours 120
ac 2 An-2, 1 PZL *Wilga*-35 **hel** 4 Robinson R-44

Forces Abroad

UN AND PEACEKEEPING

BOSNIA (SFOR II): 2 **MIDDLE EAST** (UNTSO): 1 obs

Paramilitary 2,600

BORDER GUARD (Ministry of Internal Affairs) 2,600 (170 conscripts); 1 regt, 3 rescue coy; maritime elm of Border Guard also fulfils task of Coast Guard

BASES Tallinn

PATROL CRAFT 20

PATROL, OFFSHORE 3

1 *Kou* (*Silma*), 1 *Linda* (*Kemio*), 1 *Valvas* (US *Bittersweet*)

PATROL, COASTAL 6

3 PVL-100 (*Koskelo*), 1 *Pikker*, 1 *Torm* (*Arg*), 1 *Maru* (*Viima*)

PATROL, INSHORE 11 PCI<

AVN 2 L-410 UVP-1 *Turbolet*, 5 Mi-8 (In war, subordinated to Air Force staff)

Finland SF

Total Armed Forces

ACTIVE 31,850

(incl 15,500 conscripts, some 500 women)

Terms of service 6–9–12 months (12 months for officers, NCOs and soldiers with special duties)

RESERVES some 485,000 (to be 430,000)

Total str on mob some 485,000 (all services), with 100,000 op forces, 27,000 territorial forces and 75,000 in local forces. Some 35,000 reservists a year do refresher trg: total obligation 40 days (75 for NCOs, 100 for officers) between conscript service and age 50 (NCOs and officers to age 60)

Army 24,550 (to be 315,000 on mob)

(incl 11,500 conscripts)

(all bdes reserve, some with peacetime trg role; re-org underway to be complete by 2008)

3 Mil Comd

1 with 6 mil provinces, 2 armd (1 trg), 2 *Jaeger* (trg), 7 inf bde

1 with 2 mil provinces, 3 *Jaeger* (trg) bde

1 with 4 mil provinces, 4 *Jaeger* (trg), 4 inf bde

Other units

3 AD regt, 16 engr bn

RESERVES

some 230 local bn and coy

EQUIPMENT

MBT 33 T-54, 74 T-55M, 161 T-72

AIFV 164 BMP-1PS, 110 BMP-2 (incl 'look-a-likes'), some CV9030

APC 112 BTR-60PB, 73 BTR-50PK, 655 XA-180/185/200 *Sisu*, 261 MT-LBV (incl 'look-a-likes')

TOWED ARTY 122mm: 510 H 63 (D-30); **130mm**: 127 K 54, **152mm**: 234 incl: H 55 (D-20), H 88-40, H 88-37 (ML-20), H 88-38, K 89; **155mm**: 136 K 83 (M-74), 28 K 98

SP ARTY 122mm: 72 PsH 74 (2S1); **152mm**: 18 *Telak* 91 (2S5)

MRL 122mm: 24 Rak H 76 (BM-21), 36 Rak H 89 (RM-70)

MOR 81mm: 1,416; **120mm**: 900 (some SP): incl KRH 92

ATGW PST-OHJ82 (AT-5 *Spandrel*), PST-OHJ83M (TOW 2)

RL 112mm: APILAS

RCL 66mm: 66 KES-75, 66 KES-88; **95mm**: 700 SM-58-61

AD GUNS 23mm: 1,100 ITK 61 (ZU-23); **30mm; 35mm**: 16 ITK 88, IT PSV 90 *Marksman* (GDF-005 SP); **57mm**: 47 ITK 60 (S-60), 12 IT PSV (SU-57-2SP)

SAM ITO 86M (SA-18), ITO 86 (SA-16), 21 ITO 90 (*Crotale* NG), 18 ITO 96 (SA-11)

HEL 2 Hughes 500D/E, 7 Mi-8

Navy 4,600

(incl 2,200 conscripts)

COMMANDS 2 **major**: Gulf of Finland, Archipelago Sea; **minor**: Kotka Coastal District

BASES Upinniemi (Helsinki), Turku

PATROL AND COASTAL COMBATANTS 9

MISSILE CRAFT 9

4 *Helsinki* PFM with 4 × 2 MTO-85 (Swe RBS-15SF) SSM

4 *Rauma* PFM with 2 × 2 and 2 × 1 MTO-85 (Swe RBS-15SF) SSM, 1 × 6 *Mistral* SAM

1 *Hamina* PFM with 6 RBS 15 SF SSM, 1 × 6 *Mistal* SAM

MINE WARFARE 19

MINELAYERS 6

2 *Hämeenmaa*, 150–200 mines, plus 1 × 6 Matra *Mistral* SAM

1 *Pohjanmaa*, 100–150 mines plus 2 × 5 ASW RL

3 *Pansio* aux minelayer, 50 mines

MINE COUNTERMEASURES 13

6 *Kuha* MSI<, 7 *Kiiski* MSI<

AMPHIBIOUS craft only

3 *Kampela* LCU tpt, 3 *Kala* LCU

SUPPORT AND MISCELLANEOUS 35

1 *Kustaanmiekka* command ship, 5 *Valas* tpt, 6 *Hauki* tpt, 4 *Hila* tpt, 2 *Lohi* tpt, 1 *Aranda* AGOR (Ministry of Trade control), 9 *Prisma* AGS, 7 icebreakers (Board of Navigation control)

COASTAL DEFENCE

100mm: 61 D-10T (tank turrets); **130mm**: 190 K-54 (static) arty

COASTAL SSM 5 RBS-15

Air Force 2,700

(incl 1,500 conscripts) wartime strength 35,000; 63 cbt ac, no armed hel; 3 Air Comds: Satakunta (West), Karelia (East), Lapland (North). Each Air Comd assigned to one of the 3 AD areas into which SF is divided. 3 ftr wgs, one in each AD area.

Flying hours 120

FGA 3 wg with 56 F/A-18C, 7 F/A-18D

Advanced AD/Attack Trg/Recce
50 *Hawk* 50/51A. One F-27 (ESM/*Elint*)

SURVEY 3 *Learjet* 35A (survey, ECM trg, target-towing)

TPT 1 **ac** sqn with 2 F-27, 3 Learjet-35A

TRG 28 L-70 *Vinka*

LIAISON 14 Piper (8 *Cherokee Arrow*, 6 *Chieftain*), 9 L-90 *Redigo*

UAV 1 Tactical (5 *Ranger* systems to be delivered)

AAM AA-8 *Aphid*, AIM-9 *Sidewinder*, RB-27, RB-28 (*Falcon*), AIM-120 AMRAAM

Forces Abroad

UN AND PEACEKEEPING

AFGHANISTAN (ISAF): ε50 **BOSNIA** (SFOR II): 120; 1 inf coy **CROATIA** (UNMOP): 1 obs **CYPRUS** (UNFICYP): 3 **ETHIOPIA/ERITREA** (UNMEE): 9 incl 7 obs **INDIA/PAKISTAN** (UNMOGIP): 5 obs **IRAQ/KUWAIT** (UNIKOM): 7 obs **MIDDLE EAST** (UNTSO): 4 obs **YUGOSLAVIA** (KFOR): 800

Paramilitary 3,100

FRONTIER GUARD (Ministry of Interior) 3,100

(on mob 22,000); 4 frontier, 3 Coast Guard districts, 1 air patrol sqn; 6 offshore, 2 coastal (plus 60 boats and 7 ACVs); air patrol sqn with **hel** 3 AS-332, 4 AB-206L, 4 AB-412, 1 AB-412EP **ac** 2 Do-228 (Maritime Surv)

Georgia Ga

Total Armed Forces

ACTIVE 17,500

(incl 5,800 centrally controlled staff; 10,400 conscripts; excluding 1,500 civilians)

Terms of service conscription, 18 months

RESERVES up to 250,000

with mil service in last 15 years

Army some 8,620

(incl 1,578 National Guard; 5,572 conscripts)
1 Land Forces HQ
2 MR 'bde', 1 national gd bde plus trg centre • 1 arty regt • 1 recce bn, 2 marine inf bn (1 cadre), 1 peacekeeping bn, 1 SF bn

EQUIPMENT

MBT 90: 59 T-55, 31 T-72

AIFV/APC 185: 68 BMP-1, 13 BMP-2, 11 BRM-1K, 18 BTR-70, 3 BTR-80, 72 MT-LB

TOWED ARTY 85mm: D-44; **100mm**: KS-19 (ground role); **122mm**: 60 D-30; **152mm**: 3 2A36, 10 2A65

SP ARTY 152mm: 1 2S3, 1 2S19; **203mm**: 1 2S7

MRL 122mm: 16 BM-21

MOR 120mm: 17 M-120

ATGW ε10

ATK GUNS ε40

SAM some SA-13

Navy 1,830

(incl 670 conscripts)

BASES Tbilisi (HQ), Poti

PATROL AND COASTAL COMBATANTS 11

PATROL CRAFT 11
1 *Turk* PCC, 1 *Matka* PHM, 1 *Lindau* PCC, 2 *Dilos* PCC, 1 *Stenka* PCC, 1 *Zhuk* PCI<, plus 4 other PCI<

AMPHIBIOUS craft only
2 LCT, 4 LCM

Air Force 1,250

(incl 490 conscripts)
7 cbt ac, 3 armed hel

ATTACK 7 Su-25 (1 -25, 5 - 25K, 1 -25UB), 5 Su-17 (non-operational)

TPT 4 An-2, 1 Yak-18T, 2 Yak-40, 1 Tu-134A (VIP)

HEL 3 Mi-24 (attack), 4 Mi-8/17, 8 UH-1H

TRG ac 4 Yak-52s, 9 L-29 hel 2 Mi-2

AIR DEFENCE

SAM 75 SA-2/-3/-4/-5/-7

Forces Abroad

UN AND PEACEKEEPING

YUGOSLAVIA (KFOR): 34

Opposition

ABKHAZIA ε5,000

50+ T-72, T-55 MBT, 80+ AIFV/APC, 80+ arty

SOUTH OSSETIA ε2,000

5–10 MBT, 30 AIFV/APC, 25 arty incl BM-21

Paramilitary 11,700

MINISTRY OF INTERIOR TROOPS 6,300

BORDER GUARD 5,400

COAST GUARD

2 *Zhuk* PCI

Foreign Forces

RUSSIA 4,000: **Army** 3 mil bases (each = bde+); 65 T-72 MBT, 200 ACV, 139 arty incl **122mm**: D-30, 2S1; **152mm**: 2S3; **122mm**: BM-21 MRL; **120mm**: mor

PEACEKEEPING

Abkhazia 1,600 **South Ossetia** 530

UN (UNOMIG): 108 obs from 23 countries

Ireland Irl

Total Armed Forces

ACTIVE ε10,460

(incl 200 women)

RESERVES 14,800

(obligation to age 60, officers 57–65) **Army** first-line 500, second-line 14,000 **Navy** 300 **Air Corps** 75

Army ε8,500

3 inf bde each 3 inf bn, 1 arty regt, 1 cav recce sqn, 1 engr coy

Army tps: 1 lt tk sqn, 1 AD regt, 1 Ranger coy

Total units: 9 inf bn • 1 UNIFIL bn *ad hoc* with elm from other bn, 1 lt tk sqn, 3 recce sqn, 3 fd arty regt (each of 2 bty) • 1 indep bty, 1 AD regt (1 regular, 3 reserve bty), 4 fd engr coy, 1 Ranger coy

RESERVES

4 Army gp (garrisons), 18 inf bn, 6 fd arty regt, 3 cav sqn, 3 engr sqn, 3 AD bty

EQUIPMENT

LT TK 14 *Scorpion*

RECCE 15 AML-90, 18 AML-20

APC 15 Panhard VTT/M3, 5 *Timoney* Mk 6, 2 A-180 *Sisu*, 17 *Piranha* II

TOWED ARTY 88mm: 42 25-pdr; **105mm**: 24 L-118

MOR 81mm: 400; **120mm**: 71

ATGW 21 *Milan*

RL 84mm: AT-4

RCL 84mm: 444 *Carl Gustav*

AD GUNS 40mm: 24 L/60, 2 L/70

SAM 7 RBS-70

Navy 1,100 (Naval Service)

BASE Cork, Haulbowline

PATROL AND COASTAL COMBATANTS 8

PATROL OFFSHORE 8

1 *Eithne* with 1 *Dauphin* hel PCO, 3 *Emer* PCO, 2 *Orla* (UK *Peacock*) PCO with 1 × 76mm gun, 2 *Roisin* PCO with 1 × 76mm gun

Air Corps 860

2 ops wgs, 2 sup wgs, 1 trg school

No cbt ac, no armd hel

MR 2 CN-235MP

TPT 1 *Super King Air* 200, 1 *Gulfstream* IV

LIAISON 1 sqn with 5 Cessna Reims FR-172H, 1 FR-172K

HEL 7 SA-316B (*Alouette* III), Army spt; 4 SA-365FI (*Dauphin*), Navy spt/SAR

TRG 7 SF-260WE **hel** 2 SA-342L (*Gazelle*)

Forces Abroad

UN AND PEACEKEEPING

BOSNIA (SFOR II): 50 **CROATIA** (UNMOP): 2 obs **CYPRUS** (UNFICYP): 7 **DROC** (MONUC): 2 incl 1 obs **EAST TIMOR** (UNMISET): 42 incl 1 obs **ETIOPIA/ERITREA** (UNMEE): 219 **IRAQ/KUWAIT** (UNIKOM): 6 obs **LEBANON** (UNIFIL): 3 **MIDDLE EAST** (UNTSO): 13 obs **WESTERN SAHARA** (MINURSO): 3 obs **YUGOSLAVIA** (KFOR): 104

Latvia Lat

Total Armed Forces

ACTIVE 5,500

(incl 1,600 conscripts)

Terms of service 12 months

RESERVES 14,050

National Guard

Army 4,300

(incl 1,022 conscripts)

1 mobile rifle bde with 1 inf bn • 1 recce bn • 1 HQ bn • 1 engr bn • 1 arty unit • 1 peacekeeping coy (bn to form) • 1 SF team

RESERVES

National Guard 5 bde, 32 territorial bn

EQUIPMENT

MBT 3 T-55 (trg)

RECCE 2 BRDM-2

APC 13 *Pskbil* m/42

TOWED ARTY 100mm: 26 K-53

MOR 82mm: 5; **120mm**: 32

RL 84mm: 82 AT-4

AD GUNS 14.5mm: 12 ZPU-4; **40mm**: 18 L/70

Navy 930

(incl 250 Coast Guard; 290 conscripts)
Lat, Ea and L have set up a joint Naval unit BALTRON with bases at Liepaja, Riga, Ventspils (Lat), Tallinn (Ea), Klaipeda (L)
BASES Liepaja, Riga (HQ), Ventspils

PATROL AND COASTAL COMBATANTS 4

PATROL COASTAL 4

1 *Osa* PFM (unarmed), 3 *Storm* PCC (unarmed)

MINE WARFARE 3

MINE COUNTERMEASURES 3

2 *Kondor* II MCC, 1 *Namejs* (Ge *Lindau*) MHC

SUPPORT AND MISCELLANEOUS 3

1 *Nyrat* AT, 1 *Goliat* AT, 1 diving vessel

COASTAL GUARD (250, part of Navy)

8 patrol craft: 1 *Ribnadzor* PCC, 5 KBV 236 PCI, 2 PCI<

Air Force 270

AC 13 An-2, 1 L-410, 5 PZL Wilga
HEL 3 Mi-2, 2 Mi-8

Forces Abroad

UN AND PEACEKEEPING

BOSNIA (SFOR II): 97 **YUGOSLAVIA** (KFOR): 15

Paramilitary 3,200

BORDER GUARD (Ministry of Internal Affairs) 3,200

1 bde (7 bn)

Lithuania L

Total Armed Forces

ACTIVE 13,510

(incl 1,800 centrally controlled staff and support units, 1,960 Voluntary National Defence Force; 4,200 conscripts) *Terms of service* 12 months

RESERVES 309,200

25,000 **first line** (ready 72 hrs, incl 11,700 Voluntary National Defence Service), 284,200 **second line** (age up to 59)

Army 8,100

(incl 3,027 conscripts)
2 mil region, 1 motor rifle bde (4 bn), 1 rapid reaction bde (2 mech inf, 1 mot inf, 1 arty bn) • 1 Jaeger bn, 1 trg regt (4 bn), 1 engr, 1 staff bn

EQUIPMENT

RECCE 11 BRDM-2
APC 27 BTR-60, 11 *Pskbil* m/42D, 10 MT-LB, 49 M-113A1
TOWED ARTY 105mm: 62 M-101 (being delivered)
MOR 120mm: 56 M-43
RL 73mm: 400 RPG-7; **82mm**: 210 RPG-2; **84mm**: AT-4
RCL 84mm: 119 *Carl Gustav*; **90mm**: 380 PV-1110

RESERVES

Voluntary National Defence Service: 10 Territorial Defence regt, 36 territorial def bn with 130 territorial def coy, 2 air sqn

Navy 650

(incl 300 conscripts)
Lat, Ea and L have set up a joint Naval unit BALTRON with bases at Liepaja, Riga, Ventspils (Lat), Tallinn (Ea), Klaipeda (L)
BASE Klaipeda

PATROL AND COASTAL COMBATANTS 5

CORVETTES 2

2 FSU *Grisha III* FS, with 4 × 533mm TT, 2 × 12 ASW RL

PATROL COASTAL 3

3 *Storm* PCC

MINE WARFARE 2

MINE COUNTERMEASURES 2

2 *Suduvis* (Ge *Lindau*) MHC

SUPPORT AND MISCELLANEOUS 1

1 *Valerian Uryvayev* AGOR/AG

Air Force 1,000

(no conscripts)
no cbt ac
Air Surveillance and Control Command, 2 air bases
Flying hours 90
TPT 2 L-410, 3 An-26, 22 An-2
TRG 6 L-39
HEL 8 Mi-8 (tpt/SAR), 5 Mi-2
AIRFIELD DEFENCE 1 AD bn with 18 40mm Bofors L/70. 1 reserve AD bn to be formed

Forces Abroad

UN AND PEACEKEEPING

BOSNIA (SFOR II): 95 **YUGOSLAVIA** (KFOR): 29
GEORGIA 1

Paramilitary 13,850

STATE BORDER GUARD SERVICE (Ministry of Internal Affairs) 5,000

COAST GUARD (540)

RIFLEMEN UNION 8,850

Macedonia, Former Yugoslav Republic of FYROM

Total Armed Forces

ACTIVE ε12,300
(incl about 1,000 HQ staff; 8,000 conscripts)
Terms of service 9 months

RESERVES 60,000

Army ε11,300

2 Corps HQ (cadre)
1 Guard, 1 Border bde
7 bde (4 inf, 3 mot inf)
1 mixed arty regt
1 engr regt

RESERVES
9 lt inf bde, 1 arty, 1 ATK, 1 AD regt

EQUIPMENT
MBT 94 T-55A, 31 T-72A
RECCE 10 BRDM-2, 41 HMMWV
AIFV 10 BMP-2
APC 60 BTR-70, 12 BTR-80, 30 M-113A, 10 *Leonidas*, 105 TM-170 (*Hermelin*)
TOWED ARTY 76mm: 55 M-48, 72 M-1942; **105mm**: 18 M-56, 18 M-2A1; **122mm**: 108 M-30
MRL 122mm: 6; **128mm**: 25 M-71 (single barrel), 12 M-77
MOR 450: **60mm**; **82mm**; **120mm**: 145
ATGW AT-3 *Sagger*, 12 *Milan*
RCL 57mm; **82mm**: M60A

MARINE WING (400)
5 river patrol craft

ARMY AIR FORCE (800)
4 cbt ac, 12 armed hel
ATTACK 1 sqn with 4 Su-25 (3 -25K, 1 -25UB)
SURVEILLANCE 1 Cessna 337 (op under contract)
TPT/LIAISON ac 1 Learjet, 1 *Kingair* C-12, 3 An-2
ARMED HEL 1 sqn with 10 Mi-24V, 2 Mi-24K
TPT HEL 1 sqn with 3 Mi-17, 4 Mi-8 MTV, 2 UH-1H
TRG 3 *Zlin*-242
AD GUNS 58: **20mm**; 20: **37mm**; 10: **40mm**
SAM 80 SA-7, some SA-14, 12 SA-16

Paramilitary 7,600

POLICE 7,600 (some 5,000 armed) incl 2 SF units
Equipment incl BTR, M-113A, ε100 TM-170 APC
HEL 1 Bell 412EP, 1 AB-206B, 1 AB-212

Opposition

NATIONAL LIBERATION ARMY (NLA) ε500–1,000

Foreign Forces

UN (KFOR) about 4,000 providing logistic spt for tps deployed in the FRY province of Kosovo
NATO (Op Amber Fox) some 700 tps from Nl, Fr, Ge, It, PL, Gr, Da, UK, US

Malta M

Total Armed Forces

ACTIVE 2,140

Armed Forces of Malta 2,140

Comd HQ, spt tps
No. 1 Regt (inf bn): 3 rifle, 1 spt coy
No. 2 Regt (composite regt)
1 air wg (76) with **ac** 4 0-1 *Bird Dog*, 2 BN-2B *Islander* **hel** 5 SA-316B, 2 NH-369M Hughes, 2 AB-47G2
1 maritime sqn (210) with 3 ex-GDR *Kondor* 1 PCC, 4 PCI, 3 harbour craft, 1 LCVP
1 AD bty; **14.5mm**: 50 ZPU-4; **40mm**: 40 Bofors
No. 3 Regt (Depot Regt): 1 engr sqn, 1 workshop, 1 ordnance, 1 airport coy

Foreign Forces

ITALY 47: **Air Force** 2 AB-212

Moldova Mol

Total Armed Forces

ACTIVE 7,210
(ε5,200 conscripts) incl 250 Central HQ and Command staff *Terms of service* 12 months

RESERVES some 66,000

Army 5,560

(incl ε5,200 conscripts)
3 MR bde • 1 arty bde, 1 indep MR • 1 indep gd, 1 SF,

1 indep engr, 1 indep ATK bn

EQUIPMENT

AIFV 53 BMD-1
APC 11 BTR-80, 11 BTR-D, 1 BTR-60PB, 6 MT-LB, 127 TAB-71, plus 149 'look-a-likes'
TOTAL ARTY 148
TOWED ARTY 122mm: 17 M-30; **152mm**: 31 D-20, 21 2A36
COMBINED GUN/MOR 120mm: 9 2S9
MRL 220mm: 11 9P140 *Uragan*
MOR 82mm: 54; **120mm**: 59 M-120
ATGW 70 AT-4 *Spigot*, 19 AT-5 *Spandral*, 27 AT-6 *Spiral*
RCL 73mm: SPG-9
ATK GUNS 100mm: 36 MT-12
AD GUNS 23mm: 30 ZU-23; **57mm**: 12 S-60
SURV GS-13 (arty), 1 L219/200 PARK-1 (arty), *Long Trough* ((SNAR-1) arty), *Pork Trough* ((SNAR-2/-6) veh, arty), *Small Fred/Small Yawn* (veh, arty), *Big Fred* ((SNAR-10) veh, arty)

Air Force 1,400

(incl Defence Aviation)
TPT/TRG ac 1 An-72, 5 Yak-52 **hel** 2 Mi-2, 8 Mi-8
SAM 1 bde with 25 SA-3/-5

Paramilitary 3,400

INTERNAL TROOPS (Ministry of Interior) 2,500

OPON (Ministry of Interior) 900 (riot police)

Opposition

DNIESTR ε7,500 (plus 15,000 on mob)
incl Republican Guard (Dniestr bn), Delta bn, ε1,000 Cossacks
Eqpt incl 16 tks; 43 APC; 18 122mm arty; 24 BM-21 MRL; 75 82mm and 120mm mor; 29 ac and hel incl Mi-8, Mi-2 hel

Foreign Forces

RUSSIA 1,000: 1 op gp

PEACEKEEPING

Russia 500: 1 MR bn

Romania R

Total Armed Forces

ACTIVE 99,200
(incl 10,000 in centrally controlled units; ε35,000 conscripts)
Terms of service All services 12 months

RESERVES 130,000

Army 66,000

(incl ε21,000 conscripts)
3 Army Corps HQ:
1 Rapid Reaction (forming) with 3 mech, 1 armd, 1 mtn, 1 AB, 1 arty, 1 AD, 1 engr bde
2 Territorial Defence (org varies) with on mob 1 armd, 6 mech, 2 mtn, 2 arty, 2 AD, 1 engr bde

Determining the manning state of units is difficult. The following is based on the latest available information: one-third at 100%, one-third at 50–70%, one-third at 10–20%.

EQUIPMENT

MBT 1,258: 717 T-55, 314 TR-85 M1, 227 TR-580
ASLT GUN 84 SU-100
RECCE 121 BRDM-2
AIFV 177 MLI-84
APC 1,786: 167 TAB-77, 431 TABC-79, 1,030 TAB-71, 88 MLVM, 70 TAB ZIMBRU, plus 1,119 'look-a-likes'
TOTAL ARTY 1,384
TOWED 790: **122mm**: 258 M-1938 (M-30) (A-19); **130mm**: 20 Gun 82; **150mm**: 12 Skoda (Model 1934); **152mm**: 115 Gun-how 85, 331 Model 81, 54 M-1937 (ML-20)
SP 48: **122mm**: 6 2S1, 42 Model 89
MLRS 122mm: 177 APR-40
MOR 120mm: 369 M-1982
SSM launchers: 9 FROG (in store)
ATGM 53 9P122, 120 9P133, 54 9P148
ATK GUNS 100mm: 935 Gun 77, 75 Gun 75
AD GUNS 35mm: 32 *Gepard*, GDF-003; **37mm**: 230; **57mm**: 216; **85mm**: 12; **100mm**: 213
SAM 64 SA-6/-7/-8
SURV GS-13 (arty), 1 L219/200 PARK-1 (arty), *Long Trough* ((SNAR-1) arty), *Pork Trough* ((SNAR-2/-6) veh, arty), *Small Fred/Small Yawn* (veh, arty), *Big Fred* ((SNAR-10) veh, arty)
UAV 6 *Shadow*-600

Navy 6,200

COMMAND Navy HQ with 1 Naval fleet, 1 Danube flotilla
BASES Coastal Mangalia, Constanta **Danube** Braila, Tulcea

PRINCIPAL SURFACE COMBATANTS 7

DESTROYERS 1
DDG 1 *Muntena* with 4 × 2 SS-N-2C *Styx* SSM, SA-N-5 *Grail* SAM, 4 × 76mm guns, 2 × 3 533mm ASTT, 2 IAR 316 *Alouette* III hel

FRIGATES 6
FF 6
4 *Tetal* 1 with 4 × 76mm guns, 4 ASTT, 2 ASW RL

2 *Tetal* II with 1 × 76mm gun, 4 ASTT, 2 ASW RL, 1 IAR 316 *Alouette* III hel

PATROL AND COASTAL COMBATANTS 38

MISSILE CRAFT 6

3 *Zborul* PFM (FSU *Tarantul* I) with 2 × 2 SS-N-2C *Styx* SSM, 1 × 76mm gun

3 FSU *Osa* I PFM with 4 SS-N-2A *Styx* SSM

TORPEDO CRAFT 12

6 *Epitrop* PFT with 4 × 533mm TT

6 PRC *Huchuan* PHT with 2 533mm TT†

PATROL CRAFT 20

RIVERINE 20

5 *Brutar* PCR with 1 × 100mm gun, 1 × 122mm RL, 3 *Kogalniceanu* PCR with 2 × 100mm gun, 12 VB 76 PCR<

MINE WARFARE 18

MINELAYERS 2 *Cosar*, capacity 100 mines

MINE COUNTERMEASURES 16

4 *Musca* MSO, 6 T-301 MSI, 6 VD141 MSI

SUPPORT AND MISCELLANEOUS 13

2 *Constanta* log spt with 1 *Alouette* hel, 1 AK, 3 AOT; 1 trg, 2 AT; 2 AGOR, 2 AG

NAVAL AVIATION

EQUIPMENT

7 armed hel

HELICOPTERS

3 IAR-316 *Alouette*, 4 Mi-14 PL

NAVAL INFANTRY

1 mne bn

EQUIPMENT

APC 4 TABC-79 plus 4 'look-a-likes'

Air Force 17,000

(7,000 conscripts); 202 cbt ac, 21 attack hel

Flying hours 40

Air Force HQ: 2 Air Divs, 5 air bases, 2 trg bases

FGA 5 regt with 177 MiG-21 (110 being upgraded to Lancer standard: 75 Lancer A (air-to-gd), 25 Lancer C (AD), 10 Lancer B (two-seat trainers))

FTR 1 regt with 18 MiG-29

IN STORE 4 MiG-23, 3 Il-28

TPT ac 6 An-24, 11 An-26, 2 Boeing 707, 4 C-130B **hel** 5 IAR-330, 9 Mi-8, 4 SA-365

SURVEY 3 An-30

HELICOPTERS

ATTACK 14 IAR-316A, 7 IAR-330 SOCAT

CBT SPT 61 IAR-330, 53 IAR-316, 7 Mi-8, 2 Mi-17

TRG ac 17 L-29, 20 L-39, 15 IAR-99

AAM AA-2 *Atoll*, AA-3 *Anab*, AA-7 *Apex*, AA-10b *Alamo*, AA-11 *Archer*

ASM AS-7 *Kerry*

UAV Shadow 600

AD 1 bde, 2 regt

20 SAM sites with 120 SA-2, SA-3

Forces Abroad

AFGHANISTAN (OP ENDURING FREEDOM): 475 incl 1 inf bn, 1 NBC coy

UN AND PEACEKEEPING

AFGHANISTAN (ISAF): 48 **BOSNIA** (SFOR II): 122 **DROC** (MONUC): 26 incl 25 obs **ETHIOPIA/ERITREA** (UNMEE): 8 obs **IRAQ/KUWAIT** (UNIKOM): 5 obs **YUGOSLAVIA** (KFOR): 221; 2 inf coy

Paramilitary 79,900

BORDER GUARDS (Ministry of Interior) 22,900

(incl conscripts) 9 regional formations, 3 regional maritime dets

33 TAB-71 APC, 18 SU-100 aslt gun, 12 M-1931/37 (A19) **122mm** how, 18 M-38 **120mm** mor, 7 PRC *Shanghai* II PFI

GENDARMERIE (Ministry of Interior) ε57,000

Slovakia Slvk

Total Armed Forces

ACTIVE 26,200

(incl 3,000 centrally controlled staffs, log and spt tps; 14,900 conscripts, ε1,300 women)

Terms of service 9 months (to be 6 months in 2003)

RESERVES ε20,000 on mob

National Guard Force

Army 13,000

(incl 10,400 conscripts)

1 Corps HQ

1 tri-national bde HQ (forming)

2 mech inf bde (2 mech inf, 1 tk, 1 recce, 1 arty bn)

1 arty bde

1 Rapid Reaction bn

RESERVES

1 Home Gd HQ and 4 mob bases

National Guard Force

EQUIPMENT

MBT 272 T-72M

RECCE 129 BRDM, 90 OT-65, 72 BPVZ

AIFV 321 BMP-1, 93 BMP-2

APC 113 OT-90

TOTAL ARTY 374

TOWED 122mm: 75 D-30

SP 209: **122mm**: 73 2S1; **152mm**: 136 *Dana* (M-77)

MRL 122mm: 90 RM-70

ATGW 476 (incl BMP-1/-2 and BRDM mounted): AT-3 *Sagger*, AT-5 *Spandrel*
AD GUNS 200: **30mm**: M-53/-59; **57mm**: S-60
SAM SA-7, ε48 SA-13
SURV GS-13 (veh), *Long Trough* (SNAR-1), *Pork Trough* ((SNAR-2/-6) arty), *Small Fred/Small Yawn* (veh, arty), *Big Fred* ((SNAR-10) veh, arty)

Air Force 10,200

60 cbt ac, 19 attack hel
Flying hours 45
1 Ftr wg with 24 MiG-29/UB, 16 MiG-21MF/UB
1 FGA/Recce wg 8 Su-22M4/UM3K, 12 Su-25K/UBK
1 Tpt wg 2 An-24, 2 An-26, 6 L410M, 2 Mi-8PS (VIP)
1 Hel wg 19* Mi-24V/D, 17 Mi-17, 6 Mi-2
Trg 20 L-29, 7 L-39
AAM AA-2 *Atoll*, AA-7 *Apex*, AA-8 *Aphid*, AA-10 *Alamo*, AA-11 *Archer*
2 AD bde
AD SA-3, SA-6, SA-7, SA-10B, S-125 *Neva*

Forces Abroad

UN AND PEACEKEEPING

CYPRUS (UNFICYP): 272 **EAST TIMOR** (UNMISET): 34 **ETHIOPIA/ERITREA** (UNMEE): 194 **MIDDLE EAST** (UNTSO): 2 obs **SIERRA LEONE** (UNAMSIL): 2 obs **SYRIA** (UNDOF): 97 **YUGOSLAVIA** (KFOR): 40

Paramilitary 4,700

BORDER POLICE 1,700

GUARD TROOPS 250

CIVIL DEFENCE TROOPS 1,350

RAILWAY DEFENCE TROOPS 1,400

Slovenia Slvn

Total Armed Forces

ACTIVE 9,000
(incl ε4–5,000 conscripts)
Terms of service 7 months (conscription to end in 2004)

RESERVES 20,000
Army (incl 300 maritime)

Army 9,000 (incl 5,000 reserve)

2 Force Comd • 2 mech inf, 1 inf, 1 AD, 1 Air bde, 2 arty bn

RESERVES
2 inf bde, 16 territorial regt (to be 6)

EQUIPMENT
MBT 47 M-84, 30 T-55S1, 26 T-55
RECCE 8 BRDM-2
AIFV 52 M-80
APC 20 *Valuk* (*Pandur*), 14 BOV-1, 5 BTR-50PU
TOWED ARTY 105mm: 18 M-2A1; **155mm**: 18 Model 845
SP 122mm: 8 2S1
MRL 128mm: 48 M-71 (single tube), 4 M-63
MOR 120mm: 8 M-52, 24 M-74, 56 MN-9
ATGW AT-3 *Sagger* (incl 13 BOV-3SP), AT-4 *Spigot* (incl 12 BOV-3SP)

MARITIME ELEMENT (100)
(effectively police)
BASE Koper
1 PCI

AIR ELEMENT (250)
8 armed hel
AC 12 PC-9, 8 *Zlin*-242, 1 LET L-410, 3 UTVA-75, 2 PC-6, 2 Z-143L
HEL 3 B-206, 8* B-412
SAM SA-7, 9 SA-9, 6 *Roland* II, SA-16/18
AD GUNS 20mm: 9 SP; **30mm**: 9 SP; **57mm**: 21 SP

Forces Abroad

UN AND PEACEKEEPING

BOSNIA (SFOR II): 78 **MIDDLE EAST** (UNTSO): 2 obs **YUGOSLAVIA** (KFOR): 6

Paramilitary 4,500

POLICE 4,500
armed (plus 5,000 reserve) **hel** 2 AB-206 *Jet Ranger*, 1 AB-109A, 1 AB-212, 1 AB-412

Sweden Swe

Total Armed Forces

ACTIVE 33,900
(incl 15,000 conscripts and recalled reservists)
Terms of service **Army**, **Navy** 7–15 months **Air Force** 8–12 months

RESERVES 262,000
(obligation to age 47) **Army** (incl Local Defence and Home Guard) 225,000 **Navy** 20,000 **Air Force** 17,000

Army 19,100

(incl 9,000 conscripts and active reservists)
1 Joint Forces Comd
4 Mil Districts (incl Gotland)
No active units (as defined by Vienna Document)
4 armd, 2 inf, 1 arty regt (trg establishments – on mob to form 6 mech bde with 16 mech inf, 6 rifle, 1 AB, 4 arty, 4 AA, 4 engr bn)

EQUIPMENT

MBT 160 Strv-121 (*Leopard* 2), 120 Strv-122 (*Leopard* 2 (S))
AIFV 512 Pbv-302, 327 Strf-9040, 350 Pbv-501 (BMP-1) plus 138 look-a-likes
APC 550 Pbv 401A (MT-LB), 100 XA-203 plus 293 look-a-likes
TOWED ARTY 155mm: 106 FH-77A, 48 FH-77B
SP ARTY 155mm: 26 BK-1C
MOR 81mm: 160; **120mm**: 599
ATGW 57 TOW (Pvrbv 551 SP), RB-55, RB-56 *Bill*
RL 84mm: AT-4
RCL 84mm: *Carl Gustav*; **90mm**: PV-1110
AD GUNS 40mm: 600 (incl 27 Strv 90LV)
SAM RBS-70 (incl 48 Lvrbv SP), RB-77 (I HAWK), RBS-90
SURV *Green Archer* (mor), ARTHUR (arty)
AC 1 C-212
HEL see under Air Force 'Armed Forces Helicopter Wing'
UAV 3 *Sperwer* systems

Navy 7,100

(incl 1,100 Coastal Defence, 320 Naval Avn; 2,300 conscripts)
BASES Muskö, Karlskrona, Härnösand, Göteborg (spt only)

SUBMARINES 7

SSK 7
3 *Gotland* with 4 × 533mm TT, TP-613 HWT and TP-43/45 LWT (AIP powered)
4 *Västergötland* with 6 × 533mm TT, TP-613 HWT and TP-43/45 LWT (2 being fitted with AIP)

PATROL AND COASTAL COMBATANTS 45

MISSILE CRAFT 20 PFM
4 *Göteborg* with 4 × 2 RBS-15 SSM, 4 ASW torp, 4 ASW mor
2 *Stockholm* with 4 × 2 RBS-15 SSM, 2 Type 613 HWT, 4 ASW torp, 4 ASW mor (in refit until 2002)
8 *Kaparen* with 6 RBS-12 *Penguin* SSM, ASW mor
6 *Norrköping* with 4 × 2 RBS-15 SSM, 2–6 Type 613 HWT

PATROL CRAFT 25
About 25 PCI<

MINE WARFARE 22

MINELAYERS 2
1 *Carlskrona* (200 mines) trg, 1 *Visborg* (200 mines)
(Mines can be laid by all SS classes)

MINE COUNTERMEASURES 20
4 *Styrsö* MCMV, 1 *Utö* MCMV spt, 1 *Skredsvic* MCM/diver spt, 7 *Landsort* MHC, 2 *Gassten* MSO, 1 *Vicksten* MSO, 4 *Hisingen* diver spt

AMPHIBIOUS
craft only about 120 LCU

SUPPORT AND MISCELLANEOUS 23
1 AK, 1 AR; 1 AGI, 1 ARS, 2 TRV, 8 AT, 7 icebreakers, 2 sail trg

COASTAL DEFENCE (1,100)

2 amph, 1 arty regt (trg establishments - on mob to form 1 amph bde with 3 amph, 6 coast def bn)

EQUIPMENT

APC 3 *Piranha*
GUNS 40mm, incl L/70 AA; **75mm, 105mm, 120mm** 24 CD-80 *Karin* (mobile); **120mm** *Ersta* (static)
MOR 81mm, 120mm: 70
SSM 90 RBS-17 *Hellfire*, 6 RBS-15KA
SAM RBS-70
MINELAYERS 5 inshore
PATROL CRAFT 12 PCI<
AMPH 16 LCM, 52 LCU, 123 LCA

Air Force 7,700

(incl 1,900 conscripts and 1,800 active reservists); 203 cbt ac, no armed hel
Flying hours 110–140
1 Air Force Comd, 8 air base btn
FGA/RECCE 1 sqn with 18 SAAB AJSH-37/AJSF-37, 1 OCU/EW trg with 12 SAAB SK-37E
MULTI-ROLE (FTR/FGA/RECCE) 5 sqn with 116 SAAB JAS-39 (104 -39A, 12 -39B)
FTR 2 sqn + 2 trg units with 57 SAAB JA-37. (Trg units to disband by 2003)
SIGINT 2 S-102B *Korpen* (*Gulfstream* IV)
AEW 6 S-100B *Argus* (SAAB-340B/*Erieye*)
TPT 6 sqn with 8 Tp-84 (C-130E/H) (7 tpt, 1 tkr), 3 Tp-101 (*King Air* 200), 1 Tp-100A (SAAB 340B) (VIP), 1 Tp-102A (*Gulfstream* IV) (VIP), 1 Tp-103 (Cessna 550)
ASW/MP 1 C-212
TRG 97 Sk-60
AAM RB-71 (*Skyflash*), RB-74 AIM 9L (*Sidewinder*), RB-99, AIM 120 (AMRAAM)
ASM RB-15F, RB-75 (*Maverick*), BK-39
AD 3 fighter control and air surv btn

ARMED FORCES HELICOPTER WING
(1,000 personnel from all three services and 340 conscripts)
HEL 2 btn with 14 Hkp-4 (Vertol 107) ASW/tpt/SAR, 25 Hkp-5b (Hughes 300c) trg, 19 Hkp-6a (Bell-206) utl, 10 Hkp-6b, 20 Hkp-9a (BO-105) AT, 11 Hkp-10 (*Super Puma*) SAR, 5 Hkp-11 (Bell 412) SAR

Forces Abroad

UN AND PEACEKEEPING

AFGHANISTAN (ISAF): ε45 **BOSNIA** (SFOR II): 41 **CROATIA** (UNMOP): 1 obs (SFOR): 1 **DROC** (MONUC): 2 obs **EAST TIMOR** (UNMISET): 2 obs **ETHIOPIA/ERITREA** (UNMEE): 5 obs **GEORGIA** (UNOMIG): 5 obs **INDIA/PAKISTAN** (UNMOGIP): 7 obs **IRAQ/KUWAIT** (UNIKOM): 2 obs **MIDDLE EAST** (UNTSO): 7 obs **SIERRA LEONE** (UNAMSIL): 3 obs **SYRIA** (UNDOF): 1 **YUGOSLAVIA** (KFOR): 751

Paramilitary 600

COAST GUARD 600

1 *Gotland* PCO and 1 KBV-171 PCC (fishery protection), some 65 PCI

AIR ARM 2 C-212 MR

CIVIL DEFENCE shelters for 6,300,000

All between ages 16–25 liable for civil defence duty

VOLUNTARY AUXILIARY ORGANISATIONS some 35,000

Switzerland CH

Total Armed Forces

ACTIVE about 3,500 (career officers and NCOs)

plus recruits (2 intakes in 2001 (total 24,110) each for 15 weeks only)

Terms of service 15 weeks compulsory recruit trg at age 19–20, followed by 10 refresher trg courses of 3 weeks over a 22-year period between ages 20–42. Some 186,300 attended trg in 2001

RESERVES 351,000

Army 320,400 (to be mobilised)

Armed Forces Comd (All units non-active/Reserve status)

Comd tps: 2 armd bde, 2 inf, 1 arty, 1 airport, 2 engr regt

3 fd Army Corps, each 2 fd div (3 inf, 1 arty regt), 1 armd bde, 1 engr, 1 cyclist, 1 fortress regt, 1 territorial div (5/6 regt)

1 mtn Army Corps with 3 mtn div (2 mtn inf, 1 arty regt), 3 fortress bde (each 1 mtn inf regt), 2 mtn inf, 2 fortress, 1 engr regt, 1 territorial div (6 regt), 2 territorial bde (1 regt)

EQUIPMENT

MBT 556: 186 Pz-68/88, 370 Pz-87 (*Leopard* 2)

RECCE 319 *Eagle* I/II

AIFV 435 (incl 6 in store): 120 M-63/73, 315 M-63/89 (all M-113 with **20mm**)

APC 842 M-63/73 (M-113) incl variants, 415 *Piranha*

SP ARTY 155mm: 558 PzHb 66/74/-74/-79/-88 (M-109U)

MOR 81mm: 1,224 M-33, M-72; **120mm**: 534: 402 M-87, 132 M-64 (M-113)

ATGW 2,760 *Dragon*, 303 TOW-2 SP (MOWAG *Piranha*)

RL 12,512 incl: **60mm**: *Panzerfaust*; **83mm**: M-80

SAM *Stinger*

MARINE

10 *Aquarius* patrol boats

Air Force 30,600 (to be mobilised)

(incl AD units, mil airfield guard units); 138 cbt ac, no armed hel

1 Air Force bde, 1 AD bde, 1 Air-Base bde, 1 C³I bde, AF Maintenance Service

Flying hours: 150–200; reserves approx 50

FTR 8 sqn

5 with 70 *Tiger* II/F-5E

3 with 26 F/A-18 C and 7 F/A-18D

RECCE 1 sqn with 16* *Mirage* IIIRS 2, 4* *Mirage* IIIDS (pilot trg only)

TPT 1 sqn with 16 PC-6, 1 *Learjet* 35A, 2 Do-27, 1 *Falcon*-50

HEL 6 sqn with 15 AS-332 M-1 *Super Puma*, 58 SA-316 *Alouette* III, 7 AS-532 *Cougar*

TRG 3 *Tiger* II/F-5E and 12 *Tiger* II/F-5F, 19 *Hawk* Mk 66, 38 PC-7, 11 PC-9 (tgt towing)

UAV 4 systems ADS 95 *Ranger* operational 2003. 1 UAV bn in basic trg

AAM AIM-9 *Sidewinder*, AIM-120 AMRAAM

AIR DEFENCE

1 AD bde with

1 SAM regt (3 bn, each with 2 or 3 bty; B/L-84 *Rapier*)

5 AD Regt (each with 2 bn; each bn of 3 bty; 35mm guns, Skyguard fire control radar)

Forces Abroad

UN AND PEACEKEEPING

CROATIA (UNMOP): 1 obs **DROC** (MONUC): 1 obs **ETHIOPIA/ERITREA** (UNMEE): 4 obs **GEORGIA** (UNOMIG): 4 obs **KOREA** (NNSC): 5 Staff **MIDDLE EAST** (UNTSO): 10 obs **YUGOSLAVIA** (KFOR): some 160; 1 coy

Paramilitary

CIVIL DEFENCE 280,000 (not part of Armed Forces)

Ukraine Ukr

Total Armed Forces

ACTIVE 302,300
(incl MVS and Border Guard tps – see Paramilitary; excl Black Sea Fleet and 95,000 civilian personnel)
Terms of service **Army, Air Force** 18 months **Navy** 2 years

RESERVES some 1,000,000
mil service within 5 years

Ground Forces 150,700

3 Op Comd (North, South, West), one to disband
MoD tps: 1 air mobile bde, 1 SSM bde (SS-21), 1 arty (trg), 1 engr bde

WESTERN OP COMD

Comd tps 1 arty div (1 arty, 1 MRL, 1 ATK bde), 3 SSM (SS-21) bde, 1 air mobile regt, 1 engr bde, 1 army avn regt

2 Army Corps (one to disband)
- 1 with 2 mech div (each 3 mech, 1 tk, 1 SP arty regt), 2 mech bde, 1 arty bde, 1 MRL regt
- 1 with 1 mech div (with 2 mech, 1 tk, 1 SP arty regt), 1 mech bde, 1 arty regt, 1 MRL regt

SOUTHERN OP COMD

Comd tps 1 air mobile div (1 air aslt, 1 airmobile bde, 1 arty regt), 1 arty div (1 arty, 1 MRL, 1 ATK bde), 1 air mobile, 1 SSM (*Scud*), 1 avn bde

2 Army Corps (one to form Coastguard HQ)
- 1 with 1 tank div (3 tk, 1 SP arty regt), 1 mech div (with 2 mech, 1 tk, 1 SP arty regt), 1 mech, 1 arty bde, 1 MRL, 1 engr regt
- 1 with 2 mech, 1 arty, 1 MRL, 1 engr regt

NORTHERN OP COMD

Comd tps 2 mech div (3 mech, 1 SP arty regt), 1 tk trg centre, 1 tank, 2 SSM bde (1 *Scud*, 1 SS-21), 1 army avn bde, 1 engr regt

1 Army Corps with 1 tank div (3 tk, 1 SP arty regt), 1 mech div (2 mech, 1 SP arty regt), 1 mech, 1 airmobile, 1 arty bde, 1 MRL, 1 engr regt

EQUIPMENT

MBT 3,905: 149 T-55, 2,279 T-64, 1,196 T-72, 271 T-80, 10 T-84
RECCE some 600 BRDM-2
AIFV 3,043: 1,008 BMP-1, 458 BRM-1K, 1,434 BMP-2, 4 BMP-3, 61 BMD-1, 78 BMD-2
APC 1,682: 176 BTR-60, 1,026 BTR-70, 436 BTR-80, 44 BTR-D; plus 2,090 MT-LB, 4,700 'look-a-likes'
TOTAL ARTY 3,705
TOWED 1,143: **122mm**: 443 D-30, 3 M-30; **152mm**: 216 D-20, 185 2A65, 289 2A36, 7 M-1937 (ML-20)
SP 1,298: **122mm**: 638 2S1; **152mm**: 496 2S3, 24 2S5, 40 2S19, **203mm**: 100 2S7
COMBINED GUN/MOR 120mm: 74 2S9, 2 2B16
MRL 588: **122mm**: 332 BM-21, 20 9P138; **132mm**: 3 BM-13; **220mm**: 139 9P140; **300mm**: 94 9A52
MOR 600: **120mm**: 342 2S12, 257 PM-38; **160mm**: 1 M-160
SSM 72 *Scud* B, 50 FROG, 90 SS-21
ATGW AT-4 *Spigot*, AT-5 *Spandrel*, AT-6 *Spiral*
ATK GUNS 100mm: ε500 T-12/MT-12
AD GUNS 30mm: 70 2S6 SP; **57mm**: ε400 S-60
SAM 100 SA-4, 125 SA-8, 60 SA-11, ε150 SA-13
ATTACK HEL 205 Mi-24
SPT HEL 42 Mi-6, 315 Mi-8
SURV SNAR-10 (*Big Fred*), *Small Fred* (arty)

Navy† ε13,500

(incl nearly 2,500 Naval Avn, 3,000 Naval Infantry; 2,000 conscripts)
On 31 May 1997, RF President Boris Yeltsin and Ukr President Leonid Kuchma signed an inter-governmental agreement on the status and terms of the Black Sea Fleet's deployment on the territory of Ukr and parameters for the fleet's division. The RF Fleet will lease bases in Sevastopol for the next 20 years. It is based at Sevastopol and Karantinnaya Bays and jointly with Ukr warships at Streletskaya Bay. The overall serviceability of the fleet is very low

BASES Sevastopol, Donuzlav, Odessa, Kerch, Ochakov, Chernomorskoye (Balaklava, Nikolaev construction and repair yards)

SUBMARINES 1†
SSK 1 *Foxtrot* (Type 641) (non-op)

PRINCIPAL SURFACE COMBATANTS 3
CRUISERS 1†
CG 1 *Ukraina* (RF *Slava*) (in refit)
FRIGATES 2
FFG 1
- 1 *Mikolair* (RF *Krivak* I) with 4 SS-N-14 *Silex* SSM/ASW, 2 SA-N-4 *Gecko* SAM, 4 × 76mm gun, 8 × 533mm TT†

FF 1
- 1 *Sagaidachny* (RF *Krivak* III) 3 with 2 SA-N-4 *Gecko* SAM, 1 × 100mm gun, 8 × 533mm TT, 1 KA-27 hel

PATROL AND COASTAL COMBATANTS 9
CORVETTES 3
- 3 *Grisha* II/V FS with 2 SA-N-4 *Gecko* SAM, 1 × 76mm gun, 4 × 533mm TT

TORPEDO CRAFT 2
- 2 *Pauk* 1 PFT with 4 SA-N-5 *Grail* SAM, 1 × 76mm gun, 4 × 406mm TT

MISSILE CRAFT 3
- 3 *Matka* PHM with 2 SS-N-2C *Styx* SSM, 1 × 76mm gun

PATROL CRAFT 1
- 1 *Zhuk* PCI†

MINE WARFARE 5

MINE COUNTERMEASURES 5

1 *Yevgenya* MHC, 2 *Sonya* MSC, 2 *Natya* MSC

AMPHIBIOUS 7

4 *Pomornik* ACV with 2 SA-N-5 capacity 30 tps and crew

1 *Ropucha* LST with 4 SA-N-5 SAM, 2 × 2 57mm gun, 92 mines; capacity 190 tps or 24 veh

1 *Alligator* LST with 2/3 SA-N-5 SAM capacity 300 tps and 20 tk

1 *Polnocny* LSM capacity 180 tps and 6 tk

SUPPORT AND MISCELLANEOUS 9

1 AO, 2 *Vytegrales* AK, 1 *Lama* msl spt, 1 Mod *Moma* AGI, 1 *Primore* AGI, 1 *Kashtan* buoytender, 1 *Elbrus* ASR; 1 AGOS

NAVAL AVIATION (2,500)

EQUIPMENT

13 armed hel

AIRCRAFT

TPT 8 An-26, 1 An-24, 5 An-12, 1 Il-18, 1 Tu-134

HELICOPTERS

ASW 11 Be-12, 2 Ka-27E

TPT 5 Mi-6

UTL 28 Ka-25, 42 Mi-14

NAVAL INFANTRY (3,000)

1 naval inf bde

Air Forces and Air Defence Forces 49,100

Air Forces and Air Defence Forces will merge when funds allow

499 cbt ac, no attack hel

2 air corps (5th and 14th AVK), 1 multi-role rapid reaction air gp (35th AVG), 1 trg aviation cmd

BBR 1 regt with 32 Tu-22M

FGA/BBR 3 regt with 71 Su-24

FGA 2 regt with 63 Su-25

FTR 7 regt with 217 MiG-29 (199 operational, 2 trg, 16 in store), 60 Su-27

RECCE 2 regt with 29* Su-24, 20* Su-17

CBT TRG 4* Su-24, 1* MiG-23, 2* MiG-29

TPT 3 regt with 60 Il-76, 45 An-12/An-24/An-26/Tu-134, Il-78 (tkr/tpt)

TRG 5 regt with 345 L-39, 1 regt with 16 Mi-8

SPT HEL 111 Mi-2, 23 Mi-6, 170 Mi-8

AAM AA-7, AA-8., AA-9, AA-10, AA-11

ASM AS-7, AS-9, AS-10, AS-11, AS-12, AS-13, AS-14, AS-15

SAM 825: SA-2/-3/-5/-10/-12A

Forces Abroad

UN AND PEACEKEEPING

CROATIA (UNMOP): 2 obs **DROC** (MONUC): 11 incl 10 obs **ETHIOPIA/ERITREA** (UNMEE): 6 obs **GEORGIA** (UNOMIG): 3 obs **LEBANON** (UNIFIL): 652 **SIERRA LEONE** (UNAMSIL): 630 incl 5 obs **YUGOSLAVIA** (KFOR): 325

Paramilitary

MVS (Ministry of Internal Affairs) 44,000, 4 regions, internal security tps, 85 ACV, 6 ac, 8 hel

BORDER GUARD 45,000

HQ and 3 regions, 200 ACV

MARITIME BORDER GUARD

The Maritime Border Guard is an independent subdivision of the State Commission for Border Guards, is not part of the Navy and is org with:

4 cutter, 2 river bde • 1 gunship, 1 MCM sqn • 1 aux ship gp • 1 trg div • 3 air sqn

PATROL AND COASTAL COMBATANTS 36

3 *Pauk* 1 with 4 SA-N-5 SAM, 1 76mm gun, 4 406mm TT

3 *Muravey* PHT with 1 76mm gun, 2 406mm TT

10 *Stenka* PFC with 4 30mm gun, 4 406mm TT

20 *Zhuk* PCI

AIRCRAFT

An-24, An-26, An-72, An-8, Ka-27

COAST GUARD 14,000

3 patrol boats, 1 water jet boat, 1 ACV, 1 landing ship, 1 OPV, 1 craft

CIVIL DEFENCE TROOPS (Ministry of Emergency Situations): some 9,500; 4 indep bde, 4 indep regt

Foreign Forces

Russia ε1,100 naval inf

Yugoslavia, Federal Republic of (Serbia–Montenegro) FRY

Total Armed Forces

The armed forces of FRY are subject to an arms limitation regime established under the Dayton Peace Accords. An agreement signed by BiH, its two entities, Cr and FRY on 14 June 1996, established ceilings for the holdings of the armed forces of the parties.

ACTIVE ε74,500

(ε60,000 conscripts) *Terms of service* 9 months

RESERVES some 400,000

Army (JA) ε60,000

(incl 37,000 conscripts)
6 Corps HQ • 6 armd bde • 1 gd bde (-) • 1 mech bde • 9 mot inf bde • 1 AB bde, 1 SF bde • 5 mixed arty bde

RESERVES

1 mech, 5 mot inf, 16 inf, 4 arty, 1 SAM bde

EQUIPMENT

MBT 721 T-55, 230 M-84 (T-74; mod T-72), 65 T-72
AIFV 557 M-80
APC 147 M-60P, 57 BOV VP M-86
(Total MBT, AIFV and APC reducing to 850 by end 2002)
TOWED 105mm: 243 M-56; **122mm**: 54 M-38, 304 D-30; **130mm**: 238 M-46; **152mm**: 25 D-20, 52 M-84; **155mm**: 112 M-1, 6 M-65
SP 122mm: 82 2S1
MRL 128mm: 36 M-63, 51 M-77
MOR 82mm: 1,100; **120mm**: 283 M-74, 802 M-75
(Total arty pieces reducing to 3,750 by end 2002)
SSM 4 FROG
ATGW 142 AT-3 *Sagger* incl SP (BOV-1, BRDM-1/2), AT-4 *Fagot*
RCL 57mm: 1,550; **82mm**: 1,500 M-60PB SP; **105mm**: 650 M-65
ATK GUNS 725 incl: **90mm**: M-36B2 (incl SP), M-3; **100mm**: 138 T-12, MT-12
AD GUNS 2,000: **20mm**: M-55/-75, BOV-3 SP triple; **30mm**: M-53, M-53/-59, BOV-30 SP; **57mm**: ZSU-57-2 SP
SAM 60 SA-6/-9/-13, 900 SA-7/-14/-16/-18

Navy 3,500

(incl 900 marines)
BASES Kumbor, Tivat, Bar, Novi Sad (River Comd)
(Most former Yugoslav bases are now in Cr hands)

SUBMARINES 4

SSK 1
1 *Sava* with 533mm TT
plus 3 *Una* SSI for SF ops (all non-op)

PRINCIPAL SURFACE COMBATANTS 3

FRIGATES 3

FFG 3
2 *Kotor* with 4 SS-N-2C *Styx* SSM, 1 × 2 SA-N-4 *Gecko* SAM, 2 × 3 ASTT, 2 × 12 ASW RL
1 *Split* (FSU *Koni*) with 4 SS-N-2C *Styx* SSM, 1 × 2 SA-N-4 *Gecko* SAM, 2 × 12 ASW RL

PATROL AND COASTAL COMBATANTS 31

MISSILE CRAFT 9
5 *Rade Koncar* PFM with 2 SS-N-2B *Styx* SSM (some †)
4 *Mitar Acev* (FSU *Osa* I) PFM with 4 SS-N-2A *Styx* SSM

PATROL CRAFT 22†
PATROL, INSHORE 4 *Mirna* PCI<
PATROL, RIVERINE about 18 < (some in reserve)

MINE WARFARE 10

MINE COUNTERMEASURES 10
2 *Vukov Klanac* MHC, 1 UK *Ham* MSI, 7 *Nestin* MSI

AMPHIBIOUS 1
1 *Silba* LCT/ML: capacity 6 tk or 300 tps, 1 × 4 SA-N-5 SAM, can lay 94 mines
plus craft:
8 Type 22 LCU, 6 Type 21 LCU, 4 Type 11 LCVP

SUPPORT AND MISCELLANEOUS 9
1 PO-91 *Lubin* tpt, 1 water carrier, 4 AT, 2 AK, 1 degaussing

MARINES (900)

2 mot inf 'bde' (2 regt each of 2 bn) • 1 lt inf bde (reserve) • 1 coast arty bde • 1 MP bn

Air Force 11,000

(incl 3,000 conscripts); 103 cbt ac, 44 armed hel
1 Air and 1 AD Corps
FGA 4 sqn with 21 *Orao* 2, 30 *Super Galeb* G-4
FTR 2 sqn with 28 MiG-21bis, 6 MiG-21UM, 4 MiG-29A, 1 MiG-29U
RECCE 1 sqn with 10* *Orao* 1, 3* MiG-21R
TPT 11 An-26, 2 *Falcon* 50 (VIP), 2 Yak-40, 2 Do-28D *Skyservant*
ARMED HEL 17 H-45M (SA-342) *Partizan* (*Gazelle*), 27 H-42M (SA-341) (anti-tank)
HEL 33 Mi-8, some H-42/-45 (utility), 3 HI-42 (recce/trg)
TRG ac 9 UTVA-75
AAM AA-2 *Atoll*, AA-8 *Aphid*, AA-10 *Alamo*, AA-11 *Archer*
ASM AGM-65 *Maverick*, AS-7 *Kerry*
AD 6 SAM bn (2 SA-3, 4 SA-6)
15 regt AD arty

Paramilitary

MINISTRY OF INTERIOR PERSONNEL ε40,000
internal security; eqpt incl 150 AFV, 170 mor, 16 hel (incl 3 Mi-24 *Hind*)
SPECIAL POLICE UNITS ε4,100
MONTENEGRIN MINISTRY OF INTERIOR PERSONNEL ε6,000

UN and Peacekeeping

KFOR (Kosovo Peace Implementation Force): some 34,500 (to be 32,000 by end 2002) tps from 30 countries are deployed in Kosovo, a further 6,000 provide rear area spt in Alb, FYROM and Gr

Russia

TRENDS

Russia has continued to grapple with the immense problem of military reform. There has been some criticism of the rate of progress, and the fact that Sergei Ivanov, the Minister of Defence, is seen as too disposed towards the military viewpoint in his ministry and occasionally out of step with the broader vision of President Vladimir Putin. In the immediate aftermath of 11 September, Putin and Ivanov were clearly not speaking with one voice, particularly on the issue of US bases in Central Asia. The Russian Ministry of Defence remains dominated by a largely military staff, many of whom persist in old Cold War practices and ways of thinking, and genuine civilian control of the military is some way off.

Nevertheless, there have been some changes. Increased pressure from President Putin, who is paying close attention to the military reform agenda, and from the public, has prompted the experimental professionalisation of an airborne division. The aim of this experiment is to gain a clearer idea of the costs of professionalisation and to evaluate all aspects of the creation of a fully professional armed force. Also, with the adoption of a new law by the Duma, there is progress towards 'alternative service' as an option to conscription.

The creation of the NATO–Russia Council (NRC) has brought Russia closer to cooperation with the military structures of NATO. Within the Commonwealth of Independent States (CIS) there has been progress in enhancing collective security, both in Central Asia and in the Caspian regions. Further afield, the handover of the last overseas Russian naval base has now been completed, with the return of the Cam Ranh Bay base to the Vietnamese government in July 2002.

The Caucasus remains a running sore for the Kremlin and the Ministry of Defence. Military operations continue in Chechnya. Rebel forces, despite losses among their leadership, still have significant freedom of movement. To the south, Russian–Georgian relations continue to be problematic. Tension over the issue of the Pankisi Gorge where some Chechen guerrillas are based, remains unresolved, as does disagreement over the decade-old conflict in Abkhazia. Georgia is critical of Russian peacekeeping efforts in Abkhazia.

MILITARY REFORM ISSUES

Progress in the reform of the Russian armed forces this year came mainly in the form of a plan for a fully professional force by 2012. The debate surrounding this issue centres on Russia's dilemma in not being able to support either a conscript force for demographic and social reasons, nor an expensive professional force of a sufficient size to meet perceived future requirements. The most likely outcome will be a professional force, but one which is very much smaller than some in the Ministry of Defence would want. Estimates vary as to an affordable size of force, with one estimate being 400,000. There is also the theoretical option of having a mixed conscript and professional force, but this is unlikely with all the managerial problems that it poses. A third option is to create a part-time reserve force to fill gaps in the regular force as required. In the meantime, the fact that the process has started tends to indicate that whatever the future size of the Russian armed forces, they are moving towards some kind of professional foundation.

An experiment in full professionalisation is due to start on 1 September 2002. Approximately R2.6bn has been allocated outside the annual defence budget to professionalise the 76th Airborne Division. A new garrison is to be constructed in Pskov, which will include a training centre, cultural and recreational facilities and, perhaps of most significance, new housing for servicemen and their families.

In the immediate future, two areas of particular concern are being addressed: the deficit of officers and the future readiness of the Ground Forces. The shortfall in officers is believed to be about 48,000. In an effort to correct this, pay scales are being reformed, so that from July 2002 a junior officer should receive up to twice his previous salary, with another rise of approximately 10% in January 2003. Also, the training period for officers at higher education academies is being reduced from five to four years, resulting in a greater throughput. The Deputy Minister of Defence and Commander of the Ground Forces, Colonel General Kormiltsev, announced on 2 July 2002 that the personnel in permanent readiness units will be increased significantly by 2010, mainly by making corresponding reductions in other arms and services. He also spoke about the future shape of the Ground Forces, which are to be reorganised into high-readiness units, units of reduced readiness and units that will be brought up to strength by reservists.

With conscription becoming increasingly unpopular, and the numbers meeting their draft obligations in decline, the other key question has been that of 'alternative service'. The Duma took a firm line in June and decided that those who want to opt out of military service should engage in alternative public service for a longer period than military conscripts.The alternative to the military draft is now three-and-a-half years working for social services and other organisations. Parliamentarians rejected more hard-line proposals from the Ministry of Defence that those who choose alternative service would have to provide social services at military facilities, would not be allowed to enrol in part-time higher education programmes and would have to serve away from their native towns. The subsequent compromise version of the law is regarded as unsatisfactory by both Russian human-rights groups and old-style change-averse military chiefs.

The Caucasus (see also Europe, page 31)

Chechnya remains a running sore for the Kremlin and Ministry of Defence. The lack of an effective civilian authority in the region means that the military remains the principle decision-maker. All political initiatives to start negotiations have failed, and rebel activity continues, albeit at a lower tempo than last year. Casualties among federal forces continue and retaliatory actions by both Ministry of Defence and Ministry of Interior troops are often excessive and lead to accusations of human-rights abuses. Nevertheless, there have been some notable successes for special forces, in particular, the assassination of key rebel leader Khattab in March 2002, which gave grounds for optimism that some rebel and mercenary followers would give up the struggle. However, the continuation of Russian fixed-wing and attack helicopter strikes against rebel positions indicate that the rebels are still able to move and regroup freely, and that the federal forces have little effective control over large parts of the Chechen Republic. Low intensity attacks on Russian forces, checkpoints and police positions continue. On 1 January 2002, militants attacked the Federal Security Service (FSB)'s headquarters in Grozny with grenades and automatic weapons. Rebel attacks typically involve small arms, grenades, IEDs (improvised explosive devices) and anti-tank weapons. There have also been a number of surface-to-air missile (SAM) attacks on transport helicopters and low-flying aircraft.

President Putin has stated on a number of occasions that he wants to see more authority transferred to indigenous Chechen authorities. Under current plans, local interior ministry (MVD) departments should assume limited control of their areas by October 2002, taking over from federal MVD units. More authority is likely to be transferred after the Chechen general election, to be held in winter 2002–03. Russian Ministry of Defence and Interior forces are strongly opposed to these initiatives, claiming that many Chechen police officers are former rebel fighters. The compromise agreement is that 30% of Chechen-controlled interior forces will comprise contract troops from outside the Chechen Republic. These will be on one-to-three year contracts.

One by-product of the military campaign in Chechnya has been the opportunity to test new equipment. A notable success has been the improvement to the all-weather day and night capability of attack helicopters. The commander of Russian Army Aviation, Colonel General Pavlov, said that out of some 2,000 targets identified at night during military operations in the last two years, some 1,200 had been destroyed by artillery directed by Mi-8 *Hip* MTKO helicopters carrying the GOES-321 electro-optical system along with a laser range-finder, night-vision goggles and a satellite navigation suite.

In **Georgia** the disagreement has intensified between Moscow and Tbilisi over how to deal with Chechen rebels, now acknowledged by both sides to be based in the Pankisi Gorge. Georgia is unwilling, and due to its poor military capability and lack of training, unable to enforce its authority in the area – given the risk and potential drain on its resources. At the same time, it is refusing Russia's offer of assistance in carrying out a joint military operation in the gorge and has accused Russia of a bombing attack on the border, on 2 August 2002. The OSCE observer mission, monitoring the area, confirmed the attack. Meanwhile, further demonstrating the state of relations between the two countries, Georgia placed a temporary ban on Russian daytime overflights of its territory and refused to hand over 13 named Chechen rebel suspects to the Russian authorities. The 13 had reportedly taken part in an attack on Russian border troops at Hum Kale in the Chechen Republic and were arrested by Georgian border troops when crossing the border into Georgia's Pankisi Gorge.

Another dispute between Russia and Georgia concerns the separatist region of **Abkhazia**. In April 2002, Russian peacekeepers (operating under a CIS mandate with the authority of the quadripartite Moscow Agreement of 1994) claimed to have found Georgian forces in the upper Kodori Valley. This is an area prohibited to both parties under the agreement. Russia wants a military presence in the upper valley to prevent incursions of the sort undertaken by Chechen rebel leader Ruslan Gelayev, when he entered the area with an armed force in October 2001. Subsequent to this, a UN helicopter belonging to UNOMIG was shot down.

DEFENCE COOPERATION

In **Central Asia** the Russian-led CIS Collective Rapid Reaction Force (CRDF), formed on 25 May 2001 under the CIS Collective Security Treaty Organisation, carried out its first formation-level exercise in June 2002 with battalions from Kazakhstan, Kyrgyzstan, Tajikistan and Russia. The exercise was controlled by the commander of the Volga-Ural Military District, Colonel General Baranov. The CRDF, numbering some 13,000 troops in total, has its headquarters in Bishkek, the Kyrgyz capital, and is to be given an air-mounting base at Kant, outside Bishkek.

In the **Caspian Sea** area, 60 ships, 30 aircraft – including some from the Black Sea Fleet – and some 10,000 troops from the Caspian Flotilla carried out a joint exercise with troops from Kazakhstan and Azerbaijan. This was the largest exercise ever undertaken by the Caspian Flotilla. The aim of the exercise, which started on 1 August 2002, was to practise counter-terrorist operations and anti-drug smuggling procedures. The participating countries are those which have reached agreement between themselves on the legal status of the Caspian, an issue which President Putin hoped would be resolved in 2002. However, Turkmenistan and Iran, who disagree with Russia, Kazakhstan and Azerbaijan on aspects of the Caspian's status, sent observers to the exercise. Turkmenistan and Azerbaijan continue to disagree over the 'ownership' of the Araz-Aloz–Sarq oil field block. Meanwhile Iran disagrees over its share of the seabed. According to Tehran, 20% of the Caspian seabed should be under its control, as opposed to the Russian proposition that Iran's rightful proportion is only 14%.

On 25 January 2002, Russia and **Azerbaijan** finally concluded an agreement on the status of the Gabala radar station in north Azerbaijan. The agreement allows Russia to maintain the integrity of its missile-warning system and the integrity of the CIS collective air defence system. Furthermore, showing the priority now being given to this topic in general, the Commander-in-Chief of the Russian Air Force, General Mikhailov said in August 2002 that a national aerospace defence system should be developed comprising the air defence assets of all services.

Russia is reducing its peacekeeping forces in the **Balkans**, which are attached to KFOR and SFOR. The reduction from a total of 4,200 to 360 troops is driven by practical rather than political considerations

RUSSIA–NATO (see Europe, page 28)

At the NATO Permanent Joint Council (PJC) meeting in Reykyavik on 14 May 2002, the decision was taken to create a NATO–Russia Council (NRC) in its place to reflect changes in the NATO–Russian relationship following 11 September. This decision was finalised at the **NATO** Rome Summit on 24 May 2002. The NRC allows Russia full decision-making power, although decisions are to be taken by consensus, thus preserving NATO's prerogative to act independently. Reflecting the post-11 September mood, the NRC is focusing on a number of key issues:

- counter-terrorism and threat assessments;
- crisis management;
- non-proliferation;
- arms control and confidence building;
- theatre missile defence;
- search and rescue; and
- civil emergencies.

The NRC is widely seen as a 'reward' for President Putin's practical support for the US-led war against terrorism. Moreover, the creation of the NRC has helped to soften Russia's resistance to the next wave of NATO enlargement, which is likely to include all three Baltic states. Nevertheless, there are those in the Russian administration, the Ministry of Defence and the Duma who remain opposed to NATO enlargement, particularly membership for the Baltic states (previously discussed in *The Military Balance 2001–2002*). President Putin continues to state that Russia does not believe that NATO enlargement helps to strengthen European security. Given these attitudes, and the lack of experts whom Russia could assign to work full-time within NATO, doubts remain as to the ability of NATO and Russia to forge a meaningful partnership.

Russia RF

Total Armed Forces

ACTIVE 988,100

(incl about 200,000 MoD staff, centrally controlled units for EW, trg, rear services, not incl elsewhere; perhaps 330,000 conscripts, 100,000 women)

Terms of service 18–24 months. Women with medical and other special skills may volunteer

RESERVES some 20,000,000

some 2,400,000 with service within last 5 years; Reserve obligation to age 50

Strategic Deterrent Forces ε149,000

(incl 38,000 assigned from Air Force)

NAVY (ε11,000)

216 msl in 13 operational SSBN†

SSBN 13 declared operational (all based in RF ports)

6 *Delta* IV with 16 SS-N-23 *Skiff* (96 msl)
2 *Typhoon* with 20 SS-N-20 *Sturgeon* (40 msl)
5 *Delta* III with 16 SS-N-18 *Stingray* (80 msl)

(The following non-op SSBNs remain START-accountable, with a total of 116 msl:
3 *Typhoon* with 20 SS-N-20 *Sturgeon* (60 msl)
2 *Delta* III with 16 SS-N-18 *Stingray* (32 msl)
2 *Delta* I with 12 SS-N-8 *Sawfly* (24 msl)
In the 31 Jan 2002 START I declaration, RF declared a total of 332 'deployed' SLBMs. The above figures represent holdings as of that date)

STRATEGIC MISSILE FORCE TROOPS (ε100,000 incl 50,000 conscripts)

4 rocket armies equipped with silo and mobile msl launchers. 735 launchers with 3,159 nuclear warheads org in 18 div: launcher gp normally with 10 silos (6 for SS-18) and one control centre; 12 SS-24 rail, each with 3 launchers

ICBM 735

150 SS-18 *Satan* (RS-20) at 4 fields; mostly mod 4/5, 10 MIRV per msl
150 SS-19 *Stiletto* (RS-18) at 4 fields; mostly mod 3, 6 MIRV per msl
36 SS-24 *Scalpel* (RS-22) 10 MIRV; 36 rail
360 SS-25 *Sickle* (RS-12M); mobile, single-warhead
39 SS-27 (*Topol*-M2), 3 regts

ABM 100: 36 SH-11 (mod *Galosh*), 64 SH-08 *Gazelle*, S-400

WARNING SYSTEMS

ICBM/SLBM launch-detection capability, others include photo recce and ELINT

RADARS

OVER-THE-HORIZON-BACKSCATTER (OTH-B)

2 in Ukr, at Nikolaev and Mukachevo, covering US

and polar areas, 1 near Yeniseysk, covering PRC

LONG-RANGE EARLY-WARNING ABM-ASSOCIATED

7 long-range phased-array systems operational: Moscow, Olenegorsk (Kola), Gaballa (Az), Baranovichi (Bel), Pechora (Urals), Balkhash (Kaz), Mishelevka (Irkutsk)

11 *Hen House*-series; range 6,000km, 6 locations covering approaches from the west and south-west, north-east and south-east and (partially) south. Engagement, guidance, battle management: 1 *Pill Box* phased-array at Pushkino (Moscow)

SPACE FORCES

Formations and units withdrawn from Strategic Missile and Air Defence Forces engaged in spacecraft launch and control

Army ε321,000

(incl ε190,000 conscripts)

6 Mil Districts (MD), 1 Op Strategic Gp
8 Army HQ, 2 Corps HQ
5 TD (3 tk, 1 motor rifle, 1 arty, 1 SAM regt; 1 armd recce bn; spt units)
19 MRD (3 motor rifle, 1 tk, 1 arty, 1 SAM regt; 1 indep tk, 1 ATK, 1 armd recce bn; spt units)
4 ABD (each 2/3 para, 1 arty regt) plus 1 AB trg centre (bde)
6 MG/arty div
5 arty div (each up to 6 bde incl 1 MRL, 1 ATK)
7 District trg centre (each = bde - 1 per MD)
13 indep bde (10 MR, 3 AB)
7 SF (*Spetsnaz*) bde
18 indep arty bde (incl MRL)
15 SSM bde (SS-21)
5 ATK bde, 3 ATK regt
19 SAM bde (incl 2 SA-4, 4 SA-11, 1 SA-12; all AD div disbanded)
20 hel regt (9 attack, 6 aslt tpt, 5 trg)
Other Front and Army tps
engr, pontoon-bridge, pipe-line, signals, EW, CW def, tpt, supply bde/regt/bn

RESERVES (cadre formations, on mobilisation form)

2 TD, 13 MRD, 1 hy arty bde, 4 indep arty bde, 6 MR bde, 2 tk bde

EQUIPMENT

Figures in () were reported to CFE on 1 Jan 2002 and include those held by Naval Infantry and Coastal Defence units

MBT about 21,870 (4,948), T-34 (1), 1,200 T-55 (15), 2,020 T-62 (258), 4,300 T-64A/-B (69), 9,700 T-72L/-M (1,780) 4,500 T-80/-U/UD/UM (2,818), 150 T-90 (7) (total incl ε8,000 in store – in RF)
LT TK 150 PT-76 (1)
RECCE some 2,000 BRDM-2
TOTAL AIFV/APC ε25,975 (9,175)
AIFV 14,700 (6,306): 7,500 BMP-1 (1,543), 4,600 BMP-2 (3,055), 100 BMP-3 (22), some 1,800 BMD incl BMD-1 (715), BMD-2 (361), BMD-3 (103), 700 BRM-1K (479), BTR-80A (28) (total incl 900 in store)
APC 11,275 (2,868): 1,000 BTR-50, 4,900 BTR-60/-70/-80 incl BTR-60 (17), BTR-70 (726), BTR-80 (942), 575 BTR-D (514); 4,800 MT-LB (669), plus 'look-alikes' (total incl 1,150 in store)
TOTAL ARTY 20,746 (5,695), with ε6,213 in store
TOWED 10,065 (1,717) incl: **122mm**: 1,200 M-30 (13); 3,050 D-30 (731); **130mm**: 50 M-46 (1); **152mm**: 100 ML-20 (1); 700 M-1943 (D1); 1,075 D-20 (150), 1,100 2A36 (401), 750 2A65 (420); **203mm**: 40 B-4M; also ε2,000 mainly obsolete types
SP 4,705 (2,348) incl: **122mm**: 1,725 2S1 (379); **152mm**: 1,600 2S3 (1,028), 700 2S5 (489), 550 2S19 (422); **203mm**: 130 2S7 (30)
COMBINED GUN/MOR 820+ (346): **120mm**: 790 2S9 SP (332), 2B16 (4), 30 2S23 (10)
MRL 2,606 (885) incl: **122mm**: 50 BM-13/-14/-16 (6), 1,750 BM-21 (367), 25 9P138 (7); **220mm**: 675 (412) 9P140; **300mm**: 106 (93) 9A52
MOR 2,550 (399) incl: **120mm**: 920 2S12 (143), 900 PM-38 (222); **160mm**: 300 M-160; **240mm**: 430 2S4 SP (34)
SSM (nuclear-capable) ε200 SS-21 *Scarab* (*Tochka*), (all *Scud* and FROG in store)
ATGW AT-2 *Swatter*, AT-3 *Sagger*, AT-4 *Spigot*, AT-5 *Spandrel*, AT-6 *Spiral*, AT-7 *Saxhorn*, AT-9, AT-10
RL 64mm: RPG-18; **73mm**: RPG-7/-16/-22/-26; **105mm**: RPG-27/-29
RCL 73mm: SPG-9; **82mm**: B-10
ATK GUNS 57mm: ASU-57 SP; **76mm**; **85mm**: D-44/SD-44, ASU-85 SP; **100mm**: 526 T-12/-12A/M-55 towed
AD GUNS 23mm: ZU-23, ZSU-23-4 SP; **30mm**: 2S6 SP; **37mm**; **57mm**: S-60, ZSU-57-2 SP; **85mm**: M-1939; **100mm**: KS-19; **130mm**: KS-30
SAM some 2,670
300 SA-4 A/B *Ganef* (twin) (Army/Front wpn – most in store)
350 SA-6 *Gainful* (triple) (div wpn)
550 SA-8 *Gecko* (2 triple) (div wpn)
800 SA-9 *Gaskin*/SA-13 *Gopher* (2 twin) (regt wpn)
350 SA-11 *Gadfly* (quad) (replacing SA-4/-6)
200 SA-12A/B (*Gladiator/Giant*)
120 SA-15 (replacing SA-6/SA-8)
SA-19 (2S6 SP) (8 SAM, plus twin **30mm** gun)
SA-7, SA-14 being replaced by SA-16, SA-18 (man-portable)
HELICOPTERS ε1,700 (with 600 in store) incl
ATTACK ε700 Mi-24 (517), 8 Ka-50 *Hokum* (6)
RECCE 140 Mi-24
TPT Mi-6, Mi-8/-17 (some armed), Mi-26 (hy)

Navy 171,500

(incl ε16,000 conscripts, ε11,000 Strategic Forces, ε35,000 Naval Avn, 9,500 Coastal Defence Tps/Naval Infantry)

SUBMARINES 53

STRATEGIC 13 (see p. 88)

TACTICAL 35

SSGN 6 *Oscar* II with 24 SS-N-19 *Shipwreck* USGW (VLS); T-65 HWT

SSN 16

9 *Akula* with SS-N-21 *Sampson* SLCM, T-65 HWT

1 *Sierra* with SS-N-21 *Sampson* SLCM, T-65 HWT

1 *Yankee 'Notch'* with 20+ SS-N-21 *Sampson* SLCM

5 *Victor* III with SS-N-15 *Starfish* SSM, T-65 HWT

SSK 13

9 *Kilo*, 3 *Tango*, 1 *Foxtrot* (all with T-53 HWT)

OTHER ROLES 5

3 *Uniform* SSN, 1 *Yankee* SSN, 1 *X-Ray* SSK trials

RESERVE probably some *Foxtrot*, *Tango* and *Kilo*

PRINCIPAL SURFACE COMBATANTS 32

AIRCRAFT CARRIERS† 1 *Kuznetsov* CV (67,500t) capacity 20 ac Su-33 and 15–17 ASW hel or 36 Su-33 with 12 SS-N-19 *Shipwreck* SSM, 4 × 6 SA-N-9 *Gauntlet* SAM

CRUISERS 7

CGN 2 *Kirov* with 20 SS-N-19 *Shipwreck* SSM, 12 SA-N-6 *Grumble* SAM, SA-N-4 *Gecko* SAM, 2 × 130mm gun, 10 × 533mm ASTT, SS-N-15 *Starfish* SUGW, 3 Ka-25/-27 hel

CG 5

3 *Slava* with 8 × 2 SS-N-12 *Sandbox* SSM, 8 SA-N-6 *Grumble* SAM, 2 × 130mm gun, 8 × 533mm ASTT, 1 Ka-25/-27 hel

1 *Kara* with 2 × 2 SA-N-3 *Goblet* SAM, 2 SA-N-4 *Gecko* SAM, 10 × 533mm ASTT, 2 × 4 SS-N-14 *Silex* SUGW, 1 Ka-25 hel

1 *Kynda* with 8 SS-N-3B *Sepal* SSM, 2 SA-N-1 *Goa* SAM, 4 × 76mm gun, 6 × 533mm ASTT

DESTROYERS 14

DDG 14

4 *Sovremenny* with 2 × 4 SS-N-22 *Sunburn* SSM, 2 × 1 SA-N-7 *Gadfly* SAM, 2 × 2 130mm guns, 4 × 533mm TT, 1 Ka-25 hel

1 mod *Kashin* with 8 SS-N-25 *Svezda* SSM, 2 × 2 SA-N-1 *Goa* SAM, 2 × 76mm gun, 5 × 533mm ASTT

1 *Kashin* with 2 × 2 SA-N-1 *Goa* SAM, 2 × 76mm gun, 5 × 533mm ASTT, 2 ASW RL

7 *Udaloy* with 8 SA-N-9 *Gauntlet* SAM, 2 × 100mm gun, 8 × 533mm ASTT, 2 × 4 SS-N-14 *Silex* SUGW, 2 Ka-27 hel

1 *Udaloy* II with 8 × 4 SS-N-22 *Sunburn* SSM, 8 SA-N-9 *Gauntlet* SAM, 8 SA-N-11 *Grisson* SAM, 2 CADS-N-1 CIWS, 2 × 100mm gun, 10 × 533mm ASTT

FRIGATES 10

FFG 10

2 *Krivak* II with 2 SA-N-4 *Gecko* SAM, 2 × 100mm gun, 8 × 533mm ASTT, 1 × 4 SS-N-14 *Silex* SUGW, 2 × 12 ASW RL

7 *Krivak* I (wpn as *Krivak* II, but with 2 twin 76mm guns)

1 *Neustrashimyy* with SA-N-9 *Gauntlet* SAM, 1 × 100mm gun, 6 × 533mm ASTT, 2 × 12 ASW RL

PATROL AND COASTAL COMBATANTS 88

CORVETTES 23

23 *Grisha* I, -III, -IV, -V, with SA-N-14 *Gecko* SAM, 4 × 533mm ASTT, 2 × 12 ASW RL

LIGHT FRIGATES 8

8 *Parchim* II with 2 SA-N-5 *Grail* SAM, 1 × 76mm gun, 4 × 406mm ASTT, 2 × 12 ASW RL

MISSILE CRAFT 42

25 *Tarantul* PFM, 1 -I, 5 -II, both with 2 × 2 SS-N-2C *Styx* SSM; 22 -III with 2 × 2 SS-N-22 *Sunburn* SSM

12 *Nanuchka* PFM 4 -I, 17 -III and 1 -IV with 2 × 3 SS-N-9 *Siren* SSM

2 *Dergach* PHM with 8 SS-N-22 *Sunburn* SSM, 1 SAN-4 *Gecko* SAM, 1 × 76mm gun

3 *Matka* PHM with 2 × 1 SS-N-2C *Styx* SSM

TORPEDO CRAFT 8 *Turya* PHT with 4 × 533mm TT

1 *Mukha* PHT with 8 × 406mm TT

PATROL CRAFT 6

COASTAL 6 *Pauk* PFC with 4 ASTT, 2 ASW RL

MINE WARFARE 60

MINE COUNTERMEASURES 60

OFFSHORE 15

2 *Gorya* MCO

13 *Natya* I and -II MSO

COASTAL 15 *Sonya* MSC

INSHORE 30 MSI<

AMPHIBIOUS ε22

LPD 1 *Ivan Rogov* with 4–5 Ka-27 hel, capacity 520 tps, 20 tk

LST 20

16 *Ropucha*, capacity 225 tps, 9 tk

4 *Alligator*, capacity 300 tps, 20 tk

LSM 1 *Polnocny*, capacity 180 tps, 6 tk

Plus about 21 craft: about 6 *Ondatra* LCM; about 15 LCAC (incl 4 *Pomornik*, 3 *Aist*, 3 *Tsaplya*, 1 *Lebed*, 1 *Utenok*, 2 *Orlan* WIG and 1 *Utka*)

Plus about 80 smaller craft

SUPPORT AND MISCELLANEOUS about 436

UNDER WAY SUPPORT 28

1 *Berezina*, 5 *Chilikin*, 22 other AO

MAINTENANCE AND LOGISTIC about 271

some 15 AS, 38 AR, 20 AOT, 8 msl spt/resupply, 90 AT, 9 special liquid carriers, 8 AWT, 17 AK, 46 AT/ARS, 13 ARS, 7 AR/C

SPECIAL PURPOSES about 57

some 17 AGI (some armed), 1 msl range instrumentation, 7 trg, about 24 icebreakers (civil-manned), 4 AH, 4 specialist spt vessels

SURVEY/RESEARCH about 80
some 19 naval, 61 civil AGOR

MERCHANT FLEET (aux/augmentation for sealift, RF-owned ships)

1,628 ocean-going veh over 1,000t: 340 tkr, 116 dry bulk, 33 container, 1,139 other

NAVAL AVIATION (ε35,000)

ORGANISATION

4 Fleet Air Forces, each organised in air div; each with 2–3 regt of HQ elm and 2 sqn of 9–10 ac each; recce, ASW, tpt/utl org in indep regt or sqn
Flying hours 40

EQUIPMENT

217 cbt ac; 102 armed hel
AIRCRAFT
BBR 45 Tu-22M
FGA 52 Su-24, 10 Su-25, 52 Su-27
ASW 10 Tu-142, 26 Il-38, 4 Be-12
MR/EW 18 An-12
TPT 37 An-12/An-24/An-26
HELICOPTERS
ASW 3 Mi-14, 72 Ka-27
MR/EW 8 Mi-8
CBT ASLT 12 Ka-29, 15 Mi-24
MISSILES
ASM AS-4 *Kitchen*, AS-7 *Kerry*, AS-10 *Karen*, AS-11, *Kelger*, AS-13 *Kingbolt*

COASTAL DEFENCE (9,500)

(incl Naval Infantry, Coastal Defence Troops)

NAVAL INFANTRY (Marines) (7,500)

1 inf 'div' (2,500: 3 inf, 1 tk, 1 arty bn) (Pacific Fleet)
3 indep bde (4 inf, 1 tk, 1 arty, 1 MRL, 1 ATK bn), 1 indep regt, 3 indep bn
3 fleet SF bde (1 op, 2 cadre): 2–3 underwater, 1 para bn, spt elm

EQUIPMENT

MBT 160: T-55M, T-72, T-80
RECCE 60 BRDM-2/*Sagger* ATGW
AIFV ε150 BMP-2, BMP-3, some BRM-1K
APC some 750: BTR-60/-70/-80, 250 MT-LB
TOTAL ARTY 321
TOWED 122mm: 10 D-30
SP 122mm: 102 2S1; **152mm**: 18 2S3
MRL 122mm: 96 9P138
COMBINED GUN/MOR 120mm: 70 2S9 SP, 14 2B16, 11 2S23 SP
ATGW 72 AT-3/-5
ATK GUNS 100mm: MT-12
AD GUNS 23mm: 60 ZSU-23-4 SP
SAM 250 SA-7, 20 SA-8, 50 SA-9/-13

COASTAL DEFENCE TROOPS (2,000)

(all units reserve status)
1 coastal defence div
1 coastal defence bde
1 arty regt
2 SAM regt

EQUIPMENT

MBT 350 T-64
AIFV 450 BMP
APC 280 BTR-60/-70/-80, 400 MT-LB
TOTAL ARTY 364 (152)
TOWED 280: **122mm**: 140 D-30; **152mm**: 40 D-20, 50 2A65, 50 2A36
SP 152mm: 48 2S5
MRL 122mm: 36 BM-21

NAVAL DEPLOYMENT

NORTHERN FLEET (Arctic and Atlantic)

(HQ Severomorsk)
BASES Kola peninsula, Severodovinsk
SUBMARINES 32
strategic 10 SSBN **tactical** 22 (4 SSGN, 11 SSN, 2 SSK, 5 SSN other roles)
PRINCIPAL SURFACE COMBATANTS 11
1 CV, 3 CG/CGN, 5 DDG, 2 FFG
OTHER SURFACE SHIPS about 26 patrol and coastal combatants, 18 MCMV, 8 amph, some 130 spt and misc
NAVAL AVIATION
EQUIPMENT
72 cbt ac; 30 armed hel
AIRCRAFT
BBR 25 Tu-22M • **FGA** 10 Su-25, 24 Su-27 • **ASW** 11 Il-38 • **MR/EW** 2 An-12 • **TPT** 25 An-12/An-24/An-26
HELICOPTERS
ASW 25 Ka-27 • **CBT ASLT** 5 Ka-29

BALTIC FLEET (HQ Kaliningrad)

BASES Kronstadt, Baltiysk
SUBMARINES 2 SSK
PRINCIPAL SURFACE COMBATANTS 6
2 DDG, 4 FFG
OTHER SURFACE SHIPS about 26 patrol and coastal combatants, 13 MCMV, 5 amph, some 130 spt and misc
NAVAL AVIATION
EQUIPMENT
55 cbt ac; 41 armed hel
AIRCRAFT
FGA 25 Su-24, 28 Su-27 • **MR/EW** 2 An-12 • **TPT** 12 An-12/An-24/An-26
HELICOPTERS
ASW 22 Ka-27 • **CBT ASLT** 4 Ka-29, 15 Mi-24

BLACK SEA FLEET (HQ Sevastopol)

The RF Fleet is leasing bases in Sevastopol for the next 20 years; it is based at Sevastopol and Karantinnaya Bays, and, jointly with Ukr warships, at Streletskaya Bay. The Fleet's overall serviceability is low.
BASES Sevastopol, Temryuk, Novorossiysk

SUBMARINES 10 (only one op)
9 SSK, 1 SSK other roles
PRINCIPAL SURFACE COMBATANTS 7
3 CG/CGN, 2 DDG, 2 FFG
OTHER SURFACE SHIPS about 15 patrol and coastal combatants, 14 MCMV, 5 amph, some 90 spt and misc
NAVAL AVIATION
EQUIPMENT
35 cbt ac; 13 armed hel
AIRCRAFT
FGA 27 Su-24 • **ASW** 4 Be-12 • **MR/EW** 4 An-12
HELICOPTERS
ASW 5 Ka-27 • **MR/EW** 8 Mi-8

CASPIAN SEA FLOTILLA

BASE Astrakhan (RF)
The Caspian Sea Flotilla has been divided between Az (about 25%), RF, Kaz and Tkm, which are operating a joint flotilla under RF comd currently based at Astrakhan
SURFACE COMBATANTS about 36
10 patrol and coastal combatants, 5 MCMV, some 6 amph, about 15 spt

PACIFIC FLEET (HQ Vladivostok)

BASES Vladivostok, Petropavlovsk Kamchatskiy, Magadan, Sovetskaya Gavan, Fokino
SUBMARINES 8
strategic 3 SSBN **tactical** 5 (2 SSGN, 3 SSN)
PRINCIPAL SURFACE COMBATANTS 8
1 CG/CGN, 5 DDG, 2 FFG
OTHER SURFACE SHIPS about 30 patrol and coastal combatants, 8 MCMV, 4 amph, some 57 spt and misc
NAVAL AVIATION
EQUIPMENT
55 cbt ac; 26 armed hel
AIRCRAFT
BBR 20 Tu-22M • **ASW** 10 Tu-142, 15 Il-38 • **MR/EW** 10 An-12
HELICOPTERS
ASW 20 Ka-27, 3 Mi-14 • **CBT ASLT** 3 Ka-29

Military Air Forces (VVS) ε184,600

The Military Air Forces comprise Long Range Aviation Cmd (LRA), Military Transport Aviation Comd (VTA), 7 Tactical/Air Defence Armies comprising 49 air regts. Tactical/Air Defence roles includes air defence, interdiction, recce and tactical air spt. LRA (6 div) and VTA (9 regt) are subordinated to central Air Force comd. A joint CIS Unified Air Defence System covers RF, Arm, Bel, Ga, Kaz, Kgz, Tjk, Tkm, Ukr and Uz.
Flying hours Average annual flying time for LRA is about 25 hours, for Tactical/Air Defence about 15 hours, and for VTA approximately 60 hours

LONG-RANGE AVIATION COMMAND (37th Air Army)

4 hy bbr regt (strategic), 4 hy bbr regt (non-strategic), plus 1 hy bbr trg centre
BBR (START-accountable) 63 Tu-95, 15 Tu-160 (Test ac: 7 Tu-95, 1 Tu-160)
117 Tu-22M/MR (plus others in store)
TKR 20 Il-78/Il-78M
TRG 8 Tu-22M-3, 30 Tu-134

TACTICAL AVIATION

BBR/FGA some 606: 371 Su-24, 235 Su-25
FTR some 908: 5 MiG-25, 255 MiG-29, 392 Su-27, 256 MiG-31
RECCE some 214: 70 MiG-25, 144 Su-24
AEW AND CONTROL 20 A-50/A-50U
ECM 60 Mi-8
TRG 2 centre for op conversion: some 90 ac incl 20 MiG-29, 35 Su-24, 15 Su-25
2 centre for instructor trg: 53 ac incl 16 MiG-29, 16 Su-24, 10 Su-25, 11 Su-27
AAM AA-8 *Aphid*, AA-10 *Alamo*, AA-11 *Archer*
ASM AS-4 *Kitchen*, AS-7 *Kerry*, AS-10 *Karen*, AS-11 *Kilter*, AS-12 *Kegler*, AS-13 *Kingbolt*, AS-14 *Kedge*, AS-15 *Kent*, AS-17 *Krypton*, AS-16 *Kickback*, AS-18 *Kazoo*
SAM 37 SAM regt
Some 1,900 SA-10/S-300. The first SA-20/S-400 unit reportedly deployed near Moscow

MILITARY TRANSPORT AVIATION COMMAND (VTA) (61st Air Army)

2 div, total 9 regt, 271 ac; plus 4 indep regts
EQUIPMENT
some 318 ac, incl Il-76M/MD/MF, An-12, An-124
1 An-22 regt (21 ac) directly under MoD control
CIVILIAN FLEET 1,500 medium- and long-range passenger ac, incl some 350 An-12 and Il-76

AIR FORCE AVIATION TRAINING SCHOOLS

TRG 5 mil avn institutes subordinate to Air Force HQ: some 980 ac incl L-39, Tu-134, Mig-23, MiG-29, Su-25, Su-27

OPERATIONAL COMBAT AIRCRAFT

based west of Urals (CFE totals as at 1 Jan 2002 for all air forces other than maritime)
ac 1,736: 413 Su-24 • 172 Su-25 • 296 Su-27 • 81 MiG-25 • 445 MiG-29 • 237 MiG-31 • 63 Tu-22M • 29 Tu-22. Some of these, plus 194 Su-17, 52 Su-22, 359 MiG-23, 93 MiG-27 are decommissioned ac in store. No armed hel

Deployment

Deployment of formations within the Atlantic to the Urals (ATTU) region is reported to be 2 TD, 8 MRD, perhaps 4 AB, 1 arty div, 9 indep arty, 3 MRL, 7 MR, 8 SSM, 12 SAM bde.
The manning state of RF units is difficult to determine. The following assessment of units within the ATTU

region is based on the latest available information. Above 75% – possibly 3 ABD, all MR bde and 1 AB bde; above 50% – possibly 1 TD, 6 MRD, 1 ABD, 1 arty bde. The remainder are assessed as 20–50%. Units outside the ATTU are likely to be at a lower level. All bde are maintained at or above 50%. TLE in each MD includes active and trg units and in store

KALININGRAD OPERATIONAL STRATEGIC GROUP

These forces are commanded by The Ground and Coastal Defence Forces of the Baltic Fleet.

GROUND 10,500: 1 MRD (cadre), 1 MR bde, 1 SSM bde, 1 SAM regt, 1 indep MRR (trg), 1 attack hel regt, 811 MBT, 865 ACV (plus 374 lookalikes), 345 arty/MRL/mor, 18 SS-21 *Scarab*, 16 attack hel

NAVAL INFANTRY (1,100)

1 regt (26 MBT, 220 ACV, 52 arty/MRL) (Kaliningrad)

COASTAL DEFENCE

2 arty regt (133 arty)

1 SSM regt: some 8 SS-C-1b *Sepal*

AD 1 regt: 28 Su-27 (Baltic Fleet)

SAM 50

RUSSIAN MILITARY DISTRICTS

LENINGRAD MD (HQ St Petersburg)

GROUND 34,400: 1 ABD; plus 2 indep MR bde, 2 arty bde, 1 SSM, 1 SF, 4 SAM bde; 1 ATK, 1 MRL, 1 aslt tpt hel regt. 320 MBT, 103 ACV (plus 2,250 lookalikes), 690 arty/MRL/mor, 18 SS-21 *Scarab*, 52 attack hel

NAVAL INFANTRY (1,300 – subordinate to Northern Fleet)

1 regt (74 MBT, 209 ACV, 44 arty)

COASTAL DEFENCE

1 Coastal Defence (360 MT-LB, 134 arty), 1 SAM regt

AIR 6th Air Force and AD Army has 305 combat ac. It is divided into two PVO corps, 1 bbr div (58 Su-24), 1 recce regt (28 MiG-25, 18 Su-24), 1 ftr div (116 Su-27, 85 MiG-31), 1 hel ECM sqn (35 Mi-8)

SAM 525

MOSCOW MD (HQ Moscow)

GROUND 82,400: 2 Army HQ, 2 TD, 2 MRD, 2 ABD, plus 1 arty div HQ; 4 arty bde (incl 1 trg), 3 indep arty, 3 SSM, 1 indep MR, 1 SF, 4 SAM bde; 2 attack hel regt. 2,190 MBT, 1,490 ACV (plus 1,600 lookalikes), 1,600 arty/MRL/mor, 48 SS-21 *Scarab*, 75 attack hel

AIR Moscow Air Defence and Air Army has 1 corps (32 PVO) and 16th Air Army (tactical)

395 cbt ac: 41 MiG-25, 106 MiG-29, 62 MiG-31, 34 Su-24, 16 Su-24MR, 46 Su-25, 90 Su-27 hel: 2 ECM sqn with 46 Mi-8

SAM 600

VOLGA-URAL MD (HQ Yekaterinburg)

GROUND 31,700: 1 Army HQ, 1 TD, 2 MRD; 1 indep MR, 1 AB, 3 arty bde/regt, 2 SSM, 1 SF, 1 SAM bde; 1 MRL regt, 1 indep hel regt. 530 MBT, 855 ACV, 440 arty/MRL/mor, 36 SS-21 *Scarab*, 14 attack hel

AIR 5th AF and AD Army has no ac subordinated **hel** Mi-8 comms

Air Force aviation schools (383 L-39, Mi-2), storage bases

NORTH CAUCASUS MD (HQ Rostov-on-Don) incl South Caucasus Group of Forces

GROUND 102,800: 1 Army HQ; 3 MRD, 1 ABD; 2 indep MR, 1 SF, 3 SAM bde, 2 arty bde; 1 indep MRR, 2 SSM, 2 ATK, 2 attack hel, 1 aslt tpt hel regt. 628 MBT, 2,100 ACV (plus 1,200 lookalikes), 855 arty/MRL/mor, 18 SS-21 *Scarab*, 98 attack hel

NAVAL INFANTRY (ε1,400 - subordinate to Black Sea Fleet)

1 regt (59 ACV, 14 arty)

AIR 4th AF and AD Army has 391 cbt ac; 1 bbr div (84 Su-24); 1 recce regt (30 Su-24); 1 air aslt div (99 Su-25); 1 ftr corps of 4 regt (103 MiG-29, 75 Su-27); 1 hel ECM sqn with 52 Mi-8, trg regt of tac aviation and Air Force aviation schools

SAM 125

SIBERIAN MD (HQ Chita)

GROUND 2 Army; 1 Corps HQ; 2 TD, 2 MRD, 1 arty div, 2 MG/arty div; 4 MR, 1 AB, 10 arty bde/regt, 2 SSM, 2 SAM, 2 SF bde, 4 ATK, 1 attack hel. 4,468 MBT, 6,000 ACV, 4,300 arty/MRL/mor, 36 SS-21 *Scarab*, 35 attack hel

AIR 14th AF and AD Army (HQ Novosibirsk) 200 cbt ac:

BBR/FGA 56 Su-24M, 30 Su-25

FTR 46 MiG-29, 39 MiG-31

RECCE 29 Su-24MR

FAR EASTERN MD (HQ Khabarovsk) incl Pacific Fleet and Joint Command of Troops and Forces in the Russian Northeast (These forces are commanded by the Pacific Fleet)

GROUND 2 Army; 1 Corps HQ; 10 MRD (2 trg), plus 3 MG/arty div, 1 arty div; 9 arty bde/regt, 1 MR, 3 SSM, 5 SAM, 1 SF, 1 ATK bde; 2 attack hel, 2 aslt tpt hel regt. 3,900 MBT, 6,400 ACV, 3,000 arty/MRL/mor, 54 SS-21 *Scarab*, 85 attack hel

NAVAL INFANTRY (2,500; subordinate to Pacific Fleet)

1 div HQ, 3 inf, 1 tk and 1 arty bn

COASTAL DEFENCE

1 div

AIR 11th AF and AD Army (HQ Khabarovsk) 345 cbt ac:

BBR/FGA 97 Su-24M, 60 Su-25

FTR 111 Su-27, 26 MiG-31

RECCE 51 Su-24MR

Forces Abroad

ARMENIA

GROUND 2,900; 1 mil base; 74 MBT, 17 APC, 129 ACV, 84 arty/MRL/mors
AD 1 sqn: 18 MiG-29, 2 SA-12 (S-300) bty, SA-6 bty
BORDER GUARD strength n.k.

GEORGIA

GROUND 4,000; 3 mil bases (each = bde+); 65 T-72 MBT, 200 ACV, 139 arty incl **122mm** D-30, 2S1 SP; **152mm** 2S3; **122mm** BM-21 MRL; **120mm** mor, 5 attack hel

Forces deployed in Arm and Ga are subordinate to the North Caucasus MD. Total probably excludes locally enlisted personnel.

MOLDOVA (Dniestr)

GROUND ε1,000; 1 op gp with 1 MR bde, 1 SAM regt; 108 MBT, 214 ACV, 125 arty/MRL/mor, 7 hel. These forces are subordinate to the Moscow MD

TAJIKISTAN

GROUND 7,800; 1 MRD, 128 MBT, 314 ACV, 180 arty/MRL/mor, ac 5 Su-25; plus 14,500 Frontier Forces (RF officers, Tjk conscripts). These forces are subordinate to the Volga-Ural MD

UKRAINE

NAVAL INFANTRY 1,100; 1 regt (102 ACV, 24 arty)

AFRICA 100

SYRIA 150

Peacekeeping

BOSNIA (SFOR II): 300
GEORGIA/ABKHAZIA 1,600
GEORGIA/SOUTH OSSETIA 530
MOLDOVA/TRANSDNIESTR 500; 1 MR bn
YUGOSLAVIA (KFOR): ε600

UNITED NATIONS

BOSNIA (UNMIBH): 1 **CROATIA** (UNMOP): 1 obs **DROC** (MONUC): 29 incl 28 obs **EAST TIMOR** (UNMISET): 2 obs **ETHIOPIA/ERITREA** (UNMEE): 5 obs **GEORGIA** (UNOMIG): 2 obs **IRAQ/KUWAIT** (UNIKOM): 11 obs **MIDDLE EAST** (UNTSO): 3 obs **SIERRA LEONE** (UNAMSIL): 123 incl 12 obs; 4 Mi-24 **WESTERN SAHARA** (MINURSO): 25 obs

Paramilitary ε409,100 active

FEDERAL BORDER GUARD SERVICE ε140,000

directly subordinate to the President; 10 regional directorates, 7 frontier gps

EQUIPMENT

1,000 ACV (incl BMP, BTR), 90 arty (incl 2S1, 2S9, 2S12)
ac some 70 Il-76, Tu-134, An-72, An-24, An-26, Yak-40, 16 SM-92 **hel** some 200+ Mi-8, Mi-24, Mi-26, Ka-27

PATROL AND COASTAL COMBATANTS about 237

PATROL, OFFSHORE 23
7 *Krivak*-III with 1 Ka-27 hel, 1 100mm gun; 12 *Grisha*-II; 4 *Grisha*-III

PATROL, COASTAL 35
20 *Pauk*, 15 *Svetlyak*

PATROL, INSHORE 95
65 *Stenka*, 10 *Muravey*, 20 *Zhuk*

RIVERINE MONITORS about 84
10 *Yaz*, 7 *Piyavka*, 7 *Vosh*, 60 *Shmel*

SUPPORT AND MISCELLANEOUS about 26
8 *Ivan Susanin* armed icebreakers, 18 *Sorum* armed AT/F

INTERIOR TROOPS 151,100

7 districts, some 11 'div' incl 5 indep special purpose div (ODON – 2 to 5 op regt), 29 indep bde incl 10 indep special designation bde (OBRON – 3 mech, 1 mor bn); 65 regt/bn incl special motorised units, avn

EQUIPMENT

incl 69 MBT, 1,700 ACV (incl BMP-1/-2, BTR-80), 20 D-30, 45 PM-38, 4 Mi-24

FEDERAL SECURITY SERVICE ε4,000 armed incl Alfa, Beta and Zenit cdo units

FEDERAL PROTECTION SERVICE ε10,000 to 30,000

org incl elm of Ground Forces (1 mech inf bde, 1 AB regt) and Presidential Guard regt

FEDERAL COMMUNICATIONS AND INFORMATION AGENCY ε54,000

RAILWAY TROOPS ε50,000 in 4 rly corps, 28 rly bde

REGIONAL TRENDS

The Middle East and North Africa have been more affected by the consequences of the 11 September 2001 terrorist attacks than any other region. The evident links between al-Qaeda, citizens of the regional states and non-state groups, along with a widespread anti-US sentiment, has made the support of regional governments for the US war on terrorism problematic. The recent intensification of the Israel–Palestine conflict and the increased likelihood of a US attack on Iraq has served to increase their ambivalence.

The failure of the July 2000 Camp David summit and then opposition leader Ariel Sharon's controversial visit in late September 2000 to the area known to Jews as Temple Mount and to Muslims as the Haram al-Sharif, sparked off a second *intifada*. This began on 29 September, and was followed by a rapid spread of violence. Israel responded with extensive military operations in the West Bank and Gaza, which have continued to the time of writing.

The developing situation between the US and Iraq has added to regional tensions. Most Middle Eastern states, and several extra-regional states such as Turkey, are calling for any action against Saddam Hussein to be carried out under UN authority, something that the US administration has made it clear that it does not regard as a necessary pre-condition for military action. As a result, Arab states such as Saudi Arabia and Jordan are unlikely to provide the US with the physical support and basing facilities necessary for military action to be launched from their territory. Other states have proved more cooperative. Bahrain has long been home to the US Fifth Fleet and aviation assets, while Qatar is hosting a new air operations centre. Although highlighted by the US as a country housing al-Qaeda operatives, Yemen has received US financial and training support for its armed forces, in return for cooperation in the fight against terror. Yemeni forces have carried out military operations against suspected al-Qaeda bases in the country. Morocco is also acting against terrorism, and arrested 15 al-Qaeda suspects in the period April–June 2002.

THE MIDDLE EAST

Israel

Israel's defence effort is focused on two threats: that posed by Palestinian militants; and the perceived need to bolster defences against unfriendly states such as Iran and Iraq.

The struggle against Palestinian militancy, and terrorism emanating from Palestinian groups, has intensified since October 2001. The 17 October assassination of Israel's Minister for Tourism, Rehavam Zeevi – claimed by the Popular Front for the Liberation of Palestine (PFLP) – resulted in units of the Israeli Defence Forces (IDF) entering the West Bank. An ultimatum was delivered to Palestinian Authority President Yasser Arafat to hand over the assassins. From then on, IDF punitive operations in the West Bank and Gaza became the standard response to terrorist attacks inside Israel, particularly after suicide attacks. Since October 2001, the terror campaign has been dominated by suicide bombings, mostly against civilian targets. The majority of these attacks have been attributed to the al-Aqsa Martyrs Brigade, although Hamas has also claimed responsibility for some attacks. Easy to mount and hard to prevent, suicide bombing attacks have been very effective in creating uncertainty and psychological damage among the Israeli population, lowering morale significantly. (See www.iiss.org, 'Suicide attacks – a tactical weapon system'.)

The most controversial Israeli operation in Palestinian territory was that launched, as part of *Operation Defensive Shield*, on 29 March 2002 against the refugee camp in Jenin, in the northern West Bank. The camp was believed to be at the centre of the suicide bombing campaign. Hampered by snipers and booby traps, the IDF surrounded and destroyed part of the camp using bulldozers and tank-fire. Nevertheless, the suicide attacks continued, demonstrating the ineffectiveness of conventional military force in dealing with terror – suicide bombings in particular.

Another Israeli tactic has been the 'selective targeting' of militant leaders, especially key Hamas figures. On 31 October 2002, Jamil Jadallah, a suspect in the June 2001 Tel Aviv nightclub bombing, was killed by Israeli helicopter gunships. On 22 July, key Hamas figure Salah Shehada was assassinated by an Israeli air-attack on his home in Gaza. This attack effectively brought to an end any hope that discreet, behind-the-scenes negotiations would lead to peace talks. In purely military terms, however, these 'selective' attacks were successful in showing Palestinian militants that Israeli security forces could strike when, where and at whom they wished.

Suicide attacks and shootings aside, there has been an increasing number of attacks using *Qassim* rockets, which have been attributed to Hamas. In 2002 there were reports that Hamas has developed the *Qassim* 2 variant, with a range of 10km. Further evidence of militant capability was demonstrated by the 4 January detention of the *Karine-A* vessel in the Red Sea by Israeli forces. This ship was en route to Palestinian territory and was found to be carrying a large quantity of arms, including 1,550 80mm and 129mm mortar bombs, and 345 *Katyusha* rockets. The cargo originated in Iran.

Israel's armed forces benefited from a number of additions and enhancements to materiel this year. Firstly, to boost its defences against missile – particularly *Scud* – attack, Israel is seeking to deploy additional *Arrow* 2 anti-ballistic missile batteries. With Syria having developed a *Scud*-D with a range of 700km and a possible increased Iraqi missile capability, this deployment is viewed as critical by Israel. Secondly, the addition to the ground forces of the *Merkava* 4 main battle tank, fielded with improved armour, gives Israel an increased edge over any possible regional adversary. Thirdly, Israel's air force has seen its inventory augmented by additional F-16Is, boosting its regional air supremacy. The air force – often the weapon of choice in combating terrorism – was used in March 2002 to respond to Hizbullah rocket attacks on the Golan Heights and the Galilee. Meanwhile, a US project, due for completion by October 2003, will supply Israel with 228 Joint Direct Attack Munitions (JDAMs), providing an improved means of delivering existing Israeli stocks of 450 and 900kg bombs. Finally, Israel launched its *Ofek* 5 surveillance satellite on 28 May 2002. The satellite is designed to conduct surveillance of the immediate region and detect missile launches.

Israel wishes to create a blue-water navy with a second-strike, strategic deterrent capability. It is expected that such a capability will be provided by missiles carried on the three new *Dolphin*-class diesel submarines (SSK). However it is unclear if Israel currently has, or will have in the near future, medium-range nuclear-tipped missiles for deployment on submarines. Israel's request to buy *Tomahawk* land-attack cruise missiles (which are nuclear-capable) was declined by the US and it is unlikely, although not impossible, that Israel has already developed such missiles indigenously. Israeli plans to improve surface capabilities will probably be achieved sooner rather than later, as it is developing a long-range anti-surface ship missile (ASSM) with a planned range of over 200km and hopes to buy unmanned aerial vehicles (UAV) to operate from its *Saar* 5 corvettes. Furthermore, there are plans to enhance Israel's littoral capabilities, as options exist to order up to six *Super Dvora* 2 missile craft from Israel Aircraft Industries and two *Shaldag* 2 craft from Haifa-based Israel Shipyards.

Iraq (see map opposite)

In his 1 June 2002 speech at West Point military academy, President George W. Bush publicly articulated the US desire for regime change in Iraq. However, providing a *casus belli* for action against Iraq has proved difficult, with suggestions of Iraqi links to international terrorism proving hard to verify in the eyes of world opinion. The net effect is that the original desire for prompt action has lost momentum. Another impedance on action has been resistance from otherwise friendly Arab states and European allies to armed action against Saddam's regime. Secretary of State Colin Powell's Middle East tour of 4–17 April failed to generate further support for US action. The Iraqi regime took advantage of this situation to launch its own

Balance of Forces and Groups in the Iraq Region

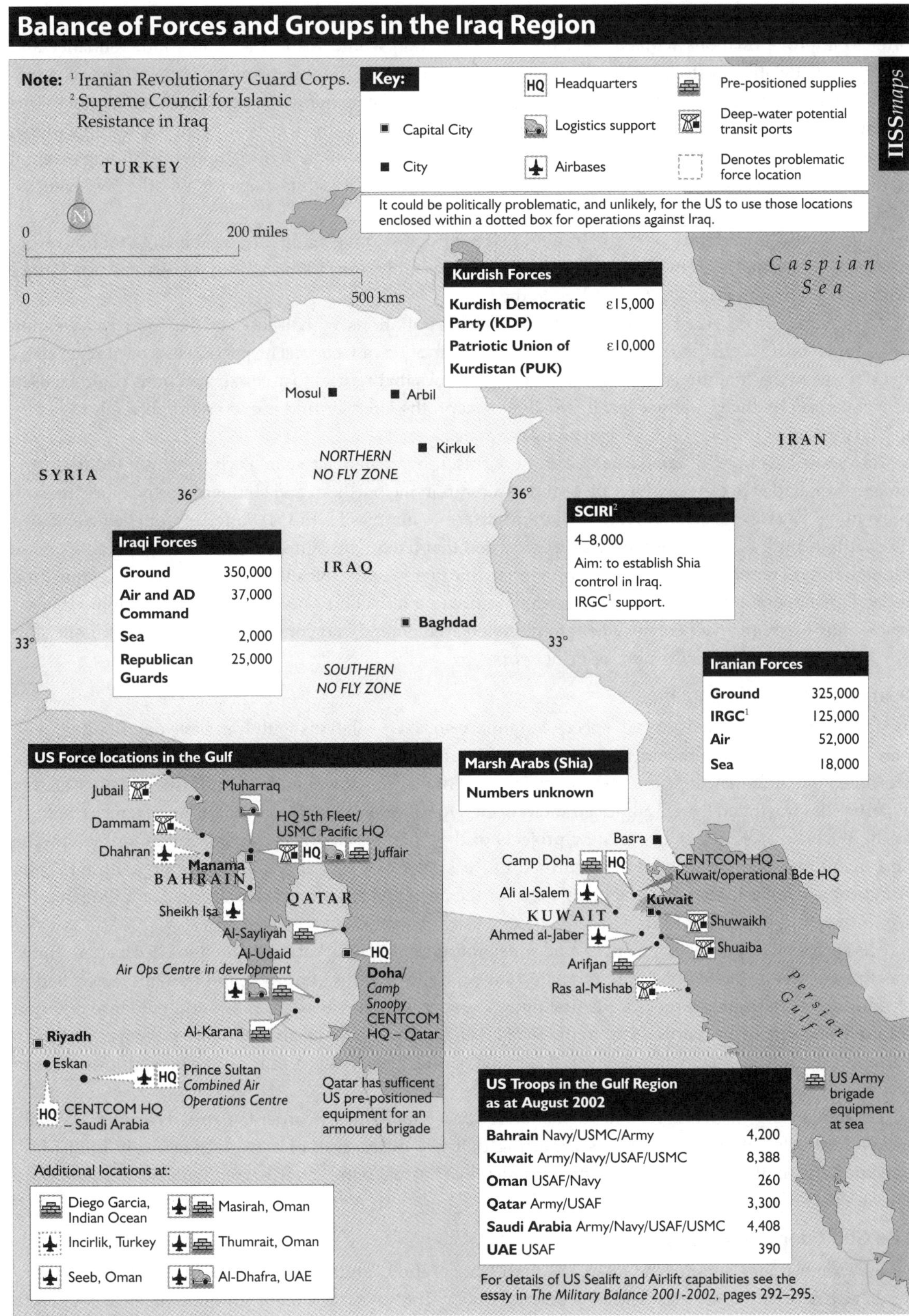

US Troops in the Gulf Region as at August 2002

Bahrain Navy/USMC/Army	4,200
Kuwait Army/Navy/USAF/USMC	8,388
Oman USAF/Navy	260
Qatar Army/USAF	3,300
Saudi Arabia Army/Navy/USAF/USMC	4,408
UAE USAF	390

For details of US Sealift and Airlift capabilities see the essay in *The Military Balance 2001-2002*, pages 292–295.

regional diplomatic initiatives. Starting at the 26 March Arab League summit in Beirut, Iraq renewed an offer to improve relations with Kuwait, declaring that Iraq would respect Kuwait's independence and sovereignty. Relations with Iran, the former enemy and neighbour have improved, as shown by exchanges of prisoners of war and remains from the Iran–Iraq War, and the opening of long-closed civil air links. This initiative, and disunity between internal opposition groups (such as the Kurds in the north, the Shia Marsh Arabs in the south, and the Iran-based Supreme Council for Revolution in Iraq), notwithstanding external opposition groups, have further complicated any plans by the US and its allies for a viable post-Saddam Iraq.

There is also uncertainty over the Iranian reaction to any move against Iraq. The fact that both were named as 'rogue states' in the 'axis of evil' by the Bush administration has in a sense given the two former adversaries a common cause – to stand up to the US.

Meanwhile, on 18 April 2002, the UN resumed negotiations with Iraq over the return of weapon inspectors. As of August 2002, Iraq's offer to allow resumption of weapons inspection had been rejected by the UN due to the conditions of the Iraqi offer. Iraq knows that refusal to accept inspections could be used as a *casus belli* by the US. However, if Iraq does accept, the US may find it even more difficult to justify military action in the eyes of European and Arab states.

Iraq's Air Defence Command has been modernised over the past year. Early warning radars in the greater Baghdad area can now identify coalition aircraft in the northern and southern no-fly zones, thereby preventing the target-acquisition radars of Iraqi surface-to-air missiles (SAM) batteries from being engaged by coalition anti-radiation missiles. Iraq has learned that fixed, undisguised military targets can increase vulnerability. Therefore SA-3 missiles, previously located in static sites with their associated acquisition radars, are now mobile. Many are now carried on rotating launchers on the back of six- or eight-wheeled trucks. Furthermore, in an enhancement to air defence command and control, SA-3 and SA-6 missile sites are said to be linked by a new fibre-optic network.

Iran (see also Russia, page 87)

Since President Bush's 'axis of evil' speech in January 2002, US relations with Iran have deteriorated, with no visible prospect of improvement. Indications of Iranian involvement in the Israel–Palestine conflict have worsened this situation, and continuing development of nuclear-power facilities at Bushehr using Russian expertise has frustrated the US administration further. Russia has refused to curtail its involvement, not just in the Bushehr project, but also in new projects of the same type, which Iran is actively pursuing. The agreement that spent fuel should be returned to Russia for disposal appears to have done little to calm American fears about such material being used for the development of nuclear weapons, or falling into the hands of would-be nuclear terrorists.

Missile tests and the development of a new generation of *Shihab* rockets has added to US concerns. In the most recent test of the *Shihab* 3 intermediate-range missile in early May 2002, the Iranians succeeded in striking a predetermined target for the first time. The success of the missile's range and guidance reflected improvements made by North Korea to the *Shihab* 3 engine, navigational and guidance system as well as in systems integration. Meanwhile a *Shihab* 4 capable of reaching Western Europe is believed to be near to testing.

The Iranian navy has continued to augment its surface capabilities, in order to patrol its territorial waters more effectively. In mid-2002, it was expecting delivery of the first of three indigenously built *Mowj* corvettes. Iran is also believed to have ordered 10 *China Cat* fast patrol craft, armed with surface-to-surface missiles (PFM), from China.

The Gulf Cooperation Council

At a December 2001 summit in Oman, the Gulf Cooperation Council (GCC) announced its intention to accelerate efforts to forge an integrated defence policy. It also established a supreme defence council to oversee the expansion of the alliance's joint defence force – named *Peninsula Shield* – from 5,000 to 20,000 troops. A major ambition of the GCC is to create a joint command, control and communications system with a view to developing a joint air defence and air traffic command-and-control structure. The first phase of this $160m project – a secure telecommunications facility and a military communications cable known as Hizam al-Taawun – has been completed. Construction of new facilities for the *Peninsula Shield* force has begun at Hafr al-Baten, in northeastern Saudi Arabia near the Iraqi border. The target date for bolstering *Peninsula Shield*, including the procurement of new equipment, is 2003. It is envisaged that 6,500 troops will be based permanently at Hafr al-Baten, while the other 13,500 will remain part of the member countries' own forces until called upon.

Oman, in order to better patrol its territorial waters and exclusive economic zones, has ordered *Super Lynx* helicopters, to be deployed from its two *Qahir* corvettes. Up to now, the Omani navy has lacked an aviation capability. The delivery of the helicopters should also increase its surface warfare capability.

Saudi Arabia accepted the first of three *al-Riyadh* (French *Lafayette*) frigates in July 2002. These ships are better armed, larger and more modern than existing Saudi frigates and all other regional surface combatants.

The UAE is also improving its surface capabilities, having ordered six *Baynunah* PFM from France – the first is expected to be delivered in late 2003. Meanwhile, the UAE's amphibious capability is due to be enhanced by the purchase of 12 landing craft, which will almost triple its current inventory of such vessels.

INTERNAL CONFLICT

Algeria

Since August 2001, approximately 2,000 people have died in Algeria in the internal conflict between the government and two Islamic militant groups: the Salafi Group for Call and Combat (GSPC); and the Armed Islamic Group (GIA). An amnesty offered to both groups by President Abdelaziz Bouteflika in 2000 was rejected by these groups, and August 2001 saw the first bomb attacks take place in the capital, Algiers, for two years.

On 25 February 2002, the Algerian government announced that parliamentary elections were to be held on 30 May. The leading pro-Berber opposition parties, the Socialist Forces Front (FFS) and the Rally for Culture and Democracy (RCD) called for an electoral boycott in protest against high unemployment and allegations of electoral fraud. As a result, the president announced, in late February, that the Berber language, Tamazight, was to be recognised as a national language – one of the key demands of the Berber community. However, tensions between the Berber people and the government continued, with Berbers protesting against heavy-handed government treatment of civilians. The death of Berber high-school student Guermah Massinissa in custody set off a wave of protests in April 2002, which were centred in the largely Berber-populated Kabyila district. A civil emergency was declared, the first since 1992.

Prime Minister Ali Benflis's National Liberation Front (FLN) won the election and the Algerian Interior Ministry said the overall turnout was 47.5%, the lowest recorded since independence in 1962. In June, protests were banned outright in Algiers.

Algeria Ag

Total Armed Forces

ACTIVE ε136,700
(incl ε75,000 conscripts)
Terms of service **Army** 18 months (6 months basic, 12 months civil projects)

RESERVES
Army some 150,000, to age 50

Army 120,000

(incl ε75,000 conscripts)
6 Mil Regions; re-org into div structure on hold
2 armd div (each 3 tk, 1 mech regt) • 2 mech div (each 3 mech, 1 tk regt) • 1 AB div (5 AB regt) • 1 indep armd bde • 4 indep mot/mech inf bde, 14 indep inf, 2 arty, 1 AD, 6 AAA bn

EQUIPMENT
- **MBT** 1,089: 288 T-54/-55, 334 T-62, 467 T-72
- **RECCE** 85 BRDM-2
- **AIFV** 700 BMP-1, 289 BMP-2
- **APC** 440 BTR-50/-60, 150 OT-64, 200 BTR-80, 100 *Fahd*
- **TOWED ARTY 122mm**: 28 D-74, 100 M-1931/37, 60 M-30 (M-1938), 198 D-30; **130mm**: 10 M-46; **152mm**: 22 ML-20 (M-1937)
- **SP ARTY** 185: **122mm**: 150 2S1; **152mm**: 35 2S3
- **MRL 122mm**: 48 BM-21; **140mm**: 48 BM-14-16; **240mm**: 30 BM-24
- **MOR 82mm**: 150 M-37; **120mm**: 120 M-1943; **160mm**: 60 M-1943
- **ATGW** AT-3 *Sagger*, AT-4 *Spigot*, AT-5 *Spandrel*
- **RCL 82mm**: 120 B-10; **107mm**: 58 B-11
- **ATK GUNS 57mm**: 156 ZIS-2; **85mm**: 37 D-44; **100mm**: 3 T-12, 50 SU-100 SP
- **AD GUNS 14.5mm**: 80 ZPU-2/-4; **20mm**: 100; **23mm**: 75 ZU-23 towed, 330 ZSU-23-4 SP; **37mm**: 145 M-1939; **57mm**: 70 S-60; **85mm**: 20 KS-12; **100mm**: 150 KS-19; **130mm**: 10 KS-30
- **SAM** SA-7/-8/-9

Navy ε6,700

(incl ε500 Coast Guard)
BASES Mers el Kebir, Algiers, Annaba, Jijel

SUBMARINES 2
SSK 2 FSU *Kilo* with 533mm TT

PRINCIPAL SURFACE COMBATANTS 3
FRIGATES 3
FF 3 *Mourad Rais* (FSU *Koni*) with SA-N-4 *Gecko* SAM, 4 × 76mm gun, 2 × 12 ASW RL

PATROL AND COASTAL COMBATANTS 17
CORVETTES 5
- 3 *Rais Hamidou* (FSU *Nanuchka* II) FSG with 4 SS-N-2C *Styx* SSM, SA-N-4 *Gecko* SAM
- 2 *Djebel Chinoise* FS with 3 × 76mm gun

MISSILE CRAFT 9 *Osa* with 4 SS-N-2 *Styx* SSM (plus 2 non-op)
PATROL CRAFT 3
- **COASTAL** 3 *El Yadekh* PCC

AMPHIBIOUS 3
- 2 *Kalaat beni Hammad* LST: capacity 240 tps, 10 tk, hel deck
- 1 *Polnocny* LSM: capacity 180 tps, 6 tk

SUPPORT AND MISCELLANEOUS 3
1 div spt, 1 *Poluchat* TRV, 1 *El Idrissi* AGHS

COAST GUARD (ε500)
Some 7 PRC *Chui-E* PCC, about 6 *El Yadekh* PCC, 16 PCI<, 1 spt, plus boats

Air Force 10,000

222 cbt ac, 63 armed hel
Flying hours 50
FGA 4 sqn
- 2 with 28 Su-24M/MK, 2 with 28 MiG-23BN

FGA/RECCE 2 sqn with 45 L-39ZA
FTR 5 sqn
- 1 with 14 MiG-25
- 4 with some 30 MiG-23B/E, 43 MiG-21MF/bis, 20+ MiG-29C/UB

RECCE 1 sqn with 4* MiG-25R
SURV/SIGINT 1 sqn with 6 *Beech* 1900D
MR 2 sqn with 15 *Super King Air* B-200T
TKR 1 sqn with 6 Il-78
TPT 2 sqn with 10 C-130H, 8 C-130H-30, 3 Il-76MD, 6 Il-76TD
VIP 2 *Falcon* 900, 3 *Gulfstream* III, 3 F-27
HELICOPTERS
- **ATTACK** 33 Mi-24, 30 Mi-8/17
- **TPT** 2 Mi-4, 5 Mi-6, 16 Mi-8/17, 2 AS 355

TRG 5 T-34C, 7 ZLIN-142, 4* MiG-21U, 5* MiG-23U, 1* MiG-25U, 7 L-39C, 35 *Safir* (ZLIN-43) hel: 25 Mi-2
UAV *Seeker*
AAM AA-2, AA-6, AA-7
ASM *Ingwe*
AD GUNS 3 bde+: 725 **85mm, 100mm, 130mm**
SAM 3 regt with 100 SA-2, SA-3, SA-6, SA-8

Forces Abroad

UN AND PEACEKEEPING
DROC (MONUC): 6 obs **ETHIOPIA/ERITREA** (UNMEE): 8 obs

Paramilitary ε181,200

GENDARMERIE 60,000 (Ministry of Defence)

6 regions; 44 Panhard AML-60/M-3, BRDM-2 recce, 200 *Fahd* APC **hel** Mi-2

NATIONAL SECURITY FORCES 20,000 (Directorate of National Security)

small arms

REPUBLICAN GUARD 1,200

AML-60, M-3 recce

LEGITIMATE DEFENCE GROUPS ε100,000

self-defence militia, communal guards

Opposition

GROUPE ISLAMIQUE ARMÉE (GIA) small gps each ε50–100; total less than 1,500

GROUPE SALAFISTE POUR LA PRÉDICATION ET LE COMBAT small gps; total less than 500

Bahrain Brn

Total Armed Forces

ACTIVE 10,700

Army 8,500

1 armd bde (-) (2 tk, 1 recce bn) • 1 inf bde (2 mech, 1 mot inf bn) • 1 arty 'bde' (1 hy, 2 med, 1 lt, 1 MRL bty) • 1 SF, 1 *Amiri* gd bn • 1 AD bn (2 SAM, 1 AD gun bty)

EQUIPMENT

MBT ε140 M-60A3
RECCE 22 AML-90, 8 *Saladin*, 8 *Ferret*, 8 Shorland
AIFV 25 YPR-765 (with **25mm**)
APC some 10 AT-105 *Saxon*, 110 Panhard M-3, 115 M-113A2
TOWED ARTY 105mm: 8 lt; **155mm**: 14 M-198
SP ARTY 203mm: 62 M-110
MRL 227mm: 9 MLRS (some ATACMS)
MOR 81mm: 12; **120mm**: 9
ATGW 15 TOW
RCL 106mm: 25 M-40A1; **120mm**: 6 MOBAT
AD GUNS 35mm: 15 Oerlikon; **40mm**: 12 L/70
SAM 60 RBS-70, 18 *Stinger*, 7 *Crotale*, 8 I HAWK

Navy 1,000

BASE Mina Salman

PRINCIPAL SURFACE COMBATANTS 1

FRIGATES 1
FFG 1 *Sabha* (US *Oliver Hazard Perry*) with 4 *Harpoon* SSM, 1 *Standard* SM-1MR SAM, 1 × 76mm gun, 2 × 3 ASTT

PATROL AND COASTAL COMBATANTS 10

CORVETTES 2 *Al Manama* (Ge Lürssen 62m) FSG with 2 × 2 MM-40 *Exocet* SSM, 1 × 76mm gun, hel deck
MISSILE CRAFT 4 *Ahmad el Fateh* (Ge Lürssen 45m) PFM with 2 × 2 MM-40 *Exocet* SSM, 1 × 76mm gun
PATROL CRAFT 4
COASTAL/INSHORE 4
2 *Al Riffa* (Ge Lürssen 38m) PFC
2 *Swift* FPB-20 PCI<

SUPPORT AND MISCELLANEOUS 5

4 *Ajeera* LCU-type spt
1 *Tiger* ACV, **hel** 2 B-105

Air Force 1,200

34 cbt ac, 40 armed hel
FGA 1 sqn with 8 F-5E, 4 F-5F
FTR 2 sqn with 18 F-16C, 4 F-16D
TPT 2 *Gulfstream* (1 -II, 1 -III; VIP), 1 Boeing 727, 1 RJ-85
HEL 1 sqn with 12 AB-212 (10 armed), 3 sqn with 24* AH-1E, 6* TAH-1P, 1 VIP unit with 3 Bo-105, 1 UH-60L (VIP), 1 S-70A (VIP)
TRG 3 Slingsby T-67M

MISSILES

ASM AS-12, AGM-65D/G *Maverick*
AAM AIM-9P *Sidewinder*, AIM-7F *Sparrow*
ATGW BGM-71 TOW

Paramilitary ε10,160

POLICE 9,000 (Ministry of Interior)

HEL 2 Hughes 500, 2 Bell 412, 1 BO-105

NATIONAL GUARD ε900

3 bn

COAST GUARD 260 (Ministry of Interior)

1 PCI, some 20 PCI<, 2 spt/landing craft, 1 hovercraft

Foreign Forces

US Air Force periodic detachments of ftr and spt ac
Navy (HQ CENTCOM and 5th Fleet): 680 **Marine** 370
UK RAF 40 (*Southern Watch*), 2 VC-10 tkr

Egypt Et

Total Armed Forces

ACTIVE 443,000
(incl ε322,000+ conscripts)
Terms of service 12 months–3 years (followed by refresher training over a period of up to 9 years)

RESERVES 254,000
Army 150,000 **Navy** 14,000 **Air Force** 20,000 **AD** 70,000

Army 320,000

(ε250,000+ conscripts)
4 Mil Districts, 2 Army HQ • 4 armd div (each with 2 armd, 1 mech, 1 arty bde) • 8 mech inf div (each with 2 mech, 1 armd, 1 arty bde) • 1 Republican Guard armd bde • 4 indep armd bde • 4 indep mech bde • 1 airmobile bde • 2 indep inf bde • 1 para bde • cdo gp • 1 SF group • 15 indep arty bde • 2 SSM bde (1 with FROG-7, 1 with *Scud*-B)

EQUIPMENT[a]

MBT 895 T-54/-55, 260 *Ramses* II (mod T-54/55), 550 T-62, 1,600 M-60 (400 M-60A1, 1,200 M-60A3), 555 M1A1 *Abrams* (plus 100 to be delivered)
RECCE 300 BRDM-2, 112 *Commando Scout*
AIFV 220 BMP-1 (in store), 265 BMR-600P, 310 YPR-765 (with **25mm**)
APC 600 *Walid*, 192 *Fahd*/-30, 1,075 BTR-50/OT-62 (most in store), 2,320 M-113A2 (incl variants), 80 YPR-765
TOWED ARTY 122mm: 36 M-1931/37, 359 M-1938, 156 D-30M; **130mm**: 420 M-46
SP ARTY 122mm: 124 SP 122, **155mm**: 164 M-109A2 (plus 179 A2/A3 to be delivered)
MRL 122mm: 96 BM-11, 60 BM-21/*as-Saqr*-10/-18/-36
MOR 82mm: 540 (some 50 SP); **120mm**: 1,800 M-1938; **160mm**: 60 M-160
SSM 9 FROG-7, *Saqr*-80 (trials), 9 *Scud*-B
ATGW 1,400 AT-3 *Sagger* (incl BRDM-2), 220 *Milan*, 200 *Swingfire*, 530 TOW (incl I-TOW, TOW-2A (with 52 on M-901, 210 on YPR-765 SP))
RCL 107mm: 520 B-11
AD GUNS 14.5mm: 200 ZPU-4; **23mm**: 280 ZU-23-2, 118 ZSU-23-4 SP, 36 *Sinai*; **37mm**: 200 M-1939; **57mm**: some S-60, 40 ZSU-57-2 SP
SAM 600+ SA-7/*'Ayn as-Saqr*, 20 SA-9, 26 M-54 SP *Chaparral*, *Stinger*, 50 *Avenger*
SURV AN/TPQ-37 (arty/mor), RASIT (veh, arty), *Cymbeline* (mor)
UAV R4E-50 *Skyeye*

[a] Most FSU eqpt now in store, incl MBT and some cbt ac

Navy 19,000

(incl ε2,000 Coast Guard and ε12,000 conscripts)
BASES Mediterranean Alexandria (HQ), Port Said, Mersa Matruh, Port Tewfig **Red Sea** Safaqa (HQ), Berenice, Hurghada, Suez

SUBMARINES 4
SSK 4 *Romeo* with *Harpoon* SSM and 533mm TT

PRINCIPAL SURFACE COMBATANTS 11
DESTROYERS 1
DD 1
1 *El Fateh* (UK 'Z') with 4 × 114mm guns, 5 × 533mm TT
FRIGATES 10
FFG 10
4 *Mubarak* (ex-US *Oliver Hazard Perry*) with 4 *Harpoon* SSM, *Standard* SM-1-MR SAM, 1 × 76mm gun, 2 hel
2 *El Suez* (Sp *Descubierta*) with 2 × 4 *Harpoon* SSM, 1 × 76mm gun, 2 × 3 ASTT, 1 × 2 ASW RL
2 *Al Zaffir* (PRC *Jianghu* I) with 2 CSS-N-2 (*HY* 2) SSM, 2 ASW RL
2 *Damyat* (US *Knox*) with 8 *Harpoon* SSM, 1 × 127mm gun, 4 × 324mm TT

PATROL AND COASTAL COMBATANTS 39
MISSILE CRAFT 25
6 *Ramadan* PFM with 4 *Otomat* SSM
5 FSU *Osa* I PFM with 4 SS-N-2A *Styx* SSM (1 may be non-op)
6 *6th October* PFM with 2 *Otomat* SSM
3 FSU *Komar* PFM with 2 SSN-2A *Styx* SSM
5 PRC *Hegu* (*Komar*-type) PFM with 2 SSN-2A *Styx* SSM
PATROL CRAFT, COASTAL 14
4 PRC *Hainan* PFC with 6 × 324mm TT, 4 ASW RL (plus 4 in reserve)
6 FSU *Shershen* PFC; 2 with 4 × 533mm TT and BM-21 (8-tube) 122mm MRL; 4 with SA-N-5 SAM and 1 BM-24 (12-tube) 240mm MRL
4 PRC *Shanghai* II PFC

MINE WARFARE 12
MINE COUNTERMEASURES 12
6 *Assiout* (FSU T-43 class) MSO
4 *Aswan* (FSU *Yurka*) MSC
2 *Swiftship* MHI
plus 1 route survey boat

AMPHIBIOUS 3
3 FSU *Polnocny* LSM, capacity 100 tps, 5 tk
plus craft: 9 *Vydra* LCU

SUPPORT AND MISCELLANEOUS 20
7 AOT (small), 5 trg, 6 AT, 1 diving spt, 1 *Tariq* (ex-UK FF) trg

NAVAL AVIATION
EQUIPMENT
24 armed hel (operated by Air Force)

HELICOPTERS
5 *Sea King* Mk 47, 9 SA-341, 10 SH-2G *Super Sea-Sprite* with Mk 46 LWT
UAV
2 Camcopter 5.1

COASTAL DEFENCE (Army tps, Navy control)

GUNS 130mm: SM-4-1
SSM *Otomat*

Air Force 29,000

(incl 10,000 conscripts); 608 cbt ac, 128 armed hel
FGA 7 sqn
2 with 41 *Alpha Jet*, 2 with 44 PRC J-6, 2 with 28 F-4E, 1 with 20 *Mirage* 5E2
FTR 22 sqn
2 with 25 F-16A/8 F-16B, 6 with 50 MiG-21, 7 with 134 F-16C/40 F-16D, 2 with 53 *Mirage* 5D/E, 3 with 53 PRC J-7, 1 with 18 *Mirage* 2000C
RECCE 2 sqn with 6* *Mirage* 5SDR, 14* MiG-21R
EW ac 2 C-130H (ELINT), 6 Beech 1900 (ELINT) **hel** 4 *Commando* 2E (ECM)
AEW 5 E-2C (6th on order)
MR 2 Beech 1900C surv ac
TPT 21 C-130H, 5 DHC-5D, 1 *Super King Air*, 2 *Gulfstream* III, 5 *Gulfstream* IV, 3 *Falcon* 20
HELICOPTERS
ASW 9* SA-342L, 5* *Sea King* 47, 10* SH-2G (with Navy)
ATTACK 6 sqn with 69 SA-342K (44 with HOT, 25 with 20mm gun), 35 AH-64A
TAC TPT hy 15 CH-47C, 14 CH-47D **med** 66 Mi-8, 25 *Commando* (3 VIP), 2 S-70 (VIP) **lt** 12 Mi-4, 15 UH-12E (trg), 2 UH-60A, 2 UH-60L (VIP), 3 AS-61
TRG incl 4 DHC-5, 49 EMB-312, 45 *Gumhuria*, 16* JJ-6, 95 L-29, 12 L-39, 30* L-59E, 24 Grob 115EG (74 on order), first of 80 K-8 being delivered to replace L-29, 20* MiG-21U, 5* *Mirage* 5SDD, 3* *Mirage* 2000B
UAV 29 Teledyne-Ryan 324 *Scarab*

MISSILES
ASM AGM-65 *Maverick*, AGM-84 *Harpoon*, *Exocet* AM-39, AS-12, AS-30, AS-30L HOT, AGM-119 *Hellfire*
ARM *Armat*
AAM AA-2 *Atoll*, AIM-7E/F/M *Sparrow*, AIM-9F/L/P *Sidewinder*, MATRA R-530, MATRA R-550 *Magic*

Air Defence Command 75,000

(incl 50,000 conscripts)
4 div: regional bde, 100 AD arty bn, 40 SA-2, 50 SA-3A, 14 SA-6 bn, 12 bty I HAWK, 12 bty *Chaparral*, 14 bty *Crotale*

EQUIPMENT
AD GUNS some 2,000: **20mm, 23mm, 37mm, 57mm, 85mm, 100mm**
SAM some 300 SA-2, 232 SA-3, 200 SA-6, 78 I HAWK, some 24 *Crotale*
AD SYSTEMS some 18 *Amoun* (*Skyguard*/RIM-7F *Sparrow*, some 36 twin **35mm** guns, some 36 quad SAM); *Sinai*-23 short-range AD (Dassault 6SD-20S radar, **23mm** guns, *'Ayn as-Saqr* SAM)

Forces Abroad

Advisers in O, Sau, DROC

UN AND PEACEKEEPING

CROATIA (UNMOP): 1 obs **DROC** (MONUC): 26 incl 24 obs **EAST TIMOR** (UNMISET): 4 incl 2 obs **GEORGIA** (UNOMIG): 3 obs **SIERRA LEONE** (UNAMSIL): 10 obs **WESTERN SAHARA** (MINURSO): 19 obs

Paramilitary ε330,000 active

CENTRAL SECURITY FORCES 250,000 (including conscripts (Ministry of Interior))
110 *Hotspur Hussar*, *Walid* APC

NATIONAL GUARD 60,000
8 bde (each of 3 bn; cadre status); lt wpns only

BORDER GUARD FORCES 20,000
19 Border Guard Regt; lt wpns only

COAST GUARD (ε2,000 incl in Naval entry)
PATROL, INSHORE 40
20 *Timsah* PCI<, 9 *Swiftships*, 5 *Nisr*†, 6 *Crestitalia* PFI<, plus some 60 boats

Opposition

AL-JIHAD 1,000+

ISLAMIC GROUP 1,000+

Foreign Forces

PEACEKEEPING
MFO Sinai: some 1,896 from **Aus, Ca, Co, Fji, Fr, Hu, It, No, NZ, Ury, US**

Iran Ir

Total Armed Forces

ACTIVE ε520,000
(perhaps 220,000 conscripts)
Terms of service 21 months

RESERVES

Army 350,000, ex-service volunteers

Army 325,000

(perhaps 220,000 conscripts)
4 Corps HQ • 4 armd div (each 3 armd, 1 mech bde, 4–5 arty bn) • 6 inf div (each 4 inf bde, 4–5 arty bn) • 2 cdo div • 1 AB bde • some indep armd, inf, cdo bde • 5 arty gps • Army avn

EQUIPMENT† (overall totals incl those held by Revolutionary Guard Corps Ground Forces)

MBT some 1,565 incl: 500 T-54/-55 and PRC Type-59, some 75 T-62, 480 T-72, 200 *Chieftain* Mk 3/5, 150 M-47/-48, 150 M-60A1, ε10 *Zulfiqar*
LT TK 80 *Scorpion*, *Towsan*
RECCE 35 EE-9 *Cascavel*
AIFV 350 BMP-1, 400 BMP-2
APC 300 BTR-50/-60, 250 M-113, ε40 *Boragh*
TOWED 2,085: **105mm**: 130 M-101A1; **122mm**: 500 D-30, 100 PRC Type-54; **130mm**: 1,100 M-46/Type-59; **152mm**: 30 D-20; **155mm**: 15 WAC-21, 70 M-114; 120 GHN-45; **203mm**: 20 M-115
SP 310: **122mm**: 60 2S1, *Thunder* 1; **155mm**: 180 M-109, *Thunder* 2; **170mm**: 10 M-1978; **175mm**: 30 M-107; **203mm**: 30 M-110
MRL 889+: **107mm**: 700 PRC Type-63; *Haseb*, *Fadjr* 1; **122mm**: 50 *Hadid/Arash/Noor*, 100 BM-21, 20 BM-11; **240mm**: 9 M-1985, ε10 *Fadjr* 3; **333mm**: *Fadjr* 5
MOR 5,000 incl: **60mm; 81mm; 82mm; 107mm**: 4.2in M-30; **120mm**: M-65
SSM ε17 *Scud*-B/-C launchers/launch vehicles (300 msl), ε30 CSS-8 (175 msl), *Oghab*, *Shahin* 1/-2, *Nazeat*, some *Shehab* 3
ATGW 75: TOW, AT-3 *Sagger* (some SP), AT-4 *Spigot*, some AT-5 *Spandrel*, *Dragon*
RL 73mm: RPG-7
RCL 75mm: M-20; **82mm**: B-10; **106mm**: ε200 M-40; **107mm**: B-11
AD GUNS 1,700: **14.5mm**: ZPU-2/-4; **23mm**: ZU-23 towed, ZSU-23-4 SP; **35mm; 37mm**: M-1939, PRC Type-55; **57mm**: ZSU-57-2 SP, S-60
SAM SA-7/-14/-16, HQ-7 (reported)
UAV *Mohajer* II/III/IV
AC 10 Cessna 185, 2 F-27, 1 *Falcon* 20, 4 Turbo Commander 690
HEL 50 AH-1J **attack**; 20 CH-47C **hy tpt**; 50 Bell 214; 40 AB-205A; 10 AB-206; 25 Mi-8/-17

Revolutionary Guard Corps (*Pasdaran Inqilab*) some 125,000

GROUND FORCES some 100,000

grouped into perhaps 16–20 div incl 2 armd, 5 mech, 10 inf, 1 SF and 15–20 indep bde, incl inf, armd, para, SF, 6 arty gp (incl SSM), engr, AD and border defence units, serve indep or with Army; eqpt incl 470 tk, 620 APC/ACV, 360 arty, 40 RL and 140 AD guns, all incl in army inventory; controls *Basij* (see *Paramilitary*) when mob

NAVAL FORCES some 20,000

BASES Al-Farsiyah, Halul (oil platform), Sirri, Abu Musa, Bandar-e Abbas, Khorramshahr, Larak
some 40 Swe Boghammar Marin boats armed with ATGW, RCL, machine guns; 10 *Houdong* with C-802 SSM; controls coast-defence elm incl arty and CSSC-3 (*HY* 2) *Seersucker* SSM bty

MARINES some 5,000 1 bde

AIR FORCES

Few details known of this org, which is commanded by a Brig Gen

Navy 18,000

(incl 2,000 Naval Avn and 2,600 Marines)
BASES Bandar-e Abbas (HQ), Bushehr, Kharg Island, Bandar-e Anzelli, Bandar-e Khomeini, Bandar-e Mahshahr, Chah Bahar

SUBMARINES 6

SSK 3 *Kilo* (RF Type 877) with 6 × 533mm TT (TEST 71/96 HWT/LWT) (only 1 fully operable)
SSI 3

PRINCIPAL SURFACE COMBATANTS 3

FRIGATES 3
FFG 3 *Alvand* (UK Vosper Mk 5) with 2 × 2 C-802 SSM, 1 × 114mm gun, 1 × 3 *Limbo* ASW RL

PATROL AND COASTAL COMBATANTS 56

CORVETTES 2 *Bayandor* (US PF-103) FS with 2 × 76mm gun
MISSILE CRAFT 10
10 *Kaman* (Fr *Combattante* II) PFM; 5 of which have 2 or 4 C-802 SSM
PATROL, COASTAL 3
3 *Parvin* PCC
PATROL, INSHORE 41
3 *Zafar* PCI<, 3 *China Cat* PCI<, some 35 PFI<, plus some 14 hovercraft< (not all op), 200+ small craft

MINE WARFARE 7

MINE LAYERS 2
2 *Hejaz* LST
MINE COUNTERMEASURES 5†
1 *Shahrokh* MSC (in Caspian Sea as trg ship)
2 292 MSC
2 *Riazi* (US *Cape*) MSI

AMPHIBIOUS 9

4 *Hengam* LST, capacity 225 tps, 9 tk, 1 hel
3 *Iran Hormuz 24* (ROK) LSM, capacity 140 tps, 9 tk
2 *Fouque* LSL
Plus craft: 3 LCT, 6 ACV

SUPPORT AND MISCELLANEOUS 23

1 *Kharg* AO with 3 hel, 2 *Bandar Abbas* AO with 1 hel; 2 AWT, 3 *Delvar* spt, 12 *Hendijan* spt; 1 AT, 2 trg craft

NAVAL AVIATION (2,000)

EQUIPMENT
5 cbt ac, 19 armed hel
AIRCRAFT
MR 5 P-3F, 5 Do-228
TPT 4 *Commander*, 4 F-27
HELICOPTERS
ASW ε10 SH-3D, 6 AB-212
MCM 3 RH-53D
TPT 3 *Falcon* 20, 5 AB 205a, 2 AB-206, 4 Mi-171

MARINES (2,600) 2 bde

Air Force ε52,000

(incl 15,000 Air Defence); some 306 cbt ac (serviceability probably about 60% for US ac types and about 80% for PRC/Russian ac); no armed hel
FGA 9 sqn
4 with some 65 F-4D/E, 4 with some 60 F-5E/F, 1 with 30 Su-24MK (including former Irq ac), 7 Su-25K (former Irq ac), 24 Mirage F-1E (former Irq ac)
FTR 7 sqn
2 with 25 F-14, 1 with 24 F-7M, 2 with 25 MiG-29A/UB (incl former Irq ac)
(Some F-7 operated by Pasdaran air arm)
MR 5* C-130H-MP
AEW 1 Il-76 (former Irq ac)
RECCE 1 sqn (det) with some 6* RF-4E
TKR/TPT 1 sqn with 3 Boeing 707, 1 Boeing 747
TPT 5 sqn with 4 Boeing 747F, 1 Boeing 727, 18 C-130E/H, 3 *Commander* 690, 10 F-27, 1 *Falcon* 20, 2 *Jetstar*, 10 PC-6B, 2 Y-7, some Il-76 (former Irq ac), 9 Y-12(II)
HEL 2 AB-206A, 30 Bell 214C, *Shabaviz* 2061 and 2-75 (indigenous versions in production), 2 CH-47, 2 Mi-17 (30 to be delivered by end 2003)
TRG incl 20 Beech F-33A/C, 15 EMB-312, 40 PC-7, 7 T-33, 15* FT-7, 20* F-5B, 8 TB-21, 4 TB-200, 22 MFI-17 *Mushshaq*

MISSILES

ASM some 3,000 AGM-65A *Maverick*, AS-10, AS-11, AS-14, C-801
AAM AIM-7 *Sparrow*, AIM-9 *Sidewinder*, AIM-54 *Phoenix*, probably AA-8, AA-10, AA-11 for MiG-29, PL-2A, PL-7
SAM 16 bn with ε150 I HAWK, 5 sqn with 30 *Rapier*, 15 *Tigercat*, 45 HQ-2J (PRC version of SA-2), 10 SA-5, FM-80 (PRC version of *Crotale*), SA-7, *Stinger*

Forces Abroad

LEBANON ε150 Revolutionary Guard
SUDAN mil advisers

Paramilitary 40,000 active

BASIJ ('Popular Mobilisation Army') (R) ε300,000
peacetime volunteers, mostly youths; str up to 1,000,000 during periods of offensive ops. Small arms only; org into ε900 bn but not currently embodied for mil ops

LAW-ENFORCEMENT FORCES (Ministry of Interior) ε40,000
incl border-guard elm **ac** Cessna 185/310 lt **hel** ε24 AB-205/-206; about 90 patrol inshore, 40 harbour craft

Opposition

NATIONAL LIBERATION ARMY (NLA) some 6–8,000
Irq based; org in bde, armed with captured eqpt. Perhaps 250+ T-54/-55, *Chieftain* MBT, BMP-1 AIFV, D-30 **122mm** arty, BM-21 **122mm** MRL, Mi-8 hel

KURDISH DEMOCRATIC PARTY OF IRAN (KDP–Iran) ε1,200–1,800

KURDISTAN ORGANISATION OF THE COMMUNIST PARTY OF IRAN (KOMALA–Iran) based in Irq ε200

Foreign Forces

some 400 mil technicians/trg staff from PRC, DPRK, RF

Iraq Irq

Total Armed Forces

ACTIVE ε389,000
Terms of service 18–24 months

RESERVES ε650,000

Army ε350,000

(incl ε100,000 recalled Reserves)
7 corps HQ • 3 armd div, 3 mech div[a] • 11 inf div[a] • 6 Republican Guard Force div (3 armd, 1 mech, 2 inf) • 4 Special Republican Guard bde • 5 cdo bde • 2 SF bde • Army avn: 5 wing with 2 ac, 21 hel sqn

[a] All divisions other than Republican Guard Force at reported 50% cbt effectiveness

EQUIPMENT[b]

MBT perhaps 2,600, incl T-55/-62 and PRC Type-59, 700 T-72
RECCE 400: BRDM-2, AML-60/-90, EE-9 *Cascavel*, EE-3 *Jararaca*
AIFV perhaps 1,200 BMP-1/-2
APC perhaps 1,800, incl BTR-50/-60/-152, OT-62/-64, MTLB, YW-701, M-113A1/A2, EE-11 *Urutu*
TOWED ARTY perhaps 1,900, incl **105mm**: incl M-56 pack; **122mm**: D-74, D-30, M-1938; **130mm**: incl M-46, Type 59-1; **155mm**: some G-5, GHN-45, M-114
SP ARTY 200, incl **122mm**: 2S1; **152mm**: 2S3; **155mm**: M-109A1/A2, AUF-1 (GCT)
MRL perhaps 200, incl **107mm; 122mm**: BM-21; **127mm**: ASTROS II; **132mm**: BM-13/-16; **400mm**: *Ababeel-100*
MOR 81mm; 120mm; 160mm: M-1943; **240mm**
SSM up to 50 FROG and 6 *Scud* launchers reported; *al-Hussein* possible
ATGW AT-3 *Sagger* (incl BRDM-2), AT-4 *Spigot* reported, SS-11, *Milan*, HOT (incl 100 VC-TH)
RCL 73mm: SPG-9; **82mm**: B-10; **107mm**: B-11
ATK GUNS 85mm; 100mm towed
HELICOPTERS 164
ATTACK 12 Mi-25, 20 SA-319, 10 SA-316, 20 SA-342
SUPPORT 20 SA-330F, 30 BO-105, 10 Mi-6, 30 Mi-8, 12 Mi-17
SURV RASIT (veh, arty), *Cymbeline* (mor)

[b] 50% of all eqpt lacks spares

Navy ε2,000

BASES Basra (limited facilities), Al Zubayr, Umm Qasr

PATROL AND COASTAL COMBATANTS 6

MISSILE CRAFT 1 FSU *Osa* I PFM with 4 SS-N-2A *Styx* SSM
PATROL, INSHORE 5†
1 FSU *Bogomol* PFI<, 3 PFI<, 1 PCI< (all non-op) plus 80 boats

MINE WARFARE 3

MINE COUNTERMEASURES 3

1 FSU *Yevgenya*, 2 *Nestin* MSI

SUPPORT AND MISCELLANEOUS 2

1 *Damen* AG, 1 yacht with hel deck

Air Force ε20,000

ε316 cbt ac, no armed hel
Serviceability of fixed-wg ac about 55%, serviceability of hel poor
Flying hours snr pilots 90–120, jnr pilots as little as 20
BBR ε6, incl H-6D, Tu-22
FGA ε130, incl MiG-23BN, *Mirage* F1EQ5, Su-20, 40 Su-22 M, 2 Su-24 MK, 2 Su-25
FTR ε180: 18 F-7, 40 MiG-21, 50 MiG-23, 12 MiG-25, 50 *Mirage* F-1EQ, 10 MiG-29
RECCE ε5 incl MiG-25
TKR incl 2 Il-76
TPT incl An-2, 3 An-12, An-24, 6 An-26, Il-76
TRG incl 20 AS-202, 50 EMB-312, some 50 L-39, *Mirage* F-1BQ, 25 PC-7, 12 PC-9
UAV some modified L-29

MISSILES

ASM AM-39, AS-4, AS-5, AS-11, AS-9, AS-12, AS-30L, C-601
AAM AA-2/-6/-7/-8/-10, R-530, R-550

Air Defence Command ε17,000

AD Comd given priority since 1991. **HQ** Baghdad/Al-Muthanna **Four regional AD centres** Kirkuk (north), Kut al Hayy (east), Basra (south), Ramadia (west)
AD GUNS ε3,000: **23mm**: ZSU-23-4 SP; **37mm**: M-1939 and twin; **57mm**: incl ZSU-57-2 SP; **85mm; 100mm; 130mm**
SAM some 850 launchers SA-2/-3/-6/-7/-8/-9/-13/-14/-16, *Roland*, *Aspide*

Paramilitary 42–44,000

SECURITY TROOPS ε15,000

BORDER GUARDS ε9,000

lt wpns and mor only

SADDAM'S *FEDAYEEN* ε18–20,000

AL QUDS VOLUNTEER FORCE str n.k.

Opposition

KURDISH DEMOCRATIC PARTY (KDP) ε15,000

(plus 25,000 tribesmen); small arms, some lt arty, MRL, mor, SAM-7

PATRIOTIC UNION OF KURDISTAN (PUK) ε10,000

(plus 22,000 tribesmen); 450 mor (**60mm, 82mm, 120mm**); **106mm** RCL; some 200 **14.5mm** AA guns; SA-7 SAM

SUPREME COUNCIL FOR ISLAMIC RESISTANCE IN IRAQ (SCIRI)

4–8,000; ε1 'bde'; Ir-based; Irq dissidents, ex-prisoners of war

Foreign Forces

UN (UNIKOM): some 904 tps and 193 mil obs from 31 countries

Israel Il

Total Armed Forces

ACTIVE ε161,500 (in addition a number of reservists have been re-called for specific ops)
(107,500 conscripts)
Terms of service **officers** 48 months **other ranks** 36 months **women** 24 months (Jews and Druze only; Christians, Circassians and Muslims may volunteer). Annual trg as cbt reservists to age 41 (some specialists to age 54) for men, 24 (or marriage) for women

RESERVES 425,000

Army 400,000 **Navy** 5,000 **Air Force** 20,000. Reserve service can be followed by voluntary service in Civil Guard or Civil Defence

Strategic Forces

Il is widely believed to have a nuclear capability with up to 100 warheads. Delivery means could include ac, *Jericho* 1 SSM (range up to 500km), *Jericho* 2 (range ε1,500–2,000km)

Army 120,000

(85,000 conscripts, male and female); some 530,000 on mob
3 territorial, 1 home front comd
4 corps HQ
2 armd div with 4 armd, 5 inf bde, 3 arty regt
5 inf div with 14 inf bde, 5 sy bn
1 air-mob div with 4 para bde (incl 3 res)
(org and structure of formations may vary according to op situations)

RESERVES

8 armd div with 25 armd, 4 inf bde, 7 arty regt

EQUIPMENT

MBT 3,750: 300 *Centurion*, 250 M-48A5, 300 M-60/A1, 600 M-60A3, 400 *Magach* 7, 200 Ti-67 (T-54/-55), 100 T-62, 1,600 *Merkava* I/II/III
RECCE about 400, incl RAMTA RBY, BRDM-2, ε8 *Fuchs*
APC 6,100 M-113A1/A2, ε400 *Nagmachon* (*Centurion*), *Puma*, *Nakpadon*, ε400 *Achzarit*, 3,500 M-2/-3 half-track (most in store)
TOWED ARTY 550: **105mm**: 70 M-101; **122mm**: 100 D-30; **130mm**: 100 M-46; **155mm**: 50 Soltam M-68/-71, 80 M-839P/-845P, 50 M-114A1, 100 Soltam M-46
SP ARTY 905: **155mm**: 150 L-33, 580 M-109A1/A2; **175mm**: 140 M-107; **203mm**: 35 M-110
MRL 198: **122mm**: 50 BM-21; **160mm**: 50 LAR-160; **227mm**: 48 MLRS; **240mm**: 30 BM-24; **290mm**: 20 LAR-290.
MOR 60mm: ε5,000; **81mm**: 700; **120mm**: 530; **160mm**: 240 (some SP)
SSM 20 *Lance* (in store), some *Jericho* 1/2
ATGW 300 TOW-2A/-B (incl *Ramta* (M-113) SP), 1,000 *Dragon*, AT-3 *Sagger*, 25 *Mapats*, *Gill*/*Spike*
RL 82mm: B-300
RCL 106mm: 250 M-40A1
SAM 250 *Stinger*, 1,000 *Redeye*, 48 *Chaparral*
SURV EL/M-2140 (veh), AN/TPQ-37 (arty), AN/PPS-15 (arty)

Navy ε6,500

(incl 2,500 conscripts), 11,500 on mob
BASES Haifa, Ashdod, Eilat

SUBMARINES 3

SSK 3 *Dolphin* (Ge Type 212 variant) with *Sub-Harpoon* USGW, 4 × 650mm ASTT, 6 × 533mm ASTT

PATROL AND COASTAL COMBATANTS 48

CORVETTES 3
3 *Eilat* (*Sa'ar* 5) FSG with 8 *Harpoon* SSM, 8 *Gabriel* II SSM, 2 *Barak* VLS SAM (2 × 32 mls), 1 × 76mm gun, 6 × 324mm ASTT, 1 SA-366G hel
MISSILE CRAFT 11
2 *Aliya* PFM with 4 *Harpoon* SSM, 4 *Gabriel* SSM, 1 SA-366G *Dauphin* hel
7 *Hetz* (*Sa'ar* 4.5) PFM with 8 *Harpoon* SSM, 6 *Gabriel* SSM, 6 *Barak* VLS SAM, 1 × 76mm gun
2 *Reshef* (*Sa'ar* 4) PFM with 8 *Harpoon* SSM, 6 *Gabriel* SSM, 1 × 76mm gun
PATROL, INSHORE 34
13 *Super Dvora* PFI<, some with 2 × 324mm TT
3 *Nashal* PCI
15 *Dabur* PFI< with 2 × 324mm TT
3 Type-1012 *Bobcat* catamaran PCC

AMPHIBIOUS craft only

1 *Ashdod* LCT, 1 US type LCM

NAVAL AVIATION

EQUIPMENT
HELICOPTERS
4 AS 565SA *Sea Panther*

NAVAL COMMANDOS ε300

Air Force 35,000

(20,000 conscripts, mainly in AD), 57,000 on mob; 454 cbt ac (plus perhaps 250 stored), 135 armed hel
Flying hours regulars: 180; reserves: 80
FGA/FTR 13 sqn
2 with 50 F-4E-2000, 20 F-4E
2 with 61 F-15 (27 -A, 7 -B, 16 -C, 11 -D)
1 with 25 F-15I
8 with 232 F-16 (90 -A, 18 -B, 75 -C, 49 -D)

FGA 1 sqn with 26 A-4N
RECCE 13* RF-4E
AEW 6 Boeing 707 with *Phalcon* system
EW 3 Boeing 707 (ELINT/ECM), 6 RC-12D, 3 IAI-200, 15 Do-28, 10 *King Air* 2000, 3 Gulfstream V on order (ELINT)
MR 3 IAI-1124 *Seascan*
TKR 5 KC-130H
TPT 1 wg incl 5 Boeing 707 (tpt/tkr), 11 C-47, 5 C-130H
LIAISON 2 *Islander*, 20 Cessna U-206, 8 *Queen Air* 80
TRG 45 CM-170 *Tzukit*, 28 *Super Cub*, 9* TA-4H, 17* TA-4J, 4 *Queen Air* 80
HELICOPTERS
ATTACK 16 AH-1E, 39 AH-1F, 33 Hughes 500MD, 42 AH-64A
ASW 5* AS-565A, 1 × SA-366G
TPT 41 CH-53D, 10 UH-60, 7 UH-60L; 15 S-70A *Blackhawk*, 54 Bell 212, 43 Bell 206
UAV *Scout*, *Searcher*, *Firebee*, *Samson*, *Delilah*, *Hunter*, *Hermes* 450, *SkyEye*, *Harpy*, *Hermes*

MISSILES
ASM AGM-45 *Shrike*, AGM-62A *Walleye*, AGM-65 *Maverick*, AGM-78D *Standard*, AGM-114 *Hellfire*, TOW, *Popeye* I + II, (GBU-31 JDAM undergoing IAF op/integration tests)
AAM AIM-7 *Sparrow*, AIM-9 *Sidewinder*, AIM-120B AMRAAM, R-530, *Shafrir*, *Python* III, *Python* IV
AD GUNS 20mm: 850: incl TCM-20, M-167 *Vulcan*, 35 M-163 *Vulcan*/M-48 *Chaparral* gun/msl, *Machbet Vulcan*/*Stinger* gun/msl SP system; **23mm**: 150 ZU-23 and 60 ZSU-23-4 SP; **37mm**: M-39; **40mm**: 150 L-70
SAM 17 bty with MIM-23 I HAWK, 3 bty *Patriot*, 1 bty Arrow 2, 8 bty *Chapparal*, *Stinger*

Forces Abroad

TURKEY occasional det of Air Force F-16 ac to Akinci air base

Paramilitary ε8,050

BORDER POLICE ε8,000
some *Walid* 1, 600 BTR-152 APC

COAST GUARD ε50
1 US PCR, 3 other patrol craft

Foreign Forces

UN (UNTSO): 139 mil obs from 23 countries

Jordan HKJ

Total Armed Forces

ACTIVE 100,240

RESERVES 35,000 (all services)
Army 30,000 (obligation to age 40)

Army 84,700

NORTHERN COMD
2 mech, 1 inf, 1 arty 1 AD bde
CENTRAL COMD
1 mech, 1 inf, 1 arty, 1 AD bde
EASTERN COMD
2 mech, 1 armd, 1 arty, 1 AD bde
1 Royal armd div with 3 armd, 1 arty, 1 AD bde
1 indep Royal Guard bde
1 Special Ops Comd with 1 Ranger, 1 AB, 1 SF bde
1 fd arty bde (4 bn)
Southern Mil Area (3 inf, 1 recce bn)

EQUIPMENT
MBT 1,179: 78 M-47/-48A5 (in store), 305 M-60 (117 -A1, 188 -A3), 274 *Khalid/Chieftain*, 281 *Tariq* (*Centurion*), ε241 *Challenger* 1 (*Al Hussein* (in total, 288 to be delivered))
LT TK 19 *Scorpion*
AIFV some 26 BMP-2
APC 1,400 M-113, 50 BTR-94 (BTR-80); ε50 *Spartan*
TOWED ARTY 113: **105mm**: 54 M-102; **155mm**: 38 M-114, 17 M-59/M-1; **203mm**: 4 M-115
SP ARTY 418: **105mm**: 35 M-52; **155mm**: 29 M-44, 234 M-109A1/A2; **203mm**: 120 M-110A2
MOR 81mm: 450 (incl 130 SP); **107mm**: 50 M-30; **120mm**: 300 Brandt
ATGW 330 TOW/-2A (incl 70 M-901 ITV), 310 *Dragon*, 30 *Javelin* (being delivered)
RL 94mm: 2,500 LAW-80; **112mm**: 2,300 APILAS
AD GUNS 416 incl: **20mm**: 100 M-163 *Vulcan* SP; **23mm**: 52 ZSU-23-4 SP
SAM SA-7B2, 52 SA-8, 92 SA-13, 300 SA-14, 240 SA-16, 260 *Redeye*
SURV AN-TPQ-36/-37 (arty, mor)

Navy ε540

BASE Aqaba

PATROL AND COASTAL COMBATANTS 3
PATROL CRAFT, INSHORE 3
3 *Al Hussein* (Vosper 30m) PFI<
plus 3 *Al Hashim* (Rotork) boats, 4 Bertram boats

Air Force 15,000

(incl 3,400 AD); 101 cbt ac, 22 armed hel
Flying hours 180
FGA/RECCE 4 sqn
3 with 55 F-5E/F
1 with 15 *Mirage* F-1EJ
FTR 2 sqn
1 with 15 *Mirage* F-1 CJ/BJ
1 with 16 F-16A/B (12 -A, 4 -B)
TPT 1 sqn with 4 C-130H, 2 C-212A, 2 CN-235, 2 TB-20, 2 CL-604
SURV 2 *Schweizer* RU-38A
VIP 1 royal flt with **ac** 2 *Gulfstream* IV, 1 L-1011, 1 Airbus A340-211 **hel** 4 S-70A
HELICOPTERS 3 sqn
ATTACK 2 with 22 AH-1F (with TOW ASM)
TPT 1 with 10 AS-332M, 50 UH-1H, 3 Bo-105 (operated on behalf of police)
TRG 3 sqn with ac: 15 *Bulldog* (being replaced by 16 T-67M *Firefly*), 13 C-101, hel: 8 Hughes 500D
AD 2 bde: 14 bty with 80 I HAWK

MISSILES

ASM TOW, AGM-65D *Maverick*, *Rockeye*
AAM AIM-7 *Sparrow*, AIM-9 *Sidewinder*, MATRA R-530, MATRA R-550 *Magic*

Forces Abroad

UN AND PEACEKEEPING

CROATIA (UNMOP): 1 obs **DROC** (MONUC): 28 incl 21 obs **EAST TIMOR** (UNMISET): 9 incl 4 obs **ETHIOPIA/ERITREA** (UNMEE): 965 incl 6 obs **GEORGIA** (UNOMIG): 6 obs **SIERRA LEONE** (UNAMSIL): 131 incl 10 obs **YUGOSLAVIA** (KFOR): 99

Paramilitary ε10,000 active

PUBLIC SECURITY DIRECTORATE (Ministry of Interior) ε10,000
(incl Police Public Sy bde); some *Scorpion* lt tk, 25 EE-11 *Urutu*, 30 *Saracen* APC

CIVIL MILITIA 'PEOPLE'S ARMY' (R) ε35,000
(to be 5,000) **men** 16–65 **women** 16–45

Kuwait Kwt

Total Armed Forces

ACTIVE 15,500
Terms of service voluntary

RESERVES 23,700
obligation to age 40; 1 month annual trg

Army 11,000

(incl 1,600 foreign personnel)
3 armd bde • 2 mech inf bde • 1 recce (mech) bde • 1 force arty bde • 1 force engr bde
1 reserve bde • 1 *Amiri* gd bde • 1 cdo bn

EQUIPMENT

MBT 150 M-84 (ε50% in store), 218 M-1A2
AIFV 76 BMP-2, 120 BMP-3, 254 *Desert Warrior* (incl variants)
APC 60 M-113A2, 40 M-577, 40 *Fahd* (in store), 11 TPz-1 *Fuchs*
SP ARTY 155mm: 23 M-109A3, 18 GCT (in store), 18 F-3, 27 PLZ 45
MRL 300mm: 27 *Smerch* 9A52
MOR 81mm: 60; **107mm**: 6 M-30; **120mm**: ε12 RT-F1
ATGW 118 TOW/TOW II (incl 8 M-901 ITV; 66 HMMWV), *Dragon*
RCL 84mm: ε200 *Carl Gustav*

Navy ε2,000

(incl 500 Coast Guard)
BASE Ras al Qalaya

PATROL AND COASTAL COMBATANTS 10

MISSILE CRAFT 10
8 *Um Almaradim* (Fr P-37 BRL) PFM with 4 *Sea Skua* SSM, 1 × 6 Sadral SAM
1 *Istiqlal* (Ge Lürssen FPB-57) PFM with 2 × 2 MM-40 *Exocet* SSM
1 *Al Sanbouk* (Ge Lürssen TNC-45) PFM with 2 × 2 MM-40 *Exocet* SSM
plus about 30 boats

SUPPORT AND MISCELLANEOUS 6

2 LCM, 4 spt

Air Force ε2,500

81 cbt ac, 20 armed hel
Flying hours 210
FTR/FGA 40 F/A-18 (-C 32, -D 8)
FTR 14 *Mirage* F1-CK/BK (non-op)
CCT 1 sqn with 11 *Hawk* 64, 16 Shorts *Tucano*
TPT ac 3 L-100-30, 1 DC-9 **hel** 4 AS-332 (tpt/SAR/attack), 8 SA-330
TRG/ATK hel 16 SA-342 (with HOT)

AIR DEFENCE

4 HAWK Phase III bty with 24 launchers
6 bty *Amoun* (each bty, 1 *Skyguard* radar, 2 *Aspide* launchers, 2 twin **35mm** Oerlikon), 48 *Starburst*

Paramilitary ε6,600 active

NATIONAL GUARD ε6,600

3 national guard bn, 1 armd car, 1 SF, 1 mil police bn; 20 VBL recce, 70 *Pandur* APC (incl variants)

COAST GUARD (500 [manpower included in naval total])

4 *Inttisar* (Aust 31.5m) PCC, 1 *Al Shaheed* PCC, 3 LCU
Plus some 30 armed boats

Foreign Forces

UN (UNIKOM): some 904 tps and 193 obs from 31 countries
UK Air Force (Southern Watch): 12 Tornado-GR1/1A
US 7,388: **Army** 5,000; prepo eqpt for 1 armd bde (2 tk, 1 mech, 1 arty bn) **Air Force** 2,000 (Southern Watch); Force structure varies with ac detachments **Navy** 10 **USMC** 378
GERMANY (OP ENDURING FREEDOM): 50

Lebanon RL

Total Armed Forces

ACTIVE 71,830 (incl 22,600 conscripts)
Terms of Service 1 year

Army 70,000 (incl conscripts)

5 regional comd
11 mech inf bde (-) • 1 Presidential Guard bde, 1 MP bde, 1 cdo/Ranger, 5 SF regt • 1 air aslt regt • 1 mne cdo regt • 2 arty regt

EQUIPMENT

MBT 115 M-48A1/A5, 212 T-54/-55
LT TK 36 AMX-13
RECCE 67 AML, 22 *Saladin*
APC 1,164 M-113A1/A2, 81 VAB-VCI, 81 AMX-VCI, 12 Panhard M3/VTT
TOWED ARTY 105mm: 13 M-101A1; **122mm**: 36 M-1938, 26 D-30; **130mm**: 20 M-46; **155mm**: 12 Model 50, 18 M-114A1, 35 M-198
MRL 122mm: 23 BM-21
MOR 81mm: 158; **82mm**: 111; **120mm**: 108 Brandt
ATGW ENTAC, *Milan*, 20 BGM-71A TOW
RL 85mm: RPG-7; **89mm**: M-65
RCL 106mm: M-40A1
AD GUNS 20mm; 23mm: ZU-23; **40mm**: 10 M-42A1

Navy 830

BASES Jounieh, Beirut

PATROL AND COASTAL COMBATANTS 7

PATROL CRAFT, INSHORE 7
5 UK *Attacker* PCI<, 2 UK *Tracker* PCI<, plus 27 armed boats

AMPHIBIOUS 2
2 *Sour* (Fr *Edic*) LST, capacity 96 tps

Air Force 1,000

All ac grounded and in store

EQUIPMENT

HEL 16 UH-1H, 1 SA-318, 3 SA-316, 5 Bell-212, 3 SA-330, 2 SA-342
TRG 3 *Bulldog*

Paramilitary ε13,000 active

INTERNAL SECURITY FORCE ε13,000 (Ministry of Interior)
(incl Regional and Beirut *Gendarmerie* coy plus Judicial Police); 30 *Chaimite* APC

CUSTOMS
2 *Tracker* PCI<, 5 *Aztec* PCI<

Opposition

MILITIAS

Most militias, except *Hizbollah*, have been substantially disbanded and hy wpn handed over to the National Army.
HIZBOLLAH ('Party of God'; Shi'a, fundamentalist, pro-Ir): ε3–500 (-) active; about 2,000 in spt
EQUIPMENT arty, 107mm/122mm MRL, RL, RCL, ATGW (AT-3 *Sagger*, AT-4 *Spigot*), AA guns, SAM

Foreign Forces

UN (UNIFIL): 3,638; 5 inf bn, 1 each from **Fji**, **Gha**, **Ind**, **PL**, **Ukr**, plus spt units from **Fr**, **It**, **Slvk**, **Irl**
IRAN ε150 Revolutionary Guard
SYRIA 18,000 **Beirut** elm 1 mech inf bde, 5 SF regt **Metn** elm 1 mech inf bde **Bekaa** 1 mech inf div HQ, elm 2 mech inf, elm 1 armd bde **Tripoli** 1 SF regt **Batrum** 1 SF Regt **Kfar Falous** elm 3 SF regt

Libya LAR

Total Armed Forces

ACTIVE 76,000
(incl ε38,000 conscripts)
Terms of service selective conscription, 1–2 years

RESERVES some 40,000

People's Militia

Army 45,000

(ε25,000 conscripts)

11 Border Def and 4 Sy Zones • 1 élite bde (regime sy force) • 10 tk bn • 22 arty bn • 18 inf bn • 7 AD arty bn • 10 mech inf bn • 6 para/cdo bn • 4 SSM bde

EQUIPMENT

MBT 560 T-55, 280 T-62, 145 T-72 (plus some 1,040 T-54/-55, 70 T-62, 115 T-72 in store†)

RECCE 166 BRDM-2, 272 EE-9 *Cascavel*

AIFV 1,000 BMP-1

APC 750 BTR-50/-60, 67 OT-62/-64, 28 M-113, 100 EE-11 *Urutu*, some BMD

TOWED ARTY some 647: **105mm**: some 42 M-101; **122mm**: 190 D-30, 60 D-74; **130mm**: 330 M-46; **152mm**: 25 M-1937

SP ARTY: 444: **122mm**: 130 2S1; **152mm**: 60 2S3, 80 DANA; **155mm**: 160 *Palmaria*, 14 M-109

MRL 107mm: ε300 Type 63; **122mm**: ε230 BM-21, ε100 RM-70, ε200 BM-11

MOR some 500 incl: **82mm; 120mm**: ε48 M-43; **160mm**: ε24 M-160

SSM launchers: 40 FROG-7, 80 *Scud*-B (SSM msl totals ε450-500) **No-dong 1** (reported)

ATGW 3,000: *Milan*, AT-3 *Sagger* (incl BRDM SP), AT-4 *Spigot*, AT-5 *Spandrel*

RL 73mm: RPG-7

RCL 84mm: *Carl Gustav*; **106mm**: 220 M-40A1

AD GUNS 600: **23mm**: ZU-23, ZSU-23-4 SP; **30mm**: M-53/59 SP; **57mm**: S-60

SAM SA-7/-9/-13, 24 quad *Crotale*

SURV RASIT (veh, arty)

Navy 8,000

(incl Coast Guard)

BASES Major Tripoli, Benghazi, Tobruk, Khums **Minor** Derna, Zuwurah, Misonhah

SUBMARINES 1†

SSK 1 *Al Badr* † (FSU *Foxtrot*) with 533mm and 406mm TT (plus 2 non-op)

PRINCIPAL SURFACE COMBATANTS 1

FRIGATES 1

FFG 1 *Al Hani* (FSU *Koni*) with 4 SS-N-2C *Styx* SSM, 4 ASTT, 2 ASW RL (plus 1 non-op)

PATROL AND COASTAL COMBATANTS 9

CORVETTES 1

1 *Ean al Gazala* (FSU *Nanuchka* II) FSG with 2 × 2 SS-N-2C *Styx* SSM (plus 1 non-op)

MISSILE CRAFT 8

5 *Sharaba* (Fr *Combattante* II) PFM with 4 *Otomat* SSM, 1 × 76mm gun (plus 4 non-op)

3 *Al Katum* (FSU *Osa* II) PFM with 4 SS-N-2C *Styx* SSM (plus 9 non-op)

MINE WARFARE 6

MINE COUNTERMEASURES 6

6 *Ras al Gelais* (FSU *Natya*) MSO (plus 6 non-op)

AMPHIBIOUS 3

2 *Ibn Ouf* LST, capacity 240 tps, 11 tk, 1 SA-316B hel

1 FSU *Polnocny* LSM, capacity 180 tps, 6 tk (plus 2 non-op)

Plus craft: 3 LCT

SUPPORT AND MISCELLANEOUS 9

1 *El Temsah* tpt, about 5 other ro-ro tpt, 1 *Zeltin* log spt; 1 ARS, 1 diving spt

NAVAL AVIATION

EQUIPMENT

7 armed hel

HELICOPTERS

7 SA-321 (Air Force assets)

COASTAL DEFENCE

1 SSC-3 *Styx* bty

Air Force 23,000

(incl Air Defence Command; ε13,000 conscripts) 400 cbt ac, 41 armed hel (many non-operational) (many ac in store) **Flying hours** 85

BBR 1 sqn with 6 Tu-22

FGA 7 sqn with 40 MiG-23BN, 15 MiG-23U, 30 *Mirage* 5D/DE, 14 *Mirage* 5DD, 14 *Mirage* F-1AD, 6 Su-24 MK, 53 Su-20/-22

FTR 9 sqn with 45 MiG-21, 75 MiG-23, 70 MiG-25, 3 -25U, 15 *Mirage* F-1ED, 3 -BD

RECCE 2 sqn with 4* *Mirage* 5DR, 7* MiG-25R

TPT 7 sqn with 23 An-26, 12 Lockheed (7 C-130H, 2 L-100-20, 3 L-100-30), 6 G-222, 25 Il-76, 15 L-410, 2 An-124

ATTACK HEL 29 Mi-25, 12 Mi-35

TPT HEL hy 17 CH-47C **med** 34 Mi-8/17 **lt** 11 SA-316, 5 AB-206

TRG ac 102 *Galeb* G-2 **hel** 50 Mi-2 **other ac** incl 1 Tu-22, 115 L-39ZO, 20 SF-260WL

MISSILES

ASM AT-2 *Swatter* ATGW (hel-borne), AS-7, AS-9, AS-11

AAM AA-2 *Atoll*, AA-6 *Acrid*, AA-7 *Apex*, AA-8 *Aphid*, R-530, R-550 *Magic*

AIR DEFENCE COMMAND

Senezh AD comd and control system

4 bde with SA-5A: each 2 bn of 6 launchers, some 4 AD arty gun bn; radar coy
5 Regions: 5–6 bde each 18 SA-2; 2–3 bde each 12 twin SA-3; ε3 bde each 20–24 SA-6/-8

Forces Abroad

CAR: ε300 (reported)

Paramilitary

CUSTOMS/COAST GUARD (Naval control)

a few patrol craft incl in naval totals, plus armed boats

Mauritania RIM

Total Armed Forces

ACTIVE ε15,750

Terms of service conscription 24 months authorised

Army 15,000

6 Mil Regions • 7 mot inf bn • 8 garrison inf bn • 1 para/cdo bn • 1 Presidential sy bn • 2 Camel Corps bn • 3 arty bn • 4 AD arty bty • 1 engr coy • 1 armd recce sqn

EQUIPMENT

MBT 35 T-54/-55
RECCE 60 AML (20 -60, 40 -90), 10 *Saladin*, 5 *Saracen*
TOWED ARTY 105mm: 35 M-101A1/HM-2; **122mm**: 20 D-30, 20 D-74
MOR 81mm: 110; **120mm**: 30 Brandt
ATGW 50 *Milan*
RL 73mm: RPG-7
RCL 75mm: ε20 M-20; **106mm**: 40 M-40A1
AD GUNS 23mm: 20 ZU-23-2; **37mm**: 10 M-1939; **57mm**: 2 S-60; **100mm**: 12 KS-19
SAM 30 SA-7, SA-9 (reported)

Navy ε500

BASES Nouadhibou, Nouakchott

PATROL AND COASTAL COMBATANTS 7

PATROL CRAFT 7
OFFSHORE 2
1 *Aboubekr Ben Amer* (Fr OPV 54) PCO
1 *N'Madi* (UK *Jura*) PCO (fishery protection)
COASTAL 1
1 *El Nasr* (Fr *Patra*) PCC
INSHORE 4
4 *Mandovi* PCI<

Air Force 250

8 cbt ac, no armed hel
CCT 5 BN-2 *Defender*, 2 FTB-337 *Milirole*, 1 Basler T-67
MR 2 *Cheyenne* II
TPT 2 Cessna F-337, 1 DHC-5D, 1 *Gulfstream* II, 2 Y-12 (II)

Paramilitary ε5,000 active

GENDARMERIE (Ministry of Interior) ε3,000

6 regional coy

NATIONAL GUARD (Ministry of Interior) 2,000

plus 1,000 auxiliaries

CUSTOMS

1 *Dah Ould Bah* (Fr *Amgram* 14)

Morocco Mor

Total Armed Forces

ACTIVE 196,300

(incl ε100,000 conscripts)
Terms of service conscription 18 months authorised; most enlisted personnel are volunteers

RESERVES

Army 150,000; obligation to age 50

Army 175,000

(ε100,000 conscripts)
2 Comd (Northern Zone, Southern Zone) • 3 mech inf bde • 1 lt sy bde • 2 para bde • 8 mech/mot inf regt • Indep units
11 armd bn • 2 cav bn • 39 inf bn • 1 mtn inf bn • 2 para bn • 3 mot (camel corps) bn • 9 arty bn • 7 engr bn • 1 AD gp • 7 cdo units

ROYAL GUARD 1,500

1 bn, 1 cav sqn

EQUIPMENT

MBT 224 M-48A5 (in store), 420 M-60 (300 -A1, 120 -A3), 100 T-72
LT TK 100 SK-105 *Kuerassier*
RECCE 16 EBR-75, 80 AMX-10RC, 190 AML-90, 38 AML-60-7
AIFV 60 *Ratel* (30 -20, 30 -90), 45 VAB-VCI, 10 AMX-10P
APC 420 M-113A1, 320 VAB-VTT
TOWED ARTY 105mm: 30 L-118, 20 M-101, 36 M-1950; **130mm**: 18 M-46; **155mm**: 20 M-114, 35 FH-70, 26 M-198

SP ARTY 105mm: 5 Mk 61; **155mm**: 98 F-3, 44 M-109A1, 20 M-44; **203mm**: 60 M-110
MRL 122mm: 26 BM-21, 14 M-1979
MOR 81mm: 870; **120mm**: 600 Brandt (incl 20 VAB SP)
ATGW 440 *Dragon*, 80 *Milan*, 150 TOW (incl 80 on M-901), 50 AT-3 *Sagger*
RL 66mm: LAW; **89mm**: 150 3.5in M-20
RCL 106mm: 350 M-40A1
ATK GUNS 90mm: 28 M-56; **100mm**: 8 SU-100 SP
AD GUNS 14.5mm: 200 ZPU-2, 20 ZPU-4; **20mm**: 40 M-167, 60 M-163 *Vulcan* SP; **23mm**: 90 ZU-23-2; **100mm**: 15 KS-19 towed
SAM 37 M-54 SP *Chaparral*, 70 SA-7
SURV RASIT (veh, arty)
UAV R4E-50 *SkyEye*

Navy 7,800

(incl 1,500 Marines)
BASES Casablanca, Agadir, Al Hoceima, Dakhla, Tangier

PRINCIPAL SURFACE COMBATANTS 2

FRIGATES 2
FFG 2
1 *Mohammed V* (Fr mod *Floreal*) with 2 MM-38 *Exocet* SSM, 1 × 76mm gun, 1 AS 565 *Panther* hel
1 *Lt Col Errhamani* (Sp *Descubierta*) with *Aspide* SAM, 1 × 76mm gun, 2 × 3 ASTT (Mk 46 LWT), 1 × 2 375mm AS mor (fitted for 4 MM-38 *Exocet* SSM)

PATROL AND COASTAL COMBATANTS 27

MISSILE CRAFT 4 *Cdt El Khattabi* (Sp *Lazaga* 58m) PFM with 4 MM-38 *Exocet* SSM, 1 × 76mm gun
PATROL CRAFT 23
COASTAL 17
2 *Okba* (Fr PR-72) PCC with 1 × 76mm gun
6 *LV Rabhi* (Sp 58m B-200D) PCC
4 *El Hahiq* (Dk *Osprey* 55) PCC (incl 2 with customs)
5 *Rais Bargach* (under control of fisheries dept)
INSHORE 6 *El Wacil* (Fr P-32) PFI< (incl 4 with customs)

AMPHIBIOUS 4

3 *Ben Aicha* (Fr *Champlain* BATRAL) LSM, capacity 140 tps, 7 tk
1 *Sidi Mohammed Ben Abdallah* (US Newport) LST, capacity 400 troops
Plus craft: 1 *Edic*-type LCT

SUPPORT AND MISCELLANEOUS 4

2 log spt, 1 tpt, 1 AGOR (US lease)

NAVAL AVIATION

EQUIPMENT
HELICOPTERS
2 AS 565 *Panther*

MARINES (1,500)

2 naval inf bn

Air Force 13,500

95 cbt ac, 24 armed hel
Flying hours F-5 and *Mirage*: over 100
FGA 8 F-5A, 3 F-5B, 24 F-5E, 4 F-5F, 14 *Mirage* F-1EH
FTR 1 sqn with 15 *Mirage* F-1CH
RECCE 2 C-130H (with side-looking radar), 4* 0V-10
EW 2 C-130 (ELINT), 2 *Falcon* 20 (ELINT)
TKR 1 Boeing 707, 2 KC-130H (tpt/tkr)
TPT 12 C-130H, 7 CN-235, 2 Do-28, 2 *Falcon 20*, 1 *Falcon 50* (VIP), 2 *Gulfstream* II (VIP), 4 *King Air* 100, 3 *King Air* 200
HELICOPTERS
ATTACK 24 SA-342 (12 with HOT, 12 with cannon)
TPT hy 7 CH-47 **med** 29 SA-330, 30 AB-205A **lt** 20 AB-206, 3 AB-212
TRG 8 AS-202, 2 CAP-10, 4 CAP-230, 10 T-34C, 14 T-37B (being replaced by K-8), 23* *Alpha Jet*
LIAISON 2 *King Air 200*, 2 UH-60 *Blackhawk*
AAM AIM-9B/D/J *Sidewinder*, R-530, R-550 *Magic*
ASM AGM-65B *Maverick* (for F-5E), HOT

Forces Abroad

UN AND PEACEKEEPING

BOSNIA (SFOR II): ε800; 1 mot inf bn **DROC** (MONUC): 619 **YUGOSLAVIA** (KFOR): 279

Paramilitary 50,000 active

GENDARMERIE ROYALE 20,000

1 bde, 4 mobile gp, 1 para sqn, air sqn, coast guard unit
EQPT 18 boats **ac** 2 *Rallye* **hel** 3 SA-315, 3 SA-316, 2 SA-318, 6 *Gazelle*, 6 SA-330, 2 SA-360

FORCE AUXILIAIRE 30,000

incl 5,000 Mobile Intervention Corps

CUSTOMS/COAST GUARD

4 *Erraid* PCI, 32 boats, 3 SAR craft

Opposition

POLISARIO FRONT ε3–6,000

Mil wing of Sahrawi People's Liberation Army, org in bn
EQPT 100 T-55, T-62 tk; 50+ BMP-1, 20–30 EE-9 *Cascavel* MICV; 25 D-30/M-30 **122mm** how; 15 BM-21 **122mm** MRL; 20 **120mm** mor; AT-3 *Sagger* ATGW; 50 ZSU-23-2, ZSU-23-4 **23mm** SP AA guns; SA-6/-7/-8/-9 SAM (Captured Mor eqpt incl AML-90, *Eland* armd recce, *Ratel* 20, Panhard APC, Steyr SK-105 *Kuerassier* lt tks)

Foreign Forces

UN (MINURSO): some 27 tps, 204 mil obs in Western Sahara from 25 countries

Oman O

Total Armed Forces

ACTIVE 41,700

(incl Royal Household tps, and some 2,000 foreign personnel)

Army 25,000

(regt are bn size)

1 armd, 2 inf bde HQ • 2 armd regt (3 tk sqn) • 1 armd recce regt (3 sqn) • 8 inf regt • 4 arty (2 fd, 1 med (2 bty), 1 AD (2 bty)) regt • 1 inf recce regt (3 recce coy), 2 indep recce coy • 1 fd engr regt (3 sqn) • 1 AB regt • Musandam Security Force (indep rifle coy)

EQUIPMENT

MBT 6 M-60A1, 73 M-60A3, 38 *Challenger* 2
LT TK 37 *Scorpion*
RECCE 50 VBL
APC 6 *Spartan*, 13 *Sultan*, 10 *Stormer*, 160 *Piranha*
TOWED ARTY 96: **105mm**: 42 ROF lt; **122mm**: 30 D-30; **130mm**: 12 M-46, 12 Type 59-1
SP ARTY 155mm: 24 G-6
MOR 81mm: 69; **107mm**: 20 4.2in M-30; **120mm**: 12 Brandt
ATGW 18 TOW/-2A (some SP), 30 *Milan*
RL 73mm: RPG-7; **94mm**: LAW-80
AD GUNS 23mm: 4 ZU-23-2; **35mm**: 10 GDF-005 with *Skyguard*; **40mm**: 12 Bofors L/60
SAM 14 *Javelin*, *Mistral* 2 (SP), 34 SA-7

Navy 4,200

BASES Seeb (HQ), Wudam (main base), Alwi, Ghanam Island, Mussandam, Salalah

PATROL AND COASTAL COMBATANTS 13

CORVETTES 2 *Qahir Al Amwaj* FSG with 8 MM-40 *Exocet* SSM, 8 *Crotale* SAM, 1 × 76mm gun, 6 × 324mm TT, hel deck
MISSILE CRAFT 4 *Dhofar* PFM, 1 with 2 × 3 MM-40 *Exocet* SSM, 3 with 2 × 4 MM-40 *Exocet* SSM
PATROL CRAFT, COASTAL/INSHORE 7
3 *Al Bushra* (Fr P-400) PCC with 1 × 76m gun, 4 × 406mm TT
4 *Seeb* (Vosper 25m) PCI<

AMPHIBIOUS 1

1 *Nasr el Bahr* LST†, capacity 240 tps, 7 tk, hel deck
Plus craft: 3 LCM, 1 LCU

SUPPORT AND MISCELLANEOUS 4

1 *Al Sultana* AK, 1 *Al Mabrukah* trg with hel deck (also used in offshore patrol role), 1 supply, 1 AGHS

Air Force 4,100

40 cbt ac, no armed hel
FGA 2 sqn, each with 8 *Jaguar* S(O) Mk 1, 4 T-2 (being progressively upgraded to (S01) GR-3 standard)
FGA/RECCE 12 *Hawk* 203
CCT 1 sqn with 12* PC-9, 4* *Hawk* 103
TPT 3 sqn
1 with 3 BAC-111
2 with 10 *Skyvan* 3M (7 radar-equipped, for MR), 3 C-130H
HEL 2 med tpt sqn with 19 AB-205, 3 AB-206, 3 AB-212, 5 AB-214
TRG 4 AS-202-18, 7 MFI-17B *Mushshak*
AD 2 sqn with 40 *Rapier* SAM, *Martello* radar, 6 *Blindfire* radar
AAM AIM-9M *Sidewinder*

Royal Household 6,400

(incl HQ staff) 2 SF regt (1,000)
Royal Guard bde (5,000) 9 VBC-90 lt tk, 14 VAB-VCI, ε50 PRC WZ-551 APC, 9 VAB-VDAA, 6 PRC Type-90A MRL, *Milan* ATGW, 14 *Javelin* SAM
Royal Yacht Squadron (based Muscat) (150) 1 Royal Yacht *Al Said*, 3,800t with hel deck, 1 *Fulk Al Salamah* tps and veh tpt with up to 2 AS-332C *Puma* hel, 1 *Zinat Al Bihaar* dhow
Royal Flight (250) **ac** 2 Boeing-747 SP, 1 DC-8-73CF, 2 *Gulfstream* IV **hel** 3 AS-330, 2 AS-332C, 1 AS-332L

Paramilitary 4,400 active

TRIBAL HOME GUARD (*Firqat*) 4,000
org in teams of ε100

POLICE COAST GUARD 400
3 CG 29 PCI<, plus 14 craft

POLICE AIR WING
ac 1 Do-228, 2 CN 235M, 1 BN-2T *Islander* **hel** 2 Bell 205A, 3 Bell 214ST

Foreign Forces

US 260 **Air Force** 200 **Navy** 60

Palestinian Autonomous Areas of Areas of Gaza and Jericho PA

Total Armed Forces

ACTIVE Nil

Paramilitary ε29,000

PUBLIC SECURITY 6,000 Gaza, 8,000 West Bank

CIVIL POLICE 4,000 Gaza, 6,000 West Bank

PREVENTIVE SECURITY 1,200 Gaza, 1,800 West Bank

General Intelligence 1,000

Military Intelligence 500

PRESIDENTIAL SECURITY ε500

Others include **Coastal Police, Civil Defence, Air Force, Customs and Excise Police Force, University Security Service**

PALESTINIAN GROUPS

All significant Palestinian factions are listed irrespective of where they are based. Est number of active 'fighters' are given; these could perhaps be doubled to give an all-told figure. In 1991, the Lebanon Armed Forces (LAF), backed by Syr, entered refugee camps in southern RL to disarm many Palestinian gps of their heavier wpns, such as tk, arty and APCs. The LAF conducted further disarming ops against *Fatah* Revolutionary Council (FRC) refugee camps in spring 1994.

PLO (Palestine Liberation Organisation) **Leader** Yasser Arafat
FATAH Political wing of the PLO
PLF (Palestine Liberation Front) ε200 **Leader** Al Abas **Based** Irq
DFLP (Democratic Front for the Liberation of Palestine) ε100 **Leader** Nayef Hawatmeh **Based** Syr, RL, elsewhere **Abd Rabbu faction** ε150–200 **Based** HKJ
PFLP (Popular Front for the Liberation of Palestine) ε1,000 **Leader** Ahmad Sadaat **Based** Syr, RL, Occupied Territories
PSF (Popular Struggle Front) ε200 **Leader** Samir Ghansha; **Based** Syr
ARAB LIBERATION FRONT ε500 **Leader** Abdel al Rahim Ahmad **Based** RL, Irq

GROUPS OPPOSED TO THE PLO

***FATAH* DISSIDENTS** (Abu Musa gp) ε1,000 **Based** Syr, RL
FRC (*Fatah* Revolutionary Council, Abu Nidal Organisation) ε300 **Based** RL, Syr, Irq, elsewhere
PFLP (GC) (Popular Front for the Liberation of Palestine (General Command)) ε500 **Leader** Ahmad Jibril
PFLP (SC) (Popular Front for the Liberation of Palestine – Special Command) 50–100 **Leader** Salim abu Salim **Based** RL, Irq, Syr
AL SAIQA ε300 **Leader** al-Khadi; **Based** Syr
IZZ AL-DIN AL-QASSEM (HAMAS MILITARY WING) ε500 **Based** Occupied Territories
PALESTINE ISLAMIC JIHAD (PIJ) ε500 all factions **Based** Occupied Territories
PALESTINE LIBERATION FRONT ε3–400 Abd al-Fatah Ghanim faction **Based** Syr
PLA (Palestine Liberation Army) ε2,000 **Based** Syr

Qatar Q

Total Armed Forces

ACTIVE ε12,400

Army 8,500

1 Royal Guard regt • 1 tk bn • 4 mech inf bn • 1 fd arty regt • 1 mor bn • 1 ATK bn • 1 SF 'bn' (coy)

EQUIPMENT

MBT 35 AMX-30
RECCE 16 VBL, 12 AMX-10RC, 8 V-150
AIFV 40 AMX-10P
LAV 36 *Piranha* II
APC 160 VAB, 30 AMX-VCI
TOWED ARTY 155mm: 12 G5
SP ARTY 155mm: 28 F-3
MRL 4 ASTROS II
MOR 81mm: 30 L16 (some SP); **120mm**: 15 Brandt
ATGW 100 *Milan*, HOT (incl 24 VAB SP)
RCL 84mm: ε40 *Carl Gustav*

Navy ε1,800

(incl Marine Police)
BASE Doha (HQ), Halul Island

PATROL AND COASTAL COMBATANTS 7

MISSILE CRAFT 7
3 *Damsah* (Fr *Combattante* III) PFM with 2 × 4 MM-40 *Exocet* SSM
4 *Barzan* (UK *Vita*) PFM with 8 MM-40 *Exocet* SSM, 6 *Mistral* SAM, 1 × 76mm gun
Plus some 20 small craft operated by Marine Police

COASTAL DEFENCE

4 × 3 *quad* MM-40 *Exocet* SSM bty

Air Force 2,100

18 cbt ac, 19 armed hel
FGA/FTR 2 sqn

1 with 6 *Alpha* jets
1 with 12 *Mirage* 2000-5 (9 EDA, 3 DDA)
TPT 1 sqn with 2 Boeing 707, 1 Boeing 727, 2 *Falcon* 900, 1 *Airbus* A340
ATTACK HEL 11 SA-342L (with HOT), 8 *Commando* Mk 3 (*Exocet*)
TPT 4 *Commando* (3 Mk 2A tpt, 1 Mk 2C VIP)

MISSILES

ASM *Exocet* AM-39, HOT, *Apache*
AAM MATRA R550 *Magic*, MATRA *Mica*
SAM 9 *Roland* 2, 24 *Mistral*, 12 *Stinger*, 20 SA-7 *Grail*, 10 *Blowpipe*

Foreign Forces

US Army ε100; prepo eqpt for 1 armd bde

Saudi Arabia Sau

Total Armed Forces

ACTIVE ε124,500
(plus 75,000 active National Guard)

Army 75,000

3 armd bde (each 3 tk, 1 mech, 1 fd arty, 1 recce, 1 AD, 1 ATK bn) • 5 mech bde (each 3 mech, 1 tk, 1 fd arty, 1 AD, 1 spt bn) • 1 AB bde (2 AB bn, 3 SF coy) • 1 Royal Guard regt (3 bn) • 8 arty bn • 1 army avn comd with 2 avn bde

EQUIPMENT

MBT 315 M-1A2 *Abrams* (ε200 in store), 290 AMX-30 (50% in store), 450 M60A3
RECCE 300 AML-60/-90
AIFV 570+ AMX-10P, 400 M-2 *Bradley*
APC 1,750 M-113 A1/A2/A3 (incl variants), 150 Panhard M-3, ε40 *Al-Fahd*
TOWED ARTY 105mm: 100 M-101/-102 (in store); **155mm**: 40 FH-70 (in store), 40 M-198, 50 M-114; **203mm**: 8 M-115 (in store)
SP ARTY 155mm: 110 M-109A1B/A2, 60 GCT
MRL 60 ASTROS II
MOR 400, incl: **81mm**: (incl 70 SP); **107mm**: 4.2in M-30 (incl 150 SP); **120mm**: 110 Brandt
SSM some 12 PRC CSS-2 (120 msl reported)
ATGW 950 TOW/-2A (incl 200 VCC-1 SP), 1,000 M-47 *Dragon*, HOT (incl 100 AMX-10P SP)
RL 112mm: ε200 APILAS
RCL 84mm: 300 *Carl Gustav*; **90mm**: 100 M-67; **106mm**: 50 M-40A1
ATTACK HEL 12 AH-64
TPT HEL 12 S-70A-1, 22 UH-60A (4 medevac), 6 SA-365N (medevac), 15 Bell 406CS
SAM *Crotale*, 500 *Stinger*, 500 *Redeye*
SURV AN/TPQ-36/-37 (arty, mor)

Navy 15,500

(incl 3,000 Marines)
BASES Riyadh (HQ Naval Forces) **Western Fleet** Jeddah (HQ), Jizan, Al Wajh **Eastern Fleet** Jubail (HQ), Dammam, Ras al Mishab, Ras al Ghar

PRINCIPAL SURFACE COMBATANTS 8

FRIGATES 4
FFG 4
4 *Madina* (Fr F-2000) with 8 *Otomat* 2 SSM, 8 *Croatale* SAM, 1 × 100mm gun, 4 × 533mm ASTT, 1 SA 365F hel
CORVETTES 4
4 *Badr* (US *Tacoma*) FSG with 2 × 4 *Harpoon* SSM, 1 × 76mm gun, 2 × 3 ASTT (Mk 46 LWT)

PATROL AND COASTAL COMBATANTS 26

MISSILE CRAFT 9 *Al Siddiq* (US 58m) PFM with 2 × 2 *Harpoon* SSM, 1 × 76mm gun
PATROL CRAFT 17 US Halter Marine PCI< (some with Coast Guard) plus 40 craft

MINE WARFARE 7

MINE COUNTERMEASURES 7
3 *Al Jawf* (UK *Sandown*) MHO
4 *Addriyah* (US *MSC-322*) MCC†

AMPHIBIOUS (craft only)

4 LCU, 4 LCM

SUPPORT AND MISCELLANEOUS 7

2 *Boraida* (mod Fr *Durance*) AO with 1 or 2 hel, 3 AT/F, 1 ARS, 1 Royal Yacht with hel deck

NAVAL AVIATION

EQUIPMENT
21 armed hel
HELICOPTERS
19 AS-565 (4 SAR, 15 with AS-15TT ASM), 12 AS-332B/F (6 tpt, 6 with AM-39 *Exocet*)

MARINES (3,000)

1 inf regt (2 bn) with 140 BMR-600P

Air Force 18,000

294 cbt ac, no armed hel
FGA 4 sqn
1 with 15 F-5B/F/RF (53 F-5E on strength, but most off-line)
3 with 85 *Tornado* IDS (incl 10 IDS recce)
FTR 9 sqn
1 with 22 *Tornado* ADV
5 with 86 F-15 (67 -C, 19 -D)

3 with 72 F-15S
AEW 1 sqn with 5 E-3A
TKR 8 KE-3A, 8 KC-130H (tkr/tpt)
OCU 2 sqn with 14* F-5B
TPT 3 sqn with 38 C-130 (7 -E, 29 -H, 2 H-30), 3 L-100-30HS (hospital ac), 4 CN-235
HEL 2 sqn with 22 AB-205, 13 AB-206A, 17 AB-212, 40 AB-41EP (SAR), 10 AS-532A2 (CSAR)

TRG 3 sqn with 43 *Hawk* (25 Mk 65, 18 Mk 65A) (incl aerobatic team), 2 sqn with 45 PC-9, 1 sqn with 1 *Jetstream* 31, 1 sqn with 13 Cessna 172

ROYAL FLT ac 2 Boeing-747SP, 1 Boeing-737-200, 4 BAe 125–800, 2 *Gulfstream* III, 2 *Learjet* 35, 4 VC-130H, 1 Cessna 310 **hel** 3 AS-61, AB-212, 1 S-70

MISSILES

ASM AGM-65 *Maverick*, *Sea Eagle*, ALARM
AAM AIM-9J/L/M/P *Sidewinder*, AIM-7F *Sparrow*, *Skyflash*

Air Defence Forces 16,000

33 SAM bty
16 with 128 I HAWK
17 with 68 *Shahine* fire units and AMX-30SA 30mm SP AA guns
73 *Shahine/Crotale* fire units as static defence

EQUIPMENT

AD GUNS 20mm: 92 M-163 *Vulcan*; **30mm**: 50 AMX-30SA; **35mm**: 128; **40mm**: 70 L/70 (in store)
SAM 141 *Shahine*, 128 MIM-23B I HAWK, 40 *Crotale*

National Guard 75,000

(75,000 active plus 25,000 tribal levies)
3 mech inf bde, each 4 all arms bn
5 inf bde
1 ceremonial cav sqn

EQUIPMENT

LAV 1,117 LAV (incl 384 LAV-25, 182 LAV-CP, 130 LAV-AG, 111 LAV-AT, 73 LAV-M, 47 LAV plus 190 spt vehs)
APC 290 V-150 *Commando* (plus 810 in store), 440 *Piranha*
TOWED ARTY 105mm: 40 M-102; **155mm**: 30 M-198
MOR 81mm; **120mm**: incl 73 on LAV-M
RCL 106mm: M-40A1
ATGW TOW incl 111 on LAV

Paramilitary 15,500+ active

FRONTIER FORCE 10,500

COAST GUARD 4,500 (base as Azizam)

EQPT 4 *Al Jouf* PFI, about 30 PCI<, 16 hovercraft, 1 trg, 1 Royal Yacht (5,000t) with 1 Bell 206B hel, about 350 armed boats

GENERAL CIVIL DEFENCE ADMINISTRATION UNITS

10 KV-107 **hel**

SPECIAL SECURITY FORCE 500

UR-416 APC

Foreign Forces

PENINSULA SHIELD FORCE ε7,000

1 inf bde (elm from all GCC states)
FRANCE (Southern Watch): 170; 5 *Mirage* 2000C, 3 F-1CR, 3 C 135FR
UK (Southern Watch): ε200; 6 *Tornado* GR-1A
US 4,408 **Army** 300 incl 1 *Patriot* SAM bty, 1 sigs unit and those on short-term duty (6 months) **Air Force** (Southern Watch) 4,050; units on rotational det, numbers vary (incl: F-15, F-16, F-117, C-130, KC-135, U-2, E-3) **Navy** 20 **USMC** 38

Syria Syr

Total Armed Forces

ACTIVE ε319,000
Terms of service conscription, 30 months

RESERVES (to age 45) 354,000
Army 280,000 **Navy** 4,000 **Air Force** 70,000

Army ε215,000

(incl conscripts)
3 corps HQ • 7 armd div (each 3 armd, 1 mech bde, 1 arty regt) • 3 mech div (-) (each 2 armd, 2 mech bde, 1 arty regt) • 1 Republican Guard div (3 armd, 1 mech bde, 1 arty regt) • 1 SF div (3 SF regt) • 4 indep inf bde • 1 Border Guard bde • 2 indep arty bde • 2 indep ATK bde • 1 indep tk regt • 10 indep SF regt • 3 SSM bde (each of 3 bn): 1 with FROG-7, 1 with *Scud*-B/-C, 1 with SS-21 • 1 coastal def SSM bde with SS-C-1B *Sepal* and SS-C-3 *Styx*

RESERVES

1 armd div HQ, 4 armd bde, 2 armd regt
31 inf, 3 arty regt

EQUIPMENT

MBT 4,700 (incl some 1,200 in static positions and in store): 2,000 T-55/MV, 1,000 T-62M/K, 1,700 T-72/-72M
RECCE 600 BRDM-2, 125 BRDM-2 Rkh
AIFV 2,600 BMP-1, 100 BMP-2, BMP-3

APC some 1,600 BTR-50/-60/-70/-152
TOWED ARTY 1,630: **122mm**: 100 M-1931/-37 (in store), 150 M-1938, 500 D-30; **130mm**: 800 M-46; **152mm**: 20 D-20, 50 M-1937; **180mm**: 10 S23
SP ARTY 122mm: 400 2S1; **152mm**: 50 2S3
MRL 107mm: 200 Type-63; **122mm**: 280 BM-21
MOR 82mm: 200; **120mm**: 350 M-1943; **160mm**: 100 M-160; **240mm**: ε9 M-240
SSM launchers: 18 FROG-7, some 18 SS-21, 26 *Scud*-B/-C; 4 SS-C-1B *Sepal*, 6 SS-C-3 *Styx* coastal (SSM msl totals ε850)
ATGW 3,500 AT-3 *Sagger* (incl 2,500 SP), 150 AT-4 *Spigot*, 200 AT-5 *Spandrel*, AT-7 *Saxhorn*, 2,000 AT-10, AT-14 *Kornet* and 200 *Milan*
RL 73mm: RPG-7; **105mm**: RPG-29
AD GUNS 2,050: **23mm**: 650 ZU-23-2 towed, 400 ZSU-23-4 SP; **37mm**: 300 M-1939; **57mm**: 675 S-60; **100mm**: 25 KS-19
SAM 4,000 SA-7, 20 SA-9, 35 SA-13

Navy 4,000

BASES Latakia, Tartus, Minet el-Baida

PRINCIPAL SURFACE COMBATANTS 2
FRIGATES 2
FF 2 FSU *Petya* III with 5 × 533mm TT, 4 ASW RL†

PATROL AND COASTAL COMBATANTS 18
MISSILE CRAFT 10
10 FSU *Osa* I and II PFM with 4 SS-N-2 *Styx* SSM
PATROL CRAFT, INSHORE 8
8 FSU *Zhuk* PFI<

MINE WARFARE 5
MINE COUNTERMEASURES 5
1 FSU T-43 MSO, 1 *Sonya* MSC, 3 *Yevgenya* MSI

AMPHIBIOUS 3
3 *Polnocny* LSM, capacity 100 tps, 5 tk

SUPPORT AND MISCellaneous 4
1 spt, 1 trg, 1 div spt, 1 AGOR

NAVAL AVIATION
EQUIPMENT
16 armed hel
HELICOPTERS
ASW 12 Mi-14, 4 Ka-28 (Air Force manpower)

Air Force 40,000

611 cbt ac; 90 armed hel (some may be in store)
Flying hours 30
FGA 10/11 sqn
5 with 90 Su-22, 2 with 44 MiG-23 BN, 2 with 20 Su-24, 1 possibly with 14 MiG-29 SMT
FTR 16 sqn
8 with 170 MiG-21, 5 with 90 MiG-23, 2 with 30 MiG-25, 1 with 22 MiG-29A
RECCE 6* MiG-25R, 8* MiG-21H/J
TPT ac 4 An-26, 2 *Falcon* 20, 6 Il-76, 6 Yak-40, 1 *Falcon* 900, 6 Tu-134 **hel** 10 Mi-2, 100 Mi-8/-17
ATTACK HEL 48 Mi-25, 42 SA-342L
TRG incl 80* L-39, 20 MBB-223, 20* MiG-21U, 6* MiG-23UM, 5* MiG-25U, 6* MiG-29UB, 6 *Mashshak*

MISSILES
ASM AT-2 *Swatter*, AS-7 *Kerry*, AS-9 *Kyle*, AS-10 *Karen*, AS-11 *Kilter*, AS-12, AS-14 *Kedge*, HOT
AAM AA-2 *Atoll*, AA-6 *Acrid*, AA-7 *Apex*, AA-8 *Aphid*, AA-10 *Alamo*

Air Defence Command ε60,000

2 AD div, 25 AD bde (some 150 SAM bty)
Some 600 SA-2/-3, 200 SA-6 and 4,000 AD arty
2 SAM regt (each 2 bn of 2 bty) with some 48 SA-5, 60 SA-8, S-300 on order

Forces Abroad

LEBANON 18,000; 1 mech div HQ, elm 1 armd, 4 mech inf bde, elm 10 SF, 2 arty regt

Paramilitary ε108,000

GENDARMERIE 8,000 (Ministry of Interior)

WORKERS' MILITIA (PEOPLE'S ARMY) (*Ba'ath* Party) ε100,000

Foreign Forces

UN (UNDOF): 1,037 tps; contingents from **A** 363 **Ca** 189 **J** 30 **Pl** 357 **Slvk** 97 **Swe** 1
RUSSIA ε150 advisers, mainly AD

Tunisia Tn

Total Armed Forces

ACTIVE ε35,000
(incl ε23,400 conscripts)
Terms of service 12 months selective

Army 27,000

(incl 22,000 conscripts)
3 mech bde (each with 1 armd, 2 mech inf, 1 arty, 1 AD regt) • 1 Sahara bde • 1 SF bde • 1 engr regt

EQUIPMENT

MBT 54 M-60A3, 30 M-60A1
LT TK 54 SK-105 *Kuerassier*
RECCE 24 *Saladin*, 45 AML-90
APC 140 M-113A1/A2, 18 EE-11 *Urutu*, 110 Fiat F-6614
TOWED ARTY 105mm: 48 M-101A1/A2; **155mm**: 12 M-114A1, 57 M-198
MOR 81mm: 95; **107mm**: 78 4.2in (some SP); **120mm**: 18 Brandt
ATGW 100 TOW (incl 35 M-901 ITV), 500 *Milan*
RL 89mm: 300 LRAC-89, 300 3.5in M-20
RCL 57mm: 140 M-18; **106mm**: 70 M-40A1
AD GUNS 20mm: 100 M-55; **37mm**: 15 Type-55/-65
SAM 48 RBS-70, 25 M-48 *Chaparral*
SURV RASIT (veh, arty)

Navy ε4,500

(incl ε700 conscripts)
BASES Bizerte, Sfax, Kelibia

PATROL AND COASTAL COMBATANTS 19

MISSILE CRAFT 6

3 *La Galite* (Fr *Combattante* III) PFM with 8 MM-40 *Exocet* SSM, 1 × 76mm gun
3 *Bizerte* (Fr *P-48*) PFM with 8 SS-12M SSM

PATROL, COASTAL/INSHORE 13

3 *Utique* (mod PRC *Shanghai* II) PCC, some 10 PCI<

SUPPORT AND MISCELLANEOUS 2

1 *Salambo* (US *Conrad*) survey/trg, 1 AGS

Air Force 3,500

(incl 700 conscripts); 29 cbt ac, 15 armed hel
FGA 12 F-5E/F
CCT 3 MB-326K, 2 MB-326L
TPT 7 C-130B, 1 C-130E, 2 C-130H, 1 *Falcon* 20, 3 LET-410, 2 G-222
LIAISON 2 S-208M
TRG 10 SF-260, 5 MB-326B, 12* L-59
ARMED HEL 5 SA-341 (attack) 10 HH-3 (ASW)
TPT HEL 1 wg with 15 AB-205, 6 AS-350B, 1 AS-365, 6 SA-313, 3 SA-316, 10 UH-1H, 2 UH-1N
AAM AIM-9J *Sidewinder*

Forces Abroad

UN AND PEACEKEEPING

DROC (MONUC): 279 incl 19 obs **ETHIOPIA/ERITREA** (UNMEE): 6 incl 3 obs

Paramilitary 12,000

NATIONAL GUARD 12,000 (Ministry of Interior)

incl Coastal Patrol with 5 (ex-GDR) *Kondor* I-class PCC, 5 (ex-GDR) *Bremse*-class PCI<, 4 *Gabes* PCI<, plus some 10 other PCI< **ac** 5 P-6B **hel** 8 SA-318/SA-319

United Arab Emirates UAE

Total Armed Forces

The Union Defence Force and the armed forces of the UAE (Abu Dhabi, Dubai, Ras Al Khaimah, Fujairah, Ajman, Umu al-Qaywayn and Sharjah) were formally merged in 1976 and centred on Abu Dhabi. Dubai still maintains independent forces, as do other emirates to a lesser degree.

ACTIVE ε41,500 (perhaps 30% expatriates)

Army 35,000

(incl **Dubai** 15,000) **GHQ** Abu Dhabi
INTEGRATED 1 Royal Guard 'bde' • 2 armd bde • 3 mech inf bde • 2 inf bde • 1 arty bde (3 regt)
NOT INTEGRATED 2 inf bde (Dubai)

EQUIPMENT

MBT 45 AMX-30, 36 OF-40 Mk 2 (*Lion*), ε300 *Leclerc*
LT TK 76 *Scorpion*
RECCE 49 AML-90, 20 *Saladin* (in store), 20 *Ferret* (in store)
AIFV 15 AMX-10P, 415 BMP-3
APC 80 VCR (incl variants), 370 Panhard M-3, 100 EE-11 *Urutu*, 136 AAPC (incl 53 engr plus other variants), 64 TPz-1 *Fuchs*
TOWED ARTY 105mm: 70 ROF lt; **130mm**: 20 PRC Type-59-1
SP ARTY 155mm: 18 Mk F-3, 78 G-6, 85 M-109A3
MRL 70mm: 18 LAU-97; **122mm**: 48 FIROS-25 (ε24 op), PRC Type-90 (reported); **300mm**: 6 *Smerch* 9A52
MOR 81mm: 114 L16, 20 Brandt; **120mm**: 21 Brandt
SSM 6 *Scud*-B
ATGW 230 *Milan*, *Vigilant* (in store), 25 TOW, 50 HOT (20 SP)
RCL 84mm: 250 *Carl Gustav*; **106mm**: 12 M-40
AD GUNS 20mm: 42 M-3VDA SP; **30mm**: 20 GCF-BM2
SAM 20+ *Blowpipe*, 20 *Mistral*

Navy ε2,500

BASE Abu Dhabi
NAVAL FACILITIES Dalma, Mina Zayed **Dubai** Mina Rashid, Mina Jabal **Ras al-Khaimah** Mina Sakr **Sharjah** Mina Khalid, Khor Fakkan

PRINCIPAL SURFACE COMBATANTS 2

FRIGATES 2
FFG 2 *Abu Dhabi* (NL *Kortenaer*) with 8 *Harpoon* SSM, 8 *Sea Sparrow* SAM, 1 × 76mm gun, 4 × 324mm TT, 2 AS565 hel

PATROL AND COASTAL COMBATANTS 16

CORVETTES 2 *Muray Jip* FSG (Ge Lürssen 62m) with 2 × 2 MM-40 *Exocet* SSM, 1 SA-316 hel
MISSILE CRAFT 8
6 *Ban Yas* (Ge Lürssen TNC-45) PFM with 2 × 2 MM-40 *Exocet* SSM, 1 × 76mm gun
2 *Mubarraz* (Ge Lürssen 45m) PFM with 2 × 2 MM-40 *Exocet* SSM, 1 × 76mm gun
PATROL, COASTAL 6
6 *Ardhana* (UK Vosper 33m) PCC

AMPHIBIOUS (craft only)

3 *Al Feyi* LCT, 2 other LCT

SUPPORT AND MISCELLANEOUS 2

1 div spt, 1 AT

NAVAL AVIATION

EQUIPMENT
HELICOPTERS
4 SA-316 *Alouette*, 6 AS 585 *Panther*

Air Force 4,000

(incl Police Air Wing) 101 cbt ac, 49 armed hel
Flying hours 110
FGA 3 sqn
1 with 9 *Mirage* 2000E
1 with 17 *Hawk* 102
1 with 17 *Hawk* Mk 63/63A/63C (FGA/trg)
FTR 1 sqn with 22 *Mirage* 2000 EAD
CCT 1 sqn with 8 MB-326 (2 -KD, 6 -LD), 5 MB-339A
OCU 5* *Hawk* Mk 61, 4* MB-339A, 6* *Mirage* 2000 DAD
RECCE 8* *Mirage* 2000 RAD
TPT incl 1 BN-2, 4 C-130H, 1 L-100-30, 4 C-212, 7 CN-235M-100, 4 Il-76 (on lease)
HELICOPTERS
ATTACK 5 AS-332F (anti-ship, 3 with *Exocet* AM-39), 10 SA-342K (with HOT), 7 SA-316/-319 (with AS-11/-12), 20 AH-64A, 7 AS-565 *Panther*
TPT 2 AS-332 (VIP), 1 AS-350, 30 Bell (8 -205, 9 -206, 5 -206L, 4 -214, 1 -407, 3 -412), 10 SA-330, 2 *King Air* 350 (VIP)
SAR 3 Bo-105, 3 *Agusta* -109 K2
TRG 30 PC-7, 5 SF-260 (4 -TP, 1 -W), 12 Grob G-115TA

MISSILES
ASM HOT, AS-11/-12, AS-15 *Exocet* AM-39, *Hellfire*, *Hydra*-70, PGM1, PGM2
AAM R-550 *Magic*, AIM 9L

AIR DEFENCE

1 AD bde (3 bn)
5 bty I HAWK
12 *Rapier*, 9 *Crotale*, 13 RBS-70, 100 *Mistral* SAM, *Javelin*, *Igla* (SA-16)

Forces Abroad

UN AND PEACEKEEPING

YUGOSLAVIA (KFOR): 380

Paramilitary

COAST GUARD (Ministry of Interior)

some 40 PCI<, plus boats

Foreign Forces

US Air Force 390

Yemen, Republic of Ye

Total Armed Forces

ACTIVE 66,500
(incl conscripts)
Terms of service conscription, 2 years

RESERVES perhaps 40,000

Army 60,000

(incl conscripts)
11 armd bde • 16 inf bde • 9 mech bde • 2 AB/cdo bde • 1 SSM bde • 7 arty bde • 1 central guard force • 1 SF bde • 2 AD bde: 4 AAA, 1 SAM bn

EQUIPMENT
MBT 790: 30 T-34, 450 T-54/-55, 200 T-62, 50 M-60A1, 60 T-72
RECCE 80 AML-90, 50 BRDM-2
AIFV 200 BMP-1/-2
APC 60 M-113, 650 BTR-40/-60/-152 (150 op)
TOWED ARTY 310: **105mm**: 25 M-101A1; **122mm**: 30 M-1931/37, 40 M-1938, 130 D-30; **130mm**: 60 M-46; **152mm**: 10 D-20; **155mm**: 15 M-114
SP ARTY 122mm: 25 2S1
ASLT GUNS 100mm: 30 SU-100
COASTAL ARTY 130mm: 36 SM-4-1

MRL 122mm: 280 BM-21 (150 op); **140mm**: 14 BM-14
MOR ε502 incl **81mm**: 200; **82mm**: 90 M-43; **107mm**: 12; **120mm**: 100; **160mm**: ε100
SSM 12 FROG-7, 10 SS-21, 6 *Scud*-B
ATGW 12 TOW, 24 *Dragon*, 35 AT-3 *Sagger*
RL 66mm: M72 LAW; **73mm**: RPG-7
RCL 75mm: M-20; **82mm**: B-10; **107mm**: B-11
ATK GUNS 85mm: D-44; **100mm**: 20 M-1944
AD GUNS 20mm: 50 M-167, 20 M-163 *Vulcan* SP; **23mm**: 100 ZSU-23-2, 50 ZSU-23-4; **37mm**: 150 M-1939; **57mm**: 120 S-60; **85mm**: 40 KS-12
SAM ε800: SA-7/-9/-13/-14

Navy 1,500

BASES Aden, Hodeida, **minor** Al Mukalla, Perim Island, Socotra (these have naval spt eqpt)

PATROL AND COASTAL COMBATANTS 11

MISSILE CRAFT 6
3 *Huangfen* with C-801 SSM (only 4 C-801 between the 3 craft)
1 *Tarantul* 1 PFM with 4 SS-N-2C *Styx* SSM (plus 1 non-op)
2 *Osa II* PFM with SS-N-2C SSM
plus 6 boats

PATROL, INSHORE 5
2 *Sana'a* (US *Broadsword* 32m) (1 non-op) PFI, 3 FSU *Zhuk* PFI<

MINE WARFARE 6

MINE COUNTERMEASURES 6
1 FSU *Natya* MSO
5 FSU *Yevgenya* MHC

AMPHIBIOUS 1
1 *Ropucha* LST, capacity 190tps/10 tks
plus craft: 2 FSU *Ondatra* LCM
4 Pl NS-717 LCU

SUPPORT AND MISCELLANEOUS 2
2 *Toplivo* AOT

Air Force 5,000 (incl Air Defence)

76 cbt ac (plus some 40 in store), 8 attack hel
FGA 10 F-5E, 30 Su-20/-22
FTR 20 MiG-21, 10 MiG-29 (8 -A, 2 -UB). 5 more MiG-29S/UB on order
TPT 2 An-12, 6 An-26, 3 C-130H, 4 IL-14, 3 IL-76
HEL 2 AB-212, 14 Mi-8, 1 AB-47, 8 Mi-35 (attack)
TRG 2* F-5B, 4* MiG-21U, 14 YAK-11, 12 L-39C, 12 Zlin 242

AIR DEFENCE 2,000
SAM some SA-2, SA-3, SA-6
AAM AA-2 *Atoll*, AIM-9 *Sidewinder*

Paramilitary 70,000

MINISTRY OF THE INTERIOR FORCES 50,000

TRIBAL LEVIES at least 20,000

COAST GUARD
(slowly being established)
5 Fr *Interceptor* PCI<

Central and South Asia

REGIONAL TRENDS

Key military and political elements of the 'war on terror' have focused on Central Asia – in recent years the hub of al-Qaeda training and planning activity. In the aftermath of 11 September, warnings were passed to the Taliban authorities in Afghanistan to surrender Osama bin Laden, the chief suspect behind the terrorist attacks, who had been based in Afghanistan since leaving Sudan in the mid-1990s.

Mullah Omar, the Taliban leader, refused to comply with these demands despite numerous entreaties, particularly by the Taliban's erstwhile backer – Pakistan. On 7 October 2001, after a three-week build-up of forces, the US-led coalition began its military campaign, codenamed *Operation Enduring Freedom*. Military operations in Afghanistan had the double objective of bringing down the Taliban regime and destroying al-Qaeda's operational capability. Although initial operations were carried out with some effectiveness from sea-based forces, the main pillars of the operation proved to be the surrounding countries of Central Asia which, together with Pakistan, gave unprecedented levels of support to coalition forces, to whose operational planning they added vital flexibility.

The anti-terrorism campaign also changed the relationship between Western and former Soviet states in Central Asia, all of which are members of NATO's Partnership for Peace programme. With Russian and CIS concurrence, US and coalition forces, for the first time, obtained basing rights in Uzbekistan, Tajikistan and Kyrgyzstan, and overflight rights and refuelling permissions in Turkmenistan (and Kazakhstan). Status of Forces Agreements of limited duration have also been signed, but it is not known how long coalition forces will remain in these locations, nor if cooperation will continue after the crisis. Although the regional states are demonstrating more willingness to cooperate among themselves, it is as yet unclear if this crisis-induced cooperation can endure on the palimpsest of Central Asian history, cultures, and traditions.

US relations with Pakistan and India, which had been strained by both countries' nuclear tests in 1998, and the 1999 military coup in Pakistan, were improving by late 2001. India's restraint over the Kargil incident in 1999 and the country's positive noises over the US decision to abandon the Anti-Ballistic Missile Treaty presaged a resumption of military-to-military ties. Meanwhile, Pakistani President Pervez Musharraf's decision to back the US line in Afghanistan led to US assistance for Pakistan's new anti-terrorist posture, while both New Delhi and Islamabad benefited from the US revocation of economic sanctions. However, relations between India and Pakistan remained hostage to the Kashmir dispute.

On 13 December 2001, a terrorist attack on the Indian parliament compound led New Delhi to renew its accusation of Islamabad's acquiescence in, and support for, terrorist actions. A further attack, on 14 May 2002 at an Indian army base at Kaluchak, near Jammu, killed 34 soldiers and civilians, provoking a major Indian military response. New Delhi deployed some 500,000 troops on the Line of Control – a number matched by Islamabad – and artillery duels and minor skirmishing intensified until June 2002, when tensions eased following heavy international pressure and firmer Pakistani action to halt terrorist infiltration. With elections in Kashmir scheduled for October 2002, there is further scope for extremist violence. In the meantime, India has appointed a new mediator for the territory.

AFGHANISTAN (see map, inside back cover)

The first phase of *Operation Enduring Freedom* was characterised by considerable US air support to the ground forces of the Northern Alliance/United Front. Extensive use of B-52 (along with B1-B and B-2) aircraft, in close coordination with ground-based target designators, was a crucial element in bringing about the collapse of the Taliban. These aircraft used a variety of munitions, including BLU-82 'daisy cutter' and BLU-118/B thermobaric bombs, along with Joint Direct Attack Munition (JDAM) tail-guidance kits, which served to give greater accuracy to previously unguided weapons.

The second phase took place in the mountains of southern Afghanistan and was more problematic. US forces, under Central Command (CENTCOM – based in Tampa, Florida), and commanded locally by the commander of the 10th Mountain Division, had the task of locating and destroying the enemy. The terrain favoured the opposition, and notwithstanding the technical advantage possessed by US forces, they lacked sufficient accurate and timely tactical information to enable carefully targeted operations to deal with the considerable numbers of enemy that remained at large. For example, *Operation Anaconda* (2–18 March 2002) comprised 1,000 US troops from the 10th Mountain Division, 101st Airborne (AB) Division, US Special Forces (SF), coalition SF and less than 1,000 Afghan troops. These forces attempted to cordon and search the Shah-e Kot area, in south-east Afghanistan near the Pakistani border. By the time the operation ended, it was clear that many opposition fighters had escaped the cordon, with significant numbers later reported in the Pakistani tribal areas. Even when US forces did produce accurate and timely tactical information, this was not always followed by prompt action. This failure has led to enhancements in command and control arrangements, along with improvements in ground-to-air communications systems.

To contribute to coalition operations, Canada provided a Light Infantry Battle Group of some 900 troops, while special forces were provided by Australia, New Zealand, Norway, Germany, France, Denmark and the United Kingdom. In April 2002, UK forces expanded their presence in Afghanistan when an operation was mounted in support of US efforts by 1,700 Royal Marines, based around a 45 Commando battlegroup. This deployment, codenamed *Operation Jacana*, was designed to locate and destroy elements of al-Qaeda and Taliban remaining in the southern region bordering Pakistan. Although there were no major engagements, two significant arms caches were found and destroyed.

In May 2002, command of US and coalition operations in Afghanistan passed to elements of HQ 18th AB Corps, to allow other regional HQs under CENTCOM to focus on activities in their own operational areas. Previously, the Kuwait-based 3rd Army HQ had controlled operations in Afghanistan. The new command HQ, entitled Combined Joint Task Force (CJTF) 180 is the first operational Joint Task Force, as envisaged in the US Quadrennial Defense Review (see page 12). The total number of US combat troops under command in Afghanistan was reported as 7,000 in May 2002, and consisted of elements from the 10th Mountain Division, 101st AB Division, and 5th SF Group, plus combat service support. Troops of the 10th Mountain Division were deployed in Mazar-e Sharif, Bagram and Kabul, while the 101st AB Division were deployed in the Bagram and Kandahar areas, subject to replacement by troops from the 82nd AB Division. Meanwhile, the 22nd Marine Expeditionary Unit remained at readiness aboard ships in the Arabian Sea.

Following the 27 November–5 December 2001 Bonn conference, which sought to establish a basis for post-Taliban governance, a UK-led International Security Assistance Force (ISAF) was authorised to support the Afghan interim administration and aid efforts to increase peace and security. ISAF does not operate as part of *Operation Enduring Freedom*. On 4 January 2002, Major-General John McColl, ISAF's British commander, signed a Military Technical Agreement with the-then Afghan Interior Minister, Yunis Qanouni. Subsequently, on 10 January, 19 countries signed a Memorandum of Understanding (MOU) laying out the parameters of their participation in ISAF, of which, in June 2002, Turkey assumed command. ISAF acts under the authority of UN Security Council Resolution (UNSCR) 1386 (2001), although it is not a UN peacekeeping operation. Under the terms of the MOU and UNSCR 1386, the force is restricted to operating in a limited area encompassing Kabul and Bagram airbase. This has become a contentious issue, and there is some international, and Afghan, pressure to expand ISAF's mandate outside these limited boundaries.

One of ISAF's key tasks has been to train what became the first battalion of the Afghan National Guard, which was operational by April 2002 – ready for the Loya Jirga. Subsequent to this, US and French forces became engaged in training lead elements of a nascent Afghan National Army. By July 2002, a brigade was ready for deployment. The aspiration is for a 68,000-strong army, comprised of 60,000 ground troops and an 8,000-strong air force. Border Guards are to number 12,000, and there is to be a paramilitary force, to include police, numbering some 70,000.

Regional cooperation

Critical support to the coalition effort in Afghanistan has been provided by the Central Asian states. At the start of operations, the timely action of Uzbekistan in allowing US troops to use its base at Khanabad was crucial in facilitating the deployment of US forces. This was followed by the reopening of the 'Friendship Bridge' across the Amu Darya river, which allowed aid to move into northern Afghanistan. Kyrgyzstan has also played a key role in supporting the coalition effort by providing basing facilities at Manas international airport and on 10 July 2002, an MOU was signed between the US and Kazakhstan allowing US aircraft to use Almaty international airport in an emergency. Meanwhile, Tajikistan is providing additional facilities at the Kulyab airbase. In Pakistan, US forces have been operating from airbases at Jacobabad in Sind province and Pasni on the coast in western Baluchistan. A third airbase at Dalbandin, within 80km of the Afghan border, has also been taken into use. These deployments are reported to consist of some 200 personnel at each base, with Marines, and more than 15 aircraft including C-130 aircraft (of differing variants) plus various rotary-wing types. Troops from the 82nd Airborne Division are providing security for these bases.

Although Central Asian states have been positive in their response to the crisis, and their support has been vital to operational success, long-standing differences between them hamper any real hope of a coordinated approach to regional security in the near future. The Shanghai Organization for Cooperation (SOC), which comprises Kazakhstan, Uzbekistan, Kyrgyzstan and Tajikistan, along with Russia and China, held a summit in St Petersburg in June 2002. This summit gave some hope of an improvement in cooperation on security issues, but not in cooperation with extra-regional states. Moreover, the SOC anti-terrorist centre, which was announced over a year ago for Bishkek in Kyrgyzstan, is still not yet operational. On the other hand, the CIS Collective Rapid Deployment Force (CRDF), which is also headquartered in Bishkek, has started low-level training, and some command-post exercises took place in early 2002, and a field training exercise in June. (See Russia, page 87.)

SOUTH ASIA

Bangladesh

Following 11 September, Bangladesh openly expressed its solidarity with the US-led anti-terrorism campaign, granting the use of its airspace, port and refueling facilities. Bangladesh also expressed a willingness to assist in military training initiatives in Afghanistan and stressed its peacekeeping experience. It is as yet unclear the extent to which such offers will be taken up.

Inside the country, there are a large number of extremist groups, shown on the list of selected non-state armed groups on page 224. In the post-11 September atmosphere, it has been easier for the government to justify an increase in internal security measures and curb the extremist groups' activities.

Bangladesh is attempting to upgrade its naval capabilities. A Korean-built *Bangabandhu* (ROK mod *Ulsan*) frigate was brought into service in late-2001, by far the most modern and powerful ship in the Bangladeshi inventory. However, serious faults were found, and the ship was returned to South Korea for repair in early 2002. A new naval base has been commissioned, at Mongla in western Bangladesh. This is primarily intended to be a base for anti-piracy patrols: despite the drop in the overall number of pirate attacks in its waters in 2001, in that year Bangladesh suffered the third-highest number of piracy attacks in the world.

The Bangladeshi air force had a mixed year, with reports suggesting that a number of recently-acquired MiG-29 aircraft were to be sold due to unsustainable maintenance costs potentially affecting the operational capability of other front-line aircraft. Support to UN peacekeeping operations has continued, with the late-2001 roulement of Bangladeshi air force helicopter support to UNIKOM (the UN Iraq/Kuwait Observer Mission).

India

The Kashmir dispute has dominated India's military year. The large-scale deployment to the Line of Control placed a considerable financial and physical burden on the armed forces. At the same time, the Indian military has remained keen to maintain its regional links and posture. In early February, the Tajik defence minister received an Indian military delegation led by the Indian air-force commander. A wide range of bilateral military and technical cooperation issues were discussed. Tajik priorities are the training of personnel for the Tajik air force, and assistance in restoring and reconstructing Ayni airfield, west of Dushanbe.

Developments continue regarding India's nuclear capability. New Delhi is establishing a separate strategic nuclear force which will incorporate all the country's nuclear assets. George Fernandes, India's defence minister, announced on 14 March 2002 that the nuclear-capable *Agni* (Fire) II SSM, with a range of 2,000km, had entered production and was undergoing 'induction' into military service. The previous January, the *Agni* family of delivery systems had also seen the launch of a short-range version of the *Agni* I missile. Conventional missile development is also proceeding, and on 5 March it was announced that a multi-target *Akash* (Sky) SAM had been successfully test-fired from a missile range in the eastern state of Orissa. Although the *Akash*, with a range of 25km, had earlier undergone several tests, the latest launch was designed to check its guidance systems. India likens the *Akash* missile (650kg) to the US *Patriot*.

The Indian navy remains the most powerful in the Central and South Asian region. However, progress remains slow towards achieving the aims set out in her naval doctrine of 2000, mainly due to financial constraints. This new doctrine stressed the need to have a fleet capable of operating in both the eastern and western Indian Ocean by having two operational aircraft carriers and highly capable submarines. Negotiations about the transfer of the Russian (mod *Kiev*-class) aircraft carrier *Admiral Gorschkov* are still ongoing, though it is believed that India cannot afford to pay for the three-year refit needed to attain operational capability. In February 2002, Fernandes announced that India would not lease, as was proposed in late 2001, two Russian nuclear-powered submarines, but would instead buy six French *Scorpene* diesel submarines, with a further six to be built in India. These should be more capable than India's present Russian *Kilo* diesel submarines, although four of these have now been upgraded and fitted with 160km range *Klub* anti-ship missiles by Russia. In November 2001, India announced plans to equip some of its principal surface combatants with the *Brahmos* supersonic anti-ship cruise missile with a range of 280km. This was seen as a partial response to China's acquisition of Russian *Sovremenny*-class destroyers, armed with Russian *Sunburn* anti-ship missiles. India has also tested a navalised version of its *Trishul* (Trident) surface-to-air missile (SAM).

The Indian air force has upgraded its capability with the Su-30 Mk1 – the only production fighter in the world with thrust-vectoring. The Su-30 Mk 1 is equivalent to the Su-37 which is being developed for the Russian air force.

Perhaps of more importance than her platform acquisitions was the February 2002 agreement, reached with the US navy, concerning anti-piracy and anti-terrorism patrols in the Malacca Strait. Under the deal, India will provide protection in the Strait from pirate and terrorist attacks on merchant shipping, with escort duties divided between both navies on a six-month basis. The Indian deployment, aimed at protecting high-value vessels, began in April. The deal illustrates two important trends. Firstly, the increasing emphasis on a naval presence in the eastern Indian Ocean and its approaches; and secondly, growing cooperation with the US navy. The Indian navy also remains a significant presence in the western Indian Ocean, with forces outnumbering Pakistan's. During both countries' April and May 2002 confrontation, the Indian navy was reportedly ready to impose a naval blockade against Karachi, having transferred five principal surface combatants from the eastern to the western Indian Ocean for this purpose.

Nepal

Maoist insurgents renewed their six year-old campaign in a series of attacks on 23 November 2001, and attempted to demonstrate increasing influence through their April 2002 order for a five-day national strike. This increase in rebel activity was shown, on 11 April alone, by incidents in which an estimated 3,000 rebels killed 84 police officers in raids across the country. In total, these raids left more than 100 people dead. The US has provided helicopters and night-vision equipment to assist the government, and the UK has allocated £20m ($29m) to facilitate anti-insurgency operations and step up anti-poverty development aid. In December 2001, Nepal bought two Mi-17 medium-lift helicopters from Kyrgyzstan and received two Hindustan Aeronautics Ltd HAS 315B *Cheetah* light utility helicopters cost-free from India.

Pakistan

Pakistan's armed forces have been deployed on two fronts. In the tribal areas neighbouring Afghanistan, the border troops in particular have borne the brunt of anti-terrorist operations. On 25 June 2002, 10 Pakistani soldiers were killed in a battle with al-Qaeda fighters near Wana in South Waziristan. Meanwhile, on the Line of Control, up to 500,000 troops faced an equivalent number of Indian troops in May 2002. These two simultaneous, but totally different operations, have been hard to sustain in Pakistan's harsh political and economic climate. However, in line with the government's anti-terror stance, an anti-terrorist task force is to be set up to combat internal threats and to prevent extremist movement across the Line of Control.

Three ballistic missiles were test-fired at the end of May – the *Ghauri*, *Ghaznavi* (*Hatf* 3) and the *Abdali* (*Hatf* 2). The missiles are not new but the coordinated firings had three political rather than developmental purposes: firstly, to subdue General Musharraf's domestic critics, who had been accusing him of neglecting the nation's defences and endangering national security; secondly, to increase pressure on the US to restrain India from launching a military strike on Pakistan; and thirdly, to proclaim that Pakistan was ready and capable of using short- and intermediate-range ballistic missiles with nuclear warheads if necessary.

Pakistan is slowly improving its naval capabilities. The second *Khalid*-class (French *Agosta* 90B) diesel submarine should enter service in late-2002 and should be at least as capable as India's *Kilo* diesel submarines. However, the projected in-service date for these submarines may be affected by the decision of the French shipbuilders, DCN, to withdraw the workers they had placed in Pakistan to assist the project. This followed an 8 May 2002 terrorist attack, in Karachi, which killed 11 French naval engineers. If Pakistan can operate these submarines to their full potential, they would pose a considerable threat to any Indian surface force attempting to impose a blockade against Pakistan. Islamabad is also still planning to replace its ageing principal surface combatants, although no contracts have yet been placed.

Sri Lanka

In Sri Lanka, violence continued until the 23 February 2002 signing of a ceasefire between the Liberation Tigers of Tamil Eelam (LTTE) and the Sri Lankan government. Under the agreement which is being supervised by Norwegian, Swedish, Danish and Finnish monitors, and was brokered by Norway, both parties pledged to halt offensive military operations and to desist from deploying armaments or munitions in their territories. Tamil paramilitary groups were also to be disarmed within a month of the treaty's signing. Although the ceasefire has largely been respected, disarmament has been slow, and there are frequent reports of attempted arms smuggling. In late February 2002, government forces seized shipments of explosives and small arms probably meant for the LTTE along routes – particularly from Thailand and Cambodia – used for such purposes in the past.

Afghanistan Afg

Proposed National Army/ Security Forces

The transitional Afg gov aims to establish control over the country by forming a national army and a national police force encompassing all ethnic and tribal gps

Army some 50–60,000

4 regional comd
9 Corps HQ
32 div (one per province – each up to 2,000 pers)

Air Force some 8,000

Border Guards some 12,000

Paramilitary some 70,000 (mostly police)

Factions and Leaders (see map, inside back)

The gps which formed the Northern Alliance or 'United Islamic Front for the Salvation of Afghanistan' are to be integrated into the proposed National Army, however this is at an early stage and regional leaders still maintain their own personal military forces.

- **ISLAMIC SOCIETY** (*Jama't-e Islami*) **str** ε18–20,000 **Leaders** Marshal Mohammed Fahim (currently Minister of Defence), General Atta Mohammad, Daoud Khan and Bismullah Khan **Area** northeast Afg **Ethnic groups** Predominately Tajik
- **NATIONAL ISLAMIC MOVEMENT (NIM)** (*Jumbesh-e Melli Islami*) **str** ε5,000 **Leader** General Abdul Rashid Dostum (Uzbek governor of Mazar-e Sharif). **Area** north Afg **Ethnic Groups** predominantly Uzbek, but also Tajik, Turkoman, Ismaili and Hazara Shi'a
- **ISLAMIC UNITY PARTY** (*Hizb-e Wahdat-e Islami – Khalili*) **Leaders** Abdul Karim Khalili and Mohaqqeq **Area** central and northern Afg
- **Leader** Ismail Khan (Tajik Governor of Herat) **Area** northwest Afg
- **Leader** Gul Agha Shirzai (Governor of Kandahar) **Area** west Afg
- **Leader** Hazrat Ali **Area** southeast Afg

Est **str** of these six gps is 90,000

A number of leaders and factions have not fully accepted the legitimacy of the transitional national gov.

- **ISLAMIC UNION FOR THE LIBERATION OF AFGHANISTAN** (*Ittihad-e Islami Bara-ye Azadi Aghanistan*) **Leader** Abdul Rasul Sayyaf
- **ISLAMIC PARTY** (*Hizb-e Islami*) faction **Leader** Yunis Khalis
- **Leader** Burhanuddin Rabbani **Area** northwest of Kabul and the Panjshir Valley
- **Leader** Padsha Khan Zadran **str** ε6,000 **Area** Khost/Gardez, southern Afg

Opponents of the transitional national government include:

- **ISLAMIC PARTY** (*Hizb-e Islami – Gulbuddin*) faction **Leader** Gulbuddin Hekmatyar
- **TALIBAN str** ε2,000, mostly loc in Pak **Leader** Mullah Mohamed Omar **Ethnic Group** Pashtun
- elements of ***al-Qaeda*** remain, incorporating amongst others ethnic Arabs, Chechens, Uzbeks and Uighurs

Equipment

It is impossible to show the division of ground force eqpt among the different regional comd. The list below represents wpn known to be in the country. Individual wpn quantities are unknown

MBT T-54/-55, T-62
LT TK PT-76
RECCE BRDM-1/-2
AIFV BMP-1/-2
APC BTR-40/-60/-70/-80/-152
TOWED ARTY 76mm: M-1938, M-1942; **85mm**: D-48; **100mm**: M-1944; **122mm**: M-30, D-30; **130mm**: M-46; **152mm**: D-1, D-20, M-1937 (ML-20)
MRL 122mm: BM-21; **140mm**: BM-14; **220mm**: 9P140 *Uragan*
MOR 82mm: M-37; **107mm; 120mm**: M-43
SSM *Scud*, FROG-7
ATGW AT-1 *Snapper*, AT-3 *Sagger*
RCL 73mm: SPG-9; **82mm**: B-10
AD GUNS: **14.5mm; 23mm**: ZU-23, ZSU-23-4 SP; **37mm**: M-1939; **57mm**: S-60; **85mm**: KS-12; **100mm**: KS-19
SAM SA-7/-13

Air Force

5 cbt ac, 5 armed hel

FGA some 5 MiG-21
TPT some An-24
HEL 5* Mi-24, 8 Mi-8/17
TRG 2 L-39

Foreign Forces

Operation Enduring Freedom – US ε7,500; Da 100; Fr; Aus ε150; Ge 100; HKJ; NZ ε50; No 70; Pl 87; R 475
UN (ISAF): Tu ε1,400; Ge 1,200; Fr 450; It 360; UK ε400; Nl 220; Alb 30; Be 20; Da 50; Por 8; A 45; SF 45; Swe 40; R 48; No 20; Gr 120; NZ 7; Cz 5; Sp 350; Bg 30

Bangladesh Bng

Total Armed Forces

ACTIVE 137,000

Army 120,000

7 inf div HQ • 17 inf bde (some 26 inf bn) • 1 armd bde (2 armd regt) • 2 armd regt • 1 arty div (6 arty regt) • 1 engr bde • 1 AD bde • 2 avn sqn

EQUIPMENT†

MBT 100 PRC Type-59/-69, 100 T-54/-55
LT TK some 40 PRC Type-62
APC 60 BTR-70, 40 BTR-80, some MT-LB, ε50 YW531
TOWED ARTY 105mm: 30 Model 56 pack, 50 M-101; **122mm**: 20 PRC Type-54; **130mm**: 40+ PRC Type-59
MOR 81mm; 82mm: PRC Type-53; **120mm**: 50 PRC Type-53
RCL 106mm: 30 M-40A1
ATK GUNS 57mm: 18 6-pdr; **76mm**: 50 PRC Type-54
AD GUNS 37mm: 16 PRC Type-55; **57mm**: PRC Type-59
SAM some HN-5A
AC 6 Cessna (4 -152, 2 -337F)

Navy† 10,500

BASES Chittagong (HQ), Dhaka, Kaptai, Khulna, Mongla

PRINCIPAL SURFACE COMBATANTS 5

FRIGATES 5
FFG 2
1 *Bangabandhu* (ROK mod *Ulsan*) with 4 *Ottomat* Mk 2 ASSM, 1 × 76mm gun, 3 × 2 TT, hel deck (in refit in ROK)†
1 *Osman* (PRC *Jianghu* I) with 2 × 2 CSS-N-2 *Hai Ying* 2 SSM, 2 × 2 100mm gun, 2 × 5 ASW mor
FF 3
1 *Umar Farooq* (UK *Salisbury*) with 1 × 2 115mm gun, 1 × 3 *Squid* ASW mor
2 *Abu Bakr* (UK *Leopard*) with 2 × 2 115mm guns

PATROL AND COASTAL COMBATANTS 33

MISSILE CRAFT 10
5 *Durdarsha* (PRC *Huangfeng*) PFM with 4 HY 2 SSM
5 *Durbar* (PRC *Hegu*) PFM< with 2 SY-1 SSM
TORPEDO CRAFT 4
4 PRC *Huchuan* PHT< with 2 × 533mm TT
PATROL, OFFSHORE 2
1 *Madhumati* (J *Sea Dragon*) PCO with 1 × 76mm gun
1 *Durjoy* (PRC *Hainan*) PCO with 4 × 5 ASW RL
PATROL, COASTAL 8
2 *Meghna* fishery protection
2 *Karnaphuli* PCC
4 *Shahead Daulat* PFC
PATROL, INSHORE 4
1 *Bishkali* PCI<, 1 *Bakarat* PCI<, 2 *Akshay* PCI<
PATROL, RIVERINE 5 *Pabna* PCR<

MINE WARFARE 4

MINE COUNTERMEASURES 4
1 *Sagar* MSO, 3 *Shapla* (UK *River*) MSI

AMPHIBIOUS craft only

7 LCU, 4 LCM, 3 LCVP

SUPPORT AND MISCELLANEOUS 8

1 coastal AOT, 1 AR, 1 AT/F, 1 AT, 2 *Yuch'in* AGHS, 1 *Shaibal* AGOR (UK *River*) (MCM capable), 1 *Shaheed Ruhul Amin* (trg)

Air Force† 6,500

83 cbt ac, no armed hel **Flying hours** 100–120
FGA/FTR 4 sqn with 8 MiG-29 (incl 2 -UB), 18 A-5C *Fantan*, 16 F-6, 23 F-7M/FT-7B *Airguard*, 1 OCU with 10 FT-6, 8 L-39ZA
TPT 3 An-32
HEL 3 sqn with 11 Bell 212, 1 Mi-8, 15 Mi-17
TRG 20 PT-6, 12 T-37B, 8 CM-170, 2 Bell 206L
AAM AA-2 *Atoll*

Forces Abroad

UN AND PEACEKEEPING

CROATIA (UNMOP): 1 obs **DROC** (MONUC): 21 incl 12 obs **EAST TIMOR** (UNMISET): 22 incl 7 obs **ETHIOPIA/ERITREA** (UNMEE): 173 incl 7 obs **GEORGIA** (UNOMIG): 8 obs **IRAQ/KUWAIT** (UNIKOM): 816 incl 6 obs **SIERRA LEONE** (UNAMSIL): 4,282 incl 15 obs **WESTERN SAHARA** (MINURSO): 8 obs

Paramilitary 63,200

BANGLADESH RIFLES 38,000 (to be 58,000)

border guard; 41 bn

ARMED POLICE 5,000

rapid action force (forming)

ANSARS (Security Guards) 20,000+

A further 180,000 unembodied

COAST GUARD 200

(HQ Chittagong and Khulma)
1 *Bishkhali* PCI<
(force in its infancy and expected to expand)

India Ind

Total Armed Forces

ACTIVE 1,298,000

RESERVES 535,000

Army 300,000 (first-line reserves within 5 years' full-time service, a further 500,000 have commitment until age 50) **Territorial Army** (volunteers) 40,000 **Air Force** 140,000 **Navy** 55,000

Army 1,100,000

HQ: 5 Regional Comd, 4 Fd Army, 12 Corps
3 armd div (each 2–3 armed, 1 SP arty (2 SP fd, 1 med regt) bde) • 4 RAPID div (each 2 inf, 1 mech bde) • 18 inf div (each 2–5 inf, 1 arty bde; some have armd regt) • 9 mtn div (each 3–4 bde, 1 or more arty regt) • 1 arty div (3 bde) • 15 indep bde: 7 armd, 5 inf, 2 mtn, 1 AB/cdo • 1 SSM regt (*Prithvi*) • 4 AD bde (plus 14 cadre) • 3 engr bde
These formations comprise
58 tk regt (bn) • 355 inf bn (incl 25 mech, 8 AB, 3 cdo) • 190 arty regt (bn) reported: incl 1 SSM, 2 MRL, 50 med (11 SP), 69 fd (3 SP), 39 mtn, 29 AD arty regt; perhaps 2 SAM gp (3–5 bty each) plus 15 SAM regt • 22 hel sqn: incl 5 ATK

RESERVES

Territorial Army 25 inf bn, plus 29 'departmental' units

EQUIPMENT

MBT ε3,898 (ε1,100 in store): some 700 T-55 (450 op), ε1,900 T-72 M1, 1,200 *Vijayanta*, ε14 *Arjun*, 84 T-90S (plus 26 to be delivered)
LT TK ε90 PT-76
RECCE ε100 BRDM-2
AIFV ε1,500 BMP-1/-2
APC 157 OT-62/-64 (in store), ε160 *Casspir*
TOWED ARTY 4,175 (perhaps 600 in store) incl: **75mm**: 900 75/24 mtn, 215 FRY M-48; **105mm**: some 1,300 IFG Mk I/II, 50 M-56; **122mm**: some 550 D-30; **130mm**: 750+ M-46; **155mm**: 410 FH-77B
SP ARTY 105mm: 80 *Abbot* (in store); **130mm**: 100 mod M-46 (ε70 in store); **152mm**: some 2S19
MRL 122mm: ε150 incl BM-21, LRAR; **214mm**: ε12 *Pinacha* (being deployed)
MOR 81mm: ε5,000 E1; **120mm**: ε1,500 incl Brandt AM-50, E1 (some SP); **160mm**: 500 M-1943
SSM *Prithvi* (3–5 launchers)
ATGW *Milan*, AT-3 *Sagger*, AT-4 *Spigot* (some SP), AT-5 *Spandrel* (some SP)
RCL 84mm: *Carl Gustav*; **106mm**: 1,000+ M-40A1
AD GUNS some 2,424: **20mm**: Oerlikon (reported); **23mm**: 300 ZU 23-2, 100 ZSU-23-4 SP; **30mm**: 24 2S6 SP; **40mm**: 1,200 L40/60, 800 L40/70
SAM 180 SA-6, 620 SA-7, 50 SA-8B, 400 SA-9, ε50 SA-11, 250 SA-13, 500 SA-16
SURV MUFAR, *Green Archer* (mor)
UAV *Searcher*, *Nishant*
HEL 100 *Chetak*, 50 *Cheetah*, 12 *Lancer*
LC 2 LCVP

DEPLOYMENT

North 3 Corps with 8 inf, 2 mtn div **West** 3 Corps with 1 armd, 5 inf div, 3 RAPID **Central** 1 Corps with 1 armd, 1 inf, 1 RAPID **East** 3 Corps with 1 inf, 7 mtn div **South** 2 Corps with 1 armd, 3 inf div

Navy 53,000

(incl 5,000 Naval Avn and 1,000 Marines; ε2,000 women)
COMMANDS Principal Western, Southern, Eastern (incl Far Eastern sub comd); **Sub Command** SS, Naval Avn
BASES Mumbai (Bombay) (HQ Western Comd), Kochi (Cochin) (HQ Southern Comd), Vishakhapatnam (HQ Eastern), Port Blair (Andaman Is, HQ Far Eastern sub Comd), Goa (HQ Naval Avn), Arakonam (Naval Avn), Calcutta, Madras, Karwar (under construction)
FLEETS Western base Bombay **Eastern base** Visakhapatnam

SUBMARINES 16

SSK 16
10 *Sindhughosh* (FSU *Kilo*) with 533mm TT (at least 1 with SS-NX-27 *Club* SSM)
4 *Shishumar* (Ge T-209/1500) with 533mm TT
2 *Kursura* (FSU *Foxtrot*)† with 533mm TT (plus 3 in reserve)

PRINCIPAL SURFACE COMBATANTS 27

AIRCRAFT CARRIERS 1 *Viraat* (UK *Hermes*) CV
Air group typically **ac** 6 *Sea Harrier* (*Sea Eagle* ASM) ftr/attack **hel** 6 *Sea King* ASW/ASUW
DESTROYERS 8
DDG 8
5 *Rajput* (FSU *Kashin*) with 4 SS-N-2C *Styx* SSM, 2 × 2 SA-N-1 *Goa* SAM, 2 × 76mm gun, 5 × 533mm ASTT, 2 ASW RL, 1 Ka-25 or 28 hel
3 *Delhi* with 16 SS-N-25 *Switchblade* SSM, 2 × SA-N-7 *Gadfly* SAM, 1 × 100mm gun, 5 × 533mm ASTT, 2 hel
FRIGATES 11
FFG 4
1 *Brahmaputra* with 16 × SS-N-25 *Switchblade* SSM, 20 SA-N-4 *Gecko* SAM, 1 × 76mm gun, 2 × 3 324mm ASTT, 1 hel
3 *Godavari* with SS-N-2D *Styx* SSM, 1 × 2 SA-N-4 *Gecko* SAM, 2 × 3 324mm ASTT, 1 *Sea King* hel
FF 7
4 *Nilgiri* (UK *Leander*) with 2 × 114mm guns, 2 × 3 ASTT, 1 × 3 *Limbo* ASW mor, 1 *Chetak* hel (2 with 1 *Sea King*)

1 *Krishna* (UK *Leander*) (trg role)
2 *Arnala* (FSU *Petya*) with 4 × 76mm gun, 3 × 533mm ASTT, 4 ASW RL

CORVETTES 7
4 *Khukri* FSG with 4 SS-N-2C *Styx* SSM, 1 × 76mm gun, hel deck
3 mod *Khukri* FSG with 16 × SS-N-25 *Switchblade* SSM, SA-N-5 *Grail* SAM, 1 × 76mm gun

PATROL AND COASTAL COMBATANTS 39

CORVETTES 17
1 *Vijay Durg* (FSU *Nanuchka* II) FSG with 4 SS-N-2C *Styx* SSM, SA-N-4 *Gecko* SAM (plus 1 non-op)
11 *Veer* (FSU *Tarantul*) FSG with 4 *Styx* SSM, SA-N-5 *Grail* SAM, 1 × 76mm gun
1 *Vibhuti* (mod *Veer*) FSG with 16 × SS-N-25 *Switchblade* SSM, SA-N-5 *Grail* SAM, 1 × 76mm gun
4 *Abhay* (FSU *Pauk* II) FS with SA-N-5 *Grail* SAM, 1 × 76mm gun, 4 × 533mm ASTT, 2 ASW mor

MISSILE CRAFT 6 *Vidyut* (FSU *Osa* II) PFM with 4 *Styx* SSM†

PATROL, OFFSHORE 5 *Sukanya* PCO

PATROL, INSHORE 11
7 SDB Mk 3 PCI
4 *Super Dvora* PCF<

MINE WARFARE 18

MINELAYERS 0
none, but all SS and *Pondicherry* MSO have minelaying capability

MINE COUNTERMEASURES 18
12 *Pondicherry* (FSU *Natya*) MSO, 6 *Mahé* (FSU *Yevgenya*) MSI<

AMPHIBIOUS 7
2 *Magar* LST, capacity 500 tps, 18 tk, 1 hel
5 *Ghorpad* (FSU *Polnocny* C) LSM, capacity 140 tps, 6 tk
Plus craft: 10 *Vasco da Gama* LCU

SUPPORT AND MISCELLANEOUS 32
1 *Aditya* (mod *Deepak*) AO, 1 *Deepak* AO, 1 *Jyoti* AO, 6 small AOT; 3 YDT, 1 *Tir* trg, 2 AWT, 3 TRV, 1 AH; 8 *Sandhayak* AGHS, 4 *Makar* AGHS, 1 *Sagardhwani* AGOR

NAVAL AVIATION (5,000)

ORGANISATION

Flying hours Sea Harrier 180

AIRCRAFT
FTR 1 sqn with *Sea Harrier* FRS Mk-1, T-60 trg*
MR 3 sqn with Il-38, Tu-142F *Bear*, Do-228, BN-2 *Defender*
COMMS 1 sqn with Do-228
TPT 1 sqn with 10 HS-748M
TRG 2 sqn with 8 HPT-32, HJT-16 Mk 1, HJT Mk 2

HELICOPTERS
ASW 6 sqn with Ka-25, Ka-28, *Sea King* Mk-42A/B, SA 319 *Alouette* III
SAR 1 sqn with *Sea King* Mk-42C

EQUIPMENT
35 cbt ac; 50 armed hel

AIRCRAFT
20 ***Sea Harrier*** FRS Mk-1 • 2 **T-60** trg* • 5 **Il-38** • 8 **Tu-142F *Bear*** • 25 **Do-228** (15 -MR, 10 -COMMS) • 15 **BN-2 *Defender*** • 8 **HPT-32** • 10 **HJ 748 M** • 6 **Kiran** 7 • 6 **Kiran** 2

HELICOPTERS
25 SA 319 *Alouette* III • 5 **Ka-25** • 8 **Ka-28** • 12 ***Sea King* Mk-42A/B** • 3 *Sea King* Mk-42C

MISSILES
AAM R-550 *Magic* 1 and 2
ASM *Sea Eagle, Sea Skua*

MARINES (1,000)
1 regt (3 gp)

Air Force 145,000

701 cbt ac, 22+ armed hel **Flying hours** 180+
Five regional air comds: **Central** (Allahabad), **Western** (New Delhi), **Eastern** (Shillong), **Southern** (Trivandrum), **South-Western** (Gandhinagar); 2 spt comds: trg and maint

FGA 30 sqn
1 with 28 Su-30 (18 -30K, 10 -MkI), 3 with 52 MiG-23 BN/UM, 4 with 35 *Jaguar* S(I), 6 with 135 MiG-27M, 4 with 55 MiG-21 MF/PFMA, 10 with 165 MiG-21bis/U (125 being upgraded), 2 with 40 *Mirage* 2000H/TH (secondary ECM role)

FTR 9 sqn
5 with 66 MiG-21 FL/U, 1 with 26 MiG-23 MF/UM, 3 with 63 MiG-29

ECM 1 sqn with some MiG-21M (ECM)

ELINT 2 Boeing 707, 2 Boeing 737

TANKER 6 IL-78

MARITIME ATTACK 1 sqn with 6 *Jaguar* S(I) with *Sea Eagle*

ATTACK HEL 2 sqn with 20+ Mi-25/35

RECCE 2 sqn
1 with 12 *Canberra* (2 PR-57, 2 PR-67, 3 B(I) 58 (ECM/tgt towing), 3 TT-18 (tgt towing), 2 T-54)
1 with 5* MiG-25R, 2* MiG-25U

MR/SURVEY 2 *Gulfstream* IV SRA, 2 *Learjet* 29

TRANSPORT
ac 6 with 105 An-32 *Sutlej*, 2 with 45 Do-228, 2 with 28 BAe-748, 2 with 25 Il-76 *Gajraj*
hel 14 sqn with 73 Mi-8/50 Mi-17, 1 sqn with 10 Mi-26 (hy tpt), 4 sqn with 40 *Cheetah/Chetak*, 2 ALH

VIP 1 HQ sqn with 2 Boeing 737-200, 7 BAe-748, 6 Mi-8

TRG ac 28 BAe-748 (trg/tpt), 120 *Kiran* I, 56 *Kiran* II, 88 HPT-32, 14* *Jaguar* B(1), 9* MiG-29UB, 44 TS-11 *Iskara*
hel 20 *Chetak*, 2 Mi-24, 2* Mi-35

UAV *Searcher*-2

MISSILES
ASM *Prithvi* SS250, AS-7 *Kerry*, AS-11B (ATGW), AS-12, AS-30, *Sea Eagle*, AM 39 *Exocet*, AS-17 *Krypton*

AAM AA-7 *Apex*, AA-8 *Aphid*, AA-10 *Alamo*, AA-11 *Archer*, R-550 *Magic*, *Super* 530D
SAM 38 sqn with 280 *Divina* V75SM/VK (SA-2), *Pechora* (SA-3), SA-5, SA-10

Forces Abroad

UN AND PEACEKEEPING

DROC (MONUC): 31 incl 22 obs **ETHIOPIA/ERITREA** (UNMEE): 1,537 incl 5 obs **IRAQ/KUWAIT** (UNIKOM): 8 obs **LEBANON** (UNIFIL): 839

Paramilitary 1,089,700 active

NATIONAL SECURITY GUARDS 7,400

(Cabinet Secretariat)

Anti-terrorism contingency deployment force, comprising elements of the armed forces, CRPF and Border Security Force

SPECIAL PROTECTION GROUP 3,000

Protection of VVIP

SPECIAL FRONTIER FORCE 9,000

(Cabinet Secretariat)

mainly ethnic Tibetans

RASHTRIYA RIFLES 40,000 (Ministry of Defence)

36 bn in 12 Sector HQ

DEFENCE SECURITY CORPS 31,000

provides security at Defence Ministry sites

INDO-TIBETAN BORDER POLICE 32,400 (Ministry of Home Affairs)

29 bn, Tibetan border security

ASSAM RIFLES 52,500 (Ministry of Home Affairs)

7 HQ, 31 bn, security within north-eastern states, mainly Army-officered; better trained than BSF

RAILWAY PROTECTION FORCES 70,000

CENTRAL INDUSTRIAL SECURITY FORCE 95,000

(Ministry of Home Affairs)[a]

guards public-sector locations

[a] Lightly armed security guards only

CENTRAL RESERVE POLICE FORCE (CRPF) 167,400

(Ministry of Home Affairs)

137 bn incl 10 rapid action, 2 *Mahila* (women); internal security duties, only lightly armed, deployable throughout the country

BORDER SECURITY FORCE (BSF) 174,000 (Ministry of Home Affairs)

some 157 bn, small arms, some lt arty, tpt/liaison air spt

HOME GUARD (R) 574,000

authorised, actual str 399,800 in all states except Arunachal Pradesh and Kerala; men on lists, no trg

STATE ARMED POLICE 400,000

For duty primarily in home state only, but can be moved to other states, incl 24 bn India Reserve Police (commando-trained)

CIVIL DEFENCE 453,000 (R)

in 135 towns in 32 states

COAST GUARD over 8,000

PATROL CRAFT 34
3 *Samar* PCO, 9 *Vikram* PCO, 19 *Jija Bai*, 3 SDB-2 plus 15 boats
AVIATION
3 sqn with **ac** 14 Do-228, **hel** 15 *Chetak*

Opposition 2,000–2,500

HIZB-UL-MUJAHIDEEN str 1,000–1,200 Operates in Ind Kashmir
HARAKAT-UL-MUJAHIDEEN str 450–500 Operates from Pak Kashmir
LASKHAR-E-ISLAMI str 300–400 Operates from Pak Kashmir
JAISH-E-MOHAMMADI str 300–400 Operates from Pak Kashmir
AL-BADR MUJAHIDEEN str 40–50 Operates in Ind Kashmir

Foreign Forces

UN (UNMOGIP): 44 mil obs from 9 countries

Kazakhstan Kaz

Total Armed Forces

ACTIVE ε60,000

Terms of service 31 months

RESERVES ε237,000

Army ε41,000

2 Mil District (plus 1 forming, 1 to form)
2 Army Corps (third to form)
1 with 1 mech div, 2 MR bde, 1 arty regt
1 with 1 mech div, 1 MR bde, 1 arty bde, 1 trg centre
1 air aslt, 1 SSM, 1 arty bde

EQUIPMENT

MBT 650 T-72, 280 T-62
RECCE 140 BRDM

AIFV 508 BMP-1/-2, 65 BRM
APC 84 BTR-70/-80, 686 MT-LB APC (plus some 1,000 in store)
TOWED ARTY 505: **122mm**: 161 D-30; **152mm**: 74 D-20, 90 2A65, 180 2A36
SP ARTY 163: **122mm**: 74 2S1; **152mm**: 89 2S3
COMBINED GUN/MOR 120mm: 26 2S9
MRL 147: **122mm**: 57 BM-21; **220mm**: 90 9P140 *Uragan*
MOR 145: **120mm**: 2B11, M-120
SSM 12 SS-21
ATGW AT-4 *Spigot*, AT-5 *Spandrel*, AT-6 *Spiral*
RL 73mm: RPG-7
ATK GUNS 100mm: 68 T-12/MT-12

In 1991, the former Soviet Union transferred some 2,680 T-64/-72s, 2,428 ACVs and 6,900 arty to storage bases in Kaz. This eqpt is under Kaz control, but has deteriorated considerably. An eqpt destruction prog is about to begin.

Air Force 19,000

(incl Air Defence)
1 Air Force div, 164 cbt ac **Flying hours** 100
FTR 1 regt with 40 MiG-29
FGA 3 regt
1 with 14 Su-25
1 with 25 Su-24
1 with 14 Su-27
RECCE 1 regt with 12 Su-24*
ACP Tu-134, Tu-154
TRG 12 L-39, 4 Yak-18
HEL numerous Mi-8, Mi-29
STORAGE some 75 MiG-27/MiG-23/MiG-23UB/MiG-25/MiG-29/SU-27
AIR DEFENCE
FTR 1 regt with 43 MiG-31, 16 MiG-25
SAM 100 SA-2, SA-3, 27 SA-4, SA-5, 20 SA-6, S-300

MISSILES

ASM AS-7 *Kerry*, AS-9 *Kyle*, S-10 *Karen*, AS-11 *Killer*
AAM AA-6 *Acrid*, AA-7 *Apex*, AA *Aphid*

Paramilitary 34,500

STATE BORDER PROTECTION FORCES ε12,000 (Ministry of Interior) incl

MARITIME BORDER GUARD (3,000)
BASE Aktau (HQ) Atyrau (Caspian)
PATROL AND COASTAL COMBATANTS 10
5 *Guardian* PCI<, 1 *Dauntless* PCI<, 4 *Almaty* PCI<, plus 5 boats†, **hel** 3 Mi-8, 6 Mi-2

INTERNAL SECURITY TROOPS ε20,000 (Ministry of Interior)

PRESIDENTIAL GUARD 2,000

GOVERNMENT GUARD 500

Kyrgyzstan Kgz

Total Armed Forces

ACTIVE 10,900
Terms of service 18 months

RESERVES 57,000

Army 8,500

1 MRD
2 indep MR bde (mtn), 1 AD bde, 1 AAA regt, 3 SF bn

EQUIPMENT

MBT 233 T-72
RECCE 30 BRDM-2
AIFV 274 BMP-1, 113 BMP-2
APC 53 BTR-70, 10 BTR-80
TOWED ARTY 141: **100mm**: 18 M-1944 (BS-3); **122mm**: 72 D-30, 35 M-30; **152mm**: 16 D-1
SP ARTY 122mm: 18 2S1
COMBINED GUN/MOR 120mm: 12 2S9
MRL 122mm: 21 BM-21
MOR 120mm: 6 2S12, 48 M-120
ATGW 26 AT-3 *Sagger*, AT-4 *Spigot*, AT-5 *Spandrel*
RL 73mm: RPG-7
RCL 73mm: SPG-9
ATK GUNS 100mm: 18 T-12/MT-12
AD GUNS 23mm: 24 ZSU-23-4SP; **57mm**: 24 S-60
SAM SA-7

Air Force 2,400

52 cbt ac, 9 attack hel
1 Ftr regt with 4 L-39, 48 MiG-21
1 Comp Avn regt with 2 An-12, 2 An-26
1 Hel regt with 9 Mi-24, 23 Mi-8
In store: 2 Mi-23, 24 L-39, 24 MiG-21

AIR DEFENCE

SAM SA-2, SA-3, 12 SA-4

Forces Abroad

UN AND PEACEKEEPING

SIERRA LEONE (UNAMSIL): 2 obs

Paramilitary ε5,000

BORDER GUARDS ε5,000 (Kgz conscripts, RF officers)

Foreign Forces

Operation Enduring Freedom – US ε700; Fr 380; Da 75; Sp 20; ROK 90

Nepal N

Total Armed Forces

ACTIVE ε51,000

Army ε51,000

1 div HQ, 1 Royal Guard bde (incl 1 MP bn) • 7 inf bde (16 inf bn) • 44 indep inf coy • 1 SF bde (incl 1 AB bn, 2 indep SF coy, 1 cav sqn (*Ferret*)) • 1 arty bde (1 arty, 1 AD regt) • 1 engr bde (4 bn)

EQUIPMENT

RECCE 40 *Ferret*
APC 130 BTR-70 (reported)
TOWED ARTY† **75mm**: 6 pack; **94mm**: 5 3.7in mtn (trg); **105mm**: 14 pack (ε6 op)
MOR 81mm; 120mm: 70 M-43 (ε12 op)
AD GUNS 14.5mm: 30 PRC Type 56; **37mm**: PRC **40mm**: 2 L/60

AIR WING (320)

no cbt ac, or armed hel
TPT ac 1 BAe-748, 1 *Skyvan* **hel** 1 HAS-315B *Cheetah*, 2 SA-316B *Chetak*, 3 Mi-17, 1 AS-332L (*Puma*), 2 AS-332L-1 (*Super Puma*), 2 Bell 206L, 1 AS-350 (*Ecureuil*)

Forces Abroad

UN AND PEACEKEEPING

CROATIA (UNMOP): 1 obs **DROC** (MONUC): 17 incl 15 obs **EAST TIMOR** (UNMISET): 162 incl 3 obs **ETHIOPIA/ERITREA** (UNMEE): 4 obs **MIDDLE EAST** (UNTSO): 2 obs **SIERRA LEONE** (UNAMSIL): 814 incl 10 obs

Paramilitary 40,000

POLICE FORCE 40,000 (incl armed police unit ε7,000)

Opposition

COMMUNIST PARTY OF NEPAL (Maoist): armed wg ε5,000

Foreign Forces

UK Army 90 (Gurkha trg org)

Pakistan Pak

Total Armed Forces

ACTIVE 620,000

RESERVES 513,000

Army ε500,000; obligation to age 45 (other ranks) or 50 (officers); active liability for 8 years after service **Navy** 5,000 **Air Force** 8,000

Army 550,000

9 Corps HQ • 2 armd div • 19 inf div • 1 area comd (div) • 9 Corps arty bde • 22 indep bde (7 armd, 6 mech, 9 inf), 7 engr bde • 3 armd recce regt • 1 SF gp (3 bn) • 1 AD comd (3 AD gp: 8 bde)
AVN 17 sqn
7 ac, 8 hel, 1 VIP, 1 obs flt

EQUIPMENT

MBT 34 M-47, 232 M-48A5, 51 T-54/-55, 1,200 PRC Type-59, 250 PRC Type-69, 250+ PRC Type-85, 320 T-80UD, ε20 *Al-Khalid*
APC 1,150+ M-113, 31 UR-416
TOWED ARTY 1,467: **85mm**: 200 PRC Type-56; **105mm**: 300 M-101, 50 M-56 pack; **122mm**: 200 PRC Type-60, 250 PRC Type-54; **130mm**: 227 PRC Type-59-1; **155mm**: 30 M-59, 60 M-114, 124 M-198; **203mm**: 26 M-115
SP ARTY 105mm: 50 M-7; **155mm**: 150 M-109A2; **203mm**: 40 M-110A2
MRL 122mm: 45 *Azar* (PRC Type-83)
MOR some 1,200 incl: **81mm**; **120mm** AM-50, M-61
SSM 80 *Hatf* 1, 50 *Hatf* 3 (PRC M-11), *Shaheen* 1, 12 *Ghauri*
ATGW 800 incl: *Cobra*, 200 TOW (incl 24 on M-901 SP), *Baktar Shikan* (PRC *Red Arrow* 8)
RL 73mm: RPG-7; **89mm**: M-20 3.5in
RCL 3,700: **75mm**: Type-52; **106mm**: M-40A1
AD GUNS 2,000+ incl: **14.5mm; 35mm**: 200 GDF-002; **37mm**: PRC Type-55/-65; **40mm**: M1, 100 L/60; **57mm**: PRC Type-59
SAM some 1,400 incl: 350 *Stinger*, HN-5A, RBS-70, 500 *Anza* Mk-1/-2
SURV RASIT (veh, arty), AN/TPQ-36 (arty, mor)

AIRCRAFT
SURVEY 1 *Commander* 840
LIAISON 1 Cessna 421, 2 *Commander* 690, 50 *Mashshaq*, 1 F-27, 2 Y-12 (II)
OBS 25 O-1E, 50 *Mashshaq*

HELICOPTERS
ATTACK 20 AH-1F (TOW)
TPT 12 Bell 47G, 6 -205, 10 -206B, 16 Mi-8, 4 Mi-17, 18 IAR/SA-315B, 24 IAR/SA-316, 25 SA-330, 6 UH-1H

UAV *Bravo*

Navy 25,000

(incl ε1,200 Marines and ε2,000 Maritime Security Agency (see *Paramilitary*))
BASE Karachi (Fleet HQ) (2 bases being built at Gwadar and Ormara)

SUBMARINES 10

SSK 7
- 1 *Khalid* (Fr *Agosta* 90B) with 533mm TT, *Exocet* SM39 USGW
- 2 *Hashmat* (Fr *Agosta* 70) with 533mm TT (F-17 HWT), *Harpoon* USGW
- 4 *Hangor* (Fr *Daphné*) with 533mm TT (L-5 HWT), *Harpoon* USGW

SSI 3 MG110 (SF delivery)

PRINCIPAL SURFACE COMBATANTS 8

FRIGATES 8
- **FFG** 6 *Tariq* (UK *Amazon*) with 4 × *Harpoon* SSM (in 3 of class), 1 × LY-60N SAM (in 3 of class), 1 × 114mm gun, 6 × 324mm ASTT, 1 *Lynx* HAS-3 hel
- **FF** 2 *Shamsher* (UK *Leander*) with 2 × 114mm guns, 1 × 3 ASW mor, 1 SA-319B hel

PATROL AND COASTAL COMBATANTS 9

MISSILE CRAFT 5
- 3 *Sabqat* (PRC *Huangfeng*) PFM with 4 HY 2 SSM
- 2 × *Jalalat* II PFM with 4 C-802 SSM

PATROL, COASTAL 3
- 1 *Larkana* PCC
- 2 *Quetta* (PRC *Shanghai*) PCC (operated by the Maritime Security Agency)

PATROL, INSHORE 1
- 1 *Rajshahi* PCI<

MINE WARFARE 3

MINE COUNTERMEASURES 3
- 3 *Munsif* (Fr *Eridan*) MHC

SUPPORT AND MISCELLANEOUS 9

1 *Fuqing* AO, 1 *Moawin* AO, 2 *Gwadar* AOT, 1 *Attock* AOT; 3 AT; 1 *Behr Paima* AGHS

NAVAL AVIATION

EQUIPMENT
6 cbt ac; 9 armed hel

AIRCRAFT
- **ASW/MR** 3 *Atlantic*, 3 P-3C *Orion* (operated by Air Force), 1 *Fokker* F27 Mk 400M
- **TPT** 3 *Fokker* F-27 Mk 200M

HELICOPTERS
- **ASW** 3 SH-2F *Sea Sprite*, 3 SH-2G *Sea Sprite*, 3 *Lynx* HAS Mk3
- **SAR** 4 SA-319 *Alouette* 3
- **TPT** 5 *Sea King* Mk-45/Mk 45C

MISSILES
- **ASM** *Exocet* AM-39

MARINES (ε1,200)

1 cdo/SF gp

Air Force 45,000

366 cbt ac, no armed hel **Flying hours** some 210
3 regional comds: **Northern** (Peshawar) **Central** (Sargodha) **Southern** (Faisal). The Composite Air Tpt Wg, Combat Cdrs School and PAF Academy are Direct Reporting Units.

FGA 6 sqn
- 1 with 16 *Mirage* (13 IIIEP (some with AM-39 ASM), 3 IIIDP (trg))
- 3 (1 OCU) with 52 *Mirage* 5 (40 -5PA/PA2, 10 5PA3 (ASuW), 2 5DPA/DPA2)
- 2 with 42 Q-5 (A-5III *Fantan*)

FTR 12 sqn
- 2 (1 OCU) with 50 F-7PG, 6 (1 OCU) with 77 F-7P/FT-7 (J-7), 2 (1 OCU) with 32 F-16 (22 -A, 10 -B), 2 with 43 *Mirage* IIIO/7-OD

RECCE 1 sqn with 11* *Mirage* IIIRP
ELINT/ECM 2 *Falcon* DA-20
SAR 7 hel sqn with SA-316
TPT ac 14 C-130 (11 B/E, 1 L-100), 2 Boeing 707, 1 *Falcon* 20, 2 F-27-200 (1 with Navy), 2 Y-12 (II), 4 Cessna 172, 1 *Piper* PA-34 *Seneca*, 4 MFI-17B *Mashshaq*
TRG 30 FT-5, 15 FT-6, 40* MFI-17B *Mashshaq*, 30 T-37B/C, 12 K-8
AD 7 SAM bty
- 6 each with 24 *Crotale*, 1 with 6 CSA-1 (SA-2), SA-16

MISSILES

- **ASM** AM-39 *Exocet*, AGM-65 *Maverick*
- **AAM** AIM-9L/P *Sidewinder*, R-530, R-550 *Magic*
- **ARM** AGM-88 *Harm*

Forces Abroad

UN AND PEACEKEEPING

CROATIA (UNMOP): 1 obs **DROC** (MONUC): 37 incl 21 obs **EAST TIMOR** (UNMISET): 142 incl 15 obs **GEORGIA** (UNOMIG): 9 obs **IRAQ/KUWAIT** (UNIKOM): 8 obs **SIERRA LEONE** (UNAMSIL): 4,285 incl 16 obs **WESTERN SAHARA** (MINURSO): 6 obs

Paramilitary ε289–294,000 active

NATIONAL GUARD 185,000

incl *Janbaz* Force, *Mujahid* Force, National Cadet Corps, Women Guards

FRONTIER CORPS up to 65,000 reported (Ministry of Interior)

11 regt (40 bn), 1 indep armd car sqn; 45 UR-416 APC

PAKISTAN RANGERS ε25,000–30,000 (Ministry of Interior)

NORTHERN LIGHT INFANTRY ε12,000; 3 bn

MARITIME SECURITY AGENCY ε2,000

1 *Alamgir* (US *Gearing* DD) (no ASROC or TT),
4 *Barkat* PCO, 2 (PRC *Shanghai*) PCC

COAST GUARD

some 23 craft

Foreign Forces

UN (UNMOGIP): 44 mil obs from 9 countries
Operation Enduring Freedom – US ε1,300

Sri Lanka Ska

Total Armed Forces

ACTIVE 157,900
(incl 42,300 recalled reservists)

RESERVES 5,500

Army 1,100 **Navy** 2,400 **Air Force** 2,000
Obligation 7 years, post regular service

Army 118,000

(incl 39,900 recalled reservists; 2,960 women)
9 div HQ • 1 air mobile bde • 33 inf bde • 1 indep SF bde • 1 cdo bde • 3 armd regt • 3 armd recce regt (bn) • 3 fd arty (2 med, 1 lt) • 3 fd engr regt

EQUIPMENT

MBT 62 T-55 A/AM2
RECCE 15 *Saladin*
AIFV 13 BMP-1, 49 BMP-2
APC 35 PRC Type-85, 31 *Buffel*, 105 *Unicorn*, 21 *Saracen*, 25 BTR-80/-80A
TOWED ARTY 85mm: 8 PRC Type-56; **88mm**: 3 25-pdr; **122mm**: 74; **130mm**: 40 PRC Type-59-1; **152mm**: 40 PRC Type-66
MRL 122mm: 22 RM-70
MOR 81mm: 520; **82mm**: 209; **120mm**: 55 M-43
RCL 105mm: ε10 M-65; **106mm**: ε30 M-40
AD GUNS 40mm: 24 L-40; **94mm**: 3 3.7in
SURV 2 AN/TPQ-36 (arty)
UAV 1 *Seeker*

Navy 20,600

(incl 2,400 recalled reservists)
BASES Colombo (HQ and Western comd), Trincomalee (main base and Eastern comd), Kankesanthurai (Northern comd), Medawachiya (North central comd), Galle (Southern comd)

PATROL AND COASTAL COMBATANTS 61
MISSILE CRAFT 2
2 *Nandimithra* (Il *Saar* 4) with 4 *Gabriel* II SSM, 1 x 76 mm gun
PATROL, OFFSHORE 3
1 *Sayura* (In *Sukanya*) PCO • 1 *Jayesagara* PCO • 1 *Parakrambahu* PCO
PATROL, COASTAL 10
2 *Ranajaya* (PRC *Haizhui*)
2 *Prathapa* (PRC mod *Haizhui*)
1 *Ranarisi* (PRC *Shanghai* II)
3 *Abeetha* (PRC mod *Shanghai*)
2 *Weeraya* (PRC *Shanghai*)
PATROL, INSHORE 46
3 *Dvora* PFI< • 9 *Super Dvora* PFI< • 3 ROK *Killer* PFI< • 19 *Colombo* PFI< • 5 *Trinity Marine* PFI< • 7 *Shaldag* PFI< • plus some 52 boats

AMPHIBIOUS 1

1 *Yuhai* LST
plus 9 craft: 2 LCM, 2 *Yunan* LCU, 1 LCAC, 4 fast personnel carrier

Air Force 19,300

22 cbt ac, 24 armed hel
FGA 1 sqn with 11 *Kfir* (8 C-2, 2 C-7, 1 TC-2), 1 sqn with 4 MiG-27M, 1 MiG-23 UB (conversion trg), 3 F-7M, 1 FT-7, 2 FT-5
ATTACK HEL 10 Bell 212, 1 Mi-24V, 13 Mi-35P
TPT 1 sqn with **ac** 2 BAe 748, 2 C-130C, 1 Cessna 421C, 1 *Super King Air* 200, 1 Y-8, 7 Y-12 (II), 7 An-32B, 5 Cessna 150 **hel** 6 Bell 412 (VIP)
UTL HEL 6 Bell 206, 3 Mi-17 (plus 4 in store)
TRG ac 5 SF-260TP, 10 PT-6, 3 K-8 **hel** 6 Bell 206
RESERVES Air Force Regt, 3 sqn; Airfield Construction, 1 sqn
UAV 1 *Scout*, 2 *Searcher*

Paramilitary ε88,600

POLICE FORCE (Ministry of Defence) 60,600

incl 30,400 reserves, 1,000 women and Special Task Force: 3,000-strong anti-guerrilla unit

NATIONAL GUARD ε15,000

HOME GUARD 13,000

Opposition

LIBERATION TIGERS OF TAMIL EELAM (LTTE) ε7,000

Eqpt incl **122mm**, **152mm** arty, **120mm** mor; some ATGW and SAM reported. 1 Robinson R-44 *Astro* lt hel plus 2 lt ac for recce and liaison
Leader Velupillai Prabhakaran

Tajikistan Tjk

Total Armed Forces

ACTIVE some 6,000

Terms of service 24 months

A number of potential officers are being trained at the Higher Army Officers and Engineers College, Dushanbe. It is planned to form an Air Force sqn and to acquire Su-25 from Bel; 5 Mi-24 and 10 Mi-8 have been procured.

Army some 6,000

2 MR bde (incl 1 trg) • 1 mtn bde • 1 arty bde • 1 SF bde • 1 SF det (ebn+) • 1 SAM regt

EQUIPMENT

MBT 35 T-72
AIFV 9 BMP-1, 25 BMP-2
APC 1 BTR-60, 2 BTR-70, 26 BTR-80
TOWED ARTY 122mm: 12 D-30
MRL 122mm: 10 BM-21
MOR 120mm: 9
SAM 20 SA-2/-3/-7, *Stinger* (reported)

AIR FORCE (some 800)

No cbt ac, 4-5 armed hel
TPT 1 Tu-134A
HEL 4-5 Mi-24, 12-14 Mi-8/17TM

Paramilitary ε1,200

BORDER GUARDS ε1,200 (Ministry of Interior)

Opposition

ISLAMIC MOVEMENT OF TAJIKISTAN some 5,000

Signed peace accord with govt on 27 Jun 1997. Integration with govt forces slowly proceeding

Foreign Forces

RUSSIA Federal Border Guard 12,000 (Tjk conscripts, RF officers) **Army** 7,800; 1 MRD

EQUIPMENT
MBT 128 T-72
AIFV/APC 314 BMP-2, BRM-1K, BTR-80
SP ARTY 122mm: 66 2S1; **152mm**: 54 2S3
MRL 122mm: 12 BM-21; **220mm**: 12 9P140
MOR 120mm: 36 PM-38
AIR DEFENCE
SAM 20 SA-8

Operation Enduring Freedom – Fr ε100

Turkmenistan Tkm

Total Armed Forces

ACTIVE 17,500

Terms of service 24 months

Army 14,500

5 Mil Districts • 4 MRD (1 trg) • 1 arty bde • 1 MRL regt • 1 ATK regt •1 engr regt • 2 SAM bde • 1 indep air aslt bn

EQUIPMENT

MBT 702 T-72
RECCE 170 BRDM/BRDM-2
AIFV 930 BMP-1/-2, 12 BRM
APC 829 BTR (-60/-70/-80)
TOWED ARTY 122mm: 180 D-30; **152mm**: 17 D-1, 72 D-20
SP ARTY 122mm: 40 2S1
COMBINED GUN/MOR 120mm: 17 2S9
MRL 122mm: 56 BM-21, 9 9P138
MOR 82mm: 31; **120mm**: 66 PM-38
ATGW 100 AT-3 *Sagger*, AT-4 *Spigot*, AT-5 *Spandrel*, AT-6 *Spiral*
RL 73mm: RPG-7
ATK GUNS 100mm: 72 T-12/MT-12
AD GUNS 23mm: 48 ZSU-23-4 SP; **57mm**: 22 S-60
SAM SA-7, 40 SA-8, 13 SA-13

Navy none

Has announced intention to form a Navy/Coast Guard and has minor base at Turkmenbashy with 5 boats. Caspian Sea Flotilla (see **Russia**) is operating as a joint RF, Kaz and Tkm flotilla under RF comd based at Astrakhan.

Air Force 3,000

(incl Air Defence)
89 cbt ac (plus 200 in store)
FGA/FTR 2 avn sqns with 24 MiG-29 (incl 2 -U), 65 Su-17
IN STORE 46 Su-25, 120 MiG-23, 10 MiG-23U, 24 MiG-25
TPT/GENERAL PURPOSE 1 composite avn sqn with 1 An-26, 10 Mi-24, 8 Mi-8
TRG 1 unit with 3 Su-7B, 2 L-39
AIR DEFENCE
SAM 50 SA-2/-3/-5

Uzbekistan Uz

Total Armed Forces

ACTIVE some 50–55,000
(incl MoD staff and centrally controlled units)
Terms of service conscription, 18 months

Army 40,000

4 Mil Districts • 2 op comd • 1 Tashkent comd • 1 tk, 10 MR, 1 lt mtn, 1 AB, 3 air aslt, 4 engr bde • 1 National Guard bde

EQUIPMENT
MBT 170 T-62, 100 T-64, 70 T-72
RECCE 13 BRDM-2
AIFV 270 BMP-2, 120 BMD-1, 9 BMD-2, 6 BRM
APC 25 BTR-70, 24 BTR-60, 210 BTR-80, 50 BTR-D
TOWED ARTY 122mm: 60 D-30; **152mm**: 140 2A36
SP ARTY 122mm: 18 2S1; **152mm**: 17 2S3, 2S5 (reported); **203mm**: 48 2S7
COMBINED GUN/MOR 120mm: 54 2S9
MRL 122mm: 36 BM-21, 24 9P138; **220mm**: 48 9P140
MOR 120mm: 18 PM-120, 19 2S12, 5 2B11
ATGW AT-3 *Sagger*, AT-4 *Spigot*
ATK GUNS 100mm: 36 T-12/MT-12
(In 1991 the former Soviet Union transferred some 2,000 tanks (T-64), 1,200 ACV and 750 arty to storage bases in Uz. This eqpt is under Uz control, but has deteriorated considerably)

Air Force some 10–15,000

7 fixed wg and hel regts
135 cbt ac (plus 30 in store), 42 attack hel
BBR/FGA 1 regt with 20 Su-25/Su-25BM, 26 Su-17MZ/Su-17UMZ, 1 regt with 23 Su-24, 11 Su-24MP (recce)
FTR 1 regt with 30 MiG-29/MiG-29UB, 1 regt with 25 Su-27/Su-27UB
IN STORE 30 MiG-29/-29UB
TPT/ELINT 1 regt with 26 An-12/An-12PP, 13 An-26/An-26RKR
TPT 1 Tu-134, 1 An-24
TRG 14 L-39 (9 in store), 1 Su-17
HELICOPTERS
1 regt with 42 Mi-24 (attack), 29 Mi-8 (aslt/tpt), 1 Mi-26 (tpt)
1 regt with 26 Mi-6 (tpt), 2 Mi-6AYa (cmd post), 29 Mi-8 (aslt/tpt)
MISSILES
AAM AA-8, AA-10, AA-11
ASM AS-7, AS-9, AS-10, AS-11, AS-12
SAM 45 SA-2/-3/-5

Paramilitary ε18–20,000

INTERNAL SECURITY TROOPS (Ministry of Interior) ε17–19,000

NATIONAL GUARD (Ministry of Defence) 1,000

1 bde

Opposition

ISLAMIC MOVEMENT OF UZBEKISTAN
ε2,000 **Leader** Tahir Yoldosh **Based** near Kunduz, Afg; supported by Juma Numangoni, warlord, based in Tjk or Afg (may be deceased)

Foreign Forces

Operation Enduring Freedom – US ε1,000

East Asia and Australasia

REGIONAL TRENDS

Military affairs in East Asia and Australasia have been largely unaffected by the events of 11 September 2001, notwithstanding Japan's defence policy review, which facilitated the deployment of elements of its self-defence forces in support of the US in its military operations in the South Asian theatre. In early November 2001, the ASEAN+3 (Japan, China and South Korea) summit adopted a resolution to act against terror. The commanders of these countries' military forces subsequently signed a joint declaration containing anti-terror measures.

The US has greatly increased its military aid to Southeast Asia. The region, where concerns about Islamic extremist militancy had been growing prior to 11 September, was quick to sign up to the anti-terrorism campaign. As a region containing large Muslim populations, and harbouring a number of militant Islamist groups, the strategic significance of Southeast Asia to US policyholders has increased. US military assistance is intended to increase the ability of indigenous forces to combat terrorism on their own territory, and has seen US troop deployments to the Philippines.

Meanwhile, independently of any perceived terrorism threat, China has continued its military transformation programme, modernising and upgrading its capabilities. Beijing remains concerned about relative military strength on both sides of the Taiwan Strait, as well as the political situation in Taiwan, particularly after Taiwanese President Chen Shui-bian talked up the possibility of a referendum on independence in August 2002. These issues add to existing strains in the relationship between Washington and Beijing. Further east, disquiet over weapons proliferation and low-level military clashes mean that the Korean Peninsula continues to give cause for concern, despite episodic diplomatic contacts between Seoul and Pyongyang.

EAST ASIA

China

After 11 September, China was quick to offer support to the US in the war on terror. Its own domestic problems with Uighur separatists in Xinjiang province motivated it to provide the US with information on the Taliban, on whose side Uighurs were known to be fighting. China hoped that their capture would yield intelligence relevant to combating separatists inside China. Although the US has publicly welcomed intelligence cooperation, it has cautioned China that the 'war on terror' should not be used as an excuse to persecute minorities. China continues to work through the Shanghai Organisation for Cooperation (SOC) to promote a regional approach to countering terror. The SOC's definition of terrorism includes separatism and extremism. Apart from this, China's only role in aiding the anti-terror coalition was its tacit acquiescence to the basing of US and coalition forces in Central Asian countries close to the Chinese western border, particularly Kyrgyzstan.

Potential difficulties for future US–China relations have been underscored by the content of three US government reports. The first of these, the Nuclear Posture Review – extracts of which were leaked in March 2002 – noted that China was 'a country that could be involved in an immediate or potential contingency', when discussing possible circumstances that may govern US nuclear strike requirements. Secondly, the US–China Security Review Commission submitted a report to Congress in June 2002, entitled 'The National Security Implications of the Economic Relationship between the United States and China'. The report noted the build-up of Chinese forces opposite Taiwan, and particularly the increase in deployment of short-range ballistic missiles (SRBM) – estimated to reach 600 by 2012. On 18 April 2002, Admiral Dennis Blair, then Commander-in-Chief of US Pacific Command, said that the current figure for SRBM's opposite Taiwan was 300, and that a further build-up could lead to the provision of US missile defence systems.

Thirdly, a Department of Defense report, issued in July 2002, argued that the reorganisation and modernisation of China's armed forces has continued at a rapid pace. Manpower changes have led to an overall reduction of some 500,000 personnel. One effect of this downsizing has been the reduction in the size of Group Armies (GA). The new GA organisation is believed to be as follows:

- 2–3 mechanised/motorised infantry divisions/brigades;
- 1 armoured division or brigade;
- 1 artillery division or brigade; and
- 1 SAM or AAA brigade.

The 2nd Artillery Corps, which operates the land-based arm of China's strategic nuclear force, carried out an exercise in March 2002 under simulated nuclear warfare conditions. Though mainly computer-based, the exercise also saw the deployment of missile units and use of anti-jamming and anti-reconnaissance hardware.

Meanwhile, China is continuing to increase its blue-water naval capabilities. It has ordered two *Sovremenny* destroyers (DDG) from Russia, to be delivered at the end of 2005, and has started building two *Luhai* DDGs. The Chinese-made destroyers will be similarly armed to the *Sovremennys*, with the best systems available to China for combating the US *Aegis* air-defence system – SS-N-22/*Sunburn* anti-ship missiles. Eight Russian built *Kilo* 636-Type diesel submarines (SSK) with anti-submarine warfare capabilities are on order, a probable response to the US's 2001 offer of eight SSKs to Taiwan. Replacements for China's *Xia* nuclear-powered ballistic-missile submarine (SSBN) and *Han*-class nuclear-powered submarine (SSN) are being built in Russia, but progress remains slow in both programmes. It has been mooted that China will release its third white paper on defence later this year. The document will be scrutinised closely for clarifications of threat perception, doctrine and general transparency (not least on spending).

Taiwan

Taiwan's ten-year defence modernisation, reform and restructuring programme – unveiled in 2000 – has been modified following the perception of an increased threat from Chinese forces across the Taiwan Strait. The July 2002 defence report stressed the need for improved C^2 capabilities, and highlighted the increased threat of an immobilising cyber attack from China, in response to which a limited information warfare capability is being developed. It has also been proposed to expand the military's anti-terrorist unit. Despite this, overall military doctrine remains unchanged, seeking to address three main operational requirements:

- maintaining air superiority over the Strait and the contiguous waters;
- conducting effective counter-blockade operations; and
- defeating an amphibious and aerial assault on Taiwan.

To address these requirements, procurement projects over the last few years have led to the introduction of Taiwan's Indigenous Defense Fighter – the *Ching Kuo*, the *Tien Kung* SAM system and foreign purchases including F-16s, French-built Mirage 2000s and *Lafayette* frigates. There are also stated aspirations to improve air defences (enhancing or replacing the *Patriot* systems already in place), anti-submarine warfare capabilities, expand military training programmes and enhance naval and air power over ground forces.

Japan

Changes to Japan's defence policy following 11 September are set out in the Japanese Defense Agency's 2002 *Defense of Japan* report. Self-defence remains the guiding-principle, and the importance of Japan's special defence relationship with the US is emphasised, in particular by reference to continuing joint US–Japanese research into ballistic missile defence systems.

On 2 November 2001, the Diet passed the 'Anti-Terrorism Special Measures Law'. This amended the Self-Defense Forces Law to permit the deployment of Japanese defence assets in support of the US in its campaign against al-Qaeda and the Taliban. On 9 November 2001, the destroyers *Kurama* and *Kirisame* left Japan for the Indian Ocean, accompanied by one supply vessel, the *Hamana*. These ships, and three additional supply vessels that were subsequently deployed, returned to Japan on 25 April 2002, to be replaced by a contingent of five ships. Prior to the Maritime Self-Defense force deployment, six C-130H aircraft from the Air Self-Defense force had deployed on 9 October 2001 to deliver humanitarian aid to Islamabad.

The Japanese Defense Agency is working on policies to cope with biological attack and has set up a biological-weapons countermeasures committee. Chemical and cyber attack also have high priority in defence planning. In terms of defence technology, the emphasis is on the development of high-technology weapon systems, cyber protection and networked C^{4}ISR systems. Japan is also designing two 13,500 tonne helicopter-carrying cruisers, which will be the most powerful ships in its inventory.

The Koreas

In **North Korea**, Kim Jong Il, in his capacity as Chairman of the National Defence Commission, controls the military which constitutes his primary power-base and continues to absorb a large portion of the country's limited resources. One result of this relationship is that the testing of the *Pekodosan*-1 missile, formerly the *Taepo-dong*, is believed to be continuing, despite the expense of this project.

North Korea's relations with the US and South Korea have remained poor, with the Bush administration including North Korea in its 'axis of evil' in January 2002. There were maritime incidents in September and October 2001, with a major clash in the Yellow Sea on 29 June 2002, in which five South Korean sailors died. There have also been exchanges of fire in the Demilitarized Zone.

Despite this, in April 2002, North Korea offered to resume talks with the US on the Agreed Framework, indicating a desire to improve its poor international standing – not least because of the continuing downward spiral of the economy and high levels of poverty. On 31 July 2002, US Secretary of State Colin Powell met the North Korean Foreign Minister, Paek Nam Sun on the fringes of the ASEAN Regional Forum meeting in Brunei – the first US–North Korea ministerial meeting since Bush's 'axis of evil' speech. On 4 August 2002, North and South Korea agreed to resume bilateral talks, and North Korea apologised for the Yellow Sea incident.

South Korea, meanwhile, is continuing its KDX destroyer programme. It has three KDX-2 destroyers in build for first delivery in 2004 and is about to order three KDX-3 destroyers. The ships will considerably enhance its blue-water capabilities, while its sub-surface capabilities will be boosted when three German Type-214 diesel submarines (SSK) are delivered in 2007–09.

The Yellow Sea incident of 29 June 2002 has caused considerable frustration in the navy, and the armed forces have requested that Rules of Engagement be changed to allow them to react more quickly to perceived North Korean provocation.

Southeast Asia and Australasia

Counter-insurgency developments

On 7 May 2002, **Indonesia**, **Malaysia** and the **Philippines** signed an anti-terrorism pact as part of Southeast Asia's battle against regional militant groups. The agreement will enable the countries to exchange intelligence and launch joint police operations. Since 11 September 2001, the governments of Indonesia and Malaysia have arrested several members of Jemaah Islamiah and the Malaysian Mujahideen Group (KMM), both believed to be fighting for a pan-Asian Islamic state. US and local officials allege that these groups have links with Osama bin Laden's al-Qaeda. Counter-terrorism measures were also discussed by regional defence ministers and their defence representatives at the June 2002 Shangri-La Dialogue, organised under the aegis of the IISS in Singapore.

On 24 April 2002, the Philippines government detained five suspects over bombings that killed 15 people earlier that month in the southern city of General Santos. In January 2002, the US expanded its campaign against terrorism and sent 1,200 troops to the southern Philippines to train Philippine troops searching for Abu Sayyaf rebels. The US and Philippine troops worked together in *Exercise Balikatan* 02-1 on the islands of Basilan and Mindanao. The exercise ended in July 2002.

The Indonesian government and separatist rebels held talks in Switzerland on 2–3 February, and again in May 2002, in a bid to find a peaceful solution to the conflict in the northern province of Aceh. The rebels, who are seeking full independence, rejected the government's offer of autonomy. No agreement has been signed and fighting continues. Since August 2001, 1,000 people have been killed.

On 11 February 2002, Christian and Muslim leaders from Indonesia's eastern Moluccan Islands signed a peace deal to end three years of bloodshed in which 5,000 people were killed. The peace deal includes: the surrender of all weapons; the return of tens of thousands of refugees; the setting up of joint security patrols; and a plan to rebuild destroyed towns and villages. Overall, security has improved, although violence and bomb attacks persist.

Australia and **New Zealand** have provided special forces personnel to operations in Afghanistan as part of the US-led *Operation Enduring Freedom* (pages 122, 123 and map, inside back cover). Australia formed a new Special Forces unit, the Tactical Assault Group, which will operate in addition to Australia's existing special forces anti-terrorism capability. **Fiji** too has formed a new anti-terrorist unit.

Defence capabilities

The **Indonesian** navy continues to deteriorate. The Chief of the Naval Staff announced in July 2002 that no vessels were combat-ready, and that only nine of the inventory of over 100 ships were under ten years old. Indonesia cannot patrol its territorial waters or Exclusive Economic Zone (EEZ) effectively. As a result, according to the International Chamber of Commerce Piracy Report, in 2001 Indonesia recorded the highest number (91) of pirate attacks in the world.

In **Malaysia** the government is to procure tanks, cannons and missiles, in an effort to upgrade and modernise its defence capabilities. It is showing a particular interest in the PT-91Z main battle tank (MBT) from Poland. Officials indicate that they would like to purchase 64–67 MBTs and associated combat support vehicles – sufficient to equip an armoured regiment. The formation of an armoured brigade is a probable long-term aim. The Malaysian defence minister, Najib Razak, announced on 10 April that a contract had been signed with Russia for the procurement of portable SAM systems, believed to be the SA-18 *Grouse.* Malaysia has also ordered the *Jernas* Area Air Defence System, the export version of the UK's *Rapier* SAM system. Delivery will begin in 2005 and a new air defence regiment will be formed to operate this equipment. An order for 22 South African G5 Mk3 155mm towed howitzers was completed by July 2002, and six more have been ordered. When delivered, these howitzers will be issued to 21 Artillery Regiment, whose 105mm guns will be re-issued to a newly formed 22 Artillery Regiment.

Australia is to issue a Strategic Review this year. New Zealand has published a naval review, which advocates the retention of a small naval combat capability (as currently represented by the two *Anzac*-class frigates) and a naval patrol force for its EEZ and territorial waters. The latter will require a future order for two or three large patrol craft.

Southwest Pacific

In **Papua New Guinea**, the surrender of weaponry as part of the Bougainville peace process continued, with some 1,034 weapons (including 222 high-velocity rifles) handed in. Preparations are moving ahead for an autonomous Bougainville government to be in place by the end of 2002, although the UN Secretary-

General's special representative has to first of all certify that weapons disposal has been completed in line with the peace agreement.

The army was called into action in July 2002, to assist police in quelling violence during the country's general election process, which ended with the election of Michael Somare to the office of prime minister. Earlier in the year, elements of the army caused concern with the seizure of a barracks at Moem, near Wewak in the north of the country, in protest at a decision to reduce the size of the army in line with defence cuts.

In the **Solomon Islands**, the December 2001 parliamentary elections passed peacefully and Allan Kemakeza, the leader of the People's Alliance Party, was elected as the new prime minister. The elections aimed to restore democracy to the Pacific nation which has been beset by three years of ethnic conflict and a coup in 2001. Fighting started in 1998 between the Isatabu Freedom Movement – natives of the main island of Guadalcanal – and the Malaita Eagle Force (MEF) – migrants from the neighbouring island of Malaita. One hundred people died in the conflict. Under a peace agreement signed in October 2000, unarmed peacekeepers from Australia and New Zealand were deployed to supervise the disarmament of the militias. However, following threats by armed gangs, three monitoring groups on Guadalcanal left their posts. It is estimated that there are still more than 500 high-powered weapons in the hands of the rebels.

Australia Aus

Total Armed Forces

ACTIVE 50,920
(incl 6,364 women)

RESERVES 20,300
Army 16,200 **Navy** 2,100 **Air Force** 2,000

Army 25,150

(incl 2,500 women)
1 Land HQ, 1 Joint Force HQ, 1 Task Force HQ (integrated), 1 bde HQ
1 armd regt (integrated), 2 recce regt (1 integrated), 1 SF (SAS) regt, 6 inf bn (incl 2 integrated mot inf, 1 mech, 1 para), 1 cdo bn (integrated), 2 indep APC sqn (1 integrated), 1 med arty regt, 2 fd arty regt (1 integrated), 1 AD regt (integrated), 3 cbt engr regt (1 integrated), 2 avn regt
3 regional force surv units (integrated)
(integrated formations/units are composed of active and reserve personnel)

RESERVES
1 div HQ, 7 bde HQ, 1 cdo, 2 recce, 1 APC, 1 med arty, 3 fd arty, 3 cbt engr, 2 engr construction regt, 13 inf bn; 1 indep fd arty bty; 1 recce, 3 fd engr sqn

EQUIPMENT
MBT 71 *Leopard* 1A3 (excl variants, plus 30 in store)
LAV 111 ASLAV-25
APC 364 M-113 (excl variants, 350 being upgraded, 119 in store)
TOWED ARTY 105mm: 240 M2A2/L5, 109 *Hamel*; **155mm**: 36 M-198
MOR 81mm: 296
RCL 84mm: 577 *Carl Gustav*; **106mm**: 74 M-40A1
SAM 18 *Rapier* B1M, 17 RBS-70
AC 3 *King Air* 200, 1 *King Air* 350, 2 DHC-6 (all on lease)
HEL 35 S-70 A-9, 38 Bell 206 B-1 *Kiowa* (to be upgraded), 25 UH-1H (armed), 6 CH-47D
MARINES 15 LCM
SURV 14 RASIT (veh, arty), AN-TPQ-36 (arty, mor)

Navy 12,570

(incl 990 Naval Avn; 1,900 women)
COMMANDS Maritime Comd, Naval Systems Comd

BASES Sydney, (Maritime Comd HQ) Stirling, Cairns, Darwin, Flinders, Jervis Bay, Noura

SUBMARINES 6

TACTICAL 6

SSK 6

6 *Collins* with *sub-Harpoon* USGW and 6 × 533mm TT (Mk 48 HWT)

PRINCIPAL SURFACE COMBATANTS 9

FRIGATES 9

FFG 6

6 *Adelaide* (US *Oliver Hazard Perry*), with *Standard* SM-1 MR SAM, *Harpoon* SSM, 1 × 76mm gun, 2 × 3 ASTT (Mk 32 LWT), 2 S-70B *Sea Hawk* hel

FF 3

3 *Anzac* (*Meko* 200) with *Sea Sparrow* VLS SAM, 1 × 127mm gun, 6 × 324mm ASTT (Mk 32 LWT), 1 S-70B-2 *Sea Hawk* hel (being replaced by SH-2GA *Super Seasprite*)

PATROL AND COASTAL COMBATANTS 15

PATROL, OFFSHORE 15 *Fremantle* PCO

MINE WARFARE 5

MINE COUNTERMEASURES 5

5 *Huon* MHC, plus 2 *Bandicoot* MSA, 1 *Brolga* MSA

AMPHIBIOUS 3

1 *Tobruk* LST, capacity 500 tps, 2 LCM, 2 LCVP

2 *Kanimbla* (US *Newport*) LPH, capacity 450 tps, 2 LCM, hel 4 Army *Blackhawk* or 3 *Sea King*, no beach-landing capability

plus 5 *Balikpapan* LCH and 4 LCM

SUPPORT AND MISCELLANEOUS 13

1 *Success* AO, 1 *Westralia* AO; 1 sail trg, 5 AT, 3 TRV; 2 *Leuwin* AGHS plus 4 craft

NAVAL AVIATION (Fleet Air Arm) (990)

EQUIPMENT

no cbt ac, 16 armed hel

AIRCRAFT

EW 2 BAe-748

HELICOPTERS

ASW 16 S-70B-2 *Sea Hawk*

UTL/SAR 7 *Sea King* Mk 50A

TRG 12 AS-350BA

Air Force 13,200

(incl 1,964 women); 156 cbt ac incl MR, no armed hel

2 Comds – Air, Trg

Flying hours F-111: 200; F/A-18: 175

AIR CBT GP

STK/RECCE WG 2 stk/recce sqn with 35 F-111 (13 F-111C, 4 F-111A (C), 14 F-111G, 4 RF-111C), 2 EP-3C, 1 EC-130H

TAC/FTR WG 3 sqn (plus 1 OCU) with 71 F/A-18 (55 -A, 16 -B)

TAC TRG WG 2 sqn with 33 *Hawk* 127 lead-in ftr trainers, 1 FAC flt with 3 PC-9A

MP GP 2 sqn with 17* AP-3C/P-3C, 3 TAP-3B

AIRLIFT GP 7 TPT/TKR sqn

2 with 24 C-130 (12 -H, 12 -J)

1 with 5 Boeing 707 (4 tkr)

2 with 14 DHC-4 (*Caribou*)

1 VIP with 2 Boeing 737 BBJ, 3 *Challenger* 604

1 with 10 HS-748 (8 for navigation trg, 2 for VIP tpt), 4 Beech-200 *Super King Air*

TRG 59 PC-9

AD *Jindalee* OTH radar: Radar 1 at Longreach (N. Queensland), Radar 2 at Laverton (W. Australia), third development site at Alice Springs, 3 control and reporting units (1 mobile)

MISSILES

ASM AGM-84A, AGM-142

AAM AIM-7 *Sparrow*, AIM-9M *Sidewinder*, ASRAAM

Forces Abroad

Advisers in **Fji**, **Indo**, **Solomon Islands**, **Th**, **Vanuatu**, **Tonga**, **Western Samoa**, **Kiribati**

MALAYSIA Army: ε115; 1 inf coy (on 3-month rotational tours) **Air Force**: 33; det with 2 P-3C **ac**

PAPUA NEW GUINEA: 38; trg unit

UN AND PEACEKEEPING

EAST TIMOR (UNMISET): 1,315 incl 15 obs and 4 SA-70A hel **ETHIOPIA/ERITREA** (UNMEE): 2 **EGYPT** (MFO): 25 obs **MIDDLE EAST** (UNTSO): 11 obs **PAPUA NEW GUINEA**: 35 (Bougainville Peace Monitoring Group)

Paramilitary

AUSTRALIAN CUSTOMS SERVICE

ac 3 DHC-8, 3 *Reims* F406, 6 BN-2B-20, 1 *Strike Aerocommander* 500 **hel** 1 Bell 206L-4; about 6 boats

Foreign Forces

US Air Force 70; **Navy** 40; joint facilities at NW Cape, Pine Gap and Nurrungar

NEW ZEALAND Air Force 9 navigation trg

SINGAPORE 230; Flying Training School with 27 S-211 **ac**

Brunei Bru

Total Armed Forces

ACTIVE 7,000

(incl 700 women)

RESERVES 700

Army 700

Army 4,900

(incl 250 women)
3 inf bn • 1 spt bn with 1 armd recce, 1 engr sqn

EQUIPMENT

LT TK 20 *Scorpion* (16 to be upgraded)
APC 39 VAB
MOR 81mm: 24
RL *Armbrust*

RESERVES

1 bn

Navy 1,000

(inc 80 women)
BASE Muara

PATROL AND COASTAL COMBATANTS 6

MISSILE CRAFT 3 *Waspada* PFM with 2 MM-38 *Exocet* SSM
PATROL, INSHORE 3 *Perwira* PFI†
PATROL, RIVERINE boats

AMPHIBIOUS craft only

4 LCU; 1 SF sqn plus boats

Air Force 1,100

(incl 75 women)
no cbt ac, 5 armed hel
HEL 2 sqn
1 with 10 Bell 212, 1 Bell 214 (SAR), 4 S-70A, 1 S-70C (VIP)
1 with 5 Bo-105 armed hel (**81mm** rockets)
TPT 1 sqn with 1 CN-235M
TRG 1 sqn with 2 SF-260W, 4 PC-7, 2 Bell 206B
AIR DEFENCE 2 sqn with 12 *Rapier* (incl *Blindfire*), 16 *Mistral*

Paramilitary ε3,750

GURKHA RESERVE UNIT ε2,000+

2 bn

ROYAL BRUNEI POLICE 1,750

7 PCI<

Foreign Forces

UK Army some 1,100; 1 Gurkha inf bn, 1 hel flt, trg school
SINGAPORE 500; trg school incl hel det (5 UH-1)

Cambodia Cam

Total Armed Forces

ACTIVE ε125,000 (to reduce)

(incl Provincial Forces, perhaps only 19,000 cbt capable)
Terms of service conscription authorised but not implemented since 1993

Army ε75,000

6 Mil Regions (incl 1 special zone for capital) • 22 inf div[a] • 3 indep inf bde • 1 protection bde (4 bn) • 9 indep inf regt • 3 armd bn • 1 AB/SF regt • 4 engr regt (3 fd, 1 construction) • some indep recce, arty, AD bn

[a] Inf div established str 3,500, actual str some 1,500 or less

EQUIPMENT

MBT 100+ T-54/-55, 50 PRC Type-59
LT TK PRC Type 62, 20 PRC Type 64
RECCE BRDM-2
AIFV some BMP-1
APC 160 BTR-60/-152, M-113, 30 OT-64 (SKOT)
TOWED ARTY some 400: **76mm**: M-1942; **122mm**: M-1938, D-30; **130mm**: Type 59
MRL 107mm: Type-63; **122mm**: 8 BM-21; **132mm**: BM-13-16; **140mm**: 20 BM-14-16
MOR 82mm: M-37; **120mm**: M-43; **160mm**: M-160
RCL 82mm: B-10; **107mm**: B-11
AD GUNS 14.5mm: ZPU 1/-2/-4; **37mm**: M-1939; **57mm**: S-60

Navy ε3,000

(incl 1,500 Naval Infantry)
BASES Ream (maritime), Prek Ta Ten (river)

PATROL AND COASTAL COMBATANTS 4

PATROL, COASTAL 2
2 FSU *Stenka* PFC plus 6 boats
RIVERINE 2
2 *Kaoh Chhlam* PCR<

NAVAL INFANTRY (1,500)

7 inf, 1 arty bn

Air Force 2,000

24 cbt ac†; no armed hel
FTR 1 sqn with 19† MiG-21 (14 -bis, 5 -UM) (up to 9 to be upgraded by IAI: 2 returned but status unclear)
TPT 1 sqn with 2 Y-12, 1 BN-2. 1 VIP sqn (reporting to Council of Ministry) with 2 An-24RV, 1 Cessna 421, 1 Falcon, 1 AS-350, 1 AS-365
HEL 1 sqn with 14 Mi-8/Mi-17 (incl 1 VIP Mi-8P), 2 Mi-26

RECCE/TRG 5* L-39 for MiG-21 lead-in trg, 5 P-92 for pilot trg/recce

Provincial Forces some 45,000

Reports of at least 1 inf regt per province, with varying numbers of inf bn with lt wpn

Paramilitary

POLICE 67,000 (incl *gendarmerie*)

China, People's Republic of PRC

Total Armed Forces

ACTIVE some 2,270,000 (being reduced)
(incl MOD staff, centrally-controlled units not included elsewhere; perhaps 1,000,000 conscripts, some 136,000 women)
Terms of service selective conscription; all services 2 years

RESERVES some 500–600,000
militia reserves being formed on a province-wide basis

Strategic Missile Forces

OFFENSIVE (100,000)+
org as 18 launch bdes within 6 msl armies; org varies by msl type; one testing and one trg base
ICBM 20+
20+ DF-5A (CSS-4)
First DF-31 (CSS-9) bde reportedly operational
IRBM 130-150
20+ DF-4 (CSS-3)
60-80 DF-3A (CSS-2)
50 DF-21 (CSS-5). At least 3 bde deployed
SLBM 1 *Xia* SSBN with 12 CSS-N-3 (JL-1)
SRBM about 25 DF-15 launchers with 160+ msl (CSS-6/M-9) (range 600km). 1 bde deployed
25 DF-11 (CSS-7/M-11) launchers with 175 msl (range 120–300+km). 2 bde deployed

DEFENSIVE
Tracking stations Xinjiang (covers Central Asia) and Shanxi (northern border)
Phased-array radar complex ballistic-msl early-warning

Army ε1,600,000

(perhaps 800,000 conscripts) (reductions continue)
7 Mil Regions (MR), 28 Provinicial Mil Districts (MD), 4 Garrison Comd
21 Integrated Group Armies (GA): str from 30–65,000, org varies, normally with 2–3 mech/mot inf div/bde, 1 armd div/bde, 1 arty div/bde, 1 SAM/AAA or AAA bde, cbt readiness category varies with 10 GA at Category A and 11 at Category B (reorg to bde structure in progress)

Summary of cbt units
Group Army (GA) 44 inf div (incl 5 mech inf and 24 mot inf) 3 with national level rapid-reaction role and at least 9 with regional rapid-reaction role ready to mobilise in 24–48 hours; 9 armd div, 12 armd bde, 1 mech inf, 22 mot inf bde, 6 arty div, 15 arty bde, 1 ATK bde, 8 SAM/AAA bde, 13 AAA bde, 3 army avn regt
Independent 5 inf div, 1 armd, 2 inf bde, 1 arty div, 3 arty bde, 1 SSM bde, 4 AAA bde, 10 army avn regt (incl 2 trg)
Local Forces (Garrison, Border, Coastal) 12 inf div, 1 mtn bde, 4 inf bde, 87 inf regt/bn
AB (manned by Air Force) ε35,000: 1 corps of 3 div
Coastal Defence Forces some indep arty, 9 SSM regt, 8 AD regt
Support Troops incl 50 engr, 50 sigs regt

EQUIPMENT
MBT some 7,010 incl: 5,000 Type-59-I/-II, 500 Type-79, 900 Type-88A/B, 550 Type-88C, 60 Type-98, some Type-96
LT TK ε1,200 incl 150 Type-63, 350 Type-63A, 700 Type-62/62I
AIFV/APC over 5,000 incl 3,000 Type-63A/I/II/C, 200 Type-77 II (BTR-50PK), 400 Type-89I (mod Type-85), 60 WZ-523, 600+ Type-92 (WZ-551), 800 Type-86A (WZ-501), 100 BMD-3 (reported)
TOWED ARTY 14,000: **100mm**: Type-59 (fd/ATK); **122mm**: Type-54-1, Type-60, Type-83; **130mm**: Type-59/-59-1; **152mm**: Type-54, Type-66; **155mm**: 90 Type-88 (WAC-21)
SP ARTY 122mm: ε1,200 incl 200 Type-70I, 500 Type-89; **152mm**: 500 Type-83
COMBINED GUN/MOR 100 2S23 *Nona-SVK*
MRL 2,400: **122mm**: Type-81, Type-89 SP; **130mm**: Type-70 SP, Type-82; **273mm**: Type-83; **320mm**: Type-96
MOR 82mm: Type-53/-67/-W87/-82 (incl SP); **100mm**: Type-71 reported; **120mm**: Type-55 (incl SP); **160mm**: Type-56
SSM HY-2/C-201/CSS-C-3, HY-4/C-401/CSS-C-7
ATGW 6,500: HJ-73 A/B/C (*Sagger*-type), HJ-8 A/C/E (TOW/*Milan*-type), 24 HJ-9
RL 62mm: Type-70-1
RCL 75mm: Type-56; **82mm**: Type-65, Type-78; **105mm**: Type-75
ATK GUNS 100mm: Type-73, Type-86; **120mm**: 300+ Type-89 SP
AD GUNS 7,700: **23mm**: Type-80; **25mm**: Type-85;

35mm: 50+ Type-90; **37mm**: Type-88SP, Type-55/-65/-74; **57mm**: Type-59, -80 SP; **85mm**: Type-56; **100mm**: Type-59

SAM HN-5A/-B/-C (SA-7 type), HQ-61A, 200 HQ-7A, 36 SA-15 (Tor-M1)

SURV *Cheetah* (arty), Type-378 (veh), RASIT (veh, arty)

HEL ε321: 30 Mi-8, 23 Mi-17, ε105 Mi-171, 3 Mi-6, 4 Z-8A, 60 Z-9A/B, 30 WZ-9, 8 SA-342 (with HOT), 22 S-70C2, 30+ Z-11, 6 SA-316

UAV ASN-104/-105

RESERVES

(undergoing major re-org on provincial basis): some 500–600,000: 70 inf, arty and AD div, 100 indep inf, arty regt

DEPLOYMENT

(GA units only)

North-east Shenyang MR (Heilongjiang, Jilin, Liaoning MD): ε250,000 with 4 GA; 2 armd, 2 mech, 3 mot, 1 arty div; 2 armd, 5 mot, 3 arty, 1 SAM/AAA, 3 AAA, 1 ATK bde

North Beijing MR (Beijing, Tianjin Garrison, Nei Mongol, Hebei, Shanxi MD): ε300,000 with 5 GA; 2 armd, 1 mech, 5 mot, 1 arty div; 3 armd, 7 mot inf, 4 arty, 2 SAM/AAA, 3 AAA bde; 1 ATK regt

West Lanzhou MR (incl Ningxia, Shaanxi, Gansu, Qing-hai, Xinjiang, South Xinjiang MD): ε220,000 with 2 GA; 1 armd, 2 mot inf div; 1 armd, 2 mot inf, 2 arty, 2 AAA bde; 1 ATK regt

South-west Chengdu MR (incl Chongqing Garrison, Sichuan, Guizhou, Yunnan, Xizang MD): ε180,000 with 2 GA; 4 mot inf, 1 arty div; 2 armd, 1 arty, 2 AAA bde

South Guangzhou MR (Hubei, Hunan, Guangdong, Guangxi, Hainan MD): ε180,000 with 2 GA; 4 mot inf, 1 arty div; 2 armd, 1 arty, 1 SAM/AAA, 1 AAA bde. Hong Kong: ε7,000 with 1 inf bde (3 inf, 1 mech inf, 1 arty regt, 1 engr bn), 1 hel unit

Centre Jinan MR (Shandong, Henan MD): ε190,000 with 3 GA; 2 armd, 1 mech inf, 3 mot inf, 1 arty div; 1 armd, 1 mech inf, 4 mot inf, 2 arty, 2 SAM/AAA, 1 AAA bde

East Nanjing MR (Shanghai Garrison, Jiangsu, Zhejiang, Fujian, Jiangxi, Anhui MD): ε250,000: 3 GA; 2 armd, 1 mech inf, 3 mot inf, 1 arty div; 1 armd, 4 mot inf, 2 arty, 2 SAM/AAA, 1 AAA bde; 1 ATK regt

Navy ε250,000

(incl Coastal Regional Defence Forces, 26,000 Naval Avn, some 10,000 Marines and 40,000 conscripts)

SUBMARINES 69

STRATEGIC 1

TACTICAL 67

SSN 5 *Han* (Type 091) with YJ-82 SSM, 6 × 533mm TT

SSG 1 mod *Romeo* (Type S5G), with 6 C-801 (YJ-6, *Exocet* derivative) ASSM; 8 × 533mm TT (test platform)

SSK 61

3 *Song* with YJ 8-2 ASSM (C-802 derivative), 6 × 533mm TT

2 *Kilo*-class (RF Type EKM 877) with 533mm TT

2 *Kilo*-class (RF Type EKM 636) with 533mm TT

3 *Ming* (Type ES5C/D) with 533mm TT

16 imp *Ming* (Type ES5E) with 533mm TT

35 *Romeo* (Type ES3B)† with 533mm TT

OTHER ROLES 1 *Golf* (SLBM trials) SS

PRINCIPAL SURFACE COMBATANTS 63

DESTROYERS 21

DDG 21

2 *Hangzhou* (RF *Sovremenny*) with 2 × 4 SS-N-22 *Sunburn* SSM, 2 SA-N-7 *Gadfly* SAM, 2 × 2 130mm guns, 2 × 2 533mm ASTT, 2 ASW mor, 1 Ka-28 hel

1 *Luhai* with 4 × 4 CSS-N-4 *Sardine* SSM, 1 × 8 *Crotale* SAM, 1 × 2 100mm guns, 2 × 3 ASTT, 2 Ka-28 hel

2 *Luhu* with 4 × 2 YJ-8/CSS-N-4 *Sardine* SSM, 1 × 8 *Crotale* SAM, 2 × 100mm guns, 2 × 3 ASTT, 2 Z-9A (Fr *Panther*) hel

1 *Luda* III with 4 × 2 YJ-8/CSS-N-4 SSM, 2 × 2 130mm gun, 2 × 3 ASTT

2 mod *Luda* with 2 × 3 HY-1/CSS-N-2 SSM, 1 × 2 130mm guns, 2 × 3 ASTT, 2 Z-9C (Fr *Panther*) hel

13 *Luda* (Type-051) with 2 × 3 CSS-N-2 or CSS-N-4 *Sardine* SSM, 2 × 2 130mm guns, 6 × 324mm ASTT, 2 × 12 ASW RL (2 also with 1 × 8 *Crotale* SAM)

FRIGATES about 42 FFG

8 *Jiangwei II* with CSS-N-4 *Sardine* SSM, 1 × 8 *Croatale* SAM, 1 × 2 100mm guns, 2 × 6 ASW mor, 1 Z-9A (Fr *Dauphin*) hel

4 *Jiangwei* I with 2 × 3 C-801 SSM, 1 × 6 × HQ-61/CSA-N-1 SAM, 1 × 2 100mm guns, 2 × 6 ASW mor, 1 Z-9C (Fr *Panther*) hel

About 30 *Jianghu*; 3 variants:

ε26 Type I, with 2 × 2 *SY*-1/CSS-N-1 SSM, 2 × 100mm guns, 4 × 5 ASW mor

ε1 Type II, with 1 × 2 *SY*-1/CSS-N-1 SSM, 1 × 2 × 100mm guns, 2 × 5 ASW RL, 1 Z-9C (Fr *Panther*) hel

ε3 Type III, with 8 CSS-N-4 *Sardine* SSM, 2 × 2 100mm guns, 4 × 5 ASW RL

PATROL AND COASTAL COMBATANTS ε368

MISSILE CRAFT ε93

5 *Huang* PFM with 6 YJ-8/CSS-N-4 SSM

20 *Houxin* PFM with 4 YJ-8/CSS-N-4 SSM

ε38 *Huangfeng/Hola* (FSU *Osa* I-Type) PFM with 4 SY-1 SSM

30 *Houku* (*Komar*-Type) PFM with 2 SY-1 SSM

TORPEDO CRAFT ε16

16 *Huchuan* PHT

PATROL CRAFT ε259

COASTAL ε118

2 *Haijui* PCC with 3 × 5 ASW RL

ε96 *Hainan* PCC with 4 ASW RL
20 *Haiqing* PCC with 2 × 6 ASW mor
INSHORE ε111
100 *Shanghai* PCI<, 11 *Haizhui* PCI<
RIVERINE ε30<

MINE WARFARE ε39

MINELAYERS 1
1 *Wolei*
In addition, *Luda* class DDG, *Hainan*, *Shanghai* PC and T-43 MSO have minelaying capability
MINE COUNTERMEASURES about 38
27 (ex-FSU T-43) MSO
7 *Wosao* MSC
3 *Wochang* and 1 *Shanghai* II MSI
plus about 50 Lienyun aux MSC, 4 drone MSI and 42 reserve drone MSI

AMPHIBIOUS 56

7 *Yukan* LST, capacity about 200 tps, 10 tk
3 *Shan* (US LST-1) LST, capacity about 165 tps, 16 tk
9 *Yuting* LST, capacity about 250 tps, 10 tk, 2 hel
1 *Yudeng* LSM, capacity about 500 tps, 9 tk
22 *Yuliang* LSM, capacity about 100 tps, 3 tk
13 *Yuhai* LSM, capacity 250 tps, 2tk
1 *Yudao* LSM
craft: 45 LCU, 10 LCAC plus over 230 LCU in reserve

SUPPORT AND MISCELLANEOUS ε163

1 *Nanchang* AO, 2 *Fuqing* AO, 33 AOT, 14 AF, 10 AS, 1 ASR, 2 AR; 6 *Qiongsha* AH, 30 tpt, 4 icebreakers, 25 AT/F, 1 hel trg, 1 trg; 33 AGOR/AGOS

NAVAL AVIATION (26,000)

EQUIPMENT
472 shore-based cbt ac, 45 armed hel
AIRCRAFT
BBR 18 H-6D reported with YJ-6/61 anti-ship ALCM; ε50 H-5 torpedo-carrying lt bbr
FGA ε30 Q-5, 18 JH-7
FTR ε250 J-6, 30 J-7, 24 J-8/8A, 12 J-8IIA, 6 J-8B, 6 J-8D
MR/ASW 4 PS-5 (SH-5), 4 Y-8X
RECCE 7 HZ-5
TKR 10 H-6D
TPT 6 An-26, 50 Y-5, 4 Y-7, 4 Y-8, 2 YAK-42,
TRG 53 PT-6, 16* JJ-6, 4* JJ-7
HELICOPTERS
ASW 15 SA-321, 8 Z-8, 6 Z-9C, 8 Ka-28, 8 AS 565
TPT 12 Mi-8
MISSILES
ALCM YJ-6/C-601, YJ-61/C-611, YJ-81/C-801K
(Naval ftr integrated into national AD system)

MERCHANT FLEET

1,957 ocean-going ships over 1,000t (incl 298 AOT, 555 dry bulk, 191 container, 913 other)

MARINES (some 10,000)

2 bde (3 marine, 1 mech inf, 1 lt tk, 1 arty bn); 2 amph recce bn
3 Army div also have amph role

EQUIPMENT
LT TK 60 Type-63A
APC 100 Type-77-II
ARTY 122mm: Type-83
MRL 107mm: Type-63
ATGW HJ-73, HJ-8
SAM HN-5

DEPLOYMENT AND BASES

NORTH SEA FLEET

coastal defence from DPRK border (Yalu River) to south of Lianyungang (approx 35°10′N); equates to Shenyang, Beijing and Jinan MR, and to seaward
BASES Qingdao (HQ), Dalian (Luda), Huludao, Weihai, Chengshan, Yuchi; 9 coastal defence districts
FORCES under review

EAST SEA FLEET

coastal defence from south of Lianyungang to Dongshan (approx 35°10′N to 23°30′N); equates to Nanjing Military Region, and to seaward
BASES HQ Dongqian Lake (Ninbo), Shanghai Naval base, Dinghai, Hangzhou, Xiangshan; 7 coastal defence districts

SOUTH SEA FLEET

coastal defence from Dongshan (approx 23°30′N) to Vn border; equates to Guangzhou MR, and to seaward (including Paracel and Spratly Islands)
BASE Hong Kong, Yulin, Guangzhou

Air Force 420,000

(incl strategic forces, 220,000 AD personnel and 160,000 conscripts); some 1,900+ cbt ac, some armed hel **Flying hours** H-6: 80; J-7 and J-8: 130; Su-27/Su-30: 180
HQ Beijing. 5 Air Corps, each equivalent to a PLA Group Army - 1 Corps (Changchun), 7 Corps (Nanning), 8 Corps (Fuzhou), 9 Corps (Urumqi), 10 Corps (Datong). 32 air divs (22 ftr, 3 bbr, 5 attack, 2 tpt). Up to 4 sqn, each with 10–15 ac, 1 maint unit, some tpt and trg ac, make up an air regt; 3 air regt form an air div. Varying numbers of air divs in the Mil Regions – many in the south-east
BBR 6 regt with 120 H-6E/F/H (1 regt (some 20 ac) nuclear ready), 1 regt with 20 H-6H (planned to carry YJ-63 cruise missile). 1 trg regt with 40 H-5
FTR 300 J-7II/IIA, 50 J-7IIH, 24 J-7 IIM, 80 J-7III, 200+ J-7E, 40 J-8IIA, 104 J-8B/D, 60 J-8E, 70 Su-27, 20 Su-27UBK
FGA 38 Su-30MKK. 300 Q-5, some 20 regt with 500+ J-6/B/D/E
RECCE/ELINT ε290: ε40 HZ-5, 100 JZ-6, some JZ-7, some 20 JZ-8, 4 Tu-154M
TPT ε513: incl some 15 Tu-154M, 2 Il-18, 20 Il-76MD,

300 Y-5, 100 Y-7/An-24/An-26, 48 Y-8/An-12, 15 Y-11, 8 Y-12, 6 Boeing 737-200 (VIP), 5 CL-601 *Challenger*

TKR 1 regt of 8 HY-6

HEL ε170: incl 6 AS-332 (VIP), 4 Bell 214, 40 Mi-8, 20 Z-9

TRG ε200: incl HJ-5, JJ-6, 50+ JJ-7, 8+ JL-8, PT-6 (CJ-6)

MISSILES

AAM PL-2, PL-5, PL-8, 250+ AA-10, 250+ AA-11, *Python* 3, 100 AA-12 on order for Su-30MKK

ASM YJ-6/C-601, YJ-61/C-611, YJ-63 expected, YJ-81K/C-801K

UAV *Chang Hong* 1

AD 3 SAM div, 1 mixed SAM/AAA div; 11 AD bde (7 SAM, 4 AAA), 16,000 **85mm** and **100mm** guns; 100+ SAM units with 500+ HQ-2/2A/2B, 60 HQ-7, 144 SA-10, 72 HQ-9

Forces Abroad

UN AND PEACEKEEPING

DROC (MONUC): 10 incl 9 obs **ETHIOPIA/ERITREA** (UNMEE): 5 obs **MIDDLE EAST** (UNTSO): 1 obs **IRAQ/KUWAIT** (UNIKOM): 11 obs **SIERRA LEONE** (UNAMSIL): 6 obs **WESTERN SAHARA** (MINURSO): 16 obs

Paramilitary ε1,500,000 active

PEOPLE'S ARMED POLICE (Ministry of Public Security) ε1,500,000

45 div (14 each with 4 regt, remainder no standard org; with 1–2 div per province) incl **Internal security** ε800,000 **Border defence** some 100,000 **Guards, Comms** ε69,000

East Timor TL

Total Armed Forces

Trg began in Jan 2001 with the aim of deploying 1,500 full time personnel and 1,500 reservists by Jan 2004

ACTIVE 636

Army 636

1 inf bn

(**NAVAL ELEMENT** 36)

Foreign Forces

UN (UNMISET): some 5,199 tps incl 117 obs from 30 countries

Fiji Fji

Total Armed Forces

ACTIVE some 3,500
(incl recalled reserves)

RESERVES some 6,000
(to age 45)

Army 3,200

(incl 300 recalled reserves)
7 inf bn (incl 4 cadre) • 1 engr bn • 1 arty bty • 1 special ops coy

EQUIPMENT

TOWED ARTY 88mm: 4 25-pdr (ceremonial)
MOR 81mm: 12
HEL 1 AS-355, 1 SA-365

Navy 300

BASES Walu Bay, Viti (trg)

PATROL AND COASTAL COMBATANTS 9

PATROL, COASTAL/INSHORE 9

3 *Kula* (*Pacific Forum*) PCC, 4 *Vai* (Il *Dabur*) PCI<, 2 *Levuka* PCI<

SUPPORT AND MISCELLANEOUS 2

1 *Cagi Donu* presidential yacht (trg), 1 *Tovutu* AGHS

Forces Abroad

UN AND PEACEKEEPING

EAST TIMOR (UNMISET): 197 **EGYPT** (MFO): 338; 1 inf bn(-) **IRAQ/KUWAIT** (UNIKOM): 7 obs **LEBANON** (UNIFIL): 583; 1 inf bn **PAPUA NEW GUINEA**: 5 (Bougainville Peace Monitoring Group)

Indonesia Indo

Total Armed Forces

ACTIVE 297,000

Terms of service 2 years selective conscription authorised

RESERVES 400,000

Army cadre units; numbers, str n.k., obligation to age 45 for officers

Army ε230,000

Strategic Reserve (KOSTRAD) (30,000)
2 inf div HQ • 3 inf bde (9 bn) • 3 AB bde (9 bn) • 2 fd arty regt (6 bn) • 1 AD arty regt (2 bn) • 2 armd bn • 2 engr bn

11 Mil Area Comd (KODAM) (150,000) (Provincial (KOREM) and District (KODIM) comd)
2 inf bde (6 bn) • 65 inf bn (incl 5 AB) • 8 cav bn • 11 fd arty, 10 AD bn • 8 engr bn • 1 composite avn sqn, 1 hel sqn

Special Forces (KOPASSUS) (e5,000); 3 SF gp (incl 2 para-cdo, 1 int, 8 counter-terrorist, 1 trg unit)

EQUIPMENT

LT TK some 275 AMX-13 (to be upgraded), 30 PT-76, 50 *Scorpion*-90
RECCE 69 *Saladin* (16 upgraded), 55 *Ferret* (13 upgraded), 18 VBL
AIFV 11 BMP-2
APC 200 AMX-VCI, 45 *Saracen* (14 upgraded), 60 V-150 *Commando*, 22 *Commando Ranger*, 80 BTR-40, 34 BTR-50PK, 40 *Stormer* (incl variants)
TOWED ARTY 76mm: 100 M-48; **105mm**: 170 M-101, 10 M-56; **155mm**: 5 FH 2000
MOR 81mm: 800; **120mm**: 75 Brandt
RCL 90mm: 90 M-67; **106mm**: 45 M-40A1
RL 89mm: 700 LRAC
AD GUNS 20mm: 125 Rh 20; **40mm**: 90 L/70; **57mm**: 200 S-60
SAM 51 *Rapier*, 42 RBS-70
AC 6 NC-212, 2 *Commander* 680, 3 DHC-5
HEL 12 Bell 205A, 13 Bo-105, 26 NB-412, 12 Hughes 300C (trg)

Navy 40,000

(incl ε1,000 Naval Avn and 12,000 Marines)
(overall serviceability of whole fleet is low)
COMMANDS Western, Eastern and Military Sealift
BASES Primary Teluk Ratai (Jakarta, HQ Western Cmd), Belawan, Surabaya (HQ Eastern Cmd), Ujung Pandang, Vayapura **Minor** 10 (in Western Cmd), 13 (in Eastern Cmd)

SUBMARINES 2

SSK 2 *Cakra* (Ge *T-209*) with 8 × 533mm TT (Ge HWT)

PRINCIPAL SURFACE COMBATANTS 17

FRIGATES 17
FFG 10
6 *Ahmad Yani* (Nl *Van Speijk*) with 2 × 4 *Harpoon* SSM, 2 × 2 *Mistral* SAM, 1 × 76mm gun, 2 × 3 ASTT, 1 *Wasp* hel
3 *Fatahillah* with 2 × 2 MM-38 *Exocet* SSM, 1 × 120mm gun, 2 × 3 ASTT (not *Nala*), 1 × 2 ASW mor, 1 *Wasp* hel (*Nala* only)
1 *Hajar Dewantara* (trg) with 2 × 2 MM-38 *Exocet* SSM, 2 × 533mm ASTT, 1 ASW mor
FF 7
4 *Samadikun* (US *Claud Jones*) with 1 × 76mm gun, 2 × 3 324mm ASTT
3 *M. K. Tiyahahu* (UK *Tribal*) with *Mistral* SAM, 2 × 114mm guns, 1 × 3 *Limbo* ASW mor, 1 *Wasp* hel

PATROL AND COASTAL COMBATANTS 36

CORVETTES 16 *Kapitan Patimura* (GDR *Parchim*) FS with SA-N-5 *Gecko* SAM (in some), 1 × 57mm gun, 4 × 400mm ASTT, 2 ASW RL
MISSILE CRAFT 4 *Mandau* (Ko *Dagger*) PFM with 4 MM-38 *Exocet* SSM
TORPEDO CRAFT 4 *Singa* (Ge Lürssen 57m) with 2 × 533mm TT
PATROL CRAFT 12
OFFSHORE 4
4 *Kakap* (Ge Lürssen 57m) PCO with hel deck
COASTAL/INSHORE 8
8 *Sibarau* (Aust *Attack*) PCC
plus 18 craft

MINE WARFARE 12

MINE COUNTERMEASURES 12
2 *Pulau Rengat* (mod Nl *Tripartite*) MCC (sometimes used for coastal patrol)
2 *Pulau Rani* (FSU T-43) MCC (mainly used for coastal patrol)
8 *Palau Rote* (GDR *Kondor* II)† MSC (mainly used for coastal patrol, 7 non-op)

AMPHIBIOUS 26

6 *Teluk Semangka* (SK *Tacoma*) LST, capacity about 200 tps, 17 tk, 2 with 3 hel
1 *Teluk Amboina* LST, capacity about 200 tps, 16 tk
7 *Teluk Langsa* (US *LST-512*) LST, capacity 200 tps, 16 tks
12 *Teluk Gilimanuk* (GDR *Frosch* I/II) LST
Plus about 65 LCM and LCVP

SUPPORT AND MISCELLANEOUS 15

1 *Sorong* AO, 1 *Arun* AO (UK *Rover*), 2 FSU *Khobi* AOT, 1 cmd/spt/replenish; 1 AR, 2 AT/F, 1 *Barakuda* (Ge *Lürssen Nav* IV) presidental yacht; 6 AGOR/AGOS

NAVAL AVIATION (ε1,000)

EQUIPMENT

no cbt ac, 17 armed hel

AIRCRAFT

MR 12 CN-235 MPA, 15 N22M *Searchmaster* B, 10 N22SL *Searchmaster* L

TPT 4 *Commander*, 4 NC-212, 2 DHC-5, 1 CN-235 M

TRG 6 PA-38 *Tomahawk*, 4 PA-34 *Seneca*

HELICOPTERS

ASW 9 *Wasp* HAS-1

TPT 26 NAS-332L *Super Puma*, 2* Bell-412, 6* NBO-105, 8 Soloy-Bell 47G, 3 EC-120B

MARINES (KORMAR) (12,000)

1 mne corps gp with 1 mne inf bde, 1 indep mne inf bde • 1 SF bn(-) • 1 cbt spt regt (arty, AD)

EQUIPMENT

LT TK 100 PT-76†
RECCE 14 BRDM
AIFV 10 AMX-10 PAC 90
APC 24 AMX-10P, 60 BTR-50P
TOWED ARTY 48: **105mm**: 20 LG-1 Mk II; **122mm**: 28 M-38
MOR 81mm
MRL 140mm: 15 BM-14
AD GUNS 50+: **40mm**: 5 L60/70; **57mm**: S-60

Air Force 27,000

90 cbt ac, no armed hel; 2 operational cmds (East and West Indo) plus trg cmd
Only 45% of ac op
FGA 4 sqn
1 with 14 A-4 (11 -E, 1 TA-4H, 2 TA-4J)
1 with 10 F-16 (7 -A, 3 -B)
2 with 7 *Hawk* Mk 109 and 28 *Hawk* Mk 209 (FGA/ftr)
FTR 1 sqn with 12 F-5 (8 -E, 4 -F)
RECCE 1 flt with 12* OV-10F (only a few op)
MR 1 sqn with 3 Boeing 737-200
TKR 2 KC-130B
TPT 5 sqn with 18 C-130 (9 -B, 3 -H, 6 -H-30), 3 L100-30, 1 Boeing 707, 4 Cessna 207, 5 Cessna 401, 2 C-402, 6 F-27-400M, 1 F-28-1000, 2 F-28-3000, 10 NC-212, 1 *Skyvan* (survey), 10 CN-235-110
HEL 3 sqn with 10 S-58T, 10 Hughes 500, 11 NAS-330, 5 NAS-332L (VIP/CSAR), 4 NBO-105CD, 8 EC-120B
TRG 3 sqn with 7 *Hawk* Mk53*, 39 AS-202, 2 Cessna 172, 20 T-34C, 6 T-41D, 19 SF-260W
MISSILES
AIM-9P *Sidewinder*, AGM-65G *Maverick*

Forces Abroad

UN AND PEACEKEEPING

CROATIA (UNMOP): 2 obs **DROC** (MONUC): 10 incl 3 obs **GEORGIA** (UNOMIG): 4 obs **IRAQ/KUWAIT** (UNIKOM): 6 obs **SIERRA LEONE** (UNAMSIL): 10 obs

Paramilitary ε195,000 active

POLICE (Ministry of Interior) ε195,000

incl 14,000 police 'mobile bde' (BRIMOB) org in 56 coy, incl counter-terrorism unit (*Gegana*)

EQUIPMENT

APC 34 *Tactica*
AC 1 *Commander*, 2 Beech 18, 2 NC-212
HEL 19 NBO-105, 3 Bell 206

MARINE POLICE (12,000)

about 10 PCC, 9 PCI and 6 PCI< (all armed)

KAMRA (People's Security) (R)

ε40,000 report for 3 weeks' basic trg each year; part-time police auxiliary

CUSTOMS

about 72 PFI<, armed

SEA COMMUNICATIONS AGENCY (responsible to Department of Communications)

5 *Kujang* PCI, 4 *Golok* PCI (SAR), plus boats

Opposition

ORGANISASI PAPUA MERDEKA (OPM) ε150 (100 armed)

FREE ACEH MOVEMENT (*Gerakan Aceh Merdeka*) armed wing (AGAM) ε2,000

Other Forces

Militia gps operating in some provinces include:

a. Muslim

Laskar Jihad (Holy war soldiers) Java-based. With ε400 based around Ambon in Maluku province.
Laskar Sabillah based west/central Java, south Sumatra
Front to Defend Islam based Java/Sumatra
Muslim Brotherhood, Laskar Mujahidin, Banser plus numerous other gps

b. Non-Muslim

Laskar Kristus based Ambon
Satgas Golkar plus 4 other gps

Japan J

Total Armed Forces

ACTIVE some 239,900
(incl 1,700 Central Staffs; some 10,400 women)
RESERVES some 47,000
READY RESERVE Army (GSDF) some 5,000
GENERAL RESERVE Army (GSDF) some 40,100 **Navy** (MSDF) some 1,100 **Air Force** (ASDF) some 800

Ground Self-Defence Force some 148,200

5 Army HQ (Regional Comds) • 1 armd div • 10 inf div (6 at 7,000, 5 at 9,000 each); 2 inf bde • 2 composite bde • 1 AB bde • 1 arty bde; 2 arty gp • 2 AD bde; 3 AD gp • 3 trg bde; 1 trg regt • 5 engr bde •1 hel bde • 5 ATK hel sqn

EQUIPMENT

MBT some 820 Type-74, some 220 Type-90
RECCE some 90 Type-87
AIFV some 60 Type-89
APC some 130 Type-60, some 340 Type-73, some 230 Type-82, some 130 Type-96
TOWED ARTY 155mm: some 480 FH-70
SP ARTY 155mm: some 190 Type-75, some Type-99; **203mm**: some 90 M-110A2
MRL 130mm: some 50 Type-75 SP; **227mm**: some 70 MLRS
MOR incl **81mm**: some 690; **107mm**: some 170; **120mm**: some 360 (some 20 SP)
SSM some 100 Type-88 coastal
ATGW some 114 Type-64, some 240 Type-79, some 320 Type-87
RL 89mm: some 1,500
RCL 84mm: some 2,720 *Carl Gustav*; **106mm**: some 190 (incl Type 60 SP)
AD GUNS 35mm: some 30 twin, some 50 Type-87 SP
SAM some 310 *Stinger*, some 60 Type 81, some 160 Type 91, some 70 Type 93, some 200 I HAWK
AC some 10 LR-1, some LR-2
ATTACK HEL some 90 AH-1S
TPT HEL 3 AS-332L (VIP), some 50 CH-47J/JA, some 150 OH-6D, some 140 UH-1H/J, some 20 UH-60JA
SURV Type-92 (mor), J/MPQ-P7 (arty)

Maritime Self-Defence Force some 44,400

(incl some 9,800 Naval Avn; and some 1,800 women)
BASES Yokosuka, Kure, Sasebo, Maizuru, Ominato
FLEET Surface units org into 4 escort flotillas of 8 DD/FF each **Bases** Yokosuka, Kure, Sasebo, Maizuru
SS org into 2 flotillas **Bases** Kure, Yokosuka
Remainder assigned to 5 regional districts

SUBMARINES 16
SSK 16
6 *Harushio* with *Harpoon* USGW, 6 × 533mm TT (J Type-89 HWT)
6 *Yuushio* with *Harpoon* USGW, 6 × 533mm TT (J Type-89 HWT)
4 *Oyashio* with *Harpoon* USGW, 6 × 533mm TT

PRINCIPAL SURFACE COMBATANTS some 54
DESTROYERS 44
DDG 39
4 *Kongou* with 2 × 4 *Harpoon* SSM, 2 VLS for *Standard* SAM and ASROC SUGW, 1 × 127mm gun, 2 × 3 ASTT, hel deck
2 *Hatakaze* with 2 × 4 *Harpoon* SSM, 1 SM-1-MR SAM, 2 × 127mm guns, 2 × 3 ASTT, 1 × 8 ASROC SUGW
3 *Tachikaze* with 2 × 4 *Harpoon* SSM, 1 SM-1-MR SAM, 1 × 127mm guns, 2 × 3 ASTT, 1 × 8 ASROC SUGW
2 *Takatsuki* (J DD) with 2 × 4 *Harpoon* SSM, *Sea Sparrow* SAM, 1 × 127mm gun, 2 × 3 ASTT, 1 × 8 ASROC SUGW, 1 × 4 ASW RL
9 *Murasame* with 2 × 4 *Harpoon* SSM, 1 VLS *Sea Sparrow* SAM, 2 × 3 ASTT, 1 VLS ASROC SUGW, 1 SH-60J hel
8 *Asagiri* (J DD) with 2 × 4 *Harpoon* SSM, *Sea Sparrow* SAM, 2 × 3 ASTT, 1 × 8 ASROC SUGW, 1 SH-60J hel
11 *Hatsuyuki* (J DD) with 2 × 4 *Harpoon* SSM, *Sea Sparrow* SAM, 2 × 3 ASTT, 1 × 8 ASROC SUGW, 1 SH-60J hel
DD 5
2 *Shirane* (J DDH) with *Sea Sparrow* SAM, 2 × 127mm guns, 2 × 3 ASTT, 1 × 8 ASROC SUGW, 3 SH-60J hel
2 *Haruna* (J DDH) with 1 x *Sea Sparrow* SAM, 2 × 127mm guns, 2 × 3 ASTT, 1 × 8 ASROC SUGW, 3 SH-60J hel
1 *Yamagumo* (J DDH) with 4 × 76mm gun, 2 × 3 ASTT, 1 × 8 ASROC SUGW, 1 × 4 ASW RL
FRIGATES 10
FFG 9
6 *Abukuma* (J DE) with 2 × 4 *Harpoon* SSM, 1 × 76mm gun, 2 × 3 ASTT, 1 × 8 ASROC SUGW
2 *Yubari* (J DE) with 2 × 4 *Harpoon* SSM, 2 × 3 ASTT, 1 × 4 ASW RL
1 *Ishikari* (J DE) with 2 × 4 *Harpoon* SSM, 2 × 3 ASTT, 1 × 4 ASW RL
FF 1
1 *Chikugo* (J DE) with 2 × 76mm guns, 2 × 3 ASTT, 1 × 8 ASROC SUGW

PATROL AND COASTAL COMBATANTS 5

MISSILE CRAFT 3 *Ichi-Go* (J PG) PHM with 4 SSM-1B, 2 *Hayabusa* PFM with 4 SSM-1B

MINE WARFARE 31

MINE COUNTERMEASURES 31

2 *Uraga* MCM spt (J MST) with hel deck; can lay mines
3 *Yaeyama* MSO
10 *Hatsushima* MSC
9 *Uwajima* MSC
5 *Sugashima* MSC
2 *Nijma* coastal MCM spt

AMPHIBIOUS 8

2 *Osumi* LST, capacity 330 tps, 10 tk, 2 LCAC, (large flight deck)
1 *Miura* LST, capacity 200 tps, 10 tk
1 *Atsumi* LST, capacity 130 tps, 5 tk
2 *Yura* and 2 *Ichi-Go* LSM
Plus craft: 2 LCAC, 11 LCM

SUPPORT AND MISCELLANEOUS 28

3 *Towada* AOE, 1 *Sagami* AOE (all with hel deck), 2 AS/ARS, 1 ARC; 2 *Yamagumo* trg, 1 *Kashima* (trg), 1 *Shimayuki* (trg), 2 trg spt, 4 AGHS, 10 AG, 1 icebreaker

NAVAL AVIATION (ε9,800)

ORGANISATION

7 Air Groups

AIRCRAFT

MR 9 sqn (1 trg) with P-3C
EW 1 sqn with EP-3
TPT 1 sqn with YS-11M
SAR 1 sqn with US-1A
TRG 4 sqn with T-5, TC-90, YS-11T

HELICOPTERS

ASW 6 land-based sqn (1 trg) with HSS-2B, 4 shipboard sqn with SH-60J
MCM 1 sqn with MH-53E
SAR 2 sqn with S-61, UH-60J
TRG 1 sqn with OH-6D, OH-6DA

EQUIPMENT

80 cbt ac; 91 armed hel

AIRCRAFT

80 **P-3C** • several **EP-3** • several **YS-11M** • some 6 **YS-11T** • 7 **US-1A** • 36 **T-5** • 26 **TC-90**

HELICOPTERS

12 **HSS-2B** • 69 **SH-60J** • 10 **MH-53E** • 3 **S-61** • 17 **UH-60J** • 7 **OH-6D** • 3 **OH-6DA**

Air Self-Defence Force some 45,600

some 280 cbt ac, no armed hel, 7 cbt air wings
Flying hours 150
FGA 1 sqn with some 20 F-1, 1 sqn with some 20 F-2
FTR 9 sqn
7 with some 130 F-15J
2 with some 50 F-4EJ
RECCE 1 sqn with some 20* RF-4E/EJ
AEW 1 sqn with some 10 E-2C, some 4 Boeing E-767 (AWACS)
EW 2 sqn with 1 EC-1, some 10 YS-11 E
TPT 4 sqn, 4 flt
3 with some 20 C-1, some 10 C-130H, a few YS-11
1 with a few 747-400 (VIP)
4 flt hy-lift hel with some 10 CH-47J
SAR 1 wg (10 det) **ac** some 10 MU-2, some 20 U-125A **hel** some 10 KV-107, some 20 UH-60J
CALIBRATION 1 sqn with a few YS-11, a few U-125-800
TRG 5 wg, 12 sqn with some 20* F-15J/DJ, some 20* T-2, some 40 T-3, some 80 T-4, some 10 T-400
LIAISON some 90 T-4, a few U-4
TEST 1 wg with a few F-15J/DJ, some 10 T-4

AIR DEFENCE

ac control and warning: 4 wg, 28 radar sites
6 SAM gp (24 sqn) with some 140 *Patriot*
Air Base Defence Gp with **20mm** *Vulcan* AA guns, Type 81 short-range SAM, Type 91 portable SAM, *Stinger* SAM
ASM ASM-1, ASM-2
AAM AAM-3, AIM-7 *Sparrow*, AIM-9 *Sidewinder*

Forces Abroad

UN AND PEACEKEEPING

EAST TIMOR (UNMISET): 690 **SYRIA/ISRAEL** (UNDOF): 30

Paramilitary 12,250

COAST GUARD 12,250 (Ministry of Transport, no cbt role)

PATROL VESSELS some 333
Offshore (over 1,000 tons) 42, incl 1 *Shikishima* with 2 *Super Puma* hel, 2 *Mizuho* with 2 Bell 212, 8 *Soya* with 1 Bell 212 hel, 2 *Izu*, 28 *Shiretok* and 1 Kojima (trg) **Coastal** (under 1,000 tons) 66 **Inshore** some 225 patrol craft most<
MISC 74: 13 AGHS, 54 nav tender, 4 buoy tenders, 3 trg, plus 86 boats
AC 5 YS-11A, 2 Saab 340, 19 *King Air*, 1 Cessna U-206G
HEL 26 Bell 212, 4 Bell 206B, 6 Bell 412, 4 *Super Puma*, 4 Sikorsky S76C

Foreign Forces

US 38,450: **Army** 1,900; 1 Corps HQ **Navy** 5,200; bases at Yokosuka (HQ 7th Fleet) and Sasebo **Marines** 20,000; 1 MEF in Okinawa **Air Force** 11,350; 1 Air Force HQ (5th Air Force), 90 cbt ac, 1 ftr wg, 2 sqn with 36 F-16, 1 wg, 3 sqn with 54 F-15C/D, 1 sqn with 15 KC-135, 1 SAR sqn with 8 HH-60, 1 sqn with 2 E-3 AWACS; 1 airlift wg with 16 C-130E/H, 4 C-21, 3 C-9; 1 special ops gp with 4 MC-130P, 4 MC-130E

Korea, Democratic People's Republic of (North) DPRK

Total Armed Forces

ACTIVE ε1,082,000

Terms of service **Army** 5–8 years **Navy** 5–10 years **Air Force** 3–4 years, followed by compulsory part-time service to age 40. Thereafter service in the Worker/Peasant Red Guard to age 60

RESERVES 4,700,000 of which

Army 600,000 **Navy** 65,000 are assigned to units (see also *Paramilitary*)

Army ε950,000

20 Corps (1 armd, 4 mech, 12 inf, 2 arty, 1 capital defence) • 27 inf div • 15 armd bde • 14 inf • 21 arty • 9 MRL bde

Special Purpose Forces Comd (88,000): 10 *Sniper* bde (incl 2 amph, 2 AB), 12 lt inf bde (incl 3 AB), 17 recce, 1 AB bn, 'Bureau of Reconnaissance SF' (8 bn)

Army tps: 6 hy arty bde (incl MRL), 1 *Scud* SSM bde, 1 FROG SSM regt

Corps tps: 14 arty bde incl 122mm, 152mm SP, MRL

RESERVES

40 inf div, 18 inf bde

EQUIPMENT

MBT some 3,500: T-34, T-54/-55, T-62, Type-59
LT TK 560 PT-76, M-1985
APC 2,500 BTR-40/-50/-60/-152, PRC Type-531, VTT-323 (M-1973), some BTR-80A
TOTAL ARTY (excl mor) 10,400
TOWED ARTY 3,500: **122mm**: M-1931/-37, D-74, D-30; **130mm**: M-46; **152mm**: M-1937, M-1938, M-1943
SP ARTY 4,400: **122mm**: M-1977, M-1981, M-1985, M-1991; **130mm**: M-1975, M-1981, M-1991; **152mm**: M-1974, M-1977; **170mm**: M-1978, M-1989
COMBINED GUN/MOR: **120mm** (reported)
MRL 2,500: **107mm**: Type-63; **122mm**: BM-21, BM-11, M-1977/-1985/-1992/-1993; **240mm**: M-1985/-1989/-1991
MOR 7,500: **82mm**: M-37; **120mm**: M-43 (some SP); **160mm**: M-43
SSM 24 FROG-3/-5/-7; some 30 *Scud*-C, ε10 *No-dong*
ATGW: AT-1 *Snapper*, AT-3 *Sagger* (some SP), AT-4 *Spigot*, AT-5 *Spandrel*
RCL 82mm: 1,700 B-10
AD GUNS 11,000: **14.5mm**: ZPU-1/-2/-4 SP, M-1984 SP; **23mm**: ZU-23, M-1992 SP; **37mm**: M-1939, M-1992; **57mm**: S-60, M-1985 SP; **85mm**: KS-12; **100mm**: KS-19
SAM ε10,000+ SA-7/-16

Navy ε46,000

BASES East Coast Toejo (HQ), Changjon, Munchon, Songjon-pardo, Mugye-po, Mayang-do, Chaho Nodongjagu, Puam-Dong, Najin **West Coast** Nampo (HQ), Pipa Got, Sagon-ni, Chodo-ri, Koampo, Tasa-ri 2 Fleet HQ

SUBMARINES 26

SSK 26
22 PRC Type-031/FSU *Romeo* with 533mm TT, 4 FSU *Whiskey*† with 533mm and 406mm TT
(Plus some 45 SSI and 21 *Sang-O* SSC mainly used for SF ops, but some with 2 TT, all †)

PRINCIPAL SURFACE COMBATANTS 3

FRIGATES 3
FF 3
1 *Soho* with 4 SS-N-2 *Styx* SSM, 1 × 100mm gun and hel deck, 4 ASW RL
2 *Najin* with 2 SS-N-2 *Styx* SSM, 2 × 100mm guns, 2 × 5 ASW RL

PATROL AND COASTAL COMBATANTS some 310

CORVETTES 6
4 *Sariwon* FS with 1 × 85mm gun
2 *Tral* FS with 1 × 85mm gun
MISSILE CRAFT 43
15 *Soju*, 8 FSU *Osa*, 4 PRC *Huangfeng* PFM with 4 SS-N-2 *Styx* SSM, 6 *Sohung*, 10 FSU *Komar* PFM with 2 SS-N-2 *Styx* SSM
TORPEDO CRAFT some 103
3 FSU *Shershen* PFT with 4 × 533mm TT
60 *Ku Song* PHT
40 *Sin Hung* PHT
PATROL CRAFT 158
COASTAL 25
6 *Hainan* PFC with 4 ASW RL, 13 *Taechong* PFC with 2 ASW RL, 6 *Chong-Ju* with 1 × 85mm gun, (2 ASW mor)
INSHORE some 133
18 SO-1<, 12 *Shanghai* II<, 3 *Chodo*<, some 100<

MINE WARFARE 23

MINE COUNTERMEASURES about 23 MSI<

AMPHIBIOUS 10

10 *Hantae* LSM, capacity 350 tps, 3 tk
plus craft 15 LCM, 15 LCU, about 100 *Nampo* LCVP, plus about 130 hovercraft

SUPPORT AND MISCELLANEOUS 7

2 AT/F, 1 AS, 1 ocean and 3 inshore AGHS

COASTAL DEFENCE

2 SSM regt: *Silkworm* in 6 sites, and probably some

mobile launchers
GUNS 122mm: M-1931/-37; **130mm**: SM-4-1, M-1992; **152mm**: M-1937

Air Force 86,000

6 air divs (3 cbt, 2 tpt, 1 trg). 1st, 2nd and 3rd Air Divs (cbt) responsible for N, E and S air defence sectors respectively. 8th Air Div (trg) responsible for NE sector. 33 regts (11 ftr/fga, 2 bbr, 7 hel, 7 tpt, 6 trg) plus 3 indep air bns (recce/EW, test and evaluation, naval spt). The AF controls the national airline
Approx 70 full time/contingency air bases
621 cbt ac, ε24 armed hel
Flying hours 20 or less
BBR 3 lt regt with 80 H-5 (Il-28)
FGA/FTR 15 regt
3 with 107 J-5 (MiG-17), 4 with 159 J-6 (MiG-19), 4 with 130 J-7 (MiG-21), 1 with 46 MiG-23, 1 with 16 MiG-29, 1 with 18 Su-7, 1 with 35 Su-25, 30 MiG-29 (25 -As, 5 -Us), and 10 more being assembled, to start replacing J-5/J-6
TPT ac ε300 An-2/Y-5 (to infiltrate 2 air force sniper brigades deep into ROK rear areas), 6 An-24, 2 Il-18, 4 Il-62M, 2 Tu-134, 4 Tu-154
HEL 306. Large hel aslt force spearheaded by 24 Mi-24*. Tpt/utility: 80 Hughes 500D, 139 Mi-2, 15 Mi-8/-17, 48 Z-5
TRG incl 10 CJ-5, 7 CJ-6, 6 MiG-21, 170 Yak-18, 35 FT-2 (MiG-15UTI)
UAV Shmel
MISSILES
AAM AA-2 *Atoll*, PL-5, PL-7, AA-7 *Apex*, AA-8 *Aphid*, AA-10 *Alamo*, AA-11 *Archer*
SAM 19 SAM bde (15 SA-2, 2 SA-3, 2 SA-5) with some 340 launchers/3,400 missiles, many thousands of SA-7/14/16

Forces Abroad

advisers in some 12 African countries

Paramilitary 189,000 active

SECURITY TROOPS (Ministry of Public Security) 189,000
incl border guards, public safety personnel

WORKER/PEASANT RED GUARD some 3,500,000 (R)
Org on a provincial/town/village basis; comd structure is bde – bn – coy – pl; small arms with some mor and AD guns (but many units unarmed)

Korea, Republic of (South) ROK

Total Armed Forces

ACTIVE 686,000
(incl ε159,000 conscripts)
Terms of service conscription **Army** 26 months **Navy** and **Air Force** 30 months; First Combat Forces (Mobilisation Reserve Forces) or Regional Combat Forces (Homeland Defence Forces) to age 33

RESERVES 4,500,000
being re-org

Army 560,000

(incl 140,000 conscripts)
HQ: 3 Army, 11 Corps (two to be disbanded)
3 mech inf div (each 3 bde: 3 mech inf, 3 tk, 1 recce, 1 engr bn; 1 fd arty bde) • 19 inf div (each 3 inf regt, 1 recce, 1 tk, 1 engr bn; 1 arty regt (4 bn)) • 2 indep inf bde • 7 SF bde • 3 counter-infiltration bde • 3 SSM bn with NHK-I/-II (*Honest John*) • 3 AD arty bde • 3 I HAWK bn (24 sites), 2 *Nike Hercules* bn (10 sites) • 1 avn comd with 1 air aslt bde

RESERVES
1 Army HQ, 23 inf div

EQUIPMENT
MBT 1,000 Type 88, 80 T-80U, 400 M-47, 850 M-48
AIFV 40 BMP-3
APC incl 1,700 KIFV, 420 M-113, 140 M-577, 200 Fiat 6614/KM-900/-901, 20 BTR-80
TOWED ARTY some 3,500: **105mm**: 1,700 M-101, KH-178; **155mm**: M-53, M-114, KH-179; **203mm**: M-115
SP ARTY 155mm: 1,040 M-109A2, ε36 K-9; **175mm**: M-107; **203mm**: 13 M-110
MRL 130mm: 156 *Kooryong* (36-tube); **227mm**: 29 MLRS (all ATACMS capable)
MOR 6,000: **81mm**: KM-29; **107mm**: M-30
SSM 12 NHK-I/-II
ATGW TOW-2A, *Panzerfaust*, AT-7 *Saxhorn*
RCL 57mm, 75mm, 90mm: M67; **106mm**: M40A2
ATK GUNS 58: **76mm**: 8 M-18; **90mm**: 50 M-36 SP
AD GUNS 600: **20mm**: incl KIFV (AD variant), 60 M-167 *Vulcan*; **30mm**: 20 B1 HO SP; **35mm**: 20 GDF-003; **40mm**: 80 L60/70, M-1
SAM 350 *Javelin*, 60 *Redeye*, ε200 *Stinger*, 170 *Mistral*, SA-16, 110 I HAWK, 200 *Nike Hercules*, *Chun Ma* (reported)
SURV RASIT (veh, arty), AN/TPQ-36 (arty, mor), AN/TPQ-37 (arty)
HEL
ATTACK 60 AH-1F/-J, 45 Hughes 500 MD, 12 BO-105

TPT 18 CH-47D, 6 MH-47E
UTL 130 Hughes 500, 20 UH-1H, 130 UH-60P, 3 AS-332L

Navy 63,000

(incl 28,000 Marines; ε19,000 conscripts)
COMMANDS 1st Tonghae (Sea of Japan); **2nd** Pyongtaek (Yellow Sea); **3rd** Chinhae (Korean Strait)
BASES Chinhae (HQ), Cheju, Mokpo, Mukho, Pohang, Pusan, Pyongtaek, Tonghae

SUBMARINES 20

SSK 9 *Chang Bogo* (Ge T-209/1200) with 8 × 533 TT
SSI 11
3 KSS-1 *Dolgorae* (175t) with 2 × 406mm TT
8 *Dolphin* (175t) with 2 × 406mm TT

PRINCIPAL SURFACE COMBATANTS 39

DESTROYERS 6
DDG 6
3 *King Kwanggaeto* with 8 *Harpoon* SSM, 1 *Sea Sparrow* SAM, 1 × 127mm gun, 1 *Super Lynx* hel
3 *Kwang Ju* (US *Gearing*) with 2 × 4 *Harpoon* SSM, 2 × 2 × 127mm guns, 2 × 3 ASTT, 1 × 8 ASROC SUGW, 1 *Alouette* III hel
FRIGATES 9
FFG 9 *Ulsan* with 2 × 4 *Harpoon* SSM, 2 × 76mm gun, 2 × 3 ASTT (Mk 46 LWT)
CORVETTES 24
24 *Po Hang* FS with 2 × 3 ASTT; some with 2 × 1 MM-38 *Exocet* SSM

PATROL AND COASTAL COMBATANTS 84

CORVETTES 4 *Dong Hae* FS with 2 × 3 ASTT
MISSILE CRAFT 5
5 *Pae Ku*-52 (US *Asheville*) PFM, 2 × 2 *Harpoon* SSM, 1 × 76mm gun
PATROL, INSHORE 75
75 *Kilurki*-11 (*Sea Dolphin*) 37m PFI

MINE WARFARE 15

MINELAYERS 1
1 *Won San* ML
MINE COUNTERMEASURES 14
6 *Kan Keong* (mod It *Lerici*) MHC
8 *Kum San* (US MSC-268/289) MSC

AMPHIBIOUS 12

4 *Alligator* (RF) LST, capacity 700
6 *Un Bong* (US LST-511) LST, capacity 200 tps, 16 tk
2 *Ko Mun* (US LSM-1) LSM, capacity 50 tps, 4 tk
Plus about 36 craft; 6 LCT, 10 LCM, about 20 LCVP

SUPPORT AND MISCELLANEOUS 14

3 AOE, 2 spt AK, 2 AT/F, 2 salv/div spt, 1 ASR, about 4 AGHS (civil-manned, Ministry of Transport-funded)

NAVAL AVIATION

EQUIPMENT
16 cbt ac; 43 armed hel
AIRCRAFT
ASW 8 S-2E, 8 P-3C *Orion*
MR 5 *Cessna* F406
HELICOPTERS
ASW 22 MD 500MD, 10 SA 316 *Alouette* III, 11 *Lynx* Mk 99
UTL 2 206B *Jetranger*

MARINES (28,000)

2 div, 1 bde • spt units

EQUIPMENT
MBT 60 M-47
AAV 60 LVTP-7, 42 AAV-7A1
TOWED ARTY 105mm, 155mm
SSM *Harpoon* (truck-mounted)

Air Force 63,000

3 Cmds (Ops, Logs, Trg), Tac Airlift Wg and Composite Wg are all responsible to ROK Air Force HQ. Ops Comd controls Anti-Aircraft Artillery Cmd, Air Traffic Centre and tac ftr wgs.
538 cbt ac, no armed hel
FTR/FGA 7 tac ftr wgs
2 with 153 F-16C/D (104 -C, 49 -D)
3 with 185 F-5E/F (150 -E, 35 -F)
2 with 130 F-4D/E (60 -D, 70 -E)
CCT 1 wg with 22* A-37B
FAC 1 wg with 20 O-1A, 10 O-2A
RECCE 1 gp with 18* RF-4C, 5* RF-5A, 3 Hawker 800RA
ELINT/SIGINT 7 Hawker 800XP
SAR 1 hel sqn, 5 UH-1H, 4 Bell-212
TAC AIRLIFT WG ac 2 BAe 748 (VIP), 1 Boeing 737-300 (VIP), 1 C-118, 10 C-130H, 20 CN-235M/-220 **hel** 6 CH-47, 3 AS-332, 3 VH-60
TRG 25* F-5B, 50 T-37, 30 T-38, 25 T-41B, 18 *Hawk* Mk-67
UAV 3 *Searcher*, 100 *Harpy*
MISSILES
ASM AGM-65A *Maverick*, AGM-88 HARM, AGM-130, AGM-142
AAM AIM-7 *Sparrow*, AIM-9 *Sidewinder*, AIM-120B AMRAAM

Forces Abroad

KYRGYZSTAN (*Op Enduring Freedom*): 90 (medical staff)

UN AND PEACEKEEPING

CYPRUS (UNFICYP): 1 **EAST TIMOR** (UNMISET): 440 **GEORGIA** (UNOMIG): 5 obs **INDIA/PAKISTAN** (UNMOGIP): 8 obs **WESTERN SAHARA** (MINURSO): 20

Paramilitary ε4,500 active

CIVILIAN DEFENCE CORPS 3,500,000 (R) (to age 50)

MARITIME POLICE ε4,500

PATROL CRAFT 81

OFFSHORE 10

3 *Mazinger* (HDP-1000) (1 CG flagship), 1 *Han Kang* (HDC-1150), 6 *Sea Dragon/Whale* (HDP-600)

COASTAL 33

22 *Sea Wolf/Shark*, 2 *Bukhansan*, 7 *Hyundai*-type, 2 *Bukhansan*

INSHORE 38

18 *Seagull*, about 20<, plus numerous boats

SUPPORT AND MISCELLANEOUS 3 salvage

HEL 9 Hughes 500

Foreign Forces

US 37,140: **Army** 29,100; 1 Army HQ, 1 inf div **Navy** 300 **Air Force** 7,600: 1 HQ (7th Air Force); 90 cbt ac, 2 ftr wg; 3 sqn with 72 F-16, 1 sqn with 6 A-10, 12 OA-10, 1 special ops sqn with 5MH -53J **USMC** 140

Laos Lao

Total Armed Forces

ACTIVE ε29,100

Terms of service conscription, 18 months minimum

Army 25,600

4 Mil Regions • 5 inf div • 7 indep inf regt • 1 armd, 5 arty, 9 AD arty bn • 3 engr (2 construction) regt • 65 indep inf coy • 1 lt ac liaison flt

EQUIPMENT

MBT 15 T-54/-55, 10 T-34/85

LT TK 10 PT-76

APC 30 BTR-40/-60, 20 BTR-152

TOWED ARTY 75mm: 20 M-116 pack; **105mm**: 20 M-101; **122mm**: 20 M-1938 and D-30; **130mm**: 10 M-46; **155mm**: 12 M-114

MOR 81mm; 82mm; 107mm: M-2A1, M-1938; **120mm**: M-43

RL 73mm: RPG-7

RCL 57mm: M-18/A1; **75mm**: M-20; **106mm**: M-40; **107mm**: B-11

AD GUNS 14.5mm: ZPU-1/-4; **23mm**: ZU-23, ZSU-23-4 SP; **37mm**: M-1939; **57mm**: S-60

SAM SA-7

(Army Marine Section ε600)

PATROL AND COASTAL COMBATANTS some 16

PATROL, RIVERINE some 16

some 12 PCR<, 4 LCM, plus about 40 boats

Air Force 3,500

ε24† cbt ac; no armed hel

FGA 2 sqn with up to 22 MiG-21bis/2-UMs (serviceability in doubt)

TPT 1 sqn with 4 An-2, 3 An-26, 1 Yak-40 (VIP), 1 An-74, 5 Y-7, 1 Y-12

HEL 1 sqn with 1 Mi-6, 9 Mi-8, 12 Mi-17, 3 SA-360, 1 Ka-32T (5 more on order), 1 Mi-26

TRG 8 Yak-18

AAM AA-2 *Atoll*†

Paramilitary

MILITIA SELF-DEFENCE FORCES 100,000+

village 'home-guard' org for local defence

Opposition

Numerous factions/groups; total armed str: ε2,000

United Lao National Liberation Front (ULNLF) largest group

Malaysia Mal

Total Armed Forces

ACTIVE 100,000

RESERVES 41,600

Army 40,000 **Navy** 1,000 **Air Force** 600

Army 80,000 (to be 60–70,000)

2 Mil Regions • 1 HQ fd comd, 4 area comd (div) • 1 mech inf, 11 inf bde • 1 AB bde (3 AB bn, 1 lt arty regt, 1 lt tk sqn – forms Rapid Deployment Force)

Summary of combat units

5 armd regt • 36 inf bn • 3 AB bn • 5 fd arty, 1 AD arty, 5 engr regt, 1 hel sqn

1 SF regt (3 bn)

RESERVES

Territorial Army 1 bde HQ; 12 inf regt, 4 highway sy bn

EQUIPMENT

LT TK 26 *Scorpion* (**90mm**)

RECCE 162 SIBMAS, 140 AML-60/-90, 92 *Ferret* (60 mod)

APC 111 Korean Infantry Fighting Vehicle (KIFV) (incl variants), some *Adnan* (being delivered) 184

V-100/-150 *Commando*, 25 *Stormer*, 459 *Condor* (150 upgraded), 37 M-3 Panhard

TOWED ARTY 105mm: 130 Model 56 pack, 40 M-102A1 († in store); **155mm**: 12 FH-70, 22 G5

MRL 127mm: some ASTROS II (being delivered)

MOR 81mm: 300

ATGW SS-11, *Eryx*, AT-7 *Saxhorn* (being delivered)

RL 89mm: M-20; **92mm**: FT5

RCL 84mm: *Carl Gustav*; **106mm**: 150 M-40

AD GUNS 35mm: 24 GDF-005; **40mm**: 36 L40/70

SAM 48 *Javelin, Starburst*

HEL 9 SA-316B

ASLT CRAFT 165 *Damen*

Navy 12,000

(incl 160 Naval Avn)

COMMANDS Naval Area 1 (peninsular), **Naval Area 2** (Sabah/Sarawak)

BASES Lumut (HQ), Labuan, Kuantan, Pengelih (new base being built at Sepanggar Bay, Sabah)

PRINCIPAL SURFACE COMBATANTS 4

FRIGATES 4

FFG 2 *Lekiu* (UK Yarrow) with 8 × MM-40 *Exocet* SSM, 1 × 16 VLS *Seawolf* SAM, 6 × 324mm ASTT

FF 2 (both used for training)

1 *Hang Tuah* (UK *Mermaid*) with 1 × 57mm gun, 1 × 3 *Limbo* ASW mor, hel deck

1 *Rahmat* with 1 × 114mm gun, 1 × 3 ASW mor, hel deck

PATROL AND COASTAL COMBATANTS 41

CORVETTES 6

4 *Laksamana* (It *Assad*) FSG with 6 OTO *Melara* SSM, 1 *Selenia* SAM, 1 × 76mm gun, 6 × 324mm ASTT

2 *Kasturi* (FS 1500) FS with 4 MM-38 *Exocet* SSM, 1 × 100mm gun, 2 × 2 ASW mor, hel deck

MISSILE CRAFT 8

4 *Handalan* (Swe *Spica*) PFM with 4 MM-38 *Exocet* SSM, 1 × 57mm gun

4 *Perdana* (Fr *Combattante* II) PFM with 2 MM-38 *Exocet* SSM, 1 × 57mm gun

PATROL CRAFT 27

OFFSHORE 2 *Musytari* PCO with 1 × 100mm gun, hel deck

COASTAL/INSHORE 25

6 *Jerong* PFC, 4 *Sabah* PCC, 14 *Kris* PCC, 1 *Kedah* PCI<

MINE WARFARE 4

MINE COUNTERMEASURES 4

4 *Mahamiru* (mod It *Lerici*) MCO

plus 1 diving tender (inshore)

AMPHIBIOUS 1

1 *Sri Inderapura* (US *Newport*) LST, capacity 400 tps, 10 tk

Plus 115 craft: LCM/LCP/LCU

SUPPORT AND MISCELLANEOUS 4

2 log/fuel spt, 2 AGOS/AGHS

NAVAL AVIATION (160)

EQUIPMENT

6 armed hel

HELICOPTERS

ASW 6 *Wasp* HAS-1 (all non-op)

SPECIAL FORCES

1 Naval Commando Unit

Air Force 8,000

95 cbt ac, no armed hel; 4 Air Div

Flying hours 60

FGA 5 sqn

3 with 8 *Hawk* 108, 17 *Hawk* 208, 9 MB-339

1 with 8 F/A-18D

FTR 2 sqn with 15 MiG-29N, 2 MiG-29U

FGA/RECCE 1 sqn with 13 F-5E/F *Tiger* II, 2 RF-5E

MR 1 sqn with 4 Beech-200T

TRANSPORT 4 sqn

1 with 6 CN-235

1 with 4 C-130H

1 with 7 C-130H-30, 1 C-130H-MP, 3 KC-130H (tkr), 9 Cessna 402B (2 modified for aerial survey)

1 with **ac** 1 *Falcon*-900 (VIP), 1 Bombardier Global Express, 1 F-28 **hel** 2 S-61N, 1 Agusta-109, 2 S-70A

HEL 3 tpt/SAR sqn with 31 S-61A, 15 SA-316A/B, 2 Mi-17 (firefighting)

UAV 3 *Eagle* 150

TRAINING

AC 20 MD3-160, 45 PC-7 (12* wpn trg), 9 PC-7-II*, 9 MB-339

HEL 8 SA-316

MISSILES

AAM AIM-7 *Sparrow*, AIM-9 *Sidewinder*, AA-10 *Alamo*, AA-11 *Archer*

ASM AGM-65 *Maverick*, AGM-84D *Harpoon*

AIRFIELD DEFENCE

1 field sqn

SAM 1 sqn with *Starburst*

Forces Abroad

UN AND PEACEKEEPING

EAST TIMOR (UNMISET): 36 incl 16 obs **ETHIOPIA/ERITREA** (UNMEE): 12 incl 7 obs **DROC** (MONUC): 18 incl 6 obs **IRAQ/KUWAIT** (UNIKOM): 7 obs **SIERRA LEONE** (UNAMSIL): 10 obs **WESTERN SAHARA** (MINURSO): 13 obs

Paramilitary ε20,100

POLICE-GENERAL OPS FORCE 18,000

5 bde HQ: 21 bn (incl 2 Aboriginal, 1 Special Ops

Force), 4 indep coy
EQPT ε100 Shorland armd cars, 140 AT-105 *Saxon*, ε30 SB-301 APC

MARINE POLICE about 2,100
BASES Kuala Kemaman, Penang, Tampoi, Kuching, Sandakan
PATROL CRAFT, INSHORE 30
15 *Lang Hitam* (38m) PFI, 6 *Sangitan* (29m) PFI, 9 improved PX PFI, plus 6 tpt, 2 tugs, 120 boats

POLICE AIR UNIT
ac 6 Cessna *Caravan* I, 4 Cessna 206, 7 PC-6 **hel** 1 Bell 206L, 2 AS-355F

AREA SECURITY UNITS (aux General Ops Force) 3,500
89 units

BORDER SCOUTS (in Sabah, Sarawak) 1,200

PEOPLE'S VOLUNTEER CORPS (RELA) 240,000
some 17,500 armed

CUSTOMS SERVICE
PATROL CRAFT, INSHORE 8
6 *Perak* (Vosper 32m) armed PFI, 2 *Combatboat 90H* PFI, plus about 36 craft

Foreign Forces

AUSTRALIA 148: **Army** 115; 1 inf coy **Air Force** 33; det with 2 P-3C **ac**

Mongolia Mgl

Total Armed Forces

ACTIVE 9,100
(incl 300 construction tps and 500 Civil Defence (see *Paramilitary*); 4,000 conscripts)
Terms of service conscription: males 18–28 years, 1 year

RESERVES 137,000
Army 137,000

Army 7,500

(incl 4,000 conscripts)
6 MR regt (all under str) • 1 arty regt • 1 lt inf bn (rapid-deployment – second bn to form) • 1 AB bn

EQUIPMENT
MBT 370 T-54/-55
RECCE 120 BRDM-2
AIFV 310 BMP-1
APC 150 BTR-60
TOWED ARTY ε300: **122mm**: M-1938/D-30; **130mm**: M-46; **152mm**: ML-20
MRL 122mm: 130 BM-21
MOR 140: **82mm, 120mm, 160mm**
ATK GUNS 200 incl: **85mm**: D-44/D-48; **100mm**: BS-3, MT-12

Air Defence 800

no cbt ac; 11 armed hel
Flying hours 22
2 AD regt
ATTACK HEL 11 Mi-24
AC IN STORE 8 MiG-21, 1 MiG-21U
TPT (Civil Registration) 6 An-2, 6 An-24, 1 An-26, 1 An-30, 2 Boeing 727, 1 Airbus A310-300, hel 2 Mi-8
AD GUNS: 150: **14.5mm**: ZPU-4; **23mm**: ZU-23, ZSU-23-4; **57mm**: S-60
SAM 250 SA-7

Paramilitary 7,200 active

BORDER GUARD 6,000 (incl 4,700 conscripts)

INTERNAL SECURITY TROOPS 1,200 (incl 800 conscripts), 4 gd units

CIVIL DEFENCE TROOPS (500)

CONSTRUCTION TROOPS (300)

Myanmar My

Total Armed Forces

ACTIVE some 444,000 reported (incl People's Police Force and People's Militia – see *Paramilitary*)

Army 325,000

10 lt inf div (each 3 tac op comd (TOC))
12 Regional Comd (each with 10 regt)
32 TOC with 145 garrison inf bn
Summary of cbt units
245 inf bn • 7 arty bn • 4 armd bn • 4 AD bn

EQUIPMENT†
MBT 100 PRC Type-69II
LT TK 105 Type-63 (ε60 serviceable)
RECCE 45 *Ferret*, 40 *Humber*, 30 *Mazda* (local manufacture)
APC 20 *Hino* (local manufacture), 250 Type-85
TOWED ARTY 76mm: 100 M-1948; **88mm**: 50 25-pdr; **105mm**: 96 M-101; **122mm**; **130mm**: 16 M-46; **140mm**: 5.5in; **155mm**: 16 Soltam

MRL 107mm: 30 Type-63; **122mm**: BM-21 (reported)
MOR 81mm; 82mm: Type-53; **120mm**: Type-53, 80 Soltam
RL 73mm: RPG-7
RCL 84mm: ε1,000 *Carl Gustav*; **106mm**: M40A1
ATK GUNS 60: **57mm**: 6-pdr; **76.2mm**: 17-pdr
AD GUNS 37mm: 24 Type-74; **40mm**: 10 M-1; **57mm**: 12 Type-80
SAM HN-5A (reported), SA-16

Navy† 10,000

(incl 800 Naval Infantry)
BASES Bassein, Mergui, Moulmein, Seikyi, Yangon (Monkey Point), Sittwe

PATROL AND COASTAL COMBATANTS 73
CORVETTES 2†
1 *Yan Taing Aung* (US PCE-827) FS† with 1 × 76mm gun
1 *Yan Gyi Aung* (US *Admirable* MSF) FS† with 1 × 76mm gun
MISSILE CRAFT 6 *Houxin* PFM with 4 C-801 SSM, 5 PRC PFM
PATROL, OFFSHORE 3 *In Daw* (UK *Osprey*) PCO
PATROL, COASTAL 10 *Yan Sit Aung* (PRC *Hainan*) PCC
PATROL, INSHORE 18
12 US PGM-401/412, 3 FRY PB-90 PFI<, 3 *Swift* PCI 421
PATROL, RIVERINE about 29
2 *Nawarat*, 2 imp FRY Y-301 and 10 FRY Y-301, about 15<, plus some 25 boats

AMPHIBIOUS craft only
1 LCU, 10 LCM

SUPPORT 9
6 coastal tpt, 1 AOT, 1 diving spt, 1 buoy tender, plus 6 boats

NAVAL INFANTRY (800) 1 bn

Air Force 9,000

113 cbt ac, 29 armed hel
FTR 3 sqn with 50 F-7, 10 FT-7
(10 MiG-29 (8 -29B, 2 -29UB) on order)
FGA 2 sqn with 22 A-5M
CCT 2 sqn with 12 PC-7, 9 PC-9, 10 *Super Galeb* G4
TPT 1 sqn with 3 F-27, 4 FH-227, 5 PC-6A/-B, 2 Y-8D
LIAISON/TRG 4 Cessna 180, 1 Cessna *Citation* II, 12 K-8
HEL 4 sqn with 12 Bell 205, 6 Bell 206, 9 SA-316, 18* Mi-2, 11* Mi-17, 10 PZL W-3 *Sokol*

Paramilitary ε100,250

PEOPLE'S POLICE FORCE 65,000

PEOPLE'S MILITIA 35,000

PEOPLE'S PEARL AND FISHERY MINISTRY ε250
11 patrol boats (3 *Indaw* (Dk *Osprey*) PCC, 3 US *Swift* PGM PCI, 5 Aus *Carpentaria* PCI<)

Opposition and Former Opposition

GROUPS WITH CEASE-FIRE AGREEMENTS
UNITED WA STATE ARMY (UWSA) ε15,000 **Area** Wa hills between Salween river and PRC border; formerly part of Communist Party of Burma (CPB)
KACHIN INDEPENDENCE ARMY (KIA) some 8,000 **Area** northern My, incl Kuman range. Reached cease-fire agreement with govt in Oct 1993
MONG THAI ARMY (MTA) (formerly Shan United Army) ε3,000+ **Area** along Th border and between Lashio and PRC border
NATIONAL DEMOCRATIC ALLIANCE ARMY (NDAA) 1,000 **Area** north-east Shan state
MON NATIONAL LIBERATION ARMY (MNLA) ε1,000 **Area** on Th border in Mon state
NATIONAL DEMOCRATIC ALLIANCE ARMY (NDAA) ε1,000 **Area** eastern corner of Shan state on PRC–Lao border; formerly part of CPB
PALAUNG STATE LIBERATION ARMY (PSLA) ε700 **Area** hill tribesmen north of Hsipaw
NEW DEMOCRATIC ARMY (NDA) ε500 **Area** along PRC border in Kachin state; former CPB
DEMOCRATIC KAREN BUDDHIST ORGANISATION (DKBO) ε100–500 armed

GROUPS STILL IN OPPOSITION
SHAN STATE ARMY (SSA) ε3,000 **Area** Shan state
KAREN NATIONAL LIBERATION ARMY (KNLA) ε4,000 **Area** based in Th border area; political wg is Karen National Union (KNU)
ALL BURMA STUDENTS DEMOCRATIC FRONT ε2,000
KARENNI ARMY (KA) >1,000 **Area** Kayah state, Th border

New Zealand NZ

Total Armed Forces

ACTIVE 8,710
(incl some 1,280 women)

RESERVES some 5,870
Regular some 3,420 **Army** 1,700 **Navy** 670 **Air Force** 1,050 *Territorial* 2,450 **Army** 2,040 **Navy** 370 **Air Force** 40

Army 4,530

(incl 570 women)
1 Land Force Comd HQ • 2 Land Force Gp HQ • 1 APC/Recce regt (-) • 2 inf bn • 1 arty regt (2 fd bty, 1 AD tp) • 1 engr regt (-) • 2 SF sqn (incl 1 reserve)

RESERVES

Territorial Force 6 Territorial Force Regional Trg regt (each responsible for providing trained individuals for top-up and round-out of deployed forces)

EQUIPMENT

LAV some LAV III (being delivered)
APC 41 M-113 (plus variants)
TOWED ARTY 105mm: 24 *Hamel*
MOR 81mm: 50
ATGW 24 *Javelin*
RL 94mm: LAW
RCL 84mm: 42 *Carl Gustav*
SAM 12 *Mistral*
SURV *Cymbeline* (mor)

Navy 1,980

(incl 360 women)
BASE Auckland (Fleet HQ)

PRINCIPAL SURFACE COMBATANTS 3

FRIGATES 3
FF 3
2 *Anzac* with 8 *Sea Sparrow* VLS SAM, 1 × 127mm gun, 6 × 324mm TT, 1 SH-2F hel
1 *Canterbury* (UK *Leander*) with 2 × 114mm guns, 6 × 324mm ASTT, 1 SH-2F hel

PATROL AND COASTAL COMBATANTS 4

4 *Moa* PCI (reserve trg)

SUPPORT AND MISCELLANEOUS 5

1 *Endeavour* AO; 1 trg, 1 diving spt; 1 *Resolution* (US *Stalwart*) AGHS, 1 inshore AGHS

NAVAL AVIATION

EQUIPMENT
3 armed hel
HELICOPTERS
5 SH-2F/G *Sea Sprite* (see Air Force)

Air Force 2,200

(incl 350 women); 6 cbt ac, no armed hel
Flying hours 180

AIR COMMAND

MR 1 sqn with 6* P-3K *Orion*
ASW/ASUW 5 SH-2F/G (Navy-assigned)
TPT 2 sqn
ac 1 with 5 C-130H, 2 Boeing 727
hel 1 with 14 UH-1H, 5 Bell 47G (trg)
TRG 1 sqn with 13 CT-4E, 5 Beech King Air (leased)

MISSILES

ASM AGM-65B/G *Maverick*

Forces Abroad

AUSTRALIA 9 navigation trg
SINGAPORE 11; spt unit

UN AND PEACEKEEPING

AFGHANISTAN (ISAF): 12 **BOSNIA** (SFOR II): 26 **CAMBODIA** (CMAC): 2 **CROATIA** (UNMOP): 1 obs **EAST TIMOR** (UNMISET): 663 incl 5 obs **EGYPT** (MFO): 26 **MIDDLE EAST** (UNTSO): 6 obs **PAPUA NEW GUINEA**: 15 (Bougainville Peace Monitoring Group) **SIERRA LEONE** (UNAMSIL): 2 obs

Papua New Guinea PNG

Total Armed Forces

ACTIVE ε3,100

Army ε2,500

2 inf bn • 1 engr bn

EQUIPMENT

MOR 81mm; **120mm**: 3

Maritime Element 400

BASES Port Moresby (HQ), Lombrum (Manus Island) (patrol boat sqn); forward bases at Kieta and Alotau

PATROL AND COASTAL COMBATANTS 4

PATROL, COASTAL 4 *Tarangau* (Aust *Pacific Forum* 32-m) PCC

AMPHIBIOUS 2

2 *Salamaua* (Aust *Balikpapan*) LCH, plus 4 landing craft, manned and op by the civil administration

Air Force 200

no cbt ac, no armed hel
TPT 2 CN-235, 3 IAI-201 *Arava*, 1 CN-212
HEL 4 UH-1H†

Foreign Forces

AUSTRALIA 38; trg unit

BOUGAINVILLE PEACE MONITORING GROUP
some 55 tps from Aus (35), NZ (15), Fji (5)

Philippines Pi

Total Armed Forces

ACTIVE 106,000

RESERVES 131,000

Army 100,000 (some 75,000 more have commitments) **Navy** 15,000 **Air Force** 16,000 (to age 49)

Army 66,000

5 Area Unified Comd (joint service) • 8 lt inf div (each with 3 inf bde, 1 arty bn) • 1 special ops comd with 1 lt armd bde ('regt'), 1 scout ranger, 1 SF regt • 5 engr bn • 1 arty regt HQ • 1 Presidential Security Group

EQUIPMENT

LT TK 40 *Scorpion*
AIFV 85 YPR-765 PRI
APC 100 M-113, 20 *Chaimite*, 100 V-150, 150 *Simba*
TOWED ARTY 105mm: 230 M-101, M-102, M-26 and M-56; **155mm**: 12 M-114 and M-68
MOR 81mm: M-29; **107mm**: 40 M-30
RCL 75mm: M-20; **90mm**: M-67; **106mm**: M-40 A1
AC 3 Cessna (1 P-206A, 1 -170, 1 -172), 1 *Queen Air*

Navy† ε24,000

(incl 7,500 Marines)
BASES Sangley Point/Cavite, Zamboanga, Cebu

PRINCIPAL SURFACE COMBATANTS 1

FRIGATES
FF 1 *Rajah Humabon* (US *Cannon*) with 3 × 76mm gun, ASW mor

PATROL AND COASTAL COMBATANTS 58

PATROL, OFFSHORE 13
2 *Rizal* (US *Auk*) PCO with 2 × 76mm gun, 3 × 2 ASTT, hel deck
3 *Emilio Jacinto* (ex-UK *Peacock*) PCO with 1 × 76mm gun
8 *Miguel Malvar* (US PCE-827) PCO with 1 × 76mm gun
PATROL, COASTAL 11
3 *Aguinaldo* PCC, 3 *Kagitingan* PCC, 5 *Thomas Batilo* (ROK *Sea Dolphin*) PCC
PATROL, INSHORE 34
22 *José Andrada* PCI< and about 12 other PCI<

AMPHIBIOUS 7

2 US *F. S. Besson*-class LST, capacity 32 tk plus 150 tps, hel deck
5 *Zamboanga del Sur* (US LST-1/511/542) LST, capacity either 16 tk or 10 tk plus 200 tps
Plus about 39 craft: 30 LCM, 3 LCU, some 6 LCVP

SUPPORT AND MISCELLANEOUS 11

2 AOT (small), 1 AR, 3 spt, 2 AWT, 3 AGOR/AGOS

NAVAL AVIATION

EQUIPMENT
no cbt ac, no armed hel
AIRCRAFT
TPT 4 BN12A *Defender*
HELICOPTER
SAR 4 Bo-105

MARINES (7,500)

3 bde (10 bn) to be 2 bde (6 bn)

EQUIPMENT

AAV 30 LVTP-5, 55 LVTP-7
LAV 24 LAV-300
TOWED ARTY 105mm: 150 M-101
MOR 4.2in (**107mm**): M-30

Air Force ε16,000

49 cbt ac, some 67 armed hel
FTR 1 sqn with 14 F-5 (10 -A/E, 4 -B)
ARMED HEL 3 sqn with 55 Bell UH-1H/M, 12 AUH-76 (S-76 gunship conversion)
MR 1 F-27M
ATTACK/RECCE 4 RT-33A, 20* OV-10 *Broncos*
SAR 1 sqn with UH-1H, Bell 205, S-76
PRESIDENTIAL AC WG ac 1 F-27, 1 F-28 **hel** 2 Bell 212, 4 Bell-412, 2 S-70A, 2 SA-330
TPT 3 sqn
1 with 2 C-130B, 3 C-130H, 4 C-130K, 3 L-100-20, 7 F-27
2 with 2 BN-2 *Islander*, 14 N-22B *Nomad Missionmaster*
HEL 2 sqn with 1 Bell 212, 1 Bell 214, 6 Bell 412, 22 MD-520
LIAISON 8 Cessna (5 -172, 2 -210, 1 -310), 5 DHC-2, 1 *Commander*, 12 U-17A/B
TRG 3 sqn
1 with 14 T-41D, 1 with 28 SF-260TP, 1 with 15* S-211
UAV 2 *Blue Horizon* II
AAM AIM-9B *Sidewinder*

Forces Abroad

UN AND PEACEKEEPING

EAST TIMOR (UNMISET): 66 incl 8 obs

Paramilitary 44,000 active

PHILIPPINE NATIONAL POLICE 40,500 (Department of Interior and Local Government)

62,000 active aux; 15 Regional, 73 Provincial Comd
ac 2 *Islander*, 3 Lancair 320

COAST GUARD 3,500

(Part of Department of Transport; but mainly funded, manned and run by the Navy)

EQUIPMENT

1 *San Juan* PCO, 3 *De Haviland* PCI, 4 *Basilan* (US PGM-39/42) PCI, plus some 35 *Swift* PCI, 3 SAR hel (by 2000)

CITIZEN ARMED FORCE GEOGRAPHICAL UNITS (CAFGU) 40,000

Militia, 56 bn; part-time units which can be called up for extended periods

Opposition and Former Opposition

Groups with Peace Agreements

BANGSA MORO ARMY (armed wing of Moro National Liberation Front (MNLF); Muslim) ε5,700 integrated into national army

MORO ISLAMIC LIBERATION FRONT (breakaway from MNLF; Muslim) 11,000 (up to 15,000 reported)

Groups Still in Opposition

NEW PEOPLE'S ARMY (NPA; communist) ε9,500 (up to 12,000 reported)

MORO ISLAMIC REFORMIST GROUP (breakaway from MNLF; Muslim) 900

ABU SAYYAF GROUP ε200

Singapore Sgp

Total Armed Forces

ACTIVE 60,500

(incl 39,800 conscripts)
Terms of service conscription 24–30 months

RESERVES ε312,500

Army ε300,000; annual trg to age 40 for male other ranks, 50 for officers **Navy** ε5,000 **Air Force** ε7,500

Army 50,000

(35,000 conscripts)

3 combined arms div (mixed active/reserve formations) each with 2 inf bde (each 3 inf bn), 1 armd bde, 1 recce, 2 arty, 1 AD, 1 engr bn
1 Rapid Deployment div (mixed active/reserve formation) with 3 inf bde (incl 1 air mob, 1 amph – each 3 bn)
1 mech bde
Summary of active units
9 inf bn • 4 lt armd/recce bn • 4 arty bn • 1 cdo (SF) bn • 4 engr bn

RESERVES

9 inf bde incl in mixed active/reserve formations listed above • 1 op reserve div with additional inf bde • 2 People's Defence Force cmd with 12 inf bn • Total cbt units ε60 inf, ε8 lt armd/recce, ε12 arty, 1 cdo (SF), ε8 engr bn

EQUIPMENT

MBT 80–100 *Centurion* (trg only)
LT TK ε350 AMX-13SM1
RECCE 22 AMX-10 PAC 90
AIFV 22 AMX-10P, 250 IFV-25
APC 750+ M-113A1/A2 (some with 40mm AGL, some with 25mm gun), 30 V-100, 250 V-150/-200 *Commando*, 250 IFV-40/50, some ATTC
TOWED ARTY 105mm: 37 LG1; **155mm**: 38 Soltam M-71S, 16 M-114A1 (may be in store), 45 M-68 (may be in store), 52 FH-88, 18 FH-2000
MOR 81mm (some SP); **120mm**: 50 (some SP in M-113); **160mm**: 12 Tampella
ATGW 30+ *Milan*, *Spike*
RL *Armbrust*; **89mm**: 3.5in M-20
RCL 84mm: ε200 *Carl Gustav*; **106mm**: 90 M-40A1 (in store)
AD GUNS 20mm: 30 GAI-CO1 (some SP)
SAM 75+: RBS-70 (some SP as the V-200) (Air Force), *Mistral* (Air Force), SA-18 (Air Force)
SURV AN/TPQ-36/-37 (arty, mor)

Navy 4,500

(incl 1,800 conscripts)
COMMANDS Fleet (1st, 3rd Flotillas and sub sqn) **Coastal**, **Naval Logistic** and **Training Command**
BASES Tuas (Jurong), Changi

SUBMARINES 2

2 *Challenger* (Swe *Sjoormen*) SSK with 4 × 533 TT

PATROL AND COASTAL COMBATANTS 24

CORVETTES 6 *Victory* (Ge Lürssen 62m) FSG with 8 *Harpoon* SSM, 1 × 2 *Barak* SAM, 1 × 76mm gun, 2 × 3 ASTT
MISSILE CRAFT 6
6 *Sea Wolf* (Ge Lürssen 45m) PFM with 2 × 4 *Harpoon* SSM, 4 × 2 *Gabriel* SSM, 1 × 2 *Mistral/Simbad* SAM, 1 × 57mm gun
PATROL CRAFT 12
12 *Fearless* PCO with 2 *Mistral/Sadral* SAM, 1 × 76mm gun (6 with 6 × 324mm TT)

MINE WARFARE 4

MINE COUNTERMEASURES 4

4 *Bedok* (Swe *Landsort*) MHC

AMPHIBIOUS 5

1 *Perseverance* (UK *Sir Lancelot*) LSL with 1 × 2 *Mistral/Simbad* SAM, capacity 340 tps, 16 tk, hel deck
4 *Endurance* LST with 2 × 2 *Mistral/Simbad* SAM, 1 × 76mm gun; capacity: 350 tps, 18 tk, 4 LCVP, 2 hel
Plus craft: 6 LCM, 30 LCU, and boats

SUPPORT AND MISCELLANEOUS 3

1 *Jupiter* diving spt and salvage, 1 *Kendrick* sub spt ship, 1 trg

Air Force 6,000

(incl 3,000 conscripts); 126 cbt ac, 28 armed hel
FGA 6 sqn
2 with 40 A-4SU
1 with 3 F-16A, 4 F-16B
1 with 8 F-16C, 10 F-16D (some SEAD), plus 24 F-16C/D in US
2 with 28 F-5S, 9 F-5T (secondary GA role)
RECCE 1 sqn with 8 RF-5S
AEW 1 sqn with 4 E-2C
TKR 1 sqn with 1 KC-135. 3 more in US
TPT/TKR/RECCE 2 sqn
1 with 4 KC-130B (tkr/tpt), 5 C-130H (2 ELINT), 1 KC-130H
1 with 9 F-50 *Enforcer* (4 tpt, 5 MR)
ARMED HEL 2 sqn with 20 AS 550A2/C2, 8 AH-64D (12 more on order)
HEL 4 sqn
1 with 19 UH-1H, 6 AB-205A, 2 with 18 AS-332M (incl 5 SAR), 12 AS-532UL
1 with 6 CH-47D
TRG
1 sqn with 27 SIAI S-211
1 trg detachment with 18 TA-4SU
UAV 1 sqn with 40 *Searcher* Mk 2, 24 *Chukar* III

AIR DEFENCE SYSTEMS DIVISION

4 field def sqn
Air Defence Bde 1 sqn with **35mm** Oerlikon, 1 sqn with 18 I-HAWK, 1 sqn with Blindfire *Rapier*
Air Force Systems Bde 1 sqn mobile radar, 1 sqn LORADS
Divisional Air Def Arty Bde (attached to Army divs) 1 bn with 36 *Mistral* (SAM), 3 bn with RBS 70 (SAM), 1 bn with SA-18 *Igla*

MISSILES

AAM AIM-7P *Sparrow*, AIM-9 N/P *Sidewinder* AIM-120 AMRAAM stored in US
ASM AGM-45 *Shrike*, AGM-65B *Maverick*, AGM-65G *Maverick*, AGM-84 *Harpoon*

Forces Abroad

AUSTRALIA 230; flying trg schools at Oakey (12 AS-332/532), and Pearce (27 S-211)
BRUNEI 500; trg school, incl hel det (with 5 UH-1H)
FRANCE 200; trg 8 A-4SU/10 TA-4SU (Cazaux AFB)
TAIWAN 3 trg camps (incl inf, arty and armd)
THAILAND 1 trg camp (arty, cbt engr)
US trg detachment some 6 CH-47D at Grand Prairie, TX, AH-64D at Marana, AZ; 12 F-16C/D (leased from USAF at Luke AFB, AZ), 12 F-16C/D (at Cannon AFB, NM); 1 KC-135 trg det at McConnell AFB, KS

UN AND PEACEKEEPING

EAST TIMOR (UNMISET): 129 **ETHIOPIA/ERITREA** (UNMEE): 2 obs **IRAQ/KUWAIT** (UNIKOM): 2 obs

Paramilitary ε96,300+ active

SINGAPORE POLICE FORCE ε12,000

(incl 3,500 conscripts, 21,000 reservists)
incl Police Coast Guard
EQUIPMENT
12 *Swift* PCI< and about 60 boats
Singapore Gurkha Contingent (1,500: 6 coy)

CIVIL DEFENCE FORCE 84,300

(incl 1,600 regulars, 3,200 conscripts, 23,000 reservists, 54,000+ volunteers); 1 construction bde (2,500 conscripts)

Foreign Forces

US 124: **Air Force** 34 **Navy** 90
NEW ZEALAND 11; spt unit

Taiwan (Republic of China) ROC

Total Armed Forces

ACTIVE ε370,000 (to be 350,000)
Terms of service 22 months

RESERVES 1,657,500

Army 1,500,000 with some obligation to age 30 **Navy** 32,500 **Marines** 35,000 **Air Force** 90,000

Army ε240,000 (to be 200,000)

(incl mil police)
3 Army, 1 AB Special Ops HQ • 10 inf div • 2 mech inf div • 2 AB bde • 6 indep armd bde • 1 tk gp • 2 AD SAM gp with 6 SAM bn: 2 with *Nike Hercules*, 4 with I HAWK • 2 avn gp, 6 avn sqn

RESERVES

7 lt inf div

EQUIPMENT

MBT 100 M-48A5, 450+ M-48H, 376 M-60A3
LT TK 230 M-24 (**90mm** gun), 675 M-41/Type 64
AIFV 225 M-113 with **20–30mm** cannon
APC 650 M-113, 300 V-150 *Commando*
TOWED ARTY 105mm: 650 M-101 (T-64); **155mm**: M-44, 90 M-59, 250 M-114 (T-65); **203mm**: 70 M-115
SP ARTY 105mm: 100 M-108; **155mm**: 20 T-69, 225 M-109A2/A5; **203mm**: 60 M-110
COASTAL ARTY 127mm: ε50 US Mk 32 (reported)
MRL 300+ incl **117mm**: KF VI; **126mm**: KF III/IV towed and SP; some RT 2000
MOR 81mm: M-29 (some SP); **107mm**
SSM *Ching Feng*
ATGW 1,000 TOW (some SP)
RCL 90mm: M-67; **106mm**: 500 M-40A1, Type 51
AD GUNS 40mm: 400 (incl M-42 SP, Bofors)
SAM 40 *Nike Hercules* (to be retired), 100 HAWK, *Tien Kung* (*Sky Bow*) -1/-2, *Stinger*, 74 *Avenger*, 2 *Chaparral*, 25 *Patriot*
HEL 3 CH-47SD, 80 UH-1H, 62 AH-1W, 30 TH-67 *Creek*, 39 OH-58D
UAV *Mastiff* III

DEPLOYMENT

Quemoy 15–20,000; 4 inf div **Matsu** 8–10,000; 1 inf div

Navy ε62,000

(incl 30,000 Marines)
3 Naval Districts
BASES Tsoying (HQ), Makung (Pescadores), Keelung, Hualien (ASW HQ) (New East Coast fleet set up and based at Suo)

SUBMARINES 4

SSK 4
2 *Hai Lung* (Nl mod *Zwaardvis*) with 533mm TT
2 *Hai Shih* (US *Guppy* II) with 533mm TT (trg only)

PRINCIPAL SURFACE COMBATANTS 32

DESTROYERS 11
DDG 11
7 *Chien Yang* (US *Gearing*) (*Wu Chin* III conversion) with 4 *Hsiung Feng* SSM, SM-1-MR SAM, 2 × 3 ASTT, 1 × 8 ASROC SUGW, 1 *Hughes* MD-500 hel
3 *Fu Yang* (US *Gearing*) with 5 *Hsiung Feng* I/*Gabriel* II SSM, 1 or 2 × 127mm guns, 2 × 3 ASTT, 1 *Hughes* MD-500 hel (1 also with 1 × 8 ASROC SUGW)
1 *Po Yang* (US *Sumner*)† with *Hsiung Feng* SSM, 1 or 2 × 127mm guns, 2 × 3 ASTT, 1 *Hughes* MD-500 hel

FRIGATES 21
FFG 21
7 *Cheng Kung* (US *Perry*) with 8 *Hsiung Feng* II SSM, 1 SM-1 MR SAM, 1 × 76mm gun, 2 × 3 ASTT, 2 S-70C hel
6 *Kang Ding* (Fr *La Fayette*) with 8 *Hsiung Feng* SSM, 4 *Sea Chaparral* SAM, 1 × 76mm gun, 6 × 324mm ASTT, 1 S-70C hel
8 *Chin Yang* (US *Knox*) with *Harpoon* SSM, 1 × 127mm gun, 4 ASTT, 1 × 8 ASROC SUGW, 1 SH-2F hel

PATROL AND COASTAL COMBATANTS 59

MISSILE CRAFT 59
2 *Lung Chiang*† PFM with 2 *Hsiung Feng I* SSM,
9 *Jinn Chiang* PFM with 4 *Hsiung Feng I* SSM,
48 *Hai Ou* (mod Il *Dvora*) PFM< with 2 *Hsiung Feng I* SSM

MINE WARFARE 12

MINE COUNTERMEASURES 12
4 (ex-US) *Aggressive* MSO
4 *Yung Chou* (US *Adjutant*) MSC
4 *Yung Feng* MSC converted from oil-rig spt ships

AMPHIBIOUS 18

1 *Shiu Hai* (US *Anchorage*) LSD
2 *Chung Ho* (US *Newport*) LST capacity 400 tps, 500 tons veh, 4 LCVP
1 *Kao Hsiung* (US LST 511) LCC
10 *Chung Hai* (US LST 511) LST, capacity 16 tk, 200 tps
4 *Mei Lo* (US LSM-1) LSM, capacity about 4 tk
Plus about 325 craft; some 20 LCU, 205 LCM, 100 LCVP and assault LCVP

SUPPORT AND MISCELLANEOUS 20

3 AO, 2 AR, 1 *Wu Yi* combat spt with hel deck, 2 *Yuen Feng* and 2 *Wu Kang* attack tpt with hel deck, 2 tpt, 7 AT/F, 1 *Te Kuan* AGOR

COASTAL DEFENCE 1

1 SSM coastal def bn with *Hsiung Feng* (*Gabriel*-type)

NAVAL AVIATION

EQUIPMENT
32 cbt ac; 20 armed hel
AIRCRAFT
MR 32 S-2 (24 -E, 8 -G)
HELICOPTERS
ASW 20* S-70C *Defender*

MARINES (30,000)

2 div, spt elm

EQUIPMENT

AAV LVTP-4/-5
TOWED ARTY 105mm, 155mm
RCL 106mm

Air Force 68,000

479 cbt ac, no armed hel
Flying hours 180
FTR 3 sqn with 57 *Mirage* 2000-5 (47 -5EI, 10 -5DI)
FGA/FTR 20 sqn
  6 with 90 F-5E/F (plus many in store)
  6 with 128 *Ching-Kuo*
  7 with 146 F-16A/B (incl one sqn recce capable)
  1 with 22 AT-3
RECCE 1 with 8 RF-5E
AEW 4 E-2T
EW 1 with 2 C-130HE, 2 CC-47
SAR 1 sqn with 17 S-70C
TPT 3 **ac** sqn
  2 with 19 C-130H (1 EW)
  1 VIP with 4 Boeing 727-100, 1 Boeing 737-800, 10 Beech 1900, 3 *Fokker* F-50
HEL 1 S-62A (VIP), 14 S-70, 3 CH-47
TRG ac incl 36* AT-3A/B, 42 T-34C

MISSILES
  ASM AGM-65A *Maverick*
  AAM AIM-4D *Falcon*, AIM-9J/P *Sidewinder*, *Shafrir*, *Sky Sword* I and II, MATRA *Mica*, MATRA R550 *Magic* 2
  ARM *Sky Sword* IIA

Forces Abroad

US F-16 conversion unit at Luke AFB, AZ

Paramilitary ε26,650

SECURITY GROUPS 25,000
National Police Administration (Ministry of Interior); **Bureau of Investigation** (Ministry of Justice); **Military Police** (Ministry of Defence); **Coast Guard Administration**

MARITIME POLICE ε1,000
about 38 armed patrol boats

CUSTOMS SERVICE (Ministry of Finance) 650
5 PCO, 2 PCC, 1 PCI, 5 PCI<; most armed

COAST GUARD ADMINISTRATION 22,000 (all civilians)
responsible for guarding the Spratly and Pratas island groups, and enforcing law and order at sea

Foreign Forces

SINGAPORE 3 trg camps

Thailand Th

Total Armed Forces

ACTIVE ε306,000
Terms of service 2 years

RESERVES 200,000

Army 190,000

(incl ε70,000 conscripts)
4 Regional Army HQ, 2 Corps HQ • 2 cav div • 3 armd inf div • 2 mech inf div • 1 lt inf div • 2 SF div • 1 arty div, 1 AD arty div (6 AD arty bn) • 1 engr div • 4 economic development div • 1 indep cav regt • 8 indep inf bn • 4 recce coy • armd air cav regt with 3 air-mobile coy • Some hel flt • Rapid Reaction Force (1 bn per region forming)

RESERVES
4 inf div HQ

EQUIPMENT
  MBT 50 PRC Type-69 (trg/in store), 105 M-48A5, 178 M-60 (125 A3, 53 A1)
  LT TK 154 *Scorpion* (ε50 in store), 200 M-41, 106 *Stingray*
  RECCE 32 Shorland Mk 3, HMMWV
  APC 340 M-113A1/A3, 138 V-150 *Commando*, 18 *Condor*, 450 PRC Type-85 (YW-531H)
  TOWED ARTY 105mm: 24 LG1 Mk 2, 285 M-101/-101 mod, 12 M-102, 32 M-618A2 (local manufacture); **130mm**: 15 PRC Type-59; **155mm**: 56 M-114, 62 M-198, 32 M-71, 42 GHN-45A1
  SP ARTY 155mm: 20 M-109A2
  MOR 1,900 incl **81mm** (incl 21 M-125A3 SP), **107mm** incl M-106A1 SP; **120mm**: 12 M-1064A3 SP
  ATGW TOW (incl 18 M-901A5), 300 *Dragon*
  RL M-72 LAW
  RCL 75mm: 30 M-20; **106mm**: 150 M-40
  AD GUNS 20mm: 24 M-163 *Vulcan*, 24 M-167 *Vulcan*; **37mm**: 122 Type-74; **40mm**: 80 M-1/M-42 SP, 48 L/70; **57mm**: 24+ PRC Type-59 (ε6 op)
  SAM *Redeye*, some *Aspide*, HN-5A
  UAV *Searcher*
  AIRCRAFT
    TPT 2 C-212, 2 Beech 1900C, 2 Short 330UTT, 2 *Beech King Air*, 2 *Jetstream* 41
    LIAISON 10 O-1A, 10 U-17B
    TRG 12 T-41B, 18 MX-7-235
  HELICOPTERS
    ATTACK 3 AH-1F
    TPT 6 CH-47D, 60 Bell (incl -206, -212, -214, -412), 92 UH-1H, 2 UH-60L

TRG 40 Hughes 300C
SURV RASIT (veh, arty), AN-TPQ-36 (arty, mor)

Navy 68,000

(incl 1,700 Naval Avn, 18,000 Marines, 7,000 Coastal Defence; incl 27,000 conscripts)
FLEETS 1st North Thai Gulf **2nd** South Thai Gulf **3rd** Andaman Sea
1 Naval Air Division
BASES Bangkok, Sattahip (Fleet HQ), Songkhla, Phang Nga, Nakhon Phanom (HQ Mekong River Operating Unit)

PRINCIPAL SURFACE COMBATANTS 13

AIRCRAFT CARRIER† 1 *Chakri Naruebet* CVS with 7 AV-8B *Matador* (*Harrier*), 6 S-70B *Seahawk* hel
FRIGATES 12
FFG 8
2 *Naresuan* with 2 × 4 *Harpoon* SSM, 8 cell *Sea Sparrow* SAM, 1 × 127mm gun, 6 × 324mm TT, 1 SH-2G hel
2 *Chao Phraya* (PRC *Jianghu* III) with 8 C-801 SSM, 2 × 2 × 100mm guns, 2 × 5 ASW RL, 1 Bell 212 hel
2 *Kraburi* (PRC *Jianghu* IV type) with 8 C-801 SSM, 1 × 2 100mm guns, 2 × 5 ASW RL and 1 Bell 212 hel
2 *Phutthayotfa Chulalok* (US *Knox*) (leased from US) with 8 *Harpoon* SSM, 1 × 127mm gun, 4 × 324 ASTT, 1 Bell 212 hel
FF 4
1 *Makut Rajakumarn* with 2 × 114mm guns, 2 × 3 ASTT
2 *Tapi* (US PF-103) with 1 × 76mm gun, 6 × 324mm ASTT (Mk 46 LWT)
1 *Pin Klao* (US *Cannon*) with 3 × 76mm gun, 6 × 324mm ASTT

PATROL AND COASTAL COMBATANTS 88

CORVETTES 5
2 *Rattanakosin* FSG with 2 × 4 *Harpoon* SSM, 8 *Aspide* SAM, 1 × 76mm gun, 2 × 3 ASTT
3 *Khamronsin* FS with 1 × 76mm gun, 2 × 3 ASTT
MISSILE CRAFT 6
3 *Ratcharit* (It Breda 50m) PFM with 4 MM-38 *Exocet* SSM
3 *Prabparapak* (Ge Lürssen 45m) PFM with 5 *Gabriel* SSM
PATROL CRAFT 77
OFFSHORE
1 *Kua Hin* PCO with 1 × 76mm gun
COASTAL 12
3 *Chon Buri* PFC, 6 *Sattahip*, 3 PCC
INSHORE 64
7 T-11 (US PGM-71), 9 T-91, about 33 PCF and 15 PCR plus boats

MINE WARFARE 7

MINE COUNTERMEASURES 7
2 *Lat Ya* (It *Gaeta*) MCMV
2 *Bang Rachan* (Ge Lürssen T-48) MCC
2 *Bangkeo* (US *Bluebird*) MSC
1 *Thalang* MCM spt with minesweeping capability
(Plus some 12 MSB)

AMPHIBIOUS 9

2 *Sichang* (Fr PS-700) LST, capacity 14 tk, 300 tps with hel deck (trg)
5 *Angthong* (US LST-511) LST, capacity 16 tk, 200 tps
2 *Kut* (US LSM-1) LSM, capacity about 4 tk
Plus about 51 craft: 9 LCU, about 24 LCM, 1 LCG, 2 LSIL, 3 hovercraft, 12 LCVP

SUPPORT AND MISCELLANEOUS 16

1 *Similan* AO (1 hel) , 1 *Chula* AO, 5 AO, 3 AGHS, 6 trg

NAVAL AVIATION (1,700)

(incl 300 conscripts)
EQUIPMENT
44 cbt ac; 8 armed hel
AIRCRAFT
FTR 8 *Harrier* (7 AV-8B, 1 TAV-8*)
STRIKE 14 A-7E *Corsair* II, 4 TA-7C *Corsair* II
ASW 4 S-2F *Tracker*, 2 US-2C *Tracker*, 2 P-3T, 1 UP-3T
MPA 2 C-212 300 *Aviocar*, 5 O-1G *Bird Dog*, 4 Cessna U-17B, 6 Dornier 228-212, 3 Fokker F.27 Mk 200, 5 N-22M *Search Master* L, 9 Sentry 02-337
TPT 2 Douglas C-47, 2 Fokker F.27 Mk 400M
SAR 2 CL-215-III
HELICOPTERS
ASW 8 Bell 212
SAR 4 UH-1H *Iroquois*, 6 S-76B
TPT 4 Bell 214 ST
MISSILES
ASM AGM-84 *Harpoon*

MARINES (18,000)

1 div HQ, 2 inf regt, 1 arty regt (3 fd, 1 AA bn); 1 amph aslt bn; recce bn

EQUIPMENT

AAV 33 LVTP-7
APC 24 V-150 *Commando*
TOWED ARTY 105mm: 36 (reported); **155mm**: 12 GC-45
ATGW TOW (incl 24 HMMWV), *Dragon*
AD GUNS 12.7mm: 14

Air Force ε48,000

4 air divs, one flying trg school
194 cbt ac, no armed hel
Flying hours 100
FGA 7 sqn
1 with 13 F-5A/B, 2 with 50 F-16 (38 -A, 12 -B), 3 with 34 L-39ZA/MP
3 sqn (1 aggressor) with 36 F-5E/F (32 being upgraded)

ARMED AC 3 sqn
1 with 22 AU-23A, 1 with 18 OV-10C, 1 with 20 *Alphajets*
ELINT 1 sqn with 3 IAI-201
RECCE 3 RF-5A
SURVEY 2 *Learjet* 35A, 3 *Merlin* IVA, 3 GAF N-22B
TPT 3 sqn
1 with 7 C-130H, 5 C-130H-30
1 with 3 Basler T-67, 19 N-22B
1 with 6 G-222, 4 BAe-748
VIP Royal flight **ac** 1 Airbus A-310-324, 1 Boeing 737-200, 3 *King Air* 200, 2 BAe-748, 3 *Merlin* IV **hel** 2 Bell 412, 2 AS-332L, 3 AS-532A2
TRG 24 CT-4 *Airtrainer*, 23 PC-9 **hel** 6 Bell 206B
LIAISON 3 *Commander*, 1 *King Air* E90, 3 Cessna 150, 2 *Queen Air*, 12 T-41D
HEL 2 sqn
1 with 15 S-58T, 1 with 19 UH-1H
AAM AIM-9B/J *Sidewinder*, *Python* 3, AIM-120 AMRAAM

AIR DEFENCE

1 AA arty bty: 4 *Skyguard*, 1 *Flycatcher* radars, each with 4 fire units of 2 30mm Mauser/Kuka guns
SAM *Blowpipe*, *Aspide*, RBS NS-70, *Starburst*

Forces Abroad

UN AND PEACEKEEPING

EAST TIMOR (UNMISET): 372 incl 6 obs **IRAQ/KUWAIT** (UNIKOM): 6 obs **SIERRA LEONE** (UNAMSIL): 5 obs

Paramilitary ε113,000 active

THAHAN PHRAN (Hunter Soldiers) ε20,000
volunteer irregular force; 13 regt of some 107 coy

PROVINCIAL POLICE ε50,000
incl ε500 Special Action Force

MARINE POLICE 2,500
3 PCO, 3 PCC, 8 PFI, some 110 PCI<

POLICE AVIATION 500
ac 6 AU-23, 3 *Skyvan*, 1 Fokker 50, 2 CN 235, 8 PC-6, 2 Short 330 **hel** 27 Bell 205A, 14 Bell 206, 20 Bell 212, 6 Bell 412

BORDER PATROL POLICE 40,000

NATIONAL SECURITY VOLUNTEER CORPS 50,000

Foreign Forces

SINGAPORE 1 trg camp (arty, cbt engr)
US Army 40 **Air Force** 30 **Navy** 10 **USMC** 28

Vietnam Vn

Total Armed Forces

ACTIVE ε484,000
(referred to as 'Main Force')
Terms of service 2 years Army and Air Defence, 3 years Air Force and Navy, specialists 3 years, some ethnic minorities 2 years

RESERVES some 3–4,000,000
'Strategic Rear Force' (see also *Paramilitary*)

Army ε412,000

8 Mil Regions (incl capital) • 14 Corps HQ • 58 inf div[a] • 3 mech inf div • 10 armd bde • 15 indep inf regt • SF incl AB bde, demolition engr regt • Some 10 fd arty bde • 8 engr div • 10–16 economic construction div • 20 indep engr bde
[a] Inf div str varies from 5,000 to 12,500

EQUIPMENT

MBT 45 T-34, 850 T-54/-55, 70 T-62, 350 PRC Type-59
LT TK 300 PT-76, 320 PRC Type-62/63
RECCE 100 BRDM-1/-2
AIFV 300 BMP-1/-2
APC 1,100 BTR-40/-50/-60/-152, 80 YW-531, 200 M-113 (to be upgraded)
TOWED ARTY 2,300: **76mm; 85mm; 100mm**: M-1944, T-12; **105mm**: M-101/-102; **122mm**: Type-54, Type-60, M-1938, D-30, D-74; **130mm**: M-46; **152mm**: D-20; **155mm**: M-114
SP ARTY 152mm: 30 2S3; **175mm**: M-107
COMBINED GUN/MOR 120mm: 2S9 reported
ASLT GUNS 100mm: SU-100; **122mm**: ISU-122
MRL 107mm: 360 Type 63; **122mm**: 350 BM-21; 140mm: BM-14-16
MOR 82mm, 120mm: M-43; **160mm**: M-43
SSM *Scud* B/C (reported)
ATGW AT-3 *Sagger*
RCL 75mm: PRC Type-56; **82mm**: PRC Type-65, B-10; **87mm**: PRC Type-51
AD GUNS 12,000: **14.5mm; 23mm**: incl ZSU-23-4 SP; **30mm; 37mm; 57mm; 85mm; 100mm**
SAM SA-7/-16/-18

Navy ε42,000

(incl 27,000 Naval Infantry)
Four Naval Regions
BASES Hanoi, Cam Ranh Bay, Da Nang, Haiphong (HQ), Ha Tou, Ho Chi Minh City, Can Tho, plus several smaller bases

SUBMARINES 2
SSI 2 DPRK *Yugo*

PRINCIPAL SURFACE COMBATANTS 6
FRIGATES 6
FF 6
1 *Barnegat* (US *Cutter*) with 1 × 127mm gun
3 FSU *Petya* II with 4 × 76mm gun, 10 × 406mm ASTT, 2 ASW RL
2 FSU *Petya* III with 4 × 76mm gun, 3 × 533mm ASTT, 2 ASW RL

PATROL AND COASTAL COMBATANTS 42
CORVETTES 1 HO-A (Type 124A) FSG with 8 SS-N-25 *Zvezda* SSM, SA-N-5 *Gecko* SAM
MISSILE CRAFT 12
8 FSU *Osa* II with 4 SS-N-2 *Styx* SSM
4 FSU *Tarantul* with 4 SS-N-2D *Styx* SSM
TORPEDO CRAFT 10
5 FSU *Turya* PHT with 4 × 533mm TT (2 without TT)
5 FSU *Shershen* PFT with 4 × 533mm TT
PATROL, INSHORE 19
4 FSU SO-1, 3 US PGM-59/71, 10 *Zhuk*<, 2 FSU *Poluchat* PCI; plus large numbers of river patrol boats

MINE WARFARE 10
MINE COUNTERMEASURES 10
2 *Yurka* MSC, 3 *Sonya* MSC, 2 PRC *Lienyun* MSC, 1 *Vanya* MSI, 2 *Yevgenya* MSI, plus 5 K-8 boats

AMPHIBIOUS 6
3 US LST-510-511 LST, capacity 200 tps, 16 tk
3 FSU *Polnocny* LSM, capacity 180 tps, 6 tk
Plus about 30 craft: 12 LCM, 18 LCU

SUPPORT AND MISCELLANEOUS 30+
incl 1 trg, 1 AGHS, 4 AO, about 12 small tpt, 2 ex-FSU floating docks and 3 div spt. Significant numbers of small merchant ships and trawlers are taken into naval service for patrol and resupply duties. Some of these may be lightly armed

NAVAL AVIATION
(see *People's Air Force*)

NAVAL INFANTRY (27,000)
(amph, cdo)

People's Air Force (PAF) 30,000

3 air divs (each with 3 regts), a tpt bde, an Air Force Academy
189 cbt ac, 26 armed hel
FGA 2 regt with 53 Su-22 M-3/M-4/MR (recce dedicated) and UM-3; 12 Su-27 SK/UBK
FTR 6 regt with 124 MiG-21bis/PF
ATTACK HEL 26 Mi-24
MR 4 Be-12
TPT 3 regt with **ac** 12 An-2, 12 An-26, 4 Yak-40 (VIP) **hel** 30 Mi-8/Mi-17, 4 Mi-6
ASW The PAF also maintains Vn naval air arm, operating 3 Ka-25s, 10 Ka-28s and 2 Ka-32s.
TRG 10 Yak-18, 10 BT-6, 18 L-39, some MiG-21UM
AAM AA-2 *Atoll*, AA-8 *Aphid*, AA-10 *Alamo*
ASM AS-9 *Kyle*
SAM some 66 sites with SA-2/-3/-6/-7/-16
AD 4 arty bde: **37mm, 57mm, 85mm, 100mm, 130mm**
People's Regional Force: e1,000 units, 6 radar bde: 100 sites

Paramilitary 40,000 active

BORDER DEFENCE CORPS ε40,000

COAST GUARD
came into effect on 1 Sep 1998

LOCAL FORCES some 4–5,000,000
incl **People's Self-Defence Force** (urban units), **People's Militia** (rural units); these comprise static and mobile cbt units, log spt and village protection pl; some arty, mor and AD guns; acts as reserve

CONFLICT

The conflict in **Colombia** continues to be the main cause for concern in the region. President Andres Pastrana's attempts to reach an accommodation with guerrilla groups finally failed and he was replaced by President Alvaro Uribe on 26 May 2002. Uribe has adopted a harder line towards guerrilla groups.

The security situation in **Mexico** has been relatively calm throughout the year, with the exception of some hit-and-run attacks by Ejército Zapatista de Liberación Nacional (EZLN). Chiapas remains the country's most troubled region as well as its poorest state. Attacks against government forces in the Chiapas region continue, with sporadic ambushes and kidnappings using assault rifles, grenades and pipe bombs.

In **Peru**, Sendero Luminoso carried out a bomb attack in Lima in March 2002, just before a visit by President George W. Bush, demonstrating that the organisation is still active and capable of mounting attacks.

PROTEST

In **Venezuela** there was a failed attempt by the military on 12 April 2002 to overthrow President Hugo Chavez. This was motivated by the government's heavy handed reaction to civil protests directed against its handling of the economy. In **Uruguay**, protests against the closure of the country's banks and the government's handling of the economy led to rioting on 1 August 2002. Rioting also occurred in Buenos Aires, **Argentina**, in June 2002, as citizens protested against the state of the economy.

MILITARY DEVELOPMENTS

Brazil now has in service the 40-year-old ex-French aircraft carrier *Sao Paolo*. At 32,000 tonnes, the ship is almost double the size of its retiring aircraft carrier – the *Minas Gerais* – and will carry 15 *Skyhawk* fighter aircraft. Brazil remains the only country in Latin America to have a carrier. It is trying to increase its power-projection capabilities even further, through an ongoing project to design and build an indigenous nuclear-powered attack submarine, but progress remains slow.

In **Chile**, the minister of defence, Michelle Bachelet, has reached agreement with Argentina on a joint methodology for calculating defence expenditure. This is a confidence-building measure which both countries hope can be used more widely in Latin America. In another development, announced in March 2002, Chile is to set up its own peacekeeping training centre. It is hoped that this will become a regional centre.

Chile's naval procurement is being reduced due to budgetary constraints: the *Tridente* frigate programme – a partnership with German shipbuilders for four frigates – was postponed indefinitely in early 2002. Two second-hand frigates, probably from a West European country, will probably be acquired in 2003–04 as a temporary measure to reinforce the elderly surface fleet. The programme to acquire two Franco-Spanish *Scorpene* diesel submarines to replace the current three remains on track, and the first submarine should be delivered in 2005–06.

In **Colombia**, since August 2001, more than 300 soldiers and 150 policemen have died fighting the Fuerzas Armadas Revolucionarios de Colombia (FARC). Attempts by President Andres Pastrana to come to an agreement with the FARC failed, and on 20 February 2002 he terminated the three-year peace talks and ordered the military to retake FARC-controlled territory. *Operation Thanatus* started on 21 February, but Pastrana's standing in the country had been irrevocably damaged, and on 26 May 2002, he lost the presidential election to Alvaro Uribe. President Uribe has adopted a tougher line towards FARC, which supplies approximately 80% of the world's cocaine, declaring that he will not allow them to continue to occupy their own enclave. Nevertheless, a multiple mortar attack which killed 17 people in Bogota on 7 August 2002 – the day of his inauguration – shows that the conflict is far from over. The attack is being linked to FARC cooperation with the Irish Republican Army (IRA). Three IRA members are currently awaiting trial in Colombia, having been arrested in August 2001. Furthermore, a US Congressional investigation has revealed FARC links to ETA, and Cuban and Iranian groups as well as the IRA.

The US Plan Colombia, as recently modified by the Bush administration, incorporates military aid to fight the guerrillas. Some of this aid has been directed to the modernisation of the military, resulting in the creation of a 5,000-strong rapid reaction force and increased professionalisation of the army.

The **Mexican** navy has purchased an upgrade for its eight C-212-200M aircraft in the shape of EADS-CASA's Fully Integrated Tactical System. This upgrade enables Mexico to patrol its extensive exclusive economic zone. The navy has acquired a DHC-8 *Dash* Q200 twin-turboprop for multi-role in-theatre operations.

Venezuela is upgrading its naval capabilities. In mid-2002 it received its first upgraded *Mariscal Sucre* frigate; a second upgraded frigate is to be delivered in late 2002. In December 2001, a supply ship – to be called *Ciudad Bolivar* – was commissioned, which should enable the navy to carry out limited regional deployments.

Antigua and Barbuda AB

Total Armed Forces

ACTIVE 170 (all services form combined **Antigua and Barbuda Defence Force**)

RESERVES 75

Army 125

Navy 45

BASE St Johns

PATROL CRAFT 3

PATROL, INSHORE 3

1 *Swift* PCI< • 1 *Dauntless* PCI< • 1 *Point* PCI<

Argentina Arg

Total Armed Forces

ACTIVE 69,900

RESERVES none formally established or trained

Army 41,400

3 Corps
- 1 with 1 mtn, 1 mech, 1 jungle bde
- 1 with 1 mtn, 2 mech bde
- 1 with 2 armd, 1 trg bde

STRATEGIC RESERVE
- 1 mech, 1 AB bde

Army tps
- 1 mot inf bn (Army HQ Escort Regt), 1 mot cav regt (Presidential Escort), 1 AD arty, 3 avn, 2 engr bn, 2 SF coy

EQUIPMENT
- **MBT** 200 TAM
- **LT TK** 50 AMX-13, 100 SK-105 *Kuerassier*
- **RECCE** 40 AML-90, 34 HMMWV
- **AIFV** 105 VCTP (incl variants)
- **APC** 120 M-5 half-track, 330 M-113
- **TOWED ARTY 105mm**: 100 M 56 *Oto Melara;* **155mm**: 100 CITEFA Models 77/-81
- **SP ARTY 155mm**: 20 Mk F3, 15 VCA (*Palmaria*)
- **MRL 105mm**: 5 SLAM *Pampero;* **127mm**: 5 SLAM SAPBA-1
- **MOR 81mm**: 1,100; **120mm**: 360 Brandt (37 SP in VCTM AIFV)
- **ATGW** SS-11/-12, *Cobra (Mamba)*
- **RL 66mm**: M-72
- **RCL 75mm**: 75 M-20; **90mm**: 100 M-67; **105mm**: 930 M-1968
- **AD GUNS 30mm**: 21; **40mm**: 76 L/60/-70
- **SAM** <40† *Tigercat*, <40† *Blowpipe*
- **SURV** RASIT also RATRAS (veh, arty), *Green Archer* (mor), *Skyguard*

AC 1 C212-200, 3 Cessna 207, 1 Cessna 500, 2 DHC-6, 3 G-222, 3 *Merlin* IIIA, 3 *Merlin* IV, 1 *Queen Air*, 1 *Sabreliner*, 5 T-41, 21 OV-1D (10 operational)
HEL 4 A-109, 3 AS-332B, 1 Bell 212, 4 FH-1100, 2 SA-315B, 37 UH-1H, 8 UH-12

Navy 16,000

(incl 2,000 Naval Avn and 2,500 Marines)
COMMANDS Surface Fleet, Submarines, Naval Avn, Marines
BASES Buenos Aires, Puerto Belgrano (HQ Centre), Mar del Plata (SS and HQ Atlantic), Ushuaio (HQ South), Trelew (naval avn), Punta Indio (naval avn trg), Rio Santiago (shipbuilding)

SUBMARINES 3
SSK 3
2 *Santa Cruz* (Ge TR-1700) with 6 × 533mm TT (SST-4 HWT)
1 *Salta* (Ge T-209/1200) with 8 × 533mm TT (SST-4 HWT)
PRINCIPAL SURFACE COMBATANTS 13
DESTROYERS 5
DDG 5
1 *Hercules* (UK Type 42) with 4 MM-38 *Exocet* SSM, 1 × 114mm gun, 2 × 3 ASTT, 1 *Sea King* hel
4 *Almirante Brown* (Ge MEKO 360) with 8 MM-40 *Exocet* SSM, 1 × 127mm gun, 2 × 3 ASTT, 1 AS-555 hel
FRIGATES 8
FFG 8
5 *Espora* (Ge MEKO 140) with 4 MM-38 *Exocet* SSM, 1 × 76mm gun, 2 × 3 ASTT, 1 SA 319B hel
3 *Drummond* (Fr A-69) with 4 MM-38 *Exocet* SSM, 1 × 100mm gun, 2 × 3 ASTT
PATROL AND COASTAL COMBATANTS 14
TORPEDO CRAFT 2 *Intrepida* (Ge Lürssen 45m) PFT with 2 × 533mm TT (SST-4 HWT) (one with 2 MM-38 SSM)
PATROL, OFFSHORE 7
1 *Teniente Olivieri* (ex-US oilfield tug) PCO
3 *Irigoyen* (US *Cherokee* AT) PCO
2 *King* (trg) with 3 × 105mm guns PCO
1 *Sobral* (US *Sotoyomo* AT) PCO
PATROL, INSHORE 5
4 *Baradero* (*Dabur*) PCI<
1 *Point* PCI<
MINE WARFARE 2
MINE COUNTERMEASURES 2
2 *Neuquen* (UK *Ton*) MHC
AMPHIBIOUS 1
1 *Bahia san Blas* tpt
plus 20 craft: 4 LCM, 16 LCVP

SUPPORT AND MISCELLANEOUS 11
1 *Durance* AO, 3 *Costa* tpt; 3 *Red* buoy tenders, 1 icebreaker, 1 sail trg, 1 AGOR, 1 AGHS (plus 2 craft)

NAVAL AVIATION (2,000)
EQUIPMENT
25 cbt ac, 23 armed hel
AIRCRAFT
ATTACK 11 *Super Etendard*
MR/ASW 5 S-2T, 4 P-3B, 5 BE-200M/G
TPT 3 F-28
TRG 10 T-34C
HELICOPTERS
ASW 7 ASH-3H *Sea King*, 4 AS-555 *Fennec*
CBT SPT 5 SA-319B, 7 UH-1H
SURVEY 2 B-200F, 1 PL-6A
TRG 6 EMB-326 *Xavante*
MISSILES
ASM AM-39 *Exocet*, AS-12, *Martín Pescador*
AAM R-550 *Magic*

MARINES (2,500)
FLEET FORCES 2
1 with 1 marine inf, 1 AAV, 1 arty, 1 AAA bn, 1 cdo gp
1 with 2 marine inf bn, 2 naval det
AMPH SPT FORCE 1 marine inf bn

EQUIPMENT
RECCE 12 ERC-90 *Lynx*
AAV 21 LVTP-7, 13 LARC-5
APC 6 MOWAG *Grenadier*, 36 Panhard VCR
TOWED ARTY 105mm: 6 M-101, 12 Model 56
MOR 81mm: 70; **120mm**: 12
ATGW 50 *Bantam*, *Cobra (Mamba)*
RL 89mm: 60 M-20
RCL 105mm: 30 1974 FMK1
AD GUNS 30mm: 12 HS-816; **35mm**: GDF-001
SAM 6 RBS-70

Air Force 12,500

130 cbt ac, 29 armed hel, 4 Major Comds – Air Operations, Personnel, Air Regions, Logistics
AIR OPERATIONS COMMAND (8 bde, 2 Air Mil Bases, 1 Airspace Surv and Control Gp, 1 EW Gp)
STRATEGIC AIR 5 sqn
2 with 23 *Dagger Nesher*
1 with 6 *Mirage* V Mara
2 with 36 A-4AR *Fightinghawk*
AIRSPACE DEFENCE 1 sqn with 13 *Mirage* III/EA, 3 TPS-43 field radars, SAM -3 *Roland*
AD GUNS 35mm: 1; 200mm: 86
TAC AIR 2 sqn
2 with 29 IA-58 *Pucara*
SURVEY/RECCE 1 sqn with 1 Boeing 707, 3 *Learjet* 35A, 2 IA-50
TPT/TKR 6 sqn
1 with 4 Boeing 707
2 with 12 C-130 *Hercules* (5 -B, 4 -H, 2 KC-H, 1 L-100-30)
1 with 7 F-27

1 with 4 F-28
1 with 6 DHC-6 *Twin Otter*
plus 3 IA-50 for misc comms

SAR
hel 10* UH-1H, 15* Hughes 369, 4*Hughes MD-500, 4 Bell 212, 1 SA-315B

PERSONNEL COMMAND

TRG
25 *Mentor* B-45 (basic), 27 *Tucano* EMB-312 (primary), 13* *Pampa* IA-63, 10* MS-760 (advanced), 8 Su-29AR **hel** 3 Hughes MD-500

MISSILES
ASM ASM-2 *Martín Pescador*
AAM R-530, R-550, *Shafrir*

Forces Abroad

UN AND PEACEKEEPING

CROATIA (UNMOP): 2 obs **CYPRUS** (UNFICYP) 381: 1 inf bn **IRAQ/KUWAIT** (UNIKOM): 80 engr, 5 obs **MIDDLE EAST** (UNTSO): 3 obs **WESTERN SAHARA** (MINURSO): 1 obs **YUGOSLAVIA** (KFOR): 113

Paramilitary 31,240

GENDARMERIE (Ministry of Interior) 18,000

5 Regional Comd, 16 bn
EQPT Shorland recce, 40 UR-416, 47 MOWAG *Grenadier*; **81mm** mor; **ac** 3 *Piper*, 3 PC-6, 1 Cessna *Stationair* **hel** 3 AS-350, 3 MD-500C/D

PREFECTURA NAVAL (Coast Guard) 13,240

7 comd
EQPT 5 *Mantilla* PCO, 1 *Delfin* PCO, 1 *Mandubi* PCO, 4 PCI, 21 PCI< plus boats; **ac** 5 C-212 **hel** 1 AS-330L, 2 AS-365, 1 AS-565MA, 2 Schweizer-300C

Bahamas Bs

Total Armed Forces

ACTIVE 860

Navy (Royal Bahamian Defence Force) 860

(incl 70 women)
BASE Coral Harbour, New Providence Island
MILITARY OPERATIONS PLATOON 1
ε120; Marines with internal and base sy duties

PATROL AND COASTAL COMBATANTS 7
PATROL, OFFSHORE 2 *Bahamas* PCO
PATROL, INSHORE 5
3 *Protector* PFC, 1 *Cape* PCI<, 1 *Keith Nelson* PCI<

SUPPORT AND MISCELLANEOUS 3
1 *Fort Montague* (AG)<, 2 *Dauntless* (AG)< plus 4 *Boston* whaler<

AIRCRAFT 4
1 Cessna 404, 1 Cessna 421C, 2 C-26

Barbados Bds

Total Armed Forces

ACTIVE 610

RESERVES 430

Army 500

1 inf bn (cadre)

Navy 110

BASES St Ann's Fort Garrison (HQ), Bridgetown
PATROL AND COASTAL COMBATANTS 5
PATROL, COASTAL 1
1 *Kebir* PCC
PATROL, INSHORE 4
1 *Dauntless* PCI< • 3 *Guardian* PCI< • plus boats

Belize Bze

Total Armed Forces

ACTIVE ε1,050

RESERVES 700

Army ε1,050

3 inf bn (each 3 inf coy), 1 spt gp, 3 Reserve coy

EQUIPMENT
MOR 81mm: 6
RCL 84mm: 8 *Carl Gustav*

MARITIME WING
PATROL CRAFT some 14 armed boats

AIR WING
No cbt ac or armed hel
MR/TPT 1 BN-2B *Defender*
TRG 1 T67-200 *Firefly*, 1 Cessna 182

Foreign Forces

UK Army 30

Bolivia Bol

Total Armed Forces

ACTIVE 31,500 (to be 35,000)
(incl some 20,000 conscripts)
Terms of service 12 months, selective

Army 25,000

(incl some 18,000 conscripts)
HQ: 6 Mil Regions
Army HQ direct control
2 armd bn • 1 mech cav regt • 1 Presidential Guard inf regt
10 'div'; org, composition varies; comprise
7 cav gp (5 horsed, 1 mot, 1 aslt) • 1 mot inf 'regt' with 2 bn • 22 inf bn (incl 5 inf aslt bn) • 10 arty 'regt' (bn) • 1 AB 'regt' (bn) • 6 engr bn

EQUIPMENT

LT TK 36 SK-105 *Kuerassier*
RECCE 24 EE-9 *Cascavel*
APC 18 M-113, 10 V-100 *Commando*, 20 MOWAG *Roland*, 24 EE-11 *Urutu*
TOWED ARTY 75mm: 70 incl M-116 pack, e10 Bofors M-1935; **105mm**: 30 incl M-101, FH-18; **122mm**: 18 PRC Type-54
MOR 81mm: 50; **107mm**: M-30
AC 1 C-212, 1 *King Air* B90, 1 *King Air* 200, 1 Cessna 210 *Centurion*

Navy 3,500

(incl 1,700 Marines)
COMMAND 6 naval districts covering Lake Titicaca and the rivers; each 1 flotilla
BASES Riberalta (HQ), Tiquina (HQ), Puerto Busch, Puerto Guayaramerín (HQ), Puerto Villaroel, Trinidad (HQ), Puerto Suárez (HQ), Cobija (HQ), Santa Cruz (HQ), Bermejo (HQ), Cochabamba (HQ), Puerto Villarroel

PATROL AND COASTAL COMBATANTS ε60<
PATROL CRAFT, RIVERINE some 60 riverine craft/boats, all<
SUPPORT AND MISCELLANEOUS some 18 logistic spt and patrol craft
MARINES (1,700)
6 bn (1 in each District)

Air Force 3,000

(incl perhaps 2,000 conscripts); 37 cbt ac, 16 armed hel
FGA 2 sqn with 18 AT-33AN
ADVANCED WPNS TRG/COIN 19 PC-7
ARMED HEL 1 anti-drug sqn with 16 Hughes 500M (UH-1H), plus 2 500M (VIP)
COMMS/SAR 1 hel sqn with 4 HB-315B, 2 SA-315B
SURVEY 1 sqn with 5 Cessna 206, 1 C-210, 1 C-402, 2 *Learjet* 25A/25D (secondary VIP role)
TPT 3 sqn with 1 *Sabreliner* 60, 9 C-130A/B/H, 3 F-27-400, 1 IAI-201, 3 *King Air*, 2 C-47, 3 *Convair* 580, 1 CASA 212, 1 L-188 in store
LIAISON 9 Cessna 152, 1 C-185, 13 C-206, 1 C-208, 2 C-402, 1 Beech *Bonanza*, 1 Beech *Baron*, 1 PA-32, 3 PA-34
TRG 1 Cessna 152, 2 C-172, 4 SF-260CB, 6 T-23, 10 T-34A, 1 *Lancair* 320
AD 1 air-base def regt† (Oerlikon twin **20mm**, 18 PRC Type-65 **37mm**, some truck-mounted guns)

Forces Abroad

UN AND PEACEKEEPING
DROC (MONUC): 204 **EAST TIMOR** (UNMISET): 2 obs **SIERRA LEONE** (UNAMSIL): 6 obs

Paramilitary 37,100

NATIONAL POLICE some 31,100
9 bde, 2 rapid action regt, 27 frontier units
NARCOTICS POLICE some 6,000

Brazil Br

Total Armed Forces

ACTIVE 287,600
(incl 48,200 conscripts)
Terms of service 12 months (can be extended to 18)
RESERVES
Trained first-line 1,115,000, 400,000 subject to immediate recall **Second-line** 225,000

Army 189,000

(incl 40,000 conscripts)
HQ: 7 Mil Comd, 12 Mil Regions; 8 div (3 with Regional HQ)
1 armd cav bde (2 armd cav, 1 armd, 1 arty bn), 3 armd inf bde (each 2 armd inf, 1 armd cav, 1 arty bn), 4 mech cav bde (each 2 mech cav, 1 armd cav, 1 arty bn) • 10 motor inf bde (26 bn) • 1 lt inf bde (3 bn) • 4 jungle bde • 1 frontier bde (6 bn) • 1 AB bde (3 AB, 1

arty bn) • 1 coast and AD arty bde (6 bn) • 3 cav guard regt • 10 arty gp (4 SP, 6 med) • 2 engr gp (9 bn) • 10 engr bn (incl 2 railway)
AVN 1 hel bde (2 bn each of 2 sqn)

EQUIPMENT

MBT 87 *Leopard* 1, 91 M-60A3
LT TK 286 M-41B/C
RECCE 409 EE-9 *Cascavel*
APC 219 EE-11 *Urutu*, 584 M-113
TOWED ARTY 105mm: 319 M-101/-102, 56 pack, 22 L118; **155mm**: 92 M-114
SP ARTY 105mm: 72 M-7/-108; **155mm**: 40 M-109A3
MRL 70mm: SBAT-70; 16 ASTROS II
MOR 81mm: 707; **107mm**: 236 M-30; **120mm**: 77 K6A3
ATGW 4 *Milan*, 18 *Eryx*
RL 84mm: ε500 AT-4
RCL 84mm: 127 *Carl Gustav*; **106mm**: 163 M-40A1
AD GUNS 134 incl **35mm**: GDF-001; **40mm**: L-60/-70 (some with BOFI)
SAM 4 *Roland* II, 40 SA-18
HEL 4 S-70A, 33 SA-365, 18 AS-550 *Fennec*, 15 AS-350 (armed), 8 AS-532 (being delivered)

Navy 48,600

(incl 1,150 Naval Avn, 13,900 Marines and 3,200 conscripts)
COMMAND 6, 5 Oceanic plus 1 Riverine
BASES Ocean Rio de Janeiro (HQ I Naval District), Salvador (HQ II District), Recife (HQ III District), Belém (HQ IV District), Floriancholis (HQ V District) **River** Ladario (HQ VI District)

SUBMARINES 4

SSK 4
4 *Tupi* (Ge T-209/1400) with 8 × 533mm TT (UK *Tigerfish* HWT)

PRINCIPAL SURFACE COMBATANTS 19

AIRCRAFT CARRIERS 1 *Sao Paolo* (Fr *Clemenceau*) CV with 15 A4 *Skyhawk* ac
FRIGATES 14
FFG 10
4 *Greenhaigh* (ex-UK *Broadsword*) with 4 MM-38 *Exocet* SSM, GWS 25 *Seawolf* SAM, 6 × 324mm ASTT (Mk 46 LWT), 2 *Super Lynx* hel
6 *Niteroi* with 2 × 2 MM 40 *Exocet* SSM, 2 × 3 *Seacat* SAM, 1 × 115mm gun, 6 × 324mm ASTT (Mk 46 LWT), 1 × 2 ASW mor, 1 *Super Lynx* hel
FF 4
4 *Para* (US *Garcia*) with 2 × 127mm guns, 2 × 3 ASTT, 1 × 8 ASROC SUGW, 1 *Super Lynx* hel
CORVETTES 4
4 *Inhauma* FSG, with 4 MM-40 *Exocet* SSM, 1 × 114mm gun, 2 × 3 ASTT, 1 *Super Lynx* hel

PATROL AND COASTAL COMBATANTS 50

PATROL, OFFSHORE 19
7 *Imperial Marinheiro* PCO with 1 × 76mm gun, 12 *Grajaü* PCO
PATROL, COASTAL 10
6 *Piratini* (US PGM) PCC, 4 *Bracui* (UK *River*) PCC
PATROL, INSHORE 16
16 *Tracker* PCI<
PATROL, RIVERINE 5
3 *Roraima* PCR and 2 *Pedro Teixeira* PCR

MINE WARFARE

MINELAYERS 0 but SSK class can lay mines
MINE COUNTERMEASURES 6
6 *Aratü* (Ge *Schütze*) MSC

AMPHIBIOUS 3

2 *Ceara* (US *Thomaston*) LSD capacity 345 tps, 21 LCM or 6 LCM and 3 LCUs
1 *Mattoso Maia* (US *Newport* LST) capacity 400 tps, 500 tons veh, 3 LCVP, 1 LCPL
Plus some 48 craft: 3 LCU, 10 LCM, 35 LCVP

SUPPORT AND MISCELLANEOUS 25

1 AO; 1 river gp of 1 AOT, 1 AK, 1 AF; 1 AK, 3 trp tpt; 2 AH, 1 ASR, 5 ATF, 4 AG; 2 polar AGOR, 2 AGOR, 1 AGHS plus 6 craft

NAVAL AVIATION (1,150)

EQUIPMENT
24 cbt ac, 54 armed hel
AIRCRAFT
FGA 24 A-4/TA-4*
HELICOPTERS
ASW 6 SH-3B, 7 SH-3D, 6 SH-3G/H
ATTACK 14 *Lynx* MK-21A
UTL 5 AS-332, 12 AS-350 (armed), 9 AS-355 (armed)
TRG 13 TH-57
MISSILES
ASM AS-11, AS-12, *Sea Skua*

MARINES (13,900)

FLEET FORCE 1 amph div (1 comd, 3 inf bn, 1 arty gp)
REINFORCEMENT COMD 5 bn incl 1 engr, 1 SF
INTERNAL SECURITY FORCE 8+ regional gp

EQUIPMENT

RECCE 6 EE-9 Mk IV *Cascavel*
AAV 11 LVTP-7A1, 13 AAV-7A1
APC 28 M-113, 5 EE-11 *Urutu*
TOWED ARTY 105mm: 15 M-101, 18 L-118; **155mm**: 6 M-114
MOR 81mm; 120mm: 8 K 6A3
ATGW RB-56 *Bill*
RL 89mm: 3.5in M-20
RCL 106mm: 8 M-40A1
AD GUNS 40mm: 6 L/70 with BOFI

Air Force 50,000

(incl 5,000 conscripts); 264 cbt ac, 29 armed hel

AIR DEFENCE COMMAND 1 gp

FTR 2 sqn with 18 *Mirage* F-103E/D (14 *Mirage* IIIE/ 4 DBR)

TACTICAL COMMAND 10 gp

FGA 3 sqn with 47 F-5E/-B/-F (all being upgraded), 33 AMX

CCT 2 sqn with 53 AT-26 (EMB-326) - 33 to be upgraded

RECCE 2 sqn with 4 RC-95, 10 RT-26, 12 *Learjet* 35 recce/VIP, 3 RC-130E

AEW/SURVEILLANCE

5 R-99A and 3 R-99B being delivered

SURVEILLANCE/CALIBRATION 4 *Hawker* 800XP for Amazon inspection/ATC calibration

LIAISON/OBS 7 sqn

1 with **ac** 8 T-27

5 with **ac** 31 U-7

1 with **hel** 29 UH-1H (armed)

MARITIME COMMAND 4 gp

MR/SAR 3 sqn with 10 EMB-110B, 20 EMB-111

TRANSPORT COMMAND

6 gp (6 sqn)

1 with 9 C-130H (delivery of 10 C-130H in progress), 2 KC-130H • 1 with 4 KC-137 (tpt/tkr) • 1 with 12 C-91 • 1 with 17 C-95A/B/C • 1 with 17 C-115 • 1 (VIP) with **ac** 1 VC-91, 12 VC/VU-93, 2 VC-96, 5 VC-97, 5 VU-9, 2 Boeing 737-200 **hel** 3 VH-4

7 regional sqn with 7 C-115, 86 C-95A/B/C, 6 EC-9 (VU-9)

HEL 6 AS-332, 8 AS-355, 4 Bell 206, 27 HB-350B

LIAISON 50 C-42, 3 C-98 Caravan (Cessna 205), 30 U-42

TRAINING COMMAND

AC 38* AT-26, 97 C-95 A/B/C, 25 T-23, 98 T-25, 61* T-27 (*Tucano*), 14* AMX-T

HEL 4 OH-6A, 25 OH-13

CAL 1 unit with 2 C-95, 1 EC-93, 4 EC-95, 1 U-93

MISSILES

AAM AIM-9B *Sidewinder*, R-530, *Magic* 2, MAA-1 *Piranha*

Forces Abroad

UN AND PEACEKEEPING

CROATIA (UNMOP): 2 obs **EAST TIMOR** (UNMISET): 13 obs, 74 tps

Paramilitary

PUBLIC SECURITY FORCES (R) some 385,600

in state mil pol org (state militias) under Army control and considered Army Reserve

Chile Chl

Total Armed Forces

ACTIVE 80,500

(incl 22,400 conscripts)

Terms of service **Army** 1 year **Navy** and **Air Force** 22 months. To be voluntary from 2005

RESERVES 50,000

Army 50,000

Army 45,000

(incl 20,700 conscripts)

7 Mil Regions, 2 Corps HQ

7 div; org, composition varies; comprise

25 inf (incl 10 mtn, 13 mot), 10 armd cav, 7 arty, 7 engr regt

Army tps: 1 avn bde, 1 engr, 1 AB regt (1 AB, 1 SF bn)

EQUIPMENT

MBT 40 AMX-30, 250 *Leopard* 1

RECCE 157 EE-9 *Cascavel*

AIFV 20 MOWAG *Piranha* with **90mm** gun, some M-113C/-R

APC 500 M-113, 118 Cardoen/MOWAG *Piranha*, ε290 EE-11 *Urutu*

TOWED ARTY 105mm: 66 M-101, 54 Model 56; **155mm**: 8 M-71, 11 M-68, 24 G-4

SP ARTY 155mm: 12 Mk F3

MOR 81mm: 300 M-29; **107mm**: 15 M-30; **120mm**: 125 FAMAE (incl 50 SP)

ATGW *Milan/Mamba, Mapats*

RL 89mm: 3.5in M-20

RCL 150 incl: **57mm**: M-18; **106mm**: M-40A1

AD GUNS 20mm: 60 incl some SP (Cardoen/ MOWAG)

SAM 50 *Blowpipe*, *Javelin*, 12 *Mistral*

AIRCRAFT

TPT 6 C-212, 1 *Citation* (VIP), 3 CN-235, 1 Beech *Baron*, 1 Beech *King Air*, 8 Cessna-208 *Caravan*

TRG 10 Cessna R-172

HEL 2 AS-332, 12 Enstrom 280 FX, 20 Hughes MD-530F (armed), 12 SA-315B (to be withdrawn from service), 10 SA-330, 6 AS-350B3 (being delivered)

Navy 23,000

(incl 600 Naval Avn, 3,800 Marines; 1,000 conscripts)

COMMAND AND BASES

MAIN COMMAND Fleet (includes DD and FF), SS flotilla, tpt. Remaining forces allocated to 4 Naval Zones **1st** 26°S–36°S approx: Valparaiso (HQ) **2nd** 36°S–43°S approx: Talcahuano (HQ), Puerto Montt **3rd** 43°S to Antarctica: Punta Arenas (HQ), Puerto Williams

4th north of 26°S approx: Iquique (HQ)

SUBMARINES 3

SSK 3

1 *O'Brien* (UK *Oberon*) with 8 × 533mm TT (Ge HWT)

2 *Thompson* (Ge T-209/1300) with 8 × 533mm TT (HWT)

PRINCIPAL SURFACE COMBATANTS 6

DESTROYERS 3

DDG 3

3 *Blanco Encalada* (UK *Norfolk*) with 2 × 8 *Barak 1* SAM, 2 × 114mm guns, 2 × 3 ASTT (Mk 44 LWT), 2 AS-332F hel

FRIGATES 3

FFG 3 *Condell* (mod UK *Leander*), with 2 × 2 MM 40 *Exocet* SSM, 2 x 114mm guns, 2 × 3 ASTT (Mk 44 LWT), 1 AS-332F hel

PATROL AND COASTAL COMBATANTS 27

MISSILE CRAFT 7

3 *Casma* (Il *Sa'ar* 4) PFM with 8 *Gabriel* SSM, 2 × 76mm gun

4 *Tiger* (Ge Type 148) PFM with 4 *Exocet* SSM, 1 × 6mm gun

PATROL, OFFSHORE 6

6 *Micalvi* PCO

PATROL, COASTAL 4

4 *Guacolda* (Ge Lürssen 36m) PCC

PATROL, INSHORE 10

10 *Grumete Diaz* (Il *Dabur*) PCI<

AMPHIBIOUS 3

2 *Maipo* (Fr *Batral*) LST, capacity 140 tps, 7 tk

1 *Valdivia* (US *Newport*) LST, capacity 400 tps, 500t veh

Plus craft: 2 *Elicura* LSM, 1 *Pisagua* LCU

SUPPORT AND MISCELLANEOUS 12

1 *Araucano* AO, 1 AK; 1 tpt, 2 AG; 1 trg ship, 3 ATF; 1 AGOR, 1 AGHS; 1 icebreaker

NAVAL AVIATION (600)

EQUIPMENT

13 cbt ac, 6 armed hel

AIRCRAFT

MR 3* EMB-110, 4* P-3A *Orion*, 8 Cessna *Skymaster* (plus 2 in store)

LIAISON 5 C-212A

TRG 6* PC-7

HELICOPTER

ASW 6 AS-532

UTL 5 MBB-905, 6 Bell 206

MISSILES

ASM AM-39 *Exocet*

MARINES (3,800)

4 gp: 4 inf, 2 trg bn, 4 cdo coy, 4 fd arty, 1 SSM bty, 4 AD arty bty • 1 amph bn

EQUIPMENT

LT TK 12 *Scorpion*

APC 25 MOWAG *Roland*

TOWED ARTY 105mm: 16 KH-178, **155mm**: 28 G-5

MOR 81mm: 50

SSM *Excalibur*

RCL 106mm: ε30 M-40A1

SAM *Blowpipe*

COAST GUARD (1,300)

(integral part of the Navy)

PATROL CRAFT 23

2 *Alacalufe* PCC, 15 *Rodman* PCI, 6 PCI, plus about 30 boats

Air Force 12,500

(incl 700 conscripts); 76 cbt ac, no armed hel

Flying hours: 100

5 Air Bde, 5 wg, 13 sqns

FGA 1 sqn with 14 *Mirage* 50 (12 M50M, 2 DCM)

FTR 1 sqn with 15 F-5 III (13 -E, 2 -F)

CCT 2 sqn with 14 A-37B, 12 A-36

FTR/RECCE 1 sqn with 21 *Mirage* 5 (16 M5MA, 4 M5MD, 1 M5BR)

RECCE 1 photo unit with 1 *King Air* A-100, 2 *Learjet* 35A, 3 DHC-6-100

AEW 1 IAI-707 *Phalcon* (*'Condor'*)

TPT ac 3 Boeing 707(2 tpt, 1 tkr), 1 Boeing 737-500 (VIP), 2 C-130H, 3 C-130B, 4 C-212, 9 Beech 99 (ELINT, tpt, trg), 3 Cessna 525 *Citation* CJ-1, 12 DHC-6 (2 -100, 10 -300), 1 *Gulfstream* IV (VIP), 1 *Beechcraft* 200 (VIP), 1 Cessna 206 (amph), 11 Piper PA-28

HEL 11 UH-1H (5 of which abandoned in Irq), 4 Bell 412 (first of 10–12 planned to replace UH-1H), 1 UH-60, 6 Bo-105, 3 SA-315B

TRG 1 wg, 3 flying schools **ac** 35 T-35A/B, 23 T-36, 5 *Extra* 300 **hel** 2 Bell 206A

MISSILES

AAM AIM-9B/J *Sidewinder, Shafrir, Python* III

AD 1 regt (5 gp) with **35mm**: Oerlikon GDF-005, MATRA *Mistral, Mygalle, Vulcan* 163/167

Forces Abroad

UN AND PEACEKEEPING

INDIA/PAKISTAN (UNMOGIP): 6 obs **MIDDLE EAST** (UNTSO): 4 obs

Paramilitary 36,800

CARABINEROS (Ministry of Defence) 36,800

13 zones, 39 districts, 174 *comisarias*

APC 20 MOWAG *Roland*

MOR 60mm, 81mm

AC 1 PA-31, PA-31T, *Citation*, Cessna 182/206/210

HEL 2 Bell 206, 8 Bo-105, EC-135, BK-117

Colombia Co

Total Armed Forces

ACTIVE 158,000
(incl some 74,700 conscripts)
Terms of service 12–18 months, varies (all services)

RESERVES 60,700
(incl 2,000 first-line) **Army** 54,700 **Navy** 4,800 **Air Force** 1,200

Army 136,000

(incl 63,800 conscripts)
5 div HQ
17 bde
6 mech each with 3 inf, 1 mech cav, 1 arty, 1 engr bn
2 air-portable each with 2 inf bn
9 inf (8 with 2 inf bn, 1 with 4 inf bn)
2 arty bn
Army tps
3 Mobile Counter Guerrilla Force (bde) (each with 1 cdo unit, 4 bn) – 2 more forming
2 trg bde with 1 Presidential Guard, 1 SF, 1 AB, 1 mech, 1 arty, 1 engr bn
1 army avn 'bde'
3 counter-narcotics bn
1 AD arty bn

EQUIPMENT
LT TK 12 M-3A1 (in store)
RECCE 5 M-8, 130 EE-9 *Cascavel*
APC 100+ M-113, 100+ EE-11 *Urutu*, 4 RG-31 *Nyala*
TOWED ARTY 75mm: 70 M-116; **105mm**: 86 M-101
MOR 81mm: 125 M-1; **107mm**: 148 M-2; **120mm**: 123 Brandt
ATGW 20 TOW (incl 8 SP)
RL 66mm: M-72; **89mm**: 15 M-20
RCL 106mm: 50 M-40A1
AD GUNS 40mm: 30 M-1A1
HEL some 100 incl 6 OH-6A, 13 UH-60, MD500/530, Bell 205/206/212, Bell 412, UH-1B, Hughes 300/500, 9 Mi-17

Navy 15,000

(incl 100 Naval Avn, 10,000 Marines; 7,000 conscripts)
BASES Ocean Cartagena (main), Buenaventura, Málaga (Pacific) **River** Puerto Leguízamo, Barrancabermeja, Puerto Carreño (tri-Service Unified Eastern Command HQ), Leticia, Puerto Orocue, Puerto Inirida

SUBMARINES 4
SSK 2 *Pijao* (Ge T-209/1200) with 8 × 533mm TT (Ge HWT)
SSI 2 *Intrepido* (It SX-506) (SF delivery)

PRINCIPAL SURFACE COMBATANTS 4
CORVETTES 4
4 *Almirante Padilla* FSG with 8 MM-40 *Exocet* SSM, 1 × 76mm gun, 2 × 3 ASTT, 1 Bo-105 hel

PATROL AND COASTAL COMBATANTS 27
PATROL, OFFSHORE 5
2 *Pedro de Heredia* (ex-US tugs) PCO with 1 × 76mm gun, 2 *Lazaga* PCO, 1 *Esperanta* (Sp *Cormoran*) PFO
PATROL, COASTAL/INSHORE 9
1 *Quito Sueno* (US *Asheville*) PFC with 1 × 76mm gun, 2 *Castillo Y Rada* PCC, 2 *José Garcia* PCC, 2 *José Palas* PCI, 2 *Jaime Gomez* PCI
PATROL, RIVERINE 13
3 *Arauca* PCR, 10 *Diligente* PCR, plus 76 craft: 9 *Tenerife*, 5 *Rio Magdalena*, 20 *Delfin*, 42 *Pirana*

SUPPORT AND MISCELLANEOUS 7
1 tpt; 1 AH, 1 sail trg; 2 AGOR, 2 AGHS

MARINES (10,000)
2 bde (each of 2 bn), 1 amph aslt, 1 river ops (15 amph patrol units), 1 SF, 1 sy bn
No hy eqpt (to get EE-9 *Cascavel* recce, EE-11 *Urutu* APC)

NAVAL AVIATION (100)
EQUIPMENT
AIRCRAFT
2 *Commander*, 2 PA-28, 2 PA-31, 2 *Cessna* 206
HELICOPTER
2 Bo-105, 2 AS 555SN *Fennec*

Air Force 7,000

(some 3,900 conscripts); 58 cbt ac, 23 armed hel

AIR COMBAT COMMAND
FGA 2 sqn
1 with 7 *Mirage* 5, 1 with 11 *Kfir* (10 -C7, 1 -TC7)

TACTICAL AIR SUPPORT COMMAND
CBT ac 4 AC-47T, 3 IA-58A, 20 A-37B, 13 OV-10
UTILITY/ARMED HEL 5 Bell 205, 13 Bell 212, 2 Bell 412, 10 UH-60A, 11 UH-60L (7*), 11 MD-500ME*, 2 MD-500D*, 3 MD-530F*
RECCE 5 *Schweizer* SA 2-37A/B, 3 C-26

MILITARY AIR TRANSPORT COMMAND
AC 1 Boeing 707, 2 Boeing 727, 7 C-130B, 2 C-130H, 1 C-117, 2 C-47, 2 CASA 212, 2 *Bandeirante*, 1 F-28, 3 CN-235
HEL 17 UH-1H, 6 Mi-17

AIR TRAINING COMMAND
AC 12 T-27 (*Tucano*), 9 T-34M, 12 T-37, 8 T-41
HEL 2 UH-1B, 4 UH-1H, 12 F-28F

MISSILES
AAM R-530, *Python* III

Forces Abroad

UN AND PEACEKEEPING
EGYPT (MFO) 358: 1 inf bn

Paramilitary 104,600

NATIONAL POLICE FORCE 104,600
ac 5 OV-10A, 12 Gavilan, 11 *Turbo Thrush* **hel** 10 Bell-206L, 9 Bell-212, 2 Hughes 500D, 33 UH-1H/H-II, 25 UH-1N, 11 UH-60L

Opposition

COORDINADORA NACIONAL GUERRILLERA SIMON BOLIVAR (CNGSB) loose coalition of guerrilla gps incl **Fuerzas Armadas Revolucionarias de Colombia (FARC)** up to 18,000 reported active plus 5,000 urban militia; **Ejercito de Liberacion Nacional (ELN)** ε3,500 plus urban militia, pro-Cuban; **Ejercito Popular de Liberacion (EPL)** ε500

Other Forces

AUTODEFENSAS UNIDAS DE COLOMBIA (AUC) ε10,600 right-wing paramilitary gp

Foreign Forces

US Army 15

Costa Rica CR

Total Armed Forces

ACTIVE Nil

Paramilitary 8,400

CIVIL GUARD 4,400
7 urban *comisaria* (reinforced coy) • 1 tac police *comisaria* • 1 special ops unit • 6 provincial *comisaria*

BORDER SECURITY POLICE 2,000
2 Border Sy Comd (8 *comisaria*)
MARITIME SURVEILLANCE UNIT (300)
BASES Pacific Golfito, Punta Arenas, Cuajiniquil, Quepos **Atlantic** Limon, Moin
PATROL CRAFT, COASTAL/INSHORE 8
1 *Isla del Coco* (US *Swift* 32m) PFC
1 *Astronauta* (US *Cape*) PCC
2 *Point* PCI<
4 PCI<; plus about 10 boats

AIR SURVEILLANCE UNIT (300)
No cbt ac
ac 1 Cessna O-2A, 1 DHC-4, 1 PA-31, 1 PA-34, 4 U206G **hel** 2 MD-500E, 1 Mi-17

RURAL GUARD (Ministry of Government and Police) 2,000
8 comd; small arms only

Cuba C

Total Armed Forces

ACTIVE 46,000
Terms of service 2 years

RESERVES
Army 39,000 **Ready Reserves** (serve 45 days per year) to fill out Active and Reserve units; see also *Paramilitary*

Army ε35,000

(incl conscripts and Ready Reserves)
HQ: 3 Regional Comd, 3 Army
4–5 armd bde • 9 mech inf bde (3 mech inf, 1 armd, 1 arty, 1 AD arty regt) • 1 AB bde • 14 reserve bde • 1 frontier bde
AD arty regt and SAM bde

EQUIPMENT † (some 75% in store)
MBT ε900 incl: T-34, T-54/-55, T-62
LT TK some PT-76
RECCE some BRDM-1/-2
AIFV some BMP-1
APC ε700 BTR-40/-50/-60/-152
TOWED ARTY 500: **76mm**: ZIS-3; **122mm**: M-1938, D-30; **130mm**: M-46; **152mm**: M-1937, D-1
SP ARTY 40: **122mm**: 2S1; **152mm**: 2S3
MRL 175: **122mm**: BM-21; **140mm**: BM-14
MOR 1,000: **82mm**: M-41/-43; **120mm**: M-38/-43
STATIC DEF ARTY JS-2 (**122mm**) hy tk, T-34 (**85mm**)
ATGW AT-1 *Snapper*, AT-3 *Sagger*
ATK GUNS 85mm: D-44; **100mm**: SU-100 SP, T-12
AD GUNS 400 incl: **23mm**: ZU-23, ZSU-23-4 SP; **30mm**: M-53 (twin)/BTR-60P SP; **37mm**: M-1939; **57mm**: S-60 towed, ZSU-57-2 SP; **85mm**: KS-12; **100mm**: KS-19
SAM some 300 incl: SA-6/-7/-8/-9/-13/-14/-16

Navy ε3,000

(incl 550+ Naval Infantry)
BASES Cabanas (HQ Western comd), Holquin (HQ Eastern comd), Cienfuegos, Havana, Mariel, Nicaro, Punta Movida

PATROL AND COASTAL COMBATANTS 5†

MISSILE CRAFT 4 FSU *Osa* II PFM

PATROL, COASTAL 1 FSU *Pauk* II PFC with 1 × 76mm gun, 4 ASTT, 2 ASW RL

MINE WARFARE 6

MINE COUNTERMEASURES 6†

2 FSU *Sonya* MSC, 4 FSU *Yevgenya* MHC

SUPPORT AND MISCELLANEOUS 1

1 AGHS†

NAVAL INFANTRY (550+)

2 amph aslt bn

COASTAL DEFENCE

ARTY 122mm: M-1931/37; **130mm**: M-46; **152mm**: M-1937

SSM 2 SS-C-3 systems, some mobile *Bandera* IV (reported)

Air Force ε8,000

(incl AD and conscripts); 130† cbt ac of which only some 25 are operational, 45 armed hel

Flying hours less than 50

FGA 2 sqn with 10 MiG-23BN

FTR 4 sqn

2 with 30 MiG-21F, 1 with 50 MiG-21bis, 1 with 20 MiG-23MF, 6 MiG-29

(Probably only some 3 MiG-29, 10 MiG-23, 5 MiG-21bis in operation)

ATTACK HEL 45 Mi-8/-17, Mi-25/35

ASW 5 Mi-14 hel

TPT 4 sqn with 8 An-2, 1 An-24, 15 An-26, 1 An-30, 2 An-32, 4 Yak-40, 2 Il-76 (Air Force ac in civilian markings)

HEL 40 Mi-8/-17

TRG 25 L-39, 8* MiG-21U, 4* MiG-23U, 2* MiG-29UB, 20 Z-326

MISSILES

ASM AS-7

AAM AA-2, AA-7, AA-8, AA-10, AA-11

SAM 13 active SA-2, SA-3 sites

CIVIL AIRLINE

10 Il-62, 7 Tu-154, 12 Yak-42, 1 An-30 used as tp tpt

Paramilitary 26,500 active

STATE SECURITY (Ministry of Interior) 20,000

BORDER GUARDS (Ministry of Interior) 6,500

about 20 FSU *Zhuk* and 3 FSU *Stenka* PFI<, plus boats

YOUTH LABOUR ARMY 70,000

CIVIL DEFENCE FORCE 50,000

TERRITORIAL MILITIA (R) ε1,000,000

Foreign Forces

US 2,039: **Air Force** 63 **Navy** 590 **Marines** 486 **Army** 900 plus Joint Task Force – ε170

Dominican Republic DR

Total Armed Forces

ACTIVE 24,500

Army 15,000

3 Defence Zones • 4 inf bde (with 8 inf, 1 arty bn, 2 recce sqn) • 1 armd, 1 Presidential Guard, 1 SF, 1 arty, 1 engr bn

EQUIPMENT

LT TK 12 AMX-13 (**75mm**), 12 M-41A1 (**76mm**)

RECCE 8 V-150 *Commando*

APC 20 M-2/M-3 half-track

TOWED ARTY 105mm: 22 M-101

MOR 81mm: M-1; **120mm**: 24 ECIA

Navy 4,000

(incl marine security unit and 1 SEAL unit)

BASES Santo Domingo (HQ), Las Calderas

PATROL AND COASTAL COMBATANTS 15

PATROL, OFFSHORE 5

2 *Cohoes* PCO with 2 × 76mm gun, 1 *Prestol* (US *Admirable*) with 1 × 76mm gun, 1 *Sotoyoma* PCO with 1 × 76mm gun, 1 *Balsam* PCO

PATROL, COASTAL/INSHORE 10

1 *Betelgeuse* (US PGM-71) PCC, 2 *Canopus* PCI<, 7 PCI<

SUPPORT AND MISCELLANEOUS 4

1 AOT (small harbour), 3 AT

Air Force 5,500

16 cbt ac, no armed hel

Flying hours probably less than 60

CCT 1 sqn with 6 A-37B

TPT 1 sqn with 1 Beech 60, 1 Beech 200, 1 Cessna 207, 2 C-212-400, 1 PA-31

MPA/SAR 1 sqn with 5 T-34B

HEL 1 Liaison/Casevac/SAR sqn with 6 UH-1H (plus 6 more by end 2002), 1 SA-365C, 1 SA-365N (VIP); trg, 1 SE-3130, 1 OH-6A

TRG 3 T-41D, 8 T-35B, 10 EMB-314*

AB 1 SF (AB) bn

AD 1 bn with 4 **20mm** guns

Paramilitary 15,000

NATIONAL POLICE 15,000

Ecuador Ec

Total Armed Forces

ACTIVE 59,500

Terms of service conscription 1 year, selective

RESERVES 100,000

Ages 18–55

Army 50,000

4 Defence Zones
5 inf bde (each 3 inf, 1 armd, 1 arty bn) • 1 armd bde (2 armd, 1 mech inf, 1 SP arty bn) • 3 jungle bde (2 with 3 jungle, 1 SF bn, 1 with 4 jungle bn)
Army tps: 1 SF (AB) bde (4 bn), 1 special ops gp, 1 AD arty gp, 1 avn gp (4 bn), 1 engr bde: 3 engr bn

EQUIPMENT

MBT 30+ T-55
LT TK 108 AMX-13
RECCE 27 AML-60/-90, 30 EE-9 *Cascavel*, 10 EE-3 *Jararaca*
APC 20 M-113, 80 AMX-VCI, 30 EE-11 *Urutu*
TOWED ARTY 105mm: 50 M2A2, 30 M-101, 24 Model 56; **155mm**: 12 M-198, 12 M-114
SP ARTY 155mm: 10 Mk F3
MRL 122mm: 6 RM-70
MOR 81mm: M-29; **107mm**: 4.2in M-30; **160mm**: 12 Soltam
RCL 90mm: 380 M-67; **106mm**: 24 M-40A1
AD GUNS 14.5mm: 128 ZPU-1/-2; **20mm**: 20 M-1935; **23mm**: 34 ZU-23; **35mm**: 30 GDF-002 twin; **37mm**: 18 Ch; **40mm**: 30 L/70
SAM 75 *Blowpipe*, *Chaparral*, SA-7/-8/-16, 90 SA-18 (reported)

AIRCRAFT

SURVEY 1 *King Air* 100, 1 Cessna *Citation*
TPT 1 CN-235, 1 DHC-5D, 5 IAI-201, 1 *King Air* 200, 1 PC-6

HELICOPTERS

TPT/LIAISON 4 AS-332, 1 AS-350B, 2 SA-315B, 20 SA-342, 5 Mi-17

Navy 5,500

(incl 250 Naval Avn and 1,700 Marines)
BASES Guayaquil (main base), Jaramijo, Galápagos Islands

SUBMARINES 2

SSK 2 *Shyri* (Ge T-209/1300) with 8 × 533mm TT (Ge SUT HWT)

PRINCIPAL SURFACE COMBATANTS 2

FRIGATES 2
FFG 2 *Presidente Eloy Alfaro* (ex-UK *Leander* batch II) with 4 MM-38 *Exocet* SSM, 1 206B hel

PATROL AND COASTAL COMBATANTS 11

CORVETTES 6 *Esmeraldas* FSG with 2 × 3 MM-40 *Exocet* SSM, 1 × 4 *Albatros* SAM, 1 × 76mm gun, 6 × 324mm ASTT, hel deck
MISSILE CRAFT 5
3 *Quito* (Ge Lürssen 45m) PFM with 4 MM-38 *Exocet* SSM, 1 × 76mm gun
2 *Manta*† (Ge Lürssen 36m) PFM with 4 *Gabriel* II SSM

AMPHIBIOUS 1

1 *Hualcopo* (US LST-512-1152) LST, capacity 150 tps

SUPPORT AND MISCELLANEOUS 7

2 AOT (small); 1 AE; 2 ATF, 1 sail trg; 1 AGOR

NAVAL AVIATION (250)

EQUIPMENT
AIRCRAFT
LIAISON 3 *Super King Air* 200, 1 *Super King Air* 300, 1 CN-235
TRG 3 T-34C
HELICOPTER
UTL 4 Bell 206, 2 Bell 412 EP, 4 Bell TH-57

MARINES (1,700)

3 bn: 2 on garrison duties, 1 cdo (no hy wpn/veh)

Air Force 4,000

79 cbt ac, no armed hel

OPERATIONAL COMMAND

2 wg, 4 sqn
FGA 3 sqn
1 with 8 *Jaguar* S (6 -A(E), 2 -B(E))
1 with 10 *Kfir* C-2 (being modernised to CE standard), 2 TC-2
1 with 20 A-37B
FTR 1 sqn with 13 *Mirage* F-1JE, 1 F-1JB
CCT 4 *Strikemaster* Mk 89A

MILITARY AIR TRANSPORT GROUP

2 civil/mil airlines:
TAME 3 Boeing 727, 2 BAe-748, 2 C-130B, 1 C-130H, 1 DHC-6, 1 F-28, 1 L-100-30
ECUATORIANA 3 Boeing 707-320, 1 DC-10-30, 2 A-310
LIAISON 1 *King Air* E90, 1 *Sabreliner*
LIAISON/SAR hel 2 AS-332, 1 Bell 212, 6 Bell-206B, 5 SA-316B, 1 SA-330

TRG incl 22 AT-33*, 20 Cessna 150, 5 C-172, 17 T-34C, 1 T-41

MISSILES

AAM R-550 *Magic*, *Super* 530, *Shafrir*, *Python* 3, *Python* 4
AB 1 AB sqn

Paramilitary 270

COAST GUARD 270

PATROL, COASTAL/INSHORE 4
2 *5 De Agosto* PCC, 1 PGM-71 PCI, 1 *Point* PCI plus some 8 boats

El Salvador EIS

Total Armed Forces

ACTIVE 16,800

Terms of service selective conscription, 1 year

RESERVES

Ex-soldiers registered

Army ε15,000

(incl 4,000 conscripts)
6 Mil Zones • 6 inf bde (each of 2 inf bn) • 1 special sy bde (4 MP, 2 border gd bn) • 8 inf det (bn) • 1 engr comd (2 engr bn) • 1 arty bde (2 fd, 1 AD bn) • 1 mech cav regt (2 bn) • 1 special ops gp (1 para bn, 1 naval inf, 1 SF coy)

EQUIPMENT

RECCE 10 AML-90 (2 in store)
APC 40 M-37B1 (mod), 8 UR-416
TOWED ARTY 105mm: 24 M-101 (in store), 36 M-102, 18 M-56
MOR 81mm: incl 300 M-29; **120mm**: 60 UB-M52, M-74 (in store)
RL 94mm: LAW; **82mm**: B-300
RCL 90mm: 400 M-67; **106mm**: 20+ M-40A1 (incl 16 SP)
AD GUNS 20mm: 36 FRY M-55, 4 TCM-20

Navy 700

(incl some 90 Naval Inf and spt forces)
BASES La Uníon, La Libertad, Acajutla, El Triunfo, Guija Lake

PATROL AND COASTAL COMBATANTS 5

PATROL, COASTAL/INSHORE 5
3 *Camcraft* 30m PCC, 2 PCI<, plus 22 river boats

NAVAL INFANTRY (some 90)
1 sy coy

Air Force 1,100

(incl AD and ε200 conscripts); 23 cbt ac, 21 armed hel
Flying hours A-37: 90
CBT AC 1 sqn with 5 A-37B, 4 OA-37B, 1 *Ouragan*, 9 O-2A, 2 O-2B (psyops), 2 CM-170
ARMED HEL 1 sqn with 1 MD-500D, 6 MD-500E, 3 UH-1M, (11 UH-1H in store)
TPT 1 sqn with **ac** 2 C-47, 6 Basler Turbo-67 (3 capable of being converted back to AC-47 gunships), 1 T-41D, 1 Cessna 337G, 1 *Merlin* IIIB, (1 C-123K and 1 OC-6B in store) **hel** 1 sqn with 18 UH-1H tpt hel (incl 4 SAR), (15 UH-1H in store)
TRG 5 *Rallye*, 5 T-35 *Pillan*, **hel** 6 Hughes 269A (of which 4 stored)
AAM *Shafrir*

Forces Abroad

UN AND PEACEKEEPING

WESTERN SAHARA (MINURSO): 4 obs

Paramilitary 12,000

NATIONAL CIVILIAN POLICE (Ministry of Public Security) some 12,000 (to be 16,000)
small arms; **ac** 1 Cessna O-2A **hel** 1 UH-1H, 2 Hughes-520N, 1 MD-500D
10 river boats

Guatemala Gua

Total Armed Forces

(National Armed Forces are combined; the Army provides log spt for Navy and Air Force)

ACTIVE ε31,400

(ε23,000 conscripts)
Terms of service conscription; selective, 30 months

RESERVES

Army ε35,000 (trained) **Navy** (some) **Air Force** 200

Army 29,200

(incl ε23,000 conscripts)
15 Mil Zones (22 inf, 1 trg bn, 6 armd sqn) • 2 strategic bde (4 inf, 1 lt armd bn, 1 recce sqn, 2 arty bty) • 1 SF gp (3 coy incl 1 trg) • 2 AB bn • 5 inf bn gp (each 1 inf bn, 1

recce sqn, 1 arty bty) • 1 Presidential Guard bn • 1 engr bn • 1 Frontier Detachment
RESERVES ε19 inf bn

EQUIPMENT

RECCE 7 M-8 (in store), 9 RBY-1
APC 10 M-113 (plus 5 in store), 7 V-100 *Commando*, 30 *Armadillo*
TOWED ARTY 105mm: 12 M-101, 8 M-102, 56 M-56
MOR 81mm: 55 M-1; **107mm**: 12 M-30 (in store); **120mm**: 18 ECIA
RL 89mm: 3.5in M-20 (in store)
RCL 57mm: M-20; **105mm**: 64 Arg M-1974 FMK-1; **106mm**: 56 M-40A1
AD GUNS 20mm: 16 M-55, 16 GAI-DO1

Navy ε1,500

(incl some 650 Marines)
BASES Atlantic Santo Tomás de Castilla **Pacific** Puerto Quetzal

PATROL AND COASTAL COMBATANTS 9

PATROL CRAFT, COASTAL/INSHORE 9
1 Kukulkan (US Broadsword 32m) PCI<, 2 *Stewart* PCI<, 6 *Cutlas* PCI<, plus 6 *Vigilante* boats
PATROL CRAFT, RIVERINE 20 boats

MARINES (some 650)

2 bn (-)

Air Force 700

10† cbt ac, 12 armed hel. Serviceability of ac is less than 50%
CBT AC 1 sqn with 4 Cessna A-37B, 1 sqn with 6 PC-7
TPT 1 sqn with 4 T-67 (mod C-47 *Turbo*), 2 F-27, 1 *Super King Air* (VIP), 1 PA 301 *Navajo*, 4 Arava 201
LIAISON 1 sqn with 2 Cessna 206, 1 Cessna 310
HEL 1 sqn with 12 armed hel (9 Bell 212, 3 Bell 412), 9 Bell 206, 3 UH-1H, 3 S-76
TRG 6 T-41, 5 T-35B, 5 Cessna R172K

TACTICAL SECURITY GROUP (Air Military Police)

3 CCT coy, 1 armd sqn, 1 AD bty (Army units for air-base sy)

Paramilitary 19,000 active

NATIONAL POLICE 19,000

21 departments, 1 SF bn, 1 integrated task force (incl mil and treasury police)

TREASURY POLICE (2,500)

Guyana Guy

Total Armed Forces

ACTIVE (combined **Guyana Defence Force**) some 1,600

RESERVES some 1,500
People's Militia (see *Paramilitary*)

Army 1,400

(incl 500 Reserves)
1 inf bn, 1 SF, 1 spt wpn, 1 engr coy

EQUIPMENT

RECCE 3 Shorland, 6 EE-9 *Cascavel* (reported)
TOWED ARTY 130mm: 6 M-46
MOR 81mm: 12 L16A1; **82mm**: 18 M-43; **120mm**: 18 M-43

Navy 100

(plus 170 reserves)
BASES Georgetown, New Amsterdam

PATROL AND COASTAL COMBATANTS 1

1 *Orwell* PCC plus 2 boats

Air Force 100

no cbt ac, no armed hel
TPT ac 1 Y-12, 1 *Skyvan* 3M **hel** 1 Bell 206, 1 Bell 412

Paramilitary

GUYANA PEOPLE'S MILITIA (GPM) some 1,500

Haiti RH

Total Armed Forces

ACTIVE Nil

Paramilitary

In 1994, the mil govt of Haiti was replaced by a civilian administration. The former armed forces and police were disbanded and a National Police Force of ε5,300 personnel has now been formed. All Army eqpt has been destroyed.

COAST GUARD 30

BASE Port-au-Prince

PATROL CRAFT boats only

Honduras Hr

Total Armed Forces

ACTIVE 8,300

RESERVES 60,000

Ex-servicemen registered

Army 5,500

6 Mil Zones

4 inf bde

3 with 3 inf, 1 arty bn • 1 with 3 inf bn

1 special tac gp with 1 inf (AB), 1 SF bn

1 armd cav regt (2 mech bn, 1 lt tk, 1 recce sqn, 1 arty, 1 AD arty bty)

1 engr bn

1 Presidential Guard coy

RESERVES

1 inf bde

EQUIPMENT

LT TK 12 *Scorpion*

RECCE 3 *Scimitar*, 1 *Sultan*, 50 *Saladin*, 13 RBY-1

TOWED ARTY 105mm: 24 M-102; **155mm**: 4 M-198

MOR 60mm; **81mm**; **120mm**: 60 FMK; **160mm**: 30 *Soltam*

RL 84mm: 120 *Carl Gustav*

RCL 106mm: 80 M-40A1

AD Guns 20mm: 24 M-55A2, 24 TCM-20

Navy 1,000

(incl 400 Marines)

BASES Atlantic Puerto Cortés, Puerto Castilla **Pacific** Amapala

PATROL AND COASTAL COMBATANTS 10

PATROL CRAFT, COASTAL/INSHORE 10

3 *Guaymuras* (US *Swiftship* 31m) PFC

2 *Copan* (US *Guardian* 32m) PFI<

5 PCI<, plus 28 riverine boats

AMPHIBIOUS craft only

1 *Punta Caxinas* LCT

MARINES (400)

3 indep coy (-)

Air Force 1,800

49 cbt ac, no armed hel

FGA 2 sqn

1 with 13 A-37B

1 with 11 F-5E/F

IN STORE 10 *Super Mystère* B2

TPT 5 C-47, 3 C-130A, 2 IAI-201, 1 IAI-1124, 1 L-188 *Electra*

LIAISON 6 C-185, 1 *Commander*, 1 PA-31, 1 PA-31T, 1 Cessna 401

HEL 9 Bell 412SP, 2 Hughes 500, 4 UH-1H, 1 A-109 (VIP)

TRG/COIN 4* C-101CC, 11* EMB-312, 6 T-41A, 2 Cessna 182

AAM *Shafrir*

Forces Abroad

UN AND PEACEKEEPING

WESTERN SAHARA (MINURSO): 12 obs

Paramilitary 6,000

PUBLIC SECURITY FORCES (Ministry of Public Security and Defence) 6,000

11 regional comd

Foreign Forces

US 356: **Army** 170 **Marines** 46 **Air Force** 140

Jamaica Ja

Total Armed Forces

ACTIVE (combined **Jamaican Defence Force**) some 2,830

RESERVES some 953

Army 877 **Coast Guard** 60 **Air Wing** 16

Army 2,500

2 inf, 1 spt bn, 1 engr regt (4 sqn)

EQUIPMENT

APC 13 V-150 *Commando* (some non-op)

MOR 81mm: 12 L16A1

RESERVES

1 inf bn

Coast Guard 190

BASE Port Royal, out stations at Discovery Bay and Pedro Cays

PATROL AND COASTAL COMBATANTS 5

PATROL COASTAL/INSHORE 5
- 1 *Fort Charles* (US 34m) PFC, 1 *Paul Bogle* (US-31m) PFI<, 1 *Holland Bay* PFI<, 2 *Point* PCI<
- plus 4 boats

Air Wing 140

3 flts plus National Reserve
no cbt ac, no armed hel. All apart from 4 AS-355 and 3 Bell 412 reported as grounded
AC 1 TPT/MPA flt with 1 BN-2A, 1 Cessna 210, 1 *King Air*
HEL 2 TPT/SAR flts with 4 Bell 206, 3 Bell 412, 4 AS-355

Mexico Mex

Total Armed Forces

ACTIVE 192,770
(60,000 conscripts)
Terms of service 1 year conscription (4 hours per week) by lottery

RESERVES 300,000

Army 144,000

(incl ε60,000 conscripts)
12 Mil Regions
44 Zonal Garrisons with 81 inf bn (1 mech), 19 mot cav, 3 arty regt plus 1 air-mobile SF unit per Garrison
3 Corps HQ each with 3 inf bde

STRATEGIC RESERVE

4 armd bde (each 2 armd recce, 1 arty regt, 1 mech inf bn, 1 ATK gp)
1 AB bde (3 bn)
1 MP bde (3 MP bn, 1 mech cav regt)

EQUIPMENT
- **RECCE** 40 M-8, 119 ERC-90F *Lynx*, 40 VBL, 25 MOWAG, 40 MAC-1
- **APC** 40 HWK-11, 32 M-2A1 half-track, 40 VCR/TT, 24 DN-3, 40 DN-4 *Caballo*, 70 DN-5 *Toro*, 495 AMX-VCI, 95 BDX, 26 LAV-150 ST, some BTR-60 (reported)
- **TOWED ARTY 75mm**: 18 M-116 pack; **105mm**: 16 M-2A1/M-3, 80 M-101, 80 M-56
- **SP ARTY 75mm**: 5 DN-5 *Bufalo*
- **MOR 81mm**: 1,500; **120mm**: 75 Brandt
- **ATGW** *Milan* (incl 8 VBL)
- **RL 82mm**: B-300
- **ATK GUNS 37mm**: 30 M-3
- **AD GUNS 12.7mm**: 40 M-55; **20mm:** 40 GAI-BO1
- **SAM** RBS-70

Navy 37,000

(incl 1,100 Naval Avn and 8,700 Marines)
COMMANDS Gulf (6 zones), **Pacific** (11 zones)
BASES Gulf Vera Cruz (HQ), Tampico, Chetumal, Ciudad del Carmen, Yukalpetén, Lerna, Frontera, Coatzacoalcos, Isla Mujéres **Pacific** Acapulco (HQ), Ensenada, La Paz, San Blas, Guaymas, Mazatlán, Manzanillo, Salina Cruz, Puerto Madero, Lázaro Cárdenas, Puerto Vallarta

PRINCIPAL SURFACE COMBATANTS 11

DESTROYERS 3
- **DD** 3
  - 2 *Ilhuicamina* (ex-*Quetzalcoatl*) (US *Gearing*) with 2 × 2 127mm guns, 1 Bo-105 hel
  - 1 *Cuitlahuac* (US *Fletcher*) with 5 × 127mm guns, 5 × 533mm ASTT

FRIGATES 8
- **FF** 8
  - 2 *Knox* with 1 × 127mm gun, 4 × 324mm ASTT, 2 × 8 ASROC SUGW, 1 × Bo 105 hel
  - 2 *H. Galeana* (US *Bronstein*) with 6 × 324mm ASTT, ASROC SUGW
  - 3 *Hidalgo* (US *Lawrence/Crosley*) with 1 × 127mm gun
  - 1 *Comodoro Manuel Azueta* (US *Edsall*) (trg) with 2 × 76mm gun

PATROL AND COASTAL COMBATANTS 109

PATROL, OFFSHORE 44
- 4 *Holzinger 2000* PCO with MD 902 hel
- 4 *S. J. Holzinger* (ex-*Uxmal*) (imp *Uribe*) PCO with Bo-105 hel
- 6 *Uribe* (Sp *'Halcon'*) PCO with Bo-105 hel
- 11 *Negrete* (US *Admirable* MSF) PCO with 1 Bo-105 hel
- 17 *Leandro Valle* (US *Auk* MSF) PCO
- 1 *Guanajuato* PCO with 2 × 102mm gun
- 1 *Centenario* PCO

PATROL, COASTAL 41
- 31 *Azteca* PCC
- 3 *Cabo* (US *Cape Higgon*) PCC
- 7 *Tamiahua* (US *Polimar*) PCC

PATROL, INSHORE 6
- 4 *Isla* (US *Halter*) XFPCI<
- 2 *Punta* (US *Point*) PCI<

PATROL, RIVERINE 18<, plus boats

AMPHIBIOUS 3
- 2 *Panuco* (US-511) LST
- 1 *Grijalva* (US-511) LST

SUPPORT AND MISCELLANEOUS 19
- 1 AOT; 4 AK, 2 log spt; 6 AT/F, 1 sail trg; 2 AGHS, 3 AGOR

NAVAL AVIATION (1,100)

EQUIPMENT

8 cbt ac, no armed hel

AIRCRAFT

MR 1 sqn with 8* C-212-200M

TPT 1 C-212, 2 C-180, 3 C-310, 1 DHC-5, 1 FH-227, 1 *King Air* 90, 1 *Learjet* 24, 1 *Commander*, 2 C-337, 2 C-402, 5 An-32, 1 Mu-2F

TRG 12 *Maule* MX-7, 10 F-33C *Bonanza*, 10 L-90 *Redigo*

HELICOPTER

UTL 3 Bell 47, 4 SA-319, 20 Mi-8/17, 4 AS-555, 2 R-22 *Mariner*, 1 R-44

MR 12 Bo-105 (8 afloat), 10 MD-902 *Explorer*

TRG 4 MD-500E

MARINES (8,700)

3 marine bde (each 3 bn), 1 AB regt (2 bn) • 1 Presidential Guard bn • 11 regional bn • 1 Coast def gp: 2 coast arty bn • 1 indep sy coy

EQUIPMENT

AAV 25 VAP-3550

TOWED ARTY 105mm: 16 M-56

MRL 51mm: 6 *Firos*

MOR 100 incl **60mm**, **81mm**

RCL 106mm: M-40A1

AD GUNS 20mm: Mk 38; **40mm**: Bofors

plus 60 Swe assault craft

Air Force 11,770

107 cbt ac, 71 armed hel

FTR 1 sqn with 8 F-5E, 2 -F

CCT 9 sqn

7 with 70 PC-7

2 with 17 AT-33

ARMED HEL 1 sqn with 1 Bell 205A, 15 Bell 206B, 7 Bell 206L-3, 24 Bell 212

RECCE 1 photo sqn with 10* *Commander* 500S, 2 SA 2-37A, 4 C-26

TPT 5 sqn with 1 Convair CV-580, 1 Lockheed L-1329 *Jetstar*, 1 Cessna 500 *Citation*, 1 C-118, 7 C-130A, 1 L-100 *Hercules*, 10 *Commander* 500S, 1 sqn with 9 IAI-201 (tpt/SAR)

HEL 6 S-70A, 1 Mi-2, 11 Mi-8, 24 Mi-17, 1 Mi-26T

PRESIDENTIAL TPT ac 1 Boeing 757, 3 Boeing 727-100

LIAISON/UTL 9 IAI *Arava*, 1 *King Air* A90, 3 *King Air* C90, 1 *Super King* 300, 1 *Musketeer*, 29 Beech *Bonanza* F-33C, 73 Cessna 182S, 11 Cessna 206, 11 Cessna 210, 4 PC-6, 6 Turbo Commander

TRG ac 6 Maule M-7, 21 Maule MXT-7-180, 12 PT-17 Stearman, 30 SF-260 **hel** 24* MD 530F (SAR/paramilitary/trg)

Paramilitary ε11,000

FEDERAL PREVENTIVE POLICE (Ministry of Interior) ε11,000

RURAL DEFENCE MILITIA (R) 14,000

COAST GUARD

4 *Mako* 295 PCI<

Opposition

ZAPATISTA ARMY OF NATIONAL LIBERATION str n.k.

POPULAR INSURGENT REVOLUTIONARY ARMY str n.k.

MEXICAN PEASANT WORKERS FRONT OF THE SOUTH EAST str n.k.

POPULAR MOVEMENT OF NATIONAL LIBERATION str n.k.

REVOLUTIONARY INSURGENT ARMY OF THE SOUTH EAST str n.k.

Nicaragua Nic

Total Armed Forces

ACTIVE ε14,000

Terms of service voluntary, 18–36 months

Army ε12,000

5 Regional Comd (9 inf, 1 tk coy) • 2 mil det (2 inf bn) • 1 lt mech bde (1 mech inf, 1 tk, 1 recce bn, 1 fd arty gp (2 bn), 1 atk gp) • 1 comd regt (1 inf, 1 sy bn) • 1 SF bde (3 SF bn) • 1 tpt regt (incl 1 APC bn) • 1 engr bn

EQUIPMENT

MBT some 127 T-55 (42 op remainder in store)

LT TK 10 PT-76 (in store)

RECCE 20 BRDM-2

APC 102 BTR-152 (in store), 64 BTR-60

TOWED ARTY 122mm: 12 D-30; **152mm**: 30 D-20 (in store)

MRL 107mm: 33 Type-63; **122mm**: 18 BM-21, 100 *Grad* 1P (single-tube rocket launcher)

MOR 82mm: 579; **120mm**: 24 M-43; **160mm**: 4 M-160 (in store)

ATGW AT-3 *Sagger* (12 on BRDM-2)

RL 73mm: RPG-7/-16

RCL 82mm: B-10

ATK GUNS 57mm: 354 ZIS-2 (90 in store); **76mm**: 83 ZIS-3; **100mm**: 24 M-1944

SAM 200+ SA-7/-14/-16

Navy ε800

BASES Corinto, Puerto Cabezzas, El Bluff

PATROL AND COASTAL COMBATANTS 5

PATROL, INSHORE 5
2 FSU *Zhuk* PFI<, 3 *Dabur* PCI<, plus boats

MINE WARFARE 2

MINE COUNTERMEASURES 2
2 *Yevgenya* MHI

Air Force 1,200

no cbt ac, 15 armed hel
TPT 1 An-2, 4 An-26, 1 Cessna 404 Titan (VIP)
HEL 15 Mi-17 (tpt/armed) (3 serviceable), 1 Mi-17 (VIP)
UTL/TRG ac 1 Cessna T-41D
ASM AT-2 *Swatter* ATGW
AD GUNS 1 air def gp, 18 ZU-23, 18 C3-*Morigla* M1

Panama Pan

Total Armed Forces

ACTIVE Nil

Paramilitary ε11,800

NATIONAL POLICE FORCE 11,000
Presidential Guard bn (-), 1 MP bn plus 8 coys, 18 Police coy, 1 SF unit (reported); no hy mil eqpt, small arms only

NATIONAL MARITIME SERVICE ε400
BASES Amador (HQ), Balboa, Colón
PATROL AND COASTAL COMBATANTS 14
PATROL CRAFT, COASTAL 5
2 *Panquiaco* (UK *Vosper* 31.5m) PCC, 3 other PCC
PATROL CRAFT, INSHORE 9
3 *Tres de Noviembre* (ex-US *Point*) PCI<, 1 *Swiftships* 65ft PCI<, 1 ex-US MSB 5 class, 1 *Negrita* PCI<, 3 ex-US PCI< (plus some 25 boats)

NATIONAL AIR SERVICE 400
TPT 1 CN-235-2A, 1 BN-2B, 1 PA-34, 3 CASA-212M *Aviocar*
TRG 6 T-35D
HEL 2 Bell 205, 6 Bell 212, 13 UH-1H

Paraguay Py

Total Armed Forces

ACTIVE 18,600 (to reduce)
(incl 11,000 conscripts)
Terms of service 12 months **Navy** 2 years

RESERVES some 164,500

Army 14,900

(incl 10,400 conscripts)
6 Mil Region, 3 corps HQ • 9 div HQ (6 inf, 3 cav) • 9 inf regt (bn) • 3 cav regt (horse) • 3 mech cav regt • Presidential Guard (1 inf, 1 MP bn, 1 arty bty) • 20 frontier det • 3 arty gp (bn) • 1 AD arty gp • 4 engr bn

RESERVES
14 inf, 4 cav regt

EQUIPMENT
MBT 12 M-4A3
RECCE 8 M-8, 5 M-3, 30 EE-9 *Cascavel*
APC 10 EE-11 *Urutu*
TOWED ARTY 75mm: 20 Model 1927/1934; **105mm**: 15 M-101; **152mm**: 6 Vickers 6in (coast)
MOR 81mm: 80
RCL 75mm: M-20
AD GUNS 30: **20mm**: 20 Bofors; **40mm**: 10 M-1A1

Navy 2,000

(incl 900 Marines, 100 Naval Avn)
BASES Asunción (Puerto Sajonia), Bahía Negra, Ciudad Del Este

PATROL AND COASTAL COMBATANTS 10

PATROL, RIVERINE 10
2 *Paraguais* PCR with 4 × 120mm guns†
2 *Nanawa* PCR
1 *Itapu* PCR
1 *Capitan Cabral* PCR
2 *Capitan Ortiz* PCR (ROC *Hai Ou*) PCR<
2 ROC PCR
plus some 20 craft

SUPPORT AND MISCELLANEOUS 5
1 tpt, 1 trg/tpt, 1 AGHS<, 2 LCT

NAVAL AVIATION (100)
EQUIPMENT
AIRCRAFT
CCT 2 AT-6G
LIAISON 2 Cessna 150, 2 C-206, 1 C-210
HELICOPTER
UTL 2 HB-350, 1 OH-13

MARINES (900)
(incl 200 conscripts); 4 bn(-)

Air Force 1,700

(incl 600 conscripts); 28 cbt ac, no armed hel
FTR/FGA 8 F-5E, 4 F-5F
CCT 6 AT-33, 6 EMB-326, 4 T-27
LIAISON 1 Cessna 185, 4 C-206, 2 C-402, 2 T-41
HEL 3 HB-350, 1 UH-1B, 2 UH-1H, 4 UH-12, 4 Bell 47G
TPT 1 sqn with 5 C-47, 4 C-212, 3 DC-6B, 1 DHC-6 (VIP), 1 C-131D
TRG 6 T-6, 10 T-23, 5 T-25, 10 T-35, 1 T-41

Forces Abroad

UN AND PEACEKEEPING
DROC (MONUC): 17 incl 1 obs **ETHIOPIA/ERITREA** (UNMEE): 2 obs

Paramilitary 14,800

SPECIAL POLICE SERVICE 14,800
(incl 4,000 conscripts)

Peru Pe

Total Armed Forces

ACTIVE 110,000
(incl 64,000 conscripts)
Terms of service 2 years, selective

RESERVES 188,000
Army only

Army 70,000

(incl 52,000 conscripts)
6 Mil Regions
Army tps
1 AB div (3 cdo, 1 para bn, 1 arty gp) • 1 Presidential Escort regt • 1 AD arty gp
Regional tps
3 armd div (each 2 tk, 1 armd inf bn,1 arty gp, 1 engr bn) • 1 armd gp (3 indep armd cav, 1 fd arty, 1 AD arty, 1 engr bn) • 1 cav div (3 mech regt, 1 arty gp) • 7 inf div (each 3 inf bn, 1 arty gp) • 1 jungle div • 2 med arty gp • 2 fd arty gp • 1 indep inf bn • 1 indep engr bn • 2 hel, 1 mixed avn sqn

EQUIPMENT
MBT 275 T-54/-55 (ε50 serviceable)
LT TK 110 AMX-13 (ε30 serviceable)
RECCE 60 M-8/-20, 10 M-3A1, 50 M-9A1, 15 Fiat 6616, 30 BRDM-2
APC 130 M-113, 12 BTR-60, 130 UR-416, Fiat 6614, *Casspir*, 4 *Repontec*
TOWED ARTY 105mm: 20 Model 56 pack, 130 M-101; **122mm**: 42 D-30; **130mm**: 36 M-46; **155mm**: 36 M-114
SP ARTY 155mm: 12 M-109A2, 12 Mk F3
MRL 122mm: 14 BM-21
MOR 700 incl: **81mm**: incl some SP; **107mm**: incl some SP; **120mm**: 300 Brandt, ECIA
ATGW 400 SS-11
RCL 106mm: M40A1
AD GUNS 23mm: 80 ZSU-23-2, 35 ZSU-23-4 SP; **30mm**: 10 2S6 SP; **40mm**: 45 M-1, 80 L60/70
SAM some 450 incl SA-7, SA-16/-18, *Javelin*
AC 1 Queen Air, 1 King Air, 1 C-208, 5 U-206 *Stationair*, 2 An-28, 4 An-32B, 4 Il-103, 1 L-410UVP, 1 PA-34 *Seneca*, 2 PA-31T
HEL 2 Mi-26, 50 Mi-8, 33 Mi-17, 10 SA-318C, 10 F-28F, 5 *Agusta* A-109K2

Navy 25,000

(incl some 800 Naval Avn, 4,000 Marines, 1,000 Coast Guard; 10,000 conscripts)
COMMANDS Pacific, Lake Titicaca, Amazon River
BASES Ocean Callao, San Lorenzo Island, Paita, Talara **Lake** Puno **River** Iquitos, Puerto Maldonado

SUBMARINES 6
SSK 6 *Casma* (Ge T-209/1200) with 533mm TT (It A184 HWT) (2 in refit)

PRINCIPAL SURFACE COMBATANTS 5
CRUISERS 1
CG 1 *Almirante Grau* (Nl *De Ruyter*) with 8 *Otomat* SSM, 4 × 2 152mm guns
FRIGATES 4
FFG 4 *Carvajal* (mod It *Lupo*) CG with 8 *Otomat* SSM, *Albatros* SAM, 1 × 127mm gun, 2 × 3 324mm ASTT (Mk 32 HWT), 1 AB-212 or SH-3D hel

PATROL AND COASTAL COMBATANTS 10
MISSILE CRAFT 6 *Velarde* PFM (Fr PR-72 64m) with 4 MM-38 *Exocet* SSM, 1 × 76mm gun
PATROL CRAFT, RIVERINE 4
2 *Marañon* PCR with 2 × 76 mm gun
2 *Amazonas* PCR with 1 × 76 mm gun
(plus 3 craft for lake patrol)

AMPHIBIOUS 3
3 *Paita* (US *Terrebonne Parish*) LST, capacity 395 tps, 2,000t

SUPPORT AND MISCELLANEOUS 9
3 AO, 1 AOT, 1 tpt; 1 AT/F (SAR); 1 AGOR, 2 AGHS

NAVAL AVIATION (some 800)
EQUIPMENT
7 cbt ac, 13 armed hel
AIRCRAFT
ASW/MR 6 *Super King Air* B 200T, 1 F-27
TPT 2 An-32B
TRG 7 T-34C
HELICOPTER
ASW/MR 6 AB-212, 7 SH-3D
LIAISON 5 Bell 206B, 4 Mi-8
MISSILES
ASM *Exocet* AM-39

MARINES (4,000)

1 Marine bde (2 inf, 1 amph veh, 1 recce bn, 1 arty gp, 1 special ops gp)
3 indep inf bn (incl 1 jungle), 1 inf gp, 1 cdo gp

EQUIPMENT
RECCE V-100
APC 15 V-200 *Chaimite*, 20 BMR-600
TOWED ARTY 122mm: D-30
MOR 81mm; **120mm** ε18
RCL 84mm: *Carl Gustav*; **106mm**: M-40A1
AD GUNS twin 20mm SP

COASTAL DEFENCE 3 bty with 18 **155mm** how

Air Force 15,000

(incl 2,000 conscripts); 116 cbt ac†, 19 armed hel
BBR 8 *Canberra*
FGA 2 gp, 6 sqn
3 with 28 Su-22 (incl 4* Su-22U), 18 Su-25A (incl 8* Su-25UB)
3 with 23 Cessna A-37B
FTR 3 sqn
1 with 10 *Mirage* 2000P, 2 -DP
2 with 9 *Mirage* 5P, 2 -DP
1 with 15 MiG-29C, 3 MiG-29SE, 2 MiG-29UB
ATTACK/ASSAULT HEL 1 sqn with 10 Mi-24/-25, 8 Mi-17TM, 1 Ka-50 (under evaluation)
RECCE 3 MiG-25RB, 1 photo-survey unit with 2 *Learjet* 25B, 2 -36A
TKR 1 Boeing KC 707-323C
TPT 3 gp, 7 sqn
ac 17 An-32, 3 AN-72, 1 C-130A, 6 -D, 5 L-100-20, 2 DC-8-62F, 12 DHC-5, 8 DHC-6, 1 FH-227, 9 PC-6, 6 Y-12 (II), 1 Boeing 737 **hel** 3 sqn with 8 Bell 206, 14 B-212, 5 B-214, 1 B-412, 10 Bo-105C, 5 Mi-6, 3 Mi-8, 35 Mi-17, 5 SA-316
PRESIDENTIAL FLT 1 F-28, 1 *Falcon* 20F
LIAISON ac 2 Beech 99, 3 Cessna 185, 1 Cessna 320, 15 *Queen Air* 80, 3 *King Air* 90, 1 PA-31T **hel** 8 UH-1D
TRG/DRUG INTERDICTION ac 2 Cessna 150, 17 EMB-312, 6 Il-103, 13 MB-339A, 20 T-37B/C, 15 T-41A/-D **hel** 12 Bell 47G

MISSILES
ASM AS-30
AAM AA-2 *Atoll*, AA-8 *Aphid*, AA-10 *Alemo*, R-550 *Magic*, AA-12 *Adder*
AD 3 SA-2, 6 SA-3 bn

Forces Abroad

UN AND PEACEKEEPING

DROC (MONUC): 3 obs **ETHIOPIA/ERITREA** (UNMEE): 2 obs

Paramilitary 77,000

NATIONAL POLICE 77,000 (100,000 reported)

General Police 43,000 **Security Police** 21,000 **Technical Police** 13,000
100+ MOWAG *Roland* APC

COAST GUARD (1,000) (personnel part of Navy)
5 *Rio Nepena* PCC, 3 *Dauntless* PCI<, 3 PCI, 10 riverine PCI<

RONDAS CAMPESINAS (peasant self-defence force)

perhaps 2,000 *rondas* 'gp', up to pl strength, some with small arms. Deployed mainly in emergency zone.

Opposition

SENDERO LUMINOSO (Shining Path) ε600
Maoist

MOVIMIENTO REVOLUCIONARIO TUPAC AMARU (MRTA) ε600
mainly urban gp

Suriname Sme

Total Armed Forces

ACTIVE ε1,840

(all services form part of the Army)

Army 1,400

1 inf bn (4 inf coy) • 1 mech cav sqn • 1 MP 'bn' (coy)

EQUIPMENT
RECCE 6 EE-9 *Cascavel*
APC 15 EE-11 *Urutu*
MOR 81mm: 6
RCL 106mm: M-40A1

Navy 240

BASE Paramaribo

PATROL AND COASTAL COMBATANTS 3

PATROL CRAFT, INSHORE 3
3 *Rodman* 100 PCI<, plus 5 boats

Air Force ε200

7 cbt ac, no armed hel
MPA 2 C-212-400
TPT/TRG 4* BN-2 *Defender*, 1* PC-7
LIAISON 1 Cessna U206
HEL 2 SA-316, 1 AB-205

Trinidad and Tobago TT

Total Armed Forces

ACTIVE ε2,700 (all services form part of the **Trinidad and Tobago Defence Force**)

Army ε2,000

2 inf bn • 1 spt bn • 1 SF unit

EQUIPMENT
MOR 60mm: ε40; **81mm**: 6 L16A1
RL 82mm: 13 B-300
RCL 82mm: B-300; **84mm**: ε24 *Carl Gustav*

Coast Guard 700

(incl 50 Air Wing)
BASE Staubles Bay (HQ), Hart's Cut, Point Fortin, Tobago, Galeota

PATROL AND COASTAL COMBATANTS 12†
PATROL CRAFT, OFFSHORE 1
1 *Nelson* (UK *Island*) PCO
PATROL CRAFT, COASTAL 2
2 *Barracuda* PFC (Sw *Karlskrona* 40m) (non-op)
PATROL CRAFT, INSHORE 9
4 *Plymouth* PCI<
3 *Point* PCI<
2 *Wasp* PCI<
plus 10 boats and 2 aux vessels

AIR WING
2 C-26, 1 Cessna 310, 1 C-402, 1 C-172, 2 *Navajos*

Uruguay Ury

Total Armed Forces

ACTIVE 23,900

Army 15,200

4 Mil Regions/div HQ • 5 inf bde (4 of 3 inf bn, 1 of 1 mech, 1 mot, 1 para bn) • 3 cav bde (10 cav bn (4 horsed, 3 mech, 2 mot, 1 armd)) • 1 arty bde (2 arty, 1 AD arty bn) • 1 engr bde (3 bn) • 3 arty, 4 cbt engr bn

EQUIPMENT
MBT 15 T-55
LT TK 17 M-24, 29 M-3A1, 22 M-41A1
RECCE 16 EE-3 *Jararaca*, 15 EE-9 *Cascavel*
AIFV 15 BMP-1
APC 15 M-113, 44 *Condor*, 43 OT-64 SKOT, 32 M-93 (MT-LB)
TOWED ARTY 75mm: 10 Bofors M-1902; **105mm**: 48 M-101A/M-102; **155mm**: 8 M-114A1
SP ARTY 122mm: 2 2S1
MRL 122mm: 3 RM-70
MOR 81mm: 93; **107mm**: 9 M-30; **120mm**: 34
ATGW 5 *Milan*
RCL 57mm: 67 M-18; **75mm**: 3; **106mm**: 30 M-40A1
AD GUNS 20mm: 9 TCM-20, 6 M-167 *Vulcan*; **40mm**: 8 L/60

Navy 5,700

(incl 300 Naval Avn, 450 Naval Infantry, 1,950 *Prefectura Naval* (Coast Guard))
BASES Montevideo (HQ), Paysando (river), La Paloma (naval avn), Laguna del Sauce (naval avn)

PRINCIPAL SURFACE COMBATANTS 3
FRIGATES 3
FFG 3 *General Artigas* (Fr *Cdt Rivière*) with 4 MM-38 *Exocet* SSM, 2 × 100mm guns, 2 × 3 ASTT, 1 × 2 ASW mor

PATROL AND COASTAL COMBATANTS 8
PATROL, COASTAL/INSHORE 8
3 *15 de Noviembre* PCC (Fr *Vigilante* 42m), 2 *Colonia* PCI< (US *Cape*), 1 *Paysandu* PCI<, 2 other PCI< plus 9 craft

MINE WARFARE 3
MINE COUNTERMEASURES 3
3 *Temerario* MSC (Ge *Kondor* II)

AMPHIBIOUS craft only
2 LCM, 2 LCVP

SUPPORT AND MISCELLANEOUS 6

1 *Vanguardia* ARS, 1 *Campbell* (US *Auk* MSF) PCO (Antarctic patrol/research), 1 AT (ex-GDR *Elbe*-Class), 1 trg, 1 AGHS, 1 AGOR

NAVAL AVIATION (300)

EQUIPMENT

1 cbt ac, no armed hel

AIRCRAFT

ASW 1 *Super King Air* 200T

TRG/LIAISON 1 *Jet Stream* TMK 2, 3 S-2G *Tracrer*, 2 T-34C

HELICOPTER

UTL 1 Wessex Mk60, 4 Wessex HC2, 1 Bell 47G

NAVAL INFANTRY (450)

1 bn

Air Force 3,000

28 cbt ac, no armed hel

Flying hours 120

CBT AC 2 sqn

1 with 10 A-37B, 1 with 5 IA-58B

SURVEY 1 EMB-110B1

HEL 1 sqn with 2 Bell 212, 6 UH-1H, 6 *Wessex* HC2

TPT 3 sqn with 3 C-212 (tpt/SAR), 3 EMB-110C, 1 F-27, 3 C-130B, 1 Cessna 310 (VIP), 1 Cessna 206

LIAISON 2 Cessna 182, 2 *Queen Air* 80, 5 U-17, 1 T-34A

TRG 13 SF-260EU*, 5 T-41D, 5 PC-7U

Forces Abroad

UN AND PEACEKEEPING

DROC (MONUC): 1,050 incl 30 obs **EAST TIMOR** (UNMISET): 5 obs **EGYPT** (MFO): 60 **ETHIOPIA/ ERITREA** (UNMEE): 6 obs **GEORGIA** (UNOMIG): 3 obs **INDIA/PAKISTAN** (UNMOGIP): 1 obs **IRAQ/ KUWAIT** (UNIKOM): 6 obs **SIERRA LEONE** (UNAMSIL): 11 obs **WESTERN SAHARA** (MINURSO): 13 obs

Paramilitary 920

GUARDIA DE GRANADEROS 450

GUARDIA DE CORACEROS 470

COAST GUARD (1,950)

Prefectura Naval (PNN) is part of the Navy operates 3 PCC, 2 LCMs plus 9 boats

Venezuela Ve

Total Armed Forces

ACTIVE 82,300

(incl National Guard; ε31,000 conscripts)

Terms of service 30 months selective, varies by region for all services

RESERVES

Army ε8,000

Army 34,000

(incl 27,000 conscripts)

6 inf div HQ • 1 armd bde • 1 cav bde • 7 inf bde (18 inf, 1 mech inf, 4 fd arty bn) • 1 AB bde • 2 Ranger bde (1 with 4 bn, 1 with 2 bn) • 1 mobile counter guerrilla bde (2 SF, 1 mot inf, 1 Civil Affairs bn) • 1 avn regt

RESERVES ε6 inf, 1 armd, 1 arty bn

EQUIPMENT

MBT 81 AMX-30

LT TK 75 M-18, 36 AMX-13, 80 *Scorpion* 90

RECCE 30 M-8

APC 25 AMX-VCI, 100 V-100, 30 V-150, 100 *Dragoon* (some with **90mm** gun), 35 EE-11 *Urutu*

TOWED ARTY 105mm: 40 Model 56, 40 M-101; **155mm**: 12 M-114

SP ARTY 155mm: 10 Mk F3

MRL 160mm: 20 LAR SP

MOR 81mm: 165; **120mm**: 60 Brandt

ATGW AS-11, 24 *Mapats*

RL 84mm: AT-4

RCL 84mm: *Carl Gustav*; **106mm**: 175 M-40A1

SURV RASIT (veh, arty)

AC 5 IAI-202, 2 Cessna 182, 2 C-206, 1 C-207, 2 M-28 *Skytruck*

ATTACK HEL 7 A-109 (ATK)

TPT HEL 4 AS-61A, 3 Bell 205, 2 Bell 412, 4 UH-1H

SPT 2 Bell 206, 4 AS-61D

Navy 18,300

(incl 500 Naval Avn, 7,800 Marines, 1,000 Coast Guard; ε4,000 conscripts)

NAVAL COMMANDS Fleet, Marines, Naval Avn, Coast Guard, Fluvial (River Forces)

BASES Main bases Caracas (HQ), Puerto Cabello (SS, FF, amph and service sqn), Punto Fijo (patrol sqn)

Minor bases Puerto de Hierro (naval avn), La Orchila (naval avn), Turiamo (naval avn), El Amparo (HQ Arauca River), Ciudad Bolivar (HQ Fluvial Forces), Maracaibo (Coast Guard), La Guaira (Coast Guard)

SUBMARINES 2

SSK 2 *Sabalo* (Ge T-209/1300) with 8 × 533mm TT (SST-4 HWT)

PRINCIPAL SURFACE COMBATANTS 6

FRIGATES 6

FFG 6 *Mariscal Sucre* (It mod *Lupo*) with 8 *Teseo* SSM, *Albatros* SAM, 1 × 127mm gun, 2 × 3 ASTT (A-244S LWT), 1 AB-212 hel

PATROL AND COASTAL COMBATANTS 6

MISSILE CRAFT 3

3 *Constitución* PFM (UK Vosper 37m), with 2 *Teseo* SSM

PATROL CRAFT, OFFSHORE 3

3 *Constitución* PCO (UK Vosper 37m) with 1 × 76mm gun

AMPHIBIOUS 4

4 *Capana* LST (FSU *Alligator*), capacity 200 tps, 12 tk
Plus craft: 2 LCU (river comd), 12 LCVP

SUPPORT AND MISCELLANEOUS 6

1 AO, 1 log spt; 1 *Punta Brava* AGOR, 2 AGHS; 1 sail trg

NAVAL AVIATION (500)

EQUIPMENT

3 cbt ac, 9 armed hel

AIRCRAFT

MR 1 sqn with 3 C-212-200 MPA
TPT 3 C-212, 2 C-212 *Aviocar*, 1 *Super King Air*, 1 *King Air*, 1 *Aerocommander* 980C, 1 DHC-7
TRG 2 Cessna 402, 1 Cessna 210, 2 Cessna 310Q

HELICOPTER

ASW 1 sqn with 8 AB-212, 1 Bell 212
SPT 4 Bell 412-EP
TRG 1 Bell 206B

MARINES (ε7,800)

1 div HQ, 2 landing, 1 river, 1 engr bde • cbt units incl: 8 inf bn (incl 2 river) • 1 arty bn (3 fd, 1 AD bty) • 1 amph veh bn • 4 engr

EQUIPMENT

AAV 11 LVTP-7 (to be mod to -7A1)
APC 25 EE-11 *Urutu*, 10 *Fuchs/Transportpanzer* 1
TOWED ARTY 105mm: 18 Model 56
AD GUNS 40mm: 6 M-42 twin SP

COAST GUARD (1,000)

BASE La Guaira; operates under Naval Comd and Control, but organisationally separate

PATROL, OFFSHORE 2

2 *Almirante Clemente* FS with 2 × 76mm guns, 3 × 2 ASTT

PATROL, INSHORE 16

4 *Petrel* (USCG *Point*-class) PCI, 12 Gairon PCI<
plus 27 river patrol craft and boats
plus 1 spt ship

Air Force 7,000

(some conscripts); 125 cbt ac, 31 armed hel
Flying hours 155
FTR/FGA 6 air gp
1 with 16 CF-5A/B (12 A, 4 B), 7 NF-5A/B
1 with 16 *Mirage* 50EV/DV
2 with 22 F-16A/B (18 A, 4 B)
2 with 20 EMB-312
RECCE 15* OV-10A
ECM 3 *Falcon* 20DC
ARMED HEL 1 air gp with 10 SA-316, 12 UH-1D, 5 UH-1H, 4 AS-532
TPT ac 7 C-123, 5 C-130H, 8 G-222, 2 HS-748, 2 B-707 (tkr) **hel** 2 Bell 214, 4 Bell 412, 7 AS-332B, 2 UH-1N, 18 Mi-8/17
PRESIDENTIAL FLT 1 Boeing 737, 1 Airbus A319CJ, 1 *Gulfstream* III, 1 *Gulfstream* IV, 1 *Learjet* 24D **hel** 1 Bell 412
LIAISON 9 Cessna 182, 1 *Citation* I, 1 *Citation* II, 2 *Queen Air* 65, 5 *Queen Air* 80, 5 *Super King Air* 200, 9 SA-316B *Alouette* III
TRG 1 air gp: 12* EMB-312, 20 T-34, 17* T-2D, 12 SF-260E

MISSILES

AAM R-530 *Magic*, AIM-9L *Sidewinder*, AIM-9P *Sidewinder*
ASM *Exocet*
AD GUNS 20mm: some IAI TC-20; **35mm**; **40mm**: 114: Bofors L/70 towed, Otobreda 40L70 towed
SAM 10 *Roland*, RBS-70

National Guard (*Fuerzas Armadas de Cooperación*) 23,000

(internal sy, customs)
8 regional comd

EQUIPMENT

20 UR-416 AIFV, 24 Fiat-6614 APC, 100 **60mm** mor, 50 **81mm** mor **ac** 1 *Baron*, 1 BN-2A, 2 Cessna 185, 5 -U206, 4 IAI-201, 1 *King Air* 90, 1 *King Air* 200C, 2 *Queen Air* 80, 6 M-28 *Skytruck* **hel** 4 A-109, 20 Bell 206, 2 Bell 212
PATROL CRAFT, INSHORE 52 craft/boats

Forces Abroad

UN AND PEACEKEEPING

IRAQ/KUWAIT (UNIKOM): 3 obs

Sub-Saharan Africa

REGIONAL TRENDS

Local and internal conflicts are the backdrop to trends and developments in the region. Famine and poverty remain ever-present handicaps to greater peace and security. However, a number of long-running conflicts have been resolved or brought close to resolution. In a sign of a greater determination amongst regional countries to solve their own security problems, the New Partnership for African Development (NEPAD) although driven largely by political and economic aims, has security elements referring to peacekeeping in its documentation. It is likely that this will develop in three main areas: peacekeeping operations; crisis early warning; and the non-proliferation of small arms. In a further development, military commentators in South Africa have discussed the creation of an Indigenous Military Peacebuilding Initiative (IMPI), promoting the idea of a regional security forum for conflict resolution and prevention, and also the restructuring and democratic control of armed forces. Both NEPAD and IMPI are at a very early stage in their development. Given the partnership inherent in the NEPAD process, Western countries involved may make any necessary investment conditional on democratic reforms, which may be unacceptable to some African partner countries.

Meanwhile **HIV/AIDS** is a growing problem, reducing the military capabilities of a number of countries in the region. For example, Zimbabwe is estimated to have a rate of infection of 75% in its armed forces. Exacerbating the problem further, troops who are affected have low standards of discipline, which can lead to a loss of combat effectiveness and even human rights abuses.

Piracy and maritime security is a growing threat to the region. In the aftermath of 11 September, there has been concern, particularly from the US government, about security at ports and on merchant shipping. These concerns are especially focused on parts of sub-Saharan Africa, where security at ports is poor. Mainly at the behest of the US, the International Maritime Organisation – a special working group of the UN – will meet in September 2002 in an attempt to reach agreement on the details of a convention on countering terrorism at sea, to be held later in the year. It is hoped that the convention will produce a code which will provide a standardised, consistent framework for assessing the risk to ships and port facilities and for taking security measures to counter these risks. However, such measures are likely to be too costly for most governments in sub-Saharan Africa, and foreign aid will be needed in order for any such measures to be implemented.

RESOLUTION OF CONFLICT

On 22 February 2002, Jonas Savimbi, the leader of the rebel União Nacional para a Independência Total de **Angola** (Union for the Total Independence of Angola) (UNITA), was killed during a battle with government forces in the central-eastern province of Moxico. Savimbi's death marked the end of the 40-year conflict, and bilateral talks started between UNITA and the government. In a process entirely run by the parties to the conflict, and without any involvement of a third party, 34 disarmament areas were established. By May 2002, some 40,000 UNITA rebels, or 80% of the rebel force, had been disarmed. Nevertheless, with an estimated 500,000 people close to starvation, the possibility of further conflict remains.

The delayed decision by an international commission to demarcate the disputed border between **Ethiopia** and **Eritrea** was taken in April 2002. In August 2002, de-mining of the border started under UN auspices. A final delineation of the border between Ethiopia and Eritrea will probably formalise Eritrea's ownership of the Red Sea port of Assab and could preclude any Ethiopian claims.

In the general context of conflict in Africa, **Sierra Leone** is a success story. In January 2002 the conflict was declared over, thus ending a decade of civil war in which 43,000 people died. 45,000 ex-combatants were disarmed, handing over 15,000 weapons, and in May 2002 the Revolutionary United Front (RUF)'s political aspirations were destroyed in the elections.

The UN Assistance Mission in Sierra Leone (UNAMSIL) is reducing troop numbers and the scale of its operations. The success of the operation, which was bolstered by the British intervention, can in large part be attributed to the leadership of Kenyan Lieutenant General Daniel Opande. However, tension still exists between the urban elite on the coast, who control most of the country's wealth, and the relatively poor population in the hinterland.

After the Sudanese People's Liberation Army (SPLA) launched a series of attacks on oil installations in Wehda province, **Sudan**'s government made significant military gains in their war on the rebels. As a result, rebel activity diminished. In July 2002, the government and the SPLA issued a joint communiqué pledging to find a peaceful resolution to the 50-year conflict. The communiqué was issued under the aegis of the Sudan Peace Committee of the Intergovernmental Authority on Development (IGAD). An agreement was signed on 20 July 2002. A second round of talks between the parties to the conflict was held in Nairobi in August 2002. The main objective was to arrange conditions for a ceasefire as well as to discuss the relationship between the state and religion.

Sudan's civil war, which has cost more than two million lives and displaced more than four million people, entered a new phase in 1999 with the successful exploitation of oil by foreign companies in the south, and the opening of a pipeline to the Red Sea. Since oil began flowing north, revenues of more than £700,000 a day have accrued. The move towards agreement is a sign of the increasing realisation by all sides that there are real prospects for prosperity in the country, particularly through oil revenues, but for these prospects to come to fruition, there is a need for stability.

Russia is aiming to replace China as Sudan's leading military supplier. Moscow has offered to maintain and upgrade Sudan's military as well as supply advanced aircraft. The deal, worth at least $120 million, would be based on Khartoum providing Russia with a licence to explore and develop Sudan's energy sector. Russia is seen as being able to provide far more equipment and services than China.

It is reported that Moscow has promised to provide Khartoum with the military capability required to end the insurgency in the south. Russian experts have offered to upgrade and train the Sudanese military in the use of modern air power against southern factions. This would include developing a fleet of attack and medium transport helicopters that could quickly strike rebel forces and deploy Sudanese commandos for special operations.

CONTINUING CONFLICT

In spite of the optimism following the August 2001 signing of the Arusha Peace and Reconciliation Agreement, which was aimed at securing the transition to peace in **Burundi**, little progress has been made toward its implementation. Plans for talks between the armed rebel groups and the government on securing a ceasefire have so far achieved very little and the ceasefire negotiations in South Africa, between the government and the various rebel factions, have not produced a result. In May 2002, the main rebel group, the National Council for the Defence of Democracy–Forces for the Defence of Democracy (Conseil National pour la Défense Démocratie–Forces pour la Défense de la Démocratie) (CNDD-FDD) faction, led by Jean-Pierre Nkurunziza, rejected the mediation of South African Vice-President Jacob Zuma, and called for the talks to be transferred to Tanzania. In late July 2002, it was reported that the Burundi peace talks planned to take place in Tanzania were suspended following intensified fighting between government forces and Hutu rebels. After the decision to put the talks on hold fighting escalated. Finally, on 12 August 2002, talks involving the Forces Nationales pour la Liberation (National Forces for Liberation) (FNL), both wings of FDD and the government started in Tanzania.

Following the October 2001 talks in Sun City, a new dialogue took place in April 2002 with the objective of assisting the peace process in the **Democratic Republic of Congo (DRC)**. The Ugandan-backed Congolese Liberation Movement (MLC), Rwandan-backed Congolese Rally for Democracy (RCD), unarmed opposition groups, political parties, civil society organisations and the government were all parties to the dialogue, which continued for seven weeks. The DRC government gained a partial agreement on a transitional power-sharing government. However, the RCD, which controls a third of the eastern part of the country, was only given a minor role in the power-sharing arrangement and rejected the agreement. Rwanda and Uganda tried to reopen discussion on a more inclusive peace deal for the DRC, as proposed by President Thato Mbeki of South Africa during the Sun City talks. The government rejected this initiative, and formed an alliance with the MLC and a majority of representatives from the political opposition and civil society. The RCD, having rejected an offer of the presidency of the National Assembly, formed its own alliance, the Alliance pour la sauvegarde du dialogue intercongolais (Alliance for the Protection of Congolese Dialogue), with five unarmed opposition parties, one of them being the Etienne Tshisekedi-led Union pour la democratie et le progres social (Union for Democracy and Social Progress) (UDPS).

In August 2002, renewed fighting broke out between the Hema and Lendu ethnic groups in the eastern Bunia province. Both groups belong to the RCD-Kisangani Liberation Movement (RCD-K/ML). They were dispersed by the forces of the UN Mission in the Democratic Republic of the Congo (MONUC).

The 2000 Arta Peace Conference in Djibouti established the Transitional Government (TNG) in **Somalia** and initiated a reconciliation process. Several of Somalia's major warlords and clans refused to acknowledge the TNG, and set up the Somali Reconciliation and Reconstruction Council (SRRC) to counteract its authority. Despite international attempts at mediation, clashes between TNG forces and the SRRC have continued, with the violence intensifying in 2002. The main areas of concern are Mogadishu and the southern part of the country.

On 5 August 2002, an attack by the Lord's Resistance Army (LRA), a rebel movement in **Uganda**, on the Acholi-Pi refugee camp (housing Sudanese refugees) caused 24,000 people to flee into the bush. The stated aim of the LRA, which is said to be a Christian fundamentalist movement, is to create a so-called Great Nile republic in northern Uganda.

MILITARY DEVELOPMENTS

South Africa is the only country in the region expanding its military capabilities in any notable way. Most significant are two major naval procurement programmes, now in progress. The first is an order for four German *Meko* A200 corvettes, to be delivered in 2004. Their 3,500t displacement means that South Africa will regain an ocean-going presence; the ships will be the most well-armed and capable in the region. The second programme is the order for three German Type 209 1400 diesel submarines, which will replace South Africa's two elderly *Daphne* diesel submarines. The new submarines should be delivered in 2005. South Africa is the only country in the region that has a sub-surface capability.

In an upgrade to its air capability, the South African Air Force (SAAF) is to receive nine dual seat, fourth generation, *Gripen* advanced light fighter aircraft by 2005, with an option for a further 19 single seat variants between 2009 and 2011. The *Gripen*'s impressive range of capabilities, its ability to use unimproved roads as runways, and its ease of maintenance will be a great boon in southern Africa. In an further enhancement to the SAAF, 12 *Hawk* trainers will be delivered by 2005 to replace the Atlas/Denel Aviation *Impala* I and II trainers, which have been in use since the 1960s. There is an option for a second batch to be delivered by 2006.

South Africa is to start production of an indigenous air defence missile in 2002. The system will enter serial production for the South African Navy in 2002. Improvements could include an extended range SHORAD missile as well as land-based versions for the SAAF and the South African Army. The SAAF at present only has a basic ground-based air defence capability. The South African defence industry is pressing for funds for an additional air-defence layer between the VSHORAD and the SAAF's fighter interceptors. This layer could either be a SHORAD, or a medium range surface-to-air missile with anti-tactical ballistic missile capabilities.

EMERGING THREATS

Piracy and the unlicensed exploitation of marine resources are of growing concern to governments throughout the region as the number of incidents increase. No country, not even South Africa, has the resources to patrol its territorial waters or exclusive economic zone adequately against this challenge. Over the past year, some have announced counter piracy measures. In October 2001, Ghana commissioned two patrol craft from the US, with the intention of using them mainly for counter-piracy operations. In December 2001 Nigeria announced that it would start to coordinate patrols with South Africa along the Atlantic coast in order to secure shipping lanes against piracy and possible terrorist attacks. Sierra Leone has received two small patrol craft from the UK to combat piracy. Other countries in the region remain unable to meet their maritime challenges. The Mozambique government, for example, has admitted that it cannot patrol its own waters due to lack of financial resources and Kenya has put up for sale two patrol craft acquired from the UK in 1995.

Angola Ang

Total Armed Forces

ACTIVE ε100,000

Army ε90,000

35 regts/dets/gps (armd and inf – str vary)

EQUIPMENT†

MBT 400 T-54/-55, ε230 T-62, ε30 T-72
RECCE some 40+ BRDM-2
AIFV ε400 BMP-1/-2
APC ε170 BTR-60/-80/-152
TOWED ARTY 400: incl **76mm**: M-1942 (ZIS-3); **85mm**: D-44; **122mm**: 24 D-30; **130mm**: 48 M-46; **152mm**: 4 D-20
SP ARTY 152mm: 4 2S3
ASLT GUNS 100mm: SU-100
MRL 122mm: 50 BM-21, 40 RM-70; **240mm**: some BM-24
MOR 82mm: 250; **120mm**: 40+ M-43
ATGW AT-3 *Sagger*
RL 73mm: RPG-7
RCL 500: **82mm**: B-10; **107mm**: B-11
AD GUNS 450+: **14.5mm**: ZPU-4; **23mm**: ZU-23-2, 20 ZSU-23-4 SP; **37mm**: M-1939; **57mm**: S-60 towed, 40 ZSU-57-2 SP
SAM ε575 SA-7/-14/-16

Navy 4,000

BASE Luanda (HQ)

PATROL AND COASTAL COMBATANTS 7
PATROL, INSHORE 7†
4 *Mandume* Type 31.6m PCI<, 3 *Patrulheiro* PCI< (all non-op)
plus 1 amph spt ship

COASTAL DEFENCE†
SS-C-1 *Sepal* at Luanda (non-op)

Air Force/Air Defence 6,000

104 cbt ac, 40 armed hel
FGA 30 MiG-23, 21 Su-22, 22 Su-25, 2 Su-27
FTR 20 MiG-21 MF/bis
CCT/RECCE 9* PC-7/9
MR 2 EMB-111, 1 F-27MPA, 1 *King Air* B-200B
ATTACK HEL 15 Mi-25/35, 5 SA-365M (guns), 6 SA-342 (HOT), 14 Mi-24B
TPT 2 An-2, 9 An-26, 6 BN-2, 2 C-212, 4 PC-6B, 2 L-100-20, 2 C-130, 8 An-12 and Il-76 leased from Ukr
HEL 8 AS-565, 30 IAR-316, 25 Mi-8/17
TRG 3 Cessna 172, 6 Yak-11, 6 Emb-312
AD 5 SAM bn, 10 bty with 40 SA-2, 12 SA-3, 25 SA-6, 15 SA-8, 20 SA-9, 10 SA-13 (mostly unserviceable)
MISSILES
ASM HOT, AT-2 *Swatter*
AAM AA-2 *Atoll*

Forces Abroad

DROC: ε2,000 reported **CONGO**: ε2,000 reported

Paramilitary 10,000

RAPID-REACTION POLICE 10,000

Opposition

FRENTE DE LIBERTACÃO DO ENCLAVE DE CABINDA (FLEC) ε600 (claims 5,000)
Small arms only

Benin Bn

Total Armed Forces

ACTIVE ε4,550
Terms of service conscription (selective), 18 months

Army 4,300

3 inf, 1 AB/cdo, 1 engr bn, 1 armd sqn, 1 arty bty

EQUIPMENT
- **LT TK** 18 PT-76 (op status uncertain)
- **RECCE** 7 M-8, 14 BRDM-2, 10 VBL
- **TOWED ARTY 105mm**: 4 M-101, 12 L-118
- **MOR 81mm**
- **RL 73mm**: RPG-7; **89mm**: LRAC

Navy† ε100

BASE Cotonou

PATROL AND COASTAL COMBATANTS 1
PATROL, INSHORE 1
1 *Patriote* PFI (Fr 38m)<

Air Force† 150

no cbt ac
AC 2 An-26, 2 C-47, 1 *Commander* 500B, 2 Do-128, 1 Boeing 707-320 (VIP), 1 F-28 (VIP), 1 DHC-6
HEL 2 AS-350B, 1 SE-3130

Forces Abroad

UN AND PEACEKEEPING
DROC (MONUC): 21 incl 19 obs
ETHIOPIA/ERITREA (UNMEE): 7 incl 5 obs

Paramilitary 2,500

GENDARMERIE 2,500
4 mobile coy

Botswana Btwa

Total Armed Forces

ACTIVE 9,000

Army 8,500 (to be 10,000)

1 armd bde(-), 2 inf bde (4 inf bn, 1 armd recce, 2 AD arty, 1 engr regt, 1 cdo unit), 1 arty bde, 1 AD bde(-)

EQUIPMENT
- **LT TK** 36 *Scorpion* (incl variants), 50 SK-105 *Kuerassier*
- **RECCE** 12 V-150 *Commando* (some with **90mm** gun), RAM-V
- **APC** 30 BTR-60, 6 *Spartan*, ε8 RAM-V-2
- **TOWED ARTY 105mm**: 12 L-118, 6 Model 56 pack; **155mm**: Soltam (reported)
- **MOR 81mm**: 12; **120mm**: 6 M-43
- **ATGW** 6 TOW (some SP on V-150)
- **RL 73mm**: RPG-7
- **RCL 84mm**: 30 *Carl Gustav*
- **AD GUNS 20mm**: 7 M-167
- **SAM** 12 SA-7, 10 SA-16, 6 *Javelin*

Air Wing 500

30 cbt ac, no armed hel
FTR/FGA 10 F-5A, 3 F-5B
TPT 2 CN-235, 2 *Skyvan* 3M, 1 BAe 125-800, 3 C-130, 2 CN-212 (VIP), 1 *Gulfstream* IV, 10* BN-2 *Defender*
TRG 2 sqn with 2 Cessna 152, 7* PC-7
HEL 4 AS-350B, 5 Bell 412

Paramilitary 1,500

POLICE MOBILE UNIT 1,500
(org in territorial coy)

Burkina Faso BF

Total Armed Forces

ACTIVE 10,200
(incl *Gendarmerie*)

Army 5,800

6 Mil Regions • 5 inf 'regt': HQ, 3 'bn' (each 1 coy of 5 pl) • 1 AB 'regt': HQ, 1 'bn', 2 coy • 1 tk 'bn': 2 pl • 1 arty 'bn': 2 tp • 1 engr 'bn'

EQUIPMENT

RECCE 15 AML-60/-90, 24 EE-9 *Cascavel*, 8 M-8, 2 M-20, 30 *Ferret*
APC 13 M-3
TOWED ARTY 105mm: 8 M-101; **122mm**: 6
MRL 107mm: ε4 PRC Type-63
MOR 81mm: Brandt
RL 89mm: LRAC, M-20
RCL 75mm: PRC Type-52; **84mm**: *Carl Gustav*
AD GUNS 14.5mm: 30 ZPU; **20mm**: 12 TCM-20
SAM SA-7

Air Force 200

5 cbt ac, no armed hel
TPT 1 *Beech Super King*, 1 *Commander* 500B, 2 HS-748, 2 N-262, 1 Boeing 727 (VIP)
LIAISON 2 Cessna 150/172, 1 SA-316B, 1 AS-350, 3 Mi-8/17
TRG 5* SF-260W/WL

Forces Abroad

UN AND PEACEKEEPING

DROC (MONUC): 11 obs

Paramilitary

GENDARMERIE 4,200

SECURITY COMPANY (CRG) 250

PEOPLE'S MILITIA (R) 45,000 trained

Burundi Bu

Total Armed Forces

ACTIVE 45,500
(incl *Gendarmerie*)

Army c40,000

7 inf bn • 2 lt armd 'bn' (sqn), 1 arty bn • 1 engr bn • some indep inf coy • 1 AD bn

RESERVES

10 bn (reported)

EQUIPMENT

RECCE 85 incl 18 AML (6-60, 12-90), 7 Shorland, 30 BRDM-2
APC 9 Panhard M-3, 20 BTR-40, 6 *Walid*, 12 RG-31 *Nyala*
TOWED ARTY 122mm: 18 D-30
MRL 122mm: 12 BM-21
MOR ε90+ incl **82mm**: 15 M-43; **120mm**
ATGW *Milan* (reported)
RL 83mm: *Blindicide*
RCL 75mm: 60 PRC Type-52
AD GUNS some 150: **14.5mm**: 15 ZPU-4; **23mm**: ZU-23; **37mm**: Type-54
SAM ε30 SA-7

AIR WING (200)

4 cbt ac, 1 armed hel
TRG 4* SF-260W/TP
TPT 2 DC-3
HEL 1* Mi-24, 3 SA-316B, 2 Mi-8

Forces Abroad

DROC ε1,000 reported

Paramilitary

GENDARMERIE ε5,500 (incl ε50 Marine Police): 16 territorial districts

BASE Bujumbura

3 *Huchan* (PRC Type 026) PHT† plus 1 LCT, 1 spt, 4 boats

GENERAL ADMINISTRATION OF STATE SECURITY
ε1,000

Opposition

FORCES POUR LA DÉFENSE DE LA DEMOCRATIE (FDD) up to 16,000 reported

FORCES FOR NATIONAL LIBERATION (FNL) ε2–3,000

Foreign Forces

SOUTH AFRICA: ε650: 1 inf bn

Cameroon Crn

Total Armed Forces

ACTIVE ε23,100
(incl *Gendarmerie*)

Army 12,500

8 Mil Regions each 1 inf bn under comd, Presidential Guard bn, 1 armd recce bn, 1 AB/cdo bn, 1 arty bn (5 bty), 6 inf bn (1 trg), 1 AA bn (6 bty), 1 engr bn

EQUIPMENT

RECCE 8 M-8, 15 *Ferret*, 8 V-150 *Commando* (**20mm** gun), 5 VBL
AIFV 14 V-150 *Commando* (**90mm** gun)
APC 21 V-150 *Commando*, 12 M-3 half-track
TOWED ARTY 75mm: 6 M-116 pack; **105mm**: 16 M-101; **130mm**: 12 Type-59, 12 Gun 82 (reported); **155mm**: 8 I1
MRL 122mm: 20 BM-21
MOR 81mm (some SP); **120mm**: 16 Brandt
ATGW 25 *Milan*, TOW (reported)
RL 89mm: LRAC
RCL 57mm: 13 PRC Type-52; **106mm**: 40 M-40A2
AD GUNS 14.5mm: 18 PRC Type-58; **35mm**: 18 GDF-002; **37mm**: 18 PRC Type-63

Navy ε1,300

BASES Douala (HQ), Limbe, Kribi

PATROL AND COASTAL COMBATANTS 3

PATROL, COASTAL 2
1 *Bakassi* (Fr P-48) PCC, 1 *L'Audacieux* (Fr P-48) PCC
PATROL, INSHORE 1
1 *Quartier* PCI<
PATROL, RIVERINE craft only
6 US *Swift*-38†, 6 *Simonneau*†

Air Force 300

15 cbt ac, 4 armed hel
1 composite sqn, 1 Presidential Fleet
FGA 4† *Alpha Jet*, 5 CM-170, 6 MB-326
MR 2 Do-128D-6
ATTACK HEL 4 SA-342L (with HOT)
TPT ac 3 C-130H/-H-30, 1 DHC-4, 4 DHC-5D, 1 IAI-201, 2 PA-23, 1 *Gulfstream* III, 1 Do-128, 1 Boeing 707
hel 3 Bell 206, 3 SE-3130, 1 SA-318, 3 SA-319, 2 AS-332, 1 SA-365

Forces Abroad

UN AND PEACEKEEPING

DROC (MONUC): 1

Paramilitary

GENDARMERIE 9,000
10 regional gp; about 6 US *Swift*-38 (see Navy)

Cape Verde CV

Total Armed Forces

ACTIVE ε1,200
Terms of service conscription (selective)

Army 1,000

2 inf bn gp

EQUIPMENT

RECCE 10 BRDM-2
TOWED ARTY 75mm: 12; **76mm**: 12
MOR 82mm: 12; **120mm**: 6 M-1943
RL 73mm: RPG-7; **89mm**: 3.5in
AD GUNS 14.5mm: 18 ZPU-1; **23mm**: 12 ZU-23
SAM 50 SA-7

Coast Guard ε100

PATROL, COASTAL AND INSHORE
1 *Kondor* I PCC
1 *Zhuk* PCI<†, 1 *Espadarte* PCI<

Air Force under 100

no cbt ac
MR 1 Do-228

Central African Republic CAR

Total Armed Forces

ACTIVE ε2,550
(incl *Gendarmerie*)
Terms of service conscription (selective), 2 years; reserve obligation thereafter, term n.k.

Army ε1,400

1 territorial defence regt (bn) • 1 combined arms regt (1 mech, 1 inf bn) • 1 spt/HQ regt

EQUIPMENT†

MBT 3 T-55
RECCE 8 *Ferret*
APC 4 BTR-152, some 10 VAB, 25+ ACMAT
MOR 81mm; **120mm**: 12 M-1943
RL 73mm: RPG-7; **89mm**: LRAC
RCL 106mm: 14 M-40
RIVER PATROL CRAFT 9<

Air Force 150

no cbt ac, no armed hel
TPT 1 Cessna 337, 1 *Mystère Falcon* 20, 1 *Caravelle*
LIAISON 6 AL-60, 6 MH-1521
HEL 1 AS-350, 1 SE-3130

Paramilitary

GENDARMERIE ε1,000
3 regional legions, 8 'bde'

Foreign Forces

LIBYA ε300 (reported) **SUDAN** (reported)

Chad Cha

Total Armed Forces

ACTIVE ε30,350
(incl Republican Guard)
Terms of service conscription authorised

Army ε25,000

(being re-organised)
7 Mil Regions
1 armd, 7 inf, 1 arty, 1 engr bn

EQUIPMENT

- **MBT** 60 T-55
- **RECCE** ε100 BRDM-2, 4 ERC-90, some 50 AML-60/-90, 9 V-150 with **90mm**
- **APC** 20 EE-9 *Cascavel*, ε20 BTR-60
- **TOWED ARTY 105mm**: 5 M-2
- **MOR 81mm**; **120mm**: AM-50
- **ATGW** *Milan*, *Eryx*
- **RL 73mm**: RPG-7; **89mm**: LRAC
- **RCL 106mm**: M-40A1; **112mm**: APILAS
- **AD GUNS 14.5mm**: ZPU-1/-2/-4; **23mm**: ZU-23

Air Force 350

2 cbt ac, 2 armed hel
ARMED HEL 2 Mi-25V
TPT ac 2 C-130, 1 An-26 **hel** 2 SA-316*, 2 Mi-17
LIAISON 2 PC-6B, 5 Reims-Cessna FTB 337
TRG 2* PC-7

Paramilitary 4,500 active

REPUBLICAN GUARD 5,000

GENDARMERIE 4,500

Opposition

WESTERN ARMED FORCES str n.k.

MOVEMENT FOR DEMOCRACY AND JUSTICE IN CHAD (MDJT) str n.k.

Foreign Forces

FRANCE 950: 2 inf coy; 1 ERC-90 recce sqn(-); 2 C-160, 1 C-130, 3 F-ICT, 2 F-ICR, 4 SA-330 hel

Congo RC

Total Armed Forces

ACTIVE ε10,000

Army 8,000

2 armd bn • 2 inf bn gp (each with lt tk tp, 76mm gun bty) • 1 inf bn • 1 arty gp (how, MRL) • 1 engr bn • 1 AB/cdo bn

EQUIPMENT†

- **MBT** 25 T-54/-55, 15 PRC Type-59 (some T-34 in store)
- **LT TK** 10 PRC Type-62, 3 PT-76
- **RECCE** 25 BRDM-1/-2
- **APC** M-3, 50 BTR (30 -60, 20 -152), 18 *Mamba*
- **TOWED ARTY 76mm**: M-1942; **100mm**: 10 M-1944; **122mm**: 10 D-30; **130mm**: 5 M-46; **152mm**: some D-20
- **SP ARTY 122mm**: 3 2S1
- **MRL 122mm**: 10 BM-21; **140mm**: BM-14-16
- **MOR 82mm**; **120mm**: 28 M-43
- **RL 73mm**: RPG-7
- **RCL 57mm**: M-18
- **ATK GUNS 57mm**: 5 M-1943
- **AD GUNS 14.5mm**: ZPU-2/-4; **23mm**: ZSU-23-4 SP; **37mm**: 28 M-1939; **57mm**: S-60; **100mm**: KS-19

Navy† ε800

BASE Pointe Noire

PATROL AND COASTAL COMBATANTS 3†
PATROL, INSHORE 3†
3 FSU *Zhuk* PFI< (all non-op) plus riverine boats

Air Force† 1,200

12 cbt ac, no armed hel
FGA 12 MiG-21
TPT 5 An-24, 1 An-26, 1 Boeing 727, 1 N-2501
TRG 4 L-39
HEL 2 SA-316, 2 SA-318, 1 SA-365, 2 Mi-8
MISSILES
AAM AA-2 *Atoll*

Paramilitary 2,000 active

GENDARMERIE 2,000

20 coy

PRESIDENTIAL GUARD

1 bn

Foreign Forces

ANGOLA: ε2,000

Côte D'Ivoire CI

Total Armed Forces

ACTIVE ε17,050

(incl Presidential Guard, *Gendarmerie*)
Terms of service conscription (selective), 18 months

RESERVES 10,000

Army 6,500

4 Mil Regions • 1 armd, 3 inf, 1 arty bn • 1 AB gp, 1 AAA, 1 engr coy

EQUIPMENT

- **LT TK** 5 AMX-13
- **RECCE** 6 ERC-90 *Sagaie*, 15 AML-60/-90, 10 *Mamba*
- **APC** 12 M-3, 13 VAB
- **TOWED ARTY 105mm**: 4 M-1950
- **MOR 81mm; 120mm**: 16 AM-50
- **RL 89mm**: LRAC
- **RCL 106mm**: ε12 M-40A1
- **AD GUNS 20mm**: 16, incl 6 M-3 VDA SP; **40mm**: 5 L/60

Navy ε900

BASE Locodjo (Abidjan)

PATROL AND COASTAL COMBATANTS 2

PATROL, COASTAL 2

- 2 *L'Ardent* (Fr *Patra*) PCC†

AMPHIBIOUS 1

- 1 *L'Eléphant* (Fr *Batral*) LST, capacity 140 tps, 7 tk, hel deck, plus some 8 craft†

Air Force 700

5† cbt ac, no armed hel
FGA 1 sqn with 5† *Alpha Jet*
TPT 1 hel sqn with 1 SA-318, 1 SA-319, 1 SA-330, 4 SA 365C
PRESIDENTIAL FLT ac 1 F-28, 1 *Gulfstream* IV, 3 Fokker 100 **hel** 1 SA-330
TRG 4 Beech F-33C, 2 Reims Cessna 150H
LIAISON 1 Cessna 421, 1 *Super King Air* 200

Paramilitary

PRESIDENTIAL GUARD 1,350

GENDARMERIE 7,600

VAB APC, 4 patrol boats

MILITIA 1,500

Foreign Forces

FRANCE 550: 1 marine inf coy (1 ERC-90 recce sqn); 1 AS-555 hel

Democratic Republic of Congo DROC

Total Armed Forces

ACTIVE ε81,400

Army ε79,000

10+ inf, 1 Presidential Guard bde
1 mech inf bde, 1 cdo bde (reported)

EQUIPMENT†

- **MBT** 20 PRC Type-59 (being refurbished), some 40 PRC Type-62
- **RECCE** some 140 AML-60/-90
- **APC** M-113, YW-531, Panhard M-3, some *Casspir*, *Wolf* Turbo 2, *Fahd*
- **TOWED ARTY** 100+: **75mm**: M-116 pack; **85mm**: Type-56; **122mm**: M-1938/D-30, Type-60; **130mm**: Type-59
- **MRL** ε30: **107mm**: Type 63; **122mm**: BM-21
- **MOR 81mm; 107mm**: M-30; **120mm**: Brandt
- **RCL 57mm**: M-18; **75mm**: M-20; **106mm**: M-40A1
- **AD GUNS** ε50: **14.5mm**: ZPU-4; **37mm**: M-1939/Type; **40mm**: L/60
- **SAM** SA-7

Navy ε900

BASES Coastal Matadi **River** Kinshasa, Boma **Lake Tanganyika** (4 boats)
PATROL AND COASTAL COMBATANTS 2†
PATROL, COASTAL/INSHORE 2

- 2 *Swiftships* PCI<, plus about 6 armed boats (most non-op)

Air Force ε1,500

Only a handful of utility and comms ac remain serviceable. **ac** 4 Su-25, with a further 6 reported on order **hel** 6-10 Mi-24

Paramilitary

NATIONAL POLICE incl Rapid Intervention Police (National and Provincial forces)

PEOPLE'S DEFENCE FORCE

Opposition

THE RALLY FOR CONGOLESE DEMOCRACY
ε23,000; split into two factions:
a. **Congolese Rally for Democracy – Liberation Movement** (RCD–ML) ε2-3,000
b. **Congolese Rally for Democracy – Goma** (RCD–Goma) up to 20,000 reported

MOVEMENT FOR THE LIBERATION OF THE CONGO (MLC) ε18,000
(The MLC and most of the RCD–ML formed an umbrella group on 16 Jan 2001: The Front for the Liberation of Congo (FLC) ε20,000)

Foreign Forces

In support of government:
ANGOLA: ε2,000 **ZIMBABWE**: up to 8,500 reported
In support of opposition:
BURUNDI: ε1,000 reported **RWANDA**: 15–20,000 reported **UGANDA**: some 3,000
UN (MONUC): 449 obs and 3,256 tps from 46 countries

Djibouti Dj

Total Armed Forces

ACTIVE ε9,850
(incl *Gendarmerie*)

Army ε8,000

3 Comd (North, Central, South) • 1 inf bn, incl mor, ATK pl • 1 arty bty • 1 armd sqn • 2 border cdo bn • 1 AB coy • 1 spt bn

EQUIPMENT
RECCE 15 VBL, 4 AML-60†
APC 12 BTR-60 (op status uncertain)
TOWED ARTY 122mm: 6 D-30
MOR 81mm: 25; **120mm**: 20 Brandt
RL 73mm: RPG-7; **89mm**: LRAC
RCL 106mm: 16 M-40A1
AD GUNS 20mm: 5 M-693 SP; **23mm**: 5 ZU-23; **40mm**: 5 L/70

Navy ε200

BASE Djibouti
PATROL AND COASTAL COMBATANTS 7
PATROL CRAFT, INSHORE 7
5 *Sawari* PCI<, 2 *Moussa Ali* PCI<, plus boats

Air Force 250

no cbt ac or armed hel
TPT 1 An-28, 1 Cessna U206G, 1 Cessna 208, 1 Cessna 402 (in store)
HEL 1 Mi-8, 1 Mi-17, 1 AS-355F (plus 1 in store)

Paramilitary ε2,500 active

GENDARMERIE (Ministry of Defence) 1,400
1 bn, 1 patrol boat

NATIONAL SECURITY FORCE (Ministry of Interior) ε2,500

Foreign Forces

FRANCE 3,200: incl 2 inf coy, 2 recce sqn, 26 ERC90 recce, 6 155mm arty, 16 AA arty, 3 amph craft: 1 sqn: **ac** 4 *Mirage* F-1C, 5 *Mirage* 2000, 1 C-160 **hel** 1 SA-330, 1 AS-555
GERMANY (OP ENDURING FREEDOM)

Equatorial Guinea EG

Total Armed Forces

ACTIVE 1,320

Army 1,100

3 inf bn

EQUIPMENT
RECCE 6 BRDM-2
APC 10 BTR-152

Navy† 120

BASES Malabo (Santa Isabel), Bata
PATROL AND COASTAL COMBATANTS 2

PATROL CRAFT, INSHORE 2 PCI<†

Air Force 100

no cbt ac or armed hel
TPT ac 1 Yak-40, 3 C-212, 1 Cessna-337 **hel** 2 SA-316

Paramilitary

GUARDIA CIVIL
2 coy

COAST GUARD
1 PCI<

Eritrea Er

Total Armed Forces

ACTIVE ε172,200
Terms of service 16 months (4 month mil trg)

RESERVES ε120,000 (reported)
Total holdings of army assets n.k.

Army ε170,000 (ε60,000 to be de-mob)

4 Corps
18 inf (incl 1 reserve), 1 cdo div, 1 mech bde

EQUIPMENT
- **MBT** ε100 T-54/-55
- **RECCE** 30 BRDM-1/-2
- **AIFV/APC** 50: BMP-1, BTR-60
- **TOWED ARTY** 100: **85mm**: D-44; **122mm**: D-30; **130mm**: 30 M-46
- **SP ARTY** 25: **122mm**: 12 2S1; **152mm**: 2S5
- **MRL 122mm**: 30 BM-21
- **MOR** 100+: **120mm**; **160mm**
- **RL 73mm**: RPG-7
- **ATGW** 200: AT-3 *Sagger*, AT-*Spandrel*
- **AD GUNS** 70+ incl **23mm**: ZU-23, ZSU-23-4
- **SAM** SA-7

Navy 1,400

BASES Massawa (HQ), Assab, Dahlak

PATROL AND COASTAL COMBATANTS 8
MISSILE CRAFT 1
1 *Osa* II PFM with 4 SS-N-2B *Styx* SSM
PATROL, INSHORE 7
4 *Super Dvora* PFI<, 3 *Swiftships* PCI

AMPHIBIOUS 2
2 *Chamo* LST (Ministry of Transport)
plus 2 *Soviet* LCU†

Air Force ε800

17† cbt ac, some armed hel
Current types and numbers are assessed as follows:
FTR/FGA 4† MiG-23, 3† MiG-21, 6 MiG-29 (1-UB)
TPT 3 Y-12(II), 1 IAI-1125
TRG 6 L-90 *Redigo*, 4* MB-339CE
HEL 4 Mi-8/-17, 1 Mi-24-4

Opposition

ALLIANCE OF ERITREAN NATIONAL FORCES (AENF)
str ε3,000 incl **Eritrean Liberation Front of Abdullah Idris (ELF-AI)** and **Eritrean Liberation Front – National Congress (ELF–NC)** str n.k.

AFAR RED SEA FRONT str n.k.

Foreign Forces

UN (UNMEE): 214 obs and 3,940 tps from 45 countries

Ethiopia Eth

Total Armed Forces

ACTIVE ε252,500
The Ethiopia armed forces were formed following Eritrea's declaration of independence in Apr 1993. Extensive demobilisation of former members of the Tigray People's Liberation Front (TPLF) has taken place. Ethiopia auctioned off its naval assets in Sep 1996. Currently 17 div reported. Peacetime re-org outlined below.

Army ε250,000

Re-org to consist of 3 Mil Regions each with corps HQ (each corps 2 divs, 1 reinforced mech bde); strategic reserve div of 6 bde will be located at Addis Ababa.
- **MBT** 300+: T-54/-55, T-62
- **RECCE/AIFV/APC** ε400, incl BRDM, BMP, BTR-60/-152
- **TOWED ARTY** ε300: **76mm**: ZIS-3; **85mm**: D-44; **122mm**: D-30/M-30; **130mm**: M-46
- **SP ARTY 122mm**: 2S1; **152mm**: 10 2S19
- **MRL** ε50 BM-21
- **MOR 81mm**: M-1/M-29; **82mm**: M-1937; **120mm**: M-1944
- **ATGW** AT-3 *Sagger*
- **RCL 82mm**: B-10; **107mm**: B-11
- **AD GUNS 23mm**: ZU-23, ZSU-23-4 SP; **37mm**:

M-1939; **57mm**: S-60
SAM ε370: SA-2, SA-3, SA-7

Air Force ε2,500

55 cbt ac, 30 armed hel
FGA 30 MiG-21MF, 17 MiG-23BN, 4 Su-25 (2 -25T, 2 -25UB), 4 Su-27
TPT 4 C-130B, 7 An-12, 2 DH-6, 1 Yak-40 (VIP), 2 Y-12
TRG 20 L-39, 10 SF-260
ATTACK HEL 30 Mi-24
TPT HEL 25 Mi-8/17

Opposition

THE UNITED LIBERATION FORCES OF OROMIA str n.k.
An alliance of six groups

OGADEN NATIONAL LIBERATION FRONT str n.k.

Foreign Forces

UN (UNMEE): 214 obs and 3,940 tps from 45 countries

Gabon Gbn

Total Armed Forces

ACTIVE ε4,700

Army 3,200

Presidential Guard bn gp (1 recce/armd, 3 inf coy, arty, AA bty), under direct presidential control
8 inf, 1 AB/cdo, 1 engr coy

EQUIPMENT
RECCE 14 EE-9 *Cascavel*, 24 AML-60/-90, 6 ERC-90 *Sagaie*, 12 EE-3 *Jararaca*, 14 VBL
AIFV 12 EE-11 *Urutu* with **20mm** gun
APC 9 V-150 *Commando*, Panhard M-3, 12 VXB-170
TOWED ARTY 105mm: 4 M-101
MRL 140mm: 8 *Teruel*
MORS 81mm: 35; **120mm**: 4 Brandt
ATGW 4 *Milan*
RL 89mm: LRAC
RCL 106mm: M40A1
AD GUNS 20mm: 4 ERC-20 SP; **23mm**: 24 ZU-23-2; **37mm**: 10 M-1939; **40mm**: 3 L/70

Navy ε500

BASE Port Gentil (HQ)

PATROL AND COASTAL COMBATANTS 2
PATROL, COASTAL 2 *General Ba'Oumar* (Fr P-400) PCC

Amphibious 1
1 *President Omar Bongo* (Fr *Batral*) LST, capacity 140 tps, 7 tk; plus craft 1 LCM

Air Force 1,000

10 cbt ac, 5 armed hel
FGA 9 *Mirage* 5 (2 -G, 4 -GII, 3 -DG)
MR 1* EMB-111
TPT 1 C-130H, 3 L-100-30, 1 EMB-110, 2 YS-11A, 1 CN-235
HELICOPTERS 5 SA-342*, 3 SA-330C/-H, 3 SA-316/-319, 2 AB-412
PRESIDENTIAL GUARD
CCT 4 CM-170, 3 T-34
TPT ac 1 ATR-42F, 1 EMB-110, 1 *Falcon* 900 **hel** 1 AS-332

Paramilitary 2,000

GENDARMERIE 2,000
3 'bde', 11 coy, 2 armd sqn, air unit with 1 AS-355, 2 AS-350

Foreign Forces

FRANCE 750: 2 mne inf coy, 1 ERC-90 recce platoon **ac** 2 C-160 **hel** 1 AS-555

The Gambia Gam

Total Armed Forces

ACTIVE 800

Gambian National Army 800

2 inf bn • Presidential Guard coy • 1 engr sqn

MARINE UNIT (about 70)
BASE Banjul

PATROL CRAFT, INSHORE 3
3 PCI<, boats

Forces Abroad

UN AND PEACEKEEPING
ETHIOPIA/ERITREA (UNMEE): 4 obs **SIERRA LEONE** (UNAMSIL): 15 obs

Ghana Gha

Total Armed Forces

ACTIVE 7,000

Army 5,000

2 Comd HQ • 2 bde (6 inf bn (incl 1 UNIFIL, 1 ECOMOG), spt unit) • 1 Presidential Guard, 1 trg bn • 1 recce regt (3 sqn) • 1 arty 'regt' (1 arty, 2 mor bty) • 2 AB/ SF coy • 1 fd engr regt (bn)

EQUIPMENT

RECCE 3 EE-9 *Cascavel*
AIFV 50 MOWAG *Piranha*
TOWED ARTY 122mm: 6 D-30
MOR 81mm: 50; **120mm**: 28 Tampella
RCL 84mm: 50 *Carl Gustav*
AD GUNS 14.5mm: 4 ZPU-2, ZPU-4; **23mm**: 4 ZU-23-2
SAM SA-7

Navy 1,000

COMMANDS Western and **Eastern**
BASES Sekondi (HQ Western), Tema (HQ Eastern)
PATROL AND COASTAL COMBATANTS 6
PATROL, COASTAL 6
2 *Achimota* (Ge Lürssen 57m) PFC
2 *Dzata* (Ge Lürssen 45m) PCC
2 *Anzole* (US) PCC

Air Force 1,000

19 cbt ac, no armed hel
TPT 5 Fokker (4 F-27, 1 F-28 (VIP)); 1 C-212, 6 *Skyvan*, 1 *Gulfstream*
HEL 4 AB-212 (1 VIP, 3 utl), 2 Mi-2, 4 SA-319
TRG 12* L-29, 2* L-39, 2* MB 339F, 3* MB-326K

Forces Abroad

UN AND PEACEKEEPING

CROATIA (UNMOP): 1 obs **DROC** (MONUC): 419 incl 17 obs **ETHIOPIA/ERITREA** (UNMEE): 18 incl 11 obs **IRAQ/KUWAIT** (UNIKOM): 6 obs **LEBANON** (UNIFIL): 802; 1 inf bn **SIERRA LEONE** (UNAMSIL): 928 incl 7 obs **WESTERN SAHARA** (MINURSO): 15 incl 8 obs

Guinea Gui

Total Armed Forces

ACTIVE 9,700
(perhaps 7,500 conscripts)
Terms of service conscription, 2 years

Army 8,500

1 armd bn • 5 inf bn • 1 cdo bn • 1 arty bn • 1 engr bn • 1 AD bn • 1 SF bn

EQUIPMENT†

MBT 30 T-34, 8 T-54
LT TK 15 PT-76
RECCE 25 BRDM-1/-2, 2 AML-90
APC 40 BTR (16 -40, 10 -50, 8 -60, 6 -152)
TOWED ARTY 76mm: 8 M-1942; **85mm**: 6 D-44; **122mm**: 12 M-1931/37
MOR 82mm: M-43; **120mm**: 20 M-1938/43
ATGW AT-3 *Sagger*
RL 73mm: RPG-7
RCL 82mm: B-10
ATK GUNS 57mm: M-1943
AD GUNS 30mm: twin M-53; **37mm**: 8 M-1939; **57mm**: 12 S-60, PRC Type-59; **100mm**: 4 KS-19
SAM SA-7

Navy† 400

BASES Conakry, Kakanda

PATROL AND COASTAL COMBATANTS 2†

PATROL, INSHORE 2†
2 US *Swiftships* 77 PCI<

Air Force† 800

8 cbt ac, no armed hel
FGA 4 MiG-17F, 4 MiG-21
TPT 4 An-14, 1 An-24
TRG 2 MiG-15UTI
HEL 1 IAR-330, 1 Mi-8, 1 SA-316B, 1 SA-330, 1 SA-342K

MISSILES

AAM AA-2 *Atoll*

Forces Abroad

UN AND PEACEKEEPING

SIERRA LEONE (UNAMSIL): 793 incl 12 obs
WESTERN SAHARA (MINURSO): 3 obs

Paramilitary 2,600 active

GENDARMERIE 1,000

REPUBLICAN GUARD 1,600

PEOPLE'S MILITIA 7,000

Opposition

MOVEMENT OF THE DEMOCRATIC FORCES OF GUINEA ε1,800

Guinea-Bissau GuB

Total Armed Forces

ACTIVE ε9,250 (all services, incl *Gendarmerie*, form part of the armed forces)

Terms of service conscription (selective)

As a result of the 1998 revolt by dissident army tps, manpower and eqpt totals should be treated with caution.

Army 6,800

1 armd 'bn' (sqn) • 5 inf, 1 arty bn • 1 recce, 1 engr coy

EQUIPMENT†

- **MBT** 10 T-34
- **LT TK** 15 PT-76
- **RECCE** 10 BRDM-2
- **APC** 35 BTR-40/-60/-152, 20 PRC Type-56
- **TOWED ARTY 85mm**: 8 D-44; **122mm**: 18 M-1938/ D-30
- **MOR 82mm**: M-43; **120mm**: 8 M-1943
- **RL 89mm**: M-20
- **RCL 75mm**: PRC Type-52; **82mm**: B-10
- **AD GUNS 23mm**: 18 ZU-23; **37mm**: 6 M-1939; **57mm**: 10 S-60
- **SAM** SA-7

Navy ε350

BASE Bissau

PATROL AND COASTAL COMBATANTS 3

PATROL, INSHORE 3

2 *Alfeite* PCI<, 1 PCI<

Air Force 100

3 cbt ac, no armed hel

FTR/FGA 3 MiG-17

HEL 1 SA-318, 2 SA-319

Paramilitary

GENDARMERIE 2,000

Kenya Kya

Total Armed Forces

ACTIVE 24,400

(incl HQ staff)

Army 20,000

1 armd bde (3 armd bn) • 2 inf bde (1 with 2, 1 with 3 inf bn) • 1 indep inf bn • 1 arty bde (2 bn) • 1 AD arty bn • 1 engr bde (2 bn) • 1 AB bn • 1 indep air cav bn

EQUIPMENT

- **MBT** 78 Vickers Mk 3
- **RECCE** 72 AML-60/-90, 12 *Ferret*, 8 Shorland
- **APC** 52 UR-416, 10 Panhard M-3 (in store)
- **TOWED ARTY 105mm**: 40 lt, 8 pack
- **MOR 81mm**: 50; **120mm**: 12 Brandt
- **ATGW** 40 *Milan*, 14 *Swingfire*
- **RCL 84mm**: 80 *Carl Gustav*
- **AD GUNS 20mm**: ε70 TCM-20, 11 Oerlikon; **40mm**: 13 L/70

Navy 1,400

BASE Mombasa

PATROL AND COASTAL COMBATANTS 4

MISSILE CRAFT 2

2 *Nyayo* (UK Vosper 57m) PFM with 4 *Ottomat* SSM, 1 × 76mm gun

PATROL, OFFSHORE 2

2 *Shujaa* PCO with 1 x 76mm gun

AMPHIBIOUS craft only

2 *Galana* LCM

SUPPORT AND MISCELLANEOUS 1

1 AT

Air Force 3,000

29 cbt ac, 34 armed hel

FGA 9 F-5E/F

TPT 7 DHC-5D, 12 Y-12 (II), 1 PA-31, 3 DHC-8, 1 Fokker 70 (VIP) (6 Do-28D-2 in store)

ATTACK HEL 11 Hughes 500MD (with TOW), 8 Hughes 500ME, 15 Hughes 500M
TPT HEL 9 IAR-330, 3 SA-330, 1 SA-342
TRG some 6 *Bulldog* 103/127, 8* *Hawk* Mk 52, 12* *Tucano*, **hel** 2 Hughes 500D

MISSILES

ASM AGM-65 *Maverick*, TOW
AAM AIM-9 *Sidewinder*

Forces Abroad

UN AND PEACEKEEPING

CROATIA (UNMOP): 1 obs **DROC** (MONUC): 29 incl 15 obs **ETHIOPIA/ERITREA** (UNMEE): 628 incl 12 obs **EAST TIMOR** (UNMISET): 2 obs **IRAQ/KUWAIT** (UNIKOM): 4 obs **SIERRA LEONE** (UNAMSIL): 1,086 incl 11 obs **WESTERN SAHARA** (MINURSO): 9 obs

Paramilitary 5,000

POLICE GENERAL SERVICE UNIT 5,000
AIR WING ac 7 Cessna lt **hel** 3 Bell (1 206L, 2 47G)
POLICE NAVAL SQN/CUSTOMS about 5 PCI< (2 Lake Victoria), some 12 boats

Foreign Forces

GERMANY (OP ENDURING FREEDOM) 150

Lesotho Ls

Total Armed Forces

ACTIVE ε2,000

Army ε2,000

7 inf coy • 1 recce coy, 1 arty bty(-), 1 spt coy (with 81mm mor) • 1 air sqn

EQUIPMENT

RECCE 10 Il *Ramta*, 8 Shorland, 4 AML-90
TOWED ARTY 105mm: 2
MOR 81mm: 10
RCL 106mm: 6 M-40

AIR WING (110)

AC 2 C-212-300, 1 C-212-400 (tpt, VIP tpt, casevac), 1 Cessna 182Q (trg)
HEL 2 Bell 412 SP, 1 Bell 412EP (tpt, VIP tpt, SAR), 2 Bo-105 LSA-3 (tpt/trg), 1 Bell 47G (adv trg)

Liberia Lb

Total Armed Forces

ACTIVE ε11–15,000 mobilised

Total includes militias supporting govt forces. No further details. Plans for new unified armed forces, to be implemented later, at an unspecified date, provide for:
Army 4,000 • **Navy** 1,000 • **Air Force** 300

Opposition

LIBERIANS UNITED FOR RECONCILIATION AND DEMOCRACY (LURD) str n.k. – several thousand reported

Madagascar Mdg

Total Armed Forces

ACTIVE some 13,500

Terms of service conscription (incl for civil purposes), 18 months

Army some 12,500

2 bn gp • 1 engr regt

EQUIPMENT

LT TK 12 PT-76
RECCE 8 M-8, ε20 M-3A1, 10 *Ferret*, ε35 BRDM-2
APC ε30 M-3A1 half-track
TOWED ARTY 76mm: 12 ZIS-3; **105mm**: 5 M-101; **122mm**: 12 D-30
MOR 82mm: M-37; **120mm**: 8 M-43
RL 89mm: LRAC
RCL 106mm: M-40A1
AD GUNS 14.5mm: 50 ZPU-4; **37mm**: 20 Type-55

Navy† 500

(incl some 100 Marines)
BASES Diégo-Suarez, Tamatave, Fort Dauphin, Tuléar, Majunga

AMPHIBIOUS craft only

1 LCT (Fr *Edic*)

SUPPORT AND MISCELLANEOUS 1

1 tpt/trg

Air Force 500

12 cbt ac, no armed hel
FGA 1 sqn with 4 MiG-17F, 8 MiG-21FL
TPT 4 An-26 (only 1 serviceable), 1 BN-2, 2 C-212, 2 Yak-40 (VIP)
HEL 1 sqn with 6 Mi-8
LIAISON 1 Cessna 310, 2 Cessna 337, 1 PA-23
TRG 4 Cessna 172

Paramilitary 8,100

GENDARMERIE 8,100
incl maritime police with some 5 PCI<

Malawi Mlw

Total Armed Forces

ACTIVE 5,300 (all services form part of the Army)

Army 5,300

3 inf bn • 1 indep para bn • 1 general spt bn (incl arty, engr) • 1 mne coy (+)

EQUIPMENT (less than 20% serviceability)
- **RECCE** 20 *Fox*, 8 *Ferret*, 13 *Eland*
- **TOWED ARTY 105mm**: 9 lt
- **MOR 81mm**: 8 L16
- **AD GUNS 14.5mm**: 40 ZPU-4
- **SAM** 15 *Blowpipe*

MARITIME WING (220)
BASE Monkey Bay (Lake Nyasa)
- **PATROL, INSHORE** 2
- 1 *Kasungu* PCI<†, 1 *Namacurra* PCI<, plus 12 boats

AMPHIBIOUS craft only
- 1 LCU

AIR WING (80)
no cbt ac, no armed hel
- **TPT AC** 1 sqn with 2 Basler T-67, 3 Do-228, 1 HS-125-800 (VIP)
- **TPT HEL** 1 SA-330F, 3 AS-350L, 1 *Super Puma* (VIP)

Forces Abroad

UN AND PEACEKEEPING
DROC (MONUC): 17 obs

Paramilitary 1,500

MOBILE POLICE FORCE (MPF) 1,500
8 Shorland armd car **ac** 3 BN-2T *Defender* (border patrol), 1 *Skyvan* 3M, 4 Cessna **hel** 2 AS-365

Mali RMM

Total Armed Forces

ACTIVE about 7,350 (all services form part of the Army)
Terms of service conscription (incl for civil purposes), 2 years (selective)

Army about 7,350

2 tk, 4 inf, 1 AB, 2 arty, 1 engr, 1 SF bn • 2 AD, 1 SAM bty

EQUIPMENT†
- **MBT** 21 T-34, 12 T-54/-55
- **LT TK** 18 Type-62
- **RECCE** 20 BRDM-2
- **APC** 30 BTR-40, 10 BTR-60, 10 BTR-152
- **TOWED ARTY 85mm**: 6 D-44; **100mm**: 6 M-1944; **122mm**: 8 D-30; **130mm**: M-46 reported
- **MRL 122mm**: 2 BM-21
- **MOR 82mm**: M-43; **120mm**: 30 M-43
- **ATGW** AT-3 *Sagger*
- **RL 73mm**: RPG-7
- **AD GUNS 37mm**: 6 M-1939; **57mm**: 6 S-60
- **SAM** SA-7, 12 SA-3

NAVY† (about 50)
BASES Bamako, Mopti, Segou, Timbuktu
PATROL, RIVERINE 3 PCR<

AIR FORCE (400)
16† cbt ac, no armed hel
FGA 5 MiG-17F
FTR 11 MiG-21
TPT 2 An-24, 1 An-26
HEL 1 Mi-8, 1 AS-350, 2 Z-9
TRG 6 L-29, 1 MiG-15UTI, 4 Yak-11, 2 Yak-18

Forces Abroad

UN AND PEACEKEEPING
DROC (MONUC): 24 incl 21 obs **SIERRA LEONE** (UNAMSIL): 8 obs

Paramilitary 4,800 active

GENDARMERIE 1,800
8 coy

REPUBLICAN GUARD 2,000

NATIONAL POLICE 1,000

MILITIA 3,000

Mauritius Ms

Total Armed Forces

ACTIVE Nil

Paramilitary 2,000

SPECIAL MOBILE FORCE ε1,500

6 rifle, 2 mob, 1 engr coy, spt tp

RECCE BRDM-2, *Ferret*
APC 11 VAB (2 with 20mm), 7 *Tactica*
MOR 81mm: 2
RL 89mm: 4 LRAC

COAST GUARD ε500

PATROL CRAFT 4
PATROL, OFFSHORE 1
1 *Vigilant* (Ca *Guardian* design) PCO, capability for 1 hel
PATROL, COASTAL 1
1 *Guardian* PCC
PATROL, INSHORE 2
2 FSU *Zhuk* PCI<, plus 4 *Mandovi* boats
MR 1 Do-228-101, 1 BN-2T *Defender*

POLICE AIR WING

2 *Alouette* III

Mozambique Moz

Total Armed Forces

ACTIVE ε10–11,150

Terms of service conscription, 2 years

Army ε9–10,000

7 inf, 3 SF, 2 engr, 1 log bn, 2–3 arty bty

EQUIPMENT† (ε10% or less serviceability)

MBT some 80 T-54/-55 (300+ T-34, T-54/-55 non-op)
RECCE 30 BRDM-1/-2
AIFV 40 BMP-1
APC 150+ BTR-60, 80 BTR-152, 5 *Casspir*
TOWED ARTY 76mm: 40 M-1942; **85mm**: 12 D-44, 6 D-48, 12 Type-56; **100mm**: 8 M-1944; **105mm**: 12 M-101; **122mm**: 12 D-30; **130mm**: 6 M-46; **152mm**: 12 D-1
MRL 122mm: 12 BM-21
MOR 82mm: M-43; **120mm**: 12 M-43
ATGW AT-3 *Sagger*, AT-4 *Spigot*
RCL 75mm; **82mm**: B-10; **107mm**: B-11
AD GUNS 20mm: M-55; **23mm**: ZU-23-2; **37mm**: M-1939; **57mm**: S-60 (towed), ZSU-57-2 SP
SAM SA-7

Navy† 150

BASES Monkey Bay, Lake Malawi
Inventory consists of some boats on Lake Malawi

Air Force 1,000

(incl AD units); no cbt ac, 4† armed hel
TPT 1 sqn with 5 An-26, 2 C-212, 4 PA-32 *Cherokee* (non-op)
TRG 1 Cessna 182, 7 ZLIN-326
HEL 4† Mi-24*, 5 Mi-8 (all non-op, with exception of 2 Mi-8)
AD SAM †SA-2, 10 SA-3 (all non-op)

Forces Abroad

UN AND PEACEKEEPING

DROC (MONUC): 2 obs **EAST TIMOR** (UNMISET): 2 obs

Namibia Nba

Total Armed Forces

ACTIVE 9,000

Army 9,000

1 Presidential Guard, 6 inf bn • 1 cbt spt bde with 1 arty, 1 AD, 1 ATK regt

EQUIPMENT

MBT some T-34, T-54/-55 (serviceability doubtful)
RECCE 12 BRDM-2
APC 20 *Casspir*, 30 *Wolf*, 10 BTR-60
TOWED ARTY 140mm: 24 G2
MRL 122mm: 5 BM-21
MOR 81mm; **82mm**
RCL 82mm: B-10
ATK GUNS 57mm; **76mm**: 12 M-1942 (ZIS-3)
AD GUNS 14.5mm: 50 ZPU-4; **23mm**: 15 *Zumlac* (ZU-23-2) SP
SAM ε50 SA-7

AIR WING

FGA 2 MiG-23 reported
TPT 1 *Falcon* 900, 1 Learjet 36, 2 Y-12
SURVEILLANCE 6 Cessna 337/02-A
HEL 2 SA-319 *Chetak*, some Mi-8, Mi-24 (on lease)
TRG 4 K-8

Coast Guard ε200

(fishery protection, part of the Ministry of Fisheries)
BASE Walvis Bay
PATROL, OFFSHORE/COASTAL 2
1 *Osprey* PCO, 1 *Oryx* PCC
AIRCRAFT
1 F406 *Caravan* ac, 1 hel

Forces Abroad

UN AND PEACEKEEPING
ETHIOPIA/ERITREA (UNMEE): 6 incl 3 obs

Paramilitary

SPECIAL FIELD FORCE 6,000 incl Border Guard and Special Reserve Force

Niger Ngr

Total Armed Forces

ACTIVE 5,300
Terms of service selective conscription (2 years)

Army 5,200

3 Mil Districts • 4 armd recce sqn • 7 inf, 2 AB, 1 engr, 1 AD coy

EQUIPMENT

RECCE 90 AML-90, 35 AML-60/20, 7 VBL
APC 22 M-3
MOR 81mm: 19 Brandt; **82mm**: 17; **120mm**: 4 Brandt
RL 89mm: 36 LRAC
RCL 75mm: 6 M-20; **106mm**: 8 M-40
AD GUNS 20mm: 39 incl 10 M-3 VDA SP

Air Force 100

no cbt ac or armed hel
TPT 1 C-130H, 1 Do-28, 1 Do-228, 1 Boeing 737-200 (VIP), 1 An-26
LIAISON 2 Cessna 337D

Forces Abroad

UN AND PEACEKEEPING
DROC (MONUC): 12 incl 11 obs

Paramilitary 5,400

GENDARMERIE 1,400

REPUBLICAN GUARD 2,500

NATIONAL POLICE 1,500

Nigeria Nga

Total Armed Forces

ACTIVE 78,500
RESERVES
planned, none org

Army 62,000

1 armd div (2 armd bde) • 1 composite div (1 mot inf, 1 amph bde, 1 AB bn) • 2 mech div (each 1 mech, 1 mot inf bde) • 1 Presidential Guard bde (2 bn) • 1 AD bde • each div 1 arty, 1 engr bde, 1 recce bn

EQUIPMENT

MBT 50 T-55†, 150 Vickers Mk 3
LT TK 100 *Scorpion*
RECCE ε120 AML-60, 60 AML-90, 55 *Fox*, 75 EE-9 *Cascavel*, 72 VBL (reported)
APC 10 *Saracen*, 250 *Steyr* 4K-7FA, 70 MOWAG *Piranha*, EE-11 *Urutu* (reported), *Saladin* Mk2
TOWED ARTY 105mm: 200 M-56; **122mm**: 200 D-30/-74; **130mm:** 7 M-46; **155mm:** 24 FH-77B (in store)
SP ARTY 155mm: 27 *Palmaria*
MRL 122mm: 25 APR-21
MOR 81mm: 200; **82mm:** 100; **120mm**: 30+
ATGW *Swingfire*
RCL 84mm: *Carl Gustav*; **106mm:** M-40A1
AD GUNS 20mm: some 60; **23mm:** ZU-23, 30 ZSU-23-4 SP; **40mm:** L/60
SAM 48 *Blowpipe*, 16 *Roland*, ε100 SA-7
SURV RASIT (veh, arty)

Navy 7,000

(incl Coast Guard)
BASES Lagos, HQ Western Comd Apapa, HQ Eastern Comd Calabar

PRINCIPAL SURFACE COMBATANTS 1

FRIGATES 1†

FFG 1 *Aradu* (Ge MEKO 360)† with 8 *Otomat* SSM, *Albatros* SAM, 1 × 127mm gun, 2 × 3 ASTT, 1 *Lynx* hel

PATROL AND COASTAL COMBATANTS 8

CORVETTES 2† *Erinomi* (UK Vosper Mk 9) FS with 1 × 3 *Seacat* SAM, 1 × 76mm gun, 1 × 2 ASW mor

MISSILE CRAFT 3

3† *Ayam* (Fr *Combattante*) PFM with 2 × 2 MM-38 *Exocet* SSM, 1 × 76mm gun

PATROL, COASTAL 3

3 *Ekpe* (Ge Lürssen 57m) PCC with 1 × 76mm gun

MINE WARFARE 2

MINE COUNTERMEASURES 2†

2 *Ohue* (mod It *Lerici*) MCC (both non-op)

AMPHIBIOUS 1

1 *Ambe* (Ge) LST, capacity 220 tps, 5 tk

SUPPORT AND MISCELLANEOUS 5

3 AT, 1 nav trg, 1 AGHS

NAVAL AVIATION

EQUIPMENT

HELICOPTERS 2†

MR/SAR 2† *Lynx* Mk 89

Air Force 9,500

86† cbt ac, 16† armed hel (only 50% serviceability)

FGA/FTR 3 sqn

1 with 19 *Alpha Jet* (FGA/trg)

1 with 5† MiG-21MF, 1† MiG-21U, 12† MiG-21B/FR

1 with 15† *Jaguar* (12 -SN, 3 -BN)

ARMED HEL 10† Bo-105D, 6 Mi-35

TPT 2 sqn with 5 C-130H, 3 -H-30, 17 Do-128-6, 16 Do-228-200 (incl 2 VIP), 5 G-222 **hel** 4 AS-332, 2 SA-330, 3 Mi-34

PRESIDENTIAL FLT ac 1 Boeing 727, 2 *Gulfstream*, 2 *Falcon* 900, 1 BAe 125-1000

TRG ac† 22* L-39MS, 12* MB-339AN, 59 *Air Beetle* **hel** 13 Hughes 300

AAM AA-2 *Atoll*

Forces Abroad

UN AND PEACEKEEPING

CROATIA (UNMOP): 1 obs **DROC** (MONUC): 26 incl 25 obs **ERITREA/ETHIOPIA** (UNMEE): 11 incl 6 obs **IRAQ/KUWAIT** (UNIKOM): 7 obs **SIERRA LEONE** (UNAMSIL): 3,335 incl 10 obs **WESTERN SAHARA** (MINURSO): 7 obs

Paramilitary ε82,000

COAST GUARD

PORT SECURITY POLICE ε2,000

about 60 boats and some 5 hovercraft

SECURITY AND CIVIL DEFENCE CORPS (Ministry of Internal Affairs)

EQUIPMENT

POLICE 80,000: UR-416, 70 AT-105 *Saxon*† APC **ac** 1 Cessna 500, 3 Piper (2 *Navajo*, 1 *Chieftain*) **hel** 4 Bell (2 -212, 2 -222)

Rwanda Rwa

Total Armed Forces

ACTIVE ε60–75,000 (all services, incl National Police; up to 90,000 reported)

Army ε49–64,000

6 inf bde, 1 mech inf regt

EQUIPMENT

MBT 12 T-54/-55

RECCE ε90 AML-60/-90/-245, 16 VBL

AIFV some BMP

APC ε50: some BTR, Panhard, 16 RG-31 *Nyala*

TOWED ARTY 35: **105mm**†; **122mm**: 6 D-30; **152mm**

MRL 122mm: 5 RM-70

MOR 250: **81mm**; **82mm**; **120mm**

AD GUNS ε150: **14.5mm**; **23mm**; **37mm**

SAM SA-7

Air Force ε1,000

At least 5 cbt ac, no armed hel

FGA At least 5 MiG-21

TPT Some An-2, 2–3 An-8, 1 B-707, 1 Bn-2A *Islander*

HEL 8-12 Mi-17MD, 3 Mi-24

TRG Some L-39

Forces Abroad

DROC: 15–20,000 reported

Paramilitary

NATIONAL POLICE up to 10,000 reported

LOCAL DEFENCE FORCES ε2,000

Opposition

ARMY FOR THE LIBERATION OF RWANDA ε15,000 Hutu rebels in DROC (incl former govt tps, *Interahamwe* and other recruits) of which ε5,000 have been integrated into DROC armed forces

Senegal Sen

Total Armed Forces

ACTIVE 9,400 (incl ε3,500 conscripts)

Terms of service conscription, 2 years selective

RESERVES n.k.

Army 8,000 (incl ε3,500 conscripts)

4 Mil Zone HQ • 3 armd bn • 6 inf bn • 1 cdo/AB bn • 1 arty bn • 1 engr bn • 1 Presidential Guard (horsed) • 3 construction coy

EQUIPMENT

RECCE 10 M-8, 4 M-20, 30 AML-60, 27 AML-90
APC some 16 Panhard M-3, 12 M-3 half-track
TOWED ARTY 75mm: 6 M-116 pack; **105mm**: 6 M-101/HM-2; **155mm**: ε6 Fr Model-50
MOR 81mm: 8 Brandt; **120mm**: 8 Brandt
ATGW 4 *Milan*
RL 89mm: 31 LRAC
AD GUNS 20mm: 21 M-693; **40mm**: 12 L/60

Navy 600

BASES Dakar, Casamance

PATROL AND COASTAL COMBATANTS 10

PATROL, COASTAL 5
1 *Fouta* (Dk *Osprey*) PCC
1 *Njambuur* (Fr SFCN 59m) PCC
3 *Saint Louis* (Fr 48m) PCC

PATROL, INSHORE 5
3 *Senegal* II PFI<, 2 *Alioune Samb* PCI<

AMPHIBIOUS craft only
2 *Edic* 700 LCT

Air Force 800

8 cbt ac, no armed hel
MR/SAR 1 EMB-111
TPT 1 sqn with 6 F-27-400M, 1 Boeing 727-200 (VIP), 1 DHC-6 *Twin Otter*
HEL 2 SA-318C, 2 SA-330, 1 SA-341H
TRG 4* CM-170, 4* R-235 *Guerrier*, 2 *Rallye* 160, 2 R-235A

Forces Abroad

UN AND PEACEKEEPING

DROC (MONUC): 495 incl 16 obs **IRAQ/KUWAIT** (UNIKOM): 6 obs

Paramilitary ε5,800

GENDARMERIE ε5,800
12 VXB-170 APC

CUSTOMS
2 PCI<, boats

Opposition

MOUVEMENT DES FORCES DÉMOCRATIQUES DE CASAMANCE (MFDC) 2–3,000 lt wpns only

Foreign Forces

FRANCE 1,150: 1 mne inf coy, 1 ERC-90 recce sqn **ac** 1 *Atlantic*, 1 C-160 **hel** 1 AS-555

Seychelles Sey

Total Armed Forces

ACTIVE 450 (all services, incl Coast Guard, form part of the Army)

Army 200

1 inf coy
1 sy unit

EQUIPMENT†

RECCE 6 BRDM-2
MOR 82mm: 6 M-43
RL RPG-7
AD GUNS 14.5mm: ZPU-2/-4; **37mm**: M-1939
SAM 10 SA-7

Paramilitary

NATIONAL GUARD 250

COAST GUARD (200)
(incl ε80 Marines)
BASE Port Victoria
PATROL, COASTAL/INSHORE 5
1 *Andromache* (It *Pichiotti* 42m) PCC, 1 *Zhuk* PCI<, 3 PCI<
plus 1 *Cinq Juin* LCT (govt owned but civilian op)

AIR WING (20)

No cbt ac, no armed hel

MR 1 BN-2 *Defender*

TPT 1 Reims-Cessna F-406/*Caravan* 11

TRG 1 Cessna 152

Sierra Leone SL

Total Armed Forces

ACTIVE ε13–14,000

The process of disarming the various factions was completed in January 2002, with over 45,000 combatants registering. A new, UK-trained, national army has formed, which has an initial strength of 13–14,000

EQUIPMENT

MOR 81mm: ε27; **82mm**: 2; **120mm**: 2

RCL 84mm: *Carl Gustav*

AD GUNS 12.7mm: 4; **14.5mm**: 3

HEL 1 Mi-24, 2† Mi-8/17 (contract flown and maintained)

Navy† ε200

BASE Freetown

PATROL AND COASTAL COMBATANTS 5

1 PRC *Shanghai* II PFI<, 1 *Swiftships* 32m† PFI<, 1 *Fairy Marine Tracker* II (all non-op)<, 2 PCI<

Foreign Forces

UK 100

UN (UNAMSIL): 258 obs and 17,017 tps from 32 countries

Somali Republic SR

Total Armed Forces

ACTIVE Nil

Following the 1991 revolution, national armed forces have yet to be formed. A Transitional National Government (TNG) has however formed with an estimated 5,000 tps but only controls northern Mogadishu. The Somali National Movement has declared northern Somalia the independent 'Republic of Somaliland', and the northeast has seen the self-proclaimed regional administration in Puntland remain autonomous, while various groups compete for local supremacy in the south. Hy mil eqpt is in poor repair or inoperable.

Clan/Movement Groupings

'SOMALILAND' (northern Somalia) Total armed forces reported to be some 7,000 in 4 'div' with 60,000 reserves

Equipment incl 20 MBT, 4 APC, 20 arty, 120 mor (81mm/120mm)

UNITED SOMALI FRONT str n.k. **clan** Issa **leader** Abdurahman Dualeh Ali

SOMALI DEMOCRATIC ALLIANCE str n.k. **clan** Gadabursi

SOMALI NATIONAL MOVEMENT 5–6,000 **clan** Issaq, 3 factions (Tur, Dhegaweyne, Kahin)

UNITED SOMALI PARTY ε75–120 **loc** South Mogadishu **clan** Midigan/Tumaal **leader** Ahmed Guure Adan

SOMALIA

SOMALI SALVATION DEMOCRATIC FRONT 3,000 **clan** Darod **leader** Abdullah Yusuf Ahmed

UNITED SOMALI CONGRESS str n.k. **clan** Hawiye **sub-clan** Habr Gidir **leaders** Hussein Mohammed Aideed/Osman Atto

ALI MAHDI FACTION 10,000(-) **clan** Abgal **leader** Mohammed Ali Mahdi

AL ITIHAAD AL ISLAMIYA ε1,500 **loc** northern 'Puntland' and far south of Somalia

SOMALI NATIONAL FRONT 2–3,000 **clan** Darod sub-clan Marehan **leader** General Omar Hagi Mohammed Hersi

SOMALI DEMOCRATIC MOVEMENT str n.k. **clan** Rahenwein/Dighil

SOMALI PATRIOTIC MOVEMENT ε450 **clan** Darod **leader** Ahmed Omar Jess

'PUNTLAND' (northeastern Somalia)

Two groups reported: Abdullahi Yusuf str ε700–1,000; Jama Ali Jama str ε750

MARITIME SECURITY FORCE (70 civilians, based at Bosaso under Puntland govt control)

1 PCO for fisheries protection

South Africa RSA

Total Armed Forces

ACTIVE 60,000

SOUTH AFRICAN NATIONAL DEFENCE FORCE (SANDF) (incl 5,500 South African Military Health Service (SAMHS); 8,681 women; excluding 16,716 civilian employees)

Terms of service voluntary service in 4 categories (full

career, up to 10 yrs, up to 6 yrs, 1 yr voluntary military service)
Racial breakdown 37,637 black, 15,191 white, 6,331 coloured, 849 Asian

RESERVES 73,438

Regular: 17,104: **Army**: 14,615 **Navy** 1,330 **Air Force** 434 (SAMHS) 725
Territorial: **Army** 56,334

Army 40,250

(incl women)

PERMANENT FORCE

Formations under direct comd and control of SANDF Chief of Joint Operations:
5 regional joint task forces (each consists of HQ, tps are provided when necessary by permanent and reserve force units from all services)
1 SF bde (2 bn)
8 'type' formations plus 2 bde HQ
Summary of combat arm units:
1 tk, 1 armd car bn
16 inf bn (incl 2 mech, 3 mot, 10 lt inf, 1 AB)
2 SF, 2 arty (incl 1 AD), 3 engr bn

RESERVE FORCE

Regular: cadre units comprising 8 armd, 28 inf (incl 1 AB), 7 arty, 5 AD, 4 engr bn
Territorial: some 183 'cdo' (bn) home defence units

EQUIPMENT

MBT some 168 *Olifant* 1A/-B (125 in store)
RECCE 242 *Rooikat-76* (94 in store)
AIFV 1,200 *Ratel* Mk III-20/-60/-90 (666 in store)
APC 429 *Casspir*, 538 *Mamba*
TOWED ARTY 140mm: 75 G-2 (in store); **155mm**: 72 G-5 (51 in store)
SP ARTY 155mm: 43 G-6 (31 in store)
MRL 127mm: 25 *Bataleur* (40 tube) (4 in store), 26 *Valkiri* (24 tube) (in store)
MOR 81mm: 1,190 (incl some SP); **120mm**: 36
ATGW 52 ZT-3 *Swift* (36 in store)
RL 92mm: FT-5
RCL 106mm: 100 M-40A1 (some SP)
AD GUNS 23mm: 36 *Zumlac* (ZU-23-2) SP; **35mm**: 40 GDF
SURV *Green Archer* (mor), *Cymbeline* (mor)
UAV some *Vulture*

Navy 5,000

(incl 560 women)
FLOTILLAS SS, strike, MCM
BASES Simon's Town (HQ), Durban (Salisbury Island)

SUBMARINES 2

SSK 2 *Spear* (Mod Fr *Daphné*) with 550mm TT

PATROL AND COASTAL COMBATANTS 7

MISSILE CRAFT 4 *Warrior* (Il *Reshef*) PFM with 6 *Skerpioen* (Il *Gabriel*) SSM
PATROL, INSHORE 3 T craft PCI<

MINE WARFARE 6

MINE COUNTERMEASURES 6
4 *River* (Ge *Navors*) MHC (incl 2 in refit)
2 *City* (Ge *Lindau*) MSC (plus 2 in reserve)

SUPPORT AND MISCELLANEOUS 36

1 *Drakensberg* AO with 2 hel and extempore amph capability (perhaps 60 tps and 2 small LCU)
1 *Outeniqua* AO with similar capability to *Drakensberg*
1 diving spt
3 AT
28 harbour patrol PCI<
1 AGHS (UK *Hecla*)
1 Antarctic tpt with 2 hel (operated by private co for Ministry of Environment)
plus craft: 8 LCU

Air Force 9,250

(incl 1,350 women); 85 cbt ac, ε8 attack and several extempore armed hel
Air Force office, Pretoria, and 4 op gps
FTR/FGA 2 sqn
1 sqn with 28 *Cheetah* C, 10 *Cheetah* D
1 sqn with 26 *Impala* Mk2, 21 *Impala* Mk1
TPT/TKR/EW 1 sqn with 5 Boeing 707-320 (EW/tkr)
TPT 5 sqn
1 with 3 *King Air* 200, 1 *King Air* 300, 13 Cessna-208 *Caravan*, 1 PC-12
1 (VIP) with 2 *Citation* II, 2 *Falcon* 50, 1 *Falcon* 900, 1 Boeing Business Jet
1 with 11 C-47 TP (5 maritime, 4 tpt, 1 PR, 1 EW trg)
1 with 12 C-130
1 with 4 CASA-212, 1 CASA-235, 11 Cessna 185
HEL 1 cbt spt sqn with 8* *Rooivalk*, 4 tpt, 1 flying school with 44 *Oryx*, 10 BK-117, 24 SA-316/319
TRG 1 flying school with 53 PC-7
UAV 3 *Seeker* with 1 control station

MISSILES

ASM *Raptor*, ZT-3, *Mokopa* ZT-6, *Mupsow*
AAM V-3C, V4
SAM *Cactus* (*Crotale*), SAHV3 limited operational

GROUND DEFENCE

RADAR 2 Air Control Sectors (Hoedspruit and Bushveld), 3 fixed and 6 mob radars (2 long-range – Ellisras and Mariepskop – and 4 tactical)
SAAF Regt: 12 security sqn

South African Military Health Service (SAMHS) 5,500

(incl ε2,700 women); a separate service within the SANDF; 3 Type, 1 spt, 1 trg formation

Forces Abroad

BURUNDI ε650: 1 inf bn

UN AND PEACEKEEPING

DROC (MONUC): 145 incl 1 obs **ETHIOPIA/ ERITREA** (UNMEE): 7 incl 5 obs

Sudan Sdn

Total Armed Forces

ACTIVE ε117,000

(incl ε20,000 conscripts)

Terms of service conscription (males 18–30), 2 years

Army ε112,500

(incl ε20,000 conscripts)

1 armd div • 1 mech inf div • 6 inf div • 1 AB div • 1 engr div • 1 border gd bde • 8 indep inf bde (incl 1 mech) • 5 SF coy

EQUIPMENT

MBT 200 T-54/-55

LT TK 100 PRC Type-62

RECCE 6 AML-90, 30 *Saladin*, 80 *Ferret*, 60 BRDM-1/-2, 42 HMMWV

AIFV 30 BMP-1/-2

APC 90 BTR-50/-152, 42 OT-62/-64, 42 M-113, 19 V-100/-150, 120 *Walid*

TOWED ARTY 450 incl: **85mm**: D-44; **105mm**: M-101; **122mm**: D-74, M-30, Type-54/D-30; **130mm**: M-46/PRC Type 59-1

SP ARTY 155mm: ε10 M-114A1, F-3

MRL 600: **107mm**: Type-63; **122mm**: BM-21, Type-81

MOR 81mm; **82mm**; **120mm**: M-43, AM-49

ATGW 4 *Swingfire*

RL 73mm: RPG-7

RCL 106mm: 40 M-40A1

ATK GUNS 40 incl: **76mm**: M-1942; **100mm**: M-1944

AD GUNS 1,000+ incl: **14.5mm**: ZPU-2/-4; **23mm**: ZU-23-2; **37mm**: M-1939/Type-63, Type-55; **57mm**: S-60, Type-59; **85mm**: M-1944

SAM 54 SA-7

SURV RASIT (veh, arty)

Navy ε1,500

BASES Port Sudan (HQ), Flamingo Bay (Red Sea), Khartoum (Nile)

PATROL AND COASTAL COMBATANTS 6

PATROL, INSHORE 2 *Kadir* PCI<

PATROL, RIVERINE 4 PCR<, about 12 armed boats

AMPHIBIOUS craft only

some 2 *Sobat* (FRY DTK-221) LCT (used for transporting stores)

Air Force 3,000

(incl Air Defence); ε42† cbt ac, 10 armed hel

FGA 6 F-5 (7 -E, 2 -F), 7 PRC J-6 (MiG-19) (GA/adv trg), 20 F-7 (MiG-21), 6 MiG-23, first of 12 MiG-29 delivered

BBR 3 An-24 modified as bombers

TPT 1 C-130H, 4 DHC-5D, 2 F-27, 3 *Falcon* 20/50

HEL 8 AB-212, 8 IAR/SA-330, 11 (1 op) Mi-8, 10* Mi-24V

TRG 6 PT-6A

AD 5 bty SA-2 SAM (18 launchers)

Forces Abroad

CAR (reported)

Paramilitary 7,000

POPULAR DEFENCE FORCE 7,000 active

85,000 reserve; mil wg of National Islamic Front; org in bn of 1,000 (to be disbanded – loyalty in doubt)

Opposition

NATIONAL DEMOCRATIC ALLIANCE

coalition of many gp, of which the main forces are:

SUDANESE PEOPLE'S LIBERATION ARMY (SPLA) 20–30,000

four factions, each org in bn, operating mainly in southern Sdn; some captured T-54/-55 tks, BM-21 MRL and arty pieces, but mainly small arms plus **60mm** and **120mm** mor, **14.5mm** AA, SA-7 SAM

SUDAN ALLIANCE FORCES ε500

based in Er, operate in border area

BEJA CONGRESS FORCES ε500

operates on Er border (composed mainly of ε250–300 'White Lion Fighters')

NEW SUDAN BRIGADE ε2,000

operates on Er border only

Tanzania Tz

Total Armed Forces

ACTIVE ε27,000

Terms of service incl civil duties, 2 years

RESERVES 80,000

Army ε23,000

5 inf bde • 1 tk bde • 6 arty bn • 2 AD arty bn • 2 mor bn • 2 ATK bn • 1 engr regt (bn)

EQUIPMENT†

- **MBT** 15 PRC Type-59, 30 T-54/-55
- **LT TK** 25 PRC Type-62, 30 *Scorpion*
- **RECCE** 10 BRDM-2
- **APC** ε10 BTR-40/-152, ε25 PRC Type-56
- **TOWED ARTY 76mm**: ε40 ZIS-3; **85mm**: 75 PRC Type-56; **122mm**: 20 D-30, 80 PRC Type-54-1; **130mm**: 30 PRC Type-59-1
- **MRL 122mm**: 58 BM-21
- **MOR 82mm**: 100 M-43; **120mm**: 50 M-43
- **RL 73mm**: RPG-7
- **RCL 75mm**: PRC Type-52

Navy† ε1,000

BASES Dar es Salaam, Zanzibar, Mwanza (Lake Victoria)

PATROL AND COASTAL COMBATANTS 6

TORPEDO CRAFT 2 PRC *Huchuan* PHT< with 2 533mm TT

PATROL, COASTAL 4

- 2 PRC *Shanghai* II PFC
- 2 Vosper Thornycroft PCC

AMPHIBIOUS craft only

- 2 *Yunnan* LCU

Air Defence Command 3,000

(incl ε2,000 AD tps); 19 cbt act, no armed hel

Virtually no air defence assets serviceable

FTR 3 sqn with 3 PRC J-5 (MiG-17), 10 J-6 (MiG-19), 6 J-7 (MiG-21)

TPT 1 sqn with 3 DHC-5D, 1 PRC Y-5, 2 Y-12(II), 3 HS-748, 2 F-28, 1 HS-125-700

HEL 4 AB-205

LIAISON ac 5 Cessna 310, 2 Cessna 404, 1 Cessna 206 **hel** 6 Bell 206B

TRG 2 MiG-15UTI, 5 PA-28

AD GUNS 14.5mm: 40† ZPU-2/-4; **23mm**: 40 ZU-23; **37mm**: 120 PRC Type-55

SAM† 20 SA-3, 20 SA-6, 120 SA-7

Forces Abroad

UN AND PEACEKEEPING

ETHIOPIA/ERITREA (UNMEE): 11 incl 8 obs

SIERRA LEONE (UNAMSIL): 12 obs

Paramilitary 1,400 active

POLICE FIELD FORCE 1,400

18 sub-units incl Police Marine Unit

- **MARINE UNIT** (100)
  - boats only
- **AIR WING**
  - **ac** 1 Cessna U-206 **hel** 2 AB-206A, 2 Bell 206L, 2 Bell 47G

Togo Tg

Total Armed Forces

ACTIVE some 9,450

Terms of service conscription, 2 years (selective)

Army some 9,000

2 inf regt

- 1 with 1 mech bn, 1 mot bn
- 1 with 2 armd sqn, 3 inf coy; spt units (trg)

1 Presidential Guard regt: 2 bn (1 cdo), 2 coy

1 para cdo regt: 3 coy

1 spt regt: 1 fd arty, 2 AD arty bty; 1 log/tpt/engr bn

EQUIPMENT

- **MBT** 2 T-54/-55
- **LT TK** 9 *Scorpion*
- **RECCE** 6 M-8, 3 M-20, 10 AML (3 -60, 7 -90), 36 EE-9 *Cascavel*, 2 VBL
- **AIFV** 20 BMP-2
- **APC** 4 M-3A1 half-track, 30 UR-416
- **TOWED ARTY 105mm**: 4 HM-2
- **SP ARTY 122mm**: 6
- **MOR 82mm**: 20 M-43
- **RCL 57mm**: 5 ZIS-2; **75mm**: 12 PRC Type-52/-56; **82mm**: 10 PRC Type-65
- **AD GUNS 14.5mm**: 38 ZPU-4; **37mm**: 5 M-39

Navy ε200

(incl Marine Infantry unit)

BASE Lomé

PATROL AND COASTAL COMBATANTS 2

PATROL, COASTAL 2

- 2 *Kara* (Fr *Esterel*) PFC

Air Force †250

16 cbt ac, no armed hel
FGA 5 *Alpha Jet*, 4 EMB-326G
TPT 2 *Baron*, 2 DHC-5D, 1 Do-27, 1 F-28-1000 (VIP), 1 Boeing 707 (VIP), 2 Reims-Cessna 337
HEL 1 AS-332, 2 SA-315, 1 SA-319, 1 SA-330
TRG 4* CM-170, 3* TB-30

Paramilitary 750

GENDARMERIE (Ministry of Interior) 750
1 trg school, 2 reg sections, 1 mob sqn

Uganda Uga

Total Armed Forces

ACTIVE ε50–60,000

Ugandan People's Defence Force ε50–60,000

4 div (each with 5 bde), 1 armd bde, 1 arty bde

EQUIPMENT†
- **MBT** ε140 T-54/-55
- **LT TK** ε20 PT-76
- **RECCE** 40 *Eland*, 60 *Ferret* (reported)
- **APC** 20 BTR-60, 4 OT-64 SKOT, 20 *Mamba*, 20 *Buffel*
- **TOWED ARTY** 225 incl: **76mm**: M-1942; **122mm**: M-1938; **130mm**; **155mm**: 4 G5
- **MRL 122mm**: BM-21
- **MOR 81mm**: L 16; **82mm**: M-43; **120mm**: 60 Soltam
- **AD GUNS 14.5mm**: ZPU-1/-2/-4; **37mm**: 20 M-1939
- **SAM** 200 SA-7

AIR WING
- **AVN** 16 cbt ac†, 2 armed hel
- **FGA** some 6 MiG-19, 6 MiG-21
- **TRG** 3†* L-39, 1 SF*-260 (non-op)
- **ARMED HEL** 2 Mi-24
- **TPT HEL** 3 Bell 206, 2 Bell 412, 4 Mi-17, 1 Mi-172 (VIP) (only 3 Mi-17, 1 Mi-24 op)

Forces Abroad

DROC: some 3,000

Paramilitary ε1,800 active

BORDER DEFENCE UNIT ε600
small arms

POLICE AIR WING ε800
hel 1 *JetRanger*

MARINES ε400
8 riverine patrol craft<, plus boats

LOCAL DEFENCE UNITS ε15,000

Opposition

LORD'S RESISTANCE ARMY ε1,500
(ε200 in Uga, remainder in Sdn)

ALLIED DEMOCRATIC FRONT ε200

Zambia Z

Total Armed Forces

ACTIVE 21,600

Army 20,000

(incl 3,000 reserves)
3 bde HQ • 1 arty regt (2 fd, 1 MRL bn) • 9 inf bn (3 reserve) • 1 engr regt • 1 armd regt (incl 1 tank, 1 armd recce bn)

EQUIPMENT†
- **MBT** 10 T-55, 20 PRC Type-59
- **LT TK** 30 PT-76
- **RECCE** 70 BRDM-1/-2 (ε30 serviceable)
- **APC** 13 BTR-60
- **TOWED ARTY 76mm**: 35 M-1942; **105mm**: 18 Model 56 pack; **122mm**: 25 D-30; **130mm**: 18 M-46
- **MRL 122mm**: 50 BM-21 (ε12 serviceable)
- **MOR 81mm**: 55; **82mm**: 24; **120mm**: 12
- **ATGW** AT-3 *Sagger*
- **RL 73mm**: RPG-7
- **RCL 57mm**: 12 M-18; **75mm**: M-20; **84mm**: *Carl Gustav*
- **AD GUNS 20mm**: 50 M-55 triple; **37mm**: 40 M-1939; **57mm**: ε30 S-60; **85mm**: 16 KS-12
- **SAM** SA-7

Air Force 1,600

63† cbt ac, some armed hel. Very low serviceability.
FGA 1 sqn with 12 F-6 (MiG-19)†, 1 sqn with 12 MiG-21 MF† (8 undergoing refurbishment)
TPT 1 sqn with 4 An-26, 4 C-47, 4 DHC-5D, 4 Y-12(II)
VIP 1 fleet with 1 HS-748, 2 Yak-40
LIAISON 5 Do-28
TRG 2*F-5T, 2* MiG-21U†, 12* *Galeb* G-2, 15* MB-326GB, 8* SF-260MZ, 8 K-8

HEL 1 sqn with 4 AB-205A, 5 AB-212, 12 Mi-8
LIAISON HEL 12 AB-47G
MISSILES
ASM AT-3 *Sagger*
SAM 1 bn; 3 bty: SA-3 *Goa*

Forces Abroad

UN AND PEACEKEEPING

DROC (MONUC): 14 incl 10 obs **ETHIOPIA/ ERITREA** (UNMEE): 14 incl 10 obs **SIERRA LEONE** (UNAMSIL): 833 incl 10 obs

Paramilitary 1,400

POLICE MOBILE UNIT (PMU) 700

1 bn of 4 coy

POLICE PARAMILITARY UNIT (PPMU) 700

1 bn of 3 coy

Zimbabwe Zw

Total Armed Forces

ACTIVE ε36,000

Army ε32,000

5 inf bde HQ, 1 mech bde HQ and Presidential Guard gp • 1 arty bde • 1 armd sqn • 21 inf bn (incl 3 guard, 1 mech, 1 cdo, 1 para) • 1 fd arty regt • 1 AD regt • 2 engr regt

EQUIPMENT
MBT 30 PRC Type-59, 10 PRC Type-69
RECCE 80 EE-9 *Cascavel* (**90mm** gun)
APC 30 PRC Type-63 (YW-531), UR-416, 50 ACMAT
TOWED ARTY 122mm: 18 PRC Type-60, 12 PRC Type-54
MRL 107mm: 18 PRC Type-63; **122mm**: 52 RM-70
MOR 81mm/82mm 502; **120mm**: 14 M-43
AD GUNS 215 incl **14.5mm**: ZPU-1/-2/-4; **23mm**: ZU-23; **37mm**: M-1939
SAM 17 SA-7

Air Force 4,000

54 cbt ac, 32 armed hel
Flying hours 100
FGA 2 sqn
1 with 11 *Hunters* (9 FGA-90, 1 -F80, 1 T-81) (in store)
1 with 5 *Hawk* Mk 60/60A (0 serviceable)
FTR 1 sqn with 11 PRC F-7 (MiG-21) (6 serviceable)
RECCE 1 sqn with 14* Reims-Cessna 337 *Lynx*
TRG/RECCE/LIAISON 1 sqn with 22 SF-260 *Genet* (9 -C, 6* -F, 5* -W, 2* TP)
TPT 1 sqn with 6 BN-2, 8 C-212-200 (1 VIP), some An-12
HEL 1 sqn with 24 SA-319, 6 Mi-35/2 Mi-35P (armed/ liaison), 1 sqn with 8 AB-412, 2 AS-532UL (VIP)

Forces Abroad

DROC: up to 8,500

Paramilitary 21,800

ZIMBABWE REPUBLIC POLICE FORCE 19,500 (incl Air Wg)

POLICE SUPPORT UNIT 2,300

Table 2 **Selected Military High Readiness Forces**

The aim of this table is to give an indication of certain countries' and international organisations' military forces that are held, or which are in development to be, at a readiness of 60 days or less to deploy for operations outside their home territory. It does not include forces held at high readiness in order to respond solely for internal operations; or special forces or pre-deployed/forward-deployed forces. As times for deployment to any actual theatre of operations is dependent on a number of varying factors (e.g. location of operation, nature of operation, availability of overseas bases, political urgency of the mission) no time is given for readiness to deploy in theatre. However, transport assets where known are stated, in order to give some indication of the speed at which the military high readiness force could be deployed from its normal location. The table forms part of a larger database on high readiness forces which is currently in development by the IISS.

Definitions

Manpower/Title The manpower figure is the total number of troops in the ground component of the military high readiness force. Generally this number is treated as a pool from which a tailor-made force can be deployed for a specific operation. Where the ground component has a specific title, it is stated.

Readiness The period of notice at which the ground component of the military high readiness force (personnel and equipment) is held to be fully ready to deploy from its normal location.

Other Commitments Details of commitments by the ground forces to other high readiness forces.

Naval/Air Component The number of naval and air force assets known to be held at specific readiness to deploy from their normal location. Does not include naval and air tpt assets.

Major Tpt Assets In the case of country entries, means the total number of major sealift and airlift assets in the country's military inventory and on extended charter to its def/tpt department; these assets are not necessarily held at a specific readiness. In the case of IOs, means total number of sealift and airlift assets committed to its 'military high readiness force' by its members and held at a specific readiness. Neither include amphibious ships. For transport assets' capacity, cf Military Airlift and Sealift table in *The Military Balance 2001–2002*.

Abbreviations

AMF (A) Allied Mobile Force (Air) **AMF (L)** Allied Mobile Force (Land) **ARRC** Allied Rapid Reaction Force **CRDF** CIS Rapid Deployment Force **CVF** Canadian Forces Vanguard **FAR** Fuerza de Accion Rapida **IO** International Organisation **IRF** Immediate Reaction Forces **JRRF** Joint Rapid Reaction Force **MCMFM** Mine Countermeasures Force Mediterranean **MCMFN** Mine Countermeasures Force North **PSC** Principal Surface Combatant **SHIRBRIG** UN Standing High Readiness Bde **SNFL** Standing Naval Force Atlantic **SNFM** Standing Naval Force Mediterranean

The **United States'** military is undergoing a period of transformation, and as part of this is developing high readiness forces for fast deployment outside the CONUS. At present, much of the US' high readiness capability is provided by routinely forward-deployed forces, particularly from the Navy, and also by the Marine Corps; details on both of which are to be found in the US section p.16. However, the US Air Force is constituting ten deployable Aerospace Expeditionary Forces (AEFs), each of which provides a pool of mixed aircraft from which a force packaged for a particular mission can be deployed from CONUS:

	Proposed deployment times		
Air Force	**24 hours** 2 Air Expeditionary Wings, each typically with a total of ε100 ac incl ε60 ftr/SEAD ac (F15/F16),ε16 bbr (B-1B) and ε20 tpt/tkr ac (C-130/KC-130)	**48 hours** 1 AEF with typically with a total of ε200 ac incl ε120 ftr/SEAD ac (F15/F16), ε16 bbr (B-1B), ε15 tpt ac (C-130), ε40 tkr ac (KC-135)	**15 days** 5 AEF

As outlined in the 2001 QDR and in associated army doctrine papers, the US Army is transforming some of its forces into flexible, high readiness deployable units. Proposed future deployment capabilities are:

	Proposed times for deployment *in theatre*		
Army	**96 hours** 1 Initial Bde Cbt Team (IBCT) of 3,700 tps; typically will be composed of 3 mech inf bn and 1 recce/int/surv/target acquisition sqn. 1 IBCT believed to be op; between 4 and 7 more to be formed if first successful	**120 hours** 1 div	**30 days** 5 div

Ground Component Manpower/Title	Units	Readiness	Other Commitments	**Naval/Air Component**	**Major Tpt Assets**
Aus					
ε3, 000 **3 Bde**	1 lt inf bde	15–30 days	Nil	Nil	24 ac (12 C-130H, 12 C-130J)
By 2010, plans to have 3 bde at readiness of 90 days or less					
Ca CVF					
2,350	1 mech bg and 1 inf bg	21 days	Mech bg earmarked for SHIRBRIG at readiness of 30 days; CVF may also be earmarked for NATO ops	2 ships: 2 PSC (2 DD/FF); ε12 ac (12 F-16)	32 ac (32 C-130 E/H)
CIS					
ε13,000 **CRDF**		n.k.	Nil	n.k. Kant Airbase for air mounting	n.k., but RF has numerous tpt ac
Contributing states are: Kaz, Kgz, Tjk, RF					
Da					
ε2,000 **Da Reaction Bde**	1 inf bde	'High'	All earmarked to ARRC, also available for UN and OSCE ops	1 or 2 ships (1 PSC or 2 PC); 16 ac (12 ftr, 4 recce)	3 ac (3 C-130H)
Forces in dev; aim to achieve op capability by 2010					
EU					
78,890 plus 11,050 offered from non-EU European states	**A** 2,000; **Be** 1,000 (plus 3,000 for 6 mths max); **SF** 2,000; **Fr** 12,000; **Ge** 18,000; **Gr** 3,500; **Irl** 850; **It** 12,500 (plus a further 2,500 for 4 mths max); **Lu** 100; **Nl** 5,000; **Por** 2,000; **Sp** 6,000; **Swe** 1,440; **UK** 12,500)	60 days	Most of the forces committed to it are also earmarked for ARRC/SHIRBRIG/national high readiness forces	100 ships incl: 7 SS (3 SSN, 4 SSK); 23 PSC (4 CVS [1 for 6 mths max], 17 DDG/FFG, 2 FSG); 5 PC (5 POC); 15 MW (2 MCCS, 13 MHC); 10 amph (1 for 6 mths max); 2 misc (1 AGOR, 1 AGHS); 18 spt. 400 ac incl: 336 cbt ac, 24 spt ac, 9 EW ac, 3 MPA	ε2 ships (2 AK); 161 ac (type n.k.)
Force not yet fully op. Due to be declared 'fully op' in 2003					
Gr					
ε16,000 **'B Corps'**	1 mech inf div, 1 army avn bde	'High'	Mech inf div is earmarked to ARRC	Nil	15 ac (10 C-130H, 5 C-130B)
NATO IRF					
5,000 **'AMF(L)'** To be dissolved in October 2002	n.k., but tps come from 14 different NATO members who generally contribute 1 bn or 1 coy	3–7 days		28 ships divided into 4 regional/type comds: SNFL (ε8 DD/FF), SNFM (ε8 DD/FF), MCMFN (ε6 MCMV), MCMFORMED (ε6 MCMV); AMF (A) has considerable forces, but detailed composition n.k.	n.k.

Table 2 **Page 3 of 3**

Ground Component Manpower/Title	Units	Readiness	Other Commitments	Naval/Air Component	Major Tpt Assets
NATO RRF					
ε160,000 cbt tps plus additional cbt service spt tps 'ARRC'	10 cbt div provided from: **Be** 1 para bde; **Cz** 1 inf bde; **Da** 1 inf bde; **Ge** 1 armd div, 1 airborne bde; **Gr** 1 mech inf div incl 1 PL bde; **Hu** 1 mech inf bde; **It** 1 mech div, 1 inf bde; **Nl** 1 airmobile bde; **Pl** 1 inf bde; **Por** 1 para bde; **Sp** 1 lt inf div; **Tu** 1 mech inf div; **UK** 1 armd div, 1 mech inf div, 1 airmobile bde; **US** 1 armd div	7–15 days	All ARRC's assigned divs are national assets, allocated on request to NATO by national governments for specific ops	Very substantial numbers of both ships and ac earmarked by members to NATO's RRF; precise details n.k.	n.k.
Nl					
4,600	1 airmobile bde	ε7–15 days	Earmarked for ARRC and in part to EU	n.k.	2 ac (2 C-130H)
NZ					
600–800	1 mech inf bn	ε60 days (1 coy at higher readiness of 30 days)	Earmarked for SHIRBRIG	Nil	5 ac (5 C-130H)
SF					
1,500 1 bn not yet fully op	2 inf bn	15-30 days	Both bn are earmarked for EU and SHIRBRIG	Nil	Nil major
Sp					
10,000 FAR	1 div, 1 AB, 1 airmob, 1 lt inf bde	5–15 days	All earmarked to ARRC; elements may also be earmarked for the EU	Nil	7 ac (C-130-H)
UK JRRF					
ε20,000 Substantial part of naval/air component also earmarked for EU	4 inf bde: 1 cdo bde, 1 mech bde, 1 armd bde, 1 airmobile bde	ε1/3 at 'very high' readiness (ε10 days), 2/3 at 'high' readiness (ε20–30 days)	Mech bde, armd bde and airmobile bde all earmarked for ARRC; may also be earmarked for EU	42 ships (ε13 PSC, ε4 SSN, ε3 amph, ε8 MW, ε14 spt); 270 ac (110 cbt, 160 other)	2 ships (2 AK); 55 ac (4 C-17A, 50 C-130)

Table 3 Operational Offensive Nuclear Delivery Systems

Systems with dedicated crews and targeting mechanisms in place. Excludes strategic defence forces. Missile range varies with payload-to-fuel ratio and firing direction. Aircraft range can be extended with in-flight fuelling.

Name/ designation	aka	Warhead ⇩	Range (km)
Land Ballistic Missiles			
US			
LGM-30G	*Minuteman* III	▲	13,000
LGM-118	MX/*Peacekeeper*	▲	9,600
RF			
SS-18	*Satan*	▲	15,000
SS-19	*Stiletto*	▲	10,000
SS-24	*Scalpel*	▲	10,000
SS-25	*Sickle*	●	10,000
SS-27	*Topol*-M	●	10,500
PRC			
CSS-2	DF-3A	●	2,800
CSS-3	DF-4	●	4,750
CSS-4	DF-5A	●▲	13,000
CSS-5	DF-21	●	2,150
CSS-5	DF-21A	●	2,500
CSS-6	DF-15/M-9	●	600
CSS-7	DF-11/M-11	●	300
CSS-9	DF-31	●▲	8,000
Pak			
Ghauri 1	*Hatf* 5	●	1,500
Il			
Jericho 1		●	500
Jericho 2		●	1,800
SLBM			
US			
UGM-96	*Trident* I C-4	▲	7,400
UGM-133	*Trident* II D-5	▲	12,000
UK			
UGM-135	*Trident* II D-5	▲	12,000
RF			
SS-N-8	*Sawfly*	▲	9,100
SS-N-18	*Stingray*	▲	6,500
SS-N-20	*Sturgeon*	▲	8,300
SS-N-23	*Skiff*	▲	8,300
Fr			
M-4		▲	4,000
M-45		▲	4,000
PRC			
CSS-N-3	JL-1	●	2,150
Aircraft			
US			
B-52H	*Stratofortress*	◆	16,000
B-2	*Spirit*	■	12,200
F-15E	*Strike Eagle*	■	2,500
F-16A/B/C/D	*Fighting Falcon*	■	2,500
F-117A	*Nighthawk*	■	2,100
RF			
Tu-95M	*Bear*	◆■	12,000
Tu-160	*Backfire*	◆■	4,000
Tu-22M-3	*Backfire*	▼	4,800
Su-24M	*Fencer*	■	2,100
Fr			
Super Etendard		◆	650
Mirage 2000N		◆	1,200
Rafale		◆	1,200
PRC			
H-6	Tu-16	■	5,000
Q-5	MiG-19	■	400
Il			
F-4E-2000	*Kurnass*	■	2,200
F-16A/B/C/D	*Fighting Falcon*	■	2,500
F-15I	*Thunder*	■	2,500
Ind			
Jaguar S(I)	*Shamsher*	■	1,600
MiG-27M	*Bahadur*	■	1,000
Mirage 2000H	*Vajra*	■	1,200
Pak			
F-16A/B	*Fighting Falcon*	■	2,500
Mirage 5		■	1,200
Q-5	MiG-19	■	1,200
DPRK			
H-5	Il-28	■	2,100
SLCM			
US			
Tomahawk	TLAM-N	●	2,500
RF			
SS-N-9	*Siren*	●	110
SS-N-12	*Sandbox*	●	550
SS-N-19	*Shipwreck*	●	550
SS-N-21	*Sampson*	●	2,400
SS-N-22	*Sunburn*	●	120
Il			
Turbo-Popeye 3		●	1,500
ALCM			
US			
AGM-86B		●	2,500
AGM-129		●	3,500
RF			
AS-4	Kh-22 *Kitchen*	●	310
AS-15A	KH-55 *Kent*	●	2,500
AS-15B	Kh-55SM *Kent*	●	3,000
AS-16	Kh-15 *Kickback*	●	150
Fr			
ASMP		●	250

Key ▲ MIRV ● Single ◆ ALCM ■ Bomb ▼ ASM

Table 4 **Operational Nuclear Warheads**

Operational warheads aligned to an in-service delivery system, excluding artillery shells and mini-nukes.

	Strategic					Sub-Strategic				
Country	**ICBM**	**IRBM**	**SLBM**	**Delivery System** ALCM/Bombs	**Strategic Total**	**SSM**	**Navy/ SLCM**	**Delivery System** Aircraft	**Sub-Strategic Total**	**Grand Total**
US	2,079		3,616	1,318	**7,013**		320	1,350	**1,670** (150 in Europe)	**8,683**
RF	3,324		1,384	898	**5,606**		660	1,730 (+ 1,200 air defence)	**3,590**	**9,196**
Fr			288	50	**338**			10	**10**	**348**
PRC	20	108	12	120	**260**	120		30	**150**	**410**
UK			185		**185**					**185**
Il						90+	Some	100	**200**	**200**
Ind						[1]		40+	**40+**	**40+**
Pak						Some [2]		40+	**40+**	**40+**
DPRK						[3]		±2	**±2**	**±2**

Strategic missiles with a range of over 5,000km, or air-launched from long-range aircraft.

ICBM intercontinental ballistic missile
IRBM intermediate-range ballistic missile
SLBM submarine-launched ballistic missile
ALCM air-launched cruise missile

SSM surface-to-surface missile
SLCM sea-launched cruise missile

Notes
[1] See page 125
[2] See page 126
[3] See page 140

Table 5 **Selected Military Satellites**

Currently in service, excludes scientific/technology demonstrators.

Country	Designation	Quantity	Role	Remarks
US				
	DSCS 3	10	Comms	
	Milstar	4	Comms	
	SDS	1	Data relay	
	UHF *Follow-On*	7	Comms	
	DSP	3	Early warning	
	GPS	32	Navigation	Nucl det syst on 24
	GFO	1	Ocean surv	
	KH-12	3	Recce/surv	
	EIS	1	Recce/surv	
	Mercury	1	Sigint	
	Trumpet	3	ELINT	EW adjunct
	Lacrosse/Onyx	2	Recce/surv	
	DMSP	3	Meteorology	
	Advanced/Orion	1	ELINT	
	New Sigint	2	Sigint	
	Wide-area surv *Follow-On*	1	Ocean surv	
RF				
	Geizer	1	Data relay	
	Globus/Raduga (Rainbow)	2	Imaging	
	Strela-3 (Arrow)	1	Comms	
	Oko (Eye)	4	Early warning	
	Tselina-2	1	ELINT	
	US-PU	1	Ocean surv	
	Kobalt	1	PR	
	Glonass	8	Navigation	
	Okean-1	1	Earth obs	
	Parus	3	Navigation	
	Cosmos 2344 (Araks)	1	Recce/surv	
	Cosmos 2392 (Araks)	1	Recce/surv	
NATO				
	NATO 4	1	Comms	
Israel				
	OFEQ-5	1	Recce/surv	
Italy				
	Sicral	1	Comms	
UK				
	***Skynet* 4**	3	Comms	
France				
	Helios	2	Recce/surv	

Table 6 Selected Non-State Armed Groups

Definition In this table, a 'non-state armed group' is an organised and armed opposition force with a recognised political goal, acting independently from state or government. Groups are only included if they have an effective command structure. The definition covers groups that might be variously described as guerrillas, militia forces, paramilitary or self-defence groups and also terrorist groups with political objectives that have caused significant damage and casualties over several years.

The table only includes non-state armed groups that are active or have recently been active and which represent, or have represented, a significant threat to states and governments. Groups operating in protracted conflicts where there is no internationally recognised government, such as in Afghanistan and Somalia, are excluded, as are armed groups with solely criminal objectives.

Notes

▲ Group known to carry out suicide attacks

[1] **A** active, **C** cease-fire, **D** dormant (inactive for the past 12 months)

[2] Distinct Kurdish gps

Origin	Organisation • aka	Established ⇩	Estimated Strength	Status[1] ⇩	Operates	Aims (Remarks)
NATO AND NON-NATO EUROPE						
Gr	**17 November Revolutionary Organisation**	1974	20+	**D**	Athens	Remove US bases from Gr; withdraw Tu tps from Cy; sever Gr ties to NATO and EU (Radical leftist)
FYROM	**National Liberation Army** (NLA)	2001	500–1,000	**C**	north FYROM	Protect ethnic Albanian rights
Mol	**Dniestr**		7,500	**D**	Dniestr	Separate state of Transdniestr
Sp	**Euskadi ta Askatasuna** (ETA)	1959	n.k.	**A**	Basque regions, Sp	Independent homeland on Marxist principles in Basque autonomous regions
Sp	**Grupa de Resistencia Anti-Fascista Primero de Octubre** (GRAPO)	1975	10	**D**	Sp	Seeks overthrow of Sp govt and a Marxist–Leninist regime in its place
Tu[3]	**Partiya Karkeren Kurdistan** (PKK) ▲	1978	4,000–5,000	**C**	Tu, Europe, Asia, M. East	Independent Kurdish state in southeast Tu (Marxist–Leninist; in 1999 'peace initiative' claimed halt to use of force)
Tu	**Revolutionary People's Liberation Party/Front** (DHKP/C) ▲	1978	n.k.	**A**	Tu	Marxist group opposed to the US and to NATO
UK	**Continuity Irish Republican Army** (CIRA) • **Continuity Army Council**	1994	50+	**A**	UK, Irl	'Reunify Irl' (Armed wing of Republican Sinn Fein. Opposes Sinn Fein's adoption of Jul 1997 cease-fire)
UK	**Irish National Liberation Army** (INLA) • **People's Liberation Army** • **People's Republican Army** • **Catholic Reaction Force**	1975	150	**C**	UK, Irl	Remove British forces from N. Ireland and unite it with Irl. Armed wing of Irish Republican Socialist Party
UK	**Irish Republican Army** (IRA) • **Provisional Irish Republican Army** (PIRA/the Provos)	1969	400–600	**C**	UK, Irl	Remove British forces from N. Ireland and unite it with Irl (Armed wing of Sinn Fein)
UK	**Loyalist Volunteer Force** (LVF)	1996	150+	**C**	UK, Irl	No political settlement with nationalists in N. Ireland (Faction of UVF)
UK	**Orange Volunteers**	1970s	20	**C**	UK, Irl	No political settlement with nationalists in N. Ireland
UK	**Real Irish Republican Army** (RIRA) • **True IRA**	1997	100+	**A**	UK, Irl	Oppose Sinn Fein's adoption of Jul 1997 cease-fire (Armed wing of 32 County Sovereignty Committee)
UK	**Red Hand Defenders** (RHD)	1998	20	**C**	UK, Irl	No political settlement with nationalists in N. Ireland

Table 6 **Page 2 of 8** NATO and Non-NATO Europe contd • **Russia** • **Middle East** and **North Africa**

Origin	Organisation • aka	Established ⇩	Estimated Strength	Status[1] ⇩	Operates	Aims (Remarks)
UK	**Ulster Defence Association** (UDA) • **Ulster Freedom Fighters** (UFF)	1971	200+	**A**	UK, Irl	Protect Loyalist community (Largest Loyalist para-military gp in N. Ireland. Backed 1998 Good Friday Agreement. Armed wing of Ulster Democratic Party)
UK	**Ulster Volunteer Force** (UVF) • **Protestant Action Force** • **Protestant Action Group**	1966	150+	**A**	UK, Irl	Safeguard N. Ireland's constitutional position within UK. Protect Loyalist community (Armed wing of Progressive Unionist Party)
FRY	**Liberation Army of Presevo, Medvedja and Bujanovac** (UCPMB)	2000	800	**D**	Presevo Valley	Annex Kosovo for ethnic Albanians from south Serbia and west and north FYROM
RUSSIA						
RF	**Chechen Rebels** ▲		2,000–3,000	**A**	Chechnya, Dagestan	Independent Islamic state (Many Muslim mercenaries)
MIDDLE EAST AND **NORTH AFRICA**						
Ag	**Armée Islamique du Salut** (AIS)	1992	n.k.	**C**	Ag	Socialist republic in Ag within framework of Islamic principles. Truce 1997. Armed wing of Front Islamique du Salut (FIS)
Ag	**Groupe Islamique Armée** (GIA) ▲	1992	1,500	**A**	Ag	Fundamentalist Islamic state in Ag (Refused Jan 2000 peace plan)
Ag	**Groupe Salafiste pour la Prédication et le Combat** (GSPC) • **al-Safayya**	1998	500	**A**	Ag	Fundamentalist Islamic state in Ag (Splinter faction of GIA)
Et	**al-Jihad** • **Egyptian Islamic Jihad** • **Jihad Group** • **Islamic Jihad** • **Vanguards of Conquest** ▲	1973	1,000+	**A**	international	Islamic state in Et. Merged with al-Qaeda in 1998
Et	**Islamic Group** • **al-Gama'at al-Islamiyya**	1970s	1,000+	**C**	south Et	Islamic state in Et (Largest militant gp in Et)
Ir[3]	**Democratic Party of Iranian Kurdistan** (DPKI) • **Kurdish Democratic Party of Iran** (KDPI)	1995	1,200–1,800	**D**	Ir	Kurdish autonomy in Ir
Ir[3]	**Kurdistan Organisation of the Communist Party of Iran** (KOMALA)	1967	200	**A**	Ir	Communist govt in Ir (Formed Communist Party of Iran in 1983)
Ir	**National Liberation Army** (NLA)	1987	6,000–8,000	**D**	Ir	'Democratic, socialist, Islamic republic in Ir' (Largest and most active armed Ir dissident gp. Armed wing of Mujahideen-e Khalq Organisation)
Irq[3]	**Kurdish Democratic Party** (KDP)	1946	15,000	**A**	Irq	Overthrow Irq govt (Ongoing conflict with PUK)
Irq[3]	**Patriotic Union of Kurdistan** (PUK)	1975	10,000	**A**	Irq	'Revitalise resistance and rebuild a democratic Kurdish society' (Evolved into a political movement)
Irq	**Ansar al Islam** • **Jun al-Islam** • **Army of Islam**	2001	500–	**A**	Irq	Pro-al-Qaeda grp, opposed to *Op Enduring Freedom*. Opposes secular Kurdish parties in Irq

Table 6 **Page 3 of 8 Middle East** and **North Africa** contd • **Central** and **South Asia**

Origin	Organisation • aka	Established ⇩	Estimated Strength	Status[1] ⇩	Operates	Aims (Remarks)
Irq	**Abu Nidal Organisation** (ANO) • **Fatah Revolutionary Council • Black September • Arab Revolutionary Brigades • Revolutionary Organisation of Socialist Muslims**	1974	300	**D**	international	Destroy Il (Ops in LAR and Et shut down by govts in 1999)
Irq	**Badr Corps**	1982	5,000	**A**	south Irq	'Oppose Irq aggression against Ir' (Shi'ite; mutual agreement signed with PUK against Irq) (Armed wg of Surpreme Council for Islamic Revolution (SCIRI)
RL	**Hizbollah (Party of God) • Islamic Jihad • Revolutionary Justice Organisation • Organisation of the Oppressed on Earth ▲**	1982	2,000+	**A**	Bekaa Valley, Beirut, south RL	Ir-style Islamic republic in RL; all non-Islamic influences removed from area (Shi'ite; formed to resist Il occupation of south RL with political representation representation in RL Assembly.)
Mor	**Sahrawi People's Liberation Army**	1973	3,000–6,000	**C**	Mor	Independent W. Sahara (Armed wing of the Frente Popular para la Liberacion de Saguia el-Hamra y del Rio de Oro (Polisario Front))
PA	**Al-Aqsa Martyrs Brigades ▲**	2000	n.k.	**A**	PA, Il	Associated, though not officially backed, by Arafat. Military offshoot of Fatah.
PA	**Al Saika**	1968	300	**A**	PA, Il	Mil wing of PA faction of Syr Ba'ath Party (Nominally part of PLO)
PA	**Arab Liberation Front**	1969	500	**D**	PA, Il	Achieve national goals of PA (Faction of PLO formed by leadership of Irq Al-Ba'ath party)
PA	**Democratic Front for the Liberation of Palestine** (DFLP)	1969	100+	**A**	PA, Il	Achieve PA national goals through revolution (Marxist–Leninist; splintered from PFLP)
PA	**Izz al-Din al-Qassam** (IDQ) **▲**	1991	500	**A**	PA, Il	Replace Il with Islamic state in PA (Armed wing of Harakat al-Muqawama al-Islamiyya (Hamas); separate from overt org)
PA	**Palestine Islamic Jihad** (PIJ) **▲**	1970s	ε500	**A**	PA, Il	Destroy Il with holy war and establish Islamic state in PA (One of the more extreme PA gps)
PA	**Palestine Liberation Front** (PLF)	1977	300–400	**D**	PA, Il	Armed struggle against Il (Splintered from PFLP)
PA	**Popular Front for the Liberation of Palestine** (PFLP)	1967	1,000	**A**	PA, Il	Armed struggle against Il (Marxist–Leninist)
PA	**Popular Front for the Liberation of Palestine – General Command** (PFLP–GC) **▲**	1968	500	**D**	PA, Il	Armed struggle against Il (Marxist–Leninist; Split from PFLP to focus on fighting rather than politics)
CENTRAL AND **SOUTH ASIA**						
Afg	**al-Qaeda ▲**	1988	1,000+	**A**	international	'Re-establish the Muslim state' worldwide (International network controlled by Osama Bin Laden)
Afg	**Harkat ul-Mujahideen** (HUM) **▲**	1985	450–500	**A**	Kashmir	Pro-Pak Islamic gp. Est 5,000 fighters worldwide, involved in Afg, BiH, My, RF, Pi, Tjk

Origin	Organisation • aka	Established ⇩	Estimated Strength	Status[1] ⇩	Operates	Aims (Remarks)
Bng	**Harkut ul-Jihad-al Islami** (HUJI) • **Bangladesh Taleban**	1992	15,000	**A**	Bng	Aims to establish Islamic rule in Bng
Bng	**Islami Chhatra Shibir** (ICS)	1941		**A**	Bng	Student wing of Jamaat-e-Islami, Bng's third biggest political party. Seeks Taliban-style regime in Bng
Bng	**Shanto Bahani • Peace Force**	1976	3,000	**D**	Bng	Armed wing of Parbatya Chattagram Jana Sanghati Samity (PCJSS). Fights for autonomy of Chittagong Hill Tracts. Disbanded 1998, though remnants may still exist
Ind	**Tripura Liberation Organisation Front** (TLOF)	1992	n.k.		Ind	Secession of Tripura from India
Ind	**All Tripura Tiger Force** (ATTF)	1990	500–600	**A**	Ind	Independent Tripura and expulsion of Bengali-speaking immigrants from Tripura
Ind	**National Liberation Front of Tripura** (NLFT)	1989	800	**A**	Ind	To establish independence for Tripura through armed struggle
Ind	**Maoist Communist Centre** (MCC)	1969	1,000+	**A**	Bihar, Jharkhaad	Seeking people's govt through armed struggle
Ind	**The Communist Party of India (Marxist–Leninist) (People's War) • People's War Group** (PWG)	1980	1,000	**A**	Ind	Maoist grp aiming to seize political power through armed struggle
Ind/Pak	**Hizbul Mujahideen** (HM)	1989	1,000–1,200	**A**	Kashmir	Pro-Pak Islamic gp (Armed wing of Jamaat-e-Islami, Pak's largest Islamic party)
Ind/Pak	**Tehrik-e-Jihad** ▲	1997	n.k.	**A**	Kashmir	Self-determination for Kashmir; Kashmir to join Pak
Ind/Pak	**Jaish-e-Mohammed** ▲	2000	300–400	**A**	Jammu, Kashmir	Seeks to expel Ind from Jammu and Kashmir
Ind/Pak	**Al-Badr Mujahideen** ▲	1998	40–50	**A**	Kashmir	Liberate' Kashmir from Ind forces (Split from Hizb-ul Mujahideen)
Ind/Pak	**Lashkar-e-Taiba** (LT) ▲	1989	300	**A**	Jammu, Kashmir	Create independent Islamic state in Kashmir (Armed wing of Markaz-ud-Dawa-wal-Irshad (MDI))
Ind	**Sanjukta Mukti Fouj** (SMF)	1996	1,500	**A**	Ind, Assam?	Establish an autonomous and socialist Assam. Armed wg of United Liberation Front of Assam (ULFA)
Ind	**National Democratic Front of Bodoland** (NDFB)	1988	1,500	**A**	Assam	Seeks autonomy for Bodoland in areas north of river Brahmaputra
Ind	**Manipur People's Liberation Front** (MPLF)	1999	n.k.	**A**	Ind	Establish independent socialist Manipur. A coalition of United National Liberation Front, the Revolutionary People's Front and the People's Revolutionary Party of Kangleipak
N	**Communist Party of Nepal (Maoist)**	1995	5,000+	**A**	N	Overthrow N's constitutional monarchy; replace with Maoist republic (Declared 'People's War' in 1996). Headed by 'Prachanda'. Armed wing of Samyukta Jana Morcha (UPF)

Table 6 **Page 5 of 8** East Asia and Australasia contd • **Caribbean** and **Latin America**

Origin	Organisation • aka	Established ⇩	Strength[1]	Status[1] ⇩	Operates	Aims (Remarks)
Ska	**Liberation Tigers of Tamil Eelam** (LTTE) • **World Tamil Association** • **World Tamil Movement** ▲	1972	7,000	**C**	north and east Ska	Independent Tamil state (Began armed conflict in 1983. Cease-fire signed 23 February 2002
Uz	**Islamic Movement of Uzbekistan** (IMU)	1997	2,000+	**A**	Uz, Tjk, Ir, Kgz, Afg	Fundamentalist Islamic state in Uz (Coalition of Islamic militants from Uz, other C. Asian states and PRC. Aka Islamic Movement of Turkestan, evolving idea of the resurrection of the state of Turkestan
EAST ASIA AND **AUSTRALASIA**						
PRC	**Uighur Separatist Movement**	1990	n.k.	**A**	north-west PRC, C. Asia	Establish separate E. Turkestan state for Uighur population. Linked to IMU
Indo	**Gerakin Aceh Merdeka** • **Free Aceh** • **Aceh Security Disturbance Movement**	1976	2,000	**A**	Aceh	Independent Islamic state in Aceh Armed wg of Free Aceh Movement (Underground since 1996)
Indo	**Laskar Jihad**	2000	500–	**A**	Indo, Maluku	Remove Christians from Maluku; Islamic state in Indo
Indo	**Organisasi Papua Merdeka** (OPM)	1962	150	**A**	Indo	Independence for W. Papua
J	**Aum Supreme Truth** • **Aum Shinrikyo**	1987	1,500–2,000	**D**	J	'Take over J and then the world' (Released Sarin on Tokyo subway in 1995 and other chemical attacks in J)
Mal	**Malaysian Mujahideen Group, Kumpulan Mujahideen Malaysia** (KMM)	1990s	200–	**D**	Mal	Overthrow Mal govt and establish an Islamic state comprising Mal, Indo and southern Pi
Mal	**Jemaah Islamiah** (JI)	1995	n.k.	**A**	Mal, Indo, Pi, Sgp, Th	Establish an independent Islamic state encompassing southern Th, Mal, Indo and southern Pi
My	**All Burma Students Democratic Front**	1988	2,000	**A**	My	'Liberate My from dictatorship, establish democracy and transform into federal union'
My	**Chin National Army** (CNA)	1988	n.k.	**A**	west My, Chin state	Overthrow My govt (Armed wing of Chin National Front)
My	**Democratic Karen Buddhist Army** (DKBA)	1994	100–500	**C**	My, Th	Independence for Karen minority (Splinter gp of Karen National Union (KNU). Armed wing of Democratic Karen Buddhist Organisation. Ongoing conflict with KNLA)
My	**Kachin Independence Army** (KIA)	1961	8,000	**C**	north My, Khmer range	Promote Buddhism (Armed wing of Kachin Independence Organisation)
My	**Karen National Liberation Army** (KNLA)	1948	4,000	**A**	Th border	Establish Karen State with right to self-determination (Armed wing of KNU. Ongoing conflict with DKBA)
My	**Karenni National Progressive Party Army** (KNPPA)	1948	2,000	**A**	north My, Kayah State	Independence of Karenni State (Armed wing of Karenni National Progressive Party)
My	**Mong Thai Army** (MTA)	1964	3,000	**C**	Th border	Protect Shan population

Origin	Organisation • aka	Established ⇩	Strength[1]	Status[1] ⇩	Operates	Aims (Remarks)
My	**Mon National Liberation Army** (MNLA)	1958	1,000	C	Th border	Represent Mon minority (Armed wing of New Mon State Party)
My	**National Democratic Alliance Army** (NDAA)	1989	1,000	C	east Shan State, PRC–Lao border	Oppose My mil rule (Formerly part of Communist Party of Burma (CPB))
My	**Palaung State Liberation Army** (PSLA)	1963	700	C	north of Hsipaw	Greater autonomy for Palaung population
My	**Shan State Army** (SSA) • **Shan State Progress Army** (SSPA)	1964	3,000	C	south Shan State	Freedom and democracy for Shan State
My	**United Wa State Army** (UWSA)	1989	15,000	C	Wa Hills	Splinter gp of CPB
Pi	**Abu Sayyaf Group** (ASG)	1991	200	A	south Pi	Independent Islamic state in west Mindanao and Sulu (Split from Moro National Liberation Front (MNLF))
Pi	**Revolutionary Proletarian Army–Alex Boncayao Brigade** (RPA–ABB)	1997	500+	A	Manila, central Pi	Urban hit squad of Philippines Communist Party
Pi	**Bangsa Moro Army**	1970s	n.k.	C	south Pi	Muslim separatist movement (Armed wing of MNLF)
Pi	**Moro Islamic Liberation Front** (MILF)	1977	11,000	C	south Pi	Independent Islamic state in Bangsa Moro and neighbouring islands (Split from MNLF. Signed cease-fire with Pi govt 7 Aug 2001)
Pi	**Moro Islamic Reformist Group**	1978	900–	A	south Pi	Independent Islamic state in south Pi (Split from MNLF)
Pi	**New People's Army** (NPA)	1969	10,000	A	rural Luzon, Visayas and Mindanao	Overthrow Pi govt (Armed wing of Philippines Communist Party. Ended peace talks with govt after 1999 Pi–US agreement to resume joint mil exercises)
CARIBBEAN AND **LATIN AMERICA**						
Co	**Autodefensas Unidas de Colombia** (AUC)	1997	10,600	A	north and north-west Co	Coordinating gp for paramilitaries (Right-wing. Co govt refused to grant same 'political status' as guerrillas)
Co	**Ejercito de Liberación Nacional** (ELN)	1964	4,000	A	north, north-east, south-west Co	Anti-US 'Maoist–Marxist–Leninist' gp (Peace talks with govt since 1999)
Co	**Ejercito Popular de Liberación** (EPL)	1967	500–	A	Co	'Rid Co of US imperialism and Co oligarchies'
Co	**Fuerzas Armadas Revolucionarias de Colombia** (FARC)	1964	18,000	A	Co	'Overthrow govt and ruling classes' (Armed wing of Colombian Communist Party) (Linked to IRA)
Pe	**Movimiento Revolucionario Tupac Amaru** (MRTA)	1983	600	D	Pe, Upper Huallaga river valley	Establish Marxist regime and 'rid Pe of imperialist elements' (Less active since Pe govt's 1999 counter-terrorist op)
Pe	**Sendero Luminoso** (SL) • **Shining Path**	1960s	600–	A	Pe, Upper Huallaga and Ene river valleys	Establish peasant revolutionary regime in Pe (Less active since Pe govt's 2000 counter-terrorist op)

Table 6 **Page 7 of 8** Sub-Saharan Africa contd

Origin	Organisation • aka	Established ⇩	Strength[1]	Status[1] ⇩	Operates	Aims (Remarks)
SUB-SAHARAN AFRICA						
Ang	**Frente de Libertacao do Enclave de Cabinda – Forcas Armadas de Cabinda** (FLEC–FAC)	1980s	300–	A	Ang, Cabinda	Independence of Cabinda region (Split from FLEC in the 1980s)
Ang	**Frente de Libertacao do Enclave de Cabinda – Renovada** (FLEC–Renovada)	1980s	300–	A	Ang, Cabinda	Independence of Cabinda region (Split from FLEC in the 1980s)
Ang	**União Nacional para Independencia Total de Angola** (UNITA)	1966	5,000–	C	Nba, Ang, DROC	Strive for govt proportionally representative of all ethnic gps, clans and classes (Signed peace agreement with govt in April 2002)
Bu	**Forces pour la Défense de la Démocratie** (FDD)	1994	16,000	A	DROC, west Tz, Bu	Restore constitution and institutions set by 1993 elections and form national army (To be disarmed under Lusaka Peace Accord but continues attacks against Bu govt and believed involved in DROC conflict. Armed wing of National Council for the Defence of Democracy)
Bu	**Parti pour la Libération du Peuple Hutu** (Palipehutu) • **Forces for National Liberation**	1980	2,000–3,000	A	Bu, Tz borders	Liberate Hutus and establish ethnic quotas based on 1930s Be census (Armed wing of Forces Nationales de Libération)
Cha	**Mouvement pour la Démocratie et la Justice au Tchad** (MDJT)	1998	n.k.	C	north Cha, Tibesti region	Overthrow Cha govt
DROC	**Mouvement de Libération Congolais** (MLC)	1998	18,000	C	north DROC	'Fight dictatorship in DROC' (First faction to break from RCD)
DROC	**Rassemblement Congolais pour la Démocratie – Mouvement de Libération** (RCD–ML)	1999	2,000–3,000	A	DROC	Overthrow DROC govt
DROC	**Rassemblement Congolais pour la Démocratie – Goma** (RCD–GOMA)	1998	20,000	A	DROC	Establish democracy in DROC
Dj	**Front pour la Restauration de l'Unité et de la Démocratie** (FRUD)	1991	n.k.	C	Dj	Represent Afar population of Dj and establish multi-party elections (Following 1994 split, one faction signed agreement with govt to become legitimate political party, joined 1995 coalition govt)
Er	**Alliance of Eritrean National Forces** (AENF)	1999	3,000	A	Er	Overthrow Er govt (Coalition of Er armed gps)
Eth	**Ogaden National Liberation Army** (ONLA)	1984	n.k.	A	Eth	Restore rights of Ogaden population and obtain right to self-determination (Armed wing of ONLF)
Eth	**Oromo Liberation Front** (OLF)	1974	200+	A	west Eth	Lead liberation struggle of Oromo population and overthrow Eth govt
Lb	**Liberians United for Reconciliation and Democracy** (LURD)	2000	n.k.	A	north Lb, south Gui	Overthrow Lb govt
Nba	**Caprivi Liberation Army** (CLA)	1998	200–	A	Nba, Caprivi Strip	Independence of Caprivi Strip

Origin	Organisation • aka	Established ⇩	Strength[1]	Status[1] ⇩	Operates	Aims (Remarks)
Nga	**Arewa People's Congress** (APC)	1999	n.k.	A	north Nga	Defend the rights of the Hausa-Fulani tribe
Nga	**Odua People's Congress** (OPC)	1999	n.k.	A	south-west Nga	Defend the rights of the Yoruba tribe
Rwa	**Interahamwe •** **Army for the Liberation of Rwanda** (ALIR)	1994	15,000–	A	DROC, Rwa	Reinstate Hutu control of Rwa (Armed wg of Party for the Liberation of Rwanda. Consists of remnants of Hutu militias and former Rwa armed forces)
Rwa	**Forces Démocratiques pour la Liberation du Rwanda** (FDLR)	2000	3,000+	A	DROC, South Kivu and Katanga	Reinstate Hutu control of Rwa (Consists of refugee survivors of genocide in DROC by the Rwandan Patriotic Army (RPA) in 1996–97
Sen	**Mouvement des Forces Démocratiques de Casamance** (MFDC)	1982	2,000–3,000	A	Sen	Independent Casamance (Involved in peace talks with govt since 2000)
SL	**Independent RUF** (RUF–)	2002	500–	A	Lb border	Against cease-fire signed between RUF and govt in Jan 2002. (Split from RUF in 2002)
SL	**Revolutionary United Front** (RUF)	1980s	n.k.	C	Gui, SL	Overthrow SL govt (Signed cease-fire agreement in Nov 2000. Disarmament programme completed in Jan 2002)
RSA	**People Against Gangsterism and Drugs** (G-Force)	1995	50	A	Cape Town area	Combat and eradicate crime, gansterism and drugs (armed wing of PAGAD)
RSA	**Qibla**	1980s	300–	A	Cape Town area	Establish an Islamic state in RSA (Allied to PAGAD)
Sdn	**The Beja Congress**	1993	500–	A	east Sdn	Overthrow Sdn govt and establish autonomous Beja state (Controls area of eastern Sdn centred around Garoura and Hamshkoraib)
Sdn	**New Sudan Brigade**	1995	2,000–	A	east Sdn	(Eastern branch of SPLA)
Sdn	**Sudan Alliance Forces**	1994	500	A	east Sdn	Overthrow Sdn govt and 'establish progressive and secular democracy' (Played major role in opening new war front in east since 1997)
Sdn	**Sudan People's Liberation Army** (SPLA)	1983	20,000–30,000	C	south Sdn	Secular and democratic Sdn (Armed wing of Sudan People's Liberation Movement (SPLM). Signed cease-fire agreement with govt in July 2002. Largely Christian and southern)
SR	**Somali National Movement** (SNM)	1982	5,000+	A	north SR	Independence of Somaliland
SR	**Rahanweyn Resistance Army** (RRA)	1996	n.k.	A	south SR	Local autonomy (Allied to SDM)
SR	**Somali Democratic Movement** (SDM)	1992	n.k.	A	south SR	Local autonomy (Allied to RRA)
SR	**Somali Salvation Democratic Front** (SSDF)	1978	3,000–	A	north-east SR	Independence of Puntland
Uga	**Allied Democratic Front •** **Uganda Allied Democratic Army**	1996	200	A	west Uga	Replace Uga govt with regime based on Sharia law
Uga	**Lord's Resistance Army** (LRA)	1989	1,500	A	Gulu and Kitgum districts	'Rule Uga according to biblical ten commandments and create Great Nile Republic in northern Uga' (Christian fundamentalist)

Countering Terror After 11 September Early Lessons, Future Challenges

Compelled by the need to re-establish its global leadership in the aftermath of 11 September's horrendous terrorist attacks on its soil, America rapidly assembled not only an unprecedented 'coalition of the willing' but brought decisive military power to bear against the al-Qaeda terrorist network in Afghanistan and its host Taliban government. Moreover, an array of offensive and defensive measures to combat terrorism, requiring substantial increases in defence and non-defence budgets alike, is slowly being assembled to fight what most analysts believe will be a long and difficult war to eradicate global terrorism. To shed light on the prospects for success in combating global terror, the following analysis has two primary objectives: first, to derive the early lessons – however preliminary and unique to the particular circumstances – from the US-dominated war in Afghanistan, while appraising allied contributions to the fight against global terrorism; and second, to examine the longer-term military, technological, organisational and analytical challenges central to success in combating international terror.

EMERGING STRATEGY

America's fight against global terror comprises, in addition to offensive military action such as that taken in Afghanistan, a mix of offensive military, intelligence and law enforcement, homeland defence, money tracking and diplomatic and economic aid measures. Among the Bush administration's chief concerns, however, is that states possessing weapons of mass destruction (WMD) could provide them to non-state perpetrators of transnational terror. The United States' counter-terrorism policy is therefore inextricably linked to, and has energised, its counter-proliferation policy. The administration's announcement of a strategy of pre-emption has reinforced the connection. At a 1 June 2002 commencement address to graduating cadets at the United States Military Academy at West Point, New York, President Bush characterised his strategy as one of decisive military action. Bush told his audience that 'We must take the battle to the enemy, disrupt his plans and confront the worst threats before they emerge'. Although Bush did not specifically refer to Iraq in his address, his reference to 'weak states' having the capacity to do catastrophic harm to great nations seemed to imply that both non-state and state actors would be potential targets of this emerging pre-emptive strategy. Indeed, former US Secretary of State George Shultz essentially articulated the same strategy in a late May 2002 address to the US Foreign Service, referring to the war on terror as one of necessitating not just 'hot pursuit' but 'hot pre-emption'.

An affinity for pre-emptive action in emerging American counter-terrorism strategy is broadly compatible with US Secretary of Defense Donald Rumsfeld's view of future American military strategy. Unlike past and even some current (notably ground) military capabilities, the future military would conduct decisive action with rapidly deployable and agile stealth forces that could respond to various contingency requirements with a minimum of logistical support. The principle measure of effectiveness would be represented less by the number of weapon platforms that could be brought to bear on the enemy than by the quality of networking between sensors and shooters. The ubiquitous employment of microprocessors throughout military systems, remote sensing technologies, advanced data-fusion software, interlinked but physically disparate databases and high-speed, high-capacity communications networks would enable the precise application of force against the most important enemy targets. And rather than employing sequential fires against these targets, which gives one's adversary time to recover or hide, networked sensors and shooters would bring simultaneous fires with significantly greater effect than ever before. However, moving from today's less than agile, slowly deployable force to tomorrow's desired force objective is fraught with impediments, not least military services reluctant to shed Cold War era platforms for a decidedly more networked, lightweight force structure oriented towards operating jointly with force packages from other services.[1] Yet, despite institutional hindrances to rapid transformation to a more preemptively oriented military, preliminary lessons drawn from the war in Afghanistan reinforce Secretary of Defense Rumsfeld's commitment to achieve a much more decisive capacity to respond to emerging threats.

LESSONS FROM *OPERATION ENDURING FREEDOM*

Any lessons from the brief military campaign against the Taliban and al-Qaeda forces must be drawn with considerable circumspection, for several reasons. First, while the Taliban and al-Qaeda elements were routed decisively and promptly in *Operation Enduring Freedom*, many of their fighters have dispersed into hidden locations in Pakistan, Afghanistan and perhaps farther afield. The more difficult challenge of finding and defeating these remaining elements will depend less on traditional military tools than on the effectiveness of intelligence collection and cooperation among many states.

Second, there is a paucity of hard information on the military campaign itself. Because no official, systematically derived analyses of the number of forces and weapons used, targets struck, weapon accuracy, or battle damage assessment are currently available, one is left with frequently self-serving press accounts from which to draw lessons.

Third, certain unique factors shaped the outcome. Most significantly, the Taliban and al-Qaeda were unpopular with the Afghan people, which forced terrorists and their supporters to concentrate forces in compounds, caves and other sanctuaries that seemingly afforded them protection from air strikes but which actually permitted American airpower to direct devastating fire against these fixed locations, and curtail the lines of communication between them, all without significant fear of collateral damage. This stands in distinct contrast with the conditions NATO faced in *Operation Allied Force* in Kosovo. There, Serb army and national police forces operated in small units, intermingling with (and 'ethnically cleansing') Albanian Kosovars. At night, they hid in villages, schools and adjacent woods, all of which contributed to nearly impossible targeting conditions, especially given the highly restrictive rules of engagement then prevailing.

Finally, the immense practical and emotional impact of the 11 September attacks furnished the US with extraordinary political and psychological advantages, which, no matter how intangible they were, made the stakes clear in *Operation Enduring Freedom*. Such a compelling cause, together with unusual Western unity, did not prevail even in Bosnia and Kosovo, and certainly would not materialise behind any prospective military campaign against Iraq.

With these critical caveats, preliminary judgments can be made on what appear to be important military-technical trends and innovations evident from the brief military campaign in Afghanistan.

US Defense Secretary Rumsfeld opined that the nineteenth century met the twenty-first at the battle for Mazar e-Sharif during *Operation Enduring Freedom*. There US Special Forces slipped behind enemy lines and called in devastatingly effective airstrikes on Taliban and al-Qaeda forces, enabling hundreds of friendly Afghan horsemen, accompanied by more American Special Forces, to ride into battle and ultimately achieve victory over a determined adversary. Besides the palpable courage of Afghan and US military forces, the key to victory was the overwhelming decisiveness of the airstrikes, which broke the front line of resistance. Central to the effectiveness of airpower was perhaps the conflict's more important tactical innovation: the fusion of targeting on the ground with precision air strikes. This tactical innovation had two principal ingredients. First, air force combat air controllers were integrated into US Army Special Forces 'A-teams' and equipped with Global Positioning System (GPS) receivers and off-the-shelf laser binoculars, know as *Viper*, fortuitously acquired from a Swiss manufacturer immediately prior to the battle for Mazir e-Sharif. Second, combat aircraft were armed with the 900kg Joint Direct Attack Munition (JDAM) – a relatively cheap modification to existing dumb bombs that enables them to be guided extremely precisely by signals from GPS satellites to their targets.

Although the JDAM was first used in Kosovo in 1999, it was far more effective in Afghanistan because its application was determined by the air combat controllers on the ground. Combat aircraft during the

Kosovo campaign merely took off from their bases with predetermined target coordinates for their JDAMs. This greatly reduced targeting effectiveness, especially against so-called time-critical targets that could move. Air combat controllers on the ground, armed with the proper equipment, were able to shrink the amount of time between identifying a target and attacking it from hours to minutes. Literally days before the battle of Mazar-e Sharif, US combat air controllers received their first allotment of *Viper* laser binoculars. *Viper* fires a laser beam on the target that provides the object's range and bearing to the device's GPS receiver. The latter translates range and bearing into latitude and longitude, which in turn is passed by the ground controller to the aircraft for translation into JDAM targeting coordinates. Thus, in less than 20 minutes, an air combat controller on the ground can request an circling aircraft in the vicinity to accept precision targeting information that can lead to a virtually instantaneous attack against a critical target from the relative safety of 10,000 metres. Prior to *Viper's* arrival in Afghanistan, combat air controllers were limited to using laser designators that 'paint' a target with their beams. These are spotted by a circling aircraft nearby, which then launches a laser-guided bomb that follows the controller's laser beam to the target. But adverse weather and low cloud cover limit the use of laser-guided bombs, while these factors do not affect *Viper*-directed JDAM weapons. US Air Force officials are so impressed with targeting innovations that they now envision a more significant air-to-ground role for the yet-to-be-deployed F-22 stealth fighter, including alternations to laser binocular systems that would permit the automatic provision of GPS coordinates directly into the precision-guided munitions. This would eliminate the possibility that combat air controllers might mistakenly send their own or incorrect coordinates to the aircraft.

Radically improved precision targeting is but one of several illustrations of the great potential of network-centric warfare (NCW) – that is, the capacity of geographically dispersed forces to perceive substantially the same battlespace. This enables them to mass effects without massing forces, which takes time and increases vulnerability. Advances in military space-based assets and unmanned aerial vehicles (UAVs) have enhanced the US military's ability to wage NCW. Satellite communications and overhead reconnaissance and surveillance systems demonstrated dramatic improvements compared to their usage in *Operation Desert Storm* more than a decade prior to *Operation Enduring Freedom*. Then space systems were essentially the exclusive domain of the national intelligence community and senior policymakers. However, critical post-war assessments and the costly absence of real-time communications from space assets in Somalia led to a radical transformation of space support to military operations. Now, near-real-time video data from *Predator* and *Global Hawk* UAVs can be relayed via orbiting communications satellites to command centres and individual controllers on the ground. This in turn relays precision-targeting coordinates via command centres halfway around the globe to strike assets in the theatre of operations. This capacity to broaden battlefield awareness through UAVs and space-based satellite reconnaissance enabled US Central Command's commander to direct the battle from his headquarters in Tampa, Florida while being instantaneously connected to his forward headquarters in Kuwait and a subordinate jump headquarters in Uzbekistan. One potent indication of the growing importance of military space is the huge increase in bandwidth over the last decade. Among key drivers of this increase is the provision of real-time video from *Predator* UAVs to AC-130 gunships, for example, thus allowing gunship crews to be briefed with live imagery well before they reach the target. During *Operation Enduring Freedom* the Pentagon leased 800 Mbps of commercial satellite support compared with 100 Mbps during *Operation Desert Storm* – seven times the bandwidth to support one-tenth the number of forces.

Taken together, developments in shared battlefield awareness and precision targeting, through greatly improved C^4ISR (command, control, computers, communications, intelligence, surveillance and reconnaissance), bespeak a true transformation in the way airpower is now delivered. Formerly, airpower was prosecuted in pre-defined sequential increments. Intelligence platforms would collect information largely on fixed targets, and a target list would be drawn up against which to task specific aircraft as part of an overall air tasking order. A wave of aircraft would then execute this order and return to their bases for subsequent pre-defined missions. The sequential nature of the air tasking order gave adversary forces time to recover or covertly move to enhance their survivability. *Operation Enduring Freedom* demonstrated for the first time how airpower can be employed in near-simultaneous rather than sequential form due to the rapid integration of sensor data into the allocation of airpower. Much like a civilian air-traffic controller, combat air controllers on the ground can call in any number of fighters or heavy bombers just outside the target area to hit targets identified and subsequently approved for targeting within minutes of their disclosure. One important measure that reflects this transformation is the number of targets than can effectively be attacked per aircraft sortie. In *Operation Desert Storm*, using unguided or 'dumb' bombs, typically 13 aircraft sorties would be needed to complete an attack on each target. Using laser-guided bombs in the same campaign, the target-to-sortie ratio dropped to two targets per aircraft sortie – or more than an order of magnitude improvement over unguided bombs. Although no statistics are available yet from *Operation Enduring Freedom*, it is conceivable that F-22 fighters carrying eight smart bombs and B-2 stealth bombers with 216 such bombs could achieve on a single sortie as many target kills as the number of bombs they carry.

As much as these innovations demonstrate the benefits of fusing information with firepower, it is important to note several qualifications. *Operation Enduring Freedom* showed the capacity of modern airpower to make the transition from targeting large numbers of fixed targets to equally large numbers of targets of opportunity (including fleeting ones). Yet operationally tougher environments than even the unforgiving terrain of Afghanistan can be readily imagined. Finding and rapidly targeting small bands of terrorists in the jungles of the Philippines would be harder than targeting al-Qaeda and Taliban fighters in mountain bunkers. Effectively delivering shock firepower effects while minimising both friendly and civilian casualties in urban settings would be more daunting still. The prediction that 85% of the world's population will be located in cities by 2015 is a sober reminder of the challenges facing counter-terrorism planners in the years ahead. These unwelcome but inevitable operating environments place a premium on the development of breakthroughs in foliage penetration radar, miniaturised missiles and drones, variable effect dial-a-yield munitions, multipurpose robots, and exceptionally agile fibre-optic missiles capable of high-G turns, just to mention a few. Even with the advantages that technological breakthroughs may offer, fighting in such hostile environments will demand the political capacity to tolerate higher casualties and more lengthy periods of uncertain engagement.

Further, to whatever extent the operational circumstances of the Afghanistan campaign provided comparative advantages over urban or jungle operating conditions, and no matter how easy it seemed for US-led forces to defeat Taliban and al-Qaeda units, military force is likely to remain an extraordinary remedy in the fight against terrorism. By no means was *Operation Enduring Freedom* the unalloyed success some made it out to be. While General Tommy Franks, commander of the US Central Command, called *Operation Anaconda* (the March assault against al-Qaeda forces) an unqualified success by every measure, what was intended to be a two-day operation turned into nearly two weeks of heavy fighting, including eight Americans combat deaths. In contrast to the rave reports about the effects of precision bombing in the battle of Mazar-e Sharif, Australian SAS troops reported that the initial phase of the *Operation Anaconda* was severely botched due to inadequate American airpower, poor intelligence and faulty technology. This may explain America's more measured use of offensive military power in responding to potential terrorist threats in Yemen, Somalia, the Philippines and Georgia, all of which entail preventive measures and training assistance rather than direct military engagement. Eliminating Iraq's WMD – highly controversial with both America's European allies and regional Arab allies – appears to stand as America's top offensive military objective.

Overall, however, while American air and missile power, enabled through C^{4}ISR capabilities, has greatly improved since *Operation Desert Storm*, American planners should not blithely conclude that their successes during *Operation Enduring Freedom* can be easily replicated against an adversary state armed with WMD. Any strategy organised around the notion of pre-emption against a WMD-armed adversary depends critically on achieving near-perfect results against three chronically difficult challenges: finding, characterising and defeating deeply buried targets; locating, identifying and attacking highly elusive targets, most notably WMD-armed mobile missiles; and shooting down those missiles that survive pre-emptive strikes.

Effectively prosecuting deeply buried targets is made difficult due to changes in the economics of underground construction. Commercially available boring equipment can readily excavate deeper and deeper tunnels and facilities at a pace greatly exceeding an opponent's capacity to develop targeting solutions using conventional penetrating munitions. It is no less daunting simply to find and adequately characterise such deeply buried facilities to facilitate precision targeting. Thus, the US is examining the use of so-called mini-nukes as a possible solution. Dealing with elusive targets that move quickly and frequently is not much easier today than it was during *Operation Desert Storm*, when coalition forces failed to destroy a single Iraqi mobile missile launcher. Breakthroughs are needed in truly wide-area surveillance (probably through a large constellation of space-based radar satellites), automated filtering of false targets from real ones (automated target recognition algorithms have not kept pace with the increasingly elusive nature of the offence), tightening decision-making (to bring the full cycle of detection to strike down to less than five minutes) and placing weapons on targets virtually instantaneously (through loitering strike vehicles nearby or hypersonic missiles from afar). Achieving rapid success in any one of these areas would be notable; doing so for all four is highly unlikely within the next decade. Finally, there is the formidable challenge of missile defence. US ballistic missile-defence programmes have experienced staggering delays, technical problems and disruptive political expectations, while insufficient funding and service unwillingness to work toward joint solutions currently hobble cruise-missile defence programs. Indeed, the mere fact that the Pentagon has directed the Defense Science Board to investigate equipping hit-to-kill missile interceptors with small-yield nuclear warheads raises suspicion about the long-term viability of non-nuclear solutions to deal with simple countermeasures. But even putting aside the nuclear question, the stark reality is that not until at least 2007 – 16 years after *Operation Desert Storm* – will there exist some modest form of theatre missile defence against regional ballistic- and cruise-missile threats. Putting aside the matter of relative stakes, these limitations in US pre-emptive capabilities, combined with uncertainties about the extent of Iraqi WMD capabilities, make any US decision to engage Iraq in the near-term future burdened with far more risk than engaging Taliban and al-Qaeda forces in Afghanistan.

DEFENSIVE MEASURES IN COUNTERING TERRORISM

On the defensive side of countering international terrorism, 11 September's attacks transformed America's longstanding sense of safety from foreign threats into a profound recognition of vulnerability.[2] And the unquestioned superiority of American global dominance bore little relationship to improving homeland security. That said, military power would certainly have important roles to play in homeland defence (notably in the areas of protecting US airspace, using National Guard units to protect critical infrastructure, and perhaps foremost, providing missile defences against ballistic and cruise missile attacks), but the bulk of new homeland security responsibilities lie outside of the Department of Defense. Initially, the Bush administration objected to the notion of creating a new cabinet department of homeland security, which a prominent bi-partisan commission had proposed prior to 11 September, and instead appointed Governor Tom Ridge of Pennsylvania to coordinate, from an office in the White House, a vast array of agencies and state and local jurisdictions and to develop a national strategy for the whole range of homeland security challenges. But in early June 2002, President Bush surprised congressional and public critics alike when he announced a legislative proposal to create a Department of Homeland Security, which would bring together responsibilities dispersed among over 100 different government organisations.

The new department would have four primary divisions, each led by an undersecretary. The Border and Transportation Security division would consolidate the functions of the Coast Guard, Customs Service,

Immigration and Naturalization Service, Border Patrol, Transportation Security Administration and the Department of Agriculture's animal, plant and safety service, and thus create a single government entity to manage entry of people and cargo into the US. These functions would be informed by a central information-sharing clearing house and compatible databases – a key missing element that helped enable al-Qaeda terrorists to enter and plan with ease the attacks of 11 September. Another division, called Emergency Preparedness and Response, would oversee federal government assistance in domestic disasters through its work with first responders (firemen, police and emergency teams) in state and local jurisdictions. A Chemical, Biological, Radiological and Nuclear Division would set national policy for state and local authorities for dealing with mass casualty threats. Finally, an Information and Infrastructure Protection Division would focus on coordinating activities relating to the protection of the nation's critical infrastructures and to threat analysis and warning.

In light of the reported failures of both the CIA and FBI to share information with each other and the White House, the new department's threat analysis and warning capability would seem critically important. Congressional concern centres on assuring that the Homeland Security Department is given access not just to so-called finished intelligence reports from the intelligence community but the raw information that forms the analytic basis for arriving at 'finished' threat assessments. Moreover, the long-acknowledged failure to share intelligence at the national level is mirrored at lower levels. No standard protocols are in place for sharing sensitive intelligence among federal, state and local officials. This hurdle has a reciprocal quality: not only are state and local officials not getting sufficient intelligence from national authorities, but they frequently fail to furnish national agencies with what could be essential information acquired about suspicious activities occurring within their jurisdictions. Finally, the largest federal reorganisation since 1947 will not affect the CIA, FBI, or other elements of the national intelligence community where many believe the primary counter-terrorism challenges lie. Whether or not a substantial shake-up in these latter agencies occurs is likely to become clear only after the conclusion of hearings by the joint congressional intelligence panel looking into the role of intelligence in the events of 11 September. These hearings will probably be held in parallel with those convening to review and approve new legislation creating the Department of Homeland Security, which should run until the mid-term congressional elections in November. Thus, precisely what reforms if any take place within the intelligence community may not become evident until well into 2003.

ALLIED CONTRIBUTIONS

The impact of 11 September's attacks on America has had lasting effects on US–European relations in two important ways. The first flows from the psychological and thus intangible benefits of 11 September's horrific attacks and the immediate appreciation on both sides of the Atlantic of a shared vulnerability to terrorism. The distinction between the 'old' ethno-nationalist terrorism that has plagued various European countries for 30 years or more and the 'new' radical Islamic transnational terrorism exemplified by al-Qaeda is by now familiar: European terrorists have practiced some restraint to maintain the prospect of political negotiation, while al-Qaeda seeks simply to produce as many casualties as possible without regard to a negotiated outcome. But however different Europe's history with terrorism may be from the United States' recent experience, the mere fact that the 'new terrorism' could ultimately spread to European targets, especially in light of the now-acknowledged presence of al-Qaeda cells in Europe, furnishes an important basis for US–European solidarity. Certainly, NATO's swift implementation of Article 5 of the Washington Treaty demonstrated this shared solidarity. On the other hand, the US decision not to use NATO as a command framework for *Operation Enduring Freedom* (relegating allied military contributions to token ones, save for the UK) probably spells the end of attempts to transform NATO into a potent and global vehicle for decisive force projection. The task remains, however, to decide on an appropriate conceptual framework for coalition operations within NATO, most especially deciding on what tasks, including counter-terrorism, allied armed forces must prepare for.

The second potentially significant outcome of the 11 September attacks is the de facto increase in transatlantic intelligence and law-enforcement cooperation – arguably the most important counter-terrorist tool now that al-Qaeda forces have dispersed in the aftermath of the military campaign in Afghanistan. Although these links are largely bilateral ones, there is some limited potential for them to become multilateral through NATO and possibly the European Union (EU). Admittedly, transatlantic differences in threat perceptions and responses could cause an unravelling of such cooperation. But the fact that al-Qaeda effectively used Europe as a launching pad for its 11 September attacks on New York and Washington, and planned attacks (which were thwarted) on US assets in Europe as well as other purely European targets, is evidence of Europe's vulnerability to terrorist infiltration. Moreover, while the US is al-Qaeda's primary focus and preferred target at the moment, this primacy could shift to Europe if America's significant investment in homeland defence begins to show signs of a substantial return. Realisation of this possibility has stimulated increased European interest in homeland defence, particularly in the United Kingdom. The British government is drawing up plans to create a 6,000-strong special defence unit (called the Civil Contingency Reaction Force) drawn from its reserve forces, and intends the unit to be in a position to bolster homeland defence in case of a major terrorist attack by the end of 2002. Other European states have made informal expressions of interest in working more closely with America's new Homeland Defense Department to be better prepared to ramp up should mass-casualty terrorism spread to European homelands.

US preference for informal 'coalitions of the willing' may well have decreased the urgency surrounding the provision of a truly robust capability for the new 60,000-strong EU rapid reaction force, which remains largely a notional despite being officially declared operational at the December 2001 EU summit in Laeken. Still, the need for creating more appreciable European counter-terrorist military capabilities has not diminished altogether. The Assembly of the Western European Union issued a call, in a 3 June 2002 report, for the EU to update its military charter to include counter-terrorism. The report urges a reappraisal of defence strategies and European military cooperation, most importantly in procurement (emphasising intelligence, communications and precision-guided weapons) and manpower policies within the armed forces. It also states that the EU's rapid-reaction force is not sufficient to engage terrorist groups or retaliate against the regimes that sponsor them. Reaction within the EU to the report was mostly dismissive, with most analysts noting that the EU does not have full authority in military matters. For the immediate future, then, NATO remains the most important European counter-terrorism instrument, and its most important challenge is arriving at a new military framework for coalition operations. But no matter what the specific outcome, it appears likely that the alliance will become less a military organisation and more a military services one, where members can draw from an array of military capabilities according to emerging requirements.

FUTURE CHALLENGES

As al-Qaeda terrorist cells disperse in the absence of a host state, the war against terror will become increasingly amorphous. The most important challenge facing American decision-makers will be to maintain cooperative links with allies, friendly states and, indeed, some not-so-friendly states in the areas of intelligence and law enforcement. Notable successes in capturing al-Qaeda operatives in Morocco, Saudi Arabia and Chicago and the US receipt of valuable intelligence from the Syrian arrest of an al-Qaeda operative there demonstrate the value of these links in this shadowy new phase of the war on terror. The general outlines of al-Qaeda's strategy have become clear: the launching of suicide attacks against Western and Jewish targets while new plots are hatched for larger and more spectacular US attacks. The fact that dirty bombs might factor into these latter plans elevates effective monitoring and disruption to the highest priority. The dilemma confronting US counter-terrorist planners, however, is that corresponding US plans to implement regime-change in Iraq through preemptive military action could very well complicate its longer-term counter-terrorism strategy around the globe. How Washington handles the details of dealing with more reluctant allies and friends in the latter regard is of paramount importance. In particular, to manage these coalition relationships effectively, Washington will have to demonstrate that renewed UN inspections will not work, and make the case more convincingly than it has done so far that Saddam Hussein's regime is close to, or already possesses, an operational WMD capability.

An even longer-term challenge – and one that perhaps is more suited to systematic research than operational implementation at the moment – is to make more explicit the growing links not only between terrorist groups of both the new and old variety but transnational criminal organisations ones as well. The latter phenomenon emerged in the 1990s with the coincidental rise of the new terrorism, violent millenarian sects and other asymmetric challenges. Intelligence and law-enforcement priorities have naturally focused on terrorist groups with the greatest potential to produce truly mass-casualty results. Yet both criminal organisations and terrorist groups leverage the same power structures created by an increasingly globalised economy. Transnational criminal organisations have assisted terrorist groups and vice-versa, in spite of decidedly different motivations. The conflict in Colombia has become a laboratory for this phenomenon. There, the left-wing Revolutionary Armed Forces of Colombia (FARC) has drawn on the lucre of drug trafficking and the know-how of old terrorist groups like the Provisional Irish Republican Army to enhance its strength, suggesting a degree of pragmatism that certainly would not rule out a relationship with al-Qaeda.

Conversely, as al-Qaeda propagates more widely around the globe and sheds its dependence on state support, it is likely to find the modus operandi of transnational criminal organisations more and more suitable to its objectives. Indeed, al-Qaeda cells in Spain linked to the 11 September attacks used mass document and credit card fraud to fund their activity, and may have had contact with members of the Basque separatist terrorist group Euskadi ta Askatasuna, or ETA. The extent to which groups with mass-casualty intentions will intermingle more closely with other transnational organisations and terrorist groups remains to be seen. However better understanding of the potential for such liaisons and being prepared to adjust appropriate intelligence and law-enforcement mechanisms to deal with such a development would certainly seem to be in order.

Footnotes

[1] For more on US military transformation see 'US Military Transformation after 11 September', *Strategic Survey 2001/2002* (Oxford: Oxford University Press for IISS, 2002), pp. 69–79.

[2] For an in-depth treatment of this subject, see 'US Homeland Security: New Focus on Vulnerability', *Strategic Survey 2001/2002* (Oxford: Oxford University Press for IISS, 2002), pp. 36–53.

United States

The Bush administration's budget request for FY2003 included the largest annual increase in national defence spending – around US$48bn – since the beginning of the Reagan administration. However, this record increase in funding did not resolve the ongoing debate about procurement levels, or the tension between military transformation and re-capitalisation. Budget shares of the army, navy and air force remain constant at 24%, 29% and 29% respectively over the next five years. In total, national defence spending is planned to increase from US$396.8bn in FY2003 to US$469.8 in FY2007. Along with recently approved tax cuts, this will be a major factor in moving the United States from a budget surplus to a widening deficit.

The FY2003 budget was widely anticipated to be the first step towards Defense Secretary Donald Rumsfeld's stated aim of transforming the US military away from costly Cold War platforms and directing funds into network-centric capabilities, including intelligence, surveillance, reconnaissance, space initiatives and missile defence. After 11 September, however, it was difficult politically to make these sweeping changes. Instead, the FY2003 budget directed funds towards urgent areas of need, such as the campaign in Afghanistan, and avoided making any controversial decisions. It was not until May 2002 that the *Crusader* heavy artillery programme, as had been widely expected, became the first 'legacy' system to be cancelled.

Despite the headlines generated by the US$48bn addition to the National Defence Request, a closer examination of the data reveals that the increase was not as straightforward as it seemed. The extra funds are proposed to be allocated as follows:

- US$8.1bn to cover expanded future healthcare benefits for current military personnel when they retire;
- US$3.3bn for increased payments to retirement accounts for current Pentagon personnel;
- US$6.7bn for inflation adjustment;
- US$2.7bn for pay rises;
- US$7.4bn for revised cost estimates of programmes such as the F-22 fighter and contracted navy ships; and
- US$19.4bn for counter-terrorism efforts, including US$10bn in an unallocated contingency fund for the continuing war in Afghanistan, and US$9.4bn for specific costs associated with ongoing operations.

At the same time, these costs were offset by various accounting changes and internal savings, as follows:

- US$9.3bn in savings from procurement programmes included in FY2002 but left out of FY2003;
- US$5.6bn received from the retiree health-care trust fund; and
- Some US$3.4bn of the counter-terrorism funds, which was already included in the FY2002 budget supplement.

Furthermore, a significant proportion of the US$9.4bn allocated for war-related costs will be used to purchase equipment, including Unmanned Aerial Vehicles (UAVs), intelligence infrastructure and communications equipment, that will be in the inventory for several years. Therefore, of the headline increase, potentially US$20bn will be available for increased funding of new investments. This is clearly a substantial amount, but not enough to repair and maintain the current inventory, push ahead with previous procurement plans and at the same time, develop transformation systems and new technologies.

Air force

The USAF has requested US$87.2bn in FY2003, a 10% increase over the previous year. Of that total, US$28.3bn is earmarked for modernisation and transformation, US$24.6bn for operations and maintenance, and US$30bn for personnel. There was little change to the Pentagon's main aircraft programmes, with the air force moving forwards with its US$5.3bn plan to buy 23 low-rate initial production F-22s, an additional

Table 7 **National Defense Budget Authority, FY2001–FY2007** US$m

	2001	2002 Estimate	2003 Request	2004 Plan	2005 Plan	2006 Plan	2007 Plan
Military personnel	76,888	81,997	94,296	103,967	108,103	113,693	117,423
Operations & maintenance	115,758	127,668	150,444	140,980	147,088	152,449	155,310
Procurement	62.607	61,120	68,710	74,658	79,123	86,851	98,906
RDT&E	41,594	48,409	53,857	57,013	60,671	58,922	57,994
Military construction	5,423	6,555	4,767	5,102	6,325	10,803	13,773
Family housing	3,683	4,050	4,220	4,322	5,066	4,895	4,814
DoD net receipts, other	7,072	3,195	2,330	1,371	1,891	1,540	2,726
Total DoD	**313,025**	**332,994**	**378,624**	**387,413**	**408,267**	**429,153**	**450,946**
DoE (defence-related)	14,416	16,009	16,458	16,500	16,600	16,800	17,100
Other (defence-related)	1,630	1,719	1,721	1,700	1,700	1,700	1,700
Total national defence	329,071	350,722	396,803	405,613	426,567	447,653	469,746

three *Global Hawk* and 22 *Predator* UAVs. The air force also requested US$4bn for 12 C-17 *Globemaster* III strategic transporters. Four of these will be the first part of a new 60-aircraft follow-on multi-year contract with Boeing. Despite the major role that air-to-air refuelling tankers played in the coalition campaign in Afghanistan, and the fact that at any one time, a third of US KC-135 tankers are facing repairs, the Pentagon has yet to finalise a contract for the lease of 100 converted Boeing 767s. There were no procurement funds requested for this purpose in FY2003.

Navy

The US Navy continued the trend of declining aircraft and shipbuilding procurement quantities, despite a marginal increase in the procurement budget, up US$500m to US$24.9bn. Just five ships will be procured in FY2003: two DDG-51-class destroyers, one *Virginia*-class nuclear submarine, one LPD-17 amphibious landing ship and one cargo ship. This remains well below the target of procuring 8–10 new vessels a year, which is necessary to maintain a 300-ship inventory that naval planners consider the minimum requirement to meet anticipated operational requirements in coming years. The forward-planning element of the budget does makes provision for the procurement of five new ships next year, rising to eleven per year in FY2007.

In June 2002 the navy made first mention of its new operational concept: *Sea Power* 21. Evidence of the new concept was, however, clear in the announcement in late April 2002 of the contract for the DD(X) ship. This ship is intended to be the foundation of a family of future surface combatants, providing a common hull and common propulsion system for a planned future cruiser, CG(X), and a future littoral combat ship (LCS). DD(X) will be armed with *Tomahawk* missiles, a gun with a range of 100nm, *Standard* and *Sea Sparrow* SAMs and two helicopters. It will have an electric drive propulsion and requires a crew of only 125. Few details are currently available about the other two ships, but the LCS would be a new capability for the USN, being specifically designed to operate and counter threats in the littoral. It is not yet known how many of these ships will be ordered: the contract, awarded in April 2002 to Northrop Grumman at a cost of US$2.9bn, was only for the company to act as the lead design agent until 2005.

Other procurement plans remain largely unaffected by either the 2001 QDR or the events of 11 September. The first delivery of the new *Virginia*-class nuclear-fuelled submarine (SSN) is expected in 2004; 30 are still on order. The *Ronald Reagan* CVN, ninth of the *Nimitz* class, should be in service in 2003. One modified *Nimitz*, the tenth and last in the class, should be in service in 2008. It is intended to be a transition ship in terms of design and technology, paving the way for the new class of aircraft carrier, the CVNX, which is expected to enter service in 2013.

Of more direct importance to US homeland security is the US Coast Guard's *Deepwater* project. It includes the replacement or upgrade of 90 Coast Guard ships, 70 aircraft and 130 helicopters at a cost of US$15bn, over a period of 30 years. The largest of the planned surface ships, the National Security Cutters, should enter service in 2005–07 and will widen the Coast Guard's range of missions.

Army

The US Army proposed a budget of US$91bn for FY2003, an increase of nearly US$10bn on funding for FY2002. Central to the programme is increased funding for counter-terrorism programmes and the Future Combat Systems (FCS) programme, a key component of the army's future war-fighting capability. The army will devote around 80% of its science and technology budget to research on FCS, with a view to moving mature FCS technologies to the systems development and demonstration phase three years earlier than planned. To fund the change in priorities, the FY2003 proposal eliminates 12 programmes, generating savings of US$537m, and a further six programmes by 2007, yielding potential total savings of US$3.4bn during the next five years.

Although it was allocated US$476m in the FY2003 budget, and has so far consumed almost US$2bn in development costs, the *Crusader* self-propelled artillery howitzer was finally cancelled in May 2002. The 38-tonne *Crusader's* association with heavy mechanised forces was always going to be a target in the drive towards lighter and more agile platforms. One of the main arguments against the controversial artillery piece was the fact that it would take 60 C-17 *Globemaster* aircraft (half the US fleet) to deploy 18 *Crusaders* and their support vehicles into the theatre of operations. In total, a further US$9bn had been budgeted for the *Crusader* programme. These funds will now be directed toward accelerating or supporting the following projects:

- M109A6 *Paladin* & *Excalibur* precision-guided extended-range munitions;
- XM777 lightweight towed howitzer;
- High Mobility Artillery Rocket System;
- Future Combat Systems non-line-of-sight platform;
- NATO-standard integrated fuze to improve precision of artillery munitions; and
- Guided Multiple-Launch Rocket System.

Missile defence

The newly formed Missile Defense Agency has requested US$8.3bn to fund its missile defence initiatives in FY2003. Of this, US$7.1bn is earmarked for continued research and development efforts to establish an integrated, multi-layer ballistic missile defence system, to be fielded later this decade (Table 10). The agency's funding profile reflects its desire to focus on a single, integrated ballistic-missile defence system and to move away from an approach that focused on independently managed elements. To this end, extra funds become available in FY2003 following the 2002 cancellation of the Navy Area Defence programme and the restructuring of the Space-Based Infrared Systems and Space-Based Laser initiatives. US$1.1bn is requested for the ballistic-missile defence terminal-phase segment, US$3.2bn for the mid-course-phase segment and US$797m for the boost-phase segment.

The war on terror

On 14 September the US Congress approved a US$40bn emergency appropriation to pay for recovery efforts and counter-terrorism in the wake of the attacks on the Pentagon and World Trade Centre. Of these funds, US$17.2bn were allocated to the Department of Defense. In addition, the department submitted a request for US$14bn as an emergency non-offset supplement to the FY2002 Defence Budget, to cover the costs of counter-terrorism and ongoing operations in Afghanistan. At the peak of operations in Central

Asia, America had around 7,000 troops deployed in Afghanistan alone, and together with supporting assets, the costs of munitions, fuel and other supplies, *Operation Enduring Freedom* is estimated to have cost approximately US$1.5bn a month at the height of operations.

As a consequence of the 11 September attacks, President Bush has proposed a new cabinet-level Department of Homeland Security to unite essential agencies that presently operate independently of each other. Around US$38bn has been requested for the new department, which will bring together elements of various agencies including the Coast Guard, the Border Patrol, the Customs Service, Immigration, the Transportation Security Administration and the Federal Emergency Management Agency. The new department will be charged with four primary tasks:

- control of US borders;
- centralise intelligence and law enforcement information;
- quick and effective response to emergencies; and
- research and development to better detect weapons of mass destruction and to treat the victims of such an attack.

Even before the events of 2001, by the end of the decade, the Department of Defense was facing a procurement log-jam due to the number and size of existing military programmes. While the FY2003 budget request and forward planning clearly heralds a new era of increased spending for national defence following 11 September, it was conceived before the serious decline in the US stock market and the value of the US dollar, which began in April 2002. At that time of planning the budget, the US economy was expected to emerge from a shallow recession created by the bursting of the technology bubble in 2000. Growth was forecast to falter and then pick up, and the new paradigm of low inflation, low unemployment and growth would continue, providing increased revenue to fund government spending programmes and tax cuts. However, the severity of the downturn in equity markets and the deflationary environment that may result has serious implications for US government spending plans in the coming years. Although it is too early to know the exact long-term consequences for growth as a result of this year's slide in the stock market, it is likely that, in order to keep the deficit at a manageable level, spending levels will be subject to close scrutiny. In this event, it is probable that the Department of Defense will find itself under even more pressure to make 'legacy' programme adjustments – in terms of platform numbers or outright cancellations – if it is to succeed in transforming US armed forces in the direction that Defense Secretary Rumsfeld has advocated.

United States US

dollar US$		2000	2001	2002	2003
GDP	US$	9.9tr	10.2tr		
per capita	US$	35,317			
Growth	%	4.1	1.2		
Inflation	%	3.4	2.8		
Publ debt	%	58.8	57.6		
National Def bdgt					
BA	US$	304.1bn	329bn	350.7bn	
Outlay	US$	294.5bn	308.5bn	347.9bn	
Request					
BA	US$				396.8bn
Outlay	US$				379.0bn

Population			**285,900,000**
Age	13–17	18–22	23–32
Men	9,702,000	9,311,000	19,206,000
Women	9,252,000	8,894,000	18,310,000

Table 8 US Agency for International Development: International Affairs Budget US$m

Selected Programmes	2000 Actual	2001 Actual	2002 Est.	2003 Req.
Assistance to the Newly Independent States of the FSU	835	808	784	755
Support for East European democracy including FY2000 supplement	1,158	674	621	495
Voluntary peacekeeping operations	149	126	135	108
Contributions to UN and other peacekeeping operations	498	844	844	726
Economic support fund	2,792	2,314	2,224	2,290
International military education and training	50	58	70	80
Foreign military financing	4,788	3,568	3,650	4,107
Non-proliferation, anti-terrorism and related programmes	216	310	314	372
Wye Accord: Middle East Peace Process with FY2000 supplement	2,325			
International narcotics and crime with FY2000 supplement (*Plan Colombia*)	1,321	325	843	929
International disaster assistance	227	299	235	235
Total	14,359	22,835	24,013	25,428

Table 9 US National Defense Budget Function and other selected budgets, 1992, 1996–2003 US$bn

	National Defense Budget Function[1]		Department of Defense		Atomic Energy Defense Activities	International Security Assistance	Veterans Administration	Total Federal Government Expenditure	Total Federal Budget Surplus
FY	BA	Outlay	BA	Outlay	Outlay	Outlay	Outlay	Outlay	Outlay
1992	295.1	302.3	282.1	286.9	10.6	7.5	33.9	1,381	-290
1996	266.0	266.0	254.4	253.2	11.6	4.6	36.9	1,560	-107
1997	270.3	271.7	258.0	258.3	11.3	4.6	39.3	1,601	-21
1998	271.3	270.2	258.5	256.1	11.3	5.1	41.8	1,652	69
1999	292.1	275.5	278.4	261.4	12.4	5.5	43.2	1,702	124
2000	304.1	294.4	290.5	281.2	12.2	5.4	46.7	1,788	236
2001	329.0	308.5	309.9	290.9	13.0	6.0	50.7	1,856	280
2002	350.7	347.9	329.8	326.7	15.8	6.2	51.7	2,032	-165
2003	396.8	379.0	378.6	360.7	16.3	6.8	55.8	2,138	-109

Notes

FY = Fiscal Year (1 October–30 September)

[1] The National Defense Budget Function subsumes funding for the DoD, the DoE Atomic Energy Defense Activities and some smaller support agencies (including Federal Emergency Management and Selective Service System). It does not include funding for International Security Assistance (under International Affairs), the Veterans Administration, the US Coast Guard (Department of Transport), nor for the National Aeronautics and Space Administration (NASA). Funding for civil projects administered by the DoD is excluded from the figures cited here.

[2] Early in each calendar year, the US government presents its defence budget to Congress for the next fiscal year which begins on 1 October. It also presents its Future Years' Defense Program (FYDP), which covers the next fiscal year plus the following five. Until approved by Congress, the Budget is called the Budget Request; after approval, it becomes the Budget Authority.

[3] Definitions of US budget terms: **Authorisation** establishes or maintains a government programme or agency by defining its scope. Authorising legislation is normally a prerequisite for appropriations and may set specific limits on the amount that may be appropriated. An authorisation, however, does not make money available. **Budget Authority** is the legal authority for an agency to enter into obligations for the provision of goods or services. It may be available for one or more years. **Appropriation** is one form of Budget Authority provided by Congress for funding an agency, department or programme for a given length of time and for specific purposes. Funds will not necessarily all be spent in the year in which they are initially provided. **Obligation** is an order placed, contract awarded, service agreement undertaken or other commitment made by federal agencies during a given period which will require outlays during the same or some future period. **Outlays** are money spent by a federal agency from funds provided by Congress. Outlays in a given fiscal year are a result of obligations that in turn follow the provision of Budget Authority.

Table 10 Missile Defence Budget Request US$m

Research, Development, Testing & Engineering	FY2001	FY2002	FY2003
Missile Defense Agency			
National Missile Defence	1,857.5		
THAAD	541.0	866.5	934.7
Support Technologies	260.2		
Navy Area	269.6	99.3	
Navy Theatre Area	456.4		
Patriot PAC-3	79.9	128.2	
MEADS	52.6		
Family of Systems	225.9		
BMD Technical Operations	308.4		
International Coop Programmes	129.7		
Technology		139.3	121.7
BMD System		808.0	1,066.0
Terminal Defence Segment		200.1	170.0
Midcourse Defence Segment		3,762.3	3,192.6
Boost Defence Segment		599.8	796.9
Sensors Segment		335.4	373.4
Other Programmes	27.2	30.5	35.4
Subtotal	**4,208.4**	**6,969.4**	**6,690.7**
Air Force	386.1		
Airborne Laser	67.5		
Space Based Laser	233.5		
SBIRS-L			
Subtotal	**687.1**		
Army			
Patriot PAC-3			150.8
Patriot Improvements	12.4	13.8	43.7
MEADS			117.2
Subtotal	**12.4**	**13.8**	**312.2**
The Joint Staff			
JTAMDO	21.2	26.9	73.1
TOTAL Missile Defence	5,037.4	7,018.3	7,099.4

Table 11 Major US Equipment Orders, FY2001–FY2003

Classification		Designation	FY 2001		FY 2002		FY 2003		Comments
			Units	Value ($m)	Units	Value ($m)	Units	Value ($m)	
DOD	BMD	**PAC-3**	40	362	72	731	72	471	
	BMD	**PAC-3 mods**		22		25		192	
Joint	trg	**JPATS**	58	214.6	46	254.3	35	211.8	
	FGA	**JSF**		682.4		1,524.9		3,471.2	
	UAV	**UAV**	11	88.4	27	451.4	37	425.6	
	hel	**V-22**	9	1,430.2	11	1,681	11	1,994	
	tpt	**C-130J**	9	728.5	10	605.7	6	528.6	
	AAM	**AMRAAM**	233	133.3	247	140.7	261	139.5	
	ASM	**JASSM**		0.2	76	44.7	100	54.2	
	ASM	**JSOW**	104	216.1	35	29.4	476	195.2	
	PGM	**JDAM**	10,976	272.7	22,800	668.4	35,000	764.9	
	AAM	**AIM-9X**			243	62.9	581	110.3	
Air Force	tpt	**C-17**	12	2,995	15	3,762.3	12	3,826.7	
	E-8C	**J-STARS**	1	286.7	1	317.8	1	279.3	
	FGA	**F-15E**	5	661.4		241.6		232.5	
	FGA	**F-16 C/D**	4	411.1		232.4		265	
	FGA	**F-22**	10	2,536.5	13	3,037.3	23	4,621	
	SFW	**Sensor Fused Weapon**	300	112	263	108.8	298	106	
	WCMD	**Wind Corrected Dispenser**	5,918	100.3	6,917	111.4	4,959	71.2	
	sat	**DSP**		102		109		114.4	
	MLV	**Medium Launch Vehicles**		39		39.5		48.2	
	sat	***NAVSTAR***		159.6		171.2		209.5	
	launcher	***Titan***		393		350.2		335.3	
	launcher	**EELV**	3	286.3	1	98	1	158.9	
Army	hel	**AH-64D**	52	755.2	60	910.8	74	895.5	
	hel	**UH-60**	18	211.3	22	344.5	12	180.2	
	hel	**OH-58D**		41.5		42.3		42.4	
	MRL	**ATACMS**	34	215.4	6	60.6	0	49.7	
	ATGW	***Javelin***	2,776	318.3	4,139	411.8	1,725	250.5	

Table 11 **Page 2 of 2**

Classification	Designation	FY 2001		FY 2002		FY 2003		Comments
		Units	Value ($m)	Units	Value ($m)	Units	Value ($m)	
ATGM	***Longbow***	2,200	282.7	2,200	240.1	1,797	184.4	
MRL	**MLRS**	66	202.6	35	137.1	35	141.1	
IAM	**Interim Armored Vehicles**	447	928.4	303	658	332	811.8	
MBT	**M1A2**		290.9		391.7		376.3	Upgrade
AIFV	**M2A3**		423.5		387		397.1	Upgrade
ground systems	**DSCS**		74.3		99.4		89.8	
veh	**FHTV**		206.2		161.5		242.8	
veh	**FMTV**	2,269	465	2,493	464.1	3,409	681.4	
veh	**MTVR**	2,001	322.4	1,959	312.2	1,862	379.5	
veh	**HMMWV**		134.6		148.8		196.8	
Navy and Marines								
hel	**MH-60S**	15	283.8	13	254	15	372.2	
ELINT	**EA-6B**		184.4		149.7		223.5	Procurement Mods
recce	**E-2C *Hawkeye***	5	312.4	5	275.2	5	295.5	
FGA	**F/A-18 E/F**	39	2,837.8	48	3,118.3	44	3,159.5	
trg	**T-45**	14	302.3	6	183.4	8	221.4	
hel	**MH-60R**		53.7		9.9		116.2	Upgrade
anti ship cruise missiles	**RAM**		22.7	90	42.7	90	58.4	
SAM	**Standard**	86	171.9	96	156.2	87	156.4	
TCM	**(Tactical Cruise Missile) Tomahawk**			32	74	106	145.8	
SLBM	***Trident* II**	12	417.2	12	529.6	12	585.8	
CVN	**CVN-77**	1	4,143.6		136		243.7	
DDG	**AEGIS Destroyer**	3	3,282.4	2	3,081	2	2,369.5	
SSN	**NSSN**	1	1,766.9	1	2,263.2	1	2,219	
LPD	**LPD-17**		593.6		155		604.5	
auxiliary dry cargo ship	**T-AKE**	1	335.8	1	360.8	1	388.8	

NATO and Non-NATO Europe

NATO

In 2001, real defence expenditure by the non-US members of NATO, when measured in constant 2000 US$, fell 5.1%, from $173bn to $164bn. This continued the decline that began following the end of the Cold War, when non-US NATO spending was $225bn (in constant 2000 prices). In recent years, however, it is important to note that in local currency terms most countries have *increased* spending, the exceptions in 2001 being Canada, Belgium and Italy, where expenditure was only marginally lower. Preliminary budgets for 2002 indicate that in local currency terms, only Greece and Portugal will not increase expenditure.

Once again there was a call from UN General Secretary George Robertson urging European nations to increase defence funding to enhance EU capabilities and to prevent the technological and capabilities gap with the United States growing wider. Given that most Europeans leaders are more concerned with domestic issues, including the demographic effect of ageing populations and the consequences of the structural changes brought about by the single currency, it is unlikely that defence will receive the budgetary priority needed to remedy the situation. The psychological shift that occurred in the population of the United States following the attacks of 11 September, lending public support to higher defence spending to combat terrorism, has not been mirrored in Europe, where several countries have faced the reality of terrorism for many years.

In the **UK**, the three-year comprehensive spending review, released in July promised an increase in the defence budget of £3.2bn between 2002 and 2005–06, providing 1.2% annual average real growth – the largest planned increase in 20 years. Of this increase, over £1bn of new capital and £500m of new resources is to be devoted to new network-centric capabilities and other equipment, which will enable the conclusions of the new Strategic Defence Review chapter commissioned by the Defence Secretary following the events of 11 September.

A report from the UK National Audit office indicated that the Ministry of Defence is improving its control of costs and delays in the procurement process. Although costs remain 6.6% over budget, good progress was made in terms of programme slippage where the combined total for the year 2001 was down to 29 months, less than half that in 2000. Only four projects let their in-service date slip further: ASRAAM, WAH-64, *Seawolf* (mid-life upgrades – MLU) and submarine (MLU). The UK is pressing ahead with upgrades to the Royal Air Force's *Harrier* GR7 ground attack aircraft, improving them to the GR9/9A configuration. The modernisation, costing around £480m, has taken on greater importance since the announcement, earlier this year, that the *Harrier* FA2 fighters will be removed from service between 2004 and 2006. Until the Joint Strike Fighter replacement arrives in 2012, the Royal Navy's three *Invincible*-class aircraft carriers will be assigned RAF aircraft from Joint Force Harrier.

The UK Ministry of Defence awarded BAE Systems and Thales (Naval) Ltd contracts to conduct second-stage assessment-phase work on the UK's £2.7bn Future Aircraft Carrier programme. The date of selection of a single contractor has been brought forward to 2003. The UK received its first *Apache* AH-64 helicopter, which will be designated WAH-64 when domestic production begins.

In **France** the defence budget for 2002 was set at €28.9bn, virtually unchanged from 2001 when adjusted for inflation. However, procurement spending was slightly lower at €12.5bn, although this figure is set to increase with the implementation of the new six year procurement plan for the period 2003–08. The new National Defence Programme Law envisages average annual military procurement of €13.3bn, with the overall defence budget being maintained at about 2.6% of GDP. A total of €80bn is available for new equipment during the six-year period. Major projects will include the first four of 17 new multi-role frigates, 50 A400M transport aircraft, 433 VBCI armoured fighting vehicles, a third *Triomphant*-class submarine and two of six *Barracuda*-class attack submarines. The frigate programme is likely to cost up to $4.4bn with the first delivery around 2008. Half of the 4,000-tonne vessels are dedicated to littoral warfare and equipped with the new SCALP naval cruise missile, while the other half are earmarked primarily for anti-submarine warfare.

The core defence budget in **Germany** for 2002 is €23.6bn, unchanged from 2002. Additional funds have been made available from a new anti-terrorism fund established after 11 September, boosting the overall total to €24.4bn. The anti-terror fund amounts to €1.5bn a year until 2006, of which the defence ministry will receive half. It is believed that the majority of the extra military funds – around €600m – will go towards new equipment, while the remaining €150m will serve as a reserve fund. The defence budget is planned to remain fixed at €24.4 until 2006.

Following months of difficulty, the German parliament was able to authorise German participation in the A400M programme. The 2002 budget contained an order for 40 of the new Airbus military transport aircraft, at a cost of €5.1bn. Extra financing for the remaining 33 aircraft is scheduled for parliamentary approval in the 2003 budget, after the national elections in September. However, should the funding for the remaining aircraft not be forthcoming in 2003, Germany has drafted a side letter to the original contract in which it agrees to pay compensation to the other six nations involved in the project.

Concern is growing that Germany is facing a procurement problem in the years ahead that can only be solved by either a substantial increase in the defence budget or the cancellation of certain programmes. The 2002 defence budget allocated just €3.5bn to procurement; however, within a few years four programmes alone – *Eurofighter*, TIGER, NH 90 and A400M – will be consuming around €3.2bn in procurement funds a year.

In line with most other European nations, the **Netherlands**' defence budget for 2002 was virtually unchanged, taking inflation into account. Despite last-minute incentives offered by Rafale of France, and to the disappointment of the European defence industry in general, the Netherlands joined the US-led Joint Strike Fighter programme as a Level 2 partner. The country will contribute around US$800m towards the Lockheed Martin-led system development and demonstration phase for the F-35 JSF. The agreement suggests that the Royal Netherlands Air Force will replace its fleet of 138 F-16s (MLU) with the new aircraft, a process due to start around 2010. It is possible that the Netherlands will only procure around 100 F-35s, replacing the rest of their current fleet with medium-altitude, long-endurance unmanned aerial vehicles. Beginning in 2010, a budget allocation of €5.5bn has been slated to fund the procurement.

Italy increased its defence budget by 7.1% in 2002 to €18.9bn. However, most of the increase will be absorbed by personnel costs generated by the transition from a predominantly conscript force to an all-volunteer force. Italy's all-professional military will ultimately have 190,000 personnel. With the move to professional forces and the need to eliminate the technology gap that exists with its allies, Italy has pledged to increase defence spending over the next 10 years from the current level of 1.5% of GDP to 2%. A stop-gap special law is planned to provide up to €7.5bn extra during this period, principally to pay for new and ongoing procurement. The latest White Book on defence makes air defence and aerospace surveillance key priorities: airborne early warning aircraft, surface-to air-missile batteries, mobile and fixed surveillance radars, and C4I are to receive immediate funding.

The Italian parliament also gave its approval for the design, development and purchase of a new class of 10 frigates. The programme, worth €5.6bn, will be funded until 2018 and it is expected that peak expenditure of €684m will occur in 2014. The project is expected to exploit, as much as possible, the development work carried out on the joint Franco-Italian *Horizon* project.

Due to overall pressure on the defence budget, Italy withdrew from the A400M project. Originally expected to take a 7.5% stake in the project and to buy 16 aircraft, Italy will make do with 22 new C-130Js and 12 C-27J *Spartans*. An order for four Boeing 767 tanker/transport aircraft squeezed the air force budget further.

Following **Turkey**'s financial crisis of 2000–01 and a re-evaluation of threats, the Ministry of Defence suspended 88 projects, giving priority to programmes including the acquisition of the US–Israeli-developed *Arrow* anti-ballistic missile system, observation satellites and airborne early warning aircraft.

The effects of the global economic downturn in 2001 on Turkey were worse than expected. Real GNP fell by 9.3%, higher than originally forecast, and the global slowdown kept economic activity subdued into 2002. Harsh economic measures taken in 2001, including a floating exchange rate and some structural reform, failed to have the desired results. Following the economic consequences of 11 September, the IMF was forced to agree to a new $12bn of funding for Turkey. The defence budget was increased from TL7,000tr to TL9,700tr. Austerity measures adopted in 2001 enabled the Turkish armed forces to save around $400m in operational expenses, most of which was added to the central procurement budget, set at just $0.5bn in 2002.

Turkey joined the JSF system development and demonstration phase of the project as a Level 3 member. It will provide 1–2% of the funding for this phase and have a seat in the JSF joint programme office. Turkey has plans to buy around 150 aircraft, with deliveries beginning in 2013.

In December 2001, the **Czech Republic** chose 24 Swedish-made *Gripen* supersonic multi-role fighter aircraft to replace their ageing MiG-21s, estimated to have cost Kc90bn. At a cost of $1.3bn, the package was to include the provision of pilot and ground-crew training, and spare parts for three years. The first aircraft squadron was due to become operational in 2005; however, following devastating floods in August 2002, the plan was scrapped and cheaper options are now being studied.

In **Portugal** the defence budget was cut by around 30%, from Esc350bn in 2001 to Esc252bn in 2002. The cuts are to be achieved by reorganisation and reducing costs and reinforcing maintenance and operations. A working group has been established to review the funding of the armed forces. Despite his pledge to restructure the armed forces and pursue much-needed equipment acquisition, Defence Minister Rui Pena was held back by a government requirement to reduce the national budget in line with constraints imposed by membership of the common European currency. He has called for a re-assessment of the plan to buy three submarines, but confirmed an intention to buy 12 EH101 utility helicopters for search-and-rescue duties and fishery protection.

Despite an increase in the defence budget for 2002 up NKr0.6bn to NKr27.6bn, due to a shortage of funds **Norway** has withdrawn from the *Viking* programme to develop a common submarine with Denmark and Sweden. Defence spending over the next four years is planned at Nkr118bn, up from the NKr114bn originally proposed by the former Labour government, but NKr5.6bn short of the defence structure plan approved by parliament in mid-2001. The shortfall will necessitate several cuts. In particular the army will be cut from four to three brigades and three landing craft will be lost.

Denmark joined the system development and demonstration (ADD) phase of the US Joint Striker Fighter as a Level 3 member and will contribute an initial $107m. No decision has been made on whether Denmark will replace its 69 F-16 with the JSF.

Poland announced a new 2001–06 defence plan, stipulating that it will spend no less than 1.95% of GDP on defence. The plan is part of an ongoing defence reorganisation that will allow the Ministry of Defence to retain any savings made through multi-year contracts, force reduction and procurement policy. At least 70 military facilities will be closed and the savings will be directed toward the expansion of ten primary bases. Procurement spending is due to rise from 8.3% in 2002 to around 22% in 2006. The major programmes identified are 220 armoured personnel carriers, 128 main battle tanks (ex-German *Leopard* 2A4), a second ex-US Navy *Perry*-class frigate, four used submarines (ex-Norwegian) and the first two of seven planned multi-role corvettes.

NON-NATO EUROPE

All three Baltic countries aspiring to become full members of NATO increased their defence budgets in 2002. In nominal terms, **Estonia** increased planned spending by 22% to kn2,019m (US$131m), **Latvia** by 44% to L68.8m (US$116m) and **Lithuania** by 21% to L808m (US$237m).

The *Eurofighter* is the chosen replacement of **Austria**'s ageing *Draken* fighter aircraft. The original deal was valued at US$1.8bn for the delivery of 24 aircraft; however, due to the financial consequences of the devastating floods in August 2002, the order was reduced from 24 to 18 single-seat aircraft. The *Eurofighter Typhoon* beat the F-16 and *Gripen* for selection, not only on its perceived technological potential but also an offsets package worth 200% of the final contract value. Seven of the new aircraft are due for delivery in 2005, with the remainder due by 2007. It is possible that in the interim, Germany may make some loan aircraft available from 2003.

In **Bulgaria** the defence budget increased from L786bn (US$360m) in 2001 to L828bn (US$431m) in 2002. In an attempt to bolster its prospects of being invited to join NATO, Bulgaria had expressed an interest in acquiring up to 22 F-16 fighter aircraft from the US; however, due to the limited funds available for procurement, the air force instead opted to upgrade its fleet of 21 MiG-29s. The work will be completed by the Russian company RSK MiG, at a cost of around US$50m.

The implementation of 'Armed Forces 21' did not change the 2002 defence budget in **Switzerland**. Under the plan, the Swiss military will shrink from 363,000 troops to 120,000 active and 80,000 reserves by 2005. Switzerland's federal council have warned that spending should not fall any further, and that procurement spending, currently Sfr1.6bn, must be increased. The major decision to be made concerns replacements for Switzerland's ageing fleet of 101 F5-E/F *Tiger* fighter jets and 16 *Mirage* III RS reconnaissance jets, whose maintenance costs increase with age.

Ukraine increased official defence spending from h3.3bn to h3.4bn, not sufficient to cover inflation, which was at least 12% in 2001. However, Ukrainian defence outlays are provided through a range of budgetary and non-budgetary avenues, including the military itself, which is expected to finance a significant proportion of expenditure through its own economic activities. Procurement plans include continued work with Russia on the AN-70 transport aircraft, completion of the cruiser *Ukrainya* and the purchase of 10 T-84 main battle tanks. Only h300m has been earmarked for these activities, and given personnel and maintenance costs, it is unlikely that extra funds will be available to implement procurement objectives fully.

Despite renewed economic growth of over 4% in 2001, real defence spending in **Georgia** continues to fall. Savings from force reductions have been inadequate to offset budget reductions. The plan to move towards fully professional armed forces has been put on hold due to the cost involved in making the transition from conscript to contracted volunteer personnel. We estimate that in PPP terms, defence spending in Georgia fell from US$290m in 2000 to US$270m in 2001 or around 1.5% of GDP.

Belgium Be

euro € (franc fr)		2000	2001	2002
GDP	fr	10.0tr	10.5tr	
	US$	243bn	227bn	
per capita	US$	23,640	22,060	
Growth	%	4.0	1.1	
Inflation	%	2.5	2.5	
Publ debt	%	109.8	105.4	
Def exp	fr	139bn	138bn	
	US$	3.4bn	3.0bn	
Def bdgt	fr	99.4bn	102.6bn	
	€			2.6bn
	US$	2.4bn	2.2bn	2.7bn
US$1=fr		43.5	46	
US$1=€				0.98

Population			**10,300,000**
Age	13–17	18–22	23–32
Men	306,000	310,000	685,000
Women	291,000	298,000	663,000

Canada Ca

dollar C$		2000	2001	2002
GDP	C$	1,065bn	1,084bn	
	US$	720bn	700bn	
per capita	US$	23,570	23,700	
Growth	%	4.4	1.5	
Inflation	%	2.7	2.5	
Publ debt	%	104.9	98.3	
Def exp	C$	12.3bn	12.2bn	
	US$	8.4bn	7.9bn	
Def bdgt	C$	11.9bn	11.4bn	11.5bn
	US$	8.0bn	7.4bn	7.6bn
US$1=C$		1.47	1.54	1.50

Population			**31,000,000**
Age	13–17	18–22	23–32
Men	1,008,000	983,000	2,022,000
Women	963,000	949,000	1,976,000

Czech Republic Cz

koruna Kc		2000	2001	2002
GDP	Kc	2.0tr	2.1tr	
	US$	52bn	55bn	
per capita	US$	4,944	5,294	
Growth	%	2.9	3.6	
Inflation	%	3.9	4.9	
Debt	US$	23.0bn	23.1bn	
Def exp	Kc	44bn	45bn	
	US$	1,148m	1,192m	
Def bdgt	Kc	44.0bn	44.7bn	48.0bn
	US$	1,138m	1,187m	1,622m
FMA (US)	US$	7.4m	10.3m	11.8m

Cz contd	2000	2001	2002
US$1=Kc	38.6	38.0	29.6

Population			**10,300,000**
Slovak 3% **Polish** 0.6% **German** 0.5%			
Age	13–17	18–22	23–32
Men	333,000	408,000	811,000
Women	317,000	392,000	783,000

Denmark Da

kroner kr		2000	2001	2002
GDP	Kr	1,283bn	1,339bn	
	US$	160bn	161bn	
per capita	US$	30,341	30,439	
Growth	%	3.0	0.9	
Inflation	%	2.9	2.5	
Publ debt	%	48.3	46.2	
Def exp	Kr	19.4bn	20.5bn	
	US$	2.4bn	2.5bn	
Def bdgt	Kr	16.5bn	17.1bn	17.2bn
	US$	2.1bn	2.1bn	2.4bn
US$1=kr		8.0	8.3	7.3

Population			**5,308,000**
Age	13–17	18–22	23–32
Men	141,000	148,000	375,000
Women	136,000	144,000	363,000

France Fr

euro € (franc fr)		2000	2001	2002
GDP	fr	9.2tr	9.6tr	
	US$	1.3tr	1.3tr	
per capita	US$	22,000	221,110	
Growth	%	3.6	2.0	
Inflation	%	1.8	1.8	
Publ debt	%	64.4	64.9	
Def exp	fr	240bn	246bn	
	US$	34.0bn	33.6bn	
Def bdgt	fr	187.9bn	189.0bn	
	€			28.9bn
	US$	26.6bn	25.8bn	29.5bn
US$1=fr		7.07	7.31	
US$1=€				0.98

Population			**59,500,000**
Age	13–17	18–22	23–32
Men	1,981,000	1,915,000	4,275,000
Women	1,892,000	1,834,000	4,090,000

Germany Ge

euro € (deutschmark DM)

		2000	2001	2002
GDP	DM	3.9tr	4.0tr	
	US$	1.8tr	1.8tr	
per capita	US$	22,600	22,700	
Growth	%	3.0	0.6	
Inflation	%	1.9	2.4	
Publ debt	%	60.8	60.9	
Def exp	DM	59.7bn	59.8bn	
	US$	27.9bn	27.5bn	
Def bdgt	DM	48.3bn	46.8bn	
	€			24.4bn
	US$	23.6bn	21.5bn	24.9bn
US$1=DM		2.14	2.23	
US$1=€				0.98

Population **82,000,000**

Age	13–17	18–22	23–32
Men	2,394,000	2,232,000	5,168,000
Women	2,266,000	2,123,000	5,019,000

Greece Gr

drachma dr

		2000	2001	2002	
GDP	dr	41.4tr	44.3tr		
	US$	113bn	114bn		
per capita	US$	10,720	11,050		
Growth	%	4.3	4.1		
Inflation	%	2.9	3.7		
Publ debt	%	103.8	99.8		
Def exp	dr	2.0tr	2.1tr		
	US$	5.5bn	5.6bn		
Def bdgt	dr	1,160bn	1,300bn		
	€			3.4bn	
	US$	3.2bn	3.4bn	3.5bn	
US$1=dr		365	378		
US$1=€				0.98	
FMA (US)	US$	0.035m	0.025m	0.5m	0.6m

Population[a] **10,600,000** Muslim 1%

Age	13–17	18–22	23–32
Men	329,000	381,000	824,000
Women	310,000	361,000	791,000

[a] Excl ε350–400,000 Albanians working in Gr in 1999

Hungary Hu

forint f

		2000	2001	2002
GDP	f	13.1tr	14.8tr	
	US$	46bn	52bn	
per capita	US$	4,665	5,245	
Growth	%	5.3	3.8	
Inflation	%	9.8	9.1	
Debt	US$	32.2bn	30.3bn	

Hu contd		2000	2001	2002
Def exp	f	226bn	265bn	
	US$	804m	926m	
Def bdgt	f	189bn	236bn	261bn
	US$	671m	823m	1,084m
US$1=f		282	286	241
FMA (US)	US$	7.4m	10.2m	11.8m

Population **9,900,000**

Romany 4% German 3% Serb 2% Romanian 1% Slovak 1%

Age	13–17	18–22	23–32
Men	304,000	386,000	721,000
Women	288,000	362,000	675,000

Iceland Icl

kronur K

		2000	2001	2002
GDP	K	668bn	750bn	
	US$	8.5bn	8bn	
per capita	US$	30,263	27,209	
Growth	%	5.0	2.1	
Inflation	%	5.0	9.2	
Publ debt	%	42.1	46.4	
Sy bdgt[a]	K	1.9bn	1.9bn	2.1bn
	US$	23.9m	20.1m	25.1m
US$1=K		78.6	97.4	83.6

[a] Icl has no Armed Forces. Sy bdgt is mainly for Coast Guard

Population **283,000**

Age	13–17	18–22	23–32
Men	11,000	11,000	22,000
Women	10,000	10,000	20,000

Italy It

euro € (lira L)

		2000	2001	2002
GDP	L	2,257tr	2,356tr	
	US$	1.1tr	1.1tr	
per capita	US$	18, 370	19,060	
Growth	%	2.7	1.8	
Inflation	%	2.6	2.7	
Publ debt	%	110.8	107.7	
Def exp	L	47tr	46tr	
	US$	22.5bn	21.4bn	
Def bdgt	L	32.8tr	34.2tr	
	€			19bn
	US$	15.7bn	15.9bn	19.4bn
US$1=L		2,090	2,150	
US$1=€				0.98

Population **57,500,000**

Age	13–17	18–22	23–32
Men	1,483,000	1,680,000	4,397,000
Women	1,409,000	1,601,000	4,242,000

Luxembourg Lu

euro € (franc fr)		2000	2001	2002
GDP	fr	826bn	854bn	
	US$	19bn	19bn	
per capita	US$	44,050	43,520	
Growth	%	7.5	5.1	
Inflation	%	3.8	2.4	
Publ debt	%	5.3	4.5	
Def exp	fr	5.6bn	6.7bn	
	US$	129m	148m	
Def bdgt	fr	4.3bn	6.6bn	
	€	98m	146m	177m
	US$	98m	146m	180m
US$1=fr		43.5	45	
US$1=€				0.98

Population 436,000 foreign citizens ε124,000

Age	13–17	18–22	23–32
Men	12,000	12,000	27,000
Women	12,000	12,200	28,000

Netherlands Nl

euro € (guilder gld)		2000	2001	2002
GDP	gld	883bn	936bn	
	US$	373bn	384bn	
per capita	US$	23,540	24,120	
Growth	%	3.5	1.1	
Inflation	%	2.3	5.1	
Publ debt	%	63.7	53.9	
Def exp	gld	14.3bn	15.6bn	
	US$	6.2bn	6.4bn	
Def bdgt	gld	14.2bn	14.0bn	
	€			6.5bn
	US$	6.0bn	5.7bn	6.6bn
US$1=gld		2.37	2.44	
US$1=€				0.98

Population 15,900,000

Age	13–17	18–22	23–32
Men	447,000	439,000	1,112,000
Women	428,000	419,000	1,053,000

Norway No

kroner kr		2000	2001	2002
GDP	kr	1,403bn	1,472bn	
	US$	159bn	164bn	
per capita	US$	35,600	36,300	
Growth	%	2.3	1.4	
Inflation	%	3.1	3.0	
Publ debt	%	28.0	27.1	
Def exp	kr	25.4bn	27.1bn	
	US$	2.9bn	3.0bn	

No contd		2000	2001	2002
Def bdgt	kr	25.3bn	27.1bn	27.6bn
	US$	2.9bn	3.0bn	3.8bn
US$1=kr		8.81	8.99	7.32

Population 4,500,000

Age	13–17	18–22	23–32
Men	138,000	134,000	327,000
Women	131,000	127,000	309,000

Poland Pl

zloty z		2000	2001	2002
GDP	z	685bn	722bn	
	US$	158bn	176bn	
per capita	US$	4,090	4,571	
Growth	%	4.1	1.1	
Inflation	%	10.1	5.6	
Debt	US$	63bn	62bn	
Def exp	z	13.4bn	14.2bn	
	US$	3.1bn	3.5bn	
Def bdgt	z	13.2bn	14.0bn	14.3bn
	US$	3.0bn	3.4bn	3.5bn
FMA (US)	US$	9.6m	13.5m	13.9m
US$1=z		4.35	4.09	4.03

Population 38,600,000

German 1.3% Ukrainian 0.6% Belarussian 0.5%

Age	13–17	18–22	23–32
Men	1,640,000	1,688,000	2,792,000
Women	1,558,000	1,611,000	2,672,000

Portugal Por

euro € (escudo esc)		2000	2001	2002
GDP	esc	22.8tr	24.6tr	
	US$	106bn	111bn	
per capita	US$	10,600	11,100	
Growth	%	3.2	1.6	
Inflation	%	2.8	4.4	
Publ debt	%	55.6	52.8	
Def exp	esc	480bn	504bn	
	US$	2.2bn	2.3bn	
Def bdgt	esc	274bn	350bn	
	€			1.3bn
	US$	1.3bn	1.6bn	1.3bn
US$1=esc		216	222	
US$1=€				0.98
FMA (US)	US$	0.7m	0.75m	0.75m

Population 10,000,000

Age	13–17	18–22	23–32
Men	317,000	365,000	808,000
Women	298,000	347,000	785,000

Spain Sp

euro € (peseta pts)		2000	2001	2002
GDP	pts	101bn	108bn	
	US$	566bn	588bn	
per capita	US$	14,220	14,730	
Growth	%	4.1	2.8	
Inflation	%	3.5	3.2	
Publ debt	%	74.4	71.4	
Def exp	pts	1.3tr	1.3tr	
	US$	7.1bn	7.1bn	
Def bdgt	pts	1,231bn	1,303bn	
	€			8.2bn
	US$	6.9bn	7.1bn	8.4bn
US$1=pts		179	184	
US$1=€				0.98

Population 39,900,000

Age	13–17	18–22	23–32
Men	1,156,000	1,435,000	3,326,000
Women	1,084,000	1,355,000	3,166,000

Turkey Tu

lira L		2000	2001	2002
GDP	L	124,000tr	181,000tr	
	US$	200bn	148bn	
per capita	US$	3,000	2,190	
Growth	%	7.4	-6.2	
Inflation	%	54.9	54.4	
Debt	US$	119bn	118bn	
Def exp	L	6,248tr	9,030tr	
	US$	10.0bn	7.4bn	
Def bdgt	L	4,742tr	7,000tr	9,700tr
	US$	7.6bn	5.7bn	5.8bn
FMA (US)	US$	1.5m	1.6m	2.7m
US$1=L		625,219	1.2m	1.6m

Population 67,600,000 **Kurds** ε20%

Age	13–17	18–22	23–32
Men	3,264,000	3,251,000	6,242,000
Women	3,196,000	3,097,000	5,886,000

United Kingdom UK

pound £		2000	2001	2002
GDP	£	944bn	989bn	
	US$	1.4tr	1.4tr	
per capita	US$	24,120	23,740	
Growth	%	3.0	2.2	
Inflation	%	2.1	2.1	
Publ debt	%	54.4		
Def exp	£	23.5bn	24.8bn	
	US$	35.6bn	35.4bn	
Def bdgt	£	22.9bn	23.5bn	24.2bn

UK contd		2000	2001	2002
	US$	34.8bn	33.6bn	38.4bn
US$1=£		0.66	0.7	0.65

Population 59,500,000

Northern Ireland 1,600,000 **Protestant** 56% **Roman Catholic** 41%

Age	13–17	18–22	23–32
Men	1,926,000	1,772,000	3,997,000
Women	1,839,000	1,690,000	3,826,000

Albania Alb

leke		2000	2001	2002
GDP	leke	536bn	597bn	
	US$	3.8bn	4.1bn	
per capita	US$	1,190	1,319	
Growth	%	7.8	7.0	
Inflation	%	-0.2	3.5	
Debt	US$	1,100m	1,100m	
Def exp	leke	16.1bn	15.5bn	
	US$	113m	108m	
Def bdgt	leke	6.0bn	6.2bn	6.3
	US$	42.2m	42.4m	
FMA[a] (US)	US$	2.2m	9.8m	4.8m
US$1=leke		143	143	136

Population 3,100,000

Muslim 70% **Albanian Orthodox** 20% **Roman Catholic** 10%; **Greek** ε3–8%

Age	13–17	18–22	23–32
Men	191,000	176,000	329,000
Women	174,000	161,000	304,000

Armenia Arm

dram d		2000	2001	2002
GDP[a]	d	1,033bn	1,128bn	
	US$	9.7bn	10bn	
per capita	US$	2,553	2,632	
Growth	%	6.0	7.5	
Inflation	%	-0.8	3.1	
Debt	US$	858m	904m	
Def exp[a]		US$	690m	650m
Def bdgt	d	38bn	35bn	35bn
	US$	72m	65m	62m
US$1=d		539	555	568

[a] = PPP estimate

Population 3,800,000

Armenian Orthodox 94% **Russian** 2% **Kurd** 1%

Age	13–17	18–22	23–32
Men	186,000	180,000	298,000
Women	182,000	176,000	288,000

Austria A

euro € (schilling ÖS)		2000	2001	2002
GDP	ÖS	2.8tr	2.9tr	
	US$	189bn	189bn	
per capita	US$	23,470	23,430	
Growth	%	3.2	1.0	
Inflation	%	2.4	2.7	
Publ Debt	%	62.9	61.5	
Def exp	ÖS	23.9bn	22.9bn	
	US$	1.6bn	1.5bn	
Def bdgt	ÖS	23.5bn	23bn	
	€			1.6bn
	US$	1.6bn	1.5bn	1.7bn
US$1=ÖS		14.86	15.27	
US$1=€				0.98

Population			8,100,000
Age	13–17	18–22	23–32
Men	245,000	237,000	577,000
Women	234,000	228,000	555,000

Azerbaijan Az

manat m		2000	2001	2002
GDP[a]	m	21tr	26tr	
	US$	22bn	23bn	
per capita	US$	2,740	2,840	
Growth	%	11.3	9.0	
Inflation	%	1.8	2.0	
Debt	US$	1,158m	1,120m	
Def exp[a]	US$	830m	850m	
Def bdgt	m	495bn	540bn	580m
	US$	110m	115m	118m
US$1=m		4,474	4,656	4,881

[a]PPP estimate

Population			8,100,000
Daghestani 3% **Russian** 2% **Armenian** 2–3% mostly in Nagorno-Karabakh			
Age	13–17	18–22	23–32
Men	413,000	372,000	618,000
Women	393,000	345,000	610,000

Belarus Bel

rubel r		2000	2001	2002
GDP[a]	r	9.1tr	17tr	
	US$	75bn	90bn	
per capita	US$	7,400	8,910	
Growth	%	6.0	4.1	
Inflation	%	169	59.8	
Debt	US$	829m	950m	
Def exp[a]	US$	2.1bn	2.0bn	
Def bdgt	r	107.3bn	170.8bn	321.3bn

Bel contd		2000	2001	2002
	US$	122m	122m	176.7m
US$1=r		876	1,390	1,818

[a] = PPP estimate

Population			10,100,000
Russian 13% **Polish** 4% **Ukrainian** 3%			
Age	13–17	18–22	23–32
Men	407,000	398,000	715,000
Women	393,000	387,000	711,000

Bosnia-Herzegovina BiH

convertible mark		2000	2001	2002
GDP	US$	5.1bn	4.7bn	
per capita	US$	1,080	1,150	
Growth	%	5.9	5.6	
Inflation	%	4.6		
Debt	US$	2.6bn	2.8bn	
Def exp	US$	164m	144m	
Def bdgt	US$	144m	130m	130m
FMA (US)	US$	0.6m	7.1m	3.0
$1=convertible mark		2.1	2.2	1.9

Population			ε4,100,000
Bosnian Muslim 44% **Serb** 33% **Croat** 17%			
Age	13–17	18–22	23–32
Men	195,000	189,000	334,000
Women	185,000	178,000	313,000

Bulgaria Bg

leva L		2000	2001	2002
GDP	L	25.4bn	29.5bn	
	US$	12.0bn	13.5bn	
per capita	US$	1,500	1,710	
Growth	%	5.8	4.5	
Inflation	%	10.4	7.4	
Debt	US$	10.4bn	9.9bn	
Def exp	L	728bn	814bn	
	US$	343m	373m	
Def bdgt	L	729bn	786bn	828bn
	US$	333m	360m	431m
FMA (US)	US$	5.8m	15.0m	9.7m
US$1=L		2.12	2.18	1.92

Population			7,900,000
Turkish 9% **Macedonian** 3% **Romany** 3%			
Age	13–17	18–22	23–32
Men	277,000	303,000	598,000
Women	263,000	287,000	571,000

Croatia Cr

kuna k		2000	2001	2002	
GDP	k	157bn	169bn		
	US$	19.1bn	20.3bn		
per capita	US$	4.036	4,309		
Growth	%	3.7	4.2		
Inflation	%	6.2	5.7		
Debt	US$	10.8bn	13.0bn		
Def exp	k	4.6bn	4.4bn		
	US$	555m	522m		
Def bdgt	k	4.7bn	4.3bn	4.3bn	
	US$	573m	522m	599m	
FMA (US)	US$	4.5m	5.0m	5.6m	6.7m
US$1=k		8.27	8.34	7.27	

Population ε4,700,000 Serb 3% Slovene 1%

Age	13–17	18–22	23–32
Men	163,000	169,000	328,000
Women	153,000	159,000	314,000

Cyprus Cy

pound C£		2000	2001	2002
GDP	C£	5.5bn	5.9bn	
	US$	8.9bn	8.9bn	
per capita	US$	10,150	9,900	
Growth	%	5.1	4.0	
Inflation	%	4.2		
Debt	US$	6.6bn	6.9bn	
Def exp	C£	224m	212m	
	US$	361m	321m	
Def bdgt	C£	266m		
	US$	429m		
US$1=C£		0.62	0.66	0.56

Population 900,000 Turkish 23%

Age	13–17	18–22	23–32
Men	33,000	30,000	53,000
Women	32,000	28,000	50,000

Estonia Ea

kroon kn		2000	2001	2002
GDP	kn	85.4bn	95.2bn	
	US$	5.0bn	5.4bn	
per capita	US$	3,550	3,872	
Growth	%	6.4	5.0	
Inflation	%	4.0	5.7	
Debt	US$	3.3bn	3.3bn	
Def exp	kn	1,319m	1,652m	
	US$	77m	94m	
Def bdgt	kn	1,332m	1,651m	2,019m
	US$	78.5m	93.9m	131m
FMA (US)	US$	4.8m	6.9m	7.2m
US$1=kn		16.9	17.5	15.4

Population 1,400,000

Russian 28% Ukrainian 3% Belarussian 2%

Age	13–17	18–22	23–32
Men	59,000	57,000	103,000
Women	56,000	55,000	100,000

Finland SF

euro € (markka m)		2000	2001	2002
GDP	m	775bn	820bn	
	US$	120bn	124bn	
per capita	US$	23,320	23,950	
Growth	%	5.2	0.7	
Inflation	%	3.4	2.7	
Publ debt	%	50	42.1	
Def exp	m	10bn	9.6bn	
	US$	1.5bn	1.4bn	
Def bdgt[a]	m	9.83bn	9.54bn	
	€			1.7bn
	US$	1.5bn	1.4bn	1.7bn
US$1=m		6.41	6.59	
US$1=€				0.98

[a] Excl supplementary multi-year budget for procurement of m6.1bn (US$1.1bn) approved in Apr 1998

Population 5,200,000

Age	13–17	18–22	23–32
Men	166,000	172,000	330,000
Women	157,000	163,000	316,000

Georgia Ga

lari		2000	2001	2002
GDP[a]	lari	9.4bn	6.5bn	
	US$	19.5bn	16bn	
per capita	US$	3,732	3,077	
Growth	%	1.9	4.5	
Inflation	%	4.0	5.6	
Debt	US$	1.9bn	1.6bn	
Def exp	US$	290m	270m	
Def bdgt	lari	43.7m	33.1m	70m
	US$	22m	16m	32m
FMA (US)	US$	0.4m	0.4m	
US$1=lari		1.98	2.07	2.21

[a] = PPP estimate

Population 5,200,000

Armenian 8% Azeri 6% Russian 6% Ossetian 3% Abkhaz 2%

Age	13–17	18–22	23–32
Men	214,000	209,000	381,000
Women	205,000	201,000	359,000

Ireland Irl

euro € (pound I£)		2000	2001	2002
GDP	I£	103bn	115bn	
	US$	112bn	129bn	
per capita	US$	29,720	34,000	
Growth	%	11.5	6.0	
Inflation	%	5.5		
Publ debt	%	39.3	32.1	
Def exp	I£	579m	566m	
	US$	629m	636m	
Def bdgt	I£	602m	707m	
	€			710m
	US$	651m	789m	724m
US$1=I£		0.83	0.89	
US$1=€				0.98

Population 3,800,000

Age	13–17	18–22	23–32
Men	151,000	167,000	338,000
Women	142,000	158,000	319,000

Latvia Lat

lats L		2000	2001	2002
GDP	L	4.3bn	4.7bn	
	US$	7.17bn	7.5bn	
per capita	US$	2,911	3,118	
Growth	%	6.6	7.0	
Inflation	%	2.7	2.4	
Debt	US$	1.12m	1.28m	
Def exp	L	42m	54.6m	
	US$	70m	87m	
Def bdgt	L	42m	48m	69m
	US$	70m	76m	116m
FMA (US)	US$	4.8m	6.0m	7.2m
US$1=L		0.60	0.63	0.59

Population 2,400,000

Russian 34% **Belarussian** 5% **Ukrainian** 3% **Polish** 2%

Age	13–17	18–22	23–32
Men	97,000	96,000	163,000
Women	94,000	92,000	160,000

Lithuania L

litas L		2000	2001	2002
GDP	L	44.8bn	47.7bn	
	US$	11.2bn	11.9bn	
per capita	US$	3,021	3,236	
Growth	%	3.9	4.5	
Inflation	%	1.0	2.0	
Debt	US$	2.5bn	2.5bn	
Def exp	L	795m	859m	
	US$	199m	215m	

L contd		2000	2001	2002
Def bdgt	L	596m	667m	808m
	US$	149m	167m	230m
FMA (US)	US$	5.1m	7.2m	7.6m
US$1=L		4.0	4.0	3.5

Population 3,700,000

Russian 8% **Polish** 7% **Belarussian** 2%

Age	13–17	18–22	23–32
Men	142,000	139,000	253,000
Women	137,000	134,000	249,000

Macedonia, Former Yugoslav Republic of FYROM

dinar d		2000	2001	2002
GDP	US$	3.27bn	3.30bn	
per capita	US$	1,608	1,661	
Growth	%	5.1	-4.6	
Inflation	%	6.7	5.3	
Debt	US$	1.5bn	1.5bn	
Def exp	d	4.6bn	5.0bn	
	US$	70.5m	74.1m	
Def bdgt	d	4.6bn	5.6bn	6.8bn
	US$	70m	82m	115m
FMA (US)	US$	0.5m	14.3m	11.0m
US$1=d		65.9	68.0	59.7

Population 2,000,000

Albanian 22% **Turkish** 4% **Romany** 3% **Serb** 2%

Age	13–17	18–22	23–32
Men	97,000	95,000	173,000
Women	87,000	86,000	160,000

Malta M

lira ML		2000	2001	2002
GDP	ML	1.5bn	1.6bn	
	US$	3.6bn	3.6bn	
per capita	US$	9,222	8,889	
Growth	%	5.4	0.4	
Inflation	%	2.4	2.9	
Debt	US$			
Def exp	ML	11.3m	11m	
	US$	27m	24m	
Def bdgt	ML	11.3m	11.5m	11.5m
	US$	27.6m	25.6m	28m
FMA (US)	US$	0.1m	3.1m	0.3m
US$1=ML		0.41	0.45	0.41

Population 400,000

Age	13–17	18–22	23–32
Men	14,000	15,000	26,000
Women	14,000	14,000	25,000

Moldova Mol

leu L		2000	2001	2002
GDP[a]	L	16bn	19bn	
	US$	9.1bn	9bn	
per capita	US$	2,112	2,090	
Growth	%	2.1	4.0	
Inflation	%	31.3	11.1	
Debt	US$	1.3bn	1.3bn	
Def exp[a]	US$	140m	150m	
Def bdgt	L	64m	76.8m	95m
	US$	5m	5.9m	6.9m
FMA (US)	US$	1.7m	2.1m	1.5m
US$1=L		12.43	12.86	13.67

[a] PPP estimate

Population 4,300,000

Moldovan/Romanian 65% **Ukrainian** 14% **Russian** 13% **Gaguaz** 4% **Bulgarian** 2% **Jewish** <1.5%

Age	13–17	18–22	23–32
Men	206,000	190,000	303,000
Women	187,000	187,000	299,000

Romania R

lei		2000	2001	2002	
GDP	lei	796tr	1,154tr		
	US$	36.7bn	39.7 bn		
per capita	US$	1,633	1,773		
Growth	%	1.8	5.3		
Inflation	%	45.7	30.3		
Debt	US$	11.5bn	12.1bn		
Def exp	lei	20.4tr	28.7tr		
	US$	940m	989m		
Def bdgt	lei	20.4tr	28.7tr	37.5tr	
	US$	940m	989m	1,146m	
FMA (US)	US$	7.0m	18.5m	10.4m	11.5m
US$1=lei		21,708	29,060	32,712	

Population 22,400,000 **Hungarian** 9%

Age	13–17	18–22	23–32
Men	846,100	911,900	1,885,800
Women	817,700	879,800	1,823,300

Slovakia Slvk

koruna Ks		2000	2001	2002
GDP	Ks	887bn	964m	
	US$	19.2bn	19.9bn	
per capita	US$	3,568	3,694	
Growth	%	2.2	3.3	
Inflation	%	12	7.4	
Debt	US$	10.8bn	9.1bn	
Def exp	Ks	15.7bn	19.0bn	
	US$	341m	394m	

Slvk contd		2000	2001	2002
Def bdgt	Ks	16.4bn	16.7bn	19.9bn
	US$	356m	345m	450m
FMA (US)	US$	3.2m	11.7m	8.8m
US$1=Ks		46.0	48.4	44.2

Population 5,400,000

Hungarian 11% **Romany** c5% **Czech** 1%

Age	13–17	18–22	23–32
Men	219,000	238,000	425,000
Women	210,000	231,000	416,000

Slovenia Slvn

tolar t		2000	2001	2002
GDP	t	4.1tr	4.5tr	
	US$	18.2bn	18.9bn	
per capita	US$	9,100	9,430	
Growth	%	4.7	3.0	
Inflation	%	8.9	8.6	
Debt	US$	6.2bn	6.7bn	
Def exp	t	60.6bn	68.5bn	
	US$	273m	283m	
Def bdgt	t	59bn	66.7bn	70bn
	US$	268m	275m	313m
FMA (US)	US$	2.6m	6.5m	4.8m
US$1=t		222	242	223

Population 2,000,000

Croat 3% **Serb** 2% **Muslim** 1%

Age	13–17	18–22	23–32
Men	67,000	75,000	147,000
Women	63,000	71,000	143,000

Sweden Swe

kronor Skr		2000	2001	2002
GDP	Skr	2.1tr	2.2tr	
	US$	229bn	209bn	
per capita	US$	26,059	23,841	
Growth	%	3.6	1.2	
Inflation	%	1.3	2.6	
Publ Debt	%	62.3	56.2	
Def exp	Skr	42.2bn	40.9bn	
	US$	4.6bn	3.9bn	
Def bdgt	Skr	42.8bn	42.6bn	41.5bn
	US$	4.7bn	4.1bn	4.5bn
US$1=Skr		9.2	10.3	9.2

Population 8,800,000

Age	13–17	18–22	23–32
Men	268,000	256,000	595,000
Women	253,000	241,000	569,000

Switzerland CH

franc fr		2000	2001	2002
GDP	fr	404bn	417bn	
	US$	241bn	247bn	
per capita	US$	33,510	34,470	
Growth	%	3.0	1.3	
Inflation	%	1.6	1.0	
Def exp	fr	4.9bn	4.9bn	
	US$	2.9bn	2.9bn	
Def bdgt	fr	4.9bn	4.7bn	4.8bn
	US$	2.9bn	2.8bn	3.3bn
US$1=fr		1.68	1.68	1.44

Population 7,200,000

Age	13–17	18–22	23–32
Men	203,000	205,000	477,000
Women	194,000	198,000	468,000

Ukraine Ukr

hryvnia h		2000	2001	2002
GDP[a]	h	174bn	208bn	
	US$	189bn	226bn	
per capita	US$	3,820	4,600	
Growth	%	6	9.1	
Inflation	%	25.8	12.5	
Debt	US$	10.4bn	11.5bn	
Def exp[a]	US$	5.1bn	5.0bn	
Def bdgt	h	2.4bn	3.3bn	3.4bn
	US$	448m	611m	631m
FMA (US)	US$	4.5m	5.4m	5.7m
US$1=h		5.44	5.37	5.32

[a] PPP estimate

Population 49,100,000

Russian 22% **Polish** ε4% **Jewish** 1%

Age	13–17	18–22	23–32
Men	1,901,000	1,877,000	3,595,000
Women	1,832,000	1,830,000	3,573,000

Yugoslavia, Federal Republic of (Serbia–Montenegro) FRY

new dinar d		2000	2001	2002
GDP	d	221bn	656bn	
	US$	18.3bn	9.8bn	
per capita	US$	1,710	930	
Growth	d	5.0	5.0	
Debt	US$	12.2bn	11.6bn	
Def exp	d	ε22.1bn	ε41.6bn	
	US$	1.8bn	622m	
Def bdgt	d	ε16.3bn	ε32.1bn	ε43.5bn
	US$	1.3bn	479m	721m
US$1=d		12.1	66.9	60.3

Population ε10,603,000

Serbia ε9,900,000 **Serb** 66% **Albanian** 17%, 90% in Kosovo **Hungarian** 4% mainly in Vojvodina

Montenegro ε700,000 **Montenegrin** 62% **Serb** 9% **Albanian** 7%

ε2,032,000 Serbs were living in the other Yugoslav republics before the civil war

Age	13–17	18–22	23–32
Men	412,000	425,000	837,000
Women	388,000	402,000	795,000

Table 12 Arms orders and deliveries, NATO Europe and Canada, 1998–2002

	Country supplier	Classification ⇩	Designation	Quantity ⇩	Order date	Delivery date	Comment ⇩
Belgium	US	FGA	**F-16**	110	1993	1998	Mid-life update. 88 AMRAAM on order
	Sgp	tpt	**A-310**	2	1996	1998	Second aircraft del. May 1998
	A	APC	***Pandur***	54	1997	1998	
	Il	UAV	***Hunter***	3	1998	2000	3 systems, 18 air vehs
	US	FGA	**F-16**	18	1999	2000	Upgrade; option on 18 exercised
	Fr	trg	***Alpha Jet***		2000		Upgrade
	Br	tpt	**ERJ-135/145**	4	2000	2001	
Canada	dom	MCMV	***Kingston***	12	1992	1996	Deliveries complete by 1999
	US	hel	**B-412EP**	100	1992	1994	Deliveries to 1998 at 3 per month
	dom	LAV	**LAV-25**	240	1996	1998	105 in 1997, 47 1998; deliveries continue
	US	APC	**M-113**	341	1997	1998	Life extension update; deliveries continue

	Country supplier	Classification ⇩	Designation	Quantity ⇩	Order date	Delivery date	Comment ⇩
	Ge	MBT	***Leopard* 1**	114	1997	1999	*Leopard* C1A5 upgrade
	dom	LAV	**LAV-25**	120	1998	2001	Follow-on order after initial 240
	UK	SSK	***Victoria***	4	1998	2000	Deliveries delayed to 2003
	col	hel	**EH-101**	15	1998	2001	Ca designation AW520; deliveries to 2002
	dom		**CP-140 *Aurora***	16	2000	2001	Upgrade
	US	FGA	**CF-18**	80	2000	2003	Upgrade to C/D status
	dom	APC	***Bison***	199	2000	2002	Upgrade
	dom	APC	***Grizzly***	246	2000	2002	
	US	SAM	***Sea Sparrow***		2001	2003	To equip *Halifax*-class FFG
Czech Republic							
	dom	MBT	**T-72**	140	1995	2000	Upgrade prog. Rescheduled in 1999
	dom	trg	**L-39**	27	1997	1999	Originally for Nga; delivery to Cz airforce delayed
	dom	FGA	**L-159**	72	1997	2000	
	col	UAV	***Sojka* 3**	8	1998	2000	Upgraded *Sojka* III. Dev with Hu
	RF	tpt	**An-70**	3	2002	2006	Part of debt payment
	RF	cbt hel	**Mi-24**	7	2002	2006	Part of debt payment
Denmark	US	FGA	**F-16**	63	1993	1998	Mid-life update; del continue 1999
	dom	AFV	**Hydrema**	12	1996	1997	Mine-clearing AFV. Del to 1998
	Ge	MBT	***Leopard* 2A4**	51	1998	2000	Ex-Ge army
	Ca	tpt	***Challenger* 604**	3	1998		
	UK	hel	***Lynx***	8	1998	2000	Upgrade to *Super Lynx* standard
	CH	APC	***Piranha* III**	2	1998	1999	Option for 20 more; UN PKO use
	Ge	APC	**M-113**	100	1999	2000	Upgrade. Deliveries until 2001
	Fr	UAV	***Sperwer***	2	1999		
	US	PGM	**JDAM**	400	2000	2000	Deliveries to 2004
	US	tpt	**C-130J**	3	2000	2003	Option on 4th
	dom	AG	***Stanflex* S3**	2	2000	2006	
	Swe	SSK	***Nacken***	1	2001	2001	
	col	hel	**EH101**	14	2001	2004	
France	col	hel	***Tiger***	215	1984	2003	With Ge; 1st batch of 60 ordered 1999
	dom	FGA	***Rafale***	60	1984	1999	Deliveries of first 10 1999–02
	dom	FGA	***Rafale***	234	1984	1999	ISD 2005
	dom	MBT	***Leclerc***	406	1985	1992	311 delivered by 2000.
	col	ASSM	**ANNG**		1985	2005	In dev with Ge
	col	radar	***Cobra***	10	1986	2002	Counter-bty radar; dev with UK, Ge
	dom	LSD	***Foudre***	2	1986	1990	2nd of class delivered 1998
	dom	SSBN	***Le Triomphant***	3	1986	1996	Deliveries to 2001; 4th order 2000 for 2007
	dom	CVN	***Charles de Gaulle***	1	1986	1999	Sea trials mid-1998. In service 2000.
	col	hel	**NH-90**	160	1987	2003	With Ge, It, Nl; prod orders delayed.
	col	ATGW	***Trigat***		1988	2004	With Ge
	col	hel	**AS-555**	44	1988	1990	Deliveries through 1990s
	col	tpt	**FLA**	52	1989	2005	Dev. Prog status uncertain
	dom	FFG	***Lafayette***	5	1990	1996	Deliveries to 2003
	col	SAM	**FSAF**		1990	2006	Future surface-to-air-family; with It, UK
	col	hel	**EC-120**		1990		In dev with PRC, Sgp

Country supplier	Classification ⇩	Designation	Quantity ⇩	Order date	Delivery date	Comment ⇩
	col	torp	**MU-90**	150	1991	2000	With It and Ge. Deliveries 2000–02
	dom	FGA	***Mirage* 2000-D**	86	1991	1994	45 delivered by Jan 1997. Del to 2000
	col	hel	**AS-532**	4	1992	1996	Battlefield radar system *Horizon;* to 1998
	dom	FGA	***Mirage* 2000-5F**	37	1993	1998	*Mirage* 2000-C upgrade, deliveries to 2002
	col	UAV	***Eagle***				Dev with UK
	col	sat	***Helios* 1A**	2	1994	1995	With Ge, It, Sp. *Helios* 1B for launch 1999
	col	sat	***Helios* 2**	1	1994	2004	Dev with Ge
	col	sat	***Horus***		1994	2005	Fr has withdrawn funding
	US	AEW	**E2-D**	3	1994	1999	1st delivered Jan 1999
	col	ALCM	**SCALP**	600	1994	2000	2 orders for delivery over 11 years
	col	hel	**AS-532**	4	1995	1999	Combat SAR, requirement for 6
	Sp	tpt	**CN 235**	7	1996	1998	Offset for Sp AS-532 purchase
	dom	SLBM	**M-51**		1996	2008	To replace M-45; devpt continues
	col	hel	**AS-565**	8	1996	1997	7 del in 1997; 1 del 1998
	dom	SAM	***Mistral***	1,130	1996	1997	To 2002
	dom	recce	***Falcon-50***	4	1997	1998	Deliveries to 2000
	col	hel	**BK-117**	32	1997	1999	
	dom	ATGW	***Eryx***		1997	1997	700 launchers delivered to 2001
	dom	RL	**LAW**	30,800	1997	1997	For delivery 1997–2002
	col	ASM	***Vesta***		1997	2005	In devpt
	col	sat	***Skynet* 5**	4	1998	2005	Comms; devpt in 1998 with Ge, UK
	dom	SSN	**SSN**	6	1998	2010	Design studies approved Oct 1998
	col	AAM	***Mica***	225	1998	1999	Further 1,537 to be delivered from 2004
	dom	APC	**VBCI**	65	1998	2005	Up to 700 req
	dom	AIFV	**AMX-10**	300	1999	2001	Upgrade
	Swe	APC	**Bv 206S**	12	1999	1999	For units serving in Kosovo
	col	FFG	**mod *Horizon***	2	1999	2005	Joint It/Fr project
	dom	LSD	**NTCD**	2	2000	2005	2 on order
	dom	MHC	***Eridan Class***	13	2000		Upgrade
	dom	arty	***Caesar***	5	2000	2002	
	dom	MBT	***Leclerc***	38	2000	2002	Upgrade to Mk2 standard
	dom	sat	***Syracuse* 3**	3	2000	2003	Comms
	dom	LHD	***Mistral***	2	2000	2005	
	dom	FFG		17	2002	2008	First 4 ordered
Germany	col	hel	***Tiger***	212	1984	2003	With Fr. 1st order for 60 in 1999
	col	FGA	**EF-2000**	180	1985	2001	With UK, It, Sp; 44 ordered late 1998
	dom	SPA	**PzH 2000**	186	1986	1998	Req 594 units; 86 delivered by 2000
	col	hel	**NH-90**	134	1987	2003	With Fr, It, Nl; prod orders delayed
	dom	MHC	**Type 332**	12	1988	1992	Deliveries completed 1998
	col	ATGW	***Trigat***		1988	2004	
	col	tpt	**FLA**	75	1989	2008	Dev. Status uncertain
	dom	SSK	**Type 212**	4	1994	2003	Deliveries to 2006
	col	recce	***Fennek***	164	1994	2000	Joint dev with Nl. Prod in 2000
	col	sat	***Helios* 1A**	2	1994	1995	With Fr, It, Sp, *Helios* 1B for launch 1999
	col	sat	***Helios* 2**	1	1994	2001	Dev with Fr, It
	col	tpt hel	**AS-532**	3	1994	1997	

	Country supplier	Classification ⇩	Designation	Quantity ⇩	Order date	Delivery date	Comment ⇩
	col	sat	***Horus***	1	1994	2005	Dev with Fr
	dom	FFG	**Type F 124**	3	1996	2002	Deliveries 2002–05.
	dom	AOE	***Berlin***	2	1996	2000	1st delivered 2000; 2nd in 2002
	UK	hel	***Lynx***	7	1996	1999	
	dom	AAA	***Gepard***	147	1996	1999	Upgrade. 1st of 147 delivered Jan 1999
	col	sat	***Skynet* 5**	4	1997	2005	With UK, Fr
	col	AAM	**IRIS-T**		1997	2003	Dev with It, Swe, Gr, Ca, No
	col	hel	**EC-135**	15	1997	1998	For Tiger hel trg. Del start mid-1998
	col	hel	**AS-365**	13	1997	1998	Delivery 1998–01
	col	APC	**GTK**	200	1998	2004	NL and UK (MRAV)
	dom	SAM	***Wiesel* 2**	50	1998	1999	
	US	SAM	***Patriot***	7	1998		Upgrade to PAC-3 configuration
	US	SAM	***Patriot***	12	1998		*Roland/Patriot* cost total $2.1bn
	US	SAM	***Roland***	21	1998		Air defence system
	dom	APC	**TPz KRK**	50	1998	1999	
	col	radar	**COBRA**	12	1998		
	UK	hel	***Lynx***	17	1998	2000	Upgrade to *Super Lynx* standard
	col	torp	**MU-90**	600	1998	2000	
	col	ASM	***Taurus***		1998	2001	Dev with Swe (KEPD-350)
	dom	FFG	**Type F 125**	8	1999	2010	Feasibility study stage
	dom	AG	**Type 751**	1	1999	2002	Defence research and test ship
	dom	AFV	***Dingo***	147	1999	2001	
	dom	MBT	***Leopard* 2 A5**	225	2000	2001	Upgrade to 2A6
	dom	MRTT	**A310**	4	2001	2002	
	dom	FSG	**Type 130K**	5	2001	2007	Deliveries to 2008
	col	recce	***Fennek***	202	2002	2003	Complete by 2007
	Swe	AFV	**Bv 206S**	31	2002	2002	
Greece	US	FGA	**F-16**	80	1985	1988	Deliveries of 2nd batch of 40 1997–99
	Ge	FFG	***Meko***	4	1988	1992	Deliveries to 1998; last 2 built in Gr
	dom	AIFV	***Kentaurus***		1994	2000	In dev; trials in late 1998
	US	hel	**CH-47D**	7	1995	2001	In addition to 9 in inventory
	US	FGA	**F-4**	38	1996	1999	Upgrade in Ge; deliveries to 2000
	Nl	FFG	***Kortenaer***	1	2002	2002	8th ordered
	Ge	SSK	**Type 214**	1	2002		
	US	MRL	**ATACM**	81	1996	1998	Del complete by 1998
	Swe	PCI	**Cb 90**	3	1996	1998	
	US	AAM	**AIM-120B**	90	1997	1999	In addition to previous 150 AMRAAM
	US	SP arty	**M-109A5**	12	1997	1999	135 delivered; option for further 12
	Ge	MBT	***Leopard* 1A5**	170	1997	1998	In addition to previous delivery of 75
	US	SAM	**Stinger**	188	1998	2000	
	US	trg	**T-6A**	45	1998	2000	Deliveries complete 2003
	US	SAM	***Patriot* PAC-3**	5	1998	2001	5 batteries, option for 1 more
	Br	AEW	**RJ-145**	4	1998	2003	
	Ge	SSK	**Type 214**	3	1998	2005	Deliveries to 2008; 4th ordered 2002
	UK	MCMV	***Hunt***	2	1998	2000	1 delivered in 2000. 1 in 2001
	It	AK	**AK *Etna***	1	1999	2003	
	Fr	hel	**AS-532**	4	1999	2002	Option on further 2
	US	MRL	**MLRS**	18	1999	2002	
	US	FGA	**F-16C/D**	50	1999	2002	Option on further 10

	Country supplier	Classification ⇩	Designation	Quantity ⇩	Order date	Delivery date	Comment ⇩
	Fr	FGA	***Mirage* 2000-5**	15	1999	2003	Option on 3 more
	Fr	FGA	***Mirage* 2000**	10	1999	2004	Upgrade 10 of existing 35
	Fr	SAM	***Crotale* NG**	11	1999	2001	9 for air force; 2 for navy
	US	hel	**S-70B**	2	2000		Option on further 2
	col	FGA	**EF-2000**	60	2000	2005	May increase to 90
	dom	PFM	***Super Vita***	3	2000	2003	Option on further 4
	dom	PCO		4	2000		
	dom	AO		1	2000	2003	
	RF	LCAC	***Zubr***	4	2000	2001	Final delivery 2001
	US	AAM	**AMRAAM**	560	2000		
	US	recce	**C-12**	2	2000		For photo-reconnaissance
	Ge	SP arty	**PzH2000**	24	2000	2003	Deliveries to 2004
	US	ACV	**HMMWV**	70	2000	2001	
	Fr	ASSM	***Exocet* MM-40**	27	2000	2001	Deliveries to 2004
	Fr	AAM	**Mica**	200	2000		To equip *Mirage*
	Fr	ALCM	**SCALP**	56	2000		To equip *Mirage*
	US	hel	**S-70B**	8	2000		Upgrade including *Penguin* AAM
	RF	SAM	**SA-15**	29	2000	2001	Aka Tor-M1; Additional 29. Original order for 21 units completed.
	Ge	SAM	***Stinger***	54	2000	2002	
	Slvk	SPG	***Zuzana***	12	2000	2001	For Rapid Deployment Force
	RF	ATGW	***Kornet***	278	2001		Two phase purchase
	dom	PCO		2	2001		
	col	tpt	**C-27J**	12	2002	2004	
	Ge	MBT	**Leopard 2A5**	170	2002		
Hungary	Fr	SAM	***Mistral***	45	1996	1998	27 launchers, 110 msl delivered 1998
	RF	FGA	**MiG-29**	14	2001		Upgrade
	Swe	FGA	***Gripen***	14	2001	2004	Leased for 12 years
Italy	dom	MBT	**C1 *Ariete***	200	1982	1995	Deliveries to 2001
	dom	AIFV	**VCC-80**	200	1982	2000	First ordered 1998; aka *Dardo*
	col	FGA	**EF-2000**	121	1985	2002	With UK, Ge, Sp; 29 ordered
	col	hel	**NH 90**	117	1987	2003	With Fr, Ge, Nl; prod order delayed
	dom	APC	***Puma***	600	1988	2001	Deliveries to 2004
	dom	hel	***AB-412***	80	1988	1990	Licence; deliveries of 10 a year 1990–97
	dom	AGHS	***Aretusa***	2		2002	Both delivered 2002
	col	tpt	**FLA**	44	1989	2008	With Fr, Ge, Sp, Be, Por, Tu, UK
	col	SAM	**FSAF**		1990	2006	Future surface-to-air-family, with Fr, UK
	dom	trg	**MB-339CD**	15	1990	1996	Deliveries to 1998
	col	hel	**EH-101**	20	1993	1999	With UK; 4 more ordered in 2002 for amph spt
	dom	PCO	***Esploratore***	4	1993	1997	Deliveries to 2000
	col	sat	***Helios* 1A**	1	1994	1995	With Fr, Ge, Sp. *Helios* 1B for launch 1999
	dom	AO	***Etna***	1	1994	1998	
	dom	CV	***Andrea Doria***	1	1996	2007	
	US	tpt	**C-130J**	22	1997	2000	Options on further 2
	Fr	tpt	***Falcon* 900EX**	2	1997	1999	
	It	tpt	**P-180**	12	1997	1998	

	Country supplier	Classification ⇩	Designation	Quantity ⇩	Order date	Delivery date	Comment ⇩
	Ge	SSK	**Type 212**	2	1997	2005	Licence-built in It; options for 2 more
	dom	AGI	**A-5353**	2	1998	2000	2nd for delivery 2001
	dom	hel	**A-129I**	15	1998	2001	New multi-role configuration
	dom	PCO	***Aliscarfi***	4	1999	2001	1st batch of 4; 2nd expected after 2003
	dom	LPD	***San Giorgio***	2	1999	2001	Upgrade to carry 4 hel
	Ge	SPA	**PzH 2000**	70	1999	2004	Joint production
	col	FFG	**mod *Horizon***	2	1999	2007	Joint It/Fr project
	dom	AT	**C-27J**	12	1999	2001	
	US	UAV	***Predator***	6	2000	2001	
	US	AAM	***Stinger***	30	2000		For use on A-129
	US	SAM	***Standard* SM-2**	50	2000		
	dom	hel	**A-129**	45	2000		Upgrade to A-129I standard
	US	FGA	**F-16**	34	2001	2003	7-year lease
	US	tkr	**Boeing 767**	4	2001		Option on further 2
	col	AAM	***Meteor***	400	2001		
	US	UAV	***Predator***	6	2001	2002	
	dom	FFG	**NGF**	10	2002	2008	Deliveries to 2017
NATO	UK	trg	***Hawk***	18	1997	1999	Option for 8 more
	US	AWACS	**E3-A**	18	1997	1999	NATO fleet upgrade
	US	trg	**T-6A**	24	1997	1999	Deliveries to 2000
	US		**ACCS**	1	1999	2005	Air Comd and Control System
	RSA	APC	***Scout***	75	1999	2000	
Netherlands	col	hel	**NH-90**	20	1987	2003	With Fr, Ge, It
	dom	LPD	***Rotterdam***	2	1993	1998	Second due to be delivered 2006
	US	FGA	**F-16**	136	1993	1997	Update programme continues to 2001
	US	hel	**AH-64D**	30	1995	1998	4 delivered 1998
	US	hel	**CH-47C**	7	1995	1999	
	dom	FFG	***De Zeven***	4	1995	2003	2 ordered 1995; 2 more ordered 1997
	SF	APC	**XA-188**	90	1996	1998	24 delivered 1998
	US	MPA	**P-3C**	7	1999	2001	Upgrade
	col	APC	**PWV**	200	2000	2006	Joint Programme
	Ge	SPA	**PzH 2000**	60	2000	2004	
	Ge	MBT	**Leopard 2A5**	180	2001		Upgrade to 2A6
	Il	ATGW	***Spike/Gil***	300	2001	2002	
	col	recce	***Fennek***	410	2002	2003	Completed by 2007
Norway	Swe	AIFV	**CV-90**	104	1990	1996	Option for 70 more. Del 1996-99
	US	FGA	**F-16A/B**	58	1993	1997	Mid-life update prog to 2001
	US	AAM	**AMRAAM**	500	1993	1995	84 delivered 1998; del to 2000
	US	MRL	**MLRS**	12	1995	1997	Deliveries to 1998
	Swe	LCA	**90-H**	16	1995	1997	Deliveries to 1998
	dom	FAC	***Skjold***	5	1996	1999	
	US	MPA	**PC-3**	4	1997	1999	Upgrade
	Ge	AFV	***Leopard* 1**	73	1998	1999	Deliveries to 2000; for mineclearing
	Sp	FFG	***Fridthof Nansen***	5	2000	2004	
	Nl	MBT	***Leopard* 2A4**	52	2000		To be modernised
	SF	APC	**XA-200**	10	2000		
	col	hel	**NH-90**	14	2001	2004	

	Country supplier	Classification ⇩	Designation	Quantity ⇩	Order date	Delivery date	Comment ⇩
Poland	dom	AIFV	**BWP 2000**		1989		Development
	dom	hel	**W-3**	11	1994	1998	1 for Navy. First 4 delivered Jul 1998
	Il	ATGW	**NT-D**		1997		For W-3 Huzar attack hel. Canc in 1999
	dom	SAR	**PLZ M-28**	3	1998	1999	
	UK	SPA	**AS-90**	80	1999	2001	Licence
	Ge	FGA	**MiG-29**	22	1999	2002	Upgrade
	US	FFG	***Oliver Hazard Perry***	2	1999	2000	2nd delivered 2002
	Il	FGA	**Su-22**	20	2000	2003	Upgrade
	US	hel	**SH-2G**	2	1999	2000	2 more due 2002
	RF	hel	**Mi-24**	40	2001	2003	To be completed by 2006
	col	tpt	**C295M**	8	2001	2003	
	Ge	MBT	**Leopard 2A4**	128	2002	2002	Secondhand; delivery end 2002
	Ge	FGA	**MiG-29G**	23	2002	2003	Secondhand
	No	SSK	***Kobben* Class**	5	2001	2002	2 in 2002, 2 in 2004, + 1 for spares
Portugal	US	FGA	**F-16**	20	2000	2003	Upgrade
	col	hel	**EC-635**	9	2000	2001	
	col	hel	**EH101**	12	2001	2004	
Spain	col	tpt	**FLA**	36	1989	2008	With Fr, Ge, It, Be, Por, Tu, UK
	col	MHC	***Segura***	4	1989	1999	Deliveries to 2000
	dom	LPD	***Galicia***	2	1991	1998	2nd delivered 2000
	dom	FFG	**F-100**	4	1992	2002	Deliveries to 2006
	US	FGA	**F/A-18A**	30	1994	1995	Ex-USN, deliveries continue to 1998
	col	FGA	**EF-2000**	87	1994	2001	With Ge, It, UK; 20 ordered late 1998
	col	sat	***Helios* 1A**	1	1994	1995	With Fr, Ge, It. *Helios* 1B 1999
	Fr	hel	**AS-532**	18	1995	1996	1st delivery 1996. Deliveries to 2003
	US	tpt	**C-130**	12	1995	1999	Upgrade programme
	Aus	AIFV	***Pizarro***	144	1996	1998	Licence. Requirement for 463
	It	SAM	***Spada* 2000**	2	1996	1998	First of 2 batteries delivered
	dom	arty	**SBT-1**		1997	2000	Dev
	dom	MPA	**P-3**	7	1997	2002	Upgrade
	US	AAM	**AIM-120B**	100	1998	1999	
	Ge	MBT	***Leopard* 2**	235	1998	2002	Built in Sp. Includes 16 ARVs
	It	AIFV	***Centuaro***	22	1999	2000	aka VCR-105
	US	ATGW	***Javelin***	12	1999		
	Fr	trg	**EC120B**	12	2000	2000	Deliveries Jul 2000–Jul 2001
	dom	AT	**C295**	9	2000		To be delivered by 2004
	col	hel	**EC120B**	15	2000	2001	Training
	No	SAM	**NASAMS**	4	2000	2002	
	US	hel	**SH-60B**	6	2000	2004	Also upgrade of existing 6
	Swe	APC	**Bv-206S**	10	2000		Total requirement of 50
	dom	MPA	**P-3B *Orion***	5	2001	2003	Upgrade
	Swe	LAV	***Piranha* III**	18	2001	2003	
	It	AIFV	***Centuaro***	62	2002	2004	
Turkey	US	FGA	**F-16**	240	1984	1987	All but 8 assembled in Tu
	Ge	FFG	***Meko*-200**	8	1985	1987	7 by 1999; final delivery 2000, 4 built in Tu
	Ge	SSK	**Type 209**	8	1987	1994	Delivery of first 5 to 2003

Country supplier	Classification ⇩	Designation	Quantity ⇩	Order date	Delivery date	Comment ⇩
US	APC	**M-113**	1698	1988	1992	Final deliveries in 1999
Sp	tpt	**CN-235**	43	1990	1992	41 delivered by 1998
Ge	PCM	**P-330**	3	1993	1998	1st built Ge; 2nd and 3rd Tu; to 1999
US	TKR AC	**KC-135R**	9	1994	1995	Deliveries in 1995 and 1998
US	tpt hel	**CH-47**	4	1996	1999	
UK	SAM	**Rapier**	78	1996	1998	Upgrade programme
US	FFG	***Oliver Hazard Perry***	6	1996	1998	Delivery of 5 1998–99. Last 2000
Il	FGA	**F-4**	54	1996	1999	Upgrade; deliveries to 2002
US	MRL	**ATACM**	72	1996	1998	36 msl delivered 1998
Fr	hel	**AS-532**	30	1996	2000	To be completed by 2003
US	AAM	**AIM-120B**	138	1997	2000	
US	ASW hel	**SH-60B**	14	1997	2000	
dom	APC	**RN-94**	5	1997		Dev
Il	AGM	***Popeye* 1**	50	1997	1999	For use with upgraded F-4 ac
Sp	MPA	**CN-235**	52	1997	2000	
Fr	MHC	**Circe**	5	1997	1998	Ex-Fr Navy. 3 in 1998, 2 in 1999
It	SAR hel	**AB-412**	5	1998	2001	
Il	FGA	**F-5**	48	1998	2001	IAI awarded contract to upgrade 48 Tu F-5
US	hel	**CH-53E**	8	1998	2003	
US	SAM	**Stinger**	208	1999	2001	
US	hel	**S-70 *Blackhawk***	50	1999	2001	
dom	PCC		10	1999	2000	For coastguard
UK	SAM	***Rapier* Mk 2**	840	1999	2000	Licence; 80 a year for 10 years
US	FGA	**F-16**	32	1999	2002	Licence; following orders of 240 in 2 batches
Ge	SSK	**Type 214**	4	2000	2006	
Ge	MHC	**Type 332**	6	2000		1st to be built in Ge, 5 in Tu. Last delivery 2008
US	hel	**S-70B *Seahawk***	8	2000		Heavy lift
US	radar	***Sentinel***	7	2000		Including HAWK missiles
Fr	FFG	**Type A69**	6	2000	2001	5 delivered by 2002
US	APC	**M-113**	551	2000	2001	Deliveries to 2004
US	AEW	**Boeing 737**	4	2000		
RF	hel	**Ka-62**	5	2001	2002	
ROK	SPA	**TUSpH**	20	2001		300 required
US	SAM	***Stinger***	146	2001		
Il	MBT	**M60 A1**	170	2002		To be modernised by Il
Fr	AG	***Centaure***	1	1999	1999	Renamed *Degirmendere*
United Kingdom						
col	hel	**EH 101**	44	1979	1999	With It; for RN; aka Merlin HM Mk 1
dom	AAM	**ASRAAM**	1300	1981	1998	
dom	SSBN	***Vanguard***	4	1982	1993	Deliveries to 1999
US	SLBM	***Trident* D-5**	48	1982	1994	Deliveries to 1999; original order 96
col	FGA	**EF-2000**	232	1984	2002	1st batch of 55 ordered end 1998
dom	UAV	**Phoenix**	50	1985	1998	Upgrade programme planned
dom	MHC	***Sandown***	12	1985	1989	All delivered by 2001
dom	FGA	***Sea Harrier***	35	1985	1994	Upgrade prog; deliveries to 1999
col	radar	***Cobra***		1986	1999	Counter-bty radar in dev with Fr, Ge
dom	SSN	***Swiftsure***	5	1988	1999	Upgrade to carry TLAM
dom	SSN	***Trafalgar***	7	1988	2000	Upgrade to carry TLAM

Country supplier	Classification ⇩	Designation	Quantity ⇩	Order date	Delivery date	Comment ⇩
dom	FGA	***Sea Harrier***	18	1990	1995	Deliveries to 1999
dom	SSN	***Astute***	3	1991	2006	Deliveries to 2008, 3 more may be ordered
dom	LPD	***Albion***	2	1991	2003	
dom	hel	***Lynx***	50	1992	1995	Upgrade. Completion 1998–99
dom	MBT	***Challenger* 2**	386	1993	2002	Last of 386 deliveries
col	sat	***Skynet* 5**	4	1993	2005	With Fr and Ge
dom	LPH	***Ocean***	1	1993	1998	Delivered 1998
col	SAM	**PAAMS**		1994	2003	Dev with Fr, It. Part of FSAF prog
US	AAM	**AIM-120**		1994	1998	
US	tpt	**C-130J**	25	1994	1999	Option for 20 more
dom	FGA	***Tornado* GR4 ID**	142	1994	1998	Upgrade; deliveries to 2003
US	hel	**CH-47**	14	1995	1997	Deliveries to 2000. Total Chinnook buy 58
US	SLCM	***Tomahawk***	65	1995	1998	Delivered. 20 fired in Kosovo conflict
dom	ASM	***Brimstone***		1996	2001	1st 12 to be delivered 2001
col	ASM	***Storm Shadow***	900	1996	2001	
dom	FGA	***Tornado* F-3**	100	1996	1998	Upgrade
dom	MPA	***Nimrod* MRA4**	21	1996	2005	To replace MRA2
US	hel	**WAH-64D**	67	1996	2000	Deliveries to 2003
dom	APC	**Stormer**	18	1996	1998	
dom	FFG	***Duke***	3	1996	1998	All delivered by 2002; last in class
dom	AO	***Wave Knight***	2	1997	2001	Both in service 2002
dom	PCI	**Archer**	2	1997	1998	
dom	AK	***Sea Chieftain***	1	1997	1998	18-month lease renewed 2001
col	AEW	**ASTOR**	5	1997	2005	Delivery slipped from 2003
col	bbr	**FOAS**		1997	2020	Future Offensive Air System, feasibility study with Fr
Ge	trg	***Grob*-115D**	85	1998	2000	
col	lt tk	**TRACER**	200	1998	2007	With US; in feasibility phase
col	APC	**MRAV**	200	1998	2006	Multi-Role Armoured Vehicle; with Nl, Ge
col	UAV	***Sender***		1999		Devpt with US
US	SLCM	***Tomahawk***	30	1999	2002	
dom	AGHS	***Echo***	2	2000	2002	Deliveries 2002 and 2003
dom	AT	**A400M**	25	2000		UK to lease 4 C-17 in interim
dom	AAM	***Meteor***		2000		To provide BVRAAM capability
US	tpt	**C-17**	4	2000	2001	To be leased
US	ASM	***Maverick***		2000	2000	
dom	ALSL	***Bay***	4	2000	2003	Alternate landing ship logistics
dom	UAV	***Watchkeeper***		2000	2006	Under dev
dom	SAM	***Sea Wolf***	21	2000	2006	Mid-life upgrade programme
dom	TKR	**FSTA**	30	2001	2004	
Swe	APC	**BvS 10**	108	2001	2003	
dom	DDG	**Type 45**	6	2001	2005	2 further batches of 3 may be ordered
US	SLCM	***Tomahawk***	48	2001	2001	Block IIIC
dom	ro-ro AK		6	2000	2002	All due to be in service in 2004

Table 13 Arms orders and deliveries, Non-NATO Europe, 1998–2002

	Country supplier	Classification ⇩	Designation	Quantity ⇩	Order date	Delivery date	Comment ⇩
Armenia	PRC	AAA	***Typhoon***	8	1998	1999	
Azerbaijan	Kaz	FGA	**MiG-25**	8	1996	1998	
	Tu	PCC	**AB-34**	1	2000	2000	
	US	PCI		1	2001	2001	
Austria	US	SPA	**M109A2**	46	1996	1998	deliveries complete
	dom	APC	***Pandur***	269	1997	1999	
	Ge	ATGW	***Jaguar***	90	1997	1998	
	Nl	MBT	***Leopard* 2A4**	114	1997	1998	79 delivered in 1998
	Swe	FGA	**J-35**	5	1999	1999	
	col	APC	**ULAN**	112	1999	2002	Delivery to 2004. aka ASCOD
	US	hel	**S-70A**	9	2000	2001	Option for 3 more
	UK	tpt	**C-130K**	3	2002	2003	
	int	FGA	***Eurofighter***	18	2002	2005	
Belarus	RF	trg	**MiG-29UB**	8	1999	1999	
	Kaz	MBT	**T-72**	53	2000	2000	
Bosnia-Herzegovina							
	US	hel	**UH-1**	15	1996	1998	Part of US-funded Equip and Train prog
	UAE	arty	**105mm**	36	1996	1998	
	Et	arty	**122mm**	12	1996	1998	
	Et	arty	**130mm**	12	1996	1998	
	Et	AD	**23mm**	18	1996	1998	
	R	arty	**122mm**	18	1996	1998	
	R	arty	**130mm**	8	1996	1998	
Bulgaria	RF	FGA	**MiG-29UB**	21	2001	2004	Upgrade
Croatia	dom	MBT	**M-84**		1992	1996	In production
	dom	MBT	***Degman***		1995	2001	
	dom	MHC	***Rhino***	1	1995	1999	
	dom	PCI		1	1996	2001	
	US	FGA	**F-16**	18	1999	2001	Ex-US inventory
	RF	FGA	**MiG-21bis**	28	1999		Upgrade
Cyprus	It	SAM	***Aspide***	44	1996	1998	24 delivered
	RF	SAM	**S-300**	48	1997	1999	msl. Delivered to Gr, based in Crete
	Gr	MBT	**AMX-30**	37	1997	1997	Last 10 delivered 1998
	RF	hel	**Mi-35**	12	2002	2003	
Estonia	SF	arty	**105mm**	18	1996	1997	105mm. Deliveries 1997–98
	SF	ML		2	1998	1999	Free transfer
	Ge	MCMV	***Lindau***	1	1999	1999	Free transfer
	US	hel	**R44**	4	2000	2000	
	Da	FSG	***Beskytteren***	1	2000	2000	Transfer
Finland	dom	APC	**XA-185**	450	1982	1983	XA180/185 series. Deliveries to 1999
	US	FGA	**F/A-18C/D**	64	1992	1995	Delivered by 2000. 57 made in SF
	dom	ACV	**RA-140**	10	1997	1998	Mine-clearing veh

	Country supplier	Classification ⇩	Designation	Quantity ⇩	Order date	Delivery date	Comment ⇩
	dom	PFM	**Hamina**	2	1997	1998	
	dom	arty	**K-98**	7	1998	2000	Additional 9 ordered 2001
	dom	AIFV	**CV 9030**	57	1998	2002	Up to 150 req
	dom	APC	**XA-200**	48	1999	1999	Deliveries to 2001
	Il	UAV	***Ranger***	3	1999	2001	9 ac and 6 ground stations
	US	ATGW	***Javelin***	242	2000		3,190 msl
	Il	ATGW	***Spike***		2000		
	dom	APC	**XA-202**	100	2000	2001	Option on further 70
	col	hel	**NH-90**	**20**	**2001**	**2004**	
Georgia	Tu	PCI	**SG-48**	1	1997	1998	Free transfer
	Ge	MSC	***Lindau***	2	1997	1998	Free transfer; deliveries to 1999
	UK	PFC		2	1998	1999	Free transfer
	Ukr	PFM	***Konotop***	1	1999	1999	
	Cz	MBT	**T-55AM2**	120	1998	2000	1st 11 Delivered 2000
	US	hel	**UH-1**	10	1999	1999	
Ireland	UK	arty	**105mm**	12	1996	1998	
	UK	PCO	***Roisin***	2	1997	1999	2nd delivered 2001
	CH	APC	***Piranha* III**	40	1999	2001	
Latvia	Ge	MSC	***Lindau***	1	1999	1999	Free transfer
	No	PCI	***Storm***	2	2001	2001	
Lithuania	Cz	trg	**L-39**	2	1997	1998	To join 4 L-39C trg ac purchased in 1992
	Ge	MSC	***Lindau***	1	1999	1999	Free transfer
	Ge	APC	**M-113**	67	1999	2000	Free transfer
	Ge	MCMV		1	2000	2000	Token price
	US	ATGW	**Javelin**	10	2001	2004	
Macedonia	Kaz	APC	**BTR-80**	12	1997	1998	
	Ge	APC	**BTR-70**	60	1998	1998	Free transfer
	Bg	arty	**152mm**	10	1998	1998	Free transfer
	Bg	arty	**76mm**	72	1998	1998	aka ZIS-3. Free transfer
	US	ACV	**HMMWV**	41	1998	1998	Free transfer
	Bg	MBT	**T-55**	150	1998	1999	36 type T-55AM2
	Bg	arty	**122mm**	142	1998	1999	Free transfer
	US	arty	**105mm**	18	1998	1999	Free transfer
	Tu	FGA	**F-5A/B**	20	1998	1999	Free transfer
	Ge	APC	***Hermelin***	105	2000	2000	
	Ukr	hel	**Mi-24**	10	2001	2001	
	Ukr	FGA	**Su-25**	4	2001	2001	
	Ukr	hel	**Mi-8MTV**	8	2001	2001	
Malta	UK	MPA	**BN2B**	2	1997	1998	
Romania	dom	FGA	**MiG-21**	110	1994	1997	Upgrade programme with Il
	US	tpt	**C-130**	5	1995	1998	
	dom	hel	**IAR-330L**	26	1995	1998	Upgrade
	Il	UAV	***Shadow***	6	1995	1998	
	US	cbt hel	**AH-1RO**	96	1997		Licence. Derivative of AH-1W. Delayed.

	Country supplier	Classification ⇩	Designation	Quantity ⇩	Order date	Delivery date	Comment ⇩
	Ge	AAA	**35mm**	43	1997	1999	
	dom	trg	**IAR-99**	33	1998	2000	6 delivered 2000
	dom	FGA	**MiG-29**	18	2001	2003	Upgrade
	UK	FFG	**Type 22**	2	2002		Second hand
Slovakia	dom	MBT	**M-2 *Moderna***		1995	2000	T-72 upgrade programme
	Cz	APC	**OT-64**	100	1997	1998	Also 2 BVP-2 from UK for delivery to Indo
	RF	trg	***Yak*-130**	12	1997	1999	RF debt repayment. Delayed or cancelled
	RF	SAM	**S-300**		1997		Part of debt repayment. Cancelled in 1999
	col	hel	**EC-135**	12	1997	1999	
	col	hel	**AS-532**	5	1997	1999	
	col	hel	**AS-550**	2	1997	1999	
	dom	arty	***Zuzana* 2000**	8	1997	1998	155mm. Deliveries 1998
Slovenia	Il	mor	**120mm**	56	1996	1998	Mortar
	Il	arty	**M845**	18	1996	1998	155mm 45 cal. towed arty
	Il	trg	**PC-9**	9	1997	1998	Upgrade
	Ch	trg	**PC-9**	2	1997	1998	
	dom	MBT	**M-55**	30	1998	1999	T-55 upgrade involving 105mm L-7 gun
	Aus	APC	***Pandur***	70	1998	1999	
	dom	MBT	**T-84**	40	1999	2002	Upgrade
	US	APC	**HMMWV**	30	2001	2001	
	col	hel	**AS 532**	2	2001	2003	
Sweden	dom	FGA	**JAS-39**	204	1981	1995	Deliveries to 2007; 112 del to date
	dom	AIFV	**CV-90**	600	1984	1993	To 2004. Extra 40 ordered 2001
	dom	SSK	**A-19 Gotland**	3	1986	1996	Deliveries to 1997
	dom	LCA		199	1988	1989	To 2001. 100 delivered by 1997
	dom	PCI	***Tapper***	12	1992	1993	Deliveries to 1999. Coastal arty
	dom	AEW	***Saab* 340**	6	1993	1997	Deliveries 1997-98
	US	AAM	**AMRAAM**	110	1994	1998	Option for a further 700
	Ge	MBT	***Leopard* 2**	120	1994	1998	New-build *Leopard* 2A5; to 2002
	Ge	MBT	***Leopard* 2**	160	1994	1997	Ex-Ge Army. Upgrade
	dom	MCM	**YSB**	4	1994	1996	Deliveries to 1998
	Ge	APC	**MT-LB**	584	1994	1995	Deliveries to 1998. Last 34 delivered 1998
	dom	FSG	***Visby***	6	1995	2001	Deliveries to 2006
	CH	APC	***Pirahna***	13	1996	1998	Command variant. Deliveries continue.
	col	AAM	**IRIS-T**		1997	2003	Dev with Ge
	col	ASM	**KEPD 350**		1997	2003	Dev with Ge to 2002. Also KEPD 150
	dom	LCA	***Transportbat***	14	1997	1999	
	dom	ACV	**M 10**	6	1997	1998	
	Fr	UAV	***Ugglan***	3	1997		
	Fr	hel	**AS532**	12	1998	2001	Deliveries 2002
	dom	SP arty	***Karelin***	50	1998		155mm. Dev
	dom	PCI	**KBV 201**	2	1999	2002	
	Ge	ARV	***Buffel***	10	1999	2002	
	dom	FSG	***Visby***	2	1999	2008	

	Country supplier	Classification ⇩	Designation	Quantity ⇩	Order date	Delivery date	Comment ⇩
	SF	APC	**XA-203**	104	2000	2001	
	dom	APC	**Bv-206S**	15	2001		
	It	hel	**A109**	20	2001	2002	
Switzerland	US	FGA	**F/A-18C/D**	34	1993	1997	Most assembled in CH, deliveries 1997–99
	US	AAM	**AIM-120**	100	1993	1998	
	Il	UAV	***Ranger***	4	1995	1998	Licensed, 28 UAVs. Deliveries to 1999
	Ca	APC	***Piranha* II**	515	1996	1997	Deliveries to 2002
	dom	AD	***Skyguard***	100	1997	1999	Upgrade
	US	SP arty	**M-109**	456	1997	1998	Upgrade, deliveries to 2000
	Fr	hel	**AS-532**	12	1997	2000	Deliveries to 2002
	dom	APC	***Eagle* II**	175	1997	1999	Final deliveries 2001
	US	AD	***Florako***	1	1999	2007	Upgrade
	Ca	APC	***Piranha* III**	10	2000	2001	Up to 120 req
	UK	AIFV	**CV-90**	186	2000	2002	Deliveries to run to 2005
	Sp	tpt	**C295**	2	2000	2003	
	dom	APC	***Eagle* III**	120	2000	2003	
	Ge	ARV	***Buffel***	25	2002	2004	
Ukraine	dom	CG	***Ukraina***	1	1990	2000	
	col	tpt	**AN-70**	5	1991	2003	Up to 65 req
	RF	FGA	**Su-24**	4	1996	2000	Final 2 delivered 2000
	dom	MBT	**T-84**	10	1999	2000	
	RF	FGA	**MiG-29**			2001	Upgrade
	RF	FGA	**Su-25**			2001	Upgrade

Russia

Russia's economic performance since the 1998 crisis continues to surprise observers. Growth has averaged 6% a year over the last three years, after almost a decade of output declines; inflation has fallen to around 20%; and the pre-crisis fiscal deficits have turned into overall surpluses of 2% of GDP. The sharp turnaround in Russia's macro-economic performance can be attributed to three main factors. Firstly, as a result of the crisis the Russian exchange rate depreciated considerably, boosting international competitiveness and helping exports, which increased by 25% between 1998 and 2001. In addition, the value of Russia's key exports, oil and gas, increased dramatically as world prices strengthened helping both the current account and increasing government tax revenues. And lastly Russia displayed considerable fiscal prudence after the crisis restraining certain expenditures and making a major effort to raise tax compliance. In the last year Russia has weathered the global slowdown, achieving growth of 5% in 2001, and although the outlook for 2002 is slightly less optimistic, continuing structural reform means Russia is well-placed to continue to be an engine of growth for the region.

THE 2002 DEFENCE BUDGET

The national defence budget rose from R246.2bn in 2001 to R283.1bn in 2002. Although this represents a reduction in the level of funds allocated from the total federal budget, 14.5% down from 17.8%, as a proportion of GDP defence spending remains constant at 2.7%, suggesting a deliberate policy of increasing defence spending at a rate corresponding to the rate of growth of the economy. The increase in personnel costs is consistent with President Vladimir Putin's intention to bolster the morale and prestige of the armed forces. His aim is to introduce a two-phase increase in military salaries, firstly in 2002 and again in 2004, that would boost pay by 50%. Opponents of the plan, including members of the Duma defence committee, want to link military salaries to those of other government employees, which would cost considerably more than the president's plan. Concern remains that if service conditions are not improved, it will become increasingly difficult to recruit and retain junior personnel. Russia's procurement strategy for the next decade was detailed in the State Armaments Programme 2001–10, adopted by Putin in January 2002. Unlike the previous programme instigated by Boris Yeltsin for the period 1995–2006, which was undermined by lack of funds (up until 2000 only 25% of the necessary funds were actually disbursed), this latest plan is expected to be fully funded. Under the new plan, research, development and engineering (RD&E) becomes the top priority. Between 2002 and 2005, this sector alone will be allocated 40% of the annual state defence order (that is, procurement funds and R&D spending combined). In 2006 RD&E funding is scheduled to drop to 15% of the state defence order, leaving the majority to be spent on weapons procurement itself. Research and development priorities are

Russia RF

rouble r		2000	2001	2002	2003
GDP[1]	r	7,302bn	9,090bn		
	US$	1,222bn	1,522bn		
per capita	US$	8,410	10,518		
Growth	%	9.0	5.0		
Inflation	%	20.8	18.6		
Debt	US$	160bn	150bn		
Def exp[1]	US$	52bn	65bn		
Def bdgt[2]	r	143bn	219bn	262bn	
	US$	5bn	7.5bn	8.3bn	
FMA[3] (US)	US$	0.7m	0.2m	0.8m	0.8m
US$1=r		28.2	29.2	31.5	

[1] PPP est

[2] Official MoD budget at market rates

[3] Under the US Cooperative Threat Reduction programme, $2.8bn has been authorised by the US to support START implementation and demilitarisation in RF, Ukr, Bel and Kaz. RF's share is 60–65%

Population 144,700,000

Tatar 4% **Ukrainian** 3% **Chuvash** 1% **Bashkir** 1% **Belarussian** 1% **Moldovan** 1% **other** 8%

Age	13–17	18–22	23–32
Men	5,967,000	5,684,000	10,034,000
Women	5,735,000	5,538,000	9,852,000

known to include the fifth-generation fighter aircraft, spacecraft and new multi-purpose nuclear submarines. The first prototype of the fifth generation tactical fighter jet is scheduled to be built by Sukhoi Military Aircraft Corporation and be completed by 2006. In 2002, the state defence order rose from R57bn to R79bn and, as in 2001, this amount is expected to be fully funded. However, the order once again does not provide for any new aircraft for the national air force; indeed, the air force will receive only 10% of the total, only enough for limited repairs, operations and maintenance. No new combat aircraft have entered service with the air force since 1994.

DEFENCE INDUSTRY

In the last ten years, all attempts to significantly reform Russia's defence industry have failed. In November 2001, Putin signed two basic documents presaging a radical overhaul of the system: a federal plan for the reform and development of the military-industrial complex in the period 2002–06; and a basic policy for developing the military-industrial complex up to 2010.

To achieve greater efficiency from the defence industry, the new initiatives calls for a halving of the current number of defence companies – from 1,700 to 800 –and reorganising them into 50 state-controlled firms and holding companies. These new entities would then receive all government orders for research, development and production of weapon systems. There would be no state funding for other defence contractors. This plan is intended to rectify the overcapacity that has existed in the defence industry since the collapse of the Soviet Union. At present, many military enterprises are only working at 5–10% of their

Table 14 Estimated official Russian defence budget by function, 2001–02 Rm

	2001	%	ε2002	%
Ministry of Defence Budget				
Personnel	91,064	41.6	112,355	42.7
Training & Supplies	37,510	17.1	48,182	18.3
Procurement	33,100	15.1	47,400	18.0
R&D	23,900	10.9	31,600	12.0
MoD	912	0.4	950	0.4
Other	32,454	14.8	22,413	8.5
MoD Adopted Budget Total	218,940	100	262,900	100
MoD Revised Budget	234,582		n.a.	
Other National Defence Programmes				
Military progs of Minatom	6,330		13,994	
Security mobilisation of troops and ex-forces training	2,278		3,166	
Collective security & peace-keeping activities	2,716		2,728	
Activities of branches of the economy for National Defence	303		303	
Total National Defence Budget	246,209		283,091	
GDP	9,090,000		ε10,620,000	
National Defence as % of GDP		2.70		2.66
Total Federal Budget Expenditure	1,376,000		1,947,000	
National Defence as % of total expenditure		17.8		14.5

production capacity. However, as a sign that reform in this area (including marketing) is beginning to work, Russia's share of the world arms market has increased significantly (see Table 15).

The plan also takes on another area that has resisted previous efforts at restructuring – the interests of regional authorities. In the past, regional authorities, fearing they would lose vital tax revenue, were reluctant to support the formation of integrated holding companies. The region of Khabarovsk, for example, funds 40% of its budget from the tax revenue gathered from KNAAPO, the makers of the Su-27 and Su-30 fighter aircraft. Changes to the federal tax regime are proposed as a means of overcoming this problem.

ESTIMATING RUSSIAN MILITARY EXPENDITURE

As ever, estimating the real scale of Russian military spending is fraught with difficulty. When taken at face value, the official National Defence budget heading for 2001 corresponds to 2.66% of GDP; however this figure excludes military pensions, funding for military reform and several other items that are clearly defence-related costs.

Taking into account military-related spending outside the National Defence budget significantly boosts the total military spend. Table 16 lists some of these additional budget areas that need to be considered. Once included, these extra funds bring overall military related expenditure to around R379bn or 4.1% of 2001 GDP. On top of this is revenue from arms exports – US$3.6bn in 2001– much of which finds its way into the military coffers, which further inflates the total.

Translated into dollars at the market exchange rate, Russia's official National Defence budget for 2001 amounts to just US$8.3bn – roughly equivalent to Canada's annual defence expenditure. Including the other defence related items listed above boosts the figure to US$12.9bn. This is significantly lower than that suggested by the size of the armed forces or the nature of the military-industrial complex, and is thus not a useful statistic for comparative analysis. For this reason, *The Military Balance* estimates actual defence expenditure in Russia based on purchasing-power parity (PPP) rates. In 2000, the World Bank estimated that Russia's GDP at PPP rates was US$1,222bn and *The Military Balance* estimated that military related expenditure was in the order of 4.0% of GDP, making defence expenditure (including funds from arms exports) around US$52bn. Using a similar approach, we estimate that at PPP rates, military expenditure in Russia in 2001 was equivalent to US$65bn.

Table 15 Russian arms deliveries, 1994–2001

	Arms exports		Domestic procurement	Arms trade as % of	Merchandise exports	Arms trade as % of
	US$bn	Rbn	Rbn	procurement	US$bn	exports
1994	1.7	3.7	8.4	44	67	2.5
1995	3.5	16.0	10.3	155	83	4.2
1996	3.1	15.9	13.2	120	91	3.4
1997	2.6	23.1	21.0	110	89	2.9
1998	2.2	21.4	17.0	125	74	3.0
1999	3.1	76.6	23.8	322	73	4.2
2000	3.5	100.1	27.3	367	105	3.3
2001	3.6	104.0	33.1	314	103	3.5

Table 16 **Additional Military Expenditure**

not appearing under National Defence Budget heading	2001	2002
Military Science	8,838	12,136
Internal Troops	10,157	13,353
Border Troops	11,943	17,323
State Security	21,191	30,915
Military Pensions	30,651	40,274
Security Sector Pensions	14,108	20,262
Liquidation of weapons	6,036	10,300
Mobilisation of economy	500	500
Military Reform	4,237	16,545
Subsidies to closed military region	13,893	13,893
Emergencies	6,333	8,693
Military Housing	ε5,000	5,400
Military Courts	n.k.	n.k.
International Treaty Obligations	–	1,417
Total Defence-related Expenditure	379,096	474,102

Rm

Middle East and North Africa

Growth in the Middle East, after holding up relatively well in 2001, is expected to fall back in 2002, largely as a result of lower oil production and the regional security situation. The curtailment of oil production, associated with OPEC agreements to limit global supply, has depressed activity in oil-exporting countries in 2002, while the security situation has also had a negative impact on other economic activity, especially tourism.

Higher oil prices during the second half of 2000 and early 2001, when prices peaked at $38 a barrel, led to an increase in regional defence spending. In 2000, total defence expenditure for the region amounted to US$60.6bn. In 2001, the figure rose to US$68.7bn.

The **Israel–Palestine** conflict has created serious economic strains in the country. Israel's GDP shrunk by about 5% in 2001 and severe budget cuts and new taxes to ease the building fiscal problems are likely. For example, the call-up of 25,000 reservists in early 2002 will cost about 600 million shekels (NS) a month. A fiscal deficit of around 3.5% is forecast for 2002. The cost of financing this has increased as ratings agencies continue to revise the credit rating of Israeli debt in the light of the war. The original defence budget for 2002 was scheduled to increase by NS3.75bn over the level of 2001; however, the delay in passing the 2002 state budget meant that in the end the additional funds could not be allocated. Therefore, the budget was set at NS41.7bn, slightly lower than in 2001. However, in April 2002, following continued military operations in the West Bank and Gaza, in particular *Operation Protective Shield*, a further NS2bn was approved for the defence ministry, bringing its budget to NS43.7bn (US$9.4bn), 20.4% of the national budget. The Israeli Air Force will benefit from an additional 52 F-16I fighters, ordered in September 2001 at a cost of around US$2bn. This is a follow-on order, in addition to a US$2.5bn contract for 50 F-16Is, signed in 1999. The new aircraft will be delivered between 2006 and 2009. Taking into account nine *Apache Longbow* helicopters due for delivery from 2004, the air force will receive more than 50% of the IDF's total procurement budget over the next decade.

The army has begun to take delivery of the new advanced main battle tank, the *Merkava* MK4, unveiled in June and estimated to cost around US$3.7m per unit. The Ministry of Defence plans to produce between 50 and 70 tanks a year for at least the next four years. The navy, traditionally receiving the least funds of the three services, is investigating the possibility of transforming itself into an effective blue-water force with a long-range strike capability. As yet no funding has been approved, although a committee is examining the idea of re-allocating defence funding to the navy for this purpose. In an effort to preserve its faltering national shipbuilding industry, the Ministry of Defence ordered a batch of eight ships for the navy's future coastal patrol fleet from local manufacturers. The first part of the programme consists of six *Super Dvora* MkII and two *Shaldag* fast attack craft to be built at a total cost of around US$32m.

Despite expectations that it would deliver a balanced budget in 2001, **Saudi Arabia** surprised observers by announcing a budget deficit of SAR25bn. Although revenues were higher than budgeted at SAR230bn, expenditures were considerably higher than forecast at SAR255bn. The budget for 2002 anticipates revenues falling to SAR175bn while outlays are reduced to SAR202bn. Saudi Arabia remains more exposed than other smaller Gulf states to volatility in the international oil market. With over half the population under 18 years old and unemployment reaching 20%, it is critical that the economy diversifies further into the non-oil sector. Despite the drop in government expenditure forecast for 2002, the defence budget is estimated to have increased by around 4% to SAR80.1bn (US$21.3bn). In a move that carries political overtones, possibly in response to rising tension throughout the region, Saudi Arabia cancelled a long held plan to procure up to 78 G-6 artillery systems from the South African state-owned defence company Denel.

Following last year's review, which placed major acquisition programmes on hold, **Kuwait** confirmed its intention to purchase 16 Boeing AH-64 *Apache* attack helicopters and associated systems. The potential US$2.1bn package, yet to receive the go ahead from the US congress, includes eight *Longbow* fire-control radars, 96 *Longbow Hellfire* missiles, 288 *Hellfire* missiles, 16 Modernised Targeting Acquisition and Designation Systems and spare engines, missile launchers and other equipment and support. The US Department of Defense originally approved an *Apache* sale to Kuwait in 1997, but this was later dropped after congressional objections to the inclusion of the sophisticated *Longbow* Fire Control Radar. Further progress was also made on Kuwait's plans to buy a low-level air-defence system from Egypt. Kuwait already has five of the *Amoun* air-defence systems, purchased from Egypt in 1988, although these are now thought to be in poor condition. The new deal is initially for two systems, with options for a further three as well as the upgrade of the older systems.

The **Iranian** economy continued to grow at around 5% a year. More recent progress in structural reform as well as a much-needed expansion of non-oil private sector activity is expected to provide significant support to growth in 2002–03. In October 2001, following the March 2001 accord between Iranian President Muhammad Khatami and Russian President Vladimir Putin, the defence ministers of the two countries signed a military-technical cooperation agreement by which Russia plans to sell arms to Iran. Iran intends to spend around US$10bn over the next 10 years to re-equip its armed forces; the agreement with Russia will account for up to US$4bn of this. Although no specific details have been made public, the Iranian defence minister, on his trip to Russia, visited manufacturing plants that produce air-defence missile systems, anti-tank guided weapons and battlefield missile systems. According to Rosoboronexport, the Russian state-owned arms-trade company, the agreement could produce sales of up to US$300m a year. Apart from the delivery of complete armaments systems, such as the S-300 air-defence system, potential military-technical cooperation could extend to the upgrade of the Iranian Air Force fleet of Russian combat aircraft; overhauling equipment previously delivered by Russia; establishing a service centre in Iran for the MiG-29 and the Su-24MK; installing a T-72S main battle tank crew training centre; collaborating in the development of space-borne communications and earth surveillance systems; as well as organising the licensed production in Iran of several Russian-designed land and naval weapon systems. In 2001, Iran received the last of 21 Mi-17 helicopters ordered in 1999 and took up the option for the US$150m purchase of a further 30 of the military transport aircraft.

Egypt was a cause of concern to Israel when its request to purchase 53 Boeing RGM-84L *Harpoon* Block II medium-range anti-ship missiles was approved by US congress. The contract, valued at US$255m, also included Raytheon *Phalanx* Block 1B close-in weapons systems and 50,000 rounds of tungsten ammunitions. Egypt's acquisition of the *Harpoon* Block II missiles, which could potentially be adapted to have a land-attack capability, was viewed by Israel as a threat. However, following an unprecedented 15 meetings, the US Defense Security Cooperation Agency revealed that the missiles would be modified in the US to prevent any future reconfiguration. In a change of policy, the US DSCA also confirmed that the US$400m upgrade of Egypt's 35 AH-64A *Apache* helicopters to AH-64D standard will not include the AN/APG-178 *Longbow* radar as previously understood.

Despite a poor economic outlook, **Yemen** continues to sign major weapons deals. In October 2001 Yemen signed a deal estimated to be worth up to US$430m for the acquisition of 15–24 MiG-29s plus an upgrade of some of its current inventory to the same standard.

Algeria Ag

dinar D		2000	2001	2002
GDP	D	4.0tr	3.9tr	
	US$	54.8bn	50.7bn	
per capita	US$	1,800	1,600	
Growth	%	2.6	3.5	
Inflation	%	0.5	4.1	
Debt	US$	25bn	23.6bn	
Def exp	D	223bn	250bn	
	US$	3.0bn	3.2bn	
Def bdgt	D	150bn	167bn	
	US$	1.9bn	2.1bn	
FMA (US)	US$	100m	100m	200m
US$1=D		74.6	77.8	79.6

Population			32,136,000
Age	13–17	18–22	23–32
Men	1,986,000	1,834,000	2,962,000
Women	1,847,000	1,709,000	2,783,000

Bahrain Brn

dinar D		2000	2001	2002
GDP	D	2.6bn	2.9bn	
	US$	6.9bn	7.7bn	
per capita	US$	10,200	11,000	
Growth	%	5.3	3.3	
Inflation	%	-0.7	-0.2	
Debt	US$	2.9bn	2.9bn	
Def exp	D	121m	140m	
	US$	322m	371m	
Def bdgt[a]	D	121m	140m	
	US$	315m	315m	
FMA (US)	US$	200m	200m	200m
US$1=D		0.38	0.38	0.38

[a] Excl procurement

Population			626,000
Nationals 63% **Asian** 13% **other Arab** 10% **Iranian** 8% **European** 1%			
Age	13–17	18–22	23–32
Men	35,000	26,000	40,000
Women	33,000	25,000	40,000

Egypt Et

pound E£		2000	2001	2002
GDP	E£	336bn	364bn	
	US$	97.7bn	93.8bn	
per capita	US$	1,500	1,300	
Growth	%	5.3	3.3	
Inflation	%	2.8	2.4	
Debt	US$	29bn	26.5bn	
Def exp	E£	14.1bn	17.1bn	
	US$	4.1bn	4.4bn	

Et contd		2000	2001	2002
Def bdgt	E£	9.6bn	12.6bn	14.1bn
	US$	2.8bn	3.2bn	3.0bn
FMA (US)	US$	2.0bn	2.0bn	2.0bn
US$1=E£		3.44	3.88	4.6

Population			70,615,000
Age	13–17	18–22	23–32
Men	3,707,000	3,313,000	5,150,000
Women	3,510,000	3,128,000	4,853,000

Iran Ir

rial r		2000	2001	2002
GDP[a]	r	582tr	651tr	
	US$	73bn	82bn	
per capita	US$	1,500	1,300	
Growth	%	4.5	5.1	
Inflation	%	12.6	11.7	
Debt	US$	10.2bn	9.8bn	
Def exp[a]	r	31.2tr	37.9tr	
	US$	4.0bn	4.8bn	
Def bdgt	r	18.3tr	22.3tr	32.7tr
	US$	2.3bn	2.8bn	4.1bn
US$1=r		7,909	7,924	7,924

[a] Excl defence industry funding

Population			68,281,000
Persian 51% **Azeri** 24% **Gilaki/Mazandarani** 8% **Kurdish** 7% **Arab** 3% **Lur** 2% **Baloch** 2% **Turkman** 2%			
Age	13–17	18–22	23–32
Men	4,735,000	3,960,000	5,959,000
Women	4,531,000	3,835,000	5,613,000

Iraq Irq

dinar D		2000	2001	2002
GDP	US$	ε15.4bn	15bn	
Growth	%	ε15		
Inflation	%	ε100		
Debt	US$	ε139bn		
Def exp	US$	ε1.4bn	ε1.4bn	
US$1=D		0.31	0.31	0.31

Population			22,300,000
Arab 75–80% (of which Shi'a Muslim 55%, Sunni Muslim 45%) **Kurdish** 20–25%			
Age	13–17	18–22	23–32
Men	1,538,000	1,324,000	1,960,000
Women	1,472,000	1,270,000	1,899,000

Israel Il

new sheqalim NS		2000	2001	2002
GDP	NS	444bn	464bn	
	US$	109bn	110bn	
per capita	US$	17,568	18,000	
Growth	%	6.4	-0.6	
Inflation	%	1.7	2.3	
Debt	US$	61bn	67bn	
Def exp	NS	39.4bn	43.8bn	
	US$	9.6bn	10.6bn	
Def bdgt	NS	39bn	42.6bn	43.7bn
	US$	9.5bn	10.2bn	9.4bn
FMA (US)	US$	4.1bn	2.8bn	2.8bn
US$1=NS		4.12	4.21	4.66

Population[b] **6,200,000**

Jewish 82% **Arab** 19% (incl Christian 3%, Druze 2%) **Circassian** ε3,000

Age	13–17	18–22	23–32
Men	284,000	272,000	535,000
Women	268,000	259,000	528,000

[b] Incl ε180,000 Jewish settlers in Gaza and the West Bank, ε217,000 in East Jerusalem and ε15,000 in Golan

Jordan HKJ

dinar D		2000	2001	2002
GDP	D	5.4bn	6.3bn	
	US$	7.6bn	8.9bn	
per capita	US$	1,524	1,737	
Growth	%	4.0	4.2	
Inflation	%	0.6	1.8	
Debt	US$	6.7bn	7.2bn	
Def exp	D	563m	540m	
	US$	792m	755m	
Def bdgt	D	563m	537m	720m
	US$	792m	755m	1.0bn
FMA (US)	US$	425m	225m	225m
US$1=D		0.71	0.71	0.71

Population **6,869,000** **Palestinian** ε50–60%

Age	13–17	18–22	23–32
Men	280,000	247,000	454,000
Women	272,000	240,000	443,000

Kuwait Kwt

dinar D		2000	2001	2002
GDP	D	10.2bn	12.9bn	
	US$	33.4bn	42.3bn	
per capita	US$	17,424	21,127	
Growth	%	1.7	2.7	
Inflation	%	1.7	2.5	
Debt	US$	9.3bn	9.3bn	

Kwt contd		2000	2001	2002
Def exp	D	1.1bn	1.5bn	
	US$	3.7bn	5.1bn	
Def bdgt	D	713m	1.2bn	1.2bn
	US$	2.3bn	4.1bn	3.9bn
US$1=D		0.31	0.31	0.31

Population **2,065,000**

Nationals 35% **other Arab** 35% **South Asian** 9% **Iranian** 4% **other** 17%

Age	13–17	18–22	23–32
Men	124,000	107,000	148,000
Women	92,000	80,000	114,000

Lebanon RL

pound LP		2000	2001	2002
GDP	LP	24.1tr	25tr	
	US$	16.0bn	16.6bn	
per capita	US$	4,363	4,611	
Growth	%	-1.6	1.3	
Inflation	%	-0.4	3.0	
Debt	US$	7.0bn	9.5bn	
Def exp	LP	871bn	886bn	
	US$	578m	588m	
Def bdgt	LP	871bn	886bn	812bn
	US$	578m	588m	536m
FMA (US)	US$	0.6m	0.5m	0.6m
US$1=LP		1,507	1,508	1,514

Population **3,600,000**

Christian 30% **Druze** 6% **Armenian** 4%, excl ε300,000 Syrian nationals and ε350,000 Palestinian refugees

Age	13–17	18–22	23–32
Men	216,000	194,000	397,000
Women	220,000	200,000	406,000

Libya LAR

dinar D		2000	2001	2002
GDP	US$	13.5bn	13.5bn	
per capita	US$	2,477	2,505	
Growth	%	4.4	0.6	
Inflation	%	-3.0	-8.5	
Debt	US$	4.6bn	4.5bn	
Def exp	US$	1.2bn	1.2bn	
US$1=D		1.42	1.22	1.22

Population **5,644,000**

Age	13–17	18–22	23–32
Men	387,000	320,000	492,000
Women	372,000	309,000	473,000

Mauritania RIM

ougiya OM		2000	2001	2002
GDP	OM	205bn	223bn	
	US$	0.8bn	0.9bn	
per capita	US$	323	326	
Growth	%	5.0	4.6	
Inflation	%	4.5		
Debt	US$	2.6bn	2.7bn	
Def exp	OM	ε5.7bn	ε6.5bn	
	US$	23.6m	26m	
Def bdgt	OM	ε5.7bn	ε6.5bn	7.1bn
	US$	23.6m	25.6m	26m
US$1=OM		242	254	273

Population			**2,753,000**
Age	13–17	18–22	23–32
Men	149,000	121,000	194,000
Women	147,000	117,000	188,000

Morocco Mor

dirham D		2000	2001	2002
GDP	D	350bn	373bn	
	US$	33bn	32bn	
per capita	US$	1,113	1,055	
Growth	%	2.4	6.3	
Inflation	%	1.9	0.5	
Debt	US$	17.9bn	16.7bn	
Def exp	D	15bn	15.6bn	
	US$	1.4bn	1.3bn	
Def bdgt	D	15bn	15.6bn	17.7bn
	US$	1.4bn	1.3bn	1.7bn
FMA (US)	US$	14m	14m	16m
US$1=D		10.5	11.6	10.4

Population			**28,476,000**
Age	13–17	18–22	23–32
Men	1,780,000	1,612,000	2,726,000
Women	1,722,000	1,559,000	2,628,000

Oman O

rial R		2000	2001	2002
GDP	R	6.8bn	7.7bn	
	US$	17.7bn	20bn	
per capita	US$	7,131	7,702	
Growth	%	4.9	6.5	
Inflation	%	-1.0	-2.6	
Debt	US$	6.2bn	6.0bn	
Def exp	R	807m	1,111m	
	US$	2.1bn	2.9bn	
Def bdgt[a]	R	673m	926m	860m
	US$	1.75bn	2.4bn	2.3bn
FMA[b] (US)	US$	0.2m	0.25m	0.5m
US$1=R		0.38	0.38	0.38

[a] Five-year plan 2001–2005 allocates R3.4bn (US$9.05bn)for defence

Population			**2,600,000** expatriates 27%
Age	13–17	18–22	23–32
Men	136,000	110,000	159,000
Women	131,000	107,000	149,000

Palestinian Autonomous Areas of Gaza and Jericho PA

		1999	2000	2001	2002
GDP	US$				
per capita	US$				
Growth	%				
Inflation	%				
Debt	US$				
Sy bdgt	US$				
FMA (US)	US$	100m	485m	85m	75m

Population **ε3,000,000**

West Bank and Gaza excluding East Jerusalem ε2,900,000 **Israeli** ε180,000 excl East Jerusalem **Gaza** ε1,200,000 **Israeli** ε6,100 **West Bank excl East Jerusalem** ε1,700,000 **Israeli** ε174,000 **East Jerusalem Israeli** ε217,000 **Palestinian** ε86–200,000

Age	13–17	18–22	23–32
Men	163,000	140,000	233,000
Women	158,000	134,000	222,000

Qatar Q

rial R		2000	2001	2002
GDP	R	59.7bn	65bn	
	US$	16.4bn	17.9bn	
per capita	US$	23,800	29,700	
Growth	%	11.6	7.2	
Inflation	%	1.7	-0.7	
Debt	US$	12.8bn	13bn	
Def exp	R	4.3bn	4.6bn	
	US$	1.2bn	1.3bn	
Def bdgt	R	4.3bn	4.6bn	ε6.0bn
	US$	1.2bn	1.3bn	1.6bn
US$1=R		3.64	3.64	3.64

Population **610,000**

nationals 25% **expatriates** 75% of which Indian 18%, Iranian 10%, Pakistani 18%

Age	13–17	18–22	23–32
Men	26,000	22,000	38,000
Women	29,000	24,000	33,000

Saudi Arabia Sau

rial R		2000	2001	2002
GDP	R	694bn	660bn	
	US$	185bn	176bn	
per capita	US$	9,000	8,392	
Growth	%	4.5	2.2	
Inflation	%	-0.6	-1.4	
Debt	US$	36bn	36bn	
Def exp	R	82.6bn	92.7bn	
	US$	22bn	24.7bn	
Def bdgt	R	74.8bn	77.1bn	80.1bn
	US$	19.9bn	20.6bn	21.3bn
US$1=R		3.75	3.75	3.75

Population **21,000,000**

nationals 73% of which Bedouin up to 10%, Shi'a 6%, **expatriates** 27% of which Asians 20%, Arabs 6%, Africans 1%, Europeans <1%

Age	13–17	18–22	23–32
Men	1,391,000	1,177,000	1,725,000
Women	1,246,000	1,051,000	1,494,000

Syria Syr

pound S£		2000	2001	2002
GDP	S£	800bn	915bn	
	US$	13.7bn	17.6bn	
per capita	US$	851	1,060	
Growth	%	2.5	3.5	
Inflation	%	-0.6	1.0	
Debt	US$	22bn	22.3bn	
Def exp	S£	ε86bn	ε100bn	
	US$	1.5bn	1.9bn	
Def bdgt	S£	42bn	50bn	53bn
	US$	729m	960m	1.0bn
US$1=S£		58	52	52

Population **16,493,000**

Age	13–17	18–22	23–32
Men	1,076,000	883,000	1,274,000

Tunisia Tn

dinar D		2000	2001	2002
GDP	D	27bn	28.5bn	
	US$	21.3bn	19.9bn	
per capita	US$	2,245	2,076	
Growth	%	4.7	5.0	
Inflation	%	3.0	1.9	
Debt	US$	11.5bn	10.3bn	
Def exp	D	ε450m	ε550m	
	US$	356m	385m	
Def bdgt	D	441m	550m	575m
	US$	349m	384m	429m
FMA (US)	US$	3.9m	4.5m	4.5m

Tn contd	2000	2001	2002
US$1=D	1.36	1.43	1.34

Population **9,697,000**

Age	13–17	18–22	23–32
Men	529,000	505,000	869,000
Women	507,000	484,000	843,000

United Arab Emirates UAE

dirham D		2000	2001	2002
GDP	D	213bn	249bn	
	US$	58bn	67bn	
per capita	US$	22,842	25,129	
Growth	%	5.0	5.0	
Inflation	%	1.4	2.2	
Debt	US$	16bn	16bn	
Def exp	D	ε11.0bn	ε11.5bn	
	US$	3.0bn	3.1bn	
Def bdgt[a]	D	6.0bn	6.0bn	6.0bn
	US$	1.6bn	1.6bn	1.6bn
US$1=D		3.67	3.67	3.67

[a] Including extra-budgetary funding for procurement

Population **2,571,000**

nationals 24% **expatriates** 76% of which Indian 30%, Pakistani 20%, other Arab 12%, other Asian 10%, UK 2%, other European 1%

Age	13–17	18–22	23–32
Men	87,000	87,000	143,000
Women	87,000	83,000	115,000

Yemen, Republic of Ye

rial R		2000	2001	2002
GDP	R	1,017bn	1,112bn	
	US$	6.4bn	6.7bn	
per capita	US$	348	351	
Growth	%	5.1	3.3	
Inflation	%	10.9	11.9	
Debt	US$	5.6bn	5.6bn	
Def exp	R	ε80bn	ε90bn	
	US$	498m	542m	
Def bdgt	R	65bn	85bn	90bn
	US$	407m	512m	515m
FMA (US)	US$	0.1m	0.1m	
US$1=R		159	166	175

Population **18,885,000** **North** 79% **South** 21%

Age	13–17	18–22	23–32
Men	1,008,000	803,000	1,328,000
Women	982,000	778,000	1,213,000

Table 17 Arms orders and deliveries, Middle East and North Africa, 1998–2002

	Country supplier	Classification ⇩	Designation	Quantity ⇩	Order date	Delivery date	Comment ⇩
Algeria	Tu	LACV	***Scorpion***	700	1995	1996	Deliveries continuing
	Ukr	MBT	**T-72**	67	1997	1998	
	Ukr	AIFV	**BMP-2**	32	1997	1998	
	Ukr	cbt hel	**Mi-24**	14	1997	1998	
	Bel	FGA	**MiG-29**	36	1998	1999	Reportedly in exchange for 120 MiG-21s
	RF	ASSM	**Kh-35**	96	1998	1999	For FACs. 2 batches of 48 ordered
	RSA	hel	**Mi-24**	33	1999	2001	Upgrade
	Cz	FGA	**L-39ZA**	17	2001		First manufactured in 1991
	RF	FGA	**Su-24**	22	2000	2001	
	US	ESM	***Beech* 1900**	6	2000		For SIGINT role
Bahrain	US	SAM	***Hawk***	8	1996	1997	Deliveries to 1998. 8 btys
	US	FGA	**F-16C/D**	10	1998	2000	AMRAAM-equipped; option for 2 more
	US	MRL	**ATACMS**	30	1999	2001	Delivered
	US	AAM	**AMRAAM**		1999		
Egypt	US	APC	**M-113**	2,000	1980	1982	Delivered throughout 1997
	US	MBT	**M1A1**	555	1988	1993	Order for 555 complete by end-1998
	US	hel	**AH-64**	36	1990	1994	24 delivered by 1995; 12 more 1997–99
	US	FF	***Oliver Hazard Perry***	4	1994	1996	Deliveries to 1998
	US	hel	**SH-2G**	10	1994	1997	Deliveries to 1999
	US	arty	**SP 122 SPG**	24	1996	2000	2nd order
	US	FGA	**F-16C/D**	21	1996	1999	
	US	hel	**CH-47D**	4	1997	1999	Also updates for 6 CH-47Cs to D
	US	SAM	***Avenger***	50	1998	2001	Delivered
	US	ARV	**M88A2**	63	1998	2002	50 delivered in 2000
	dom	APC	***Al-Akhbar***		1998	2001	Dev complete
	US	SAM	***Patriot***	384	1998	2001	384 msl; 48 launchers
	RF	SAM	***Pechora***	50	1999	2003	Upgrade to *Pechora*-2 aka SA-3A *Goa*
	US	FGA	**F-16**	24	1999	2001	12 × 1 seater; 12 × 2 seater
	PRC	trg	**K-8**		1999	2001	
	US	AEW	**E-2C**	5	1999	2002	Upgrade
	SF	arty	**GH-52**	1	1999		
	US	MBT	**M1A1**	200	1999	2001	Kits for local assembly
	Ge	trg	**G 115EG**	74	1999	2000	Deliveries to 2002
	US	SAM	**AMRAAM**		2000		Ground launched variant
	US	hel	**AH-64A**	35	2000		Upgrade to *Longbow* standard
	It	FAC	***Ramadan***	6	2000		Upgraded Comd & Control systems
	Nl	SSK	***Moray***	2	2000	2006	
	US	FM	***Ambassador* III**	4	2001	2004	
	A	UAV	***Camcopter***	2	2001	2002	
	US	rkt	**MLRS**	26	2001		Incl. 2,850 rockets
	US	SPA	**M109A**	210	2001		Refurbished prior to delivery
	US	ASM	**Harpoon**	53	2001		Block II
Iran	RF	MBT	**T-72**	100	1989	1998	Kits for local assembly
	RF	AIFV	**BMP-2**	200	1989	1998	Kits for local assembly
	dom	SSM	**Shihab-2**		1994	1998	Dom produced Scud
	dom	SSM	***Shihab*-3**		1994	1999	Reportedly based on DPRK *No-dong* 1

	Country supplier	Classification ⇩	Designation	Quantity ⇩	Order date	Delivery date	Comment ⇩
	dom	MRBM	***Shihab*-4**		1994		Dev. Reportedly based on RF SS-4
	dom	ICBM	***Shihab*-5**		1994		Dev. Possibly based on *Taepo-dong*
	PRC	tpt	**Y-7**	14	1996	1998	Deliveries 1998–2006
	PRC	FGA	**F-7**	10	1996	1998	
	dom	hel	***Shahed*-5**	20	1999		
	RF	hel	**Mi-17**	4	1999	2000	Potential for further 20
	dom	SSI	**Al-Sabehat 15**	1		2000	Mini-sub
	RF	hel	**Mi-8**	30	2001	2002	
	dom	ATGW	**Saeque-1**		2001		In development
	Ir	FGA	**MiG-29**	29	1999	1999	Held since 1990; returned by Ir 1999
Israel	col	BMD	***Arrow***	2	1986	1999	Deployment to begin 1999; with US
	dom	PFM	***Saar* 4.5**	6	1990	1994	Upgrade. 4th delivered 1998. Deliveries of last 2 pending
	dom	sat	***Ofek*-4**	1	1990	1999	Launch failed
	dom	MBT	***Merkava* 4**		1991	2002	In production
	dom	ATGW	**LAHAT**		1991	1999	Dev completed end-1999
	Ge	SSK	***Dolphin***	3	1991	1998	Final delivery 2000. Funded by Ge
	col	BMD	***Nautilus***		1992	2000	Joint dev with US
	US	MRL	**MLRS**	42	1994	1995	Deliveries: 16 in 1997, completed 1998
	Fr	hel	**AS-565**	8	1994	1997	5 delivered 1997
	US	FGA	**F-15I**	25	1994	1998	
	dom	sat	***Amos*-1**	1	1995		Dev slowed by lack of funds
	US	tpt hel	**S-70A**	15	1995	1998	1st 2 deliveries complete
	dom	UAV	***Silver Arrow***		1997		Prototype unveiled April 1998
	US	AAM	**AIM-120B**	64	1998	1999	
	US	FGA	**F-16I**	50	1999	2003	With *Popeye* 2 and *Python* 4 AAM
	US	ASM	***Hellfire***	480	1999		
	US	cbt hel	**B200**	5	2000		
	US	AAM	**AMRAAM**	57	2000		
	US		**JDAM**		2000		
	US	hel	**AH-64D**	9	2000		New purchase rather than upgrading current fleet
	dom	FGA	**F-15**				Upgrade
	US	hel	**UH-60L**	35	2000		
	US	hel	**S-70A**	24	2001	2002	
	US	FGA	**F-16I**	52	2001	2006	deliveries 2006–09
	dom	PFC	***Super Dvora* II**	6	2002	2003	Option on further five
	dom	PFC	***Shaldag***	2	2002	2003	Option on further two
Jordan	US	FGA	**F-16A/B**	16	1995	1997	Deliveries complete April 1998
	US	hel	**UH-60L**	4	1995	1998	
	US	SPA	**M-110**	18	1996	1998	
	US	MBT	**M-60A3**	50	1996		38 delivered 1997
	UK	ASSM	***Sea Skua***	60	1997	1998	
	Aus	APC	**S-600**	22	1997	1998	
	US	cbt hel	**AH-64**	16	1997	2000	*Longbow* radar not fitted
	US	SP arty	**M-109A6**	48	1998		Includes spt veh. Order frozen late 1998
	UK	MBT	***Challenger* 1**	288	1999	2001	Ex-UK Army
	UK	recce	***Scorpion***		1999	2001	Upgrade
	US	APC	**M-113**		1999		
	Tu	tpt	**CN-235**	2	1999	2001	One year lease

	Country supplier	Classification ⇩	Designation	Quantity ⇩	Order date	Delivery date	Comment ⇩
	Ukr	APC	**BTR-94**	50	1999	2000	mod BTR-80
	Be	APC	***Spartan***	100	2001	2001	2nd-hand
	US	ATGW	***Javelin***	30	2002		
	US	MBT	**M60A3**	50	2002		Upgrade
Kuwait	Fr	PFM	***Al Maradim***	8	1995	1998	Final 2 delivered 2000. Equiped with Sea Skua
	UK	ASSM	***Sea Skua***	60	1997	1998	
	US	ATGW	**TOW-2B**	728	1999		
	col	hel	**EC135**	2	1999	2001	
	PRC	arty	**PLZ45**	18	2001		
	US	hel	**AH-64D**	16	2001		
	US	FGA	**F/A-18E/F**		2001		
Mauritania	It	trg	**SF360E**	5		2000	
Morocco	Fr	FF	***Floreal***	2	1998	2001	
	Bel	MBT	**T-72**	70	2001		
Oman	Fr	APC	**VBL**	51	1995	1997	Deliveries to 1998
	UK	ftr	***Jaguar***	15	1997	1999	Upgrade to bring up to RAF standard
	UK	MBT	***Challenger 2***	20	1997	1999	Final 10 delivered 2000
	UK	radar	**S743D**		1999	2002	
	Fr	SAM	***Mistral 2***		2000	2001	
	UK	APC	***Piranha 2***	80	2000	2001	In 7 versions
	UK	recce	***Scorpion***	60	2000	2002	Upgrades
	US	FGA	**F-16**	12	2001		
	col	hel	***Super Lynx***	20	2001		
	PRC	MLRS	**Type 90**			2002	
Qatar	Fr	FGA	***Mirage* 2000-5**	12	1994	1997	3 delivered 1997, 8 1998
	UK	APC	***Piranha 2***	40	1995	1997	2 delivered 1997, 26 1998
	UK	trg	***Hawk* 100**	15	1996	1999	
	Fr	MBT	**AMX-30**	10	1997	1998	Military aid from Fr
Saudi Arabia	Ca	LAV	**LAV-25**	1,117	1990	1992	800 delivered by 1998
	UK	FGA	***Tornado* IDS**	48	1993	1996	Deliveries completed 1998
	Fr	FFG	***Al Riyadh (La Fayette)***	3	1994	2001	1st delivery 2002, 2nd 2003, 3rd 2005
	US	Construction	***Jizan***	1	1996	1999	Military city and port
	Fr	hel	**AS-532**	12	1996	1998	4 delivered 1998
	US	AWACS	**E-3**	5	1997	2000	Upgrade
	It	SAR hel	**AB-412TP**	44	1998	2001	
	US	AAM	**AMRAAM**	475	2000		
	US	ATGW	**TOW 2A**	1,827	2000		
Syria	RF	ATGW	**AT-14**	1,000	1997	1998	msl
	RF	SAM	**S-300**		1997		Unconfirmed
	RF	FGA	**Su-27**			2000	4 delivered
	RF	FGA	**MiG-29**			2000	Deliveries from previously unannounced order
Tunisia	US	hel	**HH-3**	4	1996	1998	
	Sau	MBT	**AMX-30**	30	2000		2nd-hand
UAE	UK	ALCM	***Al-Hakim***	416	1992	1998	All delivered 1998
	Fr	MBT	***Leclerc***	390	1993	1994	Also 46 ARVs. Deliveries to 2003

	Country supplier	Classification ⇩	Designation	Quantity ⇩	Order date	Delivery date	Comment ⇩
	Fr	hel	**AS-565**	6	1995	1998	For Kortenaer frigates
	Nl	FFG	***Kortenaer***	2	1996	1997	Ex-Nl, 2nd delivery 1998
	Fr	hel	**AS-332**	5	1996	1998	Upgrade of anti-ship and ASW eqpt
	RF	tpt	**Il-76**	4	1997	1998	On lease
	Tu	APC	**AAPC**	136	1997	1999	
	Indo	tpt	**CN-235**	7	1997		
	US	cbt hel	**AH-64A**	10	1997	1999	
	Fr	hel	***Gazelle***	5	1997	1999	Option for further 5
	Fr	FGA	***Mirage*** **2000-09**	30	1997	2000	
	Fr	FGA	***Mirage*** **2000**	33	1997	2000	Upgrade to 2000-9 standard
	Fr	ALCM	***Black Shahine***		1998	2000	For new and upgraded *Mirage* 2000-9
	UK	trg	***Hawk-200***	18	1998	2001	Following delivery of 26 1992–6
	Indo	MPA	**CN-235**	4	1998		
	UK	PFC	***Protector***	2	1998	1999	
	Fr	trg	***Alpha Jet***		1999		
	Fr	trg	**AS 350B**	14	1999		
	US	FGA	**F-16**	80	2000	2002	With AMRAAM, HARM and *Hakeem* msl
	Ge	APC	***Fuchs***	64	2000		recce veh
	RF	SAM	**Partzyr-S1**	50	2000	2002	
	col	MPA	**C-295**	4	2001		
	Fr	FAC		6	2001		
Yemen	Fr	PCI	***Vigilante***	6	1996	1997	Commissioning delayed
	Cz	trg	**L-39C**	12	1999	1999	Deliveries began late 1999
	RF	FGA	**Su-27**	14	1999	2001	
	Cz	MBT	**T-55**	106		2000	
	RF	MBT	**T-72**	30		2000	
	RF	FGA	**MiG-29SMT**	24	2001		
	RF	FGA	**MiG-29**	31	2001		Upgrades

Central and South Asia

Even before the 11 September terror attacks, South Asian economies were feeling the effect of reduced growth in the US and EU, in the form of weaker export markets, in particular, those for Indian software and Pakistani cotton and textiles. The attacks, together with domestic issues such as adverse weather, widening fiscal deficits, political uncertainty and lagging structural reforms, further dampened the main economies of the region. However, some of these negative factors may be partly offset by increased access to US concessional aid and foreign investment inflows following the removal of the remaining sanctions imposed following the 1998 nuclear tests. Overall real GDP growth in South Asia fell from 5.3% in 2000 to 4.2% in 2001.

In Central Asia, rising oil and gas production contributed to stronger than expected growth of 7.7% in 2001. As with their southern neighbours, the global slow-down post-11 September and the increased outlay on security and the cost of refugees will weaken growth in 2002 and put pressure on fiscal balances.

The official **Indian** defence budget rose by a nominal 4.5% in 2002, to Rs765bn from Rs732bn in 2001. However, due to under-spending in the procurement budget during 2001, actual outlays in that year amounted to only R678bn. For this reason, the 2002 budget was misleadingly reported to be an aggressive rise of 12.8% over the previous year. Originally, the 2001 procurement budget was set at Rs225bn. However, only about Rs170bn was actually spent during the financial year and the remainder was returned to the Treasury. Problems in India's cumbersome procurement procedure were exacerbated last year by the resignation of Defence Minister George Fernades in March. He was reinstated in October, but during his absence, many significant procurement projects were left unattended and thus, under the Indian budgetary system, the unspent funds had to be returned. In order to fund the increased expenditure, a 5% surcharge on all categories of tax payers was announced during the budget speech.

The biggest beneficiary of the increased defence budget is the Indian Air Force, which will receive Rs155bn an increase of 30% over its allocation in 2001, allowing the licensed production of 140 Su-30MKI to proceed as scheduled and the development of further prototypes of the indigenous multi-role fighter known as the Light Combat Aircraft (LCA), the second of which was tested in 2002. Although the LCA project is many years behind schedule, the post-11 September scrapping of US sanctions, imposed in 1998 after India's nuclear test against Pakistan, will help to speed up deliveries of much needed components, including 40 General Electric F404 engines. The Indian Aeronautical Development Agency also revealed that they have designed the naval variant, the world's first single-engine fighter developed for an aircraft carrier. The Indian Air Force has ordered an initial eight aircraft, to take delivery of the first one in 2006. Hindustani Aeronautics Limited also delivered its first Advanced Light Helicopter to the Indian Coast Guard ten years after the prototype made its maiden flight. Around 14 helicopters will be delivered during 2002, with another 34 following in 2003. Funds have also been allocated to the purchase of three Israel Aircraft Industries *Phalcon* early-warning systems; however, in a move India believes is a gesture of thanks to Pakistan for its role in the campaign in Afghanistan, the United States has requested Israel to freeze all arms sales to India. The development came only months after Israel had guaranteed that the proposed deal would not be hindered by the US. The growing defence links between India and Israel may – if the US doesn't intervene – see Israel supplying India with helicopter upgrades, UAVs and missiles. The increase in funds has also revived speculation that the urgently needed Advanced Jet Trainer may finally be ordered, possibly 66 BAE Systems *Hawk* aircraft.

The Indian Army was allocated Rs380bn in 2002 to enable the ongoing procurement of 310 T-90S main-battle tanks from Russia and the purchase of eight Raytheon AN/TPQ-37 *Firefinder* weapon-locating radars and various other artillery projects.

The Indian Navy saw a more modest increase in resources from Rs86bn to Rs98bn.

Following the deal for tanks and aircraft between Russia and India in 2000, the two countries signed three further military protocols on 8 February 2001. The protocols detail joint collaboration in warship-building and the development of land-based systems for the army, and for both civil and military aircraft projects. In particular, India agreed to jointly develop a new military transport plane to be based on the twin-engined *Ilyushin* Il-214, and expressed an interest in cooperating with Russia on the development of

Table 18 Indian defence budget by service/department, 1997–2002 constant 2000 US$m

	1997	%	1998	%	1999	%	outurn 2000	%	outurn 2001	%	outurn 2002	%
Army	5,772	57.2	5,318	52.2	5,928	48.5	7,685	52.3	7,435	52.5	7,725	51.4
Air Force	2,515	24.9	2,314	22.7	2,374	19.4	2,543	17.3	2,492	17.6	3,048	20.3
Navy	1,190	11.8	1,476	14.5	1,567	12.8	1,848	12.6	1,814	12.8	1,936	12.9
R&D	372	3.7	439	4.3	644	5.3	698	4.7	695	4.9	719	4.8
Other/Pensions	241	2.4	629	6.2	1,705	14.0	1,925	13.1	1,731	12.2	1,600	10.6
Total	10,090	100	10,176	100	12,218	100	14,699	100	14,167	100	15,028	100
% change		14.1		0.9		20.1		20.3		-3.6		6.1

Table 19 Indian defence and military-related spending by function, 2000–2002 US$m

	2000 outurn	2001 outurn	2002 budget
Personnel, Operations & Maintenance			
MoD	76	68	186
Defence pensions	2,373	2,236	2,188
Army	5,893	6,313	6,276
Navy	906	823	931
Air Force	1,642	1,496	1,674
Defence ordnance factories	1,383	1,242	1,425
Recoveries & receipts	-1,449	-1,329	-1,404
Sub-Total	10,824	10,849	11,276
R&D, Procurement and Construction			
Tri-Service Defence R&D	185	187	195
Army	1,792	1,276	1,509
Navy	942	1,029	1,086
Air Force	901	1,048	1,513
Other	55	71	70
Sub-Total	3,875	3,611	4,373
Total Defence Budget	14,699	14,460	15,649
Other military-related funding			
Paramilitary forces	953	928	1,064
Dept of Atomic Energy	461	598	791
Dept of Space	382	432	462
Intelligence Bureau	74	74	71
Total	1,870	2,032	2,388

Russia's fifth-generation fighter. The agreements also covered the testing of the Russian BM9A52 *Smerch* 300mm multiple-rocket system and the establishment of servicing facilities in India for mid-life refits of the Indian Navy's *Kilo*-class electric submarines. No agreement was reached on a price for the aircraft-carrier *Admiral Gorshkov*, the potential lease of two nuclear submarines and four long-range maritime reconnaissance aircraft. Negotiations surrounding the *Admiral Gorshkov* have been ongoing since 1995. It is believed that in the original deal, Russia was to give the carrier to India for the cost of the refit, estimated at around $750m. But cost disagreements over this and the 40 MiG-29K fighters that would equip the vessel continue to delay a final deal.

The US-led action in Afghanistan put further economic pressure on **Pakistan**, already suffering from weaker growth in key export markets. The regional uncertainty had adverse budgetary consequences, with the government incurring additional expenses associated with the increased number of refugees, maintaining law and order and increased defence preparedness. Earlier in the year, Pakistan had kept to its policy of the last three years and announced a slight reduction in defence spending for 2001–02. It is unclear what impact the war in Afghanistan and renewed tension with India will have on overall defence spending. However, in December 2002, Pakistan took delivery of its first two batches of F-7 fighter aircraft from China. It is believed that up to 50, from a probable requirement of 80 F-7s, have been ordered to replace the country's 1960s F-6 air-defence fighters. Meanwhile, the Pakistani military is determined to promote its weapons exports in an effort to make weapons production an engine for economic growth. With these ambitions in mind, Pakistan has recently hosted three international exhibitions and established a Defence Export Promotion Organisation with the goal of increasing sales from $20m a year to $120m in two years. This is a major challenge, as much of the current limited production goes directly to the armed forces, leaving little for export. Furthermore, efforts to sell to African countries have failed because of competition from South Africa, and the failure of the Pakistan Aeronautical Complex to finish the overhaul of the UAE's *Mirage* fighters within the specified time.

Continued growth in Central Asia, coupled with the regional security situation, led to increases in the defence budgets of several Central Asian countries. **Kazakhstan** achieved growth of 13.2% in 2002, primarily as a result of new pipeline capacity coming on stream, and announced an increase in defence spending of 34%. The budget also introduced a new programme to modernise arms, military hardware and communications systems, and earmarked funds to develop the state-run armoured vehicle plant so that it will be capable of major equipment overhauls and upgrades. **Kyrgyzstan** devoted extra funds to defence in 2002 and intends to modernise aircraft, buy communications equipment and increase salaries of service personnel. However, with the domestic economic situation worsening, it is hard to see how this can be achieved. Meanwhile, **Tajikistan** cited terrorist threats for a hike in its defence spending plans.

Afghanistan Afg

afghani Afs		2000	2001	2002
GDP	US$			
per capita	US$			
Growth	%			
Inflation	%			
Debt	US$			
Def exp	US$	ε250	ε250	ε250
US$1=Afs		4,750	4,750	4,750

Population[b] **ε22,567,000**

Pashtun 38% **Tajik** 25% **Hazara** 19% **Uzbek** 12% **Aimaq** 4% **Baluchi** 0.5%

Age	13–17	18–22	23–32
Men	1,499,000	1,194,000	2,053,000
Women	1,442,000	1,134,000	1,930,000

[b] Includes ε1,500,000 refugees in Pak, ε1,000,000 in Ir, ε150,000 in RF and ε50,000 in Kgz

Bangladesh Bng

taka Tk		2000	2001	2002	2003
GDP	Tk	2.4tr	2.5tr		
	US$	46.5bn	46.8		
per capita	US$	339	333		
Growth	%	5.5	4.5		
Inflation	%	2.3	1.8		
Debt	US$	15.8bn	15.1bn		
Def exp	Tk	35.3bn	35.3bn		
	US$	691m	652m		
Def bdgt	Tk	32.8bn	35.3bn	39bn	
	US$	642m	653m	678m	
FMA (US)	US$	0.4m	0.5m	0.6m	0.7m
US$1=taka		51	54	57.4	

Population **140,400,000** **Hindu** 12%

Age	13–17	18–22	23–32
Men	8,107,000	7,738,000	12,341,000
Women	7,794,000	7,257,000	11,684,000

India Ind

rupee Rs		2000	2001	2002
GDP	Rs	20.9tr	23.0tr	
	US$	471bn	490bn	
per capita	US$	461	476	
Growth	%	5.4	4.3	
Inflation	%	4.0	3.8	
Debt	US$	103bn	101bn	
Def exp[a]	Rs	655bn	678bn	
	US$	14.6bn	14.3bn	
Def bdgt	Rs	709bn	732bn	765bn
	US$	15.9n	15.5bn	15.6bn
FMA (US)	US$	0.5m	0.5m	1.0m
US$1=Rs		44.0	47.18	48.9

[a] Incl exp on paramil org

Population **1,025,100,000**

Hindu 80% **Muslim** 14% **Christian** 2% **Sikh** 2%

Age	13–17	18–22	23–32
Men	54,638,000	49,922,000	88,478,000
Women	51,292,000	46,415,000	80,937,000

Kazakhstan Kaz

tenge t		2000	2001	2002
GDP[1]	t	2.6tr	3.2tr	
	US$	93bn	100bn	
per capita	US$	5,731	6,211	
Growth	%	9.6	13.2	
Inflation	%	13.4	8.6	
Debt	US$	6.7	6.3	
Def exp[1]	US$	1.25bn	1.3bn	
Def bdgt	t	17bn	26.4bn	34.9bn
	US$	119m	180m	226m
FMA (US)	US$	0.6m	0.6m	
US$1=t		142.5	146.3	153

[1] =PPP estimate

Population **16,115,000**

Kazak 51% **Russian** 32% **Ukrainian** 5% **German** 2% **Tatar** 2% **Uzbek** 2%

Age	13–17	18–22	23–32
Men	919,000	826,000	1,379,000
Women	896,000	814,000	1,356,000

Kyrgyzstan Kgz

som s		2000	2001	2002
GDP[1]	s	62bn	70bn	
	US$	11.7bn	13bn	
per capita	US$	2,377	2,600	
Growth	%	5.0	5.0	
Inflation	%	18.7	7.6	
Debt	US$	1.7bn	1.6bn	
Def exp[1]	US$	230m	260m	
Def bdgt	s	810m	900m	1.1bn
	US$	16.9m	18.6m	23.5m
FMA (US)	US$	1.3m	2.2m	2.6m
US$1=s		48.0	48.4	45.4

[1] = PPP estimate

Population **5,000,000**

Kyrgyz 56% **Russian** 17% **Uzbek** 13% **Ukrainian** 3%

Age	13–17	18–22	23–32
Men	292,000	247,000	372,000
Women	287,000	244,000	369,000

Nepal N

rupee NR		2000	2001	2002
GDP	NR	376bn	408bn	
	US$	5.3bn	5.4bn	
per capita	US$	228	231	
Growth	%	6.5	5.3	
Inflation	%	3.4	2.4	
Debt	US$	2.5bn		
Def exp	NR	7.4bn	10.8bn	
	US$	104.8m	144.9m	
Def bdgt	NR	3.5bn	4.5bn	5.4bn
	US$	49m	60m	70m
FMA (US)	US$	0.2m	0.2m	2.4m
US$1=NR		70.2	74.9	77.3

Population 23,600,000

Hindu 90% **Buddhist** 5% **Muslim** 3%

Age	13–17	18–22	23–32
Men	1,528,000	1,270,000	1,895,000
Women	1,447,000	1,183,000	1,723,000

Pakistan Pak

rupee Rs		2000	2001	2002
GDP	Rs	3.3tr	3.4tr	
	US$	62.8bn	55.8bn	
per capita	US$	441	385	
Growth	%	3.9	3.4	
Inflation	%	4.4	3.8	
Debt	US$	31.0bn	30bn	
Def exp	Rs	131bn	149bn	
	US$	2.5bn	2.4bn	
Def bdgt	Rs	156bn	157.6bn	
	US$	3.0bn	2.6bn	
FMA (US)	US$	0m	0m	1.0m
US$1=Rs		52.0	61.2	59.6

Population 145,000,000 **Hindu** less than 3%

Age	13–17	18–22	23–32
Men	8,990 ,000	7,684,000	12,410,000
Women	8,623,000	7,008,000	10,985,000

Sri Lanka Ska

rupee Rs		2000	2001	2002
GDP	Rs	1,255bn	1,415bn	
	US$	16.7bn	15.8bn	
per capita	US$	885	826	
Growth	%	6.0	0.4	
Inflation	%	6.2	14.0	
Debt	US$	9.5bn	9.1bn	
Def exp	Rs	66bn	72bn	
	US$	880m	803bn	
Def bdgt	Rs	52bn	57bn	62bn
	US$	700m	641m	645m

Ska contd		2000	2001	2002
FMA (US)	US$	0.2m	0.2m	0.3
US$1=Rs		74.9	89.7	96.0

Population 19,100,000

Sinhalese 74% **Tamil** 18% **Moor** 7%; **Buddhist** 69% **Hindu** 15% **Christian** 8% **Muslim** 8%

Age	13–17	18–22	23–32
Men	926,000	931,000	1,601,000
Women	890,000	893,000	1,563,000

Tajikistan Tjk

rouble Tr		2000	2001	2002
GDP[1]	Tr	1,807bn	2,512	
	US$	7.1bn	7.5	
per capita	US$	1.167	1,230	
Growth	%	8.3	10.0	
Inflation	%	34	39.4	
Debt	US$	1.2bn		
Def exp[1]	US$	130m	130m	
Def bdgt	US$	14m	12.7m	14.8m
US$1=Tr		1,436	2,350	2,703

[1] = PPP estimate

Population 6,100,000

Tajik 67% **Uzbek** 25% **Russian** 2% **Tatar** 2%

Age	13–17	18–22	23–32
Men	438,000	346,000	497,000
Women	424,000	338,000	484,000

Turkmenistan Tkm

manat		2000	2001	2002
GDP[1]	US$	6.0bn	7.0bn	
per capita	US$	1,200	1,458	
Growth	%	17.6	6	
Inflation	%	8.0	11.2	
Debt	US$	2.4bn	2.3bn	
Def exp[1]	US$	290m	226m	
Def bdgt	US$	144m	163m	
FMA (US)	US$	0.3m	0.3m	
US$1=manat		5,200	5,200	5,200

[1] = PPP estimate

Population 4,450,000

Turkmen 77% **Uzbek** 9% **Russian** 7% **Kazak** 2%

Age	13–17	18–22	23–32
Men	275,000	228,000	361,000
Women	268,000	224,000	357,000

Uzbekistan Uz

som s		2000	2001	2002
GDP	s	2.5tr	3.9tr	
	US$	59bn	70bn	
per capita	US$	2,470	2,760	
Growth	%	3.8	4.5	
Inflation	%	28	26	
Debt	US$	4.3bn	4.5bn	
Def exp[a]	US$	1.75bn	1.8bn	
Def bdgt	US$	387m	207m	106m

Uz contd		2000	2001	2002
FMA (US)	US$	0.5m	0.5m	
US$1=s		133	337	750

[a] = PPP estimate

Population **24,576,000**

Uzbek 73% **Russian** 6% **Tajik** 5% **Kazak** 4% **Karakalpak** 2% **Tatar** 2% **Korean** <1% **Ukrainian** <1%

Age	13–17	18–22	23–32
Men	1,555,000	1,298,000	1,921,000
Women	1,520,000	1,281,000	1,962,000

Table 20 Arms orders and deliveries, Central and Southern Asia, 1998–2002

	Country supplier	Classification ⇩	Designation	Quantity ⇩	Order date	Delivery date	Comment ⇩
Bangladesh	FIN	PCO	***Madhumati***	1	1995	1998	
	PRC	FGA	**F-7**	24	1996	1997	
	RF	radar	**IL-117 3-D**	2	1996	1999	Requirement for 3 more
	RF	hel	**Mi-17**	4	1997	1999	Following delivery of 12 1992-96
	PRC	trg	**FT-7B**	4	1997	1999	
	US	tpt	**C-130B**	4	1997	1999	
	RF	FGA	**MiG-29B**	8	1999	1999	Order placed 1999 after delay
	ROK	FF	***Ulsan***	1	1998	2002	
	Cz	trg	**L-39ZA**	4	1999	2000	Following delivery of 8 in 1995
	ROK	FAC	**PKM-200**	2		2000	
India	dom	SSN	**ATV**	1	1982	2007	
	dom	ICBM	***Surya***		1983		Dev. 5,000km range
	dom	SLCM	***Sagarika***		1983	2003	300km range. May be ballistic
	dom	MRBM	***Agni* 1**	10	1983	1998	Range 1,200km; under test
	dom	MRBM	***Agni* 2**	5	1983	2000	Range 2,000km; under test
	dom	MRBM	***Agni* 3**		1983		Dev. Range 4,000km; under test
	dom	SSM	***Prithvi* SS150**	150	1983	1996	150km range. Low-vol prod cont. 75 delivery late 1996
	dom	SSM	***Prithvi* SS250**	50	1983	2001	Air force variant
	dom	SSM	***Prithvi***	100	1983		Naval variant aka *Danush*, still on trial
	dom	SAM	***Akash***		1983	1999	Dev. High-altitude SAM.
	dom	SAM	***Trishul***		1983	1999	In development
	dom	ATGW	***Nag***		1983	1999	Ready for prod mid-1999
	dom	AAM	***Astra***		1999	2002	Dev. 1st test planned Jul 1999
	dom	FGA	**LCA**		1983	2012	
	RF	SSK	***Kilo***	10	1983	2000	Last of 10 delivered in 2000
	dom	FFG	***Brahmaputra***	3	1989	2000	2nd delivered in 2001
	dom	hel	**ALH**	12	1984	2000	Tri-service requirement for 300 Delivery may slip to 2001
	dom	ELINT	**HS-748**		1990		Dev
	dom	FSG	***Kora***	4	1990	1998	4th delivered in 2001

	Country supplier	Classification ⇩	Designation	Quantity ⇩	Order date	Delivery date	Comment ⇩
	dom	UAV	***Nishant***	14	1991	1999	Dev. 3 prototypes built. 14 pre-prod units on order
	dom	DD	***Delhi***	3	1986	1997	1st in 1997, 2nd in 1998, 3rd in 2001
	dom	LST	***Magyar***	2	1991	1997	1 more under construction
	RF	AD	**2S6**	24	1994	1996	12 units in 1996, 12 1998-99
	dom	sat	***Ocean sat***	1	1995	1999	Remote sensing
	dom	AGHS	***Sandhayak***	2	1995	1999	Following delivery of 6 1981–93
	RF	tkr AC	**IL-78**	6	1996	1998	First 2 delivered early 1998
	RF	ASSM	**SS-N-25**	16	1996	1997	Deliveries continue
	RF	FGA	**Su-30MK**	18	1996	1997	To be upgraded to MKI standard
	RF	FGA	**Su-30MKI**	32	1996	2001	To be completed by 2003
	RF	FGA	**MiG-21BIS**	125	1996	2001	Upgrades
	Il	PFC	***Super Dvora* MK3**	6	1996	1998	2 delivered
	RF	FF	***Krivak* III**	3	1997	2002	1 for del. by 2002, 2 by 2003. 3 improved *Krivak* due from 2007.
	RF	hel	**KA-31**	12	1997	2001	To operate from *Krivak* III frigates
	US	MPA	**P-3C**	3	1997		Delay due to sanctions.
	UK	FGA	***Harrier* TMk4**	2	1997	1999	2 ex-RN ac for delivery 1999
	RSA	APC	***Casspir***	90	1998	1999	10 delivered. 80 in 1999
	RF	ASSM	**SS-N-27 *Klub***		1998	2004	For *Krivak* 3 frigate. First export
	UK	FGA	***Jaguar***	18	1998	2001	Potential upgrade for up to 60
	RF	FGA	**MiG-21**	125	1999	2003	Upgrade. Fr and Il avionics
	dom	MBT	***Arjun***	124	1999	2002	Low-rate production
	dom	trg	**HJT-36**	200	1999	2004	
	Pl	trg	**TS-11**	12	1999	2000	Option on 8 more
	dom	CV	***Viraat***	1	1999	2001	Upgrade (ex-UK *Hermes*)
	RF	CV	***Admiral Gorshkov***	1	1999		Memo. of understanding signed.
	RF	FGA	**MiG-29K**	24	1999		Possibly 60. To equip CV *Gorshkov*
	Slvk	ARV	**T-72 VT**	42	1999	2001	Original order for 85. 43 from Pl
	Pl	ARV	**WZT-3**	43	1999	2001	Original order for 85. 42 from Slvk
	Il	arty	**M-46**	35	1999	2000	Il upgrade of FSU arty supp. mid-80s
	dom	AAM	***Astra***		1999		Live firing due 2001
	dom	MPA	**Do-228**	7	1999		Deliveries completed by 2003
	RF	hel	**Mi-17iB**	40	2000	2001	
	RF	MBT	**T-90**	310	2000		186 to be built in Ind
	Il	UAV	***Searcher* 2**	20	2000		In addition to 8 delivered 1999
	Fr	FGA	***Mirage* 2000**	10	2000	2003	Originally approved 1996
	RF	FGA	**Su-30MKI**	140	2000	2002	Licensed Production
	RF	recce	**Tu-142F**	8	2000	2002	Upgrades
	Il	hel	**Mi-8/17**	80	2001		Upgrades
	dom	FGA	**MiG-27M**	40	2001	2004	Upgrades
Kazakhstan	RF	FGA	**Su-27**	16	1997	1999	+ Su-27 & Su-29 exch. for 40 Tu-95M
	RF	SAM	**S-300**		1997	2000	
Nepal	Kgz	hel	**Mi-17**	2	2001	2001	
	Ind	hel	**HAS 315B**	2	2001	2001	
Pakistan	dom	sat	***Badar 2***				Development
	dom	sat	***Badar 1***				Multi-purpose sat. In operation.
	US	APC	**M113**	775	1989	1990	Licensed prod; deliveries to 1999
	dom	MBT	***Al-Khalid***	15	1991	2000	Pre-production batch
	Fr	MHC	***Munsif***	3	1992	1992	2nd del. 1996. 3rd 1998.

	Country supplier	Classification ⇩	Designation	Quantity ⇩	Order date	Delivery date	Comment ⇩
	PRC	FGA	**FC-1/S-7**		1993	2005	In co-dev with PRC, req for up to 150
	dom	MRBM	***Ghauri***		1993	1998	Range 1,500km. Test 4/98 Aka *Hatf* 5
	dom	MRBM	***Ghauri* 2**		1993	1999	Dev. Range 2-3,000km. Test 4/99 Aka *Hatf* 6
	dom	MRBM	***Ghauri* 3**		1993		Dev. Range 3,000km. Based on *Taepo-dong* 2
	dom	SSM	***Hatf* 2**		1994	1996	Dev. Based on PRC M-11
	dom	SSM	***Hatf* 3**		1994		Dev. Range 600–800km. Based on M-9
	dom	SSM	***Shaheen* 1**		1994	1999	In prod mid-1999. Range 750Km. Based on M-9. Aka *Hatf* 4
	dom	SSM	***Shaheen* 2**		1994		Dev. Range 2,500km. Aka *Hatf* 7
	Fr	SSK	***Khalid***	3	1994	1999	1st in 1999, 2nd 2001, 3rd 2002
	Fr	FGA	***Mirage* III**	40	1996	1998	Upgrade. 8 delivered by Apr 1999
	UKr	MBT	**T-80UD**	320	1996	1996	Final 105 delivered in 1999
	dom	PFM	***Mod. Larkana***	1	1996	1997	Commissioned 14 Aug 1997. 2 more planned.
	PRC	PFM	***Shujat* 2**	1	1997	1999	
	PRC	FGA	**F-7MG**	30–50	1999	2002	Stop gap until S-7 completed
	dom	UAV	***Bravo***			2000	In service
	PRC	FFG	***Jiangwei* II**	4	2001	2006	
	Indo	tpt	**CN235-220**	4	2001		
Sri Lanka	Il	UAV	***Super Scout***				
	Ukr	cbt hel	**Mi-24**	2	1995	1996	1 delivered 1998
	UK	ACV	**M10**		1995	1999	Hovercraft
	RF	cbt hel	**Mi-35**	2	1997	1999	May be 4. 5 delivered previously
	US	tpt	**C-130**	3	1997	1999	
	Ukr	cbt hel	**Mi-24**	2	1998	1999	
	PRC	arty	**152mm**	36	1999	2000	Delivered
	UK	tpt	**C-130**	2	1999		
	Il	FGA	***Kfir***	8	2000		
	Ind	OPV	***Sukanya Class***	1		2000	Delivered 2000
	Cz	MBT	**T-55**	11	2000	2000	
	RF	APC	**BTR-80A**	10	2000	2001	
	RF	AIFV	**BMP-2**	36	2000	2001	Reconditioned
	RF	FGA	**MiG-27M**	4		2001	
	RF	FGA	**MiG-23UB**	2		2000	
	US	hel	**Bell 412**	2	2001	2001	

East Asia and Australasia

Regional countries with export-oriented economies suffered as a result of the weakness in the world economy during 2001. With export demand falling, particularly for electronic goods, Singapore and Taiwan experienced contractions in real GDP and South Korea saw growth drop from 9% in 2000 to around 3% in 2001. As a whole, ASEAN nations saw GDP growth fall to 2.6% from 5.1% in 2000 and Japan experienced negative growth once again. Indeed, of the larger economies in the region, it was only China and Australia that saw any significant growth.

Defence spending in the region was lower in 2001, falling 6% to US$134.7bn, mainly a statistical consequence as a result of a weaker yen and reduced spending by Taiwan.

In line with the commitment to increase real defence spending by 3% per annum as set out in the 2000 White Paper, **Australia** increased its 2002 defence budget to A$13.6bn from A$13.1bn in 2001. To pay for continuing operations in Afghanistan and the Arabian Gulf, an extra A$194m was set aside in addition to the A$330m provided last year. A new counter-terrorist unit to supplement the SAS's existing squadron, to be known as the Tactical Assault Group and based on the East Coast will cost A$219m. There was also funding approval for various major capital equipment projects, including new air-to-air refuelling aircraft, a new infantry shoulder-launched guided weapon, additional troop-lift helicopters, a battle-space communications system, electronic warfare self-protection for tactical aircraft, replacement of SM-1 missiles with SM-2 and anti-ship missile defence improvements for *Anzac* frigates. The green light was given to *Project Air* 6000 for new combat aircraft and *Project Sea* 4000 for new air-warfare destroyers. The government released a detailed long-term capital equipment and capability plan, replacing the previous defence acquisition guide known as the 'Pink Book'. The plan will help the domestic defence industry and overseas suppliers with their forward planning by providing greater detail and transparency about specific acquisition proposals. It reveals that expenditure in the aerospace industry is set to peak at around A$2.3bn in 2010, in the maritime industry at A$720 in 2009 and in weapons and munitions industries at A$480m in 2006.

South Korea announced a record defence budget of Swon16.5tr (US$14.1bn) for 2002, up from Swon15.4tr in 2001 (US$11.8bn) and Swon14.4tr (US$12.8bn) in 2000. Next year's budget will be the first of a five-year force improvement programme which calls for US$26.5bn in purchases of new weapons. The first and most expensive element of the programme is the procurement of 40 fighter jets. After two years of speculation, the South Korean government awarded Boeing the US$4.5bn contract for the purchase of 40 F-15K aircraft, beating off strong competition from Dassault of France. Under the terms of the agreement, the aircraft, to be fitted with the General Electric F110-GE-129 engine rather than the Pratt & Whitney F100-PW-229, will be delivered between 2005 and 2008. Boeing has also agreed to assist South Korean industry to produce an indigenously designed fighter by 2015. As a consequence of the F-15 deal, Korea has ordered a new study of its intention to purchase 48 Raytheon *Patriot* air-defence missile systems under the SAM-X programme. The SAM-X programme to replace Korea's Nike-Hercules air-defence system by 2010 has been stalled for several years over pricing problems. Fresh funds, however, are provided for the Korean Navy to continue with the KDX-III destroyer programme. In 2002, US$720m is available to the project, which will initially see three ships built at a cost of around US$2.3bn by 2010. It is also believed that funds from the five-year plan will be made available for the AH-X programme to acquire 36 attack helicopters. Boeing's AH-64D *Apache Longbow* and Bell's AH-1Z *Super Cobra* are competing for selection.

In a historic arms sale, Korea signed an agreement with Turkey to provide artillery components for their new artillery system. It is the first major export deal won by the Korean defence industry and follows intense marketing efforts by local defence companies, led by Samsung Techwin. The original contract covers the supply of components for 20 artillery systems; however, it is known that Turkey wishes to procure up to 300 new artillery pieces by 2011, in which case the supply of the subcomponents could eventually be worth around US$1bn and may open the way for further export deals to the Middle East.

Malaysia placed several new defence contracts during the past year. The largest was a RM4bn (US$1.8bn) order with Direction des Constructions Navales of France and Izar of Spain for two *Scorpene* diesel submarines, to be delivered in 2007 and 2008. The deal also includes four years of training, to take place on a refurbished *Agosta*-class diesel submarine, based at Toulon, France. In another procurement deal, Malaysia became the first customer of the MBDA *Jernas* short-range air-defence system, the export version of the Rapier Field Standard system used by the UK. The $300m contract covers *Jernas* missile launchers, surveillance radars, tracking radars and missiles as well as training and ongoing support. The Malaysian Army placed an order worth RM750m (US$197m) for an undisclosed number of AVIBRAS ASTROS II multiple rocket systems, and the Malaysian Navy awarded a contract to Eurocopter to deliver six AS-555 unarmed helicopters for training and over-the-horizon targeting.

Despite economic slowdown in the newly industrialised economies, **China,** being less dependent on exports, enjoyed growth of 7.3% in 2001. Robust domestic demand is likely to continue and growth should stay at around 7% in 2002. For the second year running, China increased its official defence budget by 17%, up from Y141bn to Y166bn. The official Chinese defence budget only represents part of actual military expenditure: proceeds from defence sales are not included and procurement, research and development, and pensions for retired personnel are funded from elsewhere within the state budget. After months of negotiation, Israel and China signed a compensation agreement for the cancellation of the proposed sale to Beijing of the Israeli Aircraft Industries *Phalcon* airborne early warning system. The deal had to be cancelled in August 2001, after the US voiced concern over China's acquisition of the advanced system. It is believed that Israel paid around US$350m in compensation. In naval development with Russia, China is to buy two more *Sovremenny*-class destroyers at a cost of over US$1bn. The ships had originally been laid down for the Russian Navy, but funding problems prevented their completion. The contract includes an option for a further two ships. It is also reported that China is to buy eight *Kilo*-class diesel submarines equipped with *Klub* long-range anti-ship missile systems, in addition to the four *Kilo*-class vessels already purchased. If the proposed acquisition goes ahead, it may well signal the end of the indigenous Type 039 SSK programme that was intended to replace China's *Romeo*-class attack submarines. Along with a new batch of S300 anti-aircraft missiles and 40 Su-30MKK fighter bombers already ordered, the total package could be worth in excess of US$4bn, making China the largest importer of Russian defence equipment. In a further demonstration of cooperation between the two countries, China's new domestic JH-7A fighter aircraft is starting trial flights, with deliveries expected to begin in 2004. The aircraft, powered by Rolls-Royce Spey Mk 202 engines, features several Russian improvements including anti radiation missiles, laser guided bombs and radar systems.

The **Japanese** economy dipped into recession for the third time in the past decade as growth dropped to -0.4%. The global slowdown, coupled with falling consumer confidence and record unemployment, are likely to depress output again in 2002. The defence budget was unchanged at ¥4.9tr (US$42.6bn) for the seventh year running. Under the new 2001–05 defence plan, the Boeing AH-64D was selected as a replacement for the Bell AH-1S. A total of 60 aircraft will be procured, some of which will be fitted with the *Longbow* fire-control radar. Boeing was also the successful bidder for the contract to deliver four air-to-air refuelling aircraft. The 767 platforms will extend the range of Japan's Air Self-Defence Force fighters, confirming the country's decision to allow its forces to move beyond their traditionally limited role of self-defence.

As a result of a sharp fall in growth, **Taiwan** announced a 2.3% cut in overall government spending for 2002. Defence spending was down 14% to NT$230bn (US$7.0bn), representing 14.4% of the total budget compared to 16.9% in 2001. Following the major weapons package offered to Taiwan by President Bush in April 2001, Taiwan confirmed that it would buy 4 *Kidd*-class destroyers from the US and requested the purchase of 30 AH-64D *Apache* helicopters. Progress on the delivery of eight diesel submarines has been less straightforward. The US has not built diesel-electric submarines for more than 40 years and designing an entirely new model is deemed too expensive. The most likely solution would involve a third foreign participant, but at present both Germany and the Netherlands, who are leaders in the field, are refusing to become involved in the project. Similarly, the delivery of 12 Lockheed Martin P-3C *Orion* maritime patrol aircraft has become stalled over high costs and delivery dates. The P-3C production line closed in April 1990 and negotiations continue over the cost of reopening it. One possible option is for Taiwan to partner another country, thus sharing the high overhead costs.

Singapore was another country to suffer contraction, with growth falling into negative territory in 2001. In late 2001, Singapore issued a Request For Information to six different manufacturers bidding to equip the Republic of Singapore Air Force with a squadron of new multi-role fighter aircraft, replacing the current fleet of A-4 *Skyhawks* from 2006–07. Singapore became the third international customer to select the next-generation AH-64 *Apache Longbow* combat helicopter, when it ordered an additional 12 aircraft to supplement the eight originally ordered in 2000. The first of these was delivered in May 2002.

In a move that would place both Thailand and Bangladesh at a disadvantage in terms of air power, **Myanmar** is seeking to obtain R-27 (NATO reporting name A-10 *Alamo*) medium- to long-range, infra-red and radar-guided air-to-air missiles for the 10 MiG-29 aircraft bought from Russia, at a cost of approximately US$130m, last year. In the past, the US has been reluctant to introduce this level of technology into the region and has withheld the sale of Raytheon AIM-120 AMRAAM missiles to other countries. Singapore has, however, obtained the missiles on condition that they are stored in the US until required and Thailand has been assured the same deal. Malaysia was offered a similar arrangement but turned down these conditions.

Australia Aus

dollar A$		2000	2001	2002
GDP	A$	655bn	690bn	
	US$	380bn	358bn	
per capita	US$	15,230	15,450	
Growth	%	3.2	2.4	
Inflation	%	4.5	2.5	
Publ Debt	%	27.0	26.2	
Def exp	A$	12.7bn	13.3bn	
	US$	7.4bn	6.9bn	
Def bdgt	A$	11.8bn	13.1bn	13.6bn
	US$	6.9bn	6.8bn	7.6bn
US$1=A$		1.72	1.93	1.8

Population **19,015,000** **Asian** 4% **Aborigines** <1%

Age	13–17	18–22	23–32
Men	697,000	680,000	1,497,000
Women	660,000	646,000	1,452,000

Brunei Bru

dollar B$		2000	2001	2002
GDP	B$	8.5bn	8.8bn	
	US$	5.0bn	5.2bn	
per capita	US$	15,228	15,452	
Growth	%	3.0	2.7	
Inflation	%	1.5	2.1	
Debt	US$	4.1bn	4.5bn	
Def exp	B$	600m	484m	
	US$	353m	285m	
Def bdgt	B$	600m	484m	455m
	US$	352m	284m	267m
US$1=B$		1.7	1.7	1.7

Population **334,000**

Muslim 71%; **Malay** 67% **Chinese** 16% **non-Malay indigenous** 6%

Age	13–17	18–22	23–32
Men	16,000	14,000	28,000
Women	15,000	15,000	26,000

Cambodia Cam

riel r		2000	2001	2002
GDP	r	12.2tr	12.9tr	
	US$	3.2bn	3.3bn	
per capita	US$	249	247	
Growth	%	5.4	5.3	
Inflation	%	-0.8	-0.6	
Debt	US$	2.4bn	–	
Def exp	r	ε750bn	ε750bn	
	US$	195m	192m	
Def bdgt	r	556bn	600bn	620bn
	US$	144m	153m	248m
FMA (US)	US$	2.6m	2.7m	

Cam contd		2000	2001	2002
FMA (Aus)	US$			
US$1=r		3,850	3,900	2,500

Population **11,450,000**

Khmer 90% **Vietnamese** 5% **Chinese** 1%

Age	13–17	18–22	23–32
Men	645,000	501,000	888,000
Women	631,000	493,000	865,000

China, People's Republic of PRC

yuan Y		2000	2001	2002
GDP	Y	8.9tr	9.7tr	
	US$	1.1tr	1.2tr	
per capita	US$	850	918	
Growth	%	7.8	7.3	
Inflation	%	0.4	0.7	
Debt	US$	149bn	146bn	
Def exp[a]	US$	ε42bn	ε47bn	
Def bdgt[b]	Y	120.5bn	141bn	166bn
	US$	14.5bn	17bn	20bn
US$1=Y		8.28	8.28	8.28

[a] PPP est incl extra-budgetary mil exp

[b] Def bdgt shows official figures at market rates

Population **1,293,239,000**

Tibetan, Uighur and other non-Han 8% **Xinjiang Muslim** ε60% of which **Uighur** ε44% **Tibet Chinese** ε60% **Tibetan** ε40%

Age	13–17	18–22	23–32
Men	52,707,000	46,251,000	119,898,000
Women	50,049,000	43,196,000	112,665,000

Fiji Fji

dollar F$		2000	2001	2002
GDP	F$	3.3bn	3.7bn	
	US$	1.5bn	1.6bn	
per capita	US$	1,920	2,020	
Growth	%	-2.8	1.5	
Inflation	%	3.0	5.0	
Debt	US$	136m	–	
Def exp	F$	70m	61m	
	US$	32m	27m	
Def bdgt	F$	50m	62m	63m
	US$	23m	27m	30m
FMA (US)	US$	0.2m	0.2m	
FMA (Aus)	US$			
US$1=F$		2.14	2.26	2.11

Population **825,000**

Fijian 51% **Indian** 44% **European/other** 5%

Age	13–17	18–22	23–32
Men	46,000	46,000	67,000
Women	44,000	43,000	64,000

Indonesia Indo

rupiah Rp		2000	2001	2002
GDP	Rp	1,332tr	1,491tr	
	US$	158bn	145bn	
per capita	US$	749	676	
Growth	%	4.8	3.3	
Inflation	%	3.8	11.5	
Debt	US$	144n	134bn	
Def exp	Rp	5.1tr	9.0tr	
	US$	607m	878m	
Def bdgt	Rp	5.4tr	7.9tr	9.8tr
	US$	642m	777m	1,125m
FMA (US)	US$	0m	0m	0.4m
FMA (Aus)	US$	5.2m		
US$1=Rp		8,320	10,261	8,775

Population 214,800,000

Muslim 87%; **Javanese** 45% **Sundanese** 14% **Madurese** 8% **Malay** 8% **Chinese** 3% **other** 22%

Age	13–17	18–22	23–32
Men	11,037,000	11,208,000	18,278,000
Women	10,556,000	10,712,000	18,275,000

Japan J

yen ¥		2000	2001	2002
GDP	¥	512tr	504tr	
	US$	4.7tr	4.1tr	
per capita	US$	37,488	32,586	
Growth	%	2.2	-0.4	
Inflation	%	-0.8	-0.7	
Publ Debt	%	123	132	
Def exp	¥	4.9tr	4.9tr	
	US$	45.6bn	40.3bn	
Def bdgt	¥	4.9tr	4.9tr	4.9tr
	US$	45.6bn	40.3bn	42.6bn
US$1=¥		108	121.5	115.9

Population 127,300,000 **Korean** <1%

Age	13–17	18–22	23–32
Men	3,585,000	3,991,000	9,647,000
Women	3,417,000	3,800,000	9,205,000

Korea, Democratic People's Republic of (North) DPRK

won		2000	2001	2002
GNP	US$	16.4bn	ε18bn	
per capita	US$	765	804	
Growth	%	9.0		
Inflation	%	2.3		
Def exp	US$	ε2.1bn	2.1bn	2.1bn
Def bdgt	won	2.9bn	2.9bn	3.2bn
	US$	1.3bn	1.3bn	1.4bn
US$1=won		2.2	2.2	2.2

Population ε24,500,000

Age	13–17	18–22	23–32
Men	1,074,000	908,000	2,504,000
Women	1,117,000	1,004,000	2,048,000

Korea, Republic of (South) ROK

won		2000	2001	2002
GDP	won	516tr	545tr	
	US$	457bn	422bn	
per capita	US$	9,630	8,970	
Growth	%	9.3	3.0	
Inflation	%	2.3	4.0	
Debt	US$	130bn	121bn	
Def exp	won	14.4tr	14.7tr	
	US$	12.8bn	11.4bn	
Def bdgt	won	14.4tr	15.3tr	16.5tr
	US$	12.8bn	11.8bn	14.1bn
US$1=won		1,129	1,297	1,170

Population 47,295,000

Age	13–17	18–22	23–32
Men	1,780,000	1,916,000	4,359,000
Women	1,672,000	1,784,000	4,088,000

Laos Lao

kip		2000	2001	2002
GDP	kip	13.4tr	15.8tr	
	US$	1.7bn	2.1bn	
per capita	US$	335	387	
Growth	%	5.8	5.2	
Inflation	%	27.1	8.0	
Def exp	kip	ε150bn	ε150bn	
	US$	19.7m	19.7m	
Def bdgt	kip	ε107bn	ε120bn	
	US$	15.5m	15.8m	
FMA (US)	US$	1.5m	1.5m	
US$1=kip		7,600	7,600	7,600

Population 5,564,000

lowland Lao Loum 68% **upland** Lao Theung 22% **highland** Lao Soung incl **Hmong** and **Yao** 9%; **Chinese** and **Vietnamese** 1%

Age	13–17	18–22	23–32
Men	325,000	253,000	389,000
Women	319,000	249,000	388,000

Malaysia Mal

ringgit RM		2000	2001	2002
GDP	RM	337bn	332bn	
	US$	88bn	87bn	
per capita	US$	3,913	3,874	
Growth	%	8.3	0.4	
Inflation	%	1.6	1.4	
Debt	US$	41bn	45bn	
Def exp[a]	RM	9.8bn	12.6bn	
	US$	2.6bn	3.3bn	
Def bdgt	RM	7.0bn	9.0bn	11.0bn
	US$	1.8bn	2.4bn	2.9bn
FMA (US)	US$	0.7m	0.7m	
US$1=RM		3.8	3.8	3.8

[a] Incl procurement and def industry exp

Population 22,092,000

Muslim 54%; **Malay and other indigenous** 64% **Chinese** 27% **Indian** 9%; **Sabah and Sarawak** non-Muslim **Bumiputras** form the majority of the population; 1m+ **Indo** and **Pi** illegal immigrants in 1997

Age	13–17	18–22	23–32
Men	1,293,000	1,056,000	1,791,000
Women	1,230,000	1,007,000	1,730,000

Mongolia Mgl

tugrik t		2000	2001	2002
GDP	t	1.0tr	1.1tr	
	US$	0.94bn	1.0bn	
per capita	US$	371	396	
Growth	%	1.1	1.1	
Inflation	%	8	6	
Debt	US$	935m	1.0bn	
Def exp	t	24bn	27bn	
	US$	22m	25m	
Def bdgt	t	25.1bn	25.5bn	27.2bn
	US$	23.1m	23.2m	24.6m
FMA (US)	US$	0.5m	2.7m	2.6m
US$1=t		1,018	1,098	1,106

Population 2,600,000

Kazak 4% **Russian** 2% **Chinese** 2%

Age	13–17	18–22	23–32
Men	161,000	142,000	237,000
Women	155,000	136,000	228,000

Myanmar My

kyat K		2000	2001	2002
GDP[a]	K	2.3tr	2.9tr	
	US$	37bn	46bn	
per capita	US$	769	950	
Growth	%	5.5	4.8	
Inflation	%	10.3	15.0	

My contd		2000	2001	2002
Debt	US$	6.0bn	5.6bn	
Def exp[a]	US$	ε1.0bn	ε1.1bn	
Def bdgt[a]	K	29bn	32bn	35bn
	US$	460m	510m	555m
US$1=K		6.51	6.67	6.40

[a] PPP est

Population 45,381,000

Burmese 68% **Shan** 9% **Karen** 7% **Rakhine** 4% **Chinese** 3+% **Other** Chin, Kachin, Kayan, Lahu, Mon, Palaung, Pao, Wa, 9%

Age	13–17	18–22	23–32
Men	2,760,000	2,426,000	4,414,000
Women	2,685,000	2,386,000	4,343,000

New Zealand NZ

dollar NZ$		2000	2001	2002	2003
GDP	NZ$	107bn	112bn		
	US$	53bn	47.5bn		
per capita	US$	14,319	12,489		
Growth	%	3.9	2.4		
Inflation	%	2.6	2.6		
Publ debt	%	31	43		
Def exp	NZ$	1.6bn	1.6bn		
	US$	804m	677m		
Def bdgt	NZ$	1.6bn	1.6bn	1.4bn	
	US$	804m	678m	697m	
US$1=NZ$		1.99	2.36	2.05	

Population 3,800,000

Maori 15% **Pacific Islander** 6%

Age	13–17	18–22	23–32
Men	132,000	126,000	291,000
Women	125,000	119,000	277,000

Papua New Guinea PNG

kina K		2000	2001	2002
GDP	K	11bn	10.3bn	
	US$	4.0bn	3.1bn	
per capita	US$	829	637	
Growth	%	-0.8	-3.4	
Inflation	%	16.2	10.0	
Debt	US$	2.7bn	2.5bn	
Def exp	K	85m	90m	
	US$	31m	27m	
Def bdgt	K	85m	90m	54m
	US$	31m	27m	13m
FMA (US)	US$	0.2m	0.2m	
FMA (Aus)	US$			
US$1=K		2.76	3.3	4.0

Population 4,899,000

Age	13–17	18–22	23–32
Men	278,000	247,000	427,000
Women	265,000	232,000	392,000

Philippines Pi

peso P		2000	2001	2002	2003
GDP	P	3.3tr	3.6tr		
	US$	75bn	72bn		
per capita	US$	992	940		
Growth	%	4.0	3.4		
Inflation	%	4.3	6.1		
Debt	US$	51bn	52.4bn		
Def exp[a]	P	59.7bn	54.6bn		
	US$	1.3bn	1.1bn		
Def bdgt[b]	P	54bn	49.5bn	69.6bn	
	US$	1.2bn	0.97bn	1.4bn	
FMA (US)	US$	2.8m	3.4m	21.0m	22.4m
FMA (Aus)	US$				
US$1=P		44.0	50.9	50.3	50.3

[a] Incl paramil exp
[b] Incl P10bn pa 2002–06

Population 77,100,000

Muslim 5–8%; **Mindanao provinces** Muslim 40–90%; Chinese 2%

Age	13–17	18–22	23–32
Men	4,366,000	3,873,000	6,424,000
Women	4,219,000	3,737,000	6,200,000

Singapore Sgp

dollar S$		2000	2001	2002
GDP	S$	153bn	153bn	
	US$	89bn	85bn	
per capita	US$	22,800	20,900	
Growth	%	10.1	-2.1	
Inflation	%	3.5	1.0	
Debt	US$	10.7bn	9.2bn	
Def exp	S$	7.4bn	7.8bn	
	US$	4.3bn	4.4bn	
Def bdgt	S$	7.4bn	7.8bn	8.2bn
	US$	4.4bn	4.3bn	4.8
FMA (Aus)	US$			
US$1=S$		1.72	1.79	1.73

Population 3,691,000

Chinese 76% Malay 15% Indian 6%

Age	13–17	18–22	23–32
Men	122,000	108,000	240,000
Women	117,000	102,000	234,000

Taiwan (Republic of China) ROC

new Taiwan dollar		2000	2001	2002
GNP	NT$	9.7tr	9.5tr	
	US$	314bn	290bn	
per capita	US$	14,330	13,130	
Growth	%	5.9	–1.9	
Inflation	%	1.7	1.0	

ROC contd		2000	2001	2002
Debt	US$	21.8bn	18.5bn	
Def exp[a]	NT$	542bn	350bn	
	US$	17.6bn	10.7bn	
Def bdgt[b]	NT$	395bn	271bn	230bn
	US$	12.8bn	8.2bn	7.0bn
US$1=NT$		30.8	32.9	33.0

[a] Incl special appropriations for procurement and infrastructure amounting to NT$301bn (US$11bn) 1993–2001.

Population 22,124,000

Taiwanese 84% **mainland Chinese** 14%

Age	13–17	18–22	23–32
Men	966,000	1,021,000	1,816,000
Women	928,000	967,000	1,713,000

Thailand Th

baht b		2000	2001	2002
GDP	b	4.9tr	5.1tr	
	US$	122bn	112bn	
per capita	US$	1,940	1,760	
Growth	%	4.4	1.8	
Inflation	%	1.5	1.7	
Debt	US$	80bn	67.9bn	
Def exp	b	97.8bn	85bn	
	US$	2.5bn	1.9bn	
Def bdgt	b	77.1bn	77.2bn	78.6bn
	US$	1.9bn	1.7bn	1.9bn
FMA (US)	US$	$1.6m	$2.8m	
US$1=b		40.1	45.4	40.4

Population 61,586,000

Thai 75% **Chinese** 14% **Muslim** 4%

Age	13–17	18–22	23–32
Men	3,135,000	3,184,000	6,203,000
Women	3,027,000	3,092,000	6,036,000

Vietnam Vn

dong d		2000	2001	2002
GDP	d	442tr	484tr	
	US$	31bn	33bn	
per capita	US$	400	420	
Growth	%	5.8	4.7	
Inflation	%	-1.7	0.1	
Debt	US$	12.8bn	13.7bn	
Def exp	US$	2.3bn	2.4bn	
Def bdgt	US$	2.3bn	2.4bn	2.4bn
US$1=d		14,081	14,725	15,300

Population 80,976,000 Chinese 3%

Age	13–17	18–22	23–32
Men	4,557,000	4,132,000	7,149,000
Women	4,403,000	3,993,000	6,950,000

Table 21 Arms orders and deliveries, East Asia and Australasia, 1998–2002

	Country supplier	Classification ⇩	Designation	Quantity ⇩	Order date	Delivery date	Comment ⇩
Australia	dom	SSK	***Collins***	6	1987	1996	Swe license. Deliveries to 2000
	dom	FGA	**F-111**	71	1990	1999	Upgrade of F/RF-111C
	Ca	LACV	**ASLAV**	276	1992	1996	2nd batch of 150 for delivery 2002–03
	dom	MHC	***Huon***	6	1994	1999	Last delivery 2002
	dom	FGA	**F-111**	36	1995	2000	Upgrade continuing
	US	MPA	**P-3C**	17	1996	1999	Upgrade to AP-3C
	US	tpt	**C-130J**	12	1996	1999	Deliveries to 2000. 2-year slippage
	US	hel	**SH-2G**	11	1997	2000	Deliveries to 2002. *Penguin* ASSM (No)
	UK	trg	***Hawk*-100**	33	1997	1999	Final delivery 2006
	US	hel	**CH-47D**	2	1997	1999	Follow-on; 4 D models delivered 1994
	UK	FGA	**F/A-18**	71	1998	2005	Upgrade. AMRAAM (US), ASRAAM (UK)
	dom	FF	***Anzac***	8	1989	1995	Deliveries to 2005
	dom	LACV	***Bushmaster***	370	1999	2000	55 delivered in 2000
	No	ASSM	***Penguin***		1999	2003	For use with SH-2G
	US	AAM	**AMRAAM**		2000		
	US	hel	**S-70B2**	16	2000		Upgrade
	US	AEWAC	**Boeing 737**	4	2000	2007	Option on further 3
	col	hel	***Tiger***	22	2001	2004	
Brunei	UK	FSG	***Brunei***	3	1995	2001	First delivered 2001
	UK	trg	***Hawk* 100/20**	10	1996	1999	
	Indo	MPA	**CN-235**	3	1996	1999	Requirement for up to 12
	Fr	ASSM	***Exocet***	59	1997	1999	
	UK	FAC	***Waspada***	3	1997	1998	Upgrade
	Fr	SAM	***Mistral***	16	1998	1999	16 launchers
Cambodia	Il	trg	L-39	8	1994	1996	Second-hand. Only 2 delivered by Jan 1998
China	dom	ICBM	**DF-41**		1985	2005	Dev; range 12,000km
	dom	ICBM	**DF-31**		1985	2005	Dev; range 8,000km. Tested Aug 1999
	dom	SLBM	**JL-2**		1985	2008	Dev; range 8,000km
	dom	SSGN	**Type 093**	1	1985	2006	Similar to RF *Victor* 3. Launch expected 2000
	dom	SSBN	**Type 094**	4	1985	2009	Dev programme
	dom	ASSM	**C701**			1999	Dev completed
	dom	bbr	**H-6**			1998	Still in production
	dom	MBT	**Type-85-III**	400	1985	1990	Dev complete 1997
	Fr	hel	**AS-365**	50	1986	1989	Local production continues
	dom	MBT	**Type-90**		1987		For export only. No prod by 1997
	dom	FGA	**JH-7**	20	1988	1993	Upgrade to FBC-2 standard has begun
	dom	SRBM	**DF-11**	100	1988	1996	Production continuing
	dom	SRBM	**DF-15**	300	1988	1996	Production continuing
	dom	FGA	**FC-1**		1990	2005	With Pak (150 units). 1st flight in 2000
	col	hel	**EC-120**		1990		In dev with Fr and Sgp
	RF	SAM	**S-300**	30	1990	1992	Continued in 1998
	dom	FGA	**F-8IIM**		1993	1996	Modernisation completed 1999
	dom	FGA	**F-10**		1993		Dev continues
	RF	SSK	***Kilo***	4	1993	1995	Deliveries to 1999. 2 Type 877, 2 Type 636

	Country supplier	Classification ⇩	Designation	Quantity ⇩	Order date	Delivery date	Comment ⇩
	dom	SSK	***Song***	2	1994	2002	2 *Song* under construction at Wuhan
	RF	SAM	**SA-15**	35	1995	1997	Orders: 15 (1995), 20 (1999). Deliveries to 2000
	dom	AGI	***Shiyan* 970**	1	1995	1999	Sea trials in 1999
	RF	FGA	**SU-27**	200	1996	1998	15 units for production 1998–2000
	dom	ATGW	***Red Arrow* 8E**		1996	1998	Modernised Red Arrow ATGW
	dom	DDG	***Luhai***	2	1996	1999	Second delivered
	RF	DDG	***Sovremenny***	2	1996	2000	Both delivered 2000
	RF	AIFV	**BMD-3**		1997		Could be BMD-1
	dom	SLCM	**C-801(mod)**		1997		Dev (also known as YJ-82)
	col	ASM	**KR-1**		1997		In dev with RF. Kh-31P variant
	UK	MPA	***Jetstream***	2	1997	1998	For Hong Kong gov
	Il	AEW	**Il-76**	4	1997		
	RF	hel	**Ka-28**	12	1998	2000	For DDG operation
	RF	SAM	**FT-2000**		1998		
	RF	tkr ac	**Il-78**	4	1998		
	RF	SSM	**SSN-24**	24	1998	2000	For *Sovremenny*
	dom	FFG	***Jiangwei* II**	8	1998	1998	All delivered by 2002
	RF	FGA	**SU-30MKK**	40	1999	2000	
	dom	IRBM	**DF-21X**		1999		Modernised DF-15
	RF	FGA	**Su-27UBK**	28	2000	2001	Trainers
	dom	sat	***Zhongxing*-22**	1		2000	Replaces *Dongfanghong*-3
	RF	AEW	**A-50**	6	2000		Part of debt settlement
	dom	lt tk	**Type 99**			2000	Replacement for Type-63?
	RF	ASM	**Kh-35**		2001		To equip Su-30MKK
	RF	DDG	***Sovremenny***	2	2002	2005	
	RF	SSK	***Kilo***	8	2002		
Indonesia	UK	lt tk	***Scorpion***	50	195	1997	In addition to previous 50. 39 delivered 1998 incl 9 stormers.
	Slvk	APC	**BVP-2**	9	1996	1998	Incl 2 BVP-2K, originally from Ukr
	Nl	tpt	**F-28**	8	1996	1998	For Armed Forces Headquarters Foundation
	UK	FGA	***Hawk* 209**	16	1996	1999	12 were to be delivered in 1999
	dom	MPA	**CN-235MP**	3	1996	1999	
	US	hel	**NB-412**	1	1996	1998	Licence-produced
	Ge	hel	**BO-105**	3	1996	1998	40 delivered between 1980-93
	Fr	SAM	***Mistral***		1996	1998	
	RF	hel	**Mi-17**	2	1997	2000	
	ROK	LST	**??**	??		2000	1st delivery 2000
	ROK	trg	**KT-1**	7	2001	2002	
	RF	hel	**Mi-2**	8	2001		
Japan	US	AEW	**B-767**	4	1991	1998	
	dom	DD	***Murasame***	9	1991	1994	All delivered by 2002
	dom	SSK	***Oyashio-class***	8	1993	2000	5 delivered by 2002
	dom	AAM	**XAAM-5**		1994	2001	Dev
	dom	LST	***Oosumi-class***	3	1994	1997	2 delivered by 2002
	dom	SP arty	**155mm**		1994	2000	Entered prod 1999. Replacing Type-75
	dom	SAR			1996		US-1 replacement in dev
	dom	BMD	**TMD**		1997		Joint dev with US from late 1998
	dom	recce	**sat**	4	1998	2002	Dev Prog. 2 optical, 2 radar
	dom	mor	**L16**	42	1999	2000	

	Country supplier	Classification ⇩	Designation	Quantity ⇩	Order date	Delivery date	Comment ⇩
	dom	mor	**120mm**	27	1999	2000	
	dom	SP arty	**Type-96**	3	1999	2000	
	dom	SP arty	**155 mm**	4	1999	2000	Replacing Type-75. Entered prod 1999
	col	arty	**FH70**		1999	2000	40 req under 1996–2000 MTDP
	dom	MRL	**MLRS**	9	1999	2000	45 req under 1996–2000 MTDP
	dom	AAA	**Type-87**	1	1999	2000	1 delivered 1998
	dom	MBT	**Type 90**	17	1999	2000	90 req under 1996–2000 MTDP
	dom	AIFV	**Type-89**	2	1999	2000	2 delivered 1998
	dom	APC	**Type-96**	28	1999	2000	157 req under 1996–2000 MTDP
	dom	APC	**Type-82**	1	1999	2000	1 delivered 1998
	dom	lt tk	**Type-87**	1	1999	2000	1 delivered 1998
	dom	hel	**AH-1S**		1999	2000	3 req under 1996–2000 MTDP
	dom	hel	**OH-1**	3	1999	2000	Cost $66m
	dom	hel	**UH-60JA**	3	1999	2000	Cost $84m
	dom	hel	**CH-47JA**	2	1999	2000	9 req under 1996–2000 MTDP
	dom	recce	**LR-2**	1	1999	2000	Cost $24m
	dom	SAM	***Hawk***		1999	2000	
	dom	ASSM	**Type-88**	4	1999	2000	24 req under 1996–2000 MTDP
	dom		**Type-96**	6	1999	2000	
	dom	MCMV	***Sugashima***	10	1999	2008	5 delivered by 2002
	dom	PCC	***Hayabusa***	6	1999	2000	2 delivered by 2002
	dom	AK		1	1999	2000	
	dom	hel	**SH-60J**	9	1999	2000	37 req under 1996–2000 MTDP
	dom	FGA	**F-2**	130	1999	2000	18 to be delivered by 2001
	dom	hel	**CH-47J**	2	1999	2000	4 req under 1996–2000 MTDP
	dom	SAR	**U-125A**	2	1999	2000	Cost $76m
	dom	hel	**UH-60J**	2	1999	2000	Cost $59m
	dom	trg	**T-4**	10	1999	2000	54 req under 1996–2000 MTDP
	dom	trg	**T-400**		1999	2000	
	dom	tpt	**U-4**		1999	2000	
	dom	trg	**T-X**	50	2000		Dev Prog. Replacing *Fuji* T-3s. Delayed
	dom	tpt	**C-X**		2000		Replacement for C-1A
	dom	MPA	**MPA-X**		2000		Replacement for P3
	US	SAM	**Standard**	16	2000		Block III
	dom	hel	**AH-64D**	10	2001	2003	Up to 50 required
	US	tkr ac	**Boeing 767**		2002		
North Korea	dom	MRBM	***Taepo-dong* 1**				Tested October 1998
	dom	MRBM	***Taepo-dong* 2**				Tested 1999
	RF	hel	**Mi-17**	5	1998	1998	
	Kaz	FGA	**MiG-21**	30	1999	1999	Also spare parts for existing fleet
	RF	FGA	**MiG-21**	10	1999	2000	
South Korea	dom	APC	**KIFV**	2,000	1981	1985	Still producing in 1998, incl exports
	dom	SSK	***Chang Bogo***	9	1987	2001	9th delivered in 2001
	US	hel	**UH-60P**	138	1988	1990	Deliveries to 1999
	US	FGA	**F-16C/D**	120	1992	1995	Licence. Deliveries to 1999.
	dom	AIFV	**M-113**	175	1993	1994	Deliveries to 1998
	dom	MBT	**K1**		1995	1996	Upgrade programme began in 1996
	dom	sat	**KITSAT-3**		1995	1999	
	RF	APC	**BTR-80**	20	1995	1996	Deliveries to 1998
	RF	AIFV	**BMP-3**	23	1995	1996	Deliveries to 1999

	Country supplier	Classification ⇩	Designation	Quantity ⇩	Order date	Delivery date	Comment ⇩
	RF	MBT	**T-80**	33	1995	1996	Deliveries to 1999
	US	sigint	***Hawker* 800**	10	1996	1999	
	US	AAM	**AMRAAM**	190	1996	1998	
	US	AAM	**Sidewinder**	284	1996	1998	
	Il	AAM	***Popeye***	100	1996	2000	Deliveries 2000–02
	dom	DDG	***Okpo* KDX-1**	3	1996	1998	3 delivered by end of 1999
	US	MRL	**MLRS**	29	1997	1999	Including 2,400 rockets
	Il	UAV	***Harpy***	100	1997	2001	
	dom	trg	**T-50**	94	1997	2005	Dev
	Fr	utl	**F-406**	5	1997	1999	
	dom	SAM	***Pegasus***		1997	1999	Dev
	Fr	SAM	***Mistral***	1,294	1997	1998	Missiles
	Il	UAV	***Searcher***	3	1997	1998	
	RF	SAM	***Igla***		1997	1999	
	RF	ATGW	***Metis***		1997	1999	
	UK	hel	***Lynx***	13	1997	1999	
	Indo	tpt	**CN-235**	8	1997	1999	Delivery delayed
	US	AEW	**B-767**	4	1998		Delivery delayed
	dom	DDG	**KDX-2**	3	1998	2003	
	dom	SAM	**M-SAM**		1998	2008	Dev
	Ge	hel	**BO-105**	12	1998	1999	
	US	AAV	**AAV7A1**	57	1998	2001	Licence. Following delivery of 103 from US
	dom	SPA	**XK9**	68	1998	1999	
	RF	tpt	**Be-200**	1	1998	2000	
	dom	SAM	**P-SAM**		1998	2003	Dev
	dom	SSM	***Hyonmu***		1999		300km and 500km variants
	US	FGA	**F-16C/D**	20	1999	2003	Follow on order after orders for 120
	RF	hel	**Ka-32**	31	1999	2000	Upgrades
	RF	hel	**Ka-32T**	3	1999	2000	Follow on order expected
	US	SAM	**RAM**	64	1999		Block I
	US	SAM	***Standard***	110	2000		
	US	SSM	***Harpoon***	96	2000		
	US	SAM	**SM-2**		2000		
	Ge	SSK	**Type 214**	3	2000	2007	
	dom	DDG	**KDX-3**	5	2000	2009	In dev
	US	SSM	**ATACMS**	111	2002	2004	
	US	FGA	**F-15K**	40	2002	2005	
Malaysia	UK	FF	***Lekiu*-class**	2	1992	1999	2 delivered in 1999
	It	FSG	***Assad***	4	1995	1997	Originally for Irq. Deliveries 1997–99
	It	ASSM	***Otomat***	4	1996	1998	
	Fr	ASSM	***Exocet***	4	1996	1998	
	Indo	tpt	**CN-235**	6	1995	1999	
	US	hel	**S-70A**	2	1996	1998	
	Ge	OPV	***Meko* A 100**	6	1997	2004	Licence built. Req for 27 over 20 yrs
	RF	FGA	**MiG-29**	18	1997	1999	Upgrade
	It	trg	**MB-339**	2	1998	1999	
	RF	hel	**Mi-17**	10	1998	1999	
	UK	hel	***Super Lynx***	6	1999	2001	
	Tu	AIFV	***Adnan***	211	2000		
	RSA	arty	**G5 155mm**	22	2000		
	RF	ATGW	***Metis*-2**		2001		

	Country supplier	Classification ⇩	Designation	Quantity ⇩	Order date	Delivery date	Comment ⇩
	col	hel	**AS 555**	6	2001	2003	
	Br	MRS	***Astros* II**		2001	2002	
	Fr	SSK	***Scopene***	2	2002	2007	
	col	SAM	***Jernas***		2002	2005	
Myanmar	PRC	FGA	**F-7**	21	1996	1998	Following deliveries of 36 1991–96
	PRC	trg	**K-8**	4	1998	2000	
	RF	FGA	**MiG-29**	10	2001		
	RF	trg	**MiG-29UB**	2	2001		
New Zealand	A	FF	***Anzac***	2	1989	1997	With Aus. 2nd delivered 1999
	US	ASW	**P3-K**	6	1995	1998	Upgrade. 1 delivered. Project abandoned in 2000
	Fr	SAM	***Mistral***	12	1996	1997	Delivery of 2 launchers in late 1997
	US	trg	**CT-4E**	13	1997	1998	11 delivered. Lease programme
	US	hel	**SH-2G**	5	1997	2000	
	US	tpt	**C-130J**	5	1999		Lease of 5 to 7. Delayed
	Ca	APC	**LAV III**	105	2000	2002	Deliveries 2002–04
	US	ATGW	***Javelin***	24	2000		
Papua New Guinea							
	Indo	hel	**BO-105**	1	1998	1999	
Philippines	US	tpt	**C-130B**	2	1995	1998	
	US	trg	**T-41**	5	1997	1998	
	ROC	FGA	**F-5A**	5	1997	1998	Ex-ROK
	ROC	FGA	**F-5E**	40	1999		
	US	tpt	**C-130B**	1	2000	2001	Excess Defence Article stock
	US	hel	**UH-1H**	8	2000	2001	
	Aus	PCC		6	2001		For Coast Guard
Singapore	dom	AIFV	**IFV**	500	1991	1999	Two batches: 300 then 200
	dom	PCO	***Fearless***	12	1993	1996	Deliveries to 1999
	US	FGA	**F-16C/D**	42	1995	1998	First order for 18, follow-on for 24
	Swe	SSK	***Sjoormen***	4	1995	2000	2nd delivered 2001
	dom	LST	***Endurance***	4	1997	1999	All delivered by 2001
	RF	SAM	**SA-16/SA-18**		1997	1998	
	US	tkr ac	**KC-135**	4	1997	2000	
	US	hel	**CH-47D**	8	1997	2000	Follow-on order after 1994 order for 6
	US	cbt hel	**AH-64D**	12	2000	2003	
	Fr	FFG	***Lafayette***	6	2000	2005	mod *Lafayette*. 1st to be built in Fr. Final delivery 2009
	US	FGA	**F-16**	20	2000	2003	
	Fr	SSM	***Exocet* MM40**		2000		
	US	AAM	**AMRAAM**	100	2000		Only to be delivered if under military threat
Taiwan	dom	FGA	**IDF**	130	1982	1994	Deliveries completed 1999
	US	FF	***Knox***	8	1989	1993	Final delivery in 1999
	Fr	FF	***LaFayette***	6	1992	1996	All delivered by 1998
	US	FGA	**F-16A/B**	150	1992	1997	60 delivered in 1997
	Fr	FGA	***Mirage* 2000**	60	1992	1997	Deliveries completed in 1999
	dom	PFM	***Jin Chiang***	12	1992	1994	8 delivered
	US	SAM	***Patriot***	6	1993	1997	Completed 1998. Upgrade to PAC-3 standard

	Country supplier	Classification ⇩	Designation	Quantity ⇩	Order date	Delivery date	Comment ⇩
	US	tpt	**C-130**	12	1993	1995	Deliveries continue
	US	SAR hel	**S-70C**	4	1994	1998	
	US	arty	**M-109A5**	28	1995	1998	
	US	SAM	***Avenger***	70	1996	1998	
	US	MPA	**P-3**		1996		With *Harpoon* SSM
	US	hel	**TH-67**	30	1996	1998	
	Sgp	recce	**RF-5E**		1996	1998	Unspecified number of F-5E entered service as RF-5E
	US	SAM	***Stinger***	1,600	1996	1998	
	dom	trg	**AT-3**	40	1997		Order resheduled
	US	ASW hel	**S-70C**	11	1997	2000	
	US	hel	**OH-58D**	13	1998	2001	Following deliveries of 26 1994–95
	US	ASSM	***Harpoon***	58	1998		
	US	hel	**CH-47SD**	9	1999	2002	Following deliveries of 7 1993–97
	US	radar	***Pave Paws***		1999	2002	
	US	LSD	***Anchorage***	1	1999	2000	USS *Pensacola* to replace existing 2 LSDs
	dom	FF	***Chengkung***	1	1999	2003	Based on US *Oliver Hazard Perry*
	US	AEW	**E-2T**	4	1999	2002	Following delivery of 4 in 1995
	US	hel	**CH-47SD**	9	2000		3 plus long lead time for further 6
	US	AAM	**AMRAAM**	200	2000		Only to be delivered if under military threat
	US	arty	**M-109A5**	146	2000		
	US	DDG	***Kidd* Class**	4	2001	2004	
Thailand	A	arty	**155mm**	36	1995	1996	18 delivered 1996, 18 in 1998
	US	MBT	**M-60**	125	1995	1996	24 delivered 1996, 101 in 1997
	US	APC	**M113**	155	1996	1998	130 APCs from US, 25 from Ge
	US	FGA	**F/A-18C/D**	8	1996		Cancelled
	Indo	tpt	**CN-235**	2	1996		Delayed
	It	MHC	***Lat Ya***	2	1996	1998	Deliveries to December 1999
	dom	corvette		3	1996	2000	2 delivered by 2000
	US	FF		1	1996	1998	
	It	MCMV	***Gaeta***	2	1996	1998	Deliveries finished
	Il	UAV	***Searcher***	4	1997		
	Fr	APC	**VAB NG**		1997		Selected to replace 300 M-113. Order delayed
	Fr	sat			1997		Order for recce sat delayed late 1997
	A	LCU		3	1997		
	US	hel	**SH-2F**	10	1999	2002	
	Ge	FGA	***Alpha Jet***		1999		Ex -Luftwaffe to replace OV-10
	US	FGA	**F-16 A**	18	2000	2002	Replacing purchase of F/A-18
	US	hel	**UH-60L**	3	2000	2002	
	Il	hel	**UH-1**	19	2001		Upgrade
	US	hel	**AH-1**	6	2001		Upgrade
Vietnam	RF	FGA	**Su-27**	6	1		
	Il	FGA	**MiG-21**		1996		Upgrade
	RF	corvette	***Taruntul* 2**	2	1997	1999	Following delivery of 2 *Taruntul* 1995
	DPRK	SSM	***Scud***		1999	1999	Probably *Scud*-Cs; quantity unknown

Caribbean and **Latin America**

Attention in Latin America has been focused on the economic crisis in Argentina and its implications for the rest of the region. Following the removal of the peg between the Argentine peso and the US dollar, and the subsequent devaluation of the peso, short-term economic prospects in **Argentina** remain uncertain. A significant contraction of output and an acceleration of inflation appears unavoidable, although exports are likely to pick up in response to the depreciating currency. So far, the economic and financial spill-over from the crisis appears to be limited to Uruguay with the rest of the region being more negatively affected by the sharp US slowdown following 11 September than with events inside Argentina. However, if there is no rapid turnaround in Argentine policies, or if confidence deteriorates further, then serious risks remain to the region as a whole.

In 2001, regional defence spending was US$33bn, down from US$36bn in 2000; however, this apparent reduction is almost entirely due to the devaluation of the Brazilian real during that period.

In **Argentina** the defence budget for 2002 has been fixed at P3.3bn, the same as last year. In dollar terms, this represents a reduction from US$3.3bn to US$940m. Until the economic position of the country is more settled, it is an IMF requirement that Argentina reduce its fiscal deficit before receiving any more IMF funds. This prevents any immediate change in defence planning or procurement. Despite these fiscal woes, the Argentine Air Force still plans to buy 12 new AT-63 jet trainers, but options on additional purchases for the air force and an order from the navy have been shelved. However, 12 IA-63 jets in the current inventory are still to be upgraded to AT-63 standard.

Brazil was affected by the global slowdown in 2001 and recorded growth of just 1.4%, compared to 4.5% in 2000. The Brazilian Congress approved a $670m package to fund the army's modernisation programme. The money, to be released over the next three years, will pay for equipment priorities, in particular command, control, communications and intelligence systems. The army is also in need of replacing aging truck, ambulance and light utility vehicles, many of which are no longer usable.

In the Andean Region, countries were affected both by the overall slowdown in global trade and the weakening of certain commodity markets, notably oil, copper and other metals. After months of delay and amid much domestic criticism and concern in the region as a whole about a new arms build-up, **Chile** agreed to the purchase of 10 F-16 fighter aircraft from the United States. The price was fixed at $660m; given current budget limitations, the Ministry of Defence has had to put navy modernisation plans on hold to fund the purchase. The decision to buy the aircraft suggests that reform of the system for financing defence spending will be delayed. Under a law inherited from the years of military rule, 10% of Chile's copper sales are automatically allocated to the armed forces. This amounted to around $210m in 2001, but it was anticipated that this arrangement would soon be changed or even scrapped to allow for a more transparent budgetary process.

In compliance with IMF targets, and despite weakening oil markets, **Colombia** has cut its fiscal deficit from 6% of GDP in 1999 to a projected figure of 2.6% in 2002. This achievement, however, is threatened by the breakdown of peace talks between the government and the Revolutionary Forces of Colombia (FARC), which was the catalyst for an increase of P570bn in Colombia's 2002 defence budget. If peace talks are not resumed, the defence budget may rise even further in coming years. The government has already announced a cut of P2,000bn in non-military spending for 2002 and it is likely that some of these funds will be redirected to the armed forces. President Andreas Pastrana would like US military aid – currently dedicated to arming and training Colombian anti-drugs forces – to be used to protect economic assets such as oil pipelines from insurgent attacks. The Colombian government has already received US$1.3bn from the United States over the previous two years for anti-drugs operations. Whereas the Clinton administration refused to allow funds from its 'Plan Colombia' to be used for anti-insurgency measures, despite the involvement of insurgents in drug trafficking, the Bush administration has been less insistent about this.

President Alejandro Toledo of **Peru** originally announced a cut of NS100m in the defence budget for 2002, bringing it down to NS2.6bn, and pledged to reduce spending further after restructuring military and police institutions, widely seen as corrupt. However, this intention was short-lived: following a bombing incident in April that coincided with the visit of President Bush, the government reversed its decision and allocated an additional NS700m to defence and security budgets.

Antigua and Barbuda AB

East Caribbean dollar		2000	2001	2002
GDP	EC$	1.8bn	1.8bn	
	US$	670m	670m	
per capita	US$	9,800	9,800	
Growth	%	2.6	-0.6	
Inflation	%	0.7	1.0	
Ext Debt	US$			
Def exp	EC$	11m	12m	
	US$	4m	4m	
Def bdgt	EC$	12m	12m	12m
	US$	4m	4m	4m
FMA	US$	0.1m	0.1m	
US$1=EC$		2.7	2.7	2.7

Population			**68,000**
Age	13–17	18–22	23–32
Men	5,000	5,000	6,000
Women	5,000	5,000	8,000

Bahamas Bs

dollar B$		2000	2001	2002
GDP	B$	4.7bn	4.7bn	
	US$	4.7bn	4.7bn	
per capita	US$	2,427	2,047	
Growth	%	5.0	-1.0	
Inflation	%	1.6	1.0	
Debt	US$	382m	372m	
Def exp	B$	30m	30m	
	US$	30m	30m	
Def bdgt	B$	30m	30m	26m
	US$	30m	30m	26m
FMA (US)	US$	0.1m	0.2m	0.2m
US$1=B$		1.0	1.0	1.0

Population			**2,272,000**
Age	13–17	18–22	23–32
Men	17,000	15,000	32,000
Women	13,000	14,000	30,000

Argentina Arg

peso P		2000	2001	2002
GDP	P	282.8bn	268.6bn	
	US$	283bn	269bn	
per capita	US$	7,656	7,166	
Growth	%	0.8	-3.7	
Inflation	%	-0.9	-1.1	
Debt	US$	158bn	145bn	
Def exp	P	4.8bn	4.5bn	
	US$	4.8bn	4.5bn	
Def bdgt	P	3.5bn	3.3bn	3.3bn
	US$	3.5bn	3.3bn	0.94bn
FMA (US)	US$	1.1m	1.8m	2.0m
US$1=P		1.0	1.0	3.6

Population			**37,500,000**
Age	13–17	18–22	23–32
Men	1,631,000	1,652,000	2,824,000
Women	1,577,000	1,602,000	2,756,000

Barbados Bds

dollar B$		2000	2001	2002
GDP	B$	5.3bn	5.3bn	
	US$	2.6bn	2.6bn	
per capita	US$	9,800	8,460	
Growth	%	3.1	-2.1	
Inflation	%	2.5	2.2	
Debt	US$	637m	615m	
Def exp	B$	26m	26m	
	US$	13m	13m	
Def bdgt	B$	26m	26m	26m
	US$	13m	13m	13m
FMA	US$	0.1m	0.1m	
US$1=B$		2.0	2.0	2.0

Population			**271,000**
Age	13–17	18–22	23–32
Men	11,000	11,000	23,000
Women	11,000	10,000	22,000

Belize Bze

dollar BZ$		2000	2001	2002
GDP	BZ$	1.3bn	1.5bn	
	US$	674m	750m	
per capita	US$	2,900	3,050	
Growth	%	9.7	2.5	
Inflation	%	0.6	1.2	
Debt	US$	499m		
Def exp	BZ$	34m	36m	
	US$	17m	18m	
Def bdgt	BZ$	35m	36m	37m
	US$	17.5m	18m	18.5m
FMA (US)	US$	0.4m	0.5m	
US$1=BZ$		2.0	2.0	2.0

Population			**246,000**
Age	13–17	18–22	23–32
Men	14,000	13,000	20,000
Women	14,000	13,000	20,000

Bolivia Bol

boliviano B		2000	2001	2002
GDP	B	52bn	52bn	
	US$	8.4bn	8.0bn	
per capita	US$	1,040	938	
Growth	%	2.4	1.0	
Inflation	%	4.6	1.6	
Debt	US$	5.8bn	4.1bn	
Def exp	B	796m	910m	
	US$	128m	138m	
Def bdgt	B	796m	917	
	US$	128m	138m	
FMA[a] (US)	US$	0.8	0.7	
US$1=B		6.2	6.6	

[a] Excl Plan Colombia allocation for 2001

Population			**8,379,000**
Age	13–17	18–22	23–32
Men	511,000	463,000	725,000
Women	502,000	460,000	744,000

Brazil Br

real R		2000	2001	2002
GDP	R	1,131bn	1,184bn	
	US$	627bn	504bn	
per capita	US$	3,673	2,920	
Growth	%	4.4	1.5	
Inflation	%	7.0	6.8	
Debt	US$	235bn	236bn	
Def exp[a]	R	25.9bn	25.2bn	
	US$	14.4bn	10.7bn	

Br contd		2000	2001	2002
Def bdgt	R	20.7bn	20.1bn	26.0bn
	US$	11.5bn	8.6bn	9.1bn
FMA (US)	US$	0.2m	0.2m	0.4m
US$1=R		1.80	2.35	2.85

[a] Incl spending on paramilitary forces

Population			**172,600,000**
Age	13–17	18–22	23–32
Men	8,873,000	8,494,000	14,685,000
Women	8,773,000	8,483,000	14,835,000

Chile Chl

peso pCh		2000	2001	2002
GDP	pCh	40.4tr	42.2tr	
	US$	75.6bn	66.4bn	
per capita	US$	4,890	4,230	
Growth	%	4.4	2.8	
Inflation	%	3.8	3.6	
Debt	US$	37bn	38bn	
Def exp[a]	pCh	1,689bn	1,841bn	
	US$	3.1bn	2.9bn	
Def bdgt	pCh	710bn	750bn	810bn
	US$	1.3bn	1.2bn	1.1bn
FMA (US)	US$	0.5m	0.5m	
US$1=pCh		535	635	700

[a] Incl spending on paramilitary forces

Population			**15,405,000**
Age	13–17	18–22	23–32
Men	725,000	640,000	1,218,000
Women	698,000	617,000	1,188,000

Colombia Co

peso pC		2000	2001	2002
GDP	pC	166tr	191tr	
	US$	79.0bn	83bn	
per capita	US$	1,917	1,950	
Growth	%	2.8	1.5	
Inflation	%	9.2	8.0	
Debt	US$	34bn	37bn	
Def exp	pC	6.4tr	6.7tr	
	US$	3.1bn	2.9bn	
Def bdgt	pC	3.5tr	3.7tr	4.3tr
	US$	1.7bn	1.6bn	1.7bn
FMA (US)	US$	820m	265m	
US$1=pC		2,087	2,299	2,527

Population			**42,800,000**
Age	13–17	18–22	23–32
Men	1,966,000	1,917,000	3,325,000
Women	1,874,000	1,840,000	3,263,000

Costa Rica CR

colon C		2000	2001	2002
GDP	C	5.1tr	5.3tr	
	US$	16.5bn	16.2bn	
per capita	US$	4,140	3,950	
Growth	%	1.7	0.4	
Inflation	%	11.5	11.0	
Debt	US$	4.5bn	4.7bn	
Sy exp[a]	C	25.6bn	25.6bn	
	US$	86m	78m	
Sy bdgt[a]	C	29.2bn	33.9bn	
	US$	89m	94m	
FMA (US)	US$	0.2m	0.2m	
US$1=C		308	328	361

[a] No defence forces. Budgetary data are for border and maritime policing and internal security.

Population			**4,146,000**
Age	**13–17**	**18–22**	**23–32**
Men	198,000	180,000	301,000
Women	190,000	174,000	292,000

Cuba C

peso P		2000	2001	2002
GDP	US$	17.1bn	18.1bn	
per capita	US$	1,530	1,620	
Growth	%	5.5	5.0	
Inflation	%	-3.0	0.5	
Debt	US$	11.9bn	11.7bn	
Def exp	US$	ε750m	ε792m	
Def bdgt	P	650m	ε692m	
	US$	31m	37.7m	
US$1=P		21	21	21

Population			**11,242,000**
Age	**13–17**	**18–22**	**23–32**
Men	419,000	358,000	1,029,000
Women	392,000	335,000	966,000

Dominican Republic DR

peso pRD		2000	2001	2002
GDP	pRD	322bn	360bn	
	US$	20.9bn	21.3bn	
per capita	US$	2,500	2,500	
Growth	%	7.8	3.2	
Inflation	%	7.7	8.9	
Debt	US$	4.6	5.1	
Def exp	pRD	ε2.6bn	ε2.7bn	
	US$	169m	159m	
Def bdgt	pRD	2.0bn	ε2.5bn	
	US$	131m	145m	
FMA (US)	US$	1.0m	1.1m	
US$1=pRD		16.4	16.9	17.1

Population			**8,653,000**
Age	**13–17**	**18–22**	**23–32**
Men	465,000	419,000	726,000
Women	453,000	410,000	717,000

Ecuador Ec

sucre ES		2000	2001	2002
GDP	ES	357tr	449tr	
	US$	14.3bn	18bn	
per capita	US$	1,120	1,400	
Growth	%	2.3	5.2	
Inflation	%	91	37	
Debt	US$	13.3bn	13.6bn	
Def exp[a]	ES	ε12tr	ε12.9tr	
	US$	480m	518m	
Def bdgt	ES	ε8.0tr	8.6tr	
	US$	320m	345m	
FMA (US)	US$	2.7m	4.0m	
US$1=ES		25,000	25,000	25,000

[a] incl extra-budgetary funding

Population			**12,831,000**
Age	**13–17**	**18–22**	**23–32**
Men	721,000	667,000	1,147,000
Women	700,000	650,000	1,123,000

El Salvador ElS

colon C		2000	2001	2002	2003
GDP	C	105bn	120bn		
	US$	11.9bn	13.7bn		
per capita	US$	1,919	2,145		
Growth	%	2.0	2.0		
Inflation	%	2.3	3.8		
Debt	US$	4.0bn	4.7bn		
Def exp	C	1.47bn	1.43bn		
	US$	168m	168m		
Def bdgt	C	980m	980m	956m	
	US$	112m	112m	109m	
FMA (US)	US$	0.5m	0.6m	1.8m	3.4m
US$1=C		8.75	8.75	8.75	

Population			**6,400,000**
Age	**13–17**	**18–22**	**23–32**
Men	370,000	360,000	559,000
Women	358,000	347,000	572,000

Guatemala Gua

quetzal q		2000	2001	2002
GDP	q	148bn	161bn	
	US$	19.1bn	20.9bn	
per capita	US$	1,650	1,750	
Growth	%	3.5	1.8	
Inflation	%	5.1	8.7	
Debt	US$	4.7bn	4.6bn	
Def exp	q	ε1.2bn	ε1.5bn	
	US$	155m	190m	
Def bdgt	q	850m	836m	1,000m
	US$	109m	102m	126m
FMA (US)	US$	3.2m	3.3m	
US$1=q		7.76	7.85	7.88

Population			**11,541,000**
Age	13–17	18–22	23–32
Men	750,000	647,000	974,000
Women	729,000	630,000	960,000

Guyana Guy

dollar G$		2000	2001	2002	2003
GDP	G$	133.5bn	136bn		
	US$	732m	700m		
per capita	US$	850	836		
Growth	%	-0.7	0.8		
Inflation	%	6.1	2.4		
Debt	US$	1.8bn	1.5bn		
Def exp	G$	ε1.2bn	ε1.2bn		
	US$	6.6m	6.4m		
Def bdgt	G$	ε950m	ε1,000m	1,020m	
	US$	5.2m	5.3m	5.7m	
FMA (US)	US$	0.3m	0.3m	0.5m	0.7m
US$1=G$		182	187	181	

Population			**868,000**
Age	13–17	18–22	23–32
Men	43,000	38,000	77,000
Women	41,000	36,000	73,000

Haiti RH

gourde G		2000	2001	2002
GDP	G	76bn	85bn	
	US$	3.5bn	3.7bn	
per capita	US$	480	450	
Growth	%	1.0	-1.7	
Inflation	%	11.5	16.7	
Debt	US$			
Sy exp	G	ε900m	ε1,000m	
	US$	43m	41m	

RH contd		2000	2001	2002
Sy bdgt	G	ε900m	ε1,000m	
	US$	43m	41m	
FMA (US)	US$	7.3m	4.8m	
US$1=G		21.1	24.4	29.5

Population			**8,448,000**
Age	13–17	18–22	23–32
Men	431,000	380,000	626,000
Women	420,000	374,000	623,000

Honduras Hr

lempira L		2000	2001	2002	2003
GDP	L	85.7bn	98.8bn		
	US$	5.7bn	6.4bn		
per capita	US$	890	986		
Growth	%	5.0	2.5		
Inflation	%	10.6	9.7		
Debt	US$	5.5bn	5.5bn		
Def exp	L	ε1,400m	ε1,500m		
	US$	94m	97m		
Def bdgt	L	ε520m	715m	1,884m	
	US$	35m	46m	115m	
FMA (US)	US$	0.5m	0.5m	0.6m	0.6m
US$1=L		14.8	15.5	16.4	

Population			**6,600,000**
Age	13–17	18–22	23–32
Men	412,000	352,000	573,000
Women	398,000	343,000	562,000

Jamaica Ja

dollar J$		2000	2001	2002
GDP	J$	329bn	358bn	
	US$	7.7bn	7.8bn	
per capita	US$	3,000	3,000	
Growth	%	1.1	3.0	
Inflation	%	6.4	5.0	
Debt	US$	4.3bn	5.2bn	
Def exp	J$	1.9bn	1.8bn	
	US$	42m	41m	
Def bdgt	J$	1.9bn	1.8m	1.8m
	US$	42m	41m	37m
FMA (US)	US$	1.7m	2.3m	
US$1=J$		42.7	45.9	48.2

Population			**2,608,000**
Age	13–17	18–22	23–32
Men	121,000	119,000	226,000
Women	121,000	116,000	226,000

Mexico Mex

new peso NP		2000	2001	2002
GDP	NP	5.5tr	5.7tr	
	US$	583bn	617bn	
per capita	US$	5,590	6,154	
Growth	%	6.6	-0.3	
Inflation	%	9.5	6.4	
Debt	US$	172bn	170bn	
Def exp[a]	NP	50bn	55bn	
	US$	5.3bn	5.9bn	
Def bdgt	NP	28.4bn	30.1bn	31.2bn
	US$	3.0bn	3.2bn	3.2bn
FMA (US)	US$	0.8m	1.0m	1.1m
US$1=NP		9.46	9.34	9.7

[a] Incl spending on paramilitary forces.

Population	100,400,000 Chiapas region 4%		
Age	13–17	18–22	23–32
Men	5,348,000	4,901,000	9,171,000
Women	5,193,000	4,795,000	9,166,000

Nicaragua Nic

Cordoba oro Co		2000	2001	2002
GDP	Co	30.4bn	33.4bn	
	US$	2.4bn	2.5bn	
per capita	US$	480	480	
Growth	%	4.3	3.0	
Inflation	%	11.6	8.3	
Debt	US$	7.0bn	6.0bn	
Def exp	Co	306m	372m	
	US$	24m	28m	
Def bdgt	Co	306m	372m	322m
	US$	24m	28m	23m
FMA (US)	US$	0.2m	0.2m	
US$1=Co		12.7	13.4	14.2

Population			5,246,000
Age	13–17	18–22	23–32
Men	339,000	287,000	366,000
Women	299,000	254,000	396,000

Panama Pan

balboa B		2000	2001	2002
GDP	B	10.2bn	10.4bn	
	US$	10.2bn	10.4bn	
per capita	US$	3,580	3,580	
Growth	%	2.5	2.0	
Inflation	%	1.4	1.8	
Debt	US$	7.0	2.6	
Sy bdgt	B	ε130m	ε135m	
	US$	130m	135m	
FMA (US)	US$	0.1m	0.1m	
US$1=B		1.0	1.0	1.0

Population			2,845,000
Age	13–17	18–22	23–32
Men	146,000	137,000	261,000
Women	139,000	131,000	252,000

Paraguay Py

guarani Pg		2000	2001	2002
GDP	Pg	26.9tr	29.0tr	
	US$	7.7bn	7.1bn	
per capita	US$	1,400	1,260	
Growth	%	-0.4	0.8	
Inflation	%	9.2	7.7	
Debt	US$	3.1bn	3.3bn	
Def exp	Pg	315bn	320bn	
	US$	90m	78m	
Def bdgt	Pg	287bn	262bn	
	US$	83m	64m	
FMA (US)	US$	0.2m	0.2m	
US$1=Pg		3,486	4,105	6,250

Population			5,607,000
Age	13–17	18–22	23–32
Men	315,000	271,000	446,000
Women	304,000	262,000	432,000

Peru Pe

new sol NS		2000	2001	2002
GDP	NS	186bn	190bn	
	US$	53bn	54bn	
per capita	US$	2,070	2,070	
Growth	%	3.1	0.2	
Inflation	%	3.8	2.0	
Debt	US$	29.5bn	28.5bn	
Def exp	NS	3.1bn	3.2bn	
	US$	888m	913m	
Def bdgt	NS	2.9bn	3.0bn	2.7bn
	US$	980m	849m	762m
FMA (US)	US$	0.5m	0.5m	0.5m
US$1=NS		3.49	3.51	3.50

Population			26,100,000
Age	13–17	18–22	23–32
Men	1,369,000	1,309,000	2,314,000
Women	1,356,000	1,300,000	2,304,000

Suriname Sme

guilder gld		2000	2001	2002
GDP	gld	360bn	380bn	
	US$	400m	500m	
per capita	US$	1,050	1,100	
Growth	%	2.9	3.4	
Inflation	%	59.1	50.2	
Debt	US$	296m		
Def exp	gld	17bn	20bn	
	US$	13m	9m	
Def bdgt	gld	17bn	20bn	20bn
	US$	12.9m	9.2m	9.2m
FMA (US)	US$	0.1m	0.1m	0.3m
US$1=gld		1,322	2,179	2,178

Population			**420,000**
Age	13–17	18–22	23–32
Men	22,000	18,000	32,000
Women	22,000	18,000	33,000

Trinidad and Tobago TT

dollar TT$		2000	2001	2002
GDP	TT$	45.7bn	52.7bn	
	US$	7.3bn	8.5bn	
per capita	US$	5,585	6,507	
Growth	%	4.8	4.5	
Inflation	%	5.6	2.5	
Debt	US$	2.9bn	2.7bn	
Def exp	TT$	ε390m	428m	
	US$	62m	69m	
Def bdgt	TT$	390m	428m	420m
	US$	62m	69m	67m
FMA (US)	US$	0.4m	0.1m	0.4m
US$1=TT$		6.3	6.2	6.3

Population			**1,300,000**
Age	13–17	18–22	23–32
Men	73,000	66,000	103,000
Women	72,000	65,000	106,000

Uruguay Ury

peso pU		2000	2001	2002
GDP	pU	242bn	244bn	
	US$	20.0bn	18.3bn	
per capita	US$	5,950	5,381	
Growth	%	-1.3	-3.1	
Inflation	%	4.8	4.4	
Debt	US$	8.2bn	8.7bn	
Def exp	pU	4.7bn	4.8bn	
	US$	378m	358m	
Def bdgt	pU	4.7bn	4.8bn	4.8bn
	US$	378m	358m	206m
FMA (US)	US$	0.3m	0.4m	1.4m
US$1=pU		12.1	13.3	23

Population			**3,400,000**
Age	13–17	18–22	23–32
Men	129,000	136,000	254,000
Women	124,000	132,000	247,000

Venezuela Ve

bolivar Bs		2000	2001	2002	2003
GDP	Bs	82.4tr	94tr		
	US$	121bn	130bn		
per capita	US$	5,030	5,284		
Growth	%	3.2	2.7		
Inflation	%	16.2	12.5		
Debt	US$	38.2bn	40.1bn		
Def exp	Bs	1.4tr	1.3tr		
	US$	1,400m	1,900m		
Def bdgt	Bs	949bn	1,400bn	1,326bn	
	US$	1,395m	1,933m	1,053m	
FMA (US)	US$	0.4m	0.5m	0.5m	0.7m
US$1=Bs		680	724	1,260	

Population			**24,600,000**
Age	13–17	18–22	23–32
Men	1,255,000	1,200,000	2,067,000
Women	1,208,000	1,160,000	2,010,000

Table 22 **Arms orders and deliveries, Caribbean and Latin America, 1998–2002**

	Country supplier	Classification ⇩	Designation	Quantity ⇩	Order date	Delivery date	Comment ⇩
Argentina	US	hel	**UH-1H**	8	1996	1998	Acquired ex US
	US	MPA	**P-3B**	8	1996	1997	Deliveries to 1999
	US	LAW	**M72**	900	1997	1999	
	US	FGA	**A-4M**	8	1997	1999	Further 11 for spares
	US	hel	**UH-1H**	8	1997	1998	
	US	tkr ac	**KC-135**	1	1998	2000	
	Fr	AO	***Durance***	1	1998	1999	
	dom	trg	**IA-63**	1	1999	1999	
	US	APC	**M113A2**	90	1999		Ex-US Army
Bahamas	US	tpt	**C-26**	2	1997	1998	
	US	PCO	***Bahamas***	2	1997	1999	Contract options for 4 more
Bolivia	dom	PCR	**PCR**	23	1997	1999	
	US	FGA	**TA-4J**	18	1997	1998	12 for op and 6 for spare parts. Ex-USN ac
Brazil	dom	AAM	**MAA-1**	40	1976	1998	
	col	FGA	**AM-X**	54	1980	1989	Deliveries continue. 2 delivered 1997
	Fr	hel	**AS-350**	77	1985	1988	Prod under licence continues at low rate
	Ge	SSK	**Type 209**	4	1985	1989	Last delivered 2000
	Ge	PCC	***Grauna***	12	1986	1993	Last 2 delivered 1999
	dom	MRL	***Astros* 2**	20	1994	1998	4 ordered 1996, 16 1998
	Be	MBT	***Leopard* 1**	87	1995	1997	55 delivered 1998–99
	dom	FF	***Niteroi***	6	1995	1999	Upgrade to 2001
	dom	trg	**AL-X**	99	1995	2003	
	dom	AEW	**EMB-145**	8	1997	2001	5 AEW, 3 Remote Sensing
	Fr	tpt	**F-406**	5	1997	1999	For delivery 1999–2001
	dom	ATGW	**MSS-1.2**	40	1997	2001	Dev
	col	FGA	**AM-X**	13	1998	2001	3rd batch
	Kwt	FGA	**A-4**	23	1998	1998	Ex-Kwt Air Force. Includes 3 TA-4
	Il	FGA	**F-5**	48	1998	2000	Upgrade
	UK	arty	**105mm**	18	1999	2001	
	Swe	HWT	**Tp-62**	50	1999	2000	For *Tupi* SSK
	US	MPA	**P-3A/B**	12	1999	2002	Plus a further 4
	col	hel	**AS532**	8	2000	2002	Surv and border patrol
	Fr	CV	***Sao Paulo* (Fr *Foch*)**	1	2000	2001	Delivered 2001
	It	tpt	**C-130H**	10	2001	2001	Second-hand
	CH	FGA	**F-5**	15	2002		Second-hand
Chile	Ge	FAC	**Type 148**	6	1995	1997	2 delivered 1997, 4 1998
	Be	APC	**M-113**	128	1995	1998	
	UK	ASSM	**MM-38 *Exocet***	4	1996	1998	*Excalibur* ASSM; refurbished in Fr
	Fr	MBT	**AMX-30B**	60	1996	1998	Ex-Fr Army. 40 delivered
	US	tpt ac	***Caravan* 1**	3	1996	1998	
	UK	arty	**M101**	100	1996	1998	Upgrade
	col	MRL	***Rayo***		1996	1999	Dev Programme
	US	tpt	**R-182**	8	1997	1998	
	RSA	arty	**M71**	24	1997	1998	
	Ge	PFM	***Tiger***	2	1997	1998	
	Fr	SSK	***Scorpene***	2	1997	2003	1st delivery 2003, 2nd 2005

	Country supplier	Classification ⇩	Designation	Quantity ⇩	Order date	Delivery date	Comment ⇩
	US	hel	**UH-60**	12	1998	1998	First delivery Jul 1998
	dom	MPA	**P-3**	2	1998	1999	Upgrade for up to 8
	Nl	MBT	***Leopard* 1**	200	1998	1999	Deliveries completed in 2000
	US	FGA	**F-16**	10	2000	2004	Possibly up to 12 req
Colombia	Sp	tpt	**CN-235**	3	1996	1998	
	dom	utl	***Gavilan***	12	1997	1998	
	US	hel	**B-212**	6	1998	1998	First 3 to arrive in Jul/Aug 1998
	US	hel	**UH-60L**	6	1998	1999	For delivery Sep 1999–Jan 2000
	US	hel	**UH-1H**	25	1998	1999	For delivery 1999
	US	hel	**MD-530F**	2	1998	1999	National Police
	US	hel	***Black Hawk***	18	2000	2001	For counter drug operations
	US	hel	**UH-1H**	42	2000	2001	For counter drug operations
	RF	hel	**Mi-17MD**	6	2001	2002	
Dominican Republic							
	Br	trg	***Super Tucano***	10	2001		
Ecuador	Il	AAM	***Python* 3**	100	1996	1999	
	US	ASW hel	**Bell 412EP**	2	1996	1998	1st delivered late 1998, 2nd early 1999
	RF	hel	**Mi-17**	7	1997	1998	
	Il	FGA	***Kfir***	2	1998	1999	Ex-IAF; also upgrade of 11
El Salvador	US	ACV	***Hummer***	2			
	US	hel	**MD-520N**	2	1997	1998	
Guatemala	dom	APC	***Danto***		1994	1998	For internal security duties
	Chl	trg	**T-35B**	10	1997	1998	Ex-Chl Air Force
Guyana	UK	PCO	***Orwell***	1	2000	2001	
Honduras	US	FGA	***Super Mystere***	11	1997	1998	
Jamaica	Fr	hel	**AS-555**	4	1997	1999	
Mexico	RF	tpt	**An-32**	2			
	dom	PCO	***Holzinger* 2000**	8	1997	1997	Final delivery 2001
	Ukr	hel	**Mi-17**	12	1995	1997	*Erint* delivered 1998
	US	FF	***Knox***	3	1996	1998	Third delivered 2000
	US	LST	***Newport***	1	1998	1999	Excess Defense Articles (EDA)
	US	hel	**MD-520N**	8	1998	1999	
	RF	hel	**Mi-26**	1	2000	2000	
	Br	MPA	**EMB-145**	3	2001		Including 1 AEW&C
Paraguay	ROC	FGA	**F-5E**	4	1997	1998	Total of 12 in all
	ROC	PCI		2	1998	1999	Free transfer
Peru	Bel	FGA	**Su-25**	18	1995	1998	
	Bel	FGA	**MiG-29**	18	1995	1996	Deliveries 1996–97
	Fr	ASSM	***Exocet***	8	1995	1997	Deliveries to 1998
	It	ASSM	***Otomat***	12	1995	1997	Deliveries to 1998
	RF	FGA	**MiG-29**	3	1998	1998	Plus spares
	Cz	arty	**D-30**	6	1998	1998	
	Cz	trg	**ZLIN-242L**	18	1998	1998	
	RF	tpt	**Il-103**	6	1999	1999	
	US	PCI		6	2000	2000	For coastguard

	Country supplier	Classification ⇩	Designation	Quantity ⇩	Order date	Delivery date	Comment ⇩
Suriname	Sp	MPA	**C-212-400**	2	1997	1998	Second delivered 1999
Uruguay	Il	MBT	**T-55**	11	1996	1997	Deliveries to 1998
	Cz	MRL	**RM-70**	1	1998	1998	
	Cz	SPA	**2S1**	6	1998	1998	
Venezuela	Pl	tpt	**M-28**	12	1996	1996	Deliveries 1996–98
	Sp	MPA	**C-212**	3	1997	1998	Plus modernisation of existing C-212-200
	US	FGA	**F-16B**	2	1997	1999	
	US	hel	**B-212**	2	1997	1999	US grant aid for counter-drug op
	Fr	hel	**AS-532**	6	1997	2000	
	US	hel	**UH-1H**	5	1997	1999	
	Swe	ATGW	**AT-4**		1997	1999	
	US	FF	***Lupo***	2	1998	2001	Upgrade and modernisation
	Swe	radar	***Giraffe***	4	1998	1999	4 truck-mounted systems
	It	trg	**SF-260E**	12	1998	1999	2nd batch of 12 possible
	US	PCI	**PCI**	12	1998	1999	Aluminium 80 foot craft
	US	PCI	**PCI**	10	1998	1999	Aluminium 54 foot craft
	It	trg	**MB-339FD**	10	1998	2000	Req for up to 24. Deliveries to 2001
	It	FGA	**AMX**	8	1998	2001	In cooperation with Br. Up to 24 req
	US	SAR hel	**AB-412EP**	4	1998	1999	Option for a further 2
	Il	SAM	***Barak*-1**	6	1999	2000	Part of Guardian Air Defence modernisation
	Swe	SAM	**RBS-70**	500	1999	2000	Includes AT-4 ATGW
	Fr	radar	***Flycatcher***	3	1999	2000	Deliveries to early 2002. Part of Guardian
	ROK	AO	***Ciudad Bolivar***	1	1998	2001	Delivered 2001

Sub-Saharan Africa

Despite the weak global economy, growth in Africa held up well in 2001, compared to other regions of the world. Although slowing slightly, African growth is expected to continue into 2002. Oil-producing countries benefited from the high price of oil throughout most of 2001, and despite falling after 11 September, oil prices returned to their previous level during the first half of 2002. The absence of the severe floods or droughts that affected many countries in 1999 and 2000 helped support agricultural output across much of the region; however, some countries were held back by the low prices of non-oil commodities and the cyclical falls in metals prices. Structural reforms are still lagging in much of the region. Prospects for growth would be enhanced by better governance and public service delivery, infrastructure improvements and liberalisation policies. Although the decrease in the number of armed conflicts has contributed to an improved forecast for growth and policies, initiatives at a multilateral level are needed to provide the basis for sounder economic recovery. Of particular importance is the New Partnership for Africa's Development. This emphasises African ownership, leadership and accountability in improving the foundation for growth and eradicating poverty. In addition, 20 of the poorest African countries are now eligible for debt relief under the enhanced IMF–World Bank Initiative for Heavily Indebted Poor Countries, and a number of others will qualify during 2002. Further ongoing international support is needed to fight HIV/AIDS, which continues to affect a huge proportion of the young and people of working age in many southern African countries including a large portion of some countries' armed forces.

South Africa, which accounts for 40% of sub-Saharan African GDP, was affected by lower commodity prices and the global slowdown. The rand weakened sharply during 2001, before stabilising somewhat in 2002 following supportive action by the central bank. Contributing to this weakness were regional uncertainties in the wake of events in Zimbabwe, delays in the domestic privatisation programme, and a general weakness in currencies where commodities comprise an important share of exports. Despite this background, South Africa increased its defence budget for 2002–03 by 15% from the previous year, about 10% higher than originally planned. The increase of around R2.4bn, over the revised 2001 budget, is primarily to pay for the South African National Defence Force's controversial arms-acquisition programme, and to fulfil its widening commitment to regional peace-keeping. The rand's weakness has increased the cost of this significantly, from an original R30.4bn to a projected total of R52.7bn. Originally, the 12-year procurement package comprising four naval corvettes, three submarines, 30 light utility helicopters, 24 trainer aircraft and 28 fighter aircraft was expected to cost R30.4bn; however, inflation-related price escalation and projected exchange-rate movements have increased the projected cost to R52.7bn. Annual payments will reach a peak of R7.7bn in 2005/06. Projected annual commitments are summarised in table 23.

Table 23 **South African 12 year arms procurement forcast**

Rand m	
2000	2,639
2001	4,047
2002	6,331
2003	7,199
2004	7,194
2005	7,704
2006	5,960
2007	4,491
2008	3,502
2009	1,314
2010	1,182
2011	1,160
Total	52,723

The fastest-growing South African budget line of recent years is the Special Defence Account from which acquisitions are funded. By contrast, annual growth for the operation of the Landward Defence, Maritime Defence and Air Defence forces has been restricted to average growth of just 1.6% p.a. The considerable growth in the Command and Control budget (illustrated in table 24) reflects the establishment of the Regional Joint Task Force headquarters, under which expenditure previously incurred by the different arms of the SANDF has been consolidated. Following reports in the domestic media suggesting that the arms-acquisition procurement process had been corrupted, a joint investigation by the Auditor-General, the

Table 24 **South African Defence Budget by Programme, 1998–2004** Rand m (US$m)

	1998	1999	2000	Revised 2001	Budget 2002	Plan 2003	Plan 2004
	Rm	Rm	Rm	Rm	Rm	Rm	Rm
Administration	347	535	463	542	538	556	583
Landward Defence	3,556	3,290	3,105	3,483	3,477	3,560	3,649
Air Defence	1,900	1,962	1,947	1,945	2,018	2,080	2,155
Maritime Defence	804	844	881	929	979	1,039	1,097
Military Health Support	939	928	971	1,095	1,144	1,184	1,237
Defence Intelligence	130	148	127	151	149	150	161
Joint Support	1,210	1,128	1,551	1,668	1,942	2,012	2,086
Command and Control	46	37	162	406	537	269	235
Special Defence Account	1,624	1,841	4,721	5,830	7,625	8,484	8,676
Total	**10,561**	**10,717**	**13,932**	**16,052**	**18,414**	**19,338**	**19,883**
Total US$m	*1,920*	*1,728*	*1,962*	*2,031*	*1,615*	*n.a.*	*n.a.*

Public Protector and the National Director of Public Prosecution found that there was no evidence of improper or unlawful conduct by the government and that there are no grounds to suggest that the governments contracting process was flawed. It was confirmed in April 2002 that South Africa will proceed with its planned acquisition of a second batch of 12 *Hawk* lead-in fighter trainers. In 2001, South African forces were involved in peace-support operations in the Democratic Republic of Congo, Burundi and the Horn of Africa.

Angola announced a total state budget of $5bn for 2002 with defence officially allocated just $250m. Actual defence spending in Angola bears little resemblance to the declared budget. In 2001, for example, defence expenditure is estimated to have been US$1.5bn compared to the official figure of just US$500m. In recent years, it is estimated that real defence spending has consumed as much as 40% of the whole budget. The cease-fire signed in April 2002, between government forces and UNITA, suggests that Angola may be able to reduce its excessive military spending and devote more money to humanitarian assistance, which claimed just 2% of the 2002 budget. The government faces the difficult job of demobilising up to 50,000 rebel troops, and despite EU aid of $117m to help facilitate the process, there is a strong chance that many of the soldiers may turn to banditry to survive.

Nigeria boosted defence spending in the 2002 budget. Funds earmarked for defence rose to N61.4bn from N59bn in 2001. The increase reflects the continuing programme to professionalise the armed forces and enhance the welfare of its personnel after years of neglect.

Despite a reduction in rebel activity in the north of the country and the decision to pull its military forces out of the Democratic Republic of Congo, **Uganda** increased its defence budget from Ush229bn ($130m) in 2001, to Ush250bn ($140m) in 2002. The increase is part of a planned modernisation of the Uganda People's Army that will result in professional forces as well as the acquisition of new military equipment. President Museveni has indicated that he is prepared to commit up to $700m to the project over the next few years. IMF officials and opposition politicians are unsupportive, however, believing that military spending is already too high. The IMF has also suggested that all defence expenditures, even those described as classified, should be audited and that failure to do so could jeopardise future funding for Uganda. This follows two high-profile cases in recent years, in which Uganda paid vastly inflated prices for 62 T-55 tanks and 4 Mi-24 helicopters that were delivered without documentation or ammunition or personnel qualified to operate or repair them.

The continuing political violence and economic mismanagement in **Zimbabwe** show no sign of easing. Invasion of white farms by 'war veterans' has hit the agricultural sector hard, and the demise of the tourist trade and threats to nationalise the country's mining industry have also contributed to the implosion of the economy. Inflation soared to 76.7% in 2001 while growth plummeted as the economy contracted by 7.3%. The value of the currency collapsed to the extent that Zimbabwe cannot cover the cost of essential imports, including fuel and electricity. The 2002 budget was optimistically labelled a 'people-oriented budget' and called for massive increases in government spending, double for the military and healthcare, and triple for agriculture. However, with government revenue likely to fall as the tax base shrinks and businesses close, there will not be enough money to meet these spending goals. Although doubled in 2002, the defence budget failed to take into account the cost of Zimbabwe's intervention in the Democratic Republic of Congo, where one third of its armed forces are deployed to shore up the DRC government against rebels at an estimated cost of US$30m a month.

There were developments in the long-running civil war in the **Sudan** as the government mounted a ground and air offensive to create a *cordon sanitaire* around the most productive oilfields, in the west. Since the successful exploration for oil by foreign companies and the opening of a pipeline, the government has seen extra revenue of over US$1m a day, much of which has been spent on the military. Rebel forces see oil production facilities as legitimate military targets and attacked facilities in the south of the country.

Sudan has acquired 12 MiG-29 fighters and several Mi-24 helicopter gunships from Russia, which is keen to replace China as Sudan's leading supplier of major weapons systems. Moscow has offered to maintain and upgrade Sudan's military equipment and supply sophisticated weapons, in exchange for a licence to explore and develop Sudan's energy sector. Sudan is largely self-sufficient in small- and medium-size armaments.

Angola Ang

kwanza		2000	2001	2002
GDP	US$	8.8bn	8.8bn	
per capita	US$	670	650	
Growth	%	3.0	3.2	
Inflation	%	325	152	
Debt	US$	10.86bn	11.0bn	
Def exp	US$	ε2,000m	ε1,500m	
Def bdgt	US$	825m	670m	250m
FMA (Fr)	US$	0.1m		
FMA (US)	US$	0m	0m	0.1m
US$1=kwanza		10	17.9	38.9

Population			**13,500,000**
Ovimbundu 37% **Kimbundu** 25% **Bakongo** 13%			
Age	**13–17**	**18–22**	**23–32**
Men	689,000	583,000	888,000
Women	691,000	587,000	906,000

Benin Bn

CFA fr		2000	2001	2002
GDP	fr	1.6tr	1.75tr	
	US$	2.3bn	2.4bn	
per capita	US$	360	370	
Growth	%	5.0	5.8	
Inflation	%	4.2	3.8	
Debt	US$	1.4bn	1.4bn	
Def exp	fr	ε21bn	ε31bn	
	US$	34m	42m	
Def bdgt	fr	ε26bn	ε31bn	ε34bn
	US$	37m	42m	47m
FMA (Fr)	US$	4m		
FMA (US)	US$	0.4m	0.4m	0.4m
US$1=fr		711	733	718

Population			**6,400,000**
Age	**13–17**	**18–22**	**23–32**
Men	386,000	320,000	449,000
Women	393,000	333,000	486,000

Botswana Btwa

pula P		2000	2001	2002
GDP	P	25.2bn	31.8bn	
	US$	4.9bn	5.5bn	
per capita	US$	3,120	3,420	
Growth	%	8.7	7.1	
Inflation	%	7.9	7.2	
Debt	US$	385m	358m	
Def exp	P	ε1,400m	ε1,200m	
	US$	249.6m	207m	
Def bdgt	P	1,243m	1,196m	1,720m
	US$	243m	206m	277m

Btwa contd		2000	2001	2002
FMA (US)	US$	0.5m	1.6m	1.6m
US$1=P		5.1	5.8	6.2

Population			**1,600,000**
Age	**13–17**	**18–22**	**23–32**
Men	107,000	90,000	140,000
Women	110,000	93,000	143,000

Burkina Faso BF

CFA fr		2000	2001	2002
GDP	fr	1.56tr	1.71tr	
	US$	2.2bn	2.3bn	
per capita	US$	190	200	
Growth	%	5.7	5.8	
Inflation	%	-0.2	3.0	
Debt	US$	1.3bn	1.3bn	
Def exp	fr	ε25.3bn	ε26.7bn	
	US$	35m	36m	
Def bdgt	fr	ε25.3bn	ε26.7bn	ε27.5bn
	US$	35m	36m	38m
FMA (Fr)	US$	3m		
FMA (US)	US$	0m	0m	0m
US$1=fr		711	733	718

Population			**11,900,000**
Age	**13–17**	**18–22**	**23–32**
Men	730,000	595,000	859,000
Women	702,000	575,000	888,000

Burundi Bu

franc fr		2000	2001	2002
GDP	fr	511bn	549bn	
	US$	710m	660m	
per capita	US$	110	100	
Growth	%	-2.3	3.3	
Inflation	%	24.3	8.0	
Debt	US$	1.1bn	1.1bn	
Def exp	fr	ε30bn	ε30bn	
	US$	42m	36m	
Def bdgt	fr	26bn	27bn	29bn
	US$	36m	32m	33m
FMA (US)	US$	0m	0m	0m
US$1=fr		720	830	868

Population	**ε6,500,000** **Hutu** 85% **Tutsi** 14%		
Age	**13–17**	**18–22**	**23–32**
Men	455,000	364,000	541,000
Women	414,000	334,000	502,000

Cameroon Crn

CFA fr		2000	2001	2002
GDP	fr	6.3tr	6.9tr	
	US$	8.8bn	9.5bn	
per capita	US$	595	624	
Growth	%	-2.3	3.3	
Inflation	%	0.8	2.8	
Debt	US$	9.2bn	9.0bn	
Def exp	fr	87.6bn	90bn	
	US$	123m	122m	
Def bdgt	fr	87.6bn	90bn	95bn
	US$	123m	122m	132m
FMA (US)	US$	0.2m	0.2m	0.2m
FMA (Fr)	US$	8m		
US$1=fr		711	733	718

Population			**15,200,000**
Age	13–17	18–22	23–32
Men	886,000	766,000	1,157,000
Women	884,000	768,000	1,175,000

Cape Verde CV

escudo E		2000	2001	2002
GDP	E	28bn	30bn	
	US$	240m	240m	
per capita	US$	570	570	
Growth	%	6.8	3.0	
Inflation	%	-2.4	3.7	
Debt	US$	300m	344m	
Def exp	E	ε500m	ε550m	
	US$	4.3m	4.5m	
Def bdgt	E	500m	550m	600m
	US$	4.3m	4.5m	5m
FMA (US)	US$	0.1m	0.1m	0.1m
FMA (Fr)	US$			
US$1=E		115	123	119

Population			**430,000**
Age	13–17	18–22	23–32
Men	27,000	24,000	37,000
Women	28,000	26,000	41,000

Central African Republic CAR

CFA fr		2000	2001	2002
GDP	fr	715bn	699bn	
	US$	1.0bn	1.0bn	
per capita	US$	269	251	
Growth	%	2.6	1.6	
Inflation	%	3.1	3.7	
Debt	US$	745m	706m	
Def exp	fr	ε10bn	ε11bn	
	US$	14m	15m	

CAR contd		2000	2001	2002
Def bdgt	fr	10bn	11bn	15bn
	US$	14m	15m	21m
FMA[a] (US)	US$	0.1m	0.1m	0.1m
FMA (Fr)	US$	4.0m		
US$1=fr		711	733	718

Population			**3,800,000**
Age	13–17	18–22	23–32
Men	216,000	170,000	304,000
Women	214,000	177,000	302,000

Chad Cha

CFA fr		2000	2001	2002
GDP	fr	1,016bn	1,236bn	
	US$	1.4bn	1.7bn	
per capita	US$	180	210	
Growth	%	1.0	8.9	
Inflation	%	3.8	12.4	
Debt	US$	1.1bn	960m	
Def exp	fr	ε10bn	ε10bn	
	US$	14m	13m	
Def bdgt	fr	ε10bn	ε10bn	ε10bn
	US$	14m	13m	14m
FMA (Fr)	US$	8m		
FMA (US)	US$	0.1m	0.2m	0.1m
US$1=fr		711	733	718

Population			**8,100,000**
Age	13–17	18–22	23–32
Men	408,000	332,000	518,000
Women	408,000	333,000	527,000

Congo RC

CFA fr		2000	2001	2002
GDP	fr	2.1tr	2.0tr	
	US$	3.0bn	2.8bn	
per capita	US$	990	890	
Growth	%	7.9	3.3	
Inflation	%	0.4	-0.5	
Debt	US$	5.3bn	9.9bn	
Def exp	fr	ε52bn	ε60bn	
	US$	73m	82m	
Def bdgt	fr	ε52bn	ε60bn	ε65bn
	US$	73m	82m	90m
FMA (US)	US$	0m	0m	0.1m
FMA (Fr)	US$	1.0m		
US$1=fr		711	733	718

Population **3,100,000**

Kongo 48% **Sangha** 20% **Teke** 17% **M'Bochi** 12% **European** mostly French 3%

Age	13–17	18–22	23–32
Men	188,000	148,000	235,000
Women	177,000	141,000	226,000

Côte D'Ivoire CI

CFA fr		2000	2001	2002
GDP	fr	6.7tr	6.8tr	
	US$	9.4bn	9.2bn	
per capita	US$	590	560	
Growth	%	-2.3	-0.9	
Inflation	%	2.4	4.4	
Debt	US$	12.1bn	11.8bn	
Def exp	fr	ε58bn	ε60bn	
	US$	81m	81m	
Def bdgt	fr	ε58bn	ε60bn	ε65bn
	US$	81m	81m	90m
FMA (US)	US$	0.1m	0m	0m
FMA (Fr)	US$	5.0m		
US$1=fr		711	733	718

Population			**16,300,000**
Age	**13–17**	**18–22**	**23–32**
Men	1,068,000	842,000	1,212,000
Women	1,063,000	845,000	1,208,000

Democratic Republic of Congo DROC

congolese franc fr		2000	2001	2002
GDP	US$	4.7bn	4.5bn	
per capita	US$	90	80	
Growth	%	-7.0	-4.0	
Inflation	%	553	299	
Debt	US$	12.8bn	13bn	
Def exp	US$	ε400m	ε400m	
Def bdgt	US$	ε400m	ε400m	
FMA (US)	US$	0m	0m	0.1m

Population **ε52,500,000**

Bantu and Hamitic 45%; **minority groups** include Hutus and Tutsis

Age	**13–17**	**18–22**	**23–32**
Men	3,150,000	2,511,000	3,620,000
Women	3,112,000	2,502,000	3,652,000

Djibouti Dj

franc fr		2000	2001	2002
GDP	fr	96bn	102bn	
	US$	540m	580m	
per capita	US$	850	915	
Growth	%	0.7	2.0	
Inflation	%	2.4	1.8	
Debt	US$	370m	381m	
Def exp	fr	ε4.0bn	ε4.0bn	
	US$	23m	23m	
Def bdgt	fr	ε4.0bn	4.0bn	ε4.0bn
	US$	23m	23m	23m

Dj contd		2000	2001	2002
FMA (US)	US$	0.4m	0.9m	
FMA (Fr)	US$	5.0m		
US$1=fr		177	177	177

Population **632,000** **Somali** 60% **Afar** 35%

Age	**13–17**	**18–22**	**23–32**
Men	42,000	35,000	57,000
Women	41,000	35,000	62,000

Equatorial Guinea EG

CFA fr		2000	2001	2002
GDP	fr	888bn	1,000bn	
	US$	1,250m	1,360m	
per capita	US$	2,750	3,030	
Growth	%	16.9	40.7	
Inflation	%	6.0	12.0	
Debt	US$	217m	101m	
Def exp	fr	ε2.8bn	ε3.0bn	
	US$	3.9m	4.1m	
Def bdgt	fr	ε2.8bn	ε3.0bn	ε3.2bn
	US$	3.9m	4.1m	4.5m
FMA (Fr)	US$	1.0m		
US$1=fr		711	733	718

Population			**450,000**
Age	**13–17**	**18–22**	**23–32**
Men	28,000	22,000	37,000
Women	28,000	23,000	37,000

Eritrea Er

nakfa		2000	2001	2002
GDP	US$	ε650m	ε840m	
per capita	US$	170	220	
Growth	%	-8.6	6.4	
Inflation	%	19.9	15.1	
Debt	US$	281m		
Def exp	US$	ε196m	ε176m	
Def bdgt	US$	ε136m	136m	120m
FMA (US)	US$	0m	0m	0.3m
US$1=nakfa		9.5	9.5	8.3

Population **ε3,800,000**

Tigrinya 50% **Tigre and Kunama** 40% **Afar** 4% **Saho** 3%

Age	**13–17**	**18–22**	**23–32**
Men	252,000	210,000	320,000
Women	249,000	209,000	319,000

Ethiopia Eth

birr EB		2000	2001	2002
GDP	EB	51.4bn	51.2bn	
	US$	6.5bn	6.1bn	
per capita	US$	110	95	
Growth	%	5.4	7.9	
Inflation	%	4.2	-7.2	
Debt	US$	5.5bn	5.4bn	
Def exp	EB	ε5.5bn	ε5.0bn	
	US$	669m	591m	
Def bdgt	EB	5.5bn	5.0bn	4.0bn
	US$	669m	591m	481m
FMA (US)	US$	0.2m	0.2m	0.6m
FMA (Fr)	US$	0.5m		
US$1=EB		8.21	8.45	8.30

Population ε64,500,000

Oromo 40% **Amhara and Tigrean** 32% **Sidamo** 9% **Shankella** 6% **Somali** 6% **Afar** 4%

Age	13–17	18–22	23–32
Men	3,977,000	3,172,000	4,780,000
Women	3,867,000	3,031,000	4,607,000

Gabon Gbn

CFA fr		2000	2001	2002
GDP	fr	3.5tr	3.7tr	
	US$	5.0bn	5.0bn	
per capita	US$	3,860	3,880	
Growth	%	-1.9	1.5	
Inflation	%	1.0	2.6	
Debt	US$	3.9bn	3.9bn	
Def exp	fr	ε89bn	ε90bn	
	US$	125m	122m	
Def bdgt	fr	ε89bn	ε90bn	ε90bn
	US$	125m	122m	125m
FMA (Fr)	US$	6.0m		
FMA (US)	US$	0.1m	0.1m	
US$1=fr		711	733	718

Population 1,300,000

Age	13–17	18–22	23–32
Men	78,000	60,000	97,000
Women	78,000	61,000	102,000

The Gambia Gam

dalasi D		2000	2001	2002
GDP	D	5.1bn	5.6bn	
	US$	400m	360m	
per capita	US$	300	260	
Growth	%	5.6	5.8	
Inflation	%	0.9	4.0	
Debt	US$	511m	538m	

Gam contd		2000	2001	2002
Def exp	D	40m	40m	
	US$	3.1m	2.6m	
Def bdgt	D	40m	40m	45m
	US$	3.1m	2.6m	2.4m
US$1=D		12.8	15.5	18.5

Population 1,400,000

Age	13–17	18–22	23–32
Men	69,000	57,000	85,000
Women	69,000	55,000	84,000

Ghana Gha

cedi C		2000	2001	2002
GDP	C	25.5tr	38.1tr	
	US$	4.7bn	5.3bn	
per capita	US$	242	270	
Growth	%	3.7	4.0	
Inflation	%	25.2	33.0	
Debt	US$	6.7bn	6.9bn	
Def exp[a]	C	219bn	250bn	
	US$	40m	35m	
Def bdgt	C	219bn	250bn	328bn
	US$	40m	35m	42m
FMA (US)	US$	0.5m	0.8m	0.9m
US$1=C		5,455	7,170	7,850

[a] Defence and security bdgt including police

Population 19,700,000

Age	13–17	18–22	23–32
Men	1,227,000	1,015,000	1,511,000
Women	1,221,000	1,013,000	1,523,000

Guinea Gui

franc fr		2000	2001	2002
GDP	fr	6.2tr	5.9tr	
	US$	3.6bn	3.0bn	
per capita	US$	450	370	
Growth	%	2.0	2.9	
Inflation	%	6.8	6.8	
Debt	US$	3.4bn	3.2bn	
Def exp	fr	ε80bn	ε90bn	
	US$	46m	46m	
Def bdg	fr	ε80bn	ε90bn	ε85bn
	US$	46m	46m	43m
FMA (US)	US$	0.2m	3.2m	0.2m
FMA (Fr)	US$	4m		
US$1=fr		1,746	1,950	1,975

Population 8,300,000

Age	13–17	18–22	23–32
Men	449,000	371,000	554,000
Women	458,000	375,000	559,000

Population			2,200,000
Age	13–17	18–22	23–32
Men	132,000	115,000	172,000
Women	130,000	115,000	173,000

Guinea-Bissau GuB

CFA fr		2000	2001	2002
GDP	fr	136bn	149bn	
	US$	190m	200m	
per capita	US$	160	170	
Growth	%	7.5	4.0	
Inflation	%	8.6	5.0	
Debt	US$	797m	700m	
Def exp	US$	3m	3m	
FMA (US)	US$	0.1m	0.1m	0.1m
US$1=fr		711	733	718

Population			1,200,000
Age	13–17	18–22	23–32
Men	67,000	59,000	97,000
Women	68,000	56,000	88,000

Kenya Kya

shilling sh		2000	2001	2002
GDP	sh	776bn	795bn	
	US$	10.2bn	10.1bn	
per capita	US$	330	320	
Growth	%	-0.2	1.1	
Inflation	%	6.2	0.8	
Debt	US$	6.0bn	6.0bn	
Def exp	sh	ε22bn	ε24.7bn	
	US$	278m	315m	
Def bdgt	sh	16.9bn	19bn	21bn
	US$	222m	242m	268m
FMA (US)[a]	US$	0.4m	1.4m	0.6m
US$1=sh		76.2	78.5	78.3

[a] Excl ACRI and East Africa Regional funding

Population	31,3005,000 Kikuyu ε22–32%		
Age	13–17	18–22	23–32
Men	2,073,000	1,791,000	2,588,000
Women	2,065,000	1,794,000	2,616,000

Lesotho Ls

maloti M		2000	2001	2002
GDP	M	5.2bn	6.8bn	
	US$	730m	800m	
per capita	US$	346	359	
Growth	%	3.2	2.9	
Inflation	%	6.1	7.8	
Debt	US$	700m	715m	
Def exp	M	190m	210m	
	US$	27.4m	24.4m	
Def bdgt	M	190m	210m	230m
	US$	27m	24m	22m
FMA (US)	US$	0.1m	0.1m	0.1m
US$1=M		7.1	8.6	10.1

Liberia Lb

dollar L$		2000	2001	2002
GDP	US$	450m	450m	
per capita	US$	150	145	
Growth	%	15.0		
Inflation	%	5.0		
Debt	US$	2.0bn	1.9bn	
Def exp	US$	ε25m	ε25m	
Def bdgt	US$	15m	15m	15m
US$1=L$[a]		1.0	1.0	1.0

Population	ε3,100,000 Americo-Liberians 5%		
Age	13–17	18–22	23–32
Men	177,000	147,000	204,000
Women	172,000	143,000	192,000

Madagascar Mdg

franc fr		2000	2001	2002
GDP	fr	26.81tr	30.9tr	
	US$	4.0bn	4.7bn	
per capita	US$	250	290	
Growth	%	4.8	6.7	
Inflation	%	11.9	5.0	
Debt	US$	4.7bn	4.6bn	
Def exp	fr	ε316bn	ε319bn	
	US$	46.7m	48.4m	
Def bdgt	fr	ε316bn	ε319bn	ε325bn
	US$	46.7m	48.4m	48.9m
FMA (US)	US$	0.2m	0.2m	0.2m
FMA (Fr)	US$	5m		
US$1=fr		6,767	6,588	6,640

Population			16,400,000
Age	13–17	18–22	23–32
Men	928,000	770,000	1,151,000
Women	905,000	752,000	1,140,000

Malawi Mlw

kwacha K		2000	2001	2002
GDP	K	97bn	127bn	
	US$	1.6bn	ε1.8bn	
per capita	US$	140	150	
Growth	%	1.7	2.8	
Inflation	%	29.6	27.2	
Debt	US$	2.8bn	2.8bn	
Def exp	K	380m	420m	
	US$	6.4m	5.8m	
Def bdgt	K	ε380m	ε420m	ε450m
	US$	6.4m	5.8m	5.9m
FMA (US)	US$	0.3m	0.4m	0.4m
US$1=K		59.5	72.1	76.4

Population			**11,600,000**
Age	**13–17**	**18–22**	**23–32**
Men	679,000	538,000	801,000
Women	673,000	531,000	829,000

Mali RMM

CFA fr		2000	2001	2002
GDP	fr	1.8tr	1.9tr	
	US$	2.5bn	2.6bn	
per capita	US$	220	220	
Growth	%	4.8	0.1	
Inflation	%	3.3	4.7	
Debt	US$	2.6bn	2.7bn	
Def exp	fr	45bn	47bn	
	US$	63m	64m	
Def bdgt	fr	45bn	47bn	50bn
	US$	63m	64m	69m
FMA (US)	US$	0.3m	0.5m	0.3m
FMA (Fr)	US$	4m	4m	
US$1=fr		711	733	718

Population		**11,700,000**	**Tuareg** 6–10%
Age	**13–17**	**18–22**	**23–32**
Men	663,000	534,000	792,000
Women	688,000	557,000	835,000

Mauritius Ms

rupee R		2000	2001	2002
GDP	R	106bn	132bn	
	US$	4.0bn	4.5bn	
per capita	US$	3,400	3,760	
Growth	%	3.6	6.7	
Inflation	%	5.3	4.4	
Debt	US$	2.3bn	2.4bn	
Def exp	R	235m	256m	
	US$	9m	9m	
Def bdgt	R	235m	256m	260m
	US$	9m	9m	9m

Ms contd		2000	2001	2002
FMA (US)	US$	0.1m	0.1m	0.1m
US$1=R		26.2	29.1	30.2

Population			**1,200,000**
Age	**13–17**	**18–22**	**23–32**
Men	51,000	55,000	99,000
Women	50,000	54,000	99,000

Mozambique Moz

metical M		2000	2001	2002
GDP	M	70.0tr	80.5tr	
	US$	4.5bn	3.9bn	
per capita	US$	270	210	
Growth	%	1.6	12.9	
Inflation	%	12.7	9.0	
Debt	US$	9.0bn	9.6bn	
Def exp	M	1.4tr	ε1.5tr	
	US$	81m	67m	69m
Def bdgt	M	1.4tr	ε1.5tr	ε1.6tr
	US$	81m	67m	69m
FMA (US)	US$	0.2m	0.2m	0.2m
US$1=M		15,447	20,703	23,117

Population			**18,600,000**
Age	**13–17**	**18–22**	**23–32**
Men	1,184,000	993,000	1,484,000
Women	1,193,000	1,008,000	1,521,000

Namibia Nba

dollar N$		2000	2001	2002
GDP	N$	24bn	26bn	
	US$	3.5bn	3.0bn	
per capita	US$	1,960	1,660	
Growth	%	3.3	2.7	
Inflation	%	9.3	9.2	
Debt	US$	313m	390m	
Def exp	N$	ε750m	ε800m	
	US$	109m	93m	
Def bdgt	N$	781m	ε800m	ε850m
	US$	113m	93m	84m
FMA (US)	US$	0.2m	0.2m	0.2m
US$1=N$		6.9	8.6	10.1

Population			**1,800,000**
Age	**13–17**	**18–22**	**23–32**
Men	115,000	95,000	144,000
Women	114,000	94,000	143,000

Niger Ngr

CFA fr		2000	2001	2002
GDP	fr	1.0tr	1.3tr	
	US$	1.9bn	1.6bn	
per capita	US$	170	140	
Growth	%	-1.4	5.1	
Inflation	%	2.9	4.0	
Debt	US$	1.6bn	1.3bn	
Def exp	fr	ε19bn	ε22bn	
	US$	27m	30m	
Def bdgt	fr	ε19bn	ε22bn	ε24bn
	US$	27m	30m	33m
FMA (US)	US$	0m	0.1m	0.1m
FMA (Fr)	US$	2m		
US$1=fr		711	733	718

Population **11,2008,000** **Tuareg** 8–10%

Age	13–17	18–22	23–32
Men	618,000	499,000	716,000
Women	621,000	506,000	745,000

Nigeria Nga

naira N		2000	2001	2002
GDP	N	ε4.0tr	ε4.4tr	
	US$	37bn	39bn	
per capita	US$	320	330	
Growth	%	3.8	4.0	
Inflation	%	6.9	18.9	
Debt	US$	29bn	31bn	
Def exp	US$	518m	526m	
Def bdgt	N	35bn	59bn	61bn
	US$	338m	517m	529m
FMA (US)	US$	10.5m	10.6m	6.7m
US$1=N		101	114	116

Population **ε116,900,000**

North Hausa and Fulani South-west Yoruba South-east Ibo; these tribes make up ε65% of population

Age	13–17	18–22	23–32
Men	7,652,000	6,693,000	10,056,000
Women	7,631,000	6,735,000	10,450,000

Rwanda Rwa

franc fr		2000	2001	2002
GDP	fr	789bn	763bn	
	US$	2.0bn	1.7bn	
per capita	US$	260	220	
Growth	%	6.0	6.2	
Inflation	%	3.9	3.5	
Debt	US$	1.3bn	1.3bn	
Def exp	fr	ε38bn	ε44bn	
	US$	98m	100m	

Rwa contd		2000	2001	2002
Def bdgt	fr	19bn	22bn	24bn
	US$	48m	505m	52m
FMA (US)	US$	0.2m	0m	0.1m
US$1=fr		389	442	457

Population **ε7,900,000** **Hutu** 80% **Tutsi** 19%

Age	13–17	18–22	23–32
Men	581,000	469,000	671,000
Women	597,000	486,000	703,000

Senegal Sen

CFA fr		2000	2001	2002
GDP	fr	3.3tr	3.4tr	
	US$	4.6bn	4.6bn	
per capita	US$	490	480	
Growth	%	5.5	5.7	
Inflation	%	0.7	3.0	
Debt	US$	3.4bn	3.4bn	
Def exp	fr	44bn	46bn	
	US$	62m	63m	
Def bdgt	fr	44bn	ε46bn	ε48bn
	US$	62m	63m	67m
FMA (US)	US$	0.8m	1.7m	1.2m
FMA (Fr)	US$	6m		
US$1=fr		711	733	718

Population **9,700,000**

Wolof 36% **Fulani** 17% **Serer** 17% **Toucouleur** 9% **Mandingo** 9% **Diola** 9%, of which 30–60% in Casamance)

Age	13–17	18–22	23–32
Men	617,000	500,000	729,000
Women	611,000	494,000	734,000

Seychelles Sey

rupee SR		2000	2001	2002
GDP	SR	3.3bn	3.6bn	
	US$	580m	620m	
per capita	US$	7,520	7,890	
Growth	%	1.4	-1.0	
Inflation	%	7.6	6.2	
Debt	US$	386m	293m	
Def exp	SR	60m	66m	
	US$	10m	11m	
Def bdgt	SR	60m	66m	64m
	US$	10m	11m	11m
FMA (US)	US$	0.1m	0.1m	0.1m
US$1=SR		5.7	5.8	5.0

Population **78,000**

Age	13–17	18–22	23–32
Men	4,000	4,000	6,000
Women	4,000	4,000	6,000
Women	2,034,000	1,696,000	2,520,000

Sierra Leone SL

leone L		2000	2001	2002
GDP	L	1,330bn	1,508bn	
	US$	640m	760m	
per capita	US$	140	160	
Growth	%	3.8	5.4	
Inflation	%	-0.9	6.0	
Debt	US$	2.0bn	1.8bn	
Def exp	US$	ε9m	ε12m	
Def bdgt	US$	9m	12m	18m
FMA (US)	US$	0m	0.1m	0.2m
FMA (UK)	US$			
US$1=L		2,092	1,986	2,035

Population			**ε4,600,000**
Age	13–17	18–22	23–32
Men	298,000	247,000	383,000
Women	298,000	246,000	387,000

Somali Republic SR

shilling sh		2000	2001	2002
GDP	US$	ε900m	ε900m	
per capita	US$	140	100	
Growth	%			
Inflation	%			
Debt	US$	3.3bn	3.0bn	
Def exp	US$	ε40m	ε40m	
Def bdgt	US$	ε15m	ε15m	ε15m
US$1=sh		2,620	2,620	2,620

Population		**ε9,200,000** Somali 85%	
Age	13–17	18–22	23–32
Men	626,000	511,000	726,000
Women	625,000	509,000	728,000

South Africa RSA

rand R		2000	2001	2002
GDP	R	887bn	971bn	
	US$	128bn	112bn	
per capita	US$	3,190	2,530	
Growt	%	3.4	2.2	
Inflation	%	5.4	5.7	
Debt	US$	38bn	40.3bn	
Def exp	R	13.9bn	16.09bn	
	US$	2.0bn	1.9bn	
Def bdgt	R	13.8bn	15.8bn	18.4bn
	US$	1.9bn	1.8bn	1.8bn
FMA (US)	US$	0.8m	2.2m	8.1m
US$1=R		6.9	8.6	10.1

Population			**43,600,000**
Age	13–17	18–22	23–32
Men	2,570,000	2,327,000	3,855,000
Women	2,537,000	2,309,000	3,870,000

Sudan Sdn

pound S£		2000	2001	2002
GDP	US$	14bn	14bn	
per capita	US$	450	440	
Growth	%	9.7	5.3	
Inflation	%	8.0	5.0	
Debt	US$	16.4bn	15.7bn	
Def exp	US$	ε580m	ε600m	
Def bdgt	US$	ε326m	ε387m	
US$1=S£		2,588	2,588	2,588

Population **ε31,800,000**

Muslim 70% mainly in North **Christian** 10% mainly in South **African** 52% mainly in South **Arab** 39% mainly in North

Age	13–17	18–22	23–32
Men	1,990,000	1,693,000	2,542,000
Women	1,904,000	1,620,000	2,441,000

Tanzania Tz

shilling sh		2000	2001	2002
GDP	sh	7.1tr	7.9tr	
	US$	8.9bn	9.1bn	
per capita	US$	250	250	
Growth	%	5.2	5.1	
Inflation	%	6.2	5.2	
Debt	US$	6.9bn	7.0bn	
Def exp	sh	ε115bn	ε125bn	
	US$	144m	142m	
Def bdgt	sh	115bn	125bn	ε140bn
	US$	144m	142m	141m
FMA (US)[a]	US$	0.2m	0.2m	0.2m
US$1=sh		800	876	987

[a] Excl ACRI and East Africa Regional funding

Population			**36,200,000**
Age	13–17	18–22	23–32
Men	1,990,000	1,601,000	2,380,000
Women	2,034,000	1,696,000	2,520,000

Togo Tg

CFA fr		2000	2001	2002
GDP	fr	929bn	919bn	
	US$	1.3bn	1.3bn	
per capita	US$	280	270	
Growth	%	-1.9	2.7	
Inflation	%	-2.5	6.5	
Debt	US$	1.0bn	962m	
Def exp	fr	ε22bn	ε23bn	
	US$	31m	31m	
Def bdgt	fr	ε22bn	ε23bn	ε24bn
	US$	31m	31m	33m
FMA (Fr)	US$	4m		
FMA (US)	US$	0m	0.1m	0.1m
US$1=fr		711	733	718

Population			4,700,000
Age	13–17	18–22	23–32
Men	316,000	239,000	348,000
Women	314,000	249,000	375,000

Uganda Uga

shilling Ush		2000	2001	2002
GDP	Ush	9.5tr	10.2tr	
	US$	5.8bn	5.8bn	
per capita	US$	250	240	
Growth	%	4.0	4.9	
Inflation	%	6.3	4.6	
Debt	US$	3.8bn	3.4bn	
Def exp	Ush	ε300bn	400bn	
	US$	182m	228m	
Def bdgt	Ush	212bn	229bn	250bn
	US$	129m	130m	140m
FMA (US)[a]	US$	0.4m	0.4m	0.4m
US$1=Ush		1,644	1,755	1,795

[a] Excl ACRI and East Africa Regional funding

Population			22,302,000
Age	13–17	18–22	23–32
Men	1,244,000	1,110,000	1,587,000
Women	1,274,000	1,083,000	1,698,000

Zambia Z

kwacha K		2000	2001	2002
GDP	K	9.52tr	13.3tr	
	US$	3.1bn	3.7bn	
per capita	US$	320	370	
Growth	%	3.5	5.0	
Inflation	%	26.1	22.5	
Debt	US$	6.3bn	6.1bn	
Def exp	K	ε90bn	ε100bn	
	US$	29m	28m	
Def bdgt	K	73bn	90bn	100bn
	US$	24m	25m	23m
FMA (US)	US$	0.1m	0.7m	0.2m
US$1=K		3,110	3,610	4,250

Population			9,800,000
Age	13–17	18–22	23–32
Men	652,000	530,000	775,000
Women	641,000	520,000	795,000

Zimbabwe Zw

dollar Z$		2000	2001	2002
GDP	Z$	ε317bn	514bn	
	US$	7.2bn	9.3bn	
per capita	US$	635	815	
Growth	%	-2.4	-7.3	
Inflation	%	55	76.7	
Debt	US$	4.0bn	3.8bn	
Def exp	Z$	ε12bn	ε15bn	
	US$	276m	273m	
Def bdgt	Z$	9bn	15bn	35bn
	US$	206m	272m	631m
FMA (US)	US$	0.3m	0m	0m
US$1=Z$		43.5	55	55.4

Population			11,400,000
Age	13–17	18–22	23–32
Men	837,000	675,000	1,023,000
Women	826,000	670,000	1,019,000

Table 25 Arms orders and deliveries, Sub-Saharan Africa, 1998–2001

	Country supplier	Classification ⇩	Designation	Quantity ⇩	Order date	Delivery date	Comment ⇩
Angola	RF	MBT	**T-72**		1997	1999	
	RF	FGA	**MiG-23**	18	1997	1997	Deliveries into 1998
	Kaz	MRL	**BM-21**	4	1997	1998	RF state of origin
	Bel	APC	**BMP-1**	7	1998	1999	
	Bel	MRL	**BM-21**		1998	1999	RF state of origin
	Bg	MBT	**T-55**	31		1999	
	Ukr	cbt hel	**Mi-24**	6	1998	1998	For UNITA
	Ukr	FGA	**MiG-23**	6	1998	1998	For UNITA
	Slvk	MBT	**T-55**	205		1999	
	Pe	LCA	**EMB-312**	6	2002	2002	
Botswana	A	lt tk	**SK-105**	50	1997	1999	30 in 1999, 20 in 2000
Burundi	RSA	APC	**RG-31**	12	1997	1998	
Cameroon	Il	arty	**155mm**	8	1996	1997	4 in 1997, 4 in 1998
Côte d'Ivoire	PRC	AF	***Atchan***	1	1994	1998	Logistic support ship
Democratic Republic of Congo							
	Pl	mor	**120mm**	18	1997	1998	With 1,000 rounds of ammunition
Eritrea	Il	tpt	**IAI-1125**	1	1997	1998	
	RF	FGA	**MiG-29**	6	1998	1998	
	SF	trg	***Rodrigo***	8	1998	1999	
	It	cbt hel	***Augusta***		1998	1998	
	Bg	MRL	**BM-21**		1998	1998	
	RF	hel	**Mi-17**	4	1998	1999	
	RF	SAM	**SA-18**	200	1999	1999	
	Mol	FGA	**MiG-21**	6	1999	1999	
	Ga	FGA	**Su-25**	8	1999	1999	
	Pl	LCU	**NS-717**	3	2001	2001	
Ethiopia	US	tpt	**C-130B**	4	1995	1998	Ex-USAF
	RF	cbt hel	**Mi-24**	4	1998	1998	
	RF	hel	**Mi-17**	8	1998	1998	
	Bg	MBT	**T-55**	140	1998	1995	50 delivered 1998. Deliveries to 1999
	R	FGA	**MiG-21/23**	10	1998	1999	
	Bel	MBT	**T-55**	40		1998	
	RF	FGA	**Su-27**	9	1998	1998	2 delivered 2000
	RF	FGA	**MiG-29**			2000	
	RF	SPA	**152mm**	10	1999	1999	
Kenya	Fr	LACV		4	1997	1998	Riot control armoured cars
Mali	PRC	hel	**Zhi-9**	2		2000	
Namibia	Br	PCI			1996	1999	
	RSA	arty	**140mm**	24	1997	1998	Free transfer
	dom	APC	***Werewolf* MK2**	30	1998	2000	Anti-mine vehicle
	PRC	trg	**K-8**	4	1999	2000	
	LAR	hel	**Mi-24**	2	2001	2001	
	LAR	hel	**Mi-8**	2	2001	2001	
	Mol	hel	**Mi-8T**	2	2001	2001	Leased

	Country supplier	Classification ⇩	Designation	Quantity ⇩	Order date	Delivery date	Comment ⇩
Rwanda	RSA	APC	**RG-31**	14	1995	1997	4 in 1997, 10 in 1998
Senegal	Fr	LACV		10	1997	1998	Fr donated to MISAB
Sierra Leone	Ukr	cbt hel	**Mi-24**	2	1996	1999	
South Africa	dom	AAM	***R-Darter***		1988	1998	Dev prog continuing, user trials 1998
	dom	FGA	***Cheetah*-C**	38	1988	1991	Upgrade with Il assistance through 1994, continuing to 1996
	dom	APC	***Mamba***	586	1993	1995	Prod ended 1998. Mk 2 in dev
	US	tpt	**C-130**	5	1995	1997	Upgrades for 12 through 2002
	dom	cbt hel	***Rooivalk***	12	1996	1999	Deliveries to 2000
	dom	arty	**155mm**		1997	2006	Dev
	Ge	FSG	***Meko* A-200**	4	1998	2002	Deliveries from 2004
	dom	arty	**LIW 35 DPG**		1998		Dev. Twin 35mm gun completed first trials
	dom	SSK	***Daphne***	2	1998	1999	Upgrade 1999–2000
	Ge	SSK	**Type 209**	3	2000	2004	Deliveries 2005–06
	It	hel	**A109**	30	2000	2003	Option on further 10
	Swe	FGA	**JAS-39**	9	2000	2007	Option on further 19
	UK	FGA	***Hawk***	24	2000	2005	
	UK	cbt hel	***Lynx***	4	2000	2002	
	Ge	MSC	**Type 351**	6	2000	2001	Second hand
Sudan	RF	FGA	**MiG-29**	12	2002		
Tanzania	RSA	hel	**SA-316**	4	1998	1998	Free transfer
Uganda	RF	FGA	**MiG-21/23**	28	1998	1998	
	Bg	MBT	**T-54**	90	1998	1998	All delivered 1998
	RSA	APC	***Chubby***		1998		Mine Clearing veh
	Pl	FGA	**MiG-21**	7	1999	1999	
	Bel	MBT	**T-55**	10		2000	
Zambia	PRC	trg	**K-8**	8	1999	2000	Purchased in kit form
Zimbabwe	Fr	ACV	**ACMAT**	23	1992	1999	
	It	trg	**SF-260F**	6	1997	1999	

Table 26 International comparisons of defence expenditure and military manpower, 1985, 2000 and 2001

constant 2000 US$

Canada • US • NATO Europe • Non-NATO Europe

	Defence Expenditure									Numbers in Armed Forces (000)		Estimated Reservists (000)	Para-military (000)
	US$m			US$ per capita			% of GDP						
	1985	2000	2001	1985	2000	2001	1985	2000	2001	1985	2001	2001	2001
Canada	11,832	8,320	7,745	466	273	250	2.2	1.2	1.1	83.0	56.8	35.4	9.3
US	390,290	304,136	322,365	1,631	1,078	1,128	6.5	3.1	3.2	2,151.6	1,367.7	1,200.6	53.0
NATO Europe													
Belgium	6,223	3,212	3,017	631	313	293	3.0	1.4	1.3	91.6	39.4	100.5	n.a.
Czech Republic	n.a.	1,148	1,167	n.a.	111	113	n.a.	2.3	2.2	n.a.	53.6	n.a.	5.6
Denmark	3,161	2,395	2,409	618	453	454	2.2	1.5	1.5	29.6	21.4	64.9	n.a.
France	49,378	34,053	32,909	895	575	553	4.0	2.6	2.6	464.3	273.7	419.0	100.7
Germany	53,303	27,924	26,902	702	341	328	3.2	1.5	1.5	478.0	308.4	363.5	n.a.
Greece	3,521	5,528	5,517	354	523	520	7.0	4.9	4.8	201.5	159.2	291.0	4.0
Hungary	3,588	805	909	337	81	92	7.2	1.7	1.8	106.0	33.8	90.3	14.0
Iceland	n.a.	n.a.	n.a.	n.a.	n.a.	n.a.	n.a.	n.a.	n.a.	n.a.	n.a.	n.a.	0.1
Italy	25,974	22,488	20,966	455	391	365	2.3	2.1	2.0	385.1	230.4	65.2	252.2
Luxembourg	96	129	145	263	299	332	0.9	0.7	0.8	0.7	0.9	n.a.	0.6
Netherlands	8,991	6,027	6,257	621	381	394	3.1	1.6	1.7	105.5	50.4	32.2	5.2
Norway	3,129	2,923	2,967	753	653	659	3.1	1.8	1.8	37.0	26.7	222.0	n.a.
Poland	8,706	3,092	3,408	234	80	88	8.1	2.0	2.0	319.0	206.0	406.0	22.0
Portugal	1,853	2,221	2,226	181	223	223	3.1	2.1	2.0	73.0	43.6	210.9	46.4
Spain	11,390	7,063	6,938	295	178	174	2.4	1.2	1.2	320.0	143.5	328.5	71.2
Turkey	3,470	9,994	7,219	69	150	107	4.5	5.0	5.0	630.0	515.1	378.7	150.0
United Kingdom	48,196	35,655	34,714	852	601	583	5.2	2.5	2.5	334.0	211.4	247.1	n.a.
Subtotal NATO Europe	**230,516**	**172,975**	**165,416**	**511**	**331**	**325**	**3.3**	**2.1**	**2.1**	**3,658.3**	**2,317.5**	**3,219.8**	**672.0**
Total NATO	**620,806**	**477,111**	**487,781**	**624**	**372**	**370**	**4.5**	**2.2**	**2.2**	**5,809.9**	**3,742.0**	**4,455.8**	**734.3**
Non-NATO Europe													
Albania	286	113	106	96	35	34	5.3	3.0	2.6	40.4	27.0	n.a.	13.5
Armenia	n.a.	690	637	n.a.	182	168	n.a.	7.1	6.5	n.a.	42.0	210.0	1.0
Austria	1,952	1,612	1,471	258	200	182	1.2	0.9	0.8	54.7	34.6	72.0	n.a.
Azerbaijan	n.a.	830	833	n.a.	103	103	n.a.	3.8	3.7	n.a.	72.1	575.7	15.0
Belarus	n.a.	2,100	1,960	n.a.	207	194	n.a.	2.8	2.2	n.a.	82.9	289.5	110.0
Bosnia	n.a.	164	141	n.a.	40	34	n.a.	3.7	3.0	n.a.	24.0	190.0	n.a.
Bulgaria	2,474	343	365	293	43	46	14.0	2.9	2.8	148.5	77.3	303.0	34.0
Croatia	n.a.	556	512	n.a.	118	109	n.a.	2.9	2.6	n.a.	58.3	140.0	10.0
Cyprus	132	361	315	198	414	350	3.6	4.1	3.6	10.0	10.0	60.0	0.8
Czechoslovakia	3,543	n.a.	n.a.	227	n.a.	n.a.	8.2	n.a.	n.a.	203.3	n.a.	n.a.	n.a.
Estonia	n.a.	78	92	n.a.	55	66	n.a.	1.5	1.7	n.a.	4.5	14.0	2.8
Finland	2,271	1,560	1,432	463	301	275	2.8	1.3	1.2	36.5	32.3	485.0	3.1
FYROM	n.a.	71	73	n.a.	35	36	n.a.	2.2	2.2	n.a.	16.0	60.0	10.0
Georgia	n.a.	290	265	n.a.	56	51	n.a.	1.5	1.7	n.a.	16.8	250.0	11.7
Ireland	484	629	623	136	167	164	1.8	0.6	0.5	13.7	10.5	14.8	n.a.
Latvia	n.a.	71	85	n.a.	29	35	n.a.	1.0	1.2	n.a.	6.5	14.4	3.5

	Defence Expenditure US$m 1985	US$m 2000	US$m 2001	US$ per capita 1985	US$ per capita 2000	US$ per capita 2001	% of GDP 1985	% of GDP 2000	% of GDP 2001	Numbers in Armed Forces (000) 1985	Numbers in Armed Forces (000) 2001	Estimated Reservists (000) 2001	Para-military (000) 2001
Lithuania	n.a.	199	211	n.a.	54	57	n.a.	1.8	1.8	n.a.	12.2	27.8	5.0
Malta	24	27	24	68	68	60	1.4	0.7	0.7	0.8	2.1	n.a.	n.a.
Moldova	n.a.	140	147	n.a.	32	34	n.a.	1.5	1.7	n.a.	8.2	66.0	3.4
Romania	2,109	940	969	93	42	43	4.5	2.6	2.5	189.5	103.0	470.0	75.9
Slovakia	n.a.	342	386	n.a.	63	71	n.a.	1.8	2.0	n.a.	33.0	20.0	4.7
Slovenia	n.a.	273	277	n.a.	137	139	n.a.	1.5	1.5	n.a.	7.6	61.0	4.5
Sweden	4,826	4,610	3,898	578	524	443	3.3	2.0	1.9	65.7	33.9	262.0	35.6
Switzerland	2,918	2,924	2,840	452	407	394	2.1	1.2	1.2	20.0	26.8	351.2	n.a.
Ukraine	n.a.	5,100	4,899	n.a.	103	100	n.a.	2.7	2.2	n.a.	303.8	1,000.0	116.6
FRY (Serbia/Montenegro)	5,05[illegible]	1,826	609	217	173	58	3.8	10.0	6.3	241.0	105.5	400.0	93.0
Total	**26,067**	**25,849**	**23,167**	**257**	**143**	**130**	**4.3**	**2.6**	**• 2.3**	**1,024.1**	**1,150.9**	**5,336.4**	**553.5**
Russia	n.a.	52,000	63,684	n.a.	358	440	n.a.	4.3	4.3	n.a.	977.1	2,400.0	409.1
Soviet Union	364,715	n.a.	n.a.	1,308	n.a.	n.a.	16.1	n.a.	n.a.	5,300.0	n.a.	n.a.	n.a.
Middle East and North Africa													
Algeria	1,44[illegible]	2,989	3,149	66	99	102	1.7	5.5	6.3	170.0	124.0	150.0	181.2
Bahrain	228	322	364	547	474	520	3.5	4.7	4.8	2.8	11.0	n.a.	10.2
Egypt	3,905	4,099	4,318	81	66	62	7.2	4.2	4.7	445.0	443.0	254.0	325.0
Gaza and Jericho	n.a.	n.a.	n.a.	n.a.	n.a.	n.a.	n.a.	n.a.	n.a.	n.a.	n.a.	n.a.	35.0
Iran	10,736	3,957	4,698	241	56	66	18.0	5.4	5.8	610.0	513.0	350.0	40.0
Iraq	14,031	1,400	1,372	916	60	58	37.9	9.1	9.3	1,000.0	424.0	650.0	43.0
Israel	7,638	9,509	10,375	1,804	1,534	1,673	21.2	8.8	9.5	142.0	163.5	425.0	8.0
Jordan	910	792	740	260	159	145	15.9	10.4	8.5	70.3	100.2	35.0	10.0
Kuwait	2,715	3,695	5,029	1,588	1,7927	2,514	9.1	11.1	12.1	12.0	15.5	23.7	5.0
Lebanon	302	578	576	113	158	160	9.0	3.6	3.5	17.4	71.8	n.a.	13.0
Libya	2,041	423	546	542	78	101	6.2	3.2	4.1	73.0	76.0	40.0	0.5
Mauritania	79	24	25	46	9	9	6.5	2.8	2.9	8.5	15.6	n.a.	5.0
Morocco	969	1,429	1,315	44	48	43	5.4	4.3	4.2	149.0	198.5	150.0	48.0
Oman	3,261	2,099	2,831	2,038	846	1,089	20.8	11.9	14.4	29.2	43.4	n.a.	4.4
Qatar	454	1,183	1,243	1,440	1,712	2,072	6.0	7.2	7.1	6.0	12.3	n.a.	n.a.
Saudi Arabia	27,156	22,050	24,266	2,353	1,070	1,156	19.6	11.9	14.1	62.5	201.2	n.a.	16.0
Syria	5,266	1,483	1,884	501	91	114	16.4	10.8	10.9	402.5	321.0	354.0	108.0
Tunisia	630	357	377	88	38	39	5.0	1.7	1.9	35.1	35.0	n.a.	12.0
UAE	3,089	2,997	3,070	2,206	1,176	1,137	7.6	5.1	4.6	43.0	65.0	n.a.	1.0
Yemen	739	499	531	73	27	28	9.9	7.8	8.1	64.1	54.0	40.0	70.0
Total	**85,589**	**59,882**	**66,707**	**787**	**507**	**584**	**11.9**	**6.8**	**7.2**	**3,342.4**	**2,888.0**	**2,471.7**	**935.3**
Central and South Asia													
Afghanistan	434	250	245	24	10	11	8.7	13.0	12.2	47.0	n.a.	n.a.	n.a.
Bangladesh	378	691	639	4	5	5	1.4	1.5	1.4	91.3	137.0	n.a.	63.2
Bhutan	8	21	19	18	12	9	4.9	5.6	3.8	3.0	n.a.	n.a.	n.a.

Central and South Asia contd • East Asia and Australasia • Caribbean

	Defence Expenditure									Numbers in Armed Forces		Estimated Reservists	Para-military
	US$m			US$ per capita			% of GDP			(000)		(000)	(000)
	1985	2000	2001	1985	2000	2001	1985	2000	2001	1985	2001	2001	2001
India	9,469	14,765	14,167	12	15	14	3.0	3.1	2.9	1,260.0	1,263.0	535.0	1,089.7
Kazakstan	n.a.	1,250	1,274	n.a.	77	79	n.a.	1.3	1.3	n.a.	64.0	237.0	34.5
Kyrgyzstan	n.a.	230	255	n.a.	47	51	n.a.	2.0	2.0	n.a.	9.0	57.0	5.0
Maldives	5	35	36	28	139	120	3.9	7.4	6.7	n.a.	n.a.	n.a.	n.a.
Nepal	54	106	142	3	5	6	1.5	2.0	2.7	25.0	46.0	n.a.	40.0
Pakistan	3,138	2,522	2,395	33	18	17	6.9	4.0	4.4	482.8	620.0	513.0	288.0
Sri Lanka	345	880	786	22	46	41	3.8	5.3	5.1	21.6	121.0	4.2	88.6
Tajikistan	n.a.	130	127	n.a.	21	21	n.a.	1.8	1.7	n.a.	6.0	n.a.	1.2
Turkmenistan	n.a.	290	222	n.a.	58	46	n.a.	4.8	3.2	n.a.	17.5	n.a.	n.a.
Uzbekistan	n.a.	1,750	1,764	n.a.	73	70	n.a.	2.9	2.6	n.a.	52.0	n.a.	20.0
Total	**13,831**	**22,919**	**22,071**	**18**	**40**	**38**	**4.3**	**4.2**	**3.8**	**1,930.7**	**2,335.5**	**1,346.2**	**1,630.2**
East Asia and Australasia													
Australia	8,232	7,384	6,752	523	386	350	3.4	1.9	1.9	70.4	50.7	21.3	1.0
Brunei	310	353	279	1,384	1,075	833	6.0	7.1	5.5	4.1	5.9	0.7	3.8
Cambodia	n.a.	195	188	n.a.	15	14	n.a.	6.1	5.8	35.0	140.0	n.a.	67.0
China	30,009	42,000	46,049	29	33	36	7.9	3.9	4.0	3,900.0	2,310.0	550.0	1,500.0
Fiji	21	33	26	30	41	33	1.2	2.1	1.6	2.7	3.5	6.0	n.a.
Indonesia	3,539	614	860	22	3	4	2.8	0.4	0.6	278.1	297.0	400.0	195.0
Japan	32,491	45,316	39,513	269	357	310	1.0	1.0	1.0	243.0	239.8	47.4	12.3
Korea, North	6,283	2,091	2,049	308	97	91	23.0	12.7	11.6	838.0	1,082.0	4,700.0	189.0
Korea, South	9,512	12,749	11,165	232	268	237	5.1	2.8	2.7	598.0	683.0	4,500.0	4.5
Laos	83	20	19	23	4	4	7.8	1.1	0.9	53.7	29.1	n.a.	100.0
Malaysia	2,667	2,579	3,249	171	114	144	5.6	2.9	3.8	110.0	100.5	42.8	20.1
Mongolia	52	23	25	27	9	9	9.0	2.3	2.4	33.0	9.1	137.0	7.2
Myanmar	1,328	1,020	1,088	36	21	22	5.1	2.8	2.4	186.0	344.0	n.a.	100.3
New Zealand	977	804	664	300	214	175	2.9	1.5	1.4	12.4	9.2	5.5	n.a.
Papua New Guinea	54	31	27	16	6	5	1.5	0.8	0.9	3.2	4.4	n.a.	n.a.
Philippines	717	1,357	1,065	13	18	14	1.4	1.8	1.5	114.8	107.0	131.0	44.0
Singapore	1,796	4,316	4,280	702	1,105	1,044	6.7	4.9	5.1	55.0	60.5	312.5	94.0
Taiwan	9,734	17,597	10,432	502	802	472	7.0	5.6	3.7	444.0	370.0	1,657.5	26.7
Thailand	2,833	2,419	1,831	55	38	29	5.0	2.0	1.7	235.3	306.0	200.0	104.0
Vietnam	3,628	2,303	2,351	59	29	30	19.4	7.3	7.2	1,027.0	484.0	3,000.0	40.0
Total	**114,267**	**143,203**	**131,911**	**247**	**232**	**193**	**6.4**	**3.5**	**3.3**	**8,243.7**	**6,635.7**	**15,711.7**	**2,508.9**
Caribbean, Central and Latin America													
Caribbean													
Antigua and Barbuda	3	4	4	43	60	64	0.5	0.6	0.7	0.1	0.2	0.1	n.a.
Bahamas	14	30	29	62	16	13	0.5	0.6	0.6	0.5	0.9	n.a.	2.3
Barbados	17	13	13	78	49	41	0.9	0.5	0.5	1.0	0.6	0.4	n.a.
Cuba	2,414	750	735	239	67	66	9.6	4.4	4.1	161.5	46.0	39.0	26.5

	Defence Expenditure US$m			US$ per capita			% of GDP			Numbers in Armed Forces (000)		Estimated Reservists (000)	Para-military (000)
	1985	2000	2001	1985	2000	2001	1985	2000	2001	1985	2001	2001	2001
Dominican Republic	77	169	156	12	20	18	1.1	0.8	0.7	22.2	24.5	n.a.	15.0
Haiti	47	43	40	8	5	5	1.5	1.2	1.1	6.9	3.0	n.a.	5.3
Jamaica	30	42	40	14	16	16	0.9	0.5	0.5	2.1	2.8	1.0	0.2
Trinidad and Tobago	110	62	67	93	48	52	1.4	0.9	0.8	2.1	2.7	n.a.	n.a.
Central America													
Belize	6	18	18	36	73	72	1.4	2.5	2.4	0.6	1.1	0.7	n.a.
Costa Rica	44	83	76	17	21	19	0.7	0.5	0.5	n.a.	n.a.	n.a.	8.4
El Salvador	381	168	165	80	27	26	4.4	1.4	1.2	41.7	16.8	11.0	12.0
Guatemala	177	155	186	22	13	16	1.8	0.8	0.9	31.7	31.4	35.0	19.0
Honduras	109	95	96	25	15	15	2.1	1.6	1.5	16.6	8.3	60.0	6.0
Mexico	1,876	5,312	5,733	24	54	57	0.7	0.9	0.9	129.1	192.8	300.0	11.0
Nicaragua	333	24	27	102	5	5	17.4	1.0	1.1	62.9	16.0	n.a.	n.a.
Panama	136	130	132	62	45	46	2.0	1.3	1.3	12.0	n.a.	n.a.	11.8
South America													
Argentina	5,474	4,776	4,408	179	129	118	3.8	1.7	1.7	108.0	70.1	n.a.	31.2
Bolivia	192	128	135	30	16	16	2.0	1.5	1.7	27.6	31.5	n.a.	37.1
Brazil	5,854	14,378	10,511	43	84	61	1.8	2.3	2.1	276.0	287.6	1,115.0	385.6
Chile	2,428	3,158	2,841	201	204	181	10.6	4.2	4.4	101.0	87.5	50.0	34.7
Colombia	641	3,062	2,861	23	74	67	1.6	3.8	3.5	66.2	158.0	60.7	104.6
Ecuador	429	480	507	46	38	39	1.8	3.4	2.9	42.5	59.5	100.0	0.3
Guyana	48	7	6	60	8	7	6.8	0.9	0.9	6.6	1.6	n.a.	1.5
Paraguay	91	90	76	25	16	14	1.3	1.2	1.1	14.4	18.6	164.5	14.8
Peru	969	888	896	52	35	34	4.5	1.7	1.7	128.0	100.0	188.0	77.0
Suriname	13	21	24	32	50	58	2.4	4.7	5.3	2.0	2.0	n.a.	n.a.
Uruguay	361	378	352	120	112	103	3.5	1.9	2.0	31.9	23.9	n.a.	0.9
Venezuela	1,246	1,397	1,896	72	58	77	2.1	1.2	1.5	49.0	82.3	8.0	23.0
Total	**23,521**	**35,862**	**32,031**	**64**	**48**	**47**	**3.2**	**1.7**	**1.7**	**1,344.2**	**1,269.7**	**2,133.4**	**828.2**
Sub-Saharan Africa													
Horn of Africa													
Djibouti	48	23	22	113	36	35	7.9	4.2	3.9	3.0	9.6	n.a.	3.0
Eritrea	n.a.	196	173	n.a.	52	45	n.a.	30.0	20.9	n.a.	171.9	120.0	n.a.
Ethiopia	675	670	580	16	11	9	17.9	10.3	9.8	217.0	252.5	n.a.	n.a.
Somali Republic	70	40	39	11	6	4	6.2	4.4	4.4	62.7	n.a.	n.a.	n.a.
Sudan	162	581	588	7	19	18	3.2	4.2	4.3	56.6	117.0	n.a.	7.0
Central Africa													
Burundi	53	42	35	11	6	5	3.0	5.9	5.5	5.2	45.5	n.a.	5.5
Cameroon	240	123	120	24	8	8	1.4	1.4	1.3	7.3	22.1	n.a.	9.0
Cape Verde	6	4	4	17	10	10	0.9	1.8	1.8	7.7	1.2	n.a.	0.1
Central African Republic	27	14	15	10	4	4	1.4	1.4	1.6	2.3	3.2	n.a.	1.0

Central Africa contd • East Africa • West Africa • Southern Africa

	Defence Expenditure									Numbers in Armed Forces		Estimated Reservists	Para-military
	US$m			US$ per capita			% of GDP			(000)		(000)	(000)
	1985	2000	2001	1985	2000	2001	1985	2000	2001	1985	2001	2001	2001
Chad	56	14	13	11	2	2	2.9	1.0	0.8	12.2	30.4	n.a.	4.5
Congo	85	73	80	45	24	26	1.9	2.4	3.0	8.7	10.0	n.a.	2.0
DROC	122	400	392	4	8	7	1.5	8.5	8.9	48.0	81.4	n.a.	n.a.
Equatorial Guinea	5	4	4	12	9	9	2.0	0.3	0.3	2.2	1.3	n.a.	0.3
Gabon	119	125	120	120	96	93	1.8	2.5	2.4	2.4	4.7	n.a.	2.0
Rwanda	50	98	98	8	12	12	1.9	4.8	5.8	5.2	70.0	n.a.	9.0
East Africa													
Kenya	387	278	308	19	9	10	3.1	2.7	3.1	13.7	24.4	n.a.	5.0
Madagascar	82	47	47	8	3	3	2.0	1.2	1.0	21.1	13.5	n.a.	8.1
Mauritius	4	9	9	4	8	7	0.3	0.2	0.2	1.0	n.a.	n.a.	1.6
Seychelles	12	11	11	186	137	142	2.1	1.8	1.8	1.2	0.2	n.a.	0.3
Tanzania	212	144	140	10	4	4	4.4	1.6	1.6	40.4	27.0	80.0	1.4
Uganda	80	135	126	5	6	5	1.8	2.3	2.2	20.0	55.0	n.a.	1.8
West Africa													
Benin	32	37	41	8	6	6	1.1	1.6	1.8	4.5	4.8	n.a.	2.5
Burkina Faso	51	36	36	7	3	3	1.1	1.6	1.6	4.0	10.0	n.a.	4.2
Côte d'Ivoire	115	82	80	11	5	5	0.8	0.9	0.9	13.2	13.9	12.0	8.0
Gambia, The	3	3	3	4	2	2	1.5	0.8	0.7	0.5	0.8	n.a.	n.a.
Ghana	95	40	34	7	2	2	1.0	0.9	0.7	15.1	7.0	n.a.	n.a.
Guinea	79	46	45	13	6	5	1.8	1.3	1.5	9.9	9.7	n.a.	7.6
Guinea Bissau	17	3	3	19	2	2	5.7	1.4	1.5	8.6	9.3	n.a.	2.0
Liberia	42	25	24	19	8	8	2.4	5.6	5.6	6.8	15.0	n.a.	n.a.
Mali	45	64	63	6	6	5	1.4	2.6	2.5	4.9	7.4	n.a.	7.8
Niger	18	27	29	3	2	3	0.5	1.4	1.8	2.2	5.3	n.a.	5.4
Nigeria	1,135	518	516	12	4	4	3.4	1.4	1.3	94.0	78.5	n.a.	82.0
Senegal	95	62	61	15	7	6	1.1	1.3	1.4	10.1	9.8	n.a.	5.8
Sierra Leone	8	10	12	2	2	3	1.0	1.5	1.7	3.1	6.0	n.a.	n.a.
Togo	29	31	31	9	7	7	1.3	2.4	2.5	3.6	9.5	n.a.	0.8
Southern Africa													
Angola	978	2,000	1,470	112	154	109	15.1	22.7	17.0	49.5	130.5	n.a.	15.0
Botswana	56	275	203	52	174	127	1.1	5.6	3.8	4.0	9.0	n.a.	1.0
Lesotho	70	27	24	45	12	11	4.6	3.7	3.1	2.0	2.0	n.a.	n.a.
Malawi	32	6	6	5	1	0	1.0	0.4	0.3	5.3	5.3	n.a.	1.5
Mozambique	361	91	71	26	5	4	8.5	2.0	1.9	15.8	11.0	n.a.	n.a.
Namibia	n.a.	109	91	n.a.	61	51	n.a.	3.1	3.1	n.a.	9.0	n.a.	6.0
South Africa	4,342	2,019	1,829	130	50	41	2.7	1.6	1.7	106.4	61.5	89.2	5.5
Zambia	60	29	27	9	3	3	1.1	0.9	0.8	16.2	21.6	n.a.	1.4
Zimbabwe	257	276	267	31	24	23	5.6	3.8	2.9	41.0	39.0	n.a.	21.8
Total	**10,413**	**8,842**	**7,891**	**28**	**24**	**21**	**3.1**	**3.8**	**3.4**	**958.5**	**1,416.8**	**301.2**	**239.9**

Global Totals

	Defence Expenditure									Numbers in Armed Forces		Estimated Reservists	Para-military
	US$m			US$ per capita			% of GDP			(000)		(000)	(000)
	1985	2000	2001	1985	2000	2001	1985	2000	2001	1985	2001	2001	2001
Global Totals													
NATO	620,806	477,111	487,781	624	372	370	4.5	2.2	2.2	5,809.9	3,742.0	4,455.8	734.4
Non-NATO Europe	26,067	25,849	23,167	257	143	130	4.3	2.6	2.3	1,024.1	1,150.9	5,336.4	553.5
Russia	n.a.	52,000	63,684	n.a.	358	440	n.a.	4.3	4.3	n.a.	977.1	2,400.0	409.1
Soviet Union	364,715	n.a.	n.a.	1,308	n.a.	n.a.	16.1	n.a.	n.a.	5,300.0	n.a.	n.a.	n.a.
Middle East and North Africa	85,589	59,882	66,707	787	507	584	11.9	6.8	7.2	3,342.4	2,888.0	2,471.7	935.3
Central and South Asia	13,831	22,919	22,071	18	40	38	4.3	4.2	3.8	1,930.7	2,335.5	1,346.2	1,630.2
East Asia and Australasia	114,267	143,203	131,911	247	232	193	6.4	3.5	3.3	8,243.7	6,635.7	15,711.7	2,508.9
Caribbean, Central and Latin America	23,521	35,862	32,031	64	48	47	3.2	1.7	1.7	1,344.2	1,269.7	2,133.4	828.2
Sub-Saharan Africa	10,413	8,842	7,891	28	24	21	3.1	3.8	3.4	958.5	1,416.8	301.2	239.9
Global Totals	**1,259,209**	**825,668**	**835,242**	**417**	**216**	**226**	**6.7**	**3.6**	**3.5**	**27,953.5**	**20,415.7**	**34,156.4**	**7,839.4**

Table 27 **Conventional Armed Forces in Europe** (CFE) **Treaty**

Manpower and Treaty Limited Equipment (TLE)
current holdings and CFE national ceilings on the forces of the Treaty members

Current holdings are derived from data declared as of 1 January 2002 and so may differ from *The Military Balance* listings

		Manpower		Tanks[2]		ACV[2]		Artillery[2]		Attack Helicopters		Combat Aircraft[3]	
		Holding	Ceiling	Holding	Ceiling	Holding	Ceiling	Holding	Ceiling	Holding	Ceiling	Holding	Ceiling
Non-NATO	**Armenia**	44,618	*60,000*	110	*220*	146	*220*	229	*285*	7	*50*	6	*100*
	Azerbaijan	69,966	*70,000*	220	*220*	210	*220*	282	*285*	15	*50*	48	*100*
	Belarus	79,870	*100,000*	1,608	*1,800*	2,507	*2,600*	1,471	*1,615*	58	*80*	212	*294*
	Bulgaria	54,495	*104,000*	1,475	*1,475*	1,885	*2,000*	1,738	*1,750*	43	*67*	232	*235*
	Georgia	40,000	*40,000*	90	*220*	114	*220*	109	*285*	3	*50*	7	*100*
	Moldova	7,227	*20,000*	0	*210*	209	*210*	148	*250*	0	*50*	0	*50*
	Romania	109,143	*230,000*	1,258	*1,375*	2,051	*2,100*	1,384	*1,475*	22	*120*	204	*430*
	Russia [5]	650,802	*1,450,000*	4,948	*6,350*	9,175	*11,280*	5,695	*6,315*	523	*855*	2,406	*3,416*
	Slovakia	32,366	*46,667*	272	*478*	534	*683*	374	*383*	19	*40*	79	*100*
	Ukraine	305,000	*450,000*	3,895	*4,080*	4,725	*5,050*	3,705	*4,040*	205	*330*	855	*1,090*
NATO	**Belgium**	39,123	*70,000*	146	*300*	743	*989*	270	*288*	46	*46*	135	*209*
	Canada	0	*10,660*	0	*77*	0	*263*	0	*32*	0	*13*	0	*90*
	Czech Republic [4]	49,491	*93,333*	622	*957*	1,241	*1,367*	585	*767*	34	*50*	112	*230*
	Denmark	25,293	*39,000*	238	*335*	311	*336*	479	*446*	12	*18*	68	*82*
	France	184,988	*325,000*	1,084	*1,226*	3,339	*3,700*	764	*1,192*	284	*374*	588	*800*
	Germany	271,806	*345,000*	2,460	*3,444*	2,382	*3,281*	1,725	*2,255*	202	*280*	386	*765*
	Greece	158,621	*158,621*	1,735	*1,735*	2,176	*2,498*	1,901	*1,920*	20	*65*	523	*650*
	Hungary [4]	33,408	*100,000*	743	*835*	1,478	*1,700*	834	*840*	49	*108*	92	*180*
	Italy	173,522	*315,000*	1,253	*1,267*	2,934	*3,172*	1,404	*1,818*	133	*142*	497	*618*
	Netherlands	37,981	*80,000*	328	*520*	689	*864*	392	*485*	14	*50*	143	*230*
	Norway	14,733	*32,000*	141	*170*	245	*275*	184	*491*	0	*24*	72	*100*
	Poland [4]	162,693	*234,000*	1,144	*1,730*	1,392	*2,150*	1,482	*1,610*	111	*130*	207	*460*
	Portugal	36,751	*75,000*	187	*300*	353	*430*	363	*450*	0	*26*	101	*160*
	Spain	160,372	*300,000*	698	*750*	1,002	*1,588*	1,054	*1,276*	28	*80*	191	*310*
	Turkey [5]	515,749	*530,000*	2,445	*2,795*	2,831	*3,120*	2,990	*3,523*	28	*130*	343	*750*
	UK	206,762	*260,000*	608	*843*	2,344	*3,017*	459	*583*	267	*350*	511	*855*
	US	98,232	*250,000*	657	*1,812*	1,639	*3,037*	327	*1,553*	132	*396*	228	*784*

Notes

1 The adaptation of the CFE abandons the group structure (North Atlantic Group, Budapest/Tashkent Group) for a system of national and territorial ceilings. The amendment enters into force when CFE States Parties have ratified the change.

2 Includes TLE with land-based maritime forces (Marines, Naval Infantry etc.)

3 Does not include land-based maritime aircraft for which a separate limit has been set.

4 Cz, Hu and Pl became NATO members on 12 March 1999.

5 Manpower and TLE is for that in the Atlantic to the Urals (ATTU) zone only.

The International Arms Trade

DELIVERIES

Once again the global value of arms deliveries fell substantially, from US$32.5bn in 2000 to US$21.3bn in 2001, the lowest in the last eight years. The declining trend that has been in evidence since the peak in deliveries in 1997, when deliveries were worth US$46.9bn, more than double last year's total, is a consequence of several factors:

- the tailing-off of large military equipment orders from the Middle East (a post-Gulf War trend);
- a fall in the value of new orders that originated from East Asia as a consequence of the 1997–98 economic crisis;
- lower demand for US systems in Europe as defence budgets fall and military re-organisation take priority over equipment procurement; and
- uncertainty in the global economy following the technology bubble of the 1990s.

As in previous years, Saudi Arabia was the largest importer of military-related equipment. In 2001, imports into Saudi Arabia were valued at US$4.8bn, down from US$7.3bn in 2000 and substantially lower than the US$11bn achieved in 1997, when post-Gulf War deliveries were at their peak. Between 1994 and 2001, Saudi Arabia imported military equipment worth US$65bn in total, considerably more than the next biggest importer Taiwan, who imported just US$20.7bn in the same period.

MARKET SHARE

The US retained its share of nearly 50% of global arms deliveries in 2001, the eighth year in a row that the United States has led global arms deliveries. The United Kingdom ranked second and Russia third. Between them, these three countries accounted for 81% of all arms deliveries in 2001, while developing nations accounted for 67.6%.

NEW TRANSFER AGREEMENTS

The value of all arms-transfer agreements (new orders for future delivery) in 2001 was US$24.6bn, significantly down from US$40bn in 2000. The United States led in arms transfer agreements in 2001, with Russia second and France third (see table 32). The fall in the value of new agreements to developing countries is a reflection of the health of the international economy and the caution of some previously aggressive buyers. Increasingly, a number of developing nations are opting to upgrade existing weapons systems rather than commit to purchasing costly new ones. Likewise, developed nations have been purchasing fewer systems from each other as each attempts to protect elements of their own national military industrial base.

Among major weapons systems sold by the United States in 2001 were 52 F-16D combat fighter aircraft and associated equipment and services for over US$1.8bn, a US$500m sale to Egypt for an M1A1 *Abrams* main battle tank co-production deal and a US$379m contract with Singapore for 12 AG-64D *Apache* helicopters.

The total of Russia's arms transfer agreements in 2001 was US$5.8bn. Major deals in 2001 included an agreement with India for the licensed production of 310 T-90 main battle tanks, a US$1.5bn

Table 28 Arms deliveries: leading suppliers, 2001

current US$m

1	**US**	9,702
2	**UK**	4,000
3	**Russia**	3,600
4	**France**	1,000
5	**China**	500
6	**Israel**	300
7	**Ukraine**	200
8	**Slovakia**	100
9	**Belgium**	100
10	**Greece**	100
11	**South Korea**	100

Table 29 Arms deliveries: leading recipients, 2001

current US$m

1	**Saudi Arabia**	4,800
2	**China**	2,200
3	**Taiwan**	1,200
4	**South Korea**	900
5	**Eqypt**	700
6	**Israel**	600
7	**India**	500
8	**Kuwait**	400
9	**Pakistan**	200
10	**Sri Lanka**	200

sale of around 40 SU-30 MKK fighter aircraft to China, a sale of approximately US$600m to South Korea of helicopters and other military-related equipment to help retire existing Russian debts, and sales of MiG-29 fighters to Burma and Yemen.

The potential exists for a series of new arms sales to nations that were formerly part of the Warsaw Pact and are now members of NATO, or have membership in prospect, although this market is somewhat limited by the prospective buyers' lack of significant financial resources. Other significant buyers from the Middle East and East Asia remain on the sidelines as the effects of the Asian financial crisis and fluctuating oil prices restrain spending. Likewise in Latin America, although there is a need for military modernisation, the economic problems of Argentina and Brazil in 2001 and 2002 suggest that major weapons orders will be limited in the near future.

Source

Richard F. Grimmett, *Conventional Arms Transfers to Developing Nations 1994–2001* (Washington DC: Congressional Research Service, August 2002).

Table 30 Value of global arms deliveries and market share, 1994–2001

constant 2001 US$m, *% in italics*

	Total	Russia		US		UK		France		Germany		China		Others	
1994	35,030	2,143	*6.1*	15,865	*45.3*	6,190	*17.7*	1,428	*4.1*	2,024	*5.8*	714	*2.0*	6,666	*19.0*
1995	42,268	4,083	*9.7*	18,587	*44.0*	6,183	*14.6*	3,500	*8.3*	2,333	*5.5*	933	*2.2*	6,649	*15.7*
1996	41,494	3,655	*8.8*	16,940	*40.8*	7,423	*17.9*	4,340	*10.5*	2,170	*5.2*	799	*1.9*	6,167	*14.9*
1997	46,967	2,794	*5.9*	18,467	*39.3*	7,600	*16.2*	7,489	*15.9*	1,341	*2.9*	1,229	*2.6*	8,047	*17.1*
1998	40,495	2,293	*5.7*	18,439	*45.5*	4,149	*10.2*	7,753	*19.1*	1,638	*4.0*	655	*1.6*	5,568	*13.7*
1999	40,540	3,200	*7.9*	19,421	*47.9*	5,333	*13.2*	3,840	*9.5*	2,240	*5.5*	427	*1.1*	6,079	*15.0*
2000	32,567	3,743	*11.5*	13,537	*41.6*	5,823	*17.9*	2,080	*6.4*	1,248	*3.8*	728	*2.2*	5,408	*16.6*
2001	21,302	3,600	*16.9*	9,702	*45.5*	4,000	*18.8*	1,000	*4.7*	100	*0.5*	500	*2.3*	1,400	*6.6*

Table 31 Regional arms deliveries by supplier, 1994–2001

constant 2001 US$m

		United States	Russia	France	UK	China	Germany	Italy	Other European	All others
Asia	1994–97	10,964	5,500	5,000	2,600	1,600	2,600	500	2,300	1,500
	1998–01	12,613	7,600	5,400	2,300	1,000	100	800	1,000	1,100
Near East	1994–97	24,617	2,800	6,900	18,100	1,100	200	100	5,600	800
	1998–01	22,596	1,900	5,500	13,300	400	1,000	200	3,400	500
Latin America	1994–97	1,743	200	300	400	100	200	-	1,100	600
	1998–01	116	600	200	100	300	-	100	300	1,000
Africa	1994–97	116	600	200	100	300	-	100	300	1,000
	1998–01	92	1,100	-	100	500	-	-	1,000	700

Table 32 Value of global arms transfer agreements and market share by supplier, 1994–2001

constant 2001 US$m, *% in italics*

	Total	Russia		US		UK		France		Germany		China		Others	
1994	36,910	4,523	*12.3*	14,771	*40.0*	833	*2.3*	10,356	*28.1*	1,666	*4.5*	952	*2.6*	3,809	*10.3*
1995	29,873	8,749	*29.3*	10,275	*34.4*	933	*3.1*	3,150	*10.5*	467	*1.6*	233	*0.8*	6,066	*20.3*
1996	35,959	5,254	*14.6*	12,204	*33.9*	5,710	*15.9*	2,855	*7.9*	228	*0.6*	1,028	*2.9*	8,680	*24.1*
1997	25,426	3,912	*15.4*	7,765	*30.5*	1,118	*4.4*	5,253	*20.7*	671	*2.6*	1,453	*5.7*	5,254	*20.7*
1998	31,222	2,621	*8.4*	11,130	*35.6*	2,184	*7.0*	3,603	*11.5*	5,460	*17.5*	1,201	*3.8*	5,023	*16.1*
1999	35,488	4,480	*12.6*	12,662	*35.7*	1,387	*3.9*	1,600	*4.5*	3,840	*10.8*	2,666	*7.5*	8,853	*24.9*
2000	40,039	8,423	*21.0*	18,930	*47.3*	624	*1.6*	4,263	*10.6*	1,144	*2.9*	624	*1.6*	6,031	*15.1*
2001	26,388	5,800	*22.0*	12,088	*45.8*	400	*1.5*	2,900	*11.0*	1,000	*3.8*	600	*2.3*	3,600	*13.6*

Table 33 Designations of aircraft

Notes

1 [Square brackets] indicate the type from which a variant was derived: 'Q-5 … [MiG-19]' indicates that the design of the Q-5 was based on that of the MiG-19.

2 (Parentheses) indicate an alternative name by which an aircraft is known, sometimes in another version: 'L-188 … *Electra* (P-3 *Orion*)' shows that in another version the Lockheed Type 188 *Electra* is known as the P-3 *Orion*.

3 Names given in 'quotation marks' are NATO reporting names, e.g., 'Su-27… *"Flanker"*'.

4 When no information is listed under 'Country of origin' or 'Maker', the primary reference given under 'Name/designation' should be looked up under 'Type'.

5 For country abbreviations, see 'Index of Countries and Territories' (pp. 319–20).

Fixed-wing

Type	Name/designation	Country of origin	Maker
A-1	AMX	**Br/It**	AMX
A-1	*Ching-Kuo*	**ROC**	AIDC
A-3	*Skywarrior*	**US**	Douglas
A-4	*Skyhawk*	**US**	MD
A-5	(Q-5)		
A-7	*Corsair* II	**US**	LTV
A-10	*Thunderbolt*	**US**	Fairchild
A-36	*Halcón* (C-101)		
A-37	*Dragonfly*	**US**	Cessna
A-50	*'Mainstay'* (Il-76)	**RF**	Beriev
A300		**UK/Fr/Ge/Sp**	Airbus Int
A310		**UK/Fr/Ge/Sp**	Airbus Int
A340		**UK/Fr/Ge/Sp**	Airbus Int
AC-47	(C-47)		
AC-130	(C-130)		
Air Beetle		**Nga**	AIEP
Airtourer		**NZ**	Victa
AJ-37	(J-37)		
Alizé	(Br 1050)	**Fr**	Breguet
Alpha Jet		**Fr/Ge**	Dassault–Breguet/Dornier
AMX		**Br/It**	Embraer/Alenia/Aermacchi
An-2	*'Colt'*	**Ukr**	Antonov
An-12	*'Cub'*	**Ukr**	Antonov
An-14	*'Clod'* (*Pchyelka*)	**Ukr**	Antonov
An-22	*'Cock'* (*Antei*)	**Ukr**	Antonov
An-24	*'Coke'*	**Ukr**	Antonov
An-26	*'Curl'*	**Ukr**	Antonov
An-28/M-28	*'Cash'*	**Ukr** / **Pl**	Antonov / PZL
An-30	*'Clank'*	**Ukr**	Antonov
An-32	*'Cline'*	**Ukr**	Antonov
An-72	*'Coaler-C'*	**Ukr**	Antonov
An-74	*'Coaler-B'*	**Ukr**	Antonov
An-124	*'Condor'* (*Ruslan*)	**Ukr**	Antonov
Andover	[HS-748]		
Arava		**Il**	IAI
AS-202	*Bravo*	**CH**	FFA
AT-3	*Tsu Chiang*	**ROC**	AIDC
AT-6	(T-6)		
AT-11		**US**	Beech
AT-26	EMB-326		
AT-33	(T-33)		
Atlantic	(*Atlantique*)	**Fr**	Dassault–Breguet
AU-23	*Peacemaker* [PC-6B]	**US**	Fairchild
AV-8	*Harrier* II	**US/UK**	MD/BAe
Aztec	PA-23	**US**	Piper
B-1	*Lancer*	**US**	Rockwell
B-2	*Spirit*	**US**	Northrop Grumman
B-5	H-5		
B-6	H-6		
B-52	*Stratofortress*	**US**	Boeing
B-65	*Queen Air*	**US**	Beech
BAC-167	*Strikemaster*	**UK**	BAe
BAe-125		**UK**	BAe
BAe-146		**UK**	BAe
BAe-748	(HS-748)	**UK**	BAe
Baron	(T-42)		
Basler T-67	(C-47)	**US**	Basler
Be-6	*'Madge'*	**RF**	Beriev
Be-12	*'Mail'* (*Tchaika*)	**RF**	Beriev
Beech 50	*Twin Bonanza*	**US**	Beech
Beech 95	*Travel Air*	**US**	Beech
BN-2	*Islander, Defender, Trislander*	**UK**	Britten-Norman
Boeing 707		**US**	Boeing
Boeing 727		**US**	Boeing
Boeing 737		**US**	Boeing
Boeing 747		**US**	Boeing
Boeing 757		**US**	Boeing
Boeing 767		**US**	Boeing
Bonanza		**US**	Beech
Bronco	(OV-10)		
BT-5	HJ-5		
Bulldog		**UK**	BAe
C-1		**J**	Kawasaki
C-2	*Greyhound*	**US**	Grumman
C-5	*Galaxy*	**US**	Lockheed
C-7	DHC-7		
C-9	*Nightingale* (DC-9)		
C-12	*Super King Air* (*Huron*)	**US**	Beech
C-17	*Globemaster* III	**US**	McDonnell Douglas
C-18	[Boeing 707]		
C-20	(*Gulfstream* III)		
C-21	(*Learjet*)		
C-22	(Boeing 727)		
C-23	(*Sherpa*)	**UK**	Shorts
C-26	*Expediter/Merlin*	**US**	Fairchild
C-27	*Spartan*	**It**	Alenia
C-32	[Boeing 757]	**US**	Boeing
C-37A	[*Gulfstream* V]	**US**	Gulfstream
C-38A	(*Astra*)	**Il**	IAI
C-42	(Neiva *Regente*)	**Br**	Embraer
C-46	*Commando*	**US**	Curtis
C-47	DC-3 (*Dakota*) (C-117 *Skytrain*)	**US**	Douglas
C-54	*Skymaster* (DC-4)	**US**	Douglas
C-91	HS-748		
C-93	HS-125		
C-95	EMB-110		
C-97	EMB-121		
C-101	*Aviojet*	**Sp**	CASA
C-115	DHC-5	**Ca**	De Havilland

Type	Name/ designation	Country of origin Maker
C-117	(C-47)	
C-118	*Liftmaster* (DC-6)	
C-123	*Provider*	**US** Fairchild
C-127	(Do-27)	**Sp** CASA
C-130	*Hercules* (L-100)	**US** Lockheed
C-131	Convair 440	**US** Convair
C-135	[Boeing 707]	
C-137	[Boeing 707]	
C-140	(*Jetstar*)	**US** Lockheed
C-141	*Starlifter*	**US** Lockheed
C-160	*Transall*	**Fr/Ge** EADS
C-212	*Aviocar*	**Sp** CASA
C-235	*Persuader*	**Sp/Indo** CASA/Airtech
C-295M		**Sp** CASA
Canberra		**UK** BAe
CAP-10		**Fr** Mudry
CAP-20		**Fr** Mudry
CAP-230		**Fr** Mudry
Caravelle	SE-210	**Fr** Aérospatiale
CC-115	DHC-5	
CC-117	(*Falcon 20*)	
CC-132	(DHC-7)	
CC-137	(Boeing 707)	
CC-138	(DHC-6)	
CC-144	CL-600/-601	**Ca** Canadair
CF-5a		**Ca** Canadair
CF-18	F/A-18	
Cheetah	[*Mirage III*]	**RSA** Atlas
Cherokee	PA-28	**US** Piper
Cheyenne	PA-31T [*Navajo*]	**US** Piper
Chieftain	PA-31-350 [*Navajo*]	**US** Piper
Ching-Kuo	A-1	**ROC** AIDC
Citabria		**US** Champion
Citation	(T-47)	**US** Cessna
CJ-5	[Yak-18]	**PRC** NAMC (Hongdu)
CJ-6	[Yak-18]	**PRC** NAMC (Hongdu)
CL-215		**Ca** Canadair
CL-415		**Ca** Canadair
CL-600/604	*Challenger*	**Ca** Canadair
CM-170	*Magister* [*Tzukit*]	**Fr** Aérospatiale
CM-175	*Zéphyr*	**Fr** Aérospatiale
CN-212		**Sp/Indo** CASA/IPTN
CN-235		**Sp/Indo** CASA/IPTN
Cochise	T-42	
Comanche	PA-24	**US** Piper
Commander	*Aero-/TurboCommander*	**US** Rockwell
Commodore	MS-893	**Fr** Aérospatiale
CP-3	P-3 *Orion*	
CP-140	*Aurora* (P-3 *Orion*)	**US** Lockheed
	Acturas	
CT-4	*Airtrainer*	**NZ** Victa
CT-114	CL-41 *Tutor*	**Ca** Canadair
CT-133	*Silver Star* [T-33]	**Ca** Canadair
CT-134	*Musketeer*	
CT-156	*Harvard* II	**US** Beech
Dagger	(*Nesher*)	
Dakota		**US** Piper
Dakota	(C-47)	
DC-3	(C-47)	**US** Douglas
DC-4	(C-54)	**US** Douglas
DC-6	(C-118)	**US** Douglas
DC-7		**US** Douglas
DC-8		**US** Douglas
DC-9		**US** MD
Deepak	(HPT-32)	
Defender	BN-2	
DHC-3	*Otter*	**Ca** DHC
DHC-4	*Caribou*	**Ca** DHC
DHC-5	*Buffalo*	**Ca** DHC
DHC-6	*Twin Otter*, CC-138	**Ca** DHC
DHC-7	*Dash-7* (*Ranger*, CC-132)	**Ca** DHC
DHC-8		**Ca** DHC
Dimona	H-36	**Ge** Hoffman
Do-27	(C-127)	**Ge** Dornier
Do-28	*Skyservant*	**Ge** Dornier
Do-128		**Ge** Dornier
Do-228		**Ge** Dornier
E-2	*Hawkeye*	**US** Grumman
E-3	*Sentry*	**US** Boeing
E-4	[Boeing 747]	**US** Boeing
E-6	*Mercury* [Boeing 707]	**US** Boeing
E-26	T-35A (*Tamiz*)	**Chl** Enear
EA-3	[A-3]	
EA-6	*Prowler* [A-6]	
EC-130	[C-130]	
EC-135	[Boeing 707]	
EF-111	*Raven* (F-111)	**US** General Dynamic
Electra	(L-188)	
EMB-110	*Bandeirante*	
EMB-111	*Maritime Bandeirante*	**Br** Embraer
EMB-120	*Brasilia*	**Br** Embraer
EMB-121	*Xingu*	**Br** Embraer
EMB-145	(R-99A/-99B)	**Br** Embraer
EMB-201	*Ipanema*	**Br** Embraer
EMB-312	*Tucano*	**Br** Embraer
EMB-314	*Super Tucano*	**Br** Embraer
EMB-326	*Xavante* (MB-326)	**Br** Embraer
EMB-810	[*Seneca*]	**Br** Embraer
EP-3	(P-3 *Orion*)	
ERJ-145		**Br** Embraer
Etendard/Super Etendard		**Fr** Dassault
EV-1	(OV-1)	
F-1	[T-2]	**J** Mitsubishi
F-4	*Phantom*	**US** MD
F-5	-A/-B *Freedom Fighter*	
	-E/-F *Tiger* II	**US** Northrop
F-6	J-6	
F-7	J-7	
F-8	J-8	
F-10	J-10	
F-11	J-11	
F-14	*Tomcat*	**US** Grumman
F-15	*Eagle*	**US** MD
F-16	*Fighting Falcon*	**US** GD
F-18	[F/A-18], *Hornet*	
F-21	*Kfir*	**Il** IAI
F-22	*Raptor*	**US** Lockheed
F-27	*Friendship*	**Nl** Fokker
F-28	*Fellowship*	**Nl** Fokker
F-35	*Draken*	**Swe** SAAB
F-50/-60		**Nl** Fokker
F-104	*Starfighter*	**US** Lockheed

Type	Name/ designation	Country of origin	Maker
F-111	EF-111	US	GD
F-117	*Nighthawk*	US	Lockheed
F-172	(Cessna 172)	Fr/US	Reims-Cessna
F-406	*Caravan*	Fr	Reims
F/A-18	*Hornet*	US	MD
Falcon	*Mystère-Falcon*		
FB-111	(F-111)		
FBC-1	*Feibao* [JH-7]		
FC-1	(*Sabre* 2, *Super-7*)	PRC/RF/Pak	CAC/MAPO/Pak
FH-227	(F-27)	US	Fairchild-Hiller
Firefly	(T-67M)	UK	Slingsby
Flamingo	MBB-233		
FT-5	JJ-5		
FT-6	JJ-6		
FT-7	JJ-7		
FTB-337	[Cessna 337]		
G-91		It	Aeritalia
G-115E	*Tutor*	Ge	Grob
G-222		It	Alenia
Galaxy	C-5		
Galeb		FRY	SOKO
Genet	SF-260W		
GU-25	(*Falcon 20*)		
Guerrier	R-235		
Gulfstream		US	Gulfstream Aviation
Gumhuria	(*Bücker* 181)	Et	Heliopolis
H-5	[Il-28]	PRC	HAF
H-6	[Tu-16]	PRC	XAC
H-36	*Dimona*		
Halcón	[C-101]		
Harrier	(AV-8)	UK	BAe
Hawk		UK	BAe
Hawker 800XP	(BAe-125)	US	Raytheon
HC-130	(C-130)		
HF-24	*Marut*	Ind	HAL
HFB-320	*Hansajet*	Ge	Hamburger FB
HJ-5	(H-5)		
HJT-16	*Kiran*	Ind	HAL
HPT-32	*Deepak*	Ind	HAL
HS-125	(*Dominie*)	UK	BAe
HS-748	[*Andover*]	UK	BAe
HT-2		Ind	HAL
HU-16	*Albatross*	US	Grumman
HU-25	(*Falcon* 20)		
Hunter		UK	BAe
HZ-5	(H-5)		
IA-50	*Guaraní*	Arg	FMA
IA-58	*Pucará*	Arg	FMA
IA-63	*Pampa*	Arg	FMA
IAI-201/-202	*Arava*	Il	IAI
IAI-1124	*Westwind, Seascan*	Il	IAI
IAI-1125	*Astra*	Il	IAI
Iak-52	(Yak-52)	R	Aerostar
IAR-28		R	IAR
IAR-93	*Orao*	FRY/R	SOKO/IAR
IAR-99	*Soim*	R	IAR
Il-14	*'Crate'*	RF	Ilyushin
Il-18	*'Coot'*	RF	Ilyushin
Il-20	*'Coot-A'* (Il-18)	RF	Ilyushin
Il-22	*'Coot-B'* (Il-18)	RF	Ilyushin
Il-28	*'Beagle'*	RF	Ilyushin
Il-38	*'May'*	RF	Ilyushin
Il-62	*'Classic'*	RF	Ilyushin
Il-76	*'Candid'* (tpt), *'Mainstay'* (AEW)	RF	Ilyushin
Il-78	*'Midas'* (tkr)	RF	Ilyushin
Il-82	*'Candid'*	RF	Ilyushin
Il-86	*'Camber'*	RF	Ilyushin
Il-87	*'Maxdome'*	RF	Ilyushin
Impala	[MB-326]	RSA	Atlas
Islander	BN-2		
J-5	[MiG-17F]	PRC	SAF
J-6	[MiG-19]	PRC	SAF
J-7	[MiG-21]	PRC	CAC/GAIC
J-8	*Finback*	PRC	SAC
J-10	[IAI *Lavi*]	PRC	SAC
J-11	[Su-27]	PRC	SAC
J-32	*Lansen*	Swe	SAAB
J-35	*Draken*	Swe	SAAB
J-37	*Viggen*	Swe	SAAB
JA-37	(J-37)		
Jaguar		Fr/UK	SEPECAT
JAS-39	*Gripen*	Swe	SAAB
Jastreb		FRY	SOKO
Jetstream		UK	BAe
JH-7	[FBC-1]	PRC	XAC
JJ-5	[J-5]	PRC	CAF
JJ-6	[J-6]	PRC	SAF
JJ-7	[J-7]	PRC	GAIC
JZ-6	(J-6)		
K-8		PRC/Pak/Et	Hongdu/E
KA-3	[A-3]		
KA-6	[A-6]		
KC-10	*Extender* [DC-10]	US	MD
KC-130	[C-130]		
KC-135	[Boeing 707]		
KE-3A	[Boeing 707]		
KF-16	(F-16)		
Kfir		Il	IAI
King Air		US	Beech
Kiran	HJT-16		
Kraguj		FRY	SOKO
L-4	*Cub*		
L-18	*Super Cub*	US	Piper
L-19	O-1		
L-21	*Super Cub*	US	Piper
L-29	*Delfin*	Cz	Aero
L-39	*Albatros*	Cz	Aero
L-59	*Albatros*	Cz	Aero
L-70	*Vinka*	SF	Valmet
L-100	C-130 (civil version)		
L-188	*Electra* (P-3 *Orion*)	US	Lockheed
L-410	*Turbolet*	Cz	LET
L-1011	*Tristar*	US	Lockheed
Learjet	(C-21)	US	Gates
LR-1	(MU-2)	J	Mitsubishi
M-28	*Skytruck/Bryza*	Pl	MIELEC
Magister	CM-170		
Marut	HF-24		
Mashshaq	MFI-17	Pak/Swe	PAC/SAAB
Matador	(AV-8)		
Maule	M-7/MXT-7	US	Maule
MB-326		It	Aermacchi

Type	Name/ designation	Country of origin Maker
MB-339	(*Veltro*)	**It** Aermacchi
MBB-233	*Flamingo*	**Ge** MBB
MC-130	(C-130)	
Mercurius	(HS-125)	
Merlin		**US** Fairchild
Mescalero	T-41	
Metro		**US** Fairchild
MFI-17	*Supporter* (T-17)	**Swe** SAAB
MiG-15	*'Midget'* trg	**RF** MiG
MiG-17	*'Fresco'*	**RF** MiG
MiG-19	*'Farmer'*	**RF** MiG
MiG-21	*'Fishbed'*	**RF** MiG
MiG-23	*'Flogger'*	**RF** MiG
MiG-25	*'Foxbat'*	**RF** MiG
MiG-27	*'Flogger D'*	**RF** MiG
MiG-29	*'Fulcrum'*	**RF** MiG
MiG-31	*'Foxhound'*	**RF** MiG
Mirage		**Fr** Dassault
Missionmaster	N-22	
Mohawk	OV-1	
MS-760	*Paris*	**Fr** Aérospatiale
MS-893	*Commodore*	
MU-2	LR-1	**J** Mitsubishi
Musketeer	*Beech 24*	**US** Beech
Mystère-Falcon		**Fr** Dassault
N-22	*Floatmaster, Missionmaster*	**Aus** GAF
N-24	*Searchmaster* B/L	**Aus** GAF
N-262	*Frégate*	**Fr** Aérospatiale
N-2501	*Noratlas*	**Fr** Aérospatiale
Navajo	PA-31	**US** Piper
NC-212	C-212	**Sp/Indo** CASA/Nurtanio
NC-235	C-235	**Sp/Indo** CASA/Nurtanio
Nesher	[*Mirage* III]	**Il** IAI
NF-5	(F-5)	
Nightingale	(C-9)	
Nimrod	[*Comet*]	**UK** BAe
Nomad		**Aus** GAF
O-1	*Bird Dog*	**US** Cessna
O-2	(Cessna 337 *Skymaster*)	**US** Cessna
OA-4	(A-4)	
OA-37	*Dragonfly*	
Orao	IAR-93	
Ouragan		**Fr** Dassault
OV-1	*Mohawk*	**US** Rockwell
OV-10	*Bronco*	**US** Rockwell
P-3	*Orion* [L-188 *Electra*]	**US** Lockheed
P-92		**It** Teenam
P-95	EMB-110	
P-166		**It** Piaggio
P-180	*Avanti*	**It** Piaggio
PA-18	*Super Cub*	**US** Piper
PA-23	*Aztec*	**US** Piper
PA-28	*Cherokee*	**US** Piper
PA-31	*Navajo*	**US** Piper
PA-32	*Cherokee Six*	**US** Piper
PA-34	*Seneca*	**US** Piper
PA-36	*Pawnee Brave*	**US** Piper
PA-38	*Tomahawk*	**US** Piper
PA-42	*Cheyenne III*	**US** Piper
PBY-5	*Catalina*	**US** Consolidated
PC-6	*Porter*	**CH** Pilatus
PC-6A/B	*Turbo Porter*	**CH** Pilatus
PC-7	*Turbo Trainer*	**CH** Pilatus
PC-9		**CH** Pilatus
PC-12		**CH** Pilatus
PD-808		**It** Piaggio
Pillán	T-35	
PL-1	*Chien Shou*	**ROC** AIDC
PLZ M-28	[An-28]	**Pl** PZL
Porter	PC-6	
PS-5	[SH-5]	
PZL M-28	M-28 [An-28]	**Pl** PZL
PZL-104	*Wilga*	**Pl** PZL
PZL-130	*Orlik*	**Pl** PZL
Q-5	A-5 *'Fantan'* [MiG-19]	**PRC** NAMC (Hongdu)
Queen Air	(U-8)	
R-99A/B	EMB-145	**Br** Embraer
R-160		**Fr** Socata
R-235	*Guerrier*	**Fr** Socata
RC-21	(C-21, *Learjet*)	
RC-47	(C-47)	
RC-95	(EMB-110)	
RC-135	[Boeing 707]	
RF-4	(F-4)	
RF-5	(F-5)	
RF-35	(F-35)	
RF-104	(F-104)	
RG-8A		**US** Schweizer
RT-26	(EMB-326)	
RT-33	(T-33)	
RU-21	(*King Air*)	
RV-1	(OV-1)	
S-2	*Tracker*	**US** Grumman
S-208		**It** SIAI
S-211		**It** SIAI
SA 2-37A		**US** Schweizer
Saab 340H		**Swe** SAAB
Sabreliner	(CT-39)	**US** Rockwell
Safari	MFI-15	
Safir	SAAB-91 (SK-50)	**Swe** SAAB
SC-7	*Skyvan*	**UK** Short
SE-210	*Caravelle*	
Sea Harrier	(*Harrier*)	
Seascan	IAI-1124	
Searchmaster	N-24 B/L	
Seneca	PA-34 (EMB-810)	**US** Piper
Sentry	(O-2)	**US** Summit
SF-37	(J-37)	
SF-260	(SF-260W *Warrior*)	**It** SIAI
SH-5	PS-5	**PRC** HAMC
SH-37	(J-37)	
Sherpa	Short 330, C-23	**UK** Short
Short 330	(*Sherpa*)	**UK** Short
Sierra **200**	(*Musketeer*)	
SK-35	(J-35)	**Swe** SAAB
SK-37	(J-37)	
SK-60	(SAAB-105)	**Swe** SAAB
SK-61	(*Bulldog*)	
Skyvan		**UK** Short
SM-90		**RF** Technoavia
SM-1019		**It** SIAI
SP-2H	*Neptune*	**US** Lockheed

Type	Name/ designation	Country of origin Maker
SR-71	*Blackbird*	US Lockheed
Su-7	*'Fitter-A'*	RF Sukhoi
Su-15	*'Flagon'*	RF Sukhoi
Su-17/-20/-22	*'Fitter-B' - '-K'*	RF Sukhoi
Su-24	*'Fencer'*	RF Sukhoi
Su-25	*'Frogfoot'*	RF Sukhoi
Su-27	*'Flanker'*	RF Sukhoi
Su-29		RF Sukhoi
Su-30	*'Flanker'*	RF Sukhoi
Su-33	(Su-27K) *'Flanker-D'*	RF Sukhoi
Su-34	(Su-27IB) *'Flanker-C2'*	RF Sukhoi
Su-35	(Su-27) *'Flanker'*	RF Sukhoi
Su-39	(Su-25T) *'Frogfoot'*	RF Sukhoi
Super		Fr Dassault
Shrike Aerocommander		US Rockwell
Super Galeb		FRY SOKO
T-1		J Fuji
T-1A	*Jayhawk*	US Beech
T-2	*Buckeye*	US Rockwell
T-2		J Mitsubishi
T-3		J Fuji
T-6A	*Texan* II	US Beech
T-17	(*Supporter*, MFI-17)	Swe SAAB
T-23	*Uirapurú*	Br Aerotec
T-25	Neiva *Universal*	Br Embraer
T-26	EMB-326	
T-27	*Tucano*	Br Embraer
T-28	*Trojan*	US North American
T-33	*Shooting Star*	US Lockheed
T-34	*Mentor*	US Beech
T-35	*Pillán* [PA-28]	Chl Enaer
T-36	(C-101)	
T-37	(A-37)	
T-38	*Talon*	US Northrop
T-39	(*Sabreliner*)	US Rockwell
T-41	*Mescalero* (Cessna 172)	US Cessna
T-42	*Cochise* (*Baron*)	US Beech
T-43	(Boeing 737)	
T-44	(*King Air*)	
T-47	(*Citation*)	
T-67M	(*Firefly*)	UK Slingsby
T-400	(T-1A)	US Beech
TB-20	*Trinidad*	Fr Aérospatiale
TB-21	*Trinidad*	Fr Socata
TB-30	*Epsilon*	Fr Aérospatiale
TB-200	*Tobago*	Fr Socata
TBM-700		Fr Socata
TC-45	(C-45, trg)	
TCH-1	*Chung Hsing*	ROC AIDC
TL-1	(KM-2)	J Fuji
Tornado		UK/Ge/It Panavia
TR-1	[U-2]	US Lockheed
Travel Air	*Beech 95*	
Trident		UK BAe
Trislander	BN-2	
Tristar	L-1011	
TS-8	*Bies*	Pl PZL
TS-11	*Iskra*	Pl PZL
Tu-16	*'Badger'*	RF Tupolev
Tu-22	*'Blinder'*	RF Tupolev
Tu-22M	*'Backfire'*	RF Tupolev
Tu-95	*'Bear'*	RF Tupolev
Tu-126	*'Moss'*	RF Tupolev
Tu-134	*'Crusty'*	RF Tupolev
Tu-142	*'Bear* F'	RF Tupolev
Tu-154	*'Careless'*	RF Tupolev
Tu-160	*'Blackjack'*	RF Tupolev
Tucano	(EMB-312/314)	Br Embraer
Turbo Porter	PC-6A/B	
Twin Bonanza	*Beech 50*	
Twin Otter	DHC-6	
Tzukit	[CM-170]	Il IAI
U-2		US Lockheed
U-3	(Cessna 310)	US Cessna
U-4	*Gulfstream* IV	US Gulfstream Aviation
U-7	(L-18)	
U-8	(*Twin Bonanza/Queen Air*)	US Beech
U-9	(EMB-121)	
U-10	*Super Courier*	US Helio
U-17	(Cessna 180, 185)	US Cessna
U-21	(*King Air*)	
U-36	(*Learjet*)	
U-42	(C-42)	
U-93	(HS-125)	
U-125	BAe 125-800	UK BAe
U-206G	*Stationair*	US Cessna
UC-12	(*King Air*)	
UP-2J	(P-2J)	
US-1		J Shin Meiwa
US-2A	(S-2A, tpt)	
US-3	(S-3, tpt)	
UTVA-66		FRY UTVA
UTVA-75		FRY UTVA
UV-18	(DHC-6)	
V-400	*Fantrainer 400*	Ge VFW
V-600	*Fantrainer 600*	Ge VFW
Vampire	DH-100	
VC-4	*Gulfstream* I	
VC-10		UK BAe
VC-11	*Gulfstream* II	
VC-25	[Boeing 747]	US Boeing
VC-91	(HS-748)	
VC-93	(HS-125)	
VC-97	(EMB-120)	
VC-130	(C-130)	
VFW-614		Ge VFW
Vinka	L-70	
VU-9	(EMB-121)	
VU-93	(HS-125)	
WC-130	[C-130]	
WC-135	[Boeing 707]	US Boeing
Westwind	IAI-1124	
Winjeel	CA-25	
Xavante	EMB-326	
Xingu	EMB-121	
Y-5	[An-2]	PRC Hua Bei
Y-7	[An-24/-26]	PRC XAC
Y-8	[An-12]	PRC STAF
Y-12	*Turbo/Twin Panda*	PRC HAMC
Yak-11	*'Moose'*	RF Yakovlev
Yak-18	*'Max'*	RF Yakovlev
Yak-28	*'Firebar'* (*'Brewer'*)	RF Yakovlev

Type	Name/designation	Country of origin	Maker
Yak-38	*'Forger'*	**RF**	Yakovlev
Yak-40	*'Codling'*	**RF**	Yakovlev
Yak-42	*'Clobber'*	**RF**	Yakovlev
Yak-52	(IAK 52)	**R**	Aerostar
Yak-55		**RF**	Yakovlev
YS-11		**J**	Nihon
Z-142/143		**Cz**	Zlin
Z-226		**Cz**	Zlin
Z-242		**Cz**	Zlin
Z-326		**Cz**	Zlin
Z-526		**Cz**	Zlin
Zéphyr	CM-175		

Tilt-Rotor Wing

Type	Name/designation	Country of origin	Maker
V-22	*Osprey*	**US**	Bell/Boeing

Helicopters

Type	Name/designation	Country of origin	Maker
A-109	*Hirundo*	**It**	Agusta
A-129	*Mangusta*	**It**	Agusta
AB-...	(Bell 204/205/206/212/214, etc.)	**It/US**	Agusta/Bell
AH-1	*Cobra/Sea Cobra*	**US**	Bell
AH-2	*Rooivalk*	**RSA**	Denel
AH-6	(Hughes 500/530)	**US**	MD
AH-64	*Apache*	**US**	Hughes
ALH	*Adv Light Hel*	**Ind**	HAL
***Alouette* II**	SA-318, SE-3130	**Fr**	Aérospatiale
***Alouette* III**	SA-316, SA-319	**Fr**	Aérospatiale
AS-61	(SH-3)	**US/It**	Sikorsky/Agusta
AS-313 – AS-365/-366	(ex-SA-313 – SA-365/-366)		
AS-332	*Super Puma*	**Fr**	Aérospatiale
AS-350	*Ecureuil*	**Fr**	Aérospatiale
AS-355	*Ecureuil* II	**Fr**	Aérospatiale
AS-365	*Dauphin*	**Fr**	Aérospatiale
AS-532	*Cougar*	**Fr**	Eurocopter
AS-550/555	*Fennec*	**Fr**	Aérospatiale
AS-565	*Panther*	**Fr**	Eurocopter
ASH-3	(*Sea King*)	**It/US**	Agusta/Sikorsky
AUH-76	(S-76)		
Bell 47	(*Sioux*)	**US**	Bell
Bell 205		**US**	Bell
Bell 206		**US**	Bell
Bell 212		**US**	Bell
Bell 214		**US**	Bell
Bell 222		**US**	Bell
Bell 406		**US**	Bell
Bell 412		**US**	Bell
Bo-105	(NBo-105)	**Ge**	MBB
CH-3	(SH-3)		
CH-34	*Choctaw*	**US**	Sikorsky
CH-46	*Sea Knight*	**US**	Boeing-Vertol
CH-47	*Chinook*	**US**	Boeing-Vertol
CH-53	*Stallion* (*Sea Stallion*)	**US**	Sikorsky
CH-54	*Tarhe*	**US**	Sikorsky
CH-113	(CH-46)		
CH-124	SH-3 (*Sea King*)		
CH-139	Bell 206		
CH-146	Bell 412	**Ca**	Bell
CH-147	CH-47		
CH-149	*Cormorant* (Merlin)		
Cheetah	[SA-315]	**Ind**	HAL
Chetak	[SA-319]	**Ind**	HAL
Commando	(SH-3)	**UK/US**	Westland/Sikorsky
EC-120B	*Colibri*	**Fr/Ge**	Eurocopter
EH-60	(UH-60)		
EH-101	*Merlin*	**UK/It**	Westland/Agusta
F-28F		**US**	Enstrom
FH-1100	(OH-5)	**US**	Fairchild-Hiller
Gazela	(SA-342)	**Fr/FRY**	Aérospatiale/SOKO
Gazelle	SA-341/-342		
H-34	(S-58)		
H-76	S-76		
HA-15	Bo-105		
HB-315	*Gavião* (SA-315)	**Br/Fr**	Helibras Aérospatiale
HB-350	*Esquilo* (AS-350)	**Br/Fr**	Helibras Aérospatiale
HD-16	SA-319		
HH-3	(SH-3)		
HH-34	(CH-34)		
HH-53	(CH-53)		
HH-65	(AS-365)	**Fr**	Eurocopter
Hkp-2	*Alouette* II/SE-3130		
Hkp-3	AB-204		
Hkp-4	KV-107		
Hkp-5	Hughes 300		
Hkp-6	AB-206		
Hkp-9	Bo-105		
Hkp-10	AS-332		
HR-12	OH-58		
HSS-1	(S-58)		
HSS-2	(SH-3)		
HT-17	CH-47		
HT-21	AS-332		
HU-1	(UH-1)	**J/US**	Fuji/Bell
HU-8	UH-1B		
HU-10	UH-1H		
HU-18	AB-212		
Hughes 300		**US**	MD
Hughes 500/520	*Defender*	**US**	MD
IAR-316/-330	(SA-316/-330)	**R/Fr**	IAR/Aérospatiale
Ka-25	*'Hormone'*	**RF**	Kamov
Ka-27/-28	*'Helix-A'*	**RF**	Kamov
Ka-29	*'Helix-B'*	**RF**	Kamov
Ka-32	*'Helix-C'*	**RF**	Kamov
Ka-50	*Hokum*	**RF**	Kamov
KH-4	(Bell 47)	**J/US**	Kawasaki/Bell
KH-300	(Hughes 269)	**J/US**	Kawasaki/MD
KH-500	(Hughes 369)	**J/US**	Kawasaki/MD
Kiowa	OH-58		
KV-107	[CH-46]	**J/US**	Kawasaki/Vertol
Lynx		**UK**	Westland
MD-500/530	*Defender*	**US**	McDonnell Douglas
Merlin	EH-101	**UK/It**	Westland/Augusta
MH-6	(AH-6)		
MH-53	(CH-53)		
Mi-2	*'Hoplite'*	**RF**	Mil
Mi-4	*'Hound'*	**RF**	Mil
Mi-6	*'Hook'*	**RF**	Mil
Mi-8	*'Hip'*	**RF**	Mil
Mi-14	*'Haze'*	**RF**	Mil
Mi-17	*'Hip-H'*	**RF**	Mil

Type	Name/ designation	Country of origin	Maker
Mi-24, -25, -35	*'Hind'*	**RF**	Mil
Mi-26	*'Halo'*	**RF**	Mil
Mi-28	*'Havoc'*	**RF**	Mil
NAS-330	(SA-330)	**Indo/Fr**	Nurtanio / Aérospatiale
NAS-332	AS-332	**Indo/Fr**	Nurtanio / Aérospatiale
NB-412	Bell 412	**Indo/US**	Nurtanio / Bell
NBo-105	Bo-105	**Indo/Ge**	Nurtanio / MBB
NH-300	(Hughes 300)	**It/US**	Nardi / MD
OH-6	*Cayuse* (Hughes 369)	**US**	MD
OH-13	(Bell 47G)		
OH-23	*Raven*	**US**	Hiller
OH-58	*Kiowa* (Bell 206)		
OH-58D	(Bell 406)		
Oryx	(SA-330)		
PAH-1	(Bo-105)		
Partizan	(*Gazela*, armed)		
RH-53	(CH-53)		
S-58	(*Wessex*)	**US**	Sikorsky
S-61	SH-3		
S-65	CH-53		
S-70	UH-60	**US**	Sikorsky
S-76		**US**	Sikorsky
S-80	CH-53		
SA-313	*Alouette* II	**Fr**	Aérospatiale
SA-315	*Lama* [*Alouette* II]	**Fr**	Aérospatiale
SA-316	*Alouette* III (SA-319)	**Fr**	Aérospatiale
SA-318	*Alouette* II (SE-3130)	**Fr**	Aérospatiale
SA-319	*Alouette* III (SA-316)	**Fr**	Aérospatiale
SA-321	*Super Frelon*	**Fr**	Aérospatiale
SA-330	*Puma*	**Fr**	Aérospatiale
SA-341/-342	*Gazelle*	**Fr**	Aérospatiale
SA-360	*Dauphin*	**Fr**	Aérospatiale
SA-365/-366	*Dauphin* II (SA-360)		
Scout	(*Wasp*)	**UK**	Westland
SE-316	(SA-316)		
SE-3130	(SA-318)		
Sea King	[SH-3]	**UK**	Westland
SH-2	*Sea Sprite*	**US**	Kaman
SH-3	(*Sea King*)	**US**	Sikorsky
SH-34	(S-58)		
SH-57	Bell 206		
SH-60	*Sea Hawk* (UH-60)		
Sokol	W3		
TH-50	Esquilo (AS-550)		
TH-55	Hughes 269		
TH-57	*Sea Ranger* (Bell 206)		
TH-67	Creek (Bell 206B-3)	**Ca**	Bell
UH-1	*Iroquois* (Bell 204/205/212)		
UH-12	(OH-23)	**US**	Hiller
UH-13	(Bell 47J)		
UH-19	(S-55)		
UH-34T	(S-58T)		
UH-46	(CH-46)		
UH-60	*Black Hawk* (SH-60)	**US**	Sikorsky
VH-4	(Bell 206)		
VH-60	(S-70)		
W-3	*Sokol*	**Pl**	PZL
Wasp	(*Scout*)	**UK**	Westland
Wessex	(S-58)	**US/UK**	Sikorsky / Westland
Z-5	[Mi-4]	**PRC**	HAF
Z-6	[Z-5]	**PRC**	CHAF
Z-8	[AS-321]	**PRC**	CHAF
Z-9	[AS-365]	**PRC**	HAMC
Z-11	[AS-352]	**PRC**	CHAF

Index of **Tables**

By table number

By list of subjects

Index of **Tables** continued

Index of Countries and Territories

Index of **Country Abbreviations**

A ... Austria
AB ... Antigua and Barbuda
Afg ... Afghanistan
Ag ... Algeria
Alb ... Albania
Ang ... Angola
Arg ... Argentina
Arm ... Armenia
Aus ... Australia
Az ... Azerbaijan

Bds ... Barbados
Be ... Belgium
Bel ... Belarus
BF ... Burkina Faso
Bg ... Bulgaria
BiH ... Bosnia-Herzegovina
Bn ... Benin
Bng ... Bangladesh
Bol ... Bolivia
Br ... Brazil
Brn ... Bahrain
Bru ... Brunei
Bs ... Bahamas
Btwa ... Botswana
Bu ... Burundi
Bze ... Belize

C ... Cuba
Ca ... Canada
Cam ... Cambodia
CAR ... Central African Republic
CH ... Switzerland
Cha ... Chad
Chl ... Chile
CI ... Côte d'Ivoire
Co ... Colombia
Cr ... Croatia
CR ... Costa Rica
Crn ... Cameroon
CV ... Cape Verde
Cy ... Cyprus
Cz ... Czech Republic

Da ... Denmark
Dj ... Djibouti
DPRK ... Korea, Democratic People's Republic of (North)
DR ... Dominican Republic
DROC ... Democratic Republic of Congo

Ea ... Estonia
Ec ... Ecuador
EG ... Equatorial Guinea
ElS ... El Salvador
Er ... Eritrea
Et ... Egypt
Eth ... Ethiopia

Fji ... Fiji
Fr ... France
FRY ... Federal Republic of Yugoslavia (Serbia–Montenegro)
FYROM ... Former Yugoslav Republic of Macedonia

Ga ... Georgia
Gam ... Gambia, The
Gbn ... Gabon
Ge ... Germany
Gha ... Ghana
Gr ... Greece
Gua ... Guatemala
GuB ... Guinea-Bissau
Gui ... Guinea
Guy ... Guyana

HKJ ... Jordan
Hr ... Honduras
Hu ... Hungary

Icl ... Iceland
Il ... Israel
Ind ... India
Indo ... Indonesia
Ir ... Iran
Irl ... Ireland
Irq ... Iraq
It ... Italy

J ... Japan
Ja ... Jamaica

Kaz ... Kazakhstan
Kgz ... Kyrgyzstan
Kwt ... Kuwait
Kya ... Kenya

L ... Lithuania
Lao ... Laos
LAR ... Libya
Lat ... Latvia
Lb ... Liberia
Ls ... Lesotho
Lu ... Luxembourg

M ... Malta
Mal ... Malaysia
Mdg ... Madagascar
Mex ... Mexico
Mgl ... Mongolia
Mlw ... Malawi
Mol ... Moldova
Mor ... Morocco
Moz ... Mozambique
Ms ... Mauritius
My ... Myanmar (Burma)

N ... Nepal
Nba ... Namibia
Nga ... Nigeria
Ngr ... Niger
Nic ... Nicaragua
Nl ... Netherlands
No ... Norway
NZ ... New Zealand

O ... Oman

PA ... Palestinian Autonomous Areas of Gaza and Jericho
Pak ... Pakistan
Pan ... Panama
Pe ... Peru
Pi ... Philippines
Pl ... Poland
PNG ... Papua New Guinea
Por ... Portugal
PRC ... China, People's Republic of
Py ... Paraguay

Q ... Qatar

R ... Romania
RC ... Congo
RF ... Russia
RH ... Haiti
RIM ... Mauritania
RL ... Lebanon
RMM ... Mali
ROC ... Taiwan
ROK ... Korea, Republic of (South)
RSA ... South Africa
Rwa ... Rwanda

Sau ... Saudi Arabia
Sdn ... Sudan
Sen ... Senegal
Sey ... Seychelles
SF ... Finland
Sgp ... Singapore
Ska ... Sri Lanka
SL ... Sierra Leone
Slvk ... Slovakia
Slvn ... Slovenia
Sme ... Suriname
Sp ... Spain
SR ... Somali Republic
Swe ... Sweden
Syr ... Syria

Tg ... Togo
Th ... Thailand
Tjk ... Tajikistan
Tkm ... Turkmenistan
TL ... East Timor
Tn ... Tunisia
TT ... Trinidad and Tobago
Tu ... Turkey
Tz ... Tanzania

UAE ... United Arab Emirates
Uga ... Uganda
UK ... United Kingdom
Ukr ... Ukraine
Ury ... Uruguay
US ... United States
Uz ... Uzbekistan
Ve ... Venezuela
Vn ... Vietnam
Ye ... Yemen, Republic of
Z ... Zambia
Zw ... Zimbabwe